CW01509004

BLUE GUIDE

GREECE
THE AEGEAN ISLANDS

Nigel McGilchrist

Editors
Heinrich Hall & Michael Metcalfe

Somerset Books • London

Xanthi Komotini
Alexandroupolis
T H R A C E
27°00'   28°00'   30°00'
TEKIRDAĞ   **ISTANBUL**   GEBZE   IZMIT

Sea of Marmara

E V R O S
Samothrace
Eros

Northern Aegean p.499

Dardanelles

Iznik

Lemnos
Gökçeada
Çanakkale
Troy
Bozcaada

A S I A

BURSA

40°00'

Bozüyük

Aghios
Efstratios
Edremit

BALIKESIR

KÜTAHYA

L E S B O S
Ayvalik
Pergamon
Bergama

A

S

I

A

T U R K E Y

39°00'

Mytilene
Lesbos
Akhisar

Simav Çayı

UŞAK   Banaz

A
e
g
e
a
n

Eastern Aegean p.430
Psara
Manisa
Turgutlu

M
I
N
O
R

C H I O S
Chios
Chios
Çesme
**IZMIR
(SMYRNA)**

Salihli
Çivril

38°00'

Andros
Ephesus
Dazkiri

Acigöl

S
e
a

Tinos
Syros
Ermoupolis
Mykonos
Delos

Kuşadaşi
Samos
Vathy
Ikaria
Fourni

AYDIN
Menderes Nehri
Büyük

DENIZLI

Serinhisar

C Y C L A D E S
Naxos
Pátmos
Lipsi
Miletus

Muğla

37°00'

Paros
Leros
Halicarnassus
Kalymnos
Bodrum
Kos

Marmaris   Dalaman

Sikinos
Ios
Folegandros
Santorini
Anaphi
Amorgos
Astypalaia
Kos
Nisyros
Cnidos
Symi
Tilos

Fethiye

D O D E C A N E S E
Chalki
Rhodes

Rhodes

Kastellorizo

36°00'

S e a   o f   C r e t e

Karpathos

HERAKLEION
Knossos
Aghios
Nikolaos
Siteia
Kasos

Dodecanese p.252

35°00'

H E R A K L E I O N   L A S I T H I

25°00'   26°00'   27°00'   28°00'   29°00'

First edition 2010

Published by Blue Guides Limited, a Somerset Books Company
Winchester House, Deane Gate Avenue, Taunton, Somerset TA1 2UH
www.blueguides.com
'Blue Guide' is a registered trademark.

Text © Blue Guides Limited 2010

All rights reserved. No part of this publication may be reproduced or used in any form or by any means—photographic, electronic or mechanical—without permission of the publisher.

ISBN 978–1–905131–35–8

A CIP catalogue record of this book is available from the British Library.

Distributed in the United States of America by
W.W. Norton & Company, Inc.
500 Fifth Avenue, New York, NY 10110.

The Greek islands were originally included in *Blue Guide Greece* (Stuart Rossiter 1st edition 1967, 2nd 1973, 3rd 1977, 4th 1981) and Robin Barber (5th 1988, 6th 1995, revised 2001). This practice ended with the 7th edition (Sherry Marker and James Pettifer, 2006). This book on the Aegean islands draws on previous editions but is largely new material.

The editors and publisher have made reasonable efforts to ensure the accuracy of all the information in *Blue Guide Greece the Aegean Islands*; however, they can accept no responsibility for any loss, injury or inconvenience sustained by any traveller as a result of information or advice contained in the guide.

Statement of editorial independence: Blue Guides, their authors and editors, are prohibited from accepting payment from any restaurant, hotel, gallery or other establishment for its inclusion in this guide, or on www.blueguides.com, or for a more favourable mention than would otherwise have been made.

All other acknowledgements, photo credits and copyright information are given on p. 680, which forms part of this copyright page.

Your views on this book would be much appreciated. We welcome not only specific comments, suggestions or corrections, but any more general views you may have: how this book enhanced your visit, how it could have been more helpful. Blue Guides authors and editorial and production team work hard to bring you what we hope are the best-researched and best-presented cultural, historical and academic guide books in the English language. Please write to us by email (editorial@blueguides.com), via the comments page on our website (www.blueguides.com) or at the address given above. We will be happy to acknowledge useful contributions in the next edition, and to offer a free copy of one of our titles.

CONTENTS

About the author and editors

Nigel McGilchrist has lived in the Mediterranean region for over 30 years, working for the Italian Ministry of Arts and then as Director of the Anglo-Italian Institute in Rome. He has taught at the University of Rome, for the University of Massachusetts, and was for seven years Dean of European Studies for a consortium of American universities. He lectures widely in art and archaeology at museums and institutions in Europe and the United States.

Heinrich Hall is an Athens-based archaeologist specialised in the Neolithic. He has been involved in archaeological excavations and surveys in several countries, with a special focus on Crete. He is also the archaeological correspondent for the English-language *Athens News*. He organises and leads archaeological and cultural tours in Turkey and Greece for Peter Sommer Travels.

Dr Michael Metcalfe also organises and leads cultural and archaeological tours for Peter Sommer Travels. He lives in Sicily and is a specialist in Ancient History and Greek Epigraphy. He has taken part in several archaeological projects in Greece and Turkey, and is currently preparing the early 19th-century notebooks of a British archaeological mission to the Eastern Aegean for publication.

A note on transliteration

The editors' aim has been to find transcriptions that help with pronunciation without stripping words of their character or creating semantic confusion. The resulting system is personal rather than ruthlessly consistent. Names familiar from the Classical world are spelled in the way most familiar from literature (Daedalus, not Dhaidhalos). The same is true of well-known names from art and history (Lysippus; Michael Palaeologus). Accents on place names indicate the stressed syllable in modern Greek. On ancient place names, and in cases where the pronunciation is either obvious or very familiar (e.g. Mykonos), the accents are omitted.

   G or Gh (used as the transliteration for Γ) should be pronounced soft, almost like the 'y' in 'young'. D (for Δ) sounds like the 'th' in 'then'; Ch (for Χ) is pronounced like the Scottish 'loch'. The diphthong ai is like the 'ai' in 'paid'; ei is pronounced 'ee', as is 'oi'.

INTRODUCTION

There are hundreds of Greek Aegean islands, many of them mere scraps of rock in an azure sea, inhabited by birds and goats and summer yachts, but not by humans year-round. Greece, in fact, has the second longest coastline in Europe; the sea and its pleasures are one of the chief reasons to visit the Aegean region, but they are far from being the only one. Some of the most sophisticated civilisations in human history have inhabited these islands, from the great cultures of the Bronze Age to the flowering of Classical Greece, followed by the Romans, the Byzantines, the Venetians and the Ottomans. All of these have left their mark; and in the Dodecanese there is also the legacy of the Knights Hospitallers and the Italians.

Putting together a book about such a diverse region is no easy task. As Lawrence Durrell noted in his *Reflections on a Marine Venus*, 'Only by a strict submission to the laws of inconsequence can one ever write about an island'. When one sets out to write about several, the problem is multiplied. Users of this book will often find that the road leads them to this or that abandoned church or deserted headland. And there it leaves them. To discover its beauty and interest for themselves. This is no bad thing. Very often there is little to be said except that the site is ancient, the views tremendous and the solitude total. The rest is up to the individual visitor.

Five years of painstaking research went into the material for this book. The full text (*McGilchrist's Greek Islands*) is available in the Travel Monographs series (see www.blueguides.com). As well as including material from their own research and experience, the editors have compiled this volume from the most pertinent parts of the original manuscript: those which are essential to an understanding of the islands both individually and as aspects of a larger whole, and those which are most likely to appeal to a Blue Guides readership: interested non-specialists keen to see as much as possible, but who are nevertheless on holiday.

Annabel Barber
Series Editor

THE ARGO-SARONIC ISLANDS

The term Argo-Saronic describes a group of six islands, four of which (Salamis, Aegina, Angístri and Poros) are located in the Saronic Gulf, the 'home sea' of Athens, while two (Hydra and Poros) lie off the southern coast of the Argolid. Their location near the modern capital has had a notable effect: Salamis has adopted a quasi-suburban character (as have parts of northern Aegina), while the other islands, scattered with the summer houses of well-to-do Athenians, are popular destinations for day-trippers between spring and autumn. Frequent ferry services connect the entire group to Piraeus, but the southern islands are also reached by shorter crossings from the Argolid.

Aegina and Salamis were settled during the Late Neolithic, Poros during the Bronze Age, by which time Aegina had developed one of the main urban trading centres in southern Greece. In Mycenaean times, Salamis appears to have been the seat of an important local dynasty. During the early historical period, Poros became the ceremonial headquarters of the Calaurian League (*see p. 33*), while Aegina grew into a one of the strongest and wealthiest maritime powers. The growing dominance of Athens, however, eventually relegated the islands to a secondary role.

In Byzantine times, Aegina appears to have flourished again, but during the Middle Ages the entire group, now controlled by Venice, suffered from massive depopulation, probably due to pirate raids. Resettled by Albanian Christians in the 16th century, the islands once again flourished under Ottoman rule, when they played an important role in maritime trade. Before 1830, the harbour cities of Aegina, Poros, Hydra and Spétses were far bigger and wealthier than Athens; they also played an important historical role as major contributors to the Greek War of Independence, when Aegina briefly served as de-facto capital of the country.

When Athens became capital of the Kingdom of Greece in 1834, the growing new metropolis once again overshadowed the Argo-Saronic islands. Nevertheless, the mercantile affluence of the 18th and 19th centuries is still clearly visible in the splendid harbour towns that dominate each of them except Angístri. Their wealth of fine architecture is one of the principal attractions of the group. Additional points of interest include the beautifully located sanctuary of Poseidon on Poros and a triad of important sites on Aegina (*see opposite*).

The smaller islands also offer distinctive and memorable impressions. A long-standing ban on motorised traffic has made Hydra a walker's paradise. Angístri remains a surprising haven of tranquillity just a stone's throw from Athens. The waters around Spétses, once frequented by Bouboulina, the celebrated female pirate whose house still survives by the port (*see p. 45*), have become a haven for the super-rich and their yachts. The relatively untouched southern coast of Salamis, an island largely ignored by modern Athenians in spite of being closer to the city than any other, may be one of Attica's best-kept secrets.

The Argo-Saronic islands are rarely chosen as a main holiday destination, except by those who own property there. Instead, they invite short excursions. The largest and most fertile of the group, Aegina, certainly rewards more intense exploration, as does Hydra—for those prepared to explore an entire island on foot. Conveniently combinable with visits to Athens or the northern Peloponnese, a trip to the Argo-Saronic group provides an authentic glimpse of Greek island life.   H.H.

AEGINA

Aegina lies at the centre of the Saronic Gulf, a pivotal position not only geographically speaking, but also historically. In the 6th century BC it was more powerful than Athens and took precedence over that city once again in 1826, as the capital of a partially liberated Greece. Far from being, as Pericles called it, 'the eyesore of the Piraeus', it is a lovely place, with a relaxed and unpretentious main town. For lovers of ruins, its main attractions are the complex and well-presented Bronze Age-to-Byzantine city at Kolonna, the finely-preserved Classical Temple of Aphaia, and a veritable treasury of Byzantine churches at Palaiochóra. For the gastronome it offers delicious pistachio nuts, which thrive in the island's mild climate and clay soil.

HISTORY OF AEGINA

In legend, Aegina was a daughter of the river god Asopus; she was kidnapped by Zeus, brought to the island, and had a son, Aeacus (Aiakos). Later, Aeacus changed the island's name to Aegina, honouring his mother.

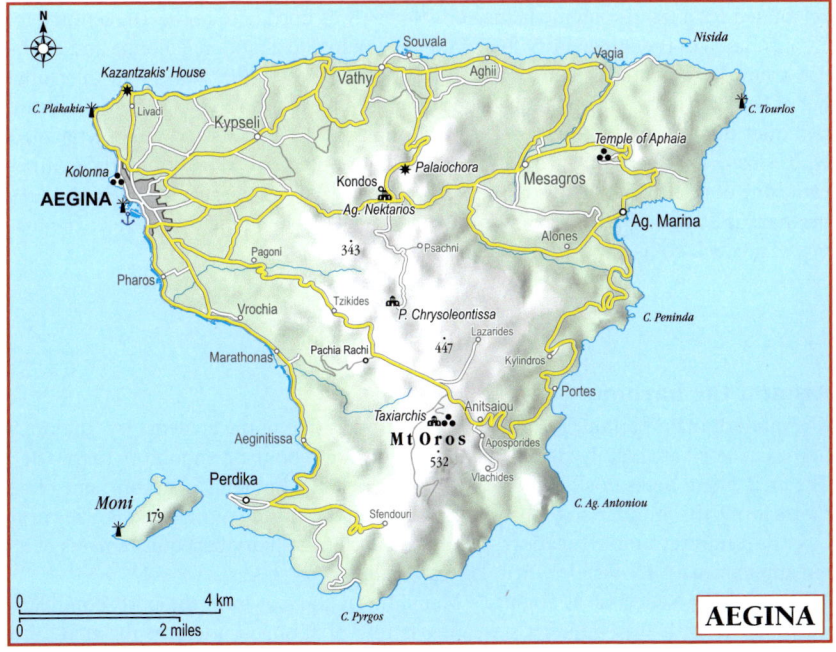

The island was inhabited in the Late Neolithic (4th millennium BC) and throughout the Bronze Age. In Mycenaean times it may have been colonised by settlers from Achaia, followed by Dorian invaders at the end of the 2nd millennium BC. Herodotus states that it was re-colonised from Epidaurus, on the mainland opposite, probably c. 950 BC. At the end of the 8th century BC, Aegina enjoyed parity with its fellow members of the Calaurian League (*see p. 33*), and by the 7th century BC, its navy held first place in the Hellenic world, plying trade from the Black Sea to Egypt, where it participated in the founding of the Greek trading station of Naucratis in the Nile Delta. Aeginetans are said to have colonised Umbria in Italy. The island was noted for pottery and especially for the quality of its bronze-founding. It was probably the first city in Greece to mint its own coins, in the mid-6th century: they were in silver and bore the image of a turtle.

Due to its trade links with Asia Minor, Aegina took an ambiguous position in the First Persian War, for which it atoned at the Battle of Salamis in 480 BC, where the Aeginetans were judged to have been the best fighters among all the Greeks. This marked the zenith of the island's power. Its wealth, naval strength and strategic position had long excited the jealousy of Athens; hostility culminated in the forcible incorporation of Aegina into the Athenian Empire in 458–457 BC and the expulsion of its ruling classes in 431 BC, replaced with Athenian settlers. Thus ended the island's independent history. It passed with the rest of Greece to Macedon and afterwards to Attalus of Pergamon. In 133 BC it was bequeathed to Rome. By 45 BC it was described as desolate and abandoned.

In Byzantine times Aegina was a joint bishopric with Keos (Kea). Paul of Aegina, celebrated for a treatise on medicine and surgery, was born here in the 7th century AD. Saracen raids in the 9th century forced the inhabitants to abandon Kolonna and establish a new island capital inland, at Palaiochóra. After 1204, the island was a personal fief of Venetian and Catalan families, until it passed to Venice in 1451. After its capture and utter devastation by Kheir ed-Din Barbarossa in 1537, the island was repopulated with Albanians. Again pillaged and recaptured for Venice by Morosini in 1654, it became one of the last Venetian strongholds in the East, ceded to the Turks only in 1718. Between 1826 and 1828, Aegina was the first capital of a fledgling free Greece. The first modern Greek coins were minted here.

AEGINA TOWN

Around the harbour

The modern main harbour is in the same location as that of the ancient city (the ruins of the city itself are plainly visible, marked by a column on the promontory to the left). The area where boats dock corresponds to the ancient commercial harbour; one of its moles forms the foundation of the present one with the church of Ághios Nikólaos near its end. A northern mole separated it from the ancient military harbour: remains of its rectangular quays are visible when the sea is calm.

The striking Neoclassical **Vogiatsís Mansion**, by the exit from the port, dominates the waterfront. It was built by a wealthy family of sponge-traders in the mid-19th

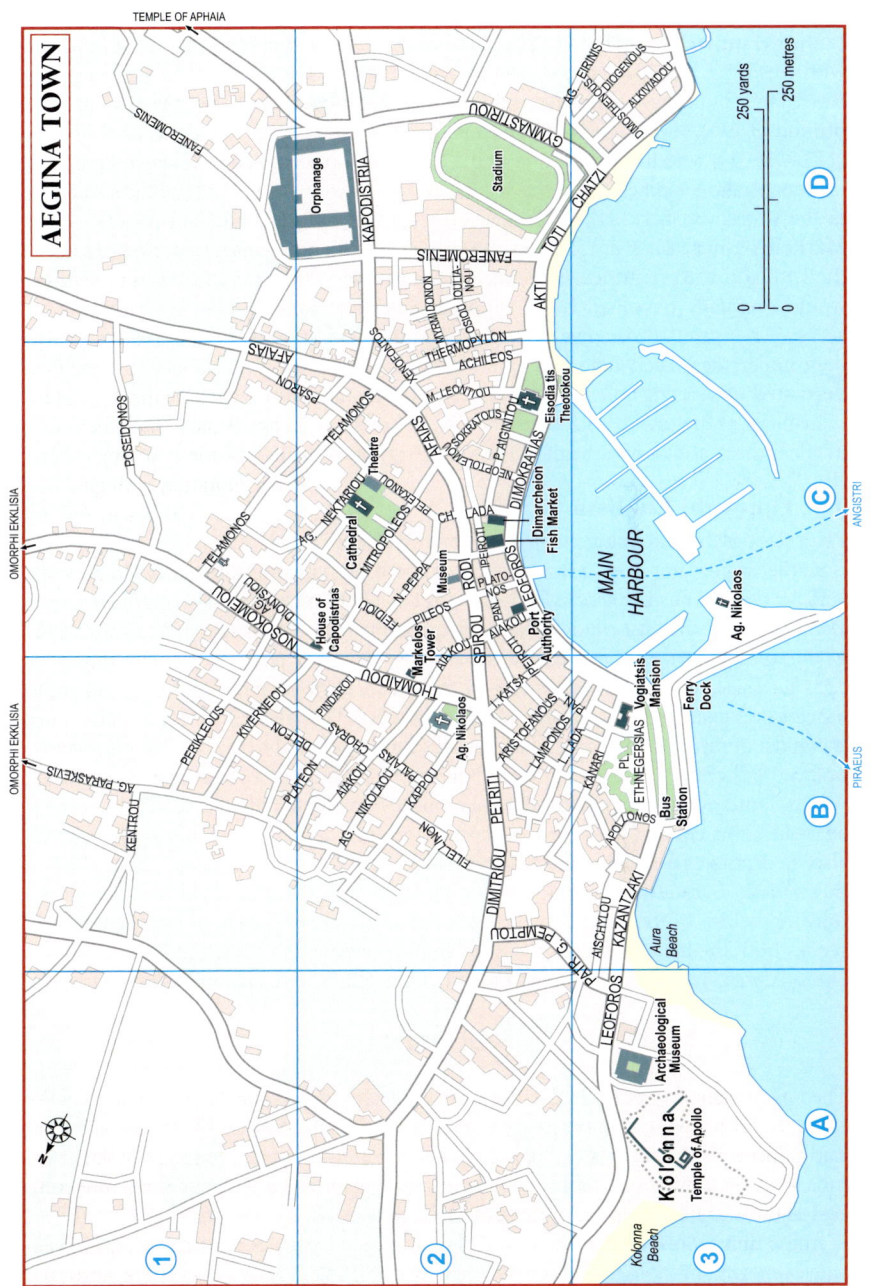

AEGINA TOWN

century. Further along the waterfront, beyond the **fish market**, small boats pull up with fresh produce, which they sell from the wharf. The gracious sweep of mostly classicising buildings is broken to the south by the **church of the Eisódia tis Theotókou** (1896). In the small square to its north stands a bust of Ioannis Capodistrias (1776–1831), who lived in Aegina as the first governor of independent Greece.

Odós Aiakoú (named after Aeacus; *see History, above*) runs east and perpendicular to the waterfront beside the Port Authority building. It leads in (four blocks) to the **Márkelos Tower** (*map p. 15, B2*), a rare survival of the Catalan presence on Aegina in the 14th and 15th centuries. Built with an eye to defence more than comfort, the tower would originally have had fewer windows, and a removable staircase or ladder for access. The turrets projecting at the upper corners still preserve the defensive slits in their undersides. The whole area uphill from here has many Neoclassical town houses, decorated in pleasing colours, with courtyards bursting with vegetation.

Just east of the tower, on Kiverneíou, is the **house of Capodistrias** (*map p. 15, B3*), in effect the seat of government of the emerging Greek state between 1826 and 1828.

The Ómorphi Ekklisía

Kiverneíou is the best point of departure for finding the church of Ághii Theódori, which is neither signed nor easy to locate, and lies about 2km inland from the port. (*From the house of Capodistrias you need to follow the street uphill/inland without turning off, until, after 1km, a busier road crosses at an oblique angle, and there is a sandstone church with a cupola on the right. By continuing here as straight as is possible, taking a narrow, concrete road to the right hand side, just around the curve on the main road, after 500m further, following straight, the church is on the right at a junction by an olive tree.*) This tiny, 13th-century church, in the midst of pistachio orchards, is sometimes simply referred to as the *Ómorphi Ekklisía*, or 'beautiful church'. It appears to be built on the podium of a small, ancient building, which stands about 40cm high from the ground, constructed of large blocks and clearly adapted on its eastern side to accommodate the apse of the church above. The church also incorporates a number of ancient blocks, one of which (northwest corner) has a fragmentary Byzantine inscription and what looks like a small part of an architectural drawing below. In the simple interior is an almost complete cycle of wall-paintings of scenes from the life of Christ (1284), which have survived in good condition. They are executed in a vigorous, stylised and rather rustic manner, with an emphasis on narrative.

KOLONNA

The low promontory north of the town is occupied by the archaeological remains of the site of Kolonna, which continues to be excavated. The Bronze Age settlement (3rd and 2nd millennia BC) here was one of the most important in Greece, but the site remained inhabited until Byzantine times. The site is complex and dense, but its small **museum**, beside the entrance, helps to understand its complex history (*open 8.30–3; closed Mon*).

In the first rooms are explanatory models and reconstructions, surrounded by excavated finds in chronological order. The Early and Middle Bronze Age pottery is painted with various patterns and motifs, including images of ships. The material from historical periods includes some fine pieces of Archaic and Classical sculpture, including a mid-5th-century BC sphinx. The courtyard displays architectural fragments. Outside the museum, beside the exit, is a fragmentary inscribed 4th-century AD mosaic from a synagogue.

The site

At the top of the first rise, the prehistoric structures which have followed the rise of the hill are revealed to the right (east). The forms of well-heads, mill-stones, doorways and ovens (under a lean-to roof) are visible, with the occasional parts of Archaic and Classical structures at a higher level above them. The site has good explanatory displays which are necessary for making sense of a complex superimposition of many layers—10 different levels in the prehistoric settlement alone, going back to the first human evidence in the 5th millennium BC. By about 2500 BC we find substantial dwellings, whose external flights of steps suggests they possessed a second floor; by 2200 BC there emerge the first clear fortifications. Development was interrupted by a conflagration c. 2050 BC, but the town soon rose again in greater strength and with renewed commercial activity (witness the presence of Minoan and Cycladic pottery); the fortifications are extended towards the east. The **burial place of a hero-warrior** from the 17th century BC lies about 20m to the southeast: when excavated it was found to contain finely-crafted weapons, a helmet and gold diadem. After this, in common with all the Mycenaean sites on the mainland, there is a clear break in habitation in 1200 BC.

To the west are the remains, built above two earlier predecessors, of the **Temple of Apollo** (c. 510 BC), a Doric temple of 6 by 11 monolithic columns, of which one from the opisthodomos remains standing (giving the site its modern name). The path crosses the stone platform surrounding the temple's high podium. A section of the temenos wall is preserved just to the north, and the temple's large altar can be seen to the east.

From the northeast corner of the temple platform there is a good view of the **fortifications** of different epochs, superimposed one above the other. In the vertical wall-facing, the rough stonework of the prehistoric (Middle Bronze Age) walls below is surmounted by later Hellenistic fortifications in regular blocks. To the left, a rectangular tower from late antiquity is built over a bastion of the prehistoric walls. The magnitude of the fortifications is best appreciated by viewing their outside face, descending from the north side of the temple, and traversing the line of the walls. Towards the eastern end, it is possible to see three periods together: the irregular stones of the prehistoric walls, set back behind the clean lines of the Archaic fortifications added in front, with Roman additions standing even further out from the city.

To the west of the Temple of Apollo, the city extends in a tight-knit web of **prehistoric houses**, with the bases of two or three later Hellenistic constructions visible above them.

Beyond Kolonna

The coast road north of Kolonna passes fine gardened villas, then turns east at Cape Plakákia. After 1km it passes the **Kapralós Museum**, devoted to the works of the sculptor and painter Christos Kapralos, whose house it was (*open Fri–Sun 10–2; June–Oct daily except Mon, 10–2 & 6–8*). A quarter of a kilometre further east, on a headland, is the **house where Nikos Kazantzakis lived** and wrote *Zorba the Greek* (1946). The next promontory to the east is the site of an ancient quarry and later necropolis.

THE NORTH OF THE ISLAND

The north of Aegina is best explored by taking Odós Faneroménis, which heads east from the southern extremity of the waterfront (*map p. 15, B4*). The road passes the former orphanage built by Capodistrias for the children orphaned by the War of Independence. A further 500m along is the ruined 18th-century basilica of the Panaghía Phaneroméni. After the town, the road climbs through olive groves and pistachio orchards.

Ághios Nektários
Four kilometres from Aegina Town, at Kondós, is the huge, modern pilgrimage church of **Ághios Nektários**, one of the largest in Greece. The neo-Byzantine octagonal church (1973) has a fine apsidal mosaic (1999) of *Christ and the Virgin*, with all the islands of the Saronic Gulf laid out below their feet. In the older monastery above, reached up a serpentine ramp, a highly decorated chapel enshrines the grave of St Nektarios (1846–1920).

Opposite the entrance to the complex, a few metres to the west, a road leads south to the isolated monastery of the **Panaghía Chrysoleóntissa**. A nunnery since 1935, it incorporates an earlier 15th-century tower. The katholikon and its wooden iconostasis date from the late 17th century.

PALAIOCHORA

Byzantine Palaiochóra was the capital of the island from the 9th–19th centuries. The inland site was chosen for its safety from coastal attack. Abandoned in the 19th century, the houses have now disappeared, leaving a multitude of churches scattered over the hillside. (*In theory, most of the churches are open all the time; the guardian at the Episkopí church has keys for any that might be locked, but he keeps no hard-and-fast hours. The following itinerary covers the site in roughly clockwise fashion.*)

Entrance to the site
The path into the main site begins at the 15th-century church of the **Tímios Stavrós (1)** beside the road, its wall-paintings retouched in the 19th century. There is a fine scene of the bound and entombed Christ in the north niche of the prothesis, behind the templon screen. Where the path divides, turn left past the ruined church of the **Panaghía tou Giánnouli (2)**, with a carved Byzantine eagle on one of the supporting pillars, and follow the path uphill to the old *plateía*.

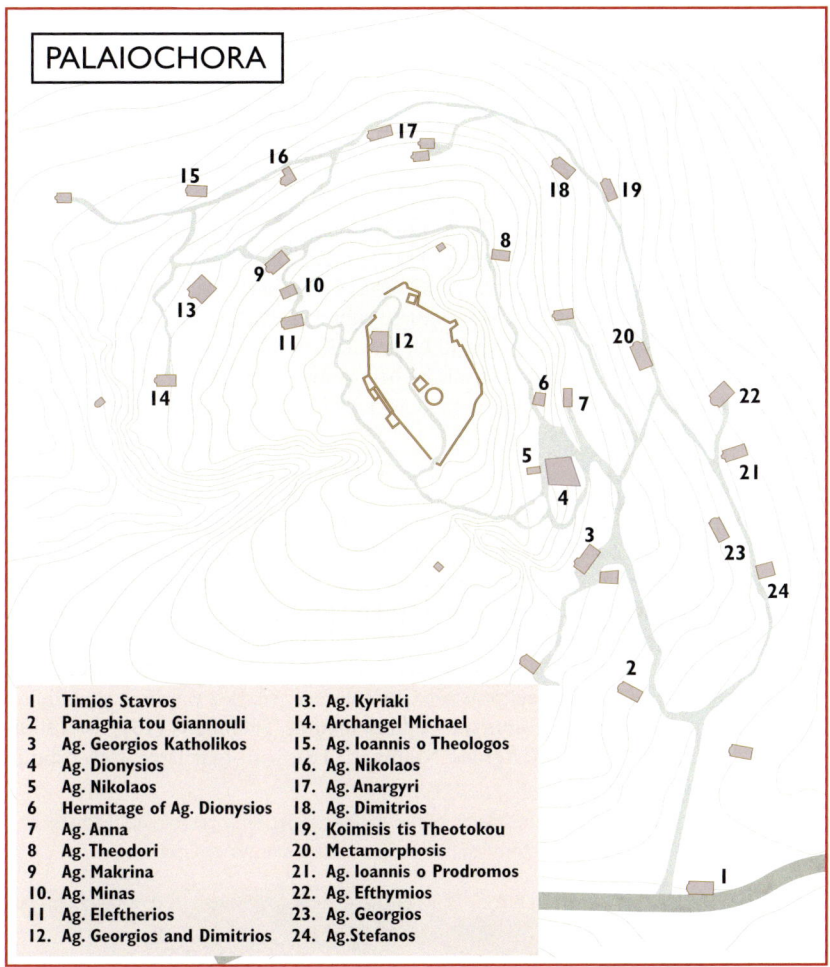

PALAIOCHORA

1	Timios Stavros	13. Ag. Kyriaki
2	Panaghia tou Giannouli	14. Archangel Michael
3	Ag. Georgios Katholikos	15. Ag. Ioannis o Theologos
4	Ag. Dionysios	16. Ag. Nikolaos
5	Ag. Nikolaos	17. Ag. Anargyri
6	Hermitage of Ag. Dionysios	18. Ag. Dimitrios
7	Ag. Anna	19. Koimisis tis Theotokou
8	Ag. Theodori	20. Metamorphosis
9	Ag. Makrina	21. Ag. Ioannis o Prodromos
10.	Ag. Minas	22. Ag. Efthymios
11	Ag. Eleftherios	23. Ag. Georgios
12.	Ag. Georgios and Dimitrios	24. Ag.Stefanos

The principal churches of Palaiochóra

The church of **Ághios Geórgios Katholikós (3)** stands on what was the only square in the settlement. The church contains a dramatic and beautiful early 15th-century *Virgin and Child* in the apse. The design of the interior is peculiar, with the long axis orientated transversely, the sanctuary in the northeast corner, and the entrance in the southwest. Perhaps this peculiarity is caused by the need to accommodate a large congregation in a building that could not be extended lengthwise due to the slope. There were once relics of St George here, but the inhabitants sold them to Venice in the 16th century.

The 15th-century church of **Ághios Dionýsios (4)**, called the 'Episkopí', a little higher up, is the principal church of the settlement. There are fine Byzantine eagles above the door. The domed interior has an aisle to the left which was added in 1610. The church can be seen in model form, held by St Peter and St Paul in the paintings on the south wall. The small church of **Ághios Nikólaos (5)** is just above and to the east.

The route to the citadel

The path continues, passing the tiny **hermitage of St Dionýsios of Zakynthos (6)**, with the church of **Aghía Ánna** below **(7)** and, further along, the church of the **Ághii Theódori (8)**: its wall-paintings include a *Crucifixion* scene on the west wall. The path turns east, and climbing past a cluster of three churches, **Aghía Makrína (9)**, **Ághios Minás (10)** and **Ághios Eleisthérios (11)**, reaches the remains of the 15th-century **Venetian citadel** on the summit. At this highest point are the remains of two cisterns and the foundations of magazines, as well as the 17th-century twin church of **Ághii Geórgios and Dimítrios (12)**.

The return route

Descending by the same path, past Aghía Makrína again, takes you to the ruined church of **Aghía Kyriakí (13)**, among the remains of a ruined monastery. A parallel nave to the north, dedicated to the Zoödóchos Pigí, has interesting 17th-century wall-paintings, including a fine *Second Coming*. The last church, beyond the monastery at the end of the path, is the church of the **Archangel Michael (14)**: above the door in its south wall are beautiful decorative details.

The lower westward path back towards the entrance passes a number of churches with interesting decorations. The first is **Ághios Ioánnis Theológos (15)**, with 14th-century paintings, followed by **Ághios Nikólaos (16)**, with four large 15th-century

Scene of the *Last Judgement* from the church of the Ághii Anárgyri. An angel rolls up the heavens like a scroll and the sea teems with terrified creatures, including four winged horses.

painted saints facing visitors on entering and arranged on a similar plan to those in Ághios Geórgios Katholikós. The next church, **Ághii Anárgyri (17)**, has (fragmentary) paintings of considerable interest. Around the west door is a fine *Christ in Majesty*, and on the south wall (by the west door) an uncommon depiction of *Abraham in Paradise*. The greatest delight lies in a tiny fragment above, which shows a ship in a sea beside a mountainous landscape: this is a Last Judgement scene, derived from St John's description of the breaking of the seals in the Book of Revelation, when 'the heaven departed as a scroll when it is rolled together; and every mountain and island were moved out of their places' (*see illustration opposite*).

After the churches of **Ághios Dimítrios (18)** and of the **Koímisis tis Theotókou (19)**, the path, turning north again, comes to the early 14th-century **church of the Metamórphosis (20)**, which has paintings—perhaps 14th century—in the sanctuary and apse. Above the *Virgin and Child* in the apse, there is a scene of the Old Testament Trinity, illustrating the episode where Abraham meets three men and gives them bread and meat, and God afterward declares that his wife Sarah shall bear a son (*Genesis 18*). Most notable is the *Last Supper* on the right side.

The other churches on this slope have less well-preserved paintings: in **Ághios Ioánnis o Pródromos** below the path **(21)**, they are possibly of the 13th century. In **Ághios Efthýmios** further below **(22)** is a 16th-century scene showing Sts Constantine and Helen with the True Cross. Just above the path, the church of **Ághios Geórgios (23)** has an interesting representation of the Prophet Elijah, with the raven and its gift of bread. Across the path and below is another lateral-axis church, **Ághios Stéfanos (24)**.

THE TEMPLE OF APHAIA

The main road after Ághios Nektários continues towards the coastal resort of **Aghía Marína**, grouped attractively around a small port amidst dense pine trees. The road passes the **Temple of Aphaia** (*open 8.30–3.30; closed Mon*), one of the most important and beautiful in Greece, famous for its late Archaic sculpted pediments (now mostly in Munich). Its site is panoramic and its well-preserved structures include not just the temple, but also other parts of the sanctuary.

There are no other temples dedicated to Aphaia, and her identity and significance remain somewhat mysterious. An ancient tradition links her with the Cretan goddess Britomartis, a daughter of Zeus. Her cult may have been related to that of Artemis. This temple appears to have been a place of predominantly female cult.

Traces of human presence on the site go as far back as c. 3000 BC, and a sanctuary appears to have been created in the Late Bronze Age. The temple standing now, completed not long after 490 BC, is the second or third stone temple at the site. A predecessor was built c. 570 BC, and burnt down c. 510 BC.

The temple is constructed out of a poor-quality local poros stone, to which a layer of plaster was applied on the columns and lower elements. This gave the building a white tone very different from the honey-colour visible today. The architectural details and sculptures were originally emphasised by being painted in strong colours.

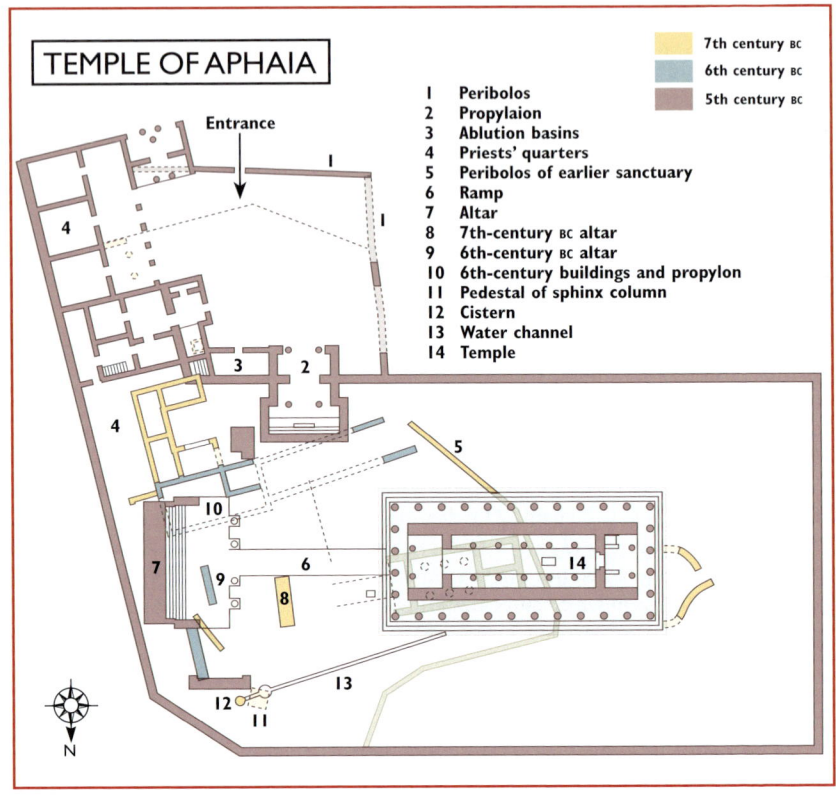

TEMPLE OF APHAIA

	7th century BC
	6th century BC
	5th century BC

Entrance

1 Peribolos
2 Propylaion
3 Ablution basins
4 Priests' quarters
5 Peribolos of earlier sanctuary
6 Ramp
7 Altar
8 7th-century BC altar
9 6th-century BC altar
10 6th-century buildings and propylon
11 Pedestal of sphinx column
12 Cistern
13 Water channel
14 Temple

The pediment sculptures

The history of the sculptural decoration is complicated by the fact that the first two series for the pediments of the existing temple, produced between 510 and 500 BC, were
removed after less than a decade and replaced by two newer series, executed c. 500 BC
(west pediment) and c. 490 BC (east pediment). The first pediment sculptures portrayed
stories from Aegina's legendary past: the fight of Telamon, son of Aeacus, and Heracles
against the Amazons in the presence of Athena (west pediment); and the abduction
of the nymph Aegina by Zeus (east pediment). When it was decided to change this
scheme, the east pediment was already in place while the west pediment may still have
been incomplete. The old pediments, still the property of the goddess, were put on display in front of the east façade. New sculpture groups were then commissioned from the
same workshop, showing scenes of Aeginetan heroes during the campaigns against Troy,
in the presiding presence of Athena: the west pediment showed Ajax, son of Telamon,
in the Trojan War; the east pediment depicted a scene from an earlier Trojan campaign
in which Aeacus himself, together with Heracles, stormed Troy. It appears that, at the

climax of their struggles with Athens around 500 BC, the Aeginetans chose to emphasise the prowess of their forefathers in battles with an earlier enemy. The stylistic changes between the two newer pediments reflect the rapid development of Greek art at the time.

Although fragments of these pediments, which are executed in Parian marble, are exhibited in the museum at Kolonna and in the National Archaeological Museum in Athens, the great majority are in the Munich Glyptothek. They were first excavated on the site by Carl von Hallerstein and Charles Robert Cockerell in 1811: they were shipped to Rome where they were purchased by Ludwig I of Bavaria.

The sanctuary

To the left on approaching the temple terrace, the base of the **peribolos (1)** is visible. Its upper section would have been of mud brick. To the right are the **foundations of the propylaion (2)**, with the stump of one of its interior octagonal columns. Further to the right are plastered **basins for ritual ablutions (3)**. Beyond them are the foundations of the **priests' quarters (4)** and those of the sanctuary's administrators

The temple terrace is built over the remains of the earlier temple and finished on top with dressed stone. A deep cut in front of the temple's south side reveals a piece of the **earlier peribolos (5)**.

The area to the east of the temple provides valuable information about the workings of a Greek sanctuary. A **paved ramp (6)** runs from the east (front) door of the temple to an **altar (7)**, the base of which survives. It was a wide, stepped structure, parallel to the temple façade and preceded by a paved area. Two square bases held dedicatory statues. Remains of **two earlier altars (8/9)** are also visible: the earliest (c. 600 BC) is in the roped-off area north of the ramp; back nearer the final altar, stones running at an obtuse angle and a lower level belong to the altar of the previous temple, c. 570 BC. The foundations to the south **(10)** were the **administrative buildings and propylon** of that earlier phase.

On the northern edge of the terrace are two more features that accompanied the 570 BC temple, but remained in place alongside its successor. A **square pedestal (11)** supported a 14-m column crowned by a sculpted sphinx. A **cistern (12)** collected rainwater from the temple roof, conducted there by a small **channel (13)** in the terrace floor.

The temple

The architectural detail of the temple **(14)** is exceptionally well preserved. It includes the perfectly clear fluting of the columns, the minimal concentric decoration on the Doric capitals, the triglyphs (originally painted dark blue, with their vertical grooves defined in black), and the clear, hanging guttae below. Grooves visible in the sides of the triglyphs held the decorated metopes (now lost), which may have been of wood or terracotta.

The building's superstructure has been reconstructed at various points, most visibly at the western end. The view inside from here reveals details of the construction and of its optical corrections, used to make its appearance seem more balanced. A slight curved rise towards the centre of the stylobate is visible, as is the increased diameter of the corner columns. The architrave also visibly consists of two parallel blocks set side by side. The roof of the naos rests on a double colonnade, with the entasis, or tapering, of the columns following through from the lower tier into the upper one. The exposed ends of the architrave of the lower colonnade display U-shaped grooves: around these a rope could be run for lifting the blocks into place.

The interior once contained two cult statues of Aphaia: a small wooden image with an ivory surface, belonging to the earlier temple, was placed in the northwest corner of the naos on a stone base; the second statue, larger than life-size, is contemporary with the existing temple, c. 505 BC. It stood in the centre of the shrine, and the holes for the posts which held a wooden barrier surrounding it can still be seen in the floor.

In various places remains of the earlier temple, smaller and at a different angle from its successor, are visible.

The museum

The tiny museum (*40m downhill of the west side of the temple*) has two floors: the ground floor relates to the existing temple, the lower floor to the 6th-century building. It displays useful explanations and models, as well as architectural elements such as marble roof tiles. The fragments of the triglyph/metope succession of the earlier entablature still retain their astonishing colouring.

THE SOUTH OF AEGINA

Two roads leave Aegina Town for the south of the island: one follows the coast, the other heads southeast across the island's central plateau, passing the charming hamlet of **Pachiá Ráchi**. About 1km further, a track leads right to the 14th-century church of the Taxiárchis, built on—and from—the massive remains of the **Sanctuary of Zeus Hellanios** ('Giver of Rain'), to whom Mt Óros was sacred. What is visible today is mainly from the 3rd century BC, although the sanctuary's origins are much older. A processional staircase, 7m wide, ascends the terrace; nothing remains of the temple that stood on it.

Mount Óros, known as Panhellenion to the ancients, dominates the view from the south. Its summit is reached in 50mins by a path from the saddle on the western side. At several points just beneath the summit, to west and to east, there are remains of walls from a 13th-century BC Mycenaean sanctuary. To the north of the chapel on the peak are traces of a later podium, possibly for a shrine. The summit commands splendid views over Aegina itself, as well as Attica, the Peloponnese and the northern Cyclades.

The coast road south from Aegina leads to the pleasant resort town of **Pérdika** in the island's southwest corner. There are good beaches between here and Aegina Town.

ANGISTRI

Angístri (*map p. 11*), ancient Pityonesos ('Island of Pines'; the modern name means 'fish-hook'), makes a delightful excursion from Aegina or Athens. A hilly protrusion on the Aegina shelf, the island features beautiful waters and a tranquil landscape.

Boats stop mostly at the harbour of Skála at the northeast corner of the island. To the south, a road leads to the more dramatic east coast, where the bays of Sklíri (0.5km) and the more untouched Chalikiáda (1km) are backed by pine-fringed cliffs. To the west, the road leads in 2km to the principal settlement of Megalochóri, passing, to the south, the island's oldest and most appealing settlement, Metóchi. Five kilometres to the south of Megalochóri is the old village of Limenária, set in a tranquil untouched landscape.

PRACTICAL INFORMATION

GETTING AROUND

Aegina is reached from Piraeus by ferry (journey time approx. 90mins) or hydrofoil (40mins), with good frequency of service. There are also services from Piraeus to Aghía Marína (one a day in winter, more in summer).

For Angístri there is a daily ferry from Piraeus, increasing to twice daily in high season. The caïque *Angistri Express* departs regularly from Aegina (15mins), with reduced frequency at weekends.

Taxis in Aegina Town will take you to the Temple of Aphaia. There is a bus to Ághios Nektários (for Palaiochóra). The taxi rank and bus station are on Dimokratías, west of the port.

WHERE TO STAY

Aegina
The **Aiginitiko Archontiko** in Aegina Town is a small hotel with great charm, in a Neoclassical house on Thomaïdou, opposite the Márkelos Tower (*T: 22970 24968, www. aeginitikoarchontiko.gr; map p. 15, B2*). This is a typical dwelling of its period, built around a courtyard and with a finely-painted ceiling in the main salon upstairs.

Angístri
One simple and comfortable solution is **Rosy's Little Village** (*T: 22970 91610; info@ rosyslittlevillage.com*) on the hillside at Sklíri Bay.

WHERE TO EAT

Aegina
The freshest fish and wine in Aegina Town is found in a simple setting with much atmosphere at the **Taverna Agora**, situated under the makeshift awnings at the back of the fish market, one block inland from the waterfront after the Dimarcheíon (*map p. 15, B3*).

At Pérdika there are many tavernas along the raised promenade: one of them, simply called '**10**', has some of the freshest produce and best-prepared dishes.

Angístri
The island has many good tavernas: for fresh home cooking, good local wines and cheeses from the Peloponnese, the traditional village tavernas **Parnassos** in Metóchi, and **Tasos** in Limenária, are highly recommended.

HYDRA

At the turn of the 19th century, when Athens had about 6,500 inhabitants, the population of Hydra (pron: *Ídra*), then an important centre of maritime trade, may have exceeded 30,000. Its sudden 17th- and 18th-century prosperity produced an extraordinary architectural flowering, endowing it with one of the most strikingly beautiful ports in the Aegean. Hydra is the only Aegean island with a total ban on motorised traffic, and this has transformed the quality of life. The interior is only accessible on foot. Hydra is most frequently visited by day-trippers, but ideally it should be visited for several days, so as to savour both its extraordinary tranquillity and to explore its uncompromised wealth of architecture.

HISTORY OF HYDRA

Hydra was substantially settled in prehistory: as many as a dozen sites of the Early Helladic II period (2800–2300 BC) have been confirmed, mostly around the coast. Its main, proto-urban centre was on the plateau of Episkopí. In late Mycenaean times the island was an outpost protecting maritime trade-routes, with a fortified citadel above Vlychós. There are few references to Hydra in early historic times, apart from Herodotus recounting that the island was purchased c. 526 BC from the people of the mainland city of Hermione by exiled Samians. Insufficient water may have been the reason for the island's lack of settlement in later antiquity, though if this is the case the names Hydra and Hydrea, which derive from the ancient Greek for water, make little sense.

During the 16th and 17th centuries, Christian refugees from Turkish rule in mainland Greece settled on Hydra, where they became practically self-governing, paying no taxes but supplying sailors to the Turkish fleet. In the late 18th century, their merchant fleet grew rapidly and prospered on the trade of corn from the Black Sea, which Hydriot ships supplied to French markets by breaking the British blockade imposed during the Napoleonic Wars. At the beginning of the Greek War of Independence in 1821, Hydra had a population of over 30,000, and one of the largest merchant fleets in the Aegean. Its council of elders at first vacillated at the outbreak of the revolutionary war, wary of imperilling their prosperity and concessions from the Ottomans. With the leadership of Lazaros Koundouriotis, however, who converted his trading fleet into men-of war at his own expense, Hydra became the largest force in the Greek revolutionary navy. Among the many Hydriot naval commanders was Andreas Miaoulis, the commander-in-chief. The war caused the depletion of Hydra's wealth, resources and manpower. A further economic blow came with the arrival of steamships, which rendered obsolete the remainder of the Hydriot sailing fleet. The commercial activity of the Aegean moved to Syros and Andros. Hydra never recovered, suffering emigration through the late 19th and early 20th centuries, its fine urban architecture crumbling, only to be revived recently by tourism and new settlement.

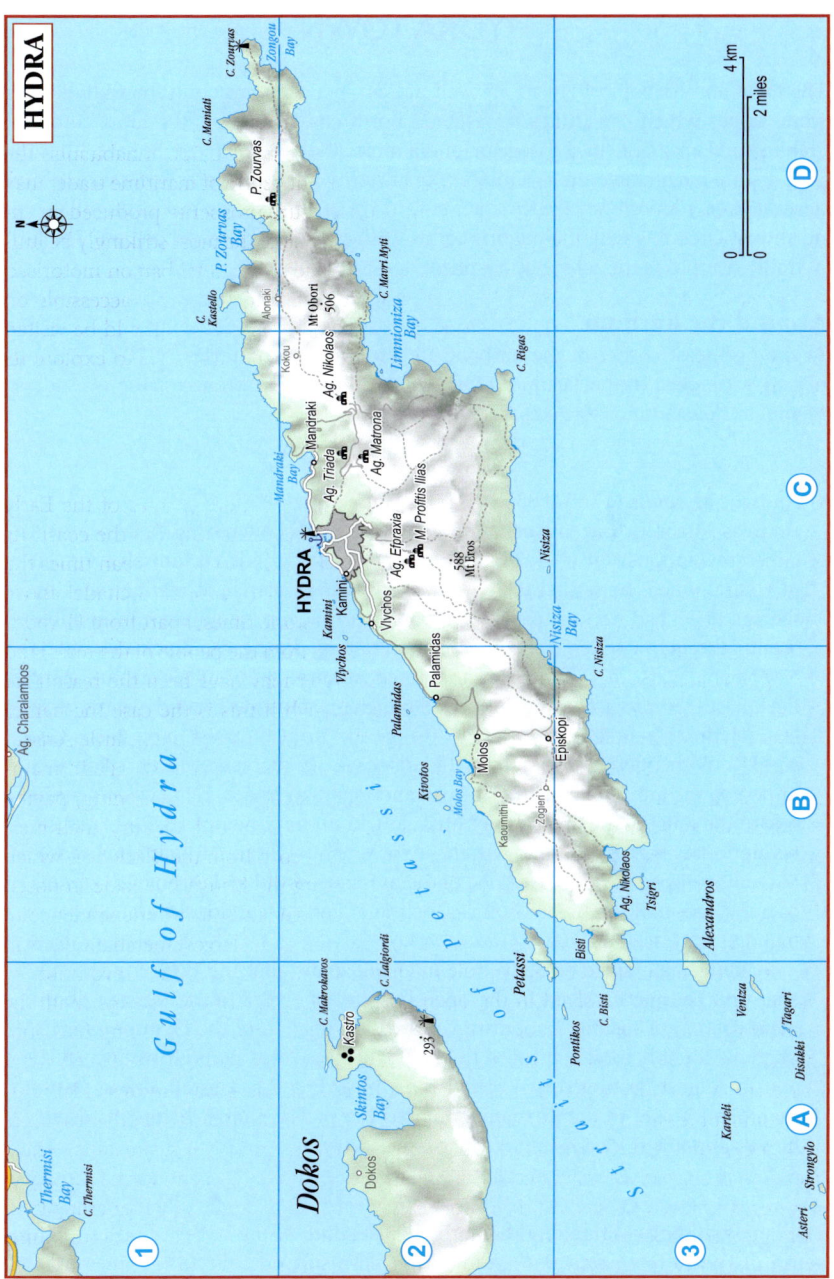

HYDRA

Thermisi Bay
C. Thermisi

Gulf of Hydra

Ag. Charalambos

C. Zoagrias
Tsongou Bay

C. Maniati

P. Zouvras
P. Zouvras Bay

C. Kastello
Alonaki
C. Mavri Myti

Mt Obori
506

Kokou
Ag. Nikolaos

Limmioniza Bay

C. Rigas

Mandraki
Mandraki Bay

Ag. Triada
Ag. Matrona

M. Profitis Ilias

HYDRA
Kamini
Kamini
Ag. Efpraxia

588
Mt Eros

Vlychos
Nisiza

Vlychos
Nisiza Bay

Palamidas
C. Nisiza

Palamidas

Kirotos
Molos Bay
Molos
Episkopi

Kaoumithi
Zoges

Ag. Nikolaos
Tsigri

Bisti
Alexandros

P e l a s s i

Dokos

Skintos Bay
C. Mavrolavos
C. Lalgiordi

Kastro
293

Dokos

C. Bisti
Pontikos

Ventza
Tigari

Karteli
Disakti
Asteri
Strongylo

S l i b r i s

0 4 km
0 2 miles

N

1
2
3

A
B
C
D

HYDRA TOWN

The town and harbour of Hydra are well hidden in a deep breach in the wall of limestone slopes which constitutes the island's north coast. Hydra is the most complete architectural ensemble in the Aegean, and almost all of its sweep can be seen from the port. Its unique architecture is a mixture of austerity and elegance, a succession of undecorated grey limestone facades, their style originating from the mountain villages of northwest Greece, where the majority of its 18th-century settlers originated. The lack of traffic completes the serene atmosphere.

Around the harbour

At the northeast corner of the harbour are the **fortified batteries** of 1821, still furnished with some of their cannon. On the upper level is a bronze statue of Andreas Miaoulis (Konstantinos Kazakos, 1892).

Andreas Miaoulis (1768–1835)

Andreas Miaoulis, one of the most sympathetic and interesting figures of the Greek revolutionary war, was born on Euboea but considered himself a citizen of Hydra, where he settled. He was a highly skilled merchant mariner, and by the age of 17 had become captain of a commercial ship, acquiring considerable wealth through a series of courageous operations during the blockades of the Napoleonic wars. In 1822 he was appointed Admiral of the Greek revolutionary fleet, hastily improvised from converted merchant ships: over half the ships were from Hydra. His first mission was to avenge the Turkish massacre on Chios (*see p. 434*). With inferior resources at his disposal, he succeeded in harrying and impeding the movements of the Turkish and Egyptian navies. He played a crucial role in the relief of the first siege of Missolonghi in the winter of 1822–23. As the revolutionary war intensified, with the involvement of Britain, Russia and France, Miaoulis stepped back to allow one of the most successful and ingenious veterans of naval action of the time, Thomas Cochrane, Earl of Dundonald, to take command of the Greek navy.

Miaoulis maintained an active role in Greek affairs after the War of Independence and became involved in the open hostility of Hydra to the Russian-dominated faction of Ioannis Capodistrias. At the instigation of the Hydriot council, Miaoulis forcibly took control of the Greek fleet in Poros harbour in July 1831, and in August destroyed two of its ships, including the flagship *Hellas*, rather than hand it over to the Russian command (*see p. 34*). Shortly before his death, he was appointed Vice-Admiral of the Greek navy.

The large building overlooking the harbour just south of the battery, houses the **Museum of Hydra** (*open daily 9–3*), a full and well-displayed collection of memorabilia of Hydra's maritime glory, including various portraits of ships and seamen, weaponry, wooden figureheads, and a silver vessel containing the heart of Andreas Miaoulis.

Next to the museum rises the tower-like **Tsamados Mansion** (c. 1790). Similar is the **Tombazis Mansion**, directly across the harbour, with several entrances on different levels along the slope. Prominently visible on the hill to the right of the Tombazis Mansion is the four-square **Voulgaris Mansion** (1810).

The cathedral and Ecclesiastical Museum

At the centre of the harbour-front is the clock-tower, behind which lies the **cathedral of the Dormition of the Virgin**, founded as an isolated nunnery in 1643, before the town existed. The present building dates from a renovation in 1776. Entered through a vestibule is a pillared courtyard on two levels. In front of the church portico stand busts of Andreas Miaoulis and Lazaros Koundouriotis. The council of notables who ran the affairs of the island in the early 19th century met in the rooms of the monastery. The interior of the katholikon is densely decorated. The monastery has a small **Ecclesiastical Museum** of liturgical items and icons of the 17th–19th centuries (*open daily except Mon, 10–5*). Of particular note are an 18th-century icon of the *Virgin of the Roses* and a delicate 16th-century image of Aghía Paraskeví. The offices of the Dimarcheíon occupy part of the monastery buildings, including its principal reception hall, which has a superbly decorated ceiling (*ask at the secretary's office on the first floor*).

The Koundouriotis Mansion

Several streets radiate uphill from the esplanade. One of them, Vótsi, passes to the west of the cathedral and opens out after 100m into Plateía Vótsi, overlooked from the south by the dignified 19th-century building of the Hydroussa Hotel, and from the west by the island's hospital.

From the south side of the hospital, steps lead up steeply to the 1780s **Koundouriotis Mansion** (*open daily April–end of Oct, 9.30–3.30. Visits at other times on request; T: 22980 52421 or 210 323 7617*). Lazaros Koundouriotis (1769–1852) was a wealthy ship-owner and the leader and political representative of the principal families of Hydra during the Greek War of Independence. From 1821 onwards he committed a large part of his wealth to the revolutionary cause, furnishing both ships and moral guidance to the independence movement. It is said that he only left Hydra on one occasion. Many of his descendants have been prominent in politics and in the Greek navy.

The mansion's main entrance leads into a courtyard below the pillared upper-floor loggia. A number of Hellenistic and Roman funerary stelae and reliefs, probably from the mainland, are immured below the staircase. A vestibule runs the width of the interior. Below its floor and that of the courtyard are large water-cisterns: the octagonal drinking-fountain above one of them stands to the right of the main door. The main rooms leading off the vestibule are characterised by high ceilings and a simplicity of furnishing in a mixture of Ottoman and Western styles. Placed above the east-facing door onto the veranda is the long panel of family icons. The upper-floor rooms are grouped around a panoramic loggia: they contain a display of furniture and (mostly female) ceremonial costumes from different parts of Greece. The bakery and cellars house an exhibition the works by the painters Pericles and Konstantinos Byzantios (father and son).

The Kiáfa area

Above the Koundouriotis Mansion, beyond the church of the Ypapantí, the street climbs to the south amongst attractive houses, past a crossroads with the main artery of the upper town, Kriezí. The Kiáfa area is the heart of the original settlement of Hydra, first occupied in the early 17th century and grouped around the town's oldest church, **Ághios Ioánnis Pródromos** (*the key is kept in the house immediately to the right of the western gate into the precinct*). The original domed-cross design is from the 17th century, but the church was renovated in 1783. It is the only church on the island to have a complete cycle of wall-paintings in its interior: they date from the late 18th century, as does the wooden iconostasis.

By climbing a short distance beyond the church and then following the main path left, it is possible to descend from Kiáfa to the east, towards a square called Kalá Pigádia ('good wells'). From the final stretch of stepped path, the large, yellow Gourogiannis Mansion (1780s) is visible in the valley below. The square is named after the two well-heads (c. 1800). From Kalá Pigádia, Odós Miaoúli leads down to the harbour; its route is lined with substantial houses of the early 19th century.

PROFITIS ILIAS & AGHIA EFPRAXIA

(*NB: Contrary to indications given by most maps and guides, this is an unrelenting 75-min climb.*) Beyond Kalá Pigádia, Odós Miaoúli rises to the south; becoming concrete, then gravel, then track, then path and finally steps, as it approaches the **monastery of Profítis Ilías** (*at any junction, take the steeper uphill turn*). The magnificent views and the serene simplicity and austerity of the architecture (1815) amply repay the climb. There is a wide range of 18th- and 19th-century icons in the katholikon. On the terrace outside stands a chapel to the island's patron saint, St Constantine of Hydra. During the civil strife of the mid-1820s Theodoros Kolokotronis was imprisoned at the monastery. A short distance below the monastery to the northwest, a stone path leads down to the sister establishment of the **convent of Aghía Efpraxía**, built in the 1860s.

The highest summit of the island, Mt Eros, rises directly to the south, and can be reached by a further 35mins' climb.

OTHER WALKS ON THE ISLAND

Hydra has no motorised vehicles; all exploration has to be undertaken on foot or by mule. The mountainous interior is grand and panoramic, but the walks are arduous and mostly shadeless, especially in the east. There are no springs, so it is important to take drinking water. (*Distances are given in terms of time on foot from the main harbour.*)

KAMINI, VLYCHOS & EPISKOPI

A stone-paved road leads from the port round the western battery to **Kamíni** (*15mins; map p. 27, C2*), an attractive fishing harbour. The route continues for **Vlychós** (*25mins*), at the mouth of a gorge. The plateau of the eastern hill was occupied by an important late Mycenaean citadel (13th–12th centuries BC). Approaching from the east, stretches of fortification wall can be seen high up on the northeast face. The summit area shows evidence of settlement, with terraces below, and a gateway on the northwest side. Archaeological evidence shows a continuation of use in historic times.

At Vlychós the path crosses an arched bridge of the late 18th century, built in dry stone. At **Palamídas** (*50mins*) is a small boatyard, overlooked by a 19th-century boathouse. The path, still a wide gravel road, rises into the interior, climbing through woods to a ridge with views down to the cove below Mólos, with the summer mansion of the Voulgaris family. Shortly after the watershed, as the road descends to the south, it reaches the half-abandoned settlement of **Episkopí** (*100mins*). The church of the Koímisis tis Theotókou has a forecourt with columns and spolia from an earlier Byzantine structure. A path continues for a further 30mins to the east of Episkopí, descending to Nísiza Bay on the south coast.

Bísti

Behind the bay of Ághios Nikólaos near Bísti (*map p. 27, B3; reached by boat*), another interesting 13th-century BC **Mycenaean installation** has been identified. On the slope of the hill are the remains of terraces and walls of considerable height, apparently designed to store water, perhaps a supply station for passing ships.

MANDRAKI & THE EASTERN MONASTERIES

Mandráki Bay (*map p. 27, C2*) was the main harbour and shipyard of the Hydriot fleet in the 19th century. The route passes the small church of the Eisódia tis Theotókou above the shore. In the hills above are three monasteries, Aghía Triáda (1704), Aghía Matróna (1865), and Ághios Nikólaos (1724), most easily approached by the wide path from the cemetery in the southeastern corner of Hydra town (*Ághios Nikólaos in 90mins, the other two in well under 1hr*). All of them were repopulated with monks or nuns in recent decades. From Ághios Nikólaos, a rough track round the north side of Mt Obóri reaches the monastery of the Panaghía Zoúrvas (1814), in a panoramic setting (*in view of the difficulty of finding the outward route and the length of the walk, 3hrs one way from the town; the monastery is best visited by taking a water taxi from Hydra to the bay of Ledéza, where a path climbs up the cliff in 40mins: the return west across the island is more easily navigated*).

DOKOS

Four kilometres north of the western tip of Hydra is the uninhabited island of Dokós, ancient Aperopia (*map p. 27, A1; access by private boat or water taxi from Hydra*). Lacking any satisfactorily sheltered port in its own coastline, Hydra used the protected bay of Skíntos, on the north coast of Dokós, as its winter anchorage. Off the northeast tip of the island, the world's oldest known shipwreck, an Early Helladic trading vessel (c. 2200 BC), its cargo carried in pottery vessels, was discovered in 1975 and excavated in 1989. Two important settlements of the mid-3rd millennium BC and two walled 13th–12th-century BC Mycenaean settlements have been excavated on the island.

PRACTICAL INFORMATION

GETTING AROUND

Hydra has typically three connections per day by hydrofoil and three by fast catamaran from Piraeus. Between mid-Oct and Easter the services are reduced. A fleet of water-taxis connect the port with outlying harbours and beaches around the island; and will also make the crossing to the mainland (Metóchi; 20mins) or to Spetses (45mins). The price-list for these services is exhibited at the water-taxi station.

WHERE TO STAY

Hydra does not have a large number of hotels, so it is a good idea to book ahead in high season; but they are of a notably higher standard and style than elsewhere. At the top end of the scale, is the **Hotel Hydroussa** ▬ in a historic mansion on Plateía Vótsi (*open Easter–Oct; T: 22980 53581/5, www.hydroussahotel.gr*). A middle-ranking hotel of great charm, in a converted private house, is **Hotel Miranda** ▬ (*open March–Nov; T: 22980 52230; www.mirandahotel.gr*). At the less expensive end of the scale is the **Piteoussa guesthouse**, simple, yet with considerable old-world charm (*T: 22980 52810; www.hydra.com.gr/piteoussa*). All are in the lower part of the town,

not far from the harbour. Since signs are very scarce on Hydra, these indications on how to find them may help. Piteoussa: first turn in to left from southeast corner of harbour, follow for 130m up to pine trees beside street; guesthouse is on left. Miranda: follow harbourfront round to right and take last turn to left before clock-tower. After the Taverna To Steki (100m), continue 50m further to Miranda, on the right. In the winter, most Hydriot hotels close: however, the Piteoussa remains open; and the more up-market **Bratsera Hotel** (*T: 22980 53971, www.bratserahotel.com*) closes only for four weeks between mid-Jan and mid-Feb.

WHERE TO EAT

Food is surprisingly unimaginative on Hydra. The nicest and most welcoming place, offering fresh and varying Greek cuisine, is **Gitoniko**, in the alleyway to the right of the long-standing and famous taverna **Xeri Elia**. **To Steki**, near Plateía Vótsi, has straightforward fare, and an attractively unreconstructed interior with folk-murals of ships on the walls. At Kamíni (15mins' walk from the main harbour) **Kontylenia's Taverna** has pleasing views and some imaginative dishes.

POROS

Separated from the Peloponnese by a narrow channel and easily accessible from Piraeus, Poros can flood with visitors during the day, but somehow manages to preserve a timeless charm, picturesque in its architectural uniformity and with the constant, unobtrusive activity of boats and caïques in its placid waters. The island is small and not very built up, making it easy to explore on foot or by bicycle; its waters are clean and its shaded coves a pleasure to swim in.

HISTORY OF POROS

Poros was already settled in the Early Bronze Age, and also saw a Late Mycenaean occupation. In historical times, its main cult was of Poseidon, and the island was the focus of the Calaurian League, an association of seven cities which included Athens, Aegina, Epidaurus and the nearby city of Troezen, to whose territory the island belonged.

The island's prosperity grew in the 17th century. In 1828, plenipotentiaries from France, Russia and Britain met on Poros to settle the terms of the new Kingdom of Greece. Three years later, the islanders adopted a stance of open hostility to the government of Capodistrias and established a Constitutional Committee. The Battle of Poros was the result (*see box overleaf*).

Sea-level changes and seismic activity have altered the geography of Poros. The island consists of two parts: the small, volcanic island of Sphaireía in the south is linked today by a swampy isthmus to the northern mountainous body of the island which the ancients called Calauria (modern Kalavreía).

THE BATTLE OF POROS

Links between Hydra and Poros were strong since both islands had prospered through their merchant fleets, which had operated in virtual autonomy under the Ottomans. Hydra used the more sheltered port of Poros extensively for its fleet. In the aftermath of the Battle of Navarino (October 1827), where the Ottoman fleet had been defeated by the combined forces of the Russians, French and British, a split had occurred between those Greeks who saw greater freedom and safety in British protection (Hydra and Poros) and the mostly mainland Greeks under Capodistrias, who favoured the protection of Orthodox Russia. Wealthy Hydra and its ally Poros saw their historic independence under threat; Capodistrias, governor of independent Greece, realised that Hydra had somehow to be neutralised.

In the summer of 1831 the small Greek navy—less than a dozen large vessels—lay in the port of Poros. Capodistrias had given orders to blockade Hydra and restore control of the waters. Hydra dispatched the veteran admiral, Andreas Miaoulis to counter-attack. On 14th July 1831, his Hydriot forces took the fleet. Capodistrias sought Russian assistance, and open hostilities broke out in late July, when the Russian admiral Richord and a detachment of Greek army regulars under Colonel Kallergis took Poros and sank one of the vessels in rebel hands. On 1st August Miaoulis, rather than handing the ships over to the Russians, detonated and sank both the corvette *Hydra* and the flagship of the fleet, the *Hellas*, then slipped through Russian lines unnoticed, returning to Hydra. In the mayhem that ensued, Poros was looted and plundered by Kallergis's men.

POROS TOWN

The elegant town of Poros is predominantly Neoclassical in style. It cascades down a steep hillside, punctuated in the centre by the clock-tower of 1927. The older houses are built in unplastered stone, exemplified by the early 19th-century Deimezis Mansion, overlooking the waterfront from a rock scarp. Many of the houses along the promenade are of a later 19th-century style, more explicitly Classicist, such as the Syngrou school building (opposite the Galatás ferry quay). Though similar in concept to one another, these houses vary enormously in detail.

Behind and above the waterfront is the **oldest part of town**, a network of narrow streets dominated by the island's principal church of Ághios Geórgios. In the square behind the church is the large, communal water-fountain and cistern (1880); on its southern side a Neoclassical shop is preserved both inside and out. At the summit of the town, 100m east of the clock-tower, is the 17th-century chapel of Ághios Ioánnis Pródromos, one of the oldest in the island.

The long **waterfront** is punctuated with small squares: the Dimarcheíon square still preserves its fine marble water-fountain. Further east is Plateía Koryzí, with the **Poros Archaeological Museum** (*open daily except Mon, 8.30–3*). The ground floor has a collection of grave stelae of various periods interspersed with a number of unusual items, including a fine Archaic relief of a hunting dog and a case with fragments of architectural elements from the Archaic temples of Aphrodite at Troezen (on the mainland; *see box below*) and of Poseidon at Calauria, preserving their vivid painted decoration. Upstairs are small finds from the area and some Mycenaean gold jewellery.

TROEZEN: THE LEGEND & THE TEMPLE

Troezen, a small, independent city-state and member of the Calaurian League (*see p. 33*), was said to be the birthplace of Theseus, the hero of Athens who slew the Cretan minotaur. When Theseus' wife Phaedra conceived a passion for her stepson Hippolytus, the youth rejected her advances, and in revenge Phaedra is said to have accused Hippolytus of rape. In his rage, Theseus called upon Poseidon, who sent a sea monster to frighten Hippolytus' horses, causing them to bolt and drag Hippolytus to his death. Remains of the city are scanty, but the deserted Palaiá Episkopí, or bishop's palace, may occupy the site of the Temple of Aphrodite Kataskopia ('Peeping Aphrodite'). Pausanias records such a temple built on the spot where the amorous Phaedra used to watch Hippolytus at his exercises.

AROUND THE ISLAND

The main road north from Poros Town leads past buildings of the former Greek naval headquarters, based here until 1878. The **Progymnastírion**, a large Neoclassical building between road and shore, originally designed as a summer residence for King Otto, is now a naval training centre.

After crossing the bridge over the artificial canal separating Sphaireía and Kalavreía, the road branches. The left branch leads to **Megálo Neório** (where there are pleasant sandy coves), passing below a russet-red Neoclassical mansion, the Villa Galini, and then by a Modernist hotel (Hotel Poros Image; *www.porosimage.gr*), constructed in 1967 by one of Greece's best-known post-war architects, Aris Konstantinidis, before reaching the 1834 **provisioning station for the Russian Navy**, consisting of two blocks: offices and quarters near the shore, and store-houses and barracks behind. The Russian Navy maintained a presence in the area until 1917.

The right branch by the canal follows the south coast east through the pleasant resort of Askéli to the 18th-century monastery of the **Zoödóchos Pigí** (*open daily 7–1.30 & 4.30–sunset*). In front of the west door of the katholikon are several gravestones to members of the Hydriot naval families, Miaoulis and Tombazis. Inside is a magnificent 17th-century wooden iconostasis.

From the junction 1km west of the monastery the road climbs through pine forests into the interior of the island. At 10km, a dirt road leads to the attractive inlet of **Vaghioniá**, where a submerged settlement is visible under the water. Due east, at the coast, is Kávo Vasíli (**Kokoréli**), a substantial Early Helladic (3rd millennium BC) settlement with the well-preserved bases of houses.

THE SANCTUARY OF POSEIDON

In the centre of the island, on a saddle between two hills with ample views, is the Sanctuary of Poseidon (*always open*). The site is beautiful, but its remains are scant.

The precinct was built on the site of a sanctuary dating back to Late Mycenaean times (11th century BC). Cult began again in the 8th century BC; by the 7th century the sanctuary became the centre of the Calaurian League (*see p. 33*). The Temple of Poseidon and the precinct walls were built at the end of the 6th century BC; its area was enlarged to the present extent in the late 4th and 3rd centuries BC. The sanctuary provided asylum: it functioned as a place of inviolable refuge for suppliants, the most famous of whom was the orator Demosthenes, who sought sanctuary here from Macedonian pursuit in 322 BC.

Layout of the site

As you stand at the entrance gate, with the sea ahead to the north, the area of the sanctuary extends to your right, with the site of the temple of Poseidon itself marked by a stand of pines in the top right-hand corner. Behind where you are standing and up the slope of the hill to your left was the ancient city of Calauria. A spring (now dry), which may have fed the town and sanctuary, can be made out, low down on the slope just above the modern road to the left. The city has not been archaeologically explored; the only part of it which has been partially excavated is to the left and ahead within the enclosure, where the remains of an important public building have been identified. The most recent excavations are under the metal roofing, immediately in front of you to the right.

A visit to the site

Ahead and to the left from the entrance is the area believed to correspond to the **agorá** of the city of Calauria; it is bounded (back left, beyond the olive trees) by a 4th-century BC **stoa** with slightly protruding wings at either end. Near its right end are many pedestals for honorific statues. Ahead and to the right of the entrance is the sanctuary itself, defined to the south by a 6th-century BC **peribolos**, obscured by a triangular building (**Building D**) placed against its south side in the 4th century BC. This structure is divided into rooms and may have functioned as a hestiatorion. The precinct was entered from a point 30m ahead of the entrance, where the rectangular **base of a propylon** (4th-century BC) is visible; placed against its inner wall is a semicircular exedra. East of the propylon was a large trapezoidal piazza, bounded to left and right by pairs of long Doric stoas. At the northern end of the area stood the **Temple of Poseidon**, built c.

520–510 BC , a Doric peripteral structure in limestone, with 6 by 12 columns. Nothing remains of its superstructure, but the foundations are visible. The surrounding, inner peribolos in rough stone, with two entrances, can be seen clearly.

PRACTICAL INFORMATION

GETTING AROUND

Poros is well connected to Piraeus, Hydra and Spétses by fast services in the summer, with typically three connections per day by hydrofoil, three by fast catamaran, and two by larger ferry. Between mid-Oct and Easter the service reduces significantly. The car and passenger ferry from Galatás on the mainland makes the 5-min crossing every 30mins, offering the opportunity for an excursion to ancient Troezen (*see box below*).

WHERE TO STAY

Hotel Dionysos (*T: 22980 23511*) on the waterfront is a simple, dignified, traditional

guesthouse in a mansion of 1826. The **Hotel Roloï** ■ (*T: 22980 25808; www.storoloi-poros. gr*) offers beautifully-appointed apartments for longer stays and is situated in the oldest part of the town above the harbour-front.

WHERE TO EAT

In the upper part of Poros Town, **Taverna Platanos**, near the church of Ághios Geór-gios, set back under a pergola, combines a peaceful setting with good traditional Greek food.

SALAMIS

Salamis (in modern Greek Salamína) is inseparably linked with the naval battle in the autumn of 480 BC, in which a fractious alliance of Greek city-states defeated Xerxes, King of Persia—a victory whose far-reaching significance even they could not fully comprehend. Today, the island, overlooked by the most industrialised stretch of the mainland coast, has essentially become a suburb of Athens. Fortunately, Salamis is large enough to have preserved some corners of tranquillity—even beauty—as well as a number of interesting archaeological sites and churches. It is probably best visited as a day excursion from Athens.

HISTORY OF SALAMIS

Salamis was first settled in the 4th millennium BC (Neolithic), when it may still have been connected to the mainland near Mégara. It had several Bronze Age settlements and an important Mycenaean urban centre. It appears to have had wide-ranging commercial connections, reaching its zenith in the 13th century BC, though by 1150 BC it was destroyed and deserted.

In historic times the island first belonged to Mégara; but its control became the object of dispute between Mégara and Athens in the 6th century BC. It was annexed to Attica as a cleruchy by Peisistratus in the late 6th century BC. At that time the capital was moved to the east coast. In the late summer of 480 BC, the Athenians evacuated their city in the face of Xerxes' advance and made Salamis their base, trusting to the 'wooden walls' of their ships, as the Delphic Oracle had advised them. The battle fought in the straits between the east coast of the island and the Attic mainland was the most significant naval victory of early Greek history. The island later remained in Athenian hands through the 5th and 4th centuries BC, until it surrendered to the Macedonian commander Cassander in 318 BC. It was restored to Athens again in c. 230 BC. The Aianteia, a cult festival in honour of Ajax, continued to be celebrated on the island into the Roman period. There appears to have been intermittent habitation in Byzantine times, but there is a lack of historical information on this and subsequent periods.

THE EAST OF THE ISLAND

Ferries land in the harbour of **Paloúkia** on the east side of the island. Paloúkia blends seamlessly across a shallow saddle with the town of **Salamína** (formerly Kouloúri), which in turn is contiguous with **Ághios Nikólaos**; all are suburban in character. The centre of morning activity is the fish-market in a custom-built structure on the north promenade. About 800m further west along the waterfront is the large church of Ághios Nikólaos; to its west is the small Archaeological Museum with Mycenaean artefacts found on the island, Classical and Hellenistic pottery from Ambelákia, and several carved grave stelae (*at the time of writing the museum was in the process of relocating to three rooms in the former First Capodistrian Public School of Salamína*). Many important finds from Salamis are displayed in the Archaeological Museum in Piraeus.

Ambelákia and ancient Salamis

The ancient city of Salamis lay 1km south of Paloúkia, beneath the modern settlement of Ambelákia, reached by taking the coast road south from the port. The city overlooked a deep bay formed by the peninsula of Poúnda to the north, and the long, straight projection of land called the Kynósoura ('dog tail') to the south. In the northwest corner the bay can be seen the partially submerged moles of the **ancient harbour**. On the southern slope of Poúnda, a section of the ancient **fortification wall**, made in mud-brick on stone, can be seen underneath a protective roof.

On the south side of the bay, as the road climbs over a low ridge, a left turn leads down the long Kynósoura peninsula, stretching over 2km out into the strait towards the Attic coast. On its north side, 1km along the headland beside the entrance to a large shipyard, is the ancient polyandrion or **grave-mound** of the Greeks who fell at the Battle of Salamis. Beyond is the islet of Psyttáleia, where the Athenians defeated a Persian infantry force during the marine battle. It now boasts Europe's largest sewage treatment plant.

South of Kynósoura is **Selínia Bay**, with a number of attractive early 20th-century Neoclassical villas.

THE BATTLE OF SALAMIS

The famous naval battle was fought in late September 480 BC, between the forces of Xerxes I and an alliance of Greek city-states, led by Sparta and Athens. Xerxes hoped to avenge the Persian defeat at the Battle of Marathon ten years before. Our primary sources for the battle are two: Herodotus (*Histories, VIII*), and Aeschylus (*The Persians*). Herodotus' account is vivid and anecdotal but short on detail. Aeschylus' dramatic version was first performed in 472 BC. Since he and most of his audience were present at the battle, we must assume his information to be accurate.

The Persian strategy: Xerxes placed his faith in numerical superiority. That superiority remained intact on land, but his naval advantage had been considerably eroded by severe losses at the Battle of Cape Artemision (*see p. 604*) in August. Though his fleet still numbered about 600 ships (twice as many as the Greeks could muster), time was against him: summer was turning to autumn and he needed to get his men and ships back to the Hellespont before the adverse winds set in. He could not delay for long, and the Greeks knew it.

The Greek strategy: Themistocles, the chief strategist of Athens, knew that a confrontation of land forces would be doomed. At sea the situation was slightly better, but since the Persians were still numerically superior, it was essential that any confrontation happened in a confined space, to make large numbers cumbersome rather than powerful. The straits of Salamis were ideal. But two problems remained: how to draw Xerxes into the narrows in the first place, and how to keep the tenuous alliance of Greeks together. The solution was to act fast. Themistocles knew that Xerxes was aware of dissent in the Greek camp. According to Herodotus, he sent a secret message to Xerxes saying that the Greeks were preparing to flee, and that if he attacked them before they left the Salamis waters, Themistocles would come to his assistance. Xerxes sailed straight into the trap.

The battle: The Greek ships were beached along the east coast from Ambelákia bay, north past the island of Ághios Geórgios, and beyond. The Persian ships grouped at the south and east of the entrance to the straits, around the island of Psyttáleia. A squadron of Egyptian ships was dispatched to circle the island and seal the western end of the straits. Under cover of darkness, Persian infantry troops were landed on Psyttáleia. According to Herodotus, Xerxes then took up a position on a throne to watch the action, on the site of modern Pérama. The Persians hoped to surprise the Greeks at dawn, but Themistocles had received news of the manoeuvres and his ships took to the water at first light. Again according to Herodotus, a squadron of Corinthian ships made a feint to the north, as if they were indeed fleeing. This drew the Persian ships deeper into the channel. As they entered, the 50 ships of Aegina and Mégara, hidden in the bay of Ambelákia, attacked them in the flank and rear. The confined space meant that the Persians had great difficulty in responding, especially as the pressure of reinforcements were entering the straits from behind. As Themistocles had wished, a large part of the Persian fleet was rendered superfluous, because it was unable to reach the theatre of action.

The battle lasted the whole day. In the late morning a wind blowing from the north increased the disarray of the crammed Persian forces, as they were pushed back on themselves, inflicting almost as much damage to their own vessels as the enemy did by advancing on them. The wind-tossed water upset the aim of the Persian archers and favoured the armed hoplites of the Greeks, who boarded and fought at close quarters. Late in the day, a Greek force landed on Psyttáleia and decimated the Persian infantry.

The consequences: The battles of Salamis and Plataea (its similarly decisive, but slightly later, counterpart on land) were seen by subsequent generations of Greeks as one of the high points of Greek history, marking as they did the decisive defeat of the Persian invasion at the hands of a unified Greek force. The inconvenient fact that many Greeks had in fact sided with the Persians was often overlooked. Useful as this collective memory was for anyone seeking to rally Greek unity in the face of other enemies, a more immediate consequence was the prestige that it bestowed on the Athenians. Athens had provided the most warships for the battle, and she went on to lead the effort to free the Greeks in the islands and western Asia Minor from Persian rule. Success in these endeavours made her the equal of Sparta, and led directly to the Peloponnesian War.

THE NORTH OF THE ISLAND

The main monument in the north of the island is the **Monastery of the Panaghía Phaneroméni** (1661; now a nunnery). Various spolia indicate the presence of earlier churches. The exterior is influenced by Western architecture but the painted interior is Byzantine (1735). The chapel of Ághios Nikólaos immediately to the south contains the tomb of Hosios Lavrentios, the founder of the monastery. On the shore below the monastery is the **solitary house of Angelos Sikelianos** (1884–1951), a popular lyric poet and playwright, and friend of the author Nikos Kazantzakis, who revived the Delphic Festival at Delphi in 1927, in an attempt to reunite modern Greek culture with its ancient roots. The house, recently restored, was his last home.

One and a half kilometres west of the Phaneroméni, on a hill south from the ferry-crossing to Néa Péramos, an ancient enclosure wall has been identified as belonging to the **fort of Boúdoron**, an Athenian stronghold during the Peloponnesian War.

There are good **beaches** where you can swim in the protected waters around Psilí Ámmos and Vasiliká Bay,

Aiántion

Aiántion lies on the south shore of the Bay of Salamis. To the west of the village centre is the 15th-century church of the Koímisis tis Theotókou; 300m west of that, at the upper extremity of the village, is the beautiful 13th-century **church of the Metamorphosis**, domed on a cross-in-square plan. It preserves 14th- and 15th-century wall-paintings, and some of its windows are still glazed with alabaster.

From here a scenic route climbs through pine forests to the monastery of **Ághios Nikólaos Limonión** (*open daily sunrise–sunset except between 1 and 4pm*). The door to its 18th-century katholikon is flanked by 12th-century templon panels. Above it is a fragment from a 4th-century BC funerary stele with a banquet scene and a sacrifice at an altar.

Kanákia

On the south side of Kanákia Bay, in the extreme southwest, archaeologists are excavating a Mycenaean centre, perhaps to be identified as the seat Ajax, hero of the Trojan War, who, according to Sophocles, dies in Troy by his own hand after the shield of Achilles is awarded to Odysseus. The excavation is along the ridge of a slope rising south of the valley behind the shore (*turn left at the waterfront, continue south along the shore; then turn left again into the pine trees before reaching the small harbour. The site is on the summit to the left as you walk inland to meet the path leading up*). The citadel and settlement, which grew into the island's principal urban centre, was continuously inhabited through the Middle and Late Bronze Age, but abandoned in the first half of the 12th century BC. It features several buildings on a megaron plan, typical of Mycenaean palaces.

Peristéria

At the southern extremity of the island, with its attractive beaches and inlets, is the bay of Peristéria. From a point shortly before its western end, a track leads inland to the so-called **Cave of Euripides** (*the track soon becomes a steep path through pines and thorn bushes; the climb takes 20mins; torch essential*). The path passes the foundations of two small shrines, perhaps related to a Hellenistic cult of Euripides and Dionysus. The cave is a short distance above, entered by a long (c. 70m), low, serpentine passageway (not for the faint-hearted). It opens eventually into a broad, low-roofed chamber, forested with thick stalagmites and stalactites. The cave was used in the Neolithic (5th millennium BC), and later as a Mycenaean burial place. Its identification with Euripides is based on a tradition that the tragedian—who may have been a native of Salamis—used it as a place of retreat. A cup bearing his name was found here, but is of 2nd-century AD date, perhaps indicating a later cult of the poet at the site.

At the western end of the bay of Peristéria, the road continues to the village of **Kolónes**. On the summit of the promontory to its west is an unusual circular funerary structure of late Classical date; in the interior are three sarcophagi sunk into the ground, still *in situ*.

PRACTICAL INFORMATION

GETTING AROUND

The port of Paloúkia is served by a frequent ferry (15mins) from Pérama, 8km northeast of Piraeus, throughout day and night. Another service links it with Piraeus between 6am and 5pm. The west of the island is linked by ferry to Néa Péramos, near the Athens–Corinth motorway. Car rental is not available on Salamis.

WHERE TO STAY

Salamis has only three, strictly utilitarian hotels. The nicest is **Hotel Votsalakia** (*T: 210 4671344*) on the waterfront at Selínia. It has its own taverna.

WHERE TO EAT

There is no shortage of good, simple tavernas: a wide variety of dishes is offered by **To**

Pirofani on the promenade from Salamína towards Ághios Nikólaos. Further east, in Ághios Nikólaos itself, the **Christos Taverna** serves good fresh fish. The **taverna of the Hotel Votsalakia** in Selínia is also to be recommended, as is the small **fish taverna in Peristéria Bay**.

FURTHER READING

The Classical sources for the Battle of Salamis are Aeschylus, *The Persians*; Herodotus, *Histories, VIII, 40*; Plutarch, *Life of Themistocles, 9*. A more recent evaluation of the conflict is Barry Strauss's *The Battle of Salamis: The Naval Encounter That Saved Greece—and Western Civilization*.

SPETSES

In summer, Spétses (*map p. 11*) is dominated by the yachts that frequent its waters, attracted by the plutocratic estates along the island's eastern shore. Much beauty and interest lies in the 18th- and 19th-century mansions of the town; Spétses was an affluent and active contributor to the Greek War of Independence, which it joined early. Its once beautiful, forested landscape was devastated by forest fires in recent decades.

HISTORY OF SPETSES

The Italians gave the island the name Spezia or Spezie ('Spiced'), probably in reference to its pungent pine- and herb-scented air. The recorded history of Spétses is confined mostly to the last 300 years; but archaeologists have revealed a flourishing Early Helladic settlement of the mid-3rd millennium BC, as well as Mycenaean occupation. In historical antiquity the island is mentioned as Pityoussa, meaning 'abundant in pines'. It was probably inhabited until the 9th century (AD) and resettled in the 15th. The island was settled on a larger scale during the 17th century by refugees from Turkish rule on the mainland. The abundance of wood both on the island and on the nearby mainland led to a flourishing boat-building industry. By the turn of the 19th century, the island's population was c. 18,000, and it possessed a large merchant fleet. In the Greek War of Independence, the first open call to arms in any island was from Spétses, on 3rd April 1821. Spétses, together with Hydra and Psará gave the uprising an all-important navy. A number of prominent naval commanders have been from Spétses, as well as Greece's best-known heroine, Laskarina Bouboulina, who led her own ships in the siege of Náfplion in 1822. After the war, the arrival of steam-ships sidelined Spétses and its fleet and the island's economy languished. At the beginning of the 20th century, a Spetsiot tobacco magnate, Sotirios Anargyros, returned to the island from America and put his wealth into many projects—afforestation, roads, aqueducts, an international hotel—laying the foundations for the tourist industry which sustains the island today.

THE TOWN

Spétses Town has developed from the 15th century onwards as a swelling amalgamation of several separate centres. Over time, its focus moved from the Kastélli hill, overlooking the ferry-port, down to the shore and then along it to the east. resulting in a sprawling settlement covering the whole northeast corner of the island. It has no clearly defined centre, but is filled with early 19th-century *archontiká* of relative simplicity, along with later elaborate Neoclassical mansions.

The Dápia and the House of Bouboulina

All the boats dock close to the harbour of the **Dápia** (from the Turkish word for a bastion), about halfway along the waterfront. At the landward end of the harbour mole, stands the so-called Chancellery, the 19th-century former town hall. The front at the Dápia is fortified, and some of its cannon emplacements remain. Overlooking the area is the stern statue of the island's heroine, Laskarina Bouboulina (*see box below*).

The **House of Bouboulina** (c. 1700), now a museum, stands just across the street from the southwest corner of the Dápia (*open daily 25 March–31 Oct; visits by guided tour only, in English or Greek, times advertised at the entrance*). It is still used by her descendants. Originally a small rural manor, it belonged to Bouboulina's second husband, Dimitrios Bouboulis. The main reception rooms on the upper floor give onto an arcaded loggia. The most ornate element is the magnificent wooden ceiling in the main room, of Florentine workmanship and Balkan-Ottoman design. Most of the furniture was French or Italian. The upstairs rooms contain memorabilia: Bouboulina's pistol, the Ottoman license for her ship, *Agamemnon*, and a headscarf she customarily wore.

Laskarina Bouboulina 1771–1825

The self-appointed commander of her own squadron of warships, the only female member of the Philikí Etaireía (the secret society of mainly expatriate Greeks who prepared Greece for its revolution), and the only Greek to be posthumously honoured with the rank of Admiral in the Russian navy, Laskarina Bouboulina is one of the most remarkable figures of the Greek Independence struggle. She was born of Hydriot parents in Constantinople, during the imprisonment of her father there for his part in the first Russo-Turkish war. After his death she grew up with her mother, on Hydra and Spétses. By the age of forty she had been married and widowed twice; she was left with seven children and a considerable inheritance from her two husbands. Although threatened with confiscation by the Turks, this was released after her appeals in person both to the Russian Ambassador at the Ottoman Court and to the mother of Sultan Mahmud II. In the capital she cultivated contacts with the Philikí Etaireía, purchased arms and ammunition, and completed the construction of her warship, the *Agamemnon*, by bribing Turkish officials to ignore the fact that it exceeded the permitted dimensions and flouted restrictions on armaments. She is said to have preceded the official declaration of war by raising and saluting her own revolutionary flag as early as 13th March 1821. In action, she and her vessels distinguished themselves against heavy odds; she also participated, together with her son, at the Siege of Tripolis (Peloponnese), where she saved the women of the harem from the slaughter and reprisals that followed the fall of the city. Three years later, however, her opposition to the imprisonment of Theodoros Kolokotronis earned her the displeasure of the new Greek government, and she returned to Spétses rather than be imprisoned herself. She was shot in May 1825, in a family feud.

The buildings of Sotirios Anargyros

To the rear of the Dápia is a small, attractively cobbled square with the church of Ághios Antónios. At the far left corner is a bronze statue to one of the island's most important benefactors, Sotirios Anargyros (*see History, above*). His house, the **Anargyros Mansion** (1904), is directly across the street. It is a curious hybrid in high Neoclassical style, with Egyptianising details.

The second of the Anárgyros projects was the **Poseidonion Hotel**, on the waterfront just northwest of the Dápia. In style, it is a northern European spa hotel transferred to the Aegean. In the 1920s, it was the most important seasonal hotel in the Balkans. To the west it another luxury hotel, Nissia, occupies a former textile factory, built in 1920. The shore beyond is fronted by simple dignified houses, interspersed with *archontiká*: the building of the current Dimarcheíon; the Economou Mansion (1851); and, in a walled enclosure further west, the Altamura Mansion.

At this point the area has ceased to be the municipality of Spétses and has become Kounoupítsa. Behind the high wall to the left of the road as it continues west is the last of the great philanthropic projects of Sotirios Anargyros, the **Anargýrios and Koryialénios School of Spétses**, completed in 1927 in a Rationalist architectural style, typical of its time. It was not intended as a school for Spetsiots, but for the wider Greek world, based on the model of Eton and Harrow and aimed at creating an educated mercantile and professional class. The concept was grand, with facilities including an observatory and an open-air theatre. When it opened in 1927, it had four students. In 1952–53 the novelist John Fowles taught there: his experiences underpinned his novel *The Magus*. The school closed in 1983. The buildings are now used for international congresses and residential courses.

East from the Dápia to the Old Harbour

Immediately east and one block in from the harbour mole is the unimpressive Plateía Rologioú ('Clock Square'), with the fish-market on its north side, overlooked by a clock-tower (1915). Uphill from the south exit of the square is the **Museum of Spétses** in the Hadji-Yannis Mexis Mansion, five blocks inland from the shore (*open daily except Mon, 8.30–2.30*). The imposing building dates from 1795–98 and has a fine arcaded loggia. In the centre of the courtyard is the bust of Hadji-Yannis Mexis (1756–1844). As a respected elder of the island, he had been named Nazir of Spétses by the sultan in 1817. In 1821 he put his personal wealth and energies behind the Greek naval insurrection.

The museum occupies the upper floor of the building, which were mostly the women's quarters and guests' rooms. Room I has maritime memorabilia including ships' portraits and figureheads. In Room II is archaeological material from the island and elsewhere, including a fine 4th-century BC circular marble offering-table. Rooms III, IV and V are dedicated to ecclesiastical material, textiles, furniture and ceramics, among them an unusual carved wooden icon of the prophet Elijah (Room III) and the **mortal remains of Laskarina Bouboulina** in a casket (Room IV). On the wall is the revolutionary flag of Spétses, a Greek cross surmounting an upturned crescent moon, symbolising a subjugated Turkey. A separate room displays the finds from the Point Íria wreck, a 12th-century BC cargo vessel excavated in the 1990s, one of the oldest shipwrecks known.

Further east along the shore is a small promontory marked by the church of Ághios Mámas. On the shoreline between it and the next promontory are a number of the finer stone houses of Spétses. They frame the compound of the **Monastery of Ághios Nikólaos**, the island's cathedral, set back above the next promontory to the east, with seaward cannon emplacements. On the esplanade outside, the uprising of Spétses was proclaimed on 3rd April 1821. Written sources for the foundation of the monastery are lacking, but it must date from c. 1700: the present complex is from a hundred years later. The katholikon incorporates an unfinished fragment of late Roman decorative frieze above the west door. The interior is covered with recent paintings and possesses a fine wooden iconostasis of c. 1805.

Beyond the promontory of Ághios Nikólaos is the deep **bay of Baltíza**, the Palaió Limáni ('Old Harbour') of Spétses, where its boatyards were—and are—located. Every year on 8th September there is a magnificent celebration here of an 1822 victory against the Turks, in which a vessel laden with fireworks, representing the Turkish flagship, blazes on the water.

Inland of the shore

Some of the town's older churches can be seen by following Odós Bótasi, which leads uphill from the left-hand side of the Anargyros Mansion, behind the Dápia. Descending to the right just beyond the three-apsed church of Ághios Geórgios, crossing a bridge below, and climbing again for 150m to the south, one reaches the church of the **Koímisis tis Theotókou** (*generally open around 4pm for cleaning; otherwise key in house across the dip to the south*). The exterior was decorated with inset ceramic dishes as trophies; those around the apse remain. The descent towards the coast passes the church of the Taxiárches to the left and the large church of the Aghía Triáda (1793) to the right.

AGHII PANDES & AROUND THE ISLAND

Ághii Pándes (*a 20-min walk to the south of the town, reached by continuing uphill from the museum*) is a peaceful 19th-century convent of nuns, with a delightful view overlooking the town and the south and east coasts. Visible below on the coast is the small church of **Aghía Marína**, reached by following the main road south out of town and turning left just at the edge of habitation. It stands on a small projection of land with bays to either side. There was a substantial settlement of the mid-3rd millennium BC here, as well as later Mycenaean habitation. South of Aghía Marína, the coast road passes a number of large estates owned by members of some of the wealthiest and most important Greek shipping families.

Spetsópoula (ancient Aristera), the pine-forested island to the east, was purchased in 1962 by Stavros Niarchos. In summer, the waters are filled with conspicuous yachts.

PRACTICAL INFORMATION

GETTING AROUND

In addition to an (all-weather) car and passenger ferry running daily from Piraeus to Spétses in summer, and five times weekly in winter, Spétses has typically three connections per day by hydrofoil and three by fast catamaran, via Poros, Hydra and Ermióni, and on to Pórto Chéli (less frequent in winter). The 15-min crossing from Kósta on the mainland is made by car-ferry four times daily. Private cars belonging to non-residents are not allowed on Spétses. Water taxis from the port will take visitors to a variety of sandy bays around the island.

WHERE TO STAY

On the seafront is the **Archontiko Economou**, providing all comforts in a restored, traditional Spetsiot house of 1851 (*T: 22980 73400; www.spetsesyc.gr/economoumansion. htm*). Simple but comfortable accommodation (medium price) is offered at the **Hotel Roumani** at Dápia (*T: 22980 72244; www. hotelroumani.gr*).

WHERE TO EAT

Two traditional tavernas stand out; the fish taverna **Patralis**, at the western end of Spétses Town in Kounoupítsa, with good service and delicious fish dishes, amongst which is the typical *psari à la spetsiota* (baked with lemon, tomato and breadcrumbs). On Bótasi, 200m from the Anargyros Mansion, **Lazaros Taverna**, behind the church of Ághios Geórgios, is one of the few traditional neighbourhood tavernas surviving in town.

Fresh goat's-milk yoghurt and a variety of natural products can be bought at **Mandragoras** store, close to the clock-tower. The cafés on the waterfront of Dápia are a good place to observe the *volta*, the traditional evening promenade.

THE CYCLADES

The Cyclades have been identified as a distinct group of islands since antiquity; their name is derived from the idealised notion that they form a circle (*kyklos*) around the sacred island of Delos, in what the poet Callimachus likened to a dance. The islands occupy the centre of the Aegean, stretching nearly 200km from Andros in the north to Anáphi in the south; or, looked at another way, for 150km from Milos in the west to Amorgós in the east. The group includes over 220 islands, of which 24 are inhabited. Some of the larger islands have airports and the region is criss-crossed by a dense network of ferry routes, connecting them with Piraeus and Rafína near Athens, but also with the Eastern Aegean, the Dodecanese and Crete.

More than any other set of islands, the Cyclades are central: not just geographically, but also to the perception of Greece, ancient and modern, internal and external. Their 'typical Greek' landscapes, with vistas of island-studded azure seas and picturesque villages of whitewashed cuboid houses and churches crowned by blue domes, have become as iconic an image of Greece as the Parthenon, infinitely reproduced on book covers (including this one), posters and in Greek restaurants all over the world. Such imagery, albeit a cliché, is not untrue; but it tends to conceal a far less uniform—and far more interesting—reality.

The Cyclades are superlative in their diversity. In number, they dwarf all other island groupings, and include an enormous variety of geologies (ranging from the bizarre products of the Aegean volcanic arc to the fine limestones created by aeon-old seabeds), of geographies (from islands located on ever-busy shipping lanes to ones isolated and exposed), of topographies (from steep rugged mountains to fertile plains) and of landscapes (from seemingly primeval wilderness to areas marked by millennia of cultivation), which have given rise to varied histories and traditions.

Early development

The Cyclades' wealth of resources—obsidian, metal ores, marble and rare minerals—as well as access to major trade routes, rich fishing grounds and, in places, to arable land, has attracted much activity throughout the ages.

The islands received at least occasional visits by humans from the Palaeolithic, but were settled more substantially in the Middle and Late Neolithic. By the Early Bronze Age, they developed what is now known as Cycladic Culture, producing the striking marble figurines that have become one of the dominant images of prehistoric creativity. These have been found in the numerous Bronze Age settlements and cemeteries across the islands, accompanied by beautiful vessels of stone or clay, including the enigmatic 'frying pans' (*for more on Bronze Age Cycladic art, see pp. 53–54*).

By the Middle Bronze Age, the Cyclades were subject to major influence (and perhaps settlement) from Minoan Crete. The Bronze Age eruption of Santorini around 1600 BC (*see p. 164*) led to the destruction of Akrotiri, an astonishingly rich, complex and well-connected Bronze Age city, one of several in the islands. The Minoan influence, also evident in the mid-2nd millennium BC settlements of Phylakopí on Milos and Aghía Eiríni on Kea, was later superseded by that of the Mycenaeans of mainland Greece.

In the early 1st millennium BC, the islands were, according to tradition, affected by the same migrations as the mainland, leading to an Ionian colonisation of the central and northern Cyclades, while the southern edge of the group, from Milos to Anáphi, accommodated Dorian settlers. Some of the Cyclades, such as Tinos and Siphnos, already flourished during Geometric times. The Archaic period saw more intense growth, with the development of about 30 separate *poleis*, or city-states, throughout the Cyclades. In most cases, an island contained a single *polis*, the exceptions being Amorgós, with three, and Kea, with four. The large and resource-rich islands of Paros and Naxos became especially affluent, playing a major role in the development of Archaic art and even founding colonies of their own, as did Santorini. At the same time, Kea underwent a phase of cultural bloom, and Delos grew into one of the most important religious centres in the Greek world. Siphnos enjoyed immense wealth for part of the 6th century, until its silver mines were exhausted.

After the Persian Wars, during which some of the islands had accepted 'barbarian' rule (although many ended up fighting on the Greek side at Salamis), most of the Cyclades joined the Delian League. Nonetheless, Naxos unsuccessfully rebelled in 473–472 BC, Santorini remained outside the League, and Milos famously resisted Athenian pressure to join until the massacre or enslavement of its entire population in 413 BC. During the Hellenistic period the islands mostly passed under Macedonian dominance and some of the *poleis* continued to thrive. Under Roman rule, most of the Cyclades were a mere backwater, occasionally used as places of exile, although Delos flourished as a major trading centre until the 1st century BC, as did Milos in the early centuries AD. Christianity had reached the islands by the 3rd century.

Later history

The Late Roman and Byzantine periods saw great instability in the region, as the power vacuum left behind by the Roman Empire caused a loss of security, leading to frequent pirate raids and a major drop in population. Only Naxos, with its large and secure interior, continued to thrive. In the aftermath of the Fourth Crusade, the Cyclades fell to the Venetian adventurer Marco Sanudo (*see p. 130*), who in 1207 founded the Duchy of the Archipelago, ruled from Naxos by him and his descendants, while certain islands were leased as fiefs to other Venetian families. Some of the islands were temporarily reconquered by Byzantium in the late 13th century. In 1383, the Sanudos lost power to the Crispi family, ending a period of relative stability. The Venetian period has left a marked influence in many of the Cyclades, including the continuing presence of Roman Catholic communities.

Most of the Cyclades were raided by Kheir ed-Din Barbarossa, the famous Turkish corsair, in the 1530s; the majority fell to the Ottomans in 1537 and 1566; but a few remained under Venetian control until 1617 (Tinos even held out until 1715). Some of the islands enjoyed partial autonomy and trading privileges under Turkish rule. In the 1770s, the Cyclades were briefly occupied by Russia. Many of the Cycladic islands participated in the Greek War of Independence; by 1835 all were part of the newly-formed Greek state.

In the 19th century, Syros and Andros in particular became important economic centres, based respectively on industry and trade. The mineral resources of Milos have been exploited by mining since the 1860s. In the difficult decades of the early and mid-20th century, the islands suffered from economic stagnation and emigration. Their intense beauty was gradually discovered: first by Greek and foreign writers and artists before the Second World War, and later by enterprising visitors seeking an untouched part of the world. These were eventually followed by travel agents and cruise operators from all over the Western world. This has led to a highly differential development, bringing some islands much wealth, but also environmental degradation and loss of traditional identity, while others have successfully maintained their local character.

Visiting the islands

Travel in the Cyclades should be planned carefully, as even adjacent islands can offer very different experiences. On many of the larger islands, the visitor has a choice between self-contained but isolated beach-side hotels offering various degrees of luxury, or simple rooms scattered throughout traditional villages and towns.

The most sustained (though not identical) forms of mass tourism have come to dominate three islands: Ios, which attracts hordes of not-so-discerning sun-and-fun-seekers each summer; Santorini (which targets cruise ships and their passengers' well-stocked wallets); and Mykonos (one of the centres of the European summer party scene and sometime gay capital of the Mediterranean). Nonetheless, each of the three still contains unique, picturesque and beautiful corners or sights. More modest levels of touristic development are found on Naxos, Paros, Milos and Andros. Some islands—usually the ones without airports—have so far escaped the more intense forms of tourism. Examples include Amorgós, far from the mainland; Anáphi, next to Santorini; or Kythnos and Kea, nearest to Athens.

Even the smaller Cycladic islands richly reward more than casual exploration, so it is advisable, depending on how much time you have, to concentrate on one alone, or to visit a smallish number in the same area, rather than attempting a general sweep. The Cyclades cannot possibly be explored in a single trip; even Athenians, only a short and inexpensive boat-trip away from the islands, tend to spend decades of holidays before claiming familiarity with the archipelago.

Many Cycladic sights have attained global fame: Santorini is renowned for its stupendous volcanic caldera, its technicolour sunsets, and the miraculously preserved Bronze Age city of Akrotiri. The dramatic cliff-top *choras*, or island capitals, of Folégandros and Amorgós are often pictured, as are the marble Portára, the surviving gateway of an Archaic temple in the harbour of Naxos, and the fine 19th-century aristocratic mansions of Andros. Delos, virtually entirely covered in ancient ruins, numbers among the most famous archaeological sites in the world, presenting the visitor with a double boon: one of the most sacred and ancient of all Greek sanctuaries, as well as the fine remains of a flourishing Hellenistic and Roman mercantile city. The Ekatontapylianí on Paros is one of the most important Byzantine churches in Greece. Greeks are also aware (respectfully) of the miracle-working icon of Tinos, object of a major pilgrimage, and (longingly) of the innumerable fine sandy beaches on Milos, perhaps the best-known subset of the thousands of Cycladic beaches, covering all gradations from coarse pebble to fine sand, and all colours between white and black.

But these star-rated attractions can easily be combined with less-trodden, more intimate and immensely memorable places scattered throughout the islands. On Kea, there are fine oak forests and a lone Archaic stone lion overlooking the sea; the churches of Kythnos contain many fine icons; Sériphos has one of the most picturesque *choras* in the islands; and the wealth of ancient Siphnos is announced to this day by its sparkling marble fortifications. The view from the highest summit on Kímolos takes in nearly all the Cyclades; and on Milos there is the most impressive Early Christian catacomb in Greece. Below the *chora* of Folégandros, a seaside cave preserves graffiti from over two millennia ago; and the church of Episkopí on Síkinos incorporates a fully-preserved Roman grave monument.

Andros is home to the excellent Goulandris Museum of Modern Greek Art; Tinos is sprinkled with exuberantly ornate dovecotes; and the attractions of Syros include not only the Bronze Age promontory fort of Kastrí, but also the melancholy charm of the decaying former industrial and commercial centre of the Cyclades, Ermoúpolis. Mykonos is host to a major collection of ancient Greek pottery; the Delos museum contains some ribald pieces of ancient art, and the cavernous marble quarries on Paros are a monument to centuries of labour.

On Naxos, unfinished Archaic sculptures are still attached to their rocks and the inland plains are scattered with painted 8th- and 9th-century churches; the Lesser Cyclades offer both intimacy and glamour; at Skárkos on Ios the streets and houses of a Bronze Age town are visible. On Amorgós, the monastery of the Chozoviótissa clings to its vertiginous cliff; in ancient Thera on Santorini, rock-carved inscriptions commemorate ancient love trysts; and on Anáphi, a whole island can be explored entirely on foot by following ancient paved tracks.

Many of the islands and their surrounding waters are also home to a rich flora and fauna. All of the Cyclades once had their own traditions of architecture, handicrafts, cuisine, dialect and song and dance. In the more remote islands, elements of this survive; in the others, folklore museums and numerous festivals give at least a glimpse of that vanishing wealth. There is no room here to list all the culinary specialities of the islands, which include the raisin wines of Santorini, chickpea croquettes from Ios, smoked pork from Kythnos, the marinaded sausages of Anáphi, the sweetened cheese pies of Tinos and the almond macaroons of Andros.   H.H.

THE CYCLADIC BRONZE AGE

Like the other groups of islands in the Aegean, the Cyclades were first settled in the Neolithic or even earlier. Settlement consolidated and grew throughout the Bronze Age. It is during the early part of this long period, here known as Early Cycladic (3100–2000 BC), that the islands played a particularly significant role, developing a civilisation that influenced developments in Crete and the mainland, areas that were later to dominate the region.

Scholarly understanding of Early Cycladic culture has improved in recent decades, but remains very fragmentary. Many of the striking works of the period are known merely as objects with no archaeological context; and among the few excavated and published sites, settlements are massively outnumbered by cemeteries. Nonetheless, it seems clear that around the turn of the 3rd millennium a network of maritime trading settlements developed in the Cyclades, and continued to flourish for many generations, subdivided by archaeologists into various cultural stages named after type sites throughout the islands: the Grotta-Pelos Culture (3100–2650 BC), its name derived from two cemetery sites on Naxos; followed by the Keros-Syros Culture (2650–2400 BC), after two islands where its remains were found; in turn followed by the Kastri Group (2400–2150 BC), named from a fortified site on Syros; and finally the Phylakopi I Culture (2150–2000 BC) at the transition to Middle Cycladic, so called on the basis of a major settlement on Milos.

The Early Cycladic culture gave rise to highly distinctive, complex and evocative artistic creations, both in clay and in marble. Among its most famous products are the marble figurines of humans, sometimes seen as the very beginning of Greek sculpture in stone and produced mostly up to 2400 BC. These figures, mostly of modest dimensions, developed from primitive origins into a highly developed, unmistakably Cycladic type, while remaining extremely stylised. They are subdivided into various chronological and regional groups; quite individualistic variations also occur. Their haunting minimalism and air of mystery make them a source of ongoing

Early Cycladic 'frying pan' from Syros, decorated with running spirals and a 'pubic triangle'. Athens, National Archaeological Museum.

fascination and they had an important influence on early 20th-century art. Unfortunately, the same qualities have led to them being highly prized by collectors: only a small proportion of the known figurines are from controlled excavations; most are the product of looting, so that reliable archaeological contexts, vital for their understanding, are rare. Their function remains mostly unclear, although recent excavations on Keros support a broadly ritual meaning or use. The majority of the figures appear to be female, and their genitals and/or breasts are often indicated. Many or all the figures were painted.

Equally well-known, and at least as enigmatic, are the so-called Cycladic 'frying pans', flat clay or stone dishes with cylindrical rims and a handle-like protrusion. Their 'back' is usually elaborately decorated with incised patterns and motifs, including spirals, wavy lines, occasional ships and female genitalia. Their meaning or functions remains a complete mystery. Other products of Early Cycladic genius include beautiful marble vessels, obsidian tools and a wide range of decorated pottery.

The islands retained a noticeably Cycladic cultural identity throughout the Bronze Age, but were increasingly overshadowed first by Minoan Crete and then by the Mycenaean mainland. Finds of the Early and Later Cycladic cultures are on display in the various museums across the islands, but especially in the National Archaeological Museum and the Goulandris Museum of Cycladic Art, both in Athens   H.H.

Early Cycladic figurine from Syros, c. 2900–2700 BC. The legs probably broke during its production, so the feet were carved at a higher than usual level. Athens, National Archaeological Museum.

SYROS

Centred on its elegant Neoclassical port, Ermoúpolis (the only true city in the Cyclades), Syros has a feel quite different from other Cycladic islands. Representing the resurgence of optimism and prosperity after hardship, Ermoúpolis is testimony to the enterprise of the Aegean islanders and to their innate genius for commerce. Outside town, the resorts of the mild southern part of the island and the dramatic panoramas of the north, with its important Bronze Age remains, provide some of the most evocative sights in the Cyclades.

HISTORY OF SYROS

Neolithic settlements (5th millennium BC) have been found in the southern half of Syros. The island's position on maritime trade routes gave rise to prosperous Early Bronze Age centres in the north, with the important sites of Kastrí and Chalandrianí.

The island has left little trace on historical antiquity. It was the birthplace, in the early 6th century BC, of Pherecydes, one of the earliest Greek philosophers. Syros was captured by Samians in the same century. It allied with the Persians during the Persian Wars, but subsequently participated in the First and Second Athenian (Delian) Leagues and minted coins (mainly during the Hellenistic period).

Throughout the Middle Ages the island was known as Souda. Following its inclusion in the Duchy of Naxos, created by Marco Sanudo (*see p. 130*) in the aftermath of the taking of Constantinople in the Fourth Crusade of 1204, a Venetian and Genoese population settled on Syros, on the hill to the northwest of the harbour, today's Ano Syros. This resulted in a Roman Catholic population, which predominated well into the 19th century and survives today as a minority. In 1633 Capuchin monks settled on the island, and in the early 18th century a Jesuit community established itself, bringing cultural links with the West. Syros had been taken in 1537 by Kheir ed-Din Barbarossa for the Ottoman sultan, but was allowed a measure of autonomy. Further privileges were accorded in 1779 when, after a short Russian occupation, Syros and Andros were given by Sultan Abdul Hamid I to his favourite niece, Sah Sultana. Syros then developed a merchant fleet and became a commercial centre, anxious to remain neutral at the outbreak of the Greek War of Independence in 1821. Its neutrality attracted refugees from other parts of the Greek world.

The 19th- and 20th-century history of Syros is marked by its absorption of large populations of refugees: in 1822 and 1824 from Chios and Psará respectively, in 1866 from Crete, and in 1923 from Asia Minor. The refugees from Chios and Psará founded the new city of Ermoúpolis, which became the premier industrial centre of Greece and the second city in importance after Athens. The city grew prosperous through commerce and shipping, and its inhabitants were Orthodox, in contrast to the Roman Catholic community in older Ano Syros. In the late 19th century, the rising importance

of the port of Piraeus and the decline in demand for wooden boats and sail-ships dealt a double blow to Ermoúpolis: it responded by moving into industrial production of leather, iron and cotton. By the 1930s, all industry had declined.

Syros was occupied by the Italians in 1941 and by the Germans from 1943; it was badly bombed in 1944. After the war it lost 20 percent of its population through emigration. After a brief closure, the shipyards re-opened in 1994. Small industries have returned, and tourism (predominantly domestic) supplements a hesitantly growing economy.

ERMOÚPOLIS & ANO SYROS

Prosperous, business-like and elegant—in parts indeed strikingly beautiful—Ermoúpolis is different from other Cycladic towns. It is the administrative capital of the Cyclades and one of the most important centres of communication and industry in the Aegean.

Although located on the site of the ancient city of Syros, Ermoúpolis was founded in the early 19th century by refugee mariners and ship-owners from Chios, who named it after Hermes, the God of trade and commerce. As viewed from the harbour, far above and behind it to the left is the medieval town of Ano Syros, a Roman Catholic neighbourhood crowned by the church of Ághios Geórgios, while along the waterfront and up the hill immediately behind extends the 19th-century city, also overlooked by a hilltop church, this time Orthodox, the Anástasi in Vrontádos. To the south of the town are the shipyards and the city's old industrial quarter. On a rise in the middle of the south shore stands the Lazareto, a former quarantine hospital, built in 1839–40.

The waterfront and main square

The harmonious Neoclassical waterfront dates from the 1820s and '30s. From the northern side of the harbour, Venizélou runs inland, crossing the market area to the city's heart, **Plateía Miaoúli** (*map p. 58, B2*), one of the most elegant and architecturally homogeneous 19th-century squares in Greece, built mainly of Cycladic marble. The square first took shape in the 1840s. Its centrepiece is a statue of the admiral and independence hero Andreas Miaoulis (*see p. 28*). On the north side is the massive Dimarcheíon (1876–89), by the German architect Ernst Ziller. Also of interest is the Hellas Club (1860s), now the library and cultural centre, its original ballroom preserved on the first floor.

West of the Dimarcheíon, a flight of steps leads to the **Archaeological Museum**, in the northwest corner of the Dimarcheíon building (*open daily except Mon, 8.30–3; free*). Especially important is the Early Bronze Age collection (Rooms II and IV), with 4th- and 3rd-millennium BC finds from Chalandrianí and Kastrí, among them figurines, metal, stone vases and pottery, including the mysterious 'frying pan' vessels (*see p. 54*). There are also Hellenistic and Roman finds, mainly sculpture, from Syros and the Cyclades (Rooms I and III).

Nisáki and Vapória

The centre of Ermoúpolis is a pleasure to explore, largely residential and dominated by fine Neoclassical architecture.

Nisáki ('Islet') is the rocky finger of land defining the eastern edge of the harbour. It offers fine views of the town, and also of Tinos and Mykonos. One of the 1830s storehouses by the port is home to the **Art Gallery of the Cyclades** (*map p. 58, C3; open 10–1 & 7–10; entrance on the east side; free*), dedicated to works by local artists.

From the Catholic Cathedral of the Annunciation (*map p. 58, C2*; 1829), Kalomenopoúlou, lined with 19th-century mansions, leads to **Vapória** ('Steamships'), its name

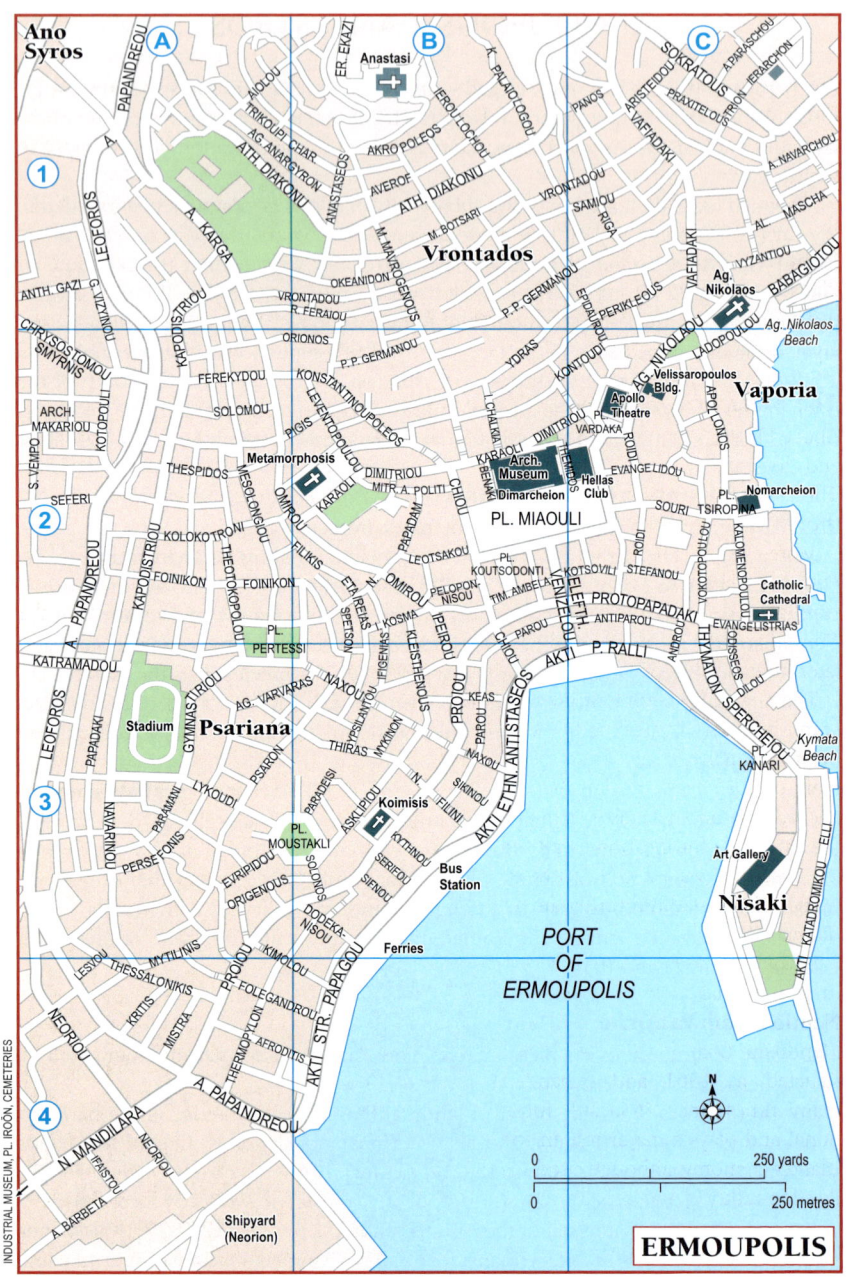

ERMOUPOLIS

a reflection of what the area's affluence was based on. Its centre is Plateía Tsiropiná, dominated by the Nomarcheíon, housed in a fine Neoclassical residence (1883–84). From here, Apóllonos, in similar grandeur, leads to the church of **Ághios Nikólaos o Ploúsios** (St Nicholas 'the Rich' or 'Magnificent', so as to differentiate it from the older church of Ághios Nikólaos o Ptochós, St Nicholas 'the Poor' in Ano Syros), begun in 1848, but constructed and decorated over the subsequent 60 years. The triple-aisled basilica with its Neoclassical façade contains an iconostasis of Pentelic marble (1871). In front of the west entrance, a small park surrounds an 1858 **monument to the Unburied Warrior** of the Greek revolution. On Aghíou Nikoláou (heading towards Plateía Miaoúli) is the impressive **Velissaropoulos Building** (1871), with fine decorative paintings inside. The **Apollo Theatre** (1862) just beyond was modelled on the great Italian theatres, symbolising the cultural aspirations of Ermoúpolis.

The Metamorphosis and Psarianá

Above Plateía Miaoúli lies Psarianá, founded by refugees from Psará (*see p. 471*) in 1822 and dominated by the **Cathedral of the Metamorphosis** (*map p. 58, B2*; 1824–31). The easternmost pair of monolithic marble columns separating its aisles are ancient (from Delos).

More elegant is the church of the **Koímisis tis Theotókou** (*map p. 58, B3*; 1828) on Proíou, its shell in marble, the roof and interior columns in wood. The church's treasure is the patronal icon (c. 1562), beside the doorway in the atrium, an image of the *Dormition of the Virgin*, painted by the barely 20-year-old Domenikos Theotokopoulos, later known in the West as El Greco. It was probably brought by refugees from Psará.

The heart of the **ancient city of Syros** (or Syra) would have been in this area. The scant remains include some seats from an ancient theatre in a basement on the corner of Kleisthénous and Kosmá and a small section of the ancient fortification wall in the base of a wall at the southeast corner of the stadium on Paramáni (*map p. 58, A3*).

Beyond Proíou is the 19th-century industrial area, including the **Neórion** (shipyard), accessed from Mandilará (*map p. 58, A4*). Constructed in 1861 and expanded many times since, it is still functional and plays a major role in the island's economy, although used today for refitting and repairs rather

El Greco: *Dormition of the Virgin*, c. 1562.

than for construction. Further along, Mandilará and then Iróön Polytechníou pass many disused warehouses and factories. The island's former industrial culture is commemorated in the **Industrial Museum** on G. Papandréou, in a former paint factory just west of Plateía Iróön (*open daily except Tues, 10–2; Thurs–Sun also 6–9; reduced hours in winter*).

The cemeteries

Less than a kilometre from Plateía Iróön, to the west side of the main road north, are the city's three cemeteries: Orthodox, Catholic and British. The first and largest is the Orthodox one, with some fine examples of 19th-century funerary sculpture. A short distance beyond is the inconspicuous entrance to the British Cemetery, with graves of early British residents and of the fallen from the First World War. Further still is the Catholic Cemetery, with the graves of French, Italian and Greek Catholic families.

ANO SYROS

Ano Syros ('upper' or old Syros) is northwest of Ermoúpolis, a 30–40-min walk uphill from the harbour, along a path accessed up Odós Omírou. By car, it is entered at its highest point, via the Epáno Térma entrance.

Ano Syros was probably first inhabited as a refuge from sea-borne Saracen raids in the 8th–9th centuries. Its present semi-fortified appearance was created by 13th-century Italian settlers. The community remains predominantly Roman Catholic. The houses are usually constructed on two floors against the steep slope: the living and sleeping rooms are on the upper floor, and the utilitarian or commercial spaces on the ground floor. The streets are narrow and often stepped, and pass frequently beneath covered passages called *steádia*.

Just outside the Epáno Térma entrance is a small 17th-century **Jesuit chapel**. Beyond the entrance, a narrow street leads directly to the summit, dominated by the church of Ághios Geórgios, built in the 1830s on the site of an earlier church.

A path descends southwards behind the Jesuit convent, founded in 1744, leading to the Neoclassical marble façade (1824) of the church of the **Madonna of Mount Carmel**, incorporating a 17th-century door frame. Further south, past the 18th-century churches of Ághios Antónios and Ághios Nikólaos 'the Poor', is the Kamára Gate. From here the Piatsa, or main street, runs to the Portára Gate in the west. To the left at a junction just beyond the Town Hall is a **museum dedicated to Markos Vamvakaris** (*open June–Sept daily 10–2.30 & 7–11.30*), one of the pioneering masters of rebétiko music and of the bouzouki. He was born on Syros in 1905.

THE SOUTH OF THE ISLAND

West of Ermoúpolis

The road west from Plateía Iróön in Ermoúpolis climbs swiftly into the interior. A left turn leads in 3km to **Episkopío**, a village of gardens and villas. **Alithiní** affords panoramic views, particularly striking at night. It is one of the two spots on the island where Pherecydes is believed to have lived a hermitic existence in a cave. Ancient architectural elements found in the area of the village have led scholars to suggest that the sanctuary to the Cabeiri (*see p. 532*), alluded to frequently in the image repertoire of Hellenistic coinage from Syros, may have been here.

Kíni is a coastal resort from where boats can be arranged to points of interest (such as Grámmata; *see overleaf*) in the north. From the waterfront at Galissás, at the head of a deep inlet on the west coast, it is possible to take a boat to visit the attractive **cave-church of Ághios Stéfanos**, 1km along the coast to the west. The chapel is built under the lee of an overhanging rock beside the entrance to a natural grotto a few metres above the water level. To the north, on the westernmost rise of Cape Kataképhalos, is a ruined medieval fortress. Near the small headland of **Aghía Pakoú**, immediately south of the bay, are two natural acropoleis, the first crowned by the church of Aghía Pakoú, the second, higher one to the south. Excavated ancient buildings lie on the saddle between.

Fínikas and Poseidonía

South of Galissás, the landscape changes rapidly becoming lower and more fertile as the road drops down to **Fínikas**, which is set in a wider and shallower bay, dotted with outlying islands. The particularly sheltered position of the harbour was appreciated in antiquity, something which has been confirmed by underwater exploration, which has revealed not only deposits of Classical, Hellenistic and Byzantine amphorae, but also the remains of an ancient harbour mole.

The tranquillity of both sea and landscape attracted the wealthy 19th-century families of Ermoúpolis, who created the summer resort of Dellagratsia, now renamed **Poseidonía**. At the height of its fashion (1880), there was even talk of linking it to Ermoúpolis by steam railway. Many of the villas still survive, built in an eclectic architectural style. Of particular note are the Poseidonia Club (1913); the Tsiropinas Villa, set amid a park of pine trees and palms; the Municipality (ex-Villa Daskou); the Valmas Villa with its conspicuous red tower; the more Neoclassical Aranghis Villa; and the grandiloquent, turreted Ladopoulos and Georgiadis villas.

More villas, predominantly Neoclassical in style, some landscaped and terraced in mature parks, are to be found scattered through the villages of the interior: at **Parakopí** (Velissaropoulos Villa); at **Chroússa** (Vafiadakis and Papadakis villas); and at **Vári** and **Áno Mánna**: their exploration constitutes one of the pleasures of a visit to Syros.

THE NORTH OF THE ISLAND

The road to the north leaves Ermoúpolis from Plateía Iróōn. It climbs up a deep cleft in the island to the watershed at Mýttakas. The branch road west leads steeply down to the remote and panoramic cluster of houses at **Chartianá**, from where a path leads to the delightful **beach at Delfíni**. Less than a kilometre beyond Mýttakas is a track leading right to Rychopós, above the east coast. From here, a clear footpath leads north to Platý Vouní (*see below*) via the **Cave of Pherecydes** (*unsigned, hidden from view, and easily missed. After 15mins, where the path levels out, there is a wall of rock to its left side: a steep scramble over the rocks here up to a ledge leads to the cave*). It is said to have been the ascetic dwelling of the 6th-century BC philosopher.

Chalandriani and Kastrí

Beyond Mýttakas, at Papoúri, a right turn leads to the strategically located Chalandriani plateau, site of **Chalandriani**, a very important Bronze Age settlement and cemetery of the Early Cycladic II period (2700–2300 BC). Little remains to be seen of the site, which lies near the church of the Panaghía. The rich pottery assemblage found here is now mostly in the National Museum in Athens.

An arduous steep path (*1hr on foot from the asphalt road at Chalandriani, first descending to sea-level to cross a torrent bed, then up across unstable scree to the acropolis, just below the summit*) leads north to **Kastrí**, one of the most remarkable Early Cycladic settlements, with imposing stone fortifications (c. 2300–2200 BC). The northern edge of the hill is defended with an outwork and semicircular wall (c. 55m long and 2m high) with six horseshoe bastions. Within the walls, one- or two-room dwellings are grouped in blocks, separated by streets. Some houses have stone hearths. Crucibles, moulds and bronze objects indicate an important metal industry.

Platý Vouní and Sýringas

Platý Vouní is one of the most traditional villages of northern Syros. Panoramic **Sýringas** has views across the Cyclades and as far as Attica.

The far north

The northern extremity of the island is also known as Epáno Meriá, the 'Uplands', and comprises a number of panoramic settlements high in the hills above the sea. The northernmost is **San Michális**, with a church of Ághios Michális, built beside a curious outcrop of rocks. Some distance below, the road ends at a final cluster of dwellings at **Kámbos**, from where it is an hour's walk down to one of the most evocative curiosities in the Cyclades, the site of **Grámmata** (literally, 'Letters'), a remote spit of rock, covered since antiquity by graffiti and divine invocations carved by generations of sailors (*the path is clear at first down to the shore, but subsequently becomes hard to trace as it follows the shoreline, about 10–15m above water-level, round two headlands, as far as the last, westernmost bay. The site can also be reached by boat from Kíni*). On the promontory of rock closing the west side of the bay, three smooth, natural ramps are visible, covered with inscriptions. Some of them are modern, some 19th-century, but the majority are ancient. They include interjections of salvation, offerings of thanks, one-word votives, and detailed records of journeys. A number of the later Hellenistic inscriptions are meticulously enclosed by a rectangular frame with two 'wings'. There also are rudimentary drawings of boats and Poseidon's trident. This unusually sheltered bay, with a small and delightful sandy beach, appears to have been the site of shrine to Asclepius.

PRACTICAL INFORMATION

GETTING AROUND

There are five weekly flights (two in winter) from Athens. The airport is 3km from Ermoúpolis. From Piraeus there are two daily connections by car ferry (4hrs) or catamaran (2hrs); from Rafína three per week. Syros also lies on ferry routes to Chios and Lesbos, Tinos and Mykonos, Naxos and Paros, and Rhodes. Local ferries join Syros with the Western Cyclades three times per week.

WHERE TO STAY

Ermoúpolis has several stylish hotels in converted Neoclassical mansions in the Vapória district. Three of them are along Babagiótou, overlooking the waterfront. The **Syrou Melathron Hotel** (*Babagiótou 5, T: 22810 85963, www.syroumelathron.gr; map p. 58, C1*) has some grand public rooms and a number of the bedrooms have painted ceilings. The **Archontiko Vourli** ■ (*Mavrogordátou 5, the extension of Babagiótou, T: 22810 81682*) has beautifully furnished rooms and good breakfasts. Simpler and less expensive is the delightful **Guesthouse Ypatia** (*Babagiótou 3, T: 22810 83575; ipatiaguest@yahoo.com; map p. 58, C1*).

For a simple beach-side hotel outside the city, the **Hotel Poseidonion** (*T: 22810 42100*) at Poseidonía is an unpretentious solution, with pleasant rooms in the new extension behind the hotel. For unusual and panoramic lodgings, the converted windmill **Anemomylos** (with air-conditioning and kitchen) high up above Ano Syros, can be rented (*T: 22810 80083 or 6944 515366*).

WHERE TO EAT

In Ermoúpolis, the taverna **Stin Ithaki tou Aï**, hidden in a side-street just east of Plateía Miaoúli, has imaginative local dishes. Just off the square, at the south end near the cinema, **Eikosipenderaki** serves good *mezédes* and has live rebétiko music on occasion. At the east end of the harbour on Plateía Kanári (*map p. 58, C3*), **Ta Giannena** has fresh and well-prepared traditional dishes: it represents a type of mid-20th-century traditional city restaurant which is fast disappearing in the islands.

Taverna San Michalis ■ in Epáno Meriá has stunning sunset views as well as good local food and wine. **Mitsos** in Alithiní, outside the town, but with a magnificent panorama over it (north off the road to Kíni) serves fresh, traditional food and is particularly popular with locals, especially at weekends.

DELOS & RHENEIA

Minute Delos (pron: *Dílos; map p. 49*) was one of the most sacred places in ancient Greece, the birthplace of the divine twins Apollo and Artemis, favoured early as central, but neutral, territory, leading to the establishment of a major sanctuary. This later led to its development as one of the most important Hellenistic and Roman mercantile centres, home to an international bourgeoisie of wealthy traders, who shipped all kinds of merchandise—from wine to slaves—around the Mediterranean, and dwelt in richly furnished and decorated houses.

Nowhere else in the Greek world have the remains of a whole city and a sanctuary of such wide-ranging importance been preserved undisturbed by modern building. Delos is a grand and instructive site that merits several days of exploration. Its museum has one of the best collections of Greek Archaic sculptures and offers delightful insights into ancient domestic life.

The island is only c. 5km long by c. 1.3km wide. The landscape is eroded and treeless: the only seasonal torrent is the ancient Ínopos, which drains the plain to the north of Mt Kýnthos into the Bay of Skardaná (northwest), forming a small circular lake along the way, where once the sacred grove of palm trees grew. The island's two harbours in the middle of the west coast are protected by two reefs, Megálos and Mikrós Rematiáris.

THE DELIAN FESTIVALS

Festivals called Delia, in honour of Apollo and Artemis and their mother Leto, were celebrated in Delos from remote antiquity. The Athenians took part, sending ambassadors called Deliastai, later Theoroi. The sacred vessel in which they sailed, the *Theoris*, was said to be the very craft which Theseus had sent after his adventures in Crete. In the course of time the festival lapsed, but was revived in 426 BC by the Athenians, who also instituted the Delian Games, held every four years. By virtue of their leadership of the Delian League, the Athenians took the most prominent part in the ceremonies. Though the islanders shared in providing choruses and animal victims for the sacrifices, the leader, or *Architheoros*, was always an Athenian. On arrival in the island, the embassy from Athens processed to the temple, singing the *Prosodion*, the hymn recounting the story of Leto and the birth of the divine twins.

After the sacrifice of the animals the games began, comprising athletic sports, horse-racing and musical contests. The *Geranos*, or Crane Dance, was performed before the altar of Apollo. Proceedings ended with theatrical plays and banquets. The Lesser Delia was a smaller annual festival.

HISTORY OF DELOS

Delos was also called Ortygia, or 'Quail Island', in remote antiquity. Remains of pre-historic settlement indicate that Delos was inhabited at the end of the 3rd millennium BC. The Mycenaean period saw the first organised settlement in the harbour area and the establishment of a cult. The Ionians who colonised the Cyclades in the 10th–9th centuries BC brought the cult of Leto, who was said to have given birth to both Artemis and Apollo on the island. In the 7th century, the sacred island, under the protection of Naxos, became the headquarters of a league of Aegean Ionians who held a great festival, the Delia, celebrated in the Homeric *Hymn to Apollo*. In this period the island was embellished first by Naxos, later by Paros. Later on the Athenians entered the league and became its ruling spirit. They sent religious embassies annually to Delos and on more than one occasion rendered the sanctuary sacred by a ritual purification (*katharsis*).

At the outbreak of the Persian Wars in 490 BC, the Delians fled from their island to Tinos, but the Persians left Delos untouched. After the Persian defeats in 480–479 BC the island became the centre of the Delian (or First Athenian) League, founded in 478 BC. Its treasury was established on the island until its transfer to Athens in 454. In 426–425 BC the Athenians ordered a second purification of Delos, on the instigation of the Delphic Oracle, following an outbreak of plague. They removed to Rheneia all the remains of the dead which were on Delos and passed a decree that thenceforward no one should die or give birth on the sacred island. After the purification the Athenians restored the Delian Festival and instituted the Delian Games. Athens actively settled the island with its citizens, and in 422 BC it banished the remaining Delians on the pretext that they were impure. They were later allowed to return, at the bidding of the Delphic Oracle.

In 404 BC Athens was defeated by Sparta in the Peloponnesian War, and from 401 to 394 BC Delos enjoyed a short period of independence until the Athenians regained possession of the island and instituted the Second Athenian League in 378 BC. By 315 BC, maritime command of the Aegean had passed to Egypt. Delos, again independent, became the centre of an island confederacy, and entered on the most prosperous and cosmopolitan period of its history (the presence of Egyptians, Syrians, Phoenicians, Palestinians and Jews is attested). Rich offerings flowed into the sanctuary. Honours decreed to foreign benefactors show the variety and importance of the island's diplomatic and commercial relations.

By 250 BC the first Romans had settled in Delos, and Roman merchants soon predominated. In 166 BC the Roman senate allowed the Athenians to reoccupy the island and made Delos a tax-free port. Once again the Delians were expelled, never to return, and the island became an Athenian cleruchy. The Romans, however, remained the true masters of the island. In 146 BC merchants from Corinth moved to Delos from their city which had been sacked by Rome. By now the great religious festival was in essence a trade fair, and Delos became the slave-market of Greece, with as many as 10,000 slaves changing hands in a single day. The sanctuary still functioned, but it was trade that filled the island's coffers. An association of Italian merchants, with the backing of Rome, was formed under the title of Hermaists. Commercial syndicates of merchants from Tyre, Beirut, Alexandria and elsewhere formed trade associations, and the fine houses of a prosperous bourgeoisie began to develop.

In 88 BC, during the First Mithridatic War, in which Athens had supported Mithridates and Delos repudiated Athens in favour of Rome, Menophanes, a general of Mithridates, descended on the island and razed the city to the ground, killing natives and foreigners alike, enslaving the women and children, seizing the sanctuary treasure and looting the markets. Regained the following year by Sulla, Delos was returned to the Athenians and partly rebuilt with Roman aid. In 69 BC the island was again sacked by the pirate Athenodorus. About 66 BC the city was walled to protect it from further attacks, but it was too late to stop its decline; by the 2nd century AD the island was virtually uninhabited. Ravaged by successive masters of the Cyclades—barbarians, pirates, Knights of St John of Jerusalem—and used as a marble quarry by the Venetians and Turks and even by the inhabitants of Mykonos and Tinos, the sacred island sank into insignificance.

In 1445 the Italian antiquarian Cyriac of Ancona visited the island. Under the Turks, who took Delos in 1566, the island's name was Sdili. In the 17th century Sir Kenelm Digby removed marbles from the island for the collection of Charles I of England. The first excavations by French and Greek archaeologists date from as early as 1873 and have continued until the present day.

Replica statues of Cleopatra and Dioscourides, in the House of Cleopatra (see p. 77).

THE SITE

Open daily except Mon and holidays, 9–3. Boat fare does not include admission to the site.
Shuttle-boats moor on a mole in the centre of the ancient harbour, roughly on a dividing line
between the sacred area to the left and the residential and commercial area to the right.

DRAMATIS PERSONAE: THE MYTH IN BRIEF

After Zeus impregnated the beautiful Leto, his wife Hera, fearful that Leto would bear Zeus a son who would supersede Ares, her own son, in his affections, forbade every place in the world to give Leto shelter. As her time came, Leto wandered the world seeking a place to give birth: but nowhere wished to incur the wrath of Hera. The single exception was a barren, insignificant, floating island called Ortygia. The island accepted Leto on condition that her children did not forswear the island because of its poverty, but would make it one of their favourite abodes. Leto's birth pains lasted nine days: Hera had detained Eileithyia, the divine midwife, on Mount Olympus. Eventually, by promising her a reward, Iris persuaded Eileithyia to attend, and Leto, clinging to a palm tree, was delivered of twins, first Artemis and then Apollo. The floating island was thereafter fixed to the sea-bed and became Delos.

Both Artemis and Apollo are aloof deities, pitiless and unsentimental. They embody different aspects, female and male, of purity and clarity: Artemis, the moon's crystalline light; Apollo, the sun's brilliance. The cerebral is uppermost in both their worlds: Artemis is ruthlessly chaste; Apollo is the god of reason and oracular clairvoyance.

THE HARBOURS & SACRED WAY

The harbour area

The ancient Sacred Harbour, where visitors and pilgrims arrived, lies to the north of the disembarkation mole, with the Commercial Harbour to its south. Both have filled with sand. They were protected by an Archaic breakwater of granite blocks, now mostly underwater. The Commercial Harbour, extending to the south and dating from Hellenistic times, was divided by moles into five basins. Some of the mooring stones are still visible.

Functioning like a vestibule for the Sanctuary, at the landward end of the modern mole, is an irregular open space called the **Agora of the Competaliasts (1)** (*see box on p. 70*). Its wide space was articulated by a circular shrine in its centre and (to the south) a larger, square-based Doric structure, both of which were offerings by another association, the Hermaists, to Hermes and his mother, Maia. On the north side of the square is an Ionic naïskos (c. 150 BC), in front of which stands a marble offertory box, adorned with a relief of snakes on its upper face.

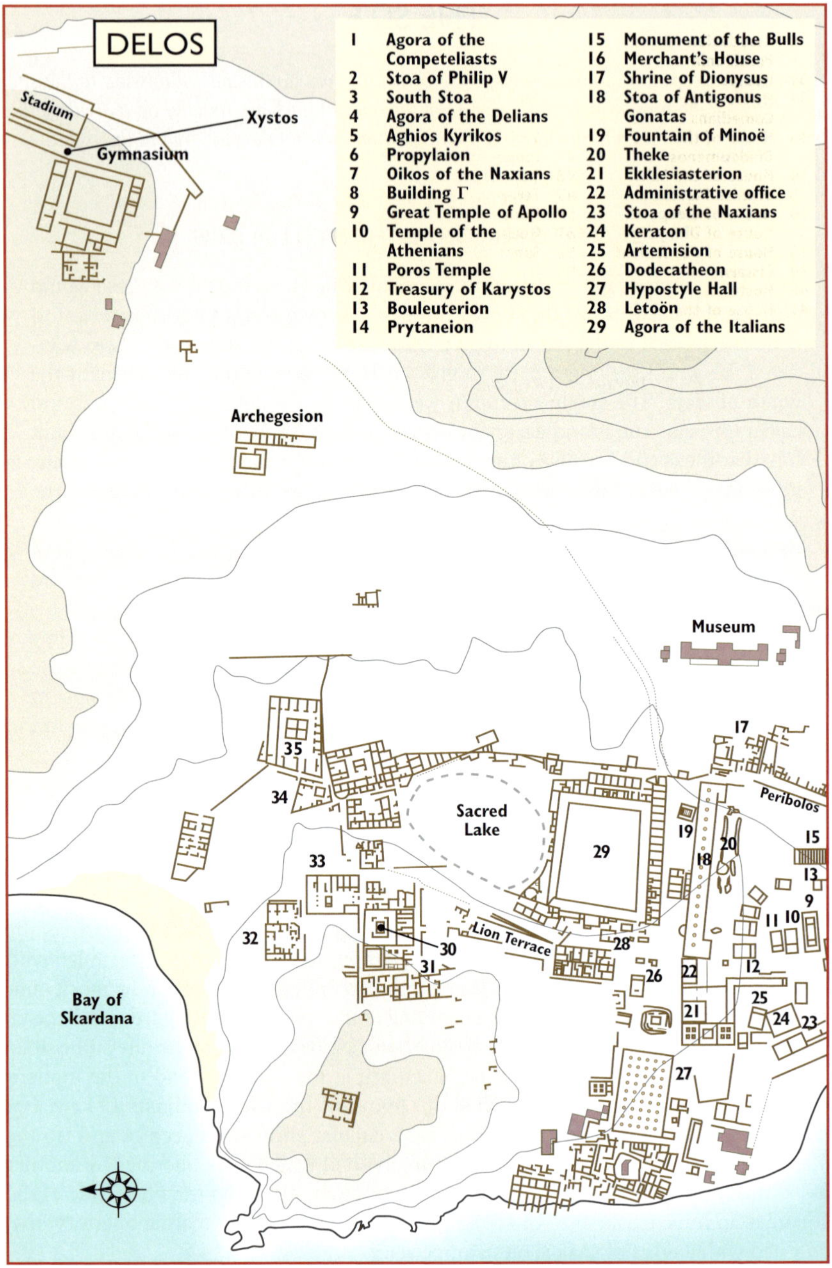

DELOS

1	Agora of the Competeliasts	15	Monument of the Bulls
2	Stoa of Philip V	16	Merchant's House
3	South Stoa	17	Shrine of Dionysus
4	Agora of the Delians	18	Stoa of Antigonus Gonatas
5	Aghios Kyrikos	19	Fountain of Minoë
6	Propylaion	20	Theke
7	Oikos of the Naxians	21	Ekklesiasterion
8	Building Γ	22	Administrative office
9	Great Temple of Apollo	23	Stoa of the Naxians
10	Temple of the Athenians	24	Keraton
11	Poros Temple	25	Artemision
12	Treasury of Karystos	26	Dodecatheon
13	Bouleuterion	27	Hypostyle Hall
14	Prytaneion	28	Letoön
		29	Agora of the Italians

Stadium

Xystos

Gymnasium

Archegesion

Museum

Sacred Lake

Peribolos

Lion Terrace

Bay of Skardana

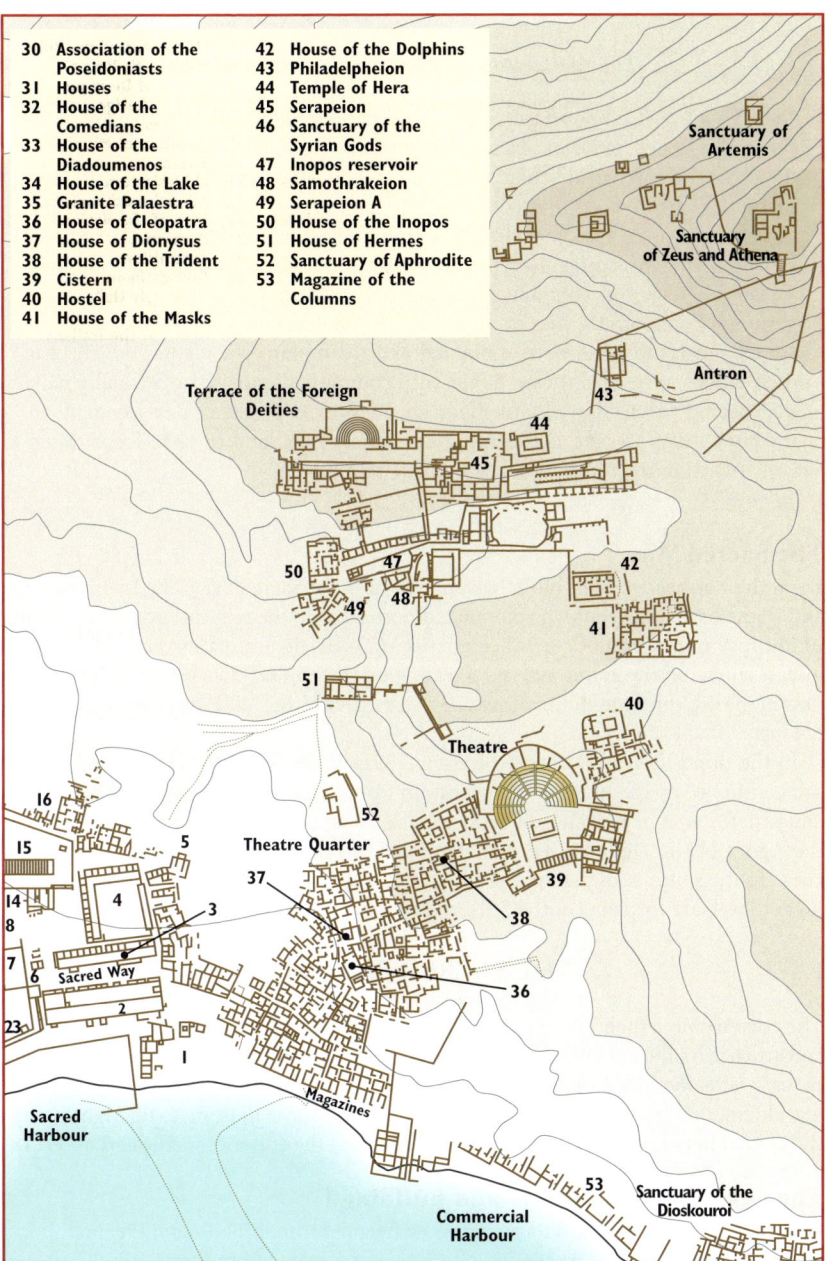

30 Association of the
   Poseidoniasts
31 Houses
32 House of the
   Comedians
33 House of the
   Diadoumenos
34 House of the Lake
35 Granite Palaestra
36 House of Cleopatra
37 House of Dionysus
38 House of the Trident
39 Cistern
40 Hostel
41 House of the Masks
42 House of the Dolphins
43 Philadelpheion
44 Temple of Hera
45 Serapeion
46 Sanctuary of the
   Syrian Gods
47 Inopos reservoir
48 Samothrakeion
49 Serapeion A
50 House of the Inopos
51 House of Hermes
52 Sanctuary of Aphrodite
53 Magazine of the
   Columns

Sanctuary of
Artemis

Sanctuary
of Zeus and Athena

Antron

Terrace of the Foreign
Deities

43

44

45

50

47

49 48

42

41

51

40

Theatre

16

52

15

5

Theatre Quarter

14

4

37

39

8

3

38

7

6 Sacred Way

36

23

2

I

Magazines

Sacred
Harbour

53 Sanctuary of the
    Dioskouroi

Commercial
Harbour

THE MERCHANT ASSOCIATIONS OF DELOS

Names such as 'Competaliasts', 'Hermaists' or 'Poseidoniasts' are associated with certain buildings on Delos. They refer to what were in effect guilds, dating from the arrival of foreign merchants from the Levant, Italy and Sicily who, though present on Delos from as far back as the 3rd century BC, settled in increasing numbers from c. 125 BC onwards. These foreigners, both citizens and freedmen as well their slaves, organised themselves in societies or groups of a combined social, religious and commercial nature under the patronage of particular divinities—Poseidon, Hermes or the Lares Compitales (Roman ancestral guardian-spirits). Yearly officials were appointed and the buildings or agoras which bear their names were constructed either with communal funds or occasionally with the specific benefaction of a member; they represent the latest developments in the city's urban design, constituting an entirely new kind of civic focus, often constructed over earlier buildings of a different nature.

The Sacred Way

From the northeast corner of the paved area runs the Sacred Way, lined with exedrae and statue bases between two colonnaded porticoes. To the seaward side was the **Stoa of Philip V of Macedon** (late 3rd century BC) **(2)**. His dedicatory inscription to Apollo in vast letters on the architrave (now resting on the ground) has survived. The thickness of the building was doubled some 30 years later by the addition of another (slightly longer) stoa facing the sea.

To the opposite (east) side of the Sacred Way is the **South Stoa (3)**, built in the 3rd century BC by the kings of Pergamon. In front of its southern end is the base of an equestrian statue of Epigenes of Teos, general of Attalus I of Pergamon. Behind it lies the **Agora of the Delians (4)**, once bounded to north and east by two-storey porticoes. To the south and east are the ruins of houses; beyond the southeast corner, at a higher level, are the ruins of the 5th-century apsidal **basilica of Ághios Kýrikos (5)**.

THE SACRED PRECINCT

The Sacred Way enters the Sacred Precinct through a monumental **Propylaion (6)**, constructed by the Athenians in the 2nd century BC to replace an earlier predecessor. Its base is marked by a three-stepped platform on which the Doric structure in white marble stood. It had four columns defining three gateways. In front, to the right, stands the eroded figure of Hermes Propylaios, guardian of the entrance, dedicated in 341 BC.

The Oikos of the Naxians and Building Γ

In its ruined state, it is hard to pick out the overall form of the Sacred Precinct. It is a large area of temples, altars, votive offerings and remains from a millennium of worship, grown organically around the earliest focus of cult. The two oldest buildings are the **Oikos of the Naxians (7)**, a 6th-century BC building with a central axis of columns; and, to its east, the smaller 8th-century BC **Building Γ (8)** (now little more than a small rectangular depression in the ground). They represent the earliest constructed places of the cult of Apollo on Delos.

The Oikos of the Naxians is based on a building completed in the same spot 50 years before. This first building appears to have been a temple to Apollo. Around 575 BC it was modified: a single, axial row of very slender marble columns almost 4.5m high now supported long, marble cross-beams, which in turn held a pitched roof tiled in marble, the first full marble roof we know. At the same time a tetrastyle porch was added to the east. This structure was eventually superseded by other temples and was later downgraded to an oikos (house), implying a functional use, for storing offerings or as a ritual meeting place for the Naxians who had originally dedicated it. It may take its orientation from that of the Geometric structure, Building Γ was possibly also a temple, the position of which was respected throughout antiquity.

Against the north wall of the Oikos stood the colossal **Statue of Apollo**, approximately four times life-size, carved from Naxian marble around the turn of the 7th century BC. The massive base (broken) is still *in situ*. The remains of the monolithic statue are now scattered in the Artemision (*see p. 73*). The statue is the largest known piece of Archaic Greek sculpture. The eastern side of the base bears the 6th-century BC epigram: 'I am of the same stone, both figure and base', probably subtly indicating that they were of Naxian marble, i.e. had been donated by Naxos, a statement made more clearly by a 4th-century inscription on its western side.

The temples of Apollo

To the right of the Sacred Way are the remains of three important temples, close together in a line facing west. First is the **Great Temple of Apollo (9)**, begun around the same time as the foundation of the Delian League in 477 BC. After the transfer to Athens of the treasury in 454 BC, construction ceased, to be completed two centuries later. Erected on a high base of granite blocks, approached by marble steps, it was a Doric hexastyle with 13 columns at the sides, the only full peripteral temple on Delos.

The **Temple of the Athenians (10)** was the last of the three to be erected, in Pentelic marble, between 425 and 417 BC. It was a Doric amphiprostyle building with six columns in front. Behind the columns is a prodromos, or entrance hall, with four columns in antis. Inside the naos were seven chryselephantine statues with Apollo in the centre, which gave the temple its alternative name, the 'House of the Seven'. They were placed on a semicircular pedestal of Eleusinian marble. The roof was pitched so as to accommodate the Archaic statue of Apollo, previously located in the older temple to its north.

Of this northernmost temple, the **Poros Temple (11)** from the 6th century BC, only the foundations (in poros stone) remain. It was here that the treasure of the Delian League was originally lodged, until its removal to Athens in 454 BC.

It is notable that none of these three relatively small temples has an altar in front and that all three, most unusually, open to the west. They all seem to be orientated towards the empty space just outside, which the temples of Artemis and Leto also look towards, suggesting that it was a location of major sacred significance. In front of the last two temples is the base of an honorific dedication to Philetairus, founder of the dynasty of Pergamon in the 3rd century BC.

The buildings arranged in an arc round the north side of the temples are probably treasuries. The first is the 6th-century BC **Treasury of Kárystos (12)**, with four columns in antis and an axial row of columns. The four remaining treasuries (to the east) were built a century later on a similar plan.

The east of the Sacred Precinct

To the south of the treasuries are the low remains of two public buildings. The northern one, of the 6th century BC, is considered to have been a **bouleuterion (13)**; its southern neighbour, of the 4th century BC, was the **prytaneion (14)**, comprising a porticoed vestibule with marble benches, a small courtyard, a sacred area with an altar to Hestia in the northwest corner, and a banquet-room and archives in the northeast corner. Grouped in front of the building to the west are several altars, dedicated to Athena Polias and Zeus Polieus ('of the city').

East of the prytaneion is the south end of a long hall (69m by 10m) known as the **Monument of the Bulls (15)** from its decoration with bulls' heads. Only foundations survive of this unusual 2nd-century BC building, entered by a pronaos from the south. It housed a military trireme dedicated to Apollo after a naval victory, probably by Demetrius Poliorcetes or his son, Antigonus Gonatas.

East of the hall is a 3rd-century BC peribolos wall, marking the edge of the Sacred Precinct. Beyond its southern end is a **merchant's house (16)** with two peristyle courts. Beyond the northern end an exedra, decorated with outsized phallic symbols, marks a small **Shrine of Dionysus (17)**, built c. 300 BC. Its reliefs (rearranged) display various Dionysiac imagery, including Dionysus, maenads, Silenus and Pan.

The north of the Sacred Precinct

The northern boundary of the Sacred Precinct is marked by the 120-m long **Stoa of Antigonus Gonatas (18)**, erected in the second half of the 3rd century BC. The stoa, with a frieze of triglyphs decorated with bulls' heads, has two longitudinal galleries with a small wing at either end: in the east wing a statue of the early 1st-century BC Roman general Caius Billienus has been replaced on its base. In front of the portico are two parallel lines of pedestals on which stood 20 statues of the ancestors of Antigonus.

In the northeast corner, just outside the back wall of the stoa, is the **Fountain of Minoë (19)**, a stepped rectangular cistern, built in the mid-6th century BC. In front of the centre of the stoa is a small, roughly circular burial area, incorporating a Mycenaean grave, later identified as the **Theke of Arge and Opis (20)**, commemorating two Hyperborean maidens (*see box opposite*).

The **Ekklesiasterion (21)** is an assembly building erected in the early 5th century BC and remodelled in Hellenistic times, with marble seats along the north wall flanking an aedicule; and, next to it, a small rectangular edifice of the late 5th century, referred to generally as an **administrative office (22)**. Between the two, a tiny passageway leads towards the Dodecatheon (*see overleaf*).

APOLLO & THE HYPERBOREANS

The Hyperboreans ('from beyond the North Wind') were a legendary race of Apollo-worshippers who lived in the far north of the world as it was imagined by the Greeks. They are mentioned in passing by Hesiod and Pindar; a fragment by the poet Alcaeus suggests that Apollo left Greece each year after the winter solstice and wintered in the land of the Hyperboreans. Other than the god, only heroes could reach their land. By the time Herodotus wrote in the 5th century BC, the arrival of the yearly offerings sent by the Hyperboreans to the sanctuary at Delos was a long established tradition. What exactly these offerings were is unclear, but we know that they were carefully wrapped in straw. Where they ultimately came from is equally unclear, but their route, described by Herodotus, was precise and unchanging. The offerings came from the Hyperboreans to the Scythians (who inhabited parts of Eastern Europe), whence they were passed between neighbouring peoples, until they arrived at Dodona in the mountainous northwest of Greece, from where they were passed to Euboea over the Malian Gulf; from Kárystos on Euboea they were then transferred to the people of Tinos, who finally delivered them to the Delians. The first maidens who made this journey to accompany the offerings were Hyperoche and Laodike; they died in Delos and are remembered here, close by the Temple of Artemis. Herodotus mentions two other maidens, Opis and Arge, who came to Delos even earlier, 'at the same time as Artemis and Apollo'.

The west of the Sacred Precinct

The Sacred Precinct is bordered by the L-shaped **Stoa of the Naxians (23)**, part of the 6th-century BC series of Naxian embellishments. In its southeast corner stand the granite foundations, with a cylindrical hollow in the middle, of the base of a bronze palm tree dedicated by Nikias in 417 BC. On one of the fragments (replaced) of the lower marble course, the name Nikias is inscribed.

Northwest of the stoa, abutting the Temple of Artemis, is a square structure **(24)** erected by the Athenians in the 4th century BC. It protected the keraton, an altar made of goat horns, said to have been built by Apollo himself and to be the location where Theseus first performed the *Geranos* ('Crane Dance'). Nothing survives of it.

Northeast of the keraton, an L-shaped Ionic portico surrounded one of the most sacred parts of the sanctuary, the **Artemision (25)**. There was a Mycenaean cult place here, probably dedicated to a female deity (*finds in the museum*). On top of it, an Archaic temple to Artemis was built in the 7th century BC, replaced by the Hellenistic temple whose remains are visible today. Near its west side stand the two imposing fragments of the colossal statue of Apollo (*see p. 71*).

THE TERRACE OF THE LIONS, THE SACRED LAKE & BEYOND

The passageway by the Ekklesiasterion leads north to two important sacred structures. Immediately to the left is the Sanctuary of the Twelve Gods or **Dodecatheon (26)**, attested since Archaic times and dedicated probably to four triads of deities: Zeus, Hera and Athena; Apollo, Artemis and Leto; Hades, Demeter and Kore; and Poseidon, Aphrodite and Hermes. The base of the temple and marble elements of its superstructure at the west end are visible, and a number of its dozen altars are clustered to the east.

West of the Dodecatheon is a large esplanade overlooking the harbour, known as the Agora of Theophrastus, erected in the 120s BC. It is overlooked from the north by the large **Hypostyle Hall (27)**, a vast 3rd-century BC closed building with a single southern entrance, and 44 columns in the interior. It may have served both sacred (festival of Poseidon) and secular (meeting-hall) functions.

The Letoön and Agora of the Italians

To the northeast is the **Letoön (28)**, or shrine of Leto, constructed c. 540 BC in a veined, white marble. The temple is built over a widely protruding rounded marble crepis in Parian marble, on which offerings were laid. A vestibule gave access to the naos.

East of the Letoön is the **Agora of the Italians (29)**, an open market-place surrounded with shops. The vast open space (100m by 70m) was surrounded by Doric porticoes, surmounted by a second tier in the Ionic order. It was donated by the Hermaists (*see p. 66*) and gives some sense of the importance and wealth which the community of merchants from the Italian peninsula had achieved on Delos by the 2nd century BC through banking and trade in slaves and other commodities. Begun c. 110 BC, it was repaired after the sack of Delos by Mithridates, but then left unfinished c. 50 BC. Its rooms contain various commemorative statues to Roman dignitaries. The room of Publius Satricanius on the north side has a fine mosaic.

Around the Sacred Lake

The avenue leading north from the Letoön begins to open out and is bordered to the west by the celebrated **Terrace of the Lions**, a ceremonial entry influenced by the avenues in Egyptian sanctuaries (the original sculptures are now in the museum). Before the construction of the Sacred Harbour, this line of magnificent creatures, made in the 7th century BC by the Naxians, of marble from their island, formed the main entranceway to the Sacred Precinct. Although five lions are visible *in situ*, their original number was at least nine, and could even have been more. One now stands by the Arsenale in Venice. The lion was traditionally associated with Artemis, perhaps reflecting a greater prominence of the goddess in early Archaic Delos.

The lions look onto the **Sacred Lake**, formed by an overflow of the Ínopos torrent but drained in 1925. Its shape is indicated by a modern wall, which represents its extent in Hellenistic times. In it were kept the sacred swans and geese of Apollo. A palm tree has been planted in the centre in memory of the grove which grew here in antiquity and of the sacred palm to which Leto clung when giving birth to the twins (*see p. 67*).

The extensive remains that lie beyond, on the hill of Skardaná, all date from Hellenistic times and after. Beyond them, the land drops steeply to the Bay of Skardaná, which was the island's harbour until the building of the Sacred Harbour in the 6th century BC.

North of the Sacred Lake

The erected columns visible to the northwest of the Lion Terrace belong to the large edifice of the **Association of the Poseidoniasts of Berytos** (modern Beirut) **(30)**, a guild of Syrian ship-owners and merchants who worshipped Baal, whom they identified with Poseidon. It was built in 110 BC and destroyed in 69 BC. The vestibule leads into a court bounded on the west by a portico onto which opened four 'chapels'. One of these, later than the others, was dedicated to the goddess Roma, a popular cult in the late 2nd century BC, and contains her statue. On the east side a colonnade leads to a peristyle court with a cistern. Further west is another court with a mosaic, probably used as a meeting-place. To the south were reception rooms and, in the basement below them, a series of shops.

West of the Building of the Poseidoniasts a road runs north–south along the side of **four houses (31)**, some of which bear apotropaic symbols carved beside their doorways: a phallus, a man holding an animal, a cutlass, etc. There are floors in attractive chequerboard mosaic in the southern houses.

To the north, along a straight east–west street, two entire blocks of houses have been excavated: their urban plan, their functional furnishings (latrines and ample cisterns), their two-storey marble peristyles (**House of the Comedians**; **32**) and their decoration with reliefs and mosaics, give a sense of the comfortable life of Hellenistic Delos. The easternmost building, known as the **House of the Diadoumenos (33)**, from a replica of the celebrated statue by Polyclitus found here, had an elaborate water-supply system. The **House of the Lake (34)**, occupying a whole block, has an especially well-preserved peristyle of monolithic columns with a mosaic impluvium.

The Granite Palaestra

The **Granite Palaestra** (mid-2nd century BC) **(35)** lies directly beyond the older and more ruined Lake Palaestra. In the middle is a large cistern in four compartments, with a roof in poros stone, which was surrounded by a Doric peristyle. Extending due south and northwest are well-preserved **stretches of the city wall**. The enceinte was built by the Roman legate Triarius in 69–66 BC to protect Delos from the attacks of the pirate Athenodorus. It was partly built over demolished houses and shops. Its southern stretch was removed for excavations in 1925–26.

THE NORTHEAST OF THE ISLAND

A hundred metres northeast of the lake (*NB: the area is not properly cleared and often closed off*) is the 6th-century BC **Archegesion**, sacred to the worship of Apollo in the person of Anius (Anios), the legendary first settler and king of Delos. A further 100m on is the Ionic peristyle of the Hellenistic **gymnasium**, and beyond it the **stadium**; both built before the **xystos** was added c. 200 BC. Beyond the stadium is a cluster of houses. Near the island's eastern shore are the remains of a mid-1st-century BC **synagogue**. The remains of a murex workshop for the production of purple dye are close to the shore, about 800m south of the synagogue.

THE MUSEUM

Many important sculptures from Delos are in the National Museum in Athens. The core of the museum here is a magnificent collection of Archaic sculpture from the 7th and early 6th centuries BC, all produced by the great sculpting centres of Naxos and Paros.

Central Hall (Galleries I and II): Archaic sculpture, including a fine assembly of fragmentary Apollonian kouroi, a Parian sphinx (early 6th century BC) and a pair of lions from the Temple of Artemis, with small perforations along the spine for affixing gilded bronze manes.

Gallery III: Among more Archaic statuary are the original lions from the Terrace of the Lions. There is also Classical material, including the acroterion of the eastern pediment of the Temple of the Athenians (c. 420 BC), depicting an Athenian legend in which Boreas, god of the North Wind, abducts Oreithyia, the daughter of King Erechtheus of Athens.

Gallery IV (northeast corner): Hellenistic sculpture, among it a beautiful 4th-century BC piece of Artemis taking a stag in the hunt. Some pieces here preserve traces of their original paint. The north wall of the gallery shows one of the finest Delian mosaic floors, with a sumptuous border of fruit and flora.

Galleries V–VI (north side): Gallery V is dominated by an enormous statue of Caius Ofellius Ferus, carved around 115 BC by two Athenian sculptors. In the arch between Galleries VI and VII is a rare votive stele preserving its bronze plaque depicting Artemis (3rd century BC). In Gallery VI are fine Roman portrait busts.

Gallery VII (returning to the main entrance) is filled with a fascinating selection of domestic objects and decorations, including votive terracotta figurines and moulds for their production, mosaic emblemata, remarkably fine jewellery, fragments of wall-paintings, a showcase of erotic and phallic objects, advertisements and graffiti from external walls of houses, glass and tableware.

Gallery VIII (right of main entrance; *frequently closed*) exhibits the finds from earliest antiquity, and the museum's vase collection. Of particular note and refinement are the carved Mycenaean ivory tablets of the 13th century BC found below the Artemision. The wide provenance of the vases—Rhodes, Chios, Milos, Corinth—reflects Delos' wide trading links.

THE COMMERCIAL & THEATRE QUARTER

In contrast to the area of the Sanctuary of Apollo, the degree of preservation of streets and dwellings in the southern sector of the city is remarkable, at times comparable with Pompeii. The beauty and sophistication of the houses provides a vivid picture of civil and domestic life in Hellenistic Greece.

A typical Delian house of the Hellenistic and Roman periods had its rooms grouped around a central courtyard, reached from the street by a short corridor. In the absence of external windows, this was the sole light-source for the interiors, keeping them cool during the summer. Richer homes had a peristyle court and interior walls were plastered, painted and polished, so as to maximise the light. The so-called Rhodian Peristyle is also found on Delos, consisting of a large hall rising the full height of the building and fronted by a taller colonnade occupying one side and one or two storeys of rooms constituting the others. The central court usually had a mosaic floor: this served as an impluvium to catch rainwater for the cistern beneath. Some houses possessed wells.

The main street

From the southeast corner of the Agora of the Competaliasts, at the head of the embarkation mole, the well-paved and drained main street of the Theatre Quarter ascends between houses and shops, some furnished with marble windows for dispensing sales. Occasional niches held lamps to light the street at night. To the right is a house with a stove and built-in basins, probably a **dyer's workshop**. A small passage and steps lead (right) up, past a dolphin mosaic, into the **House of Cleopatra (36)**. The marble colonnade has been restored; in the courtyard stand replicas of two elegant statues (originals in the museum) representing Cleopatra and Dioscourides, the 2nd-century BC Athenian owners. On the opposite side of the road (left) is the **House of Dionysus (37)**, preserving part of the staircase to an upper floor. The courtyard contains an elegant mosaic of Dionysus mounted on a tiger. Farther along, the **House of the Trident (38)**, one of the largest on the island, has a Rhodian peristyle and striking mosaics, including a Panathenaic amphora, suggesting that a member of the household had won a victory in a chariot-race.

The theatre and Hellenistic houses

At the top of the first rise, the street emerges into the space before the 3rd-century BC **theatre**. It held around 5,500 spectators. The cavea also served as a large water-catchment area during rainstorms: two well-preserved drain-mouths can be seen to either side of the semicircular orchestra, which conducted the water into the vaulted **cistern (39)** below. This could hold around 500,000 litres of water for communal use.

The cavea is partly cut into the hill and partly built up with bulwarks of fine isodomic blocks. Only in the lowest tier are the backs of the seats preserved. The large and once elaborate skene was in the form of a rectangle with colonnades on all four sides, a unique design. On the side facing the audience it would have had engaged Doric columns, flanked by paraskenia. Twenty metres to the south of the cistern are the large foundations of the **Altar of Dionysus** with, behind it, remains of a small **Temple of Apollo**, dated by an inscription to 110–109 BC. Two adjacent shrines were dedicated to Artemis-Hecate (west) and Dionysus, Hermes and Pan (east).

Beside the theatre to the southeast, entered through a fine marble doorway, is a building known as the **Hostel (40)**. It had three floors and a very large cistern, almost 20m deep, with a feed-pipe visible in the southwest corner. The building is thought to have provided accommodation for visitors to the Delian festivals.

The ruins of the theatre at Delos, with the large cistern in front of it and the building called the Hostel in the foreground. Between the theatre and the coast stretches the Theatre Quarter.

The House of the Masks and House of the Dolphins

The path east from the theatre passes between two of the best-preserved Hellenistic houses on Delos: to the right is the **House of the Masks (41)**, a large merchant's house consisting of shops, workshops and living-quarters. The side looking onto the street consists of shops which were rented out by the owner; the residence (*entered from around the west side*) is set back to the south, around a peristyle beside a deep, rock-cut cistern, originally covered by a wing of the house. Well-preserved reception rooms look onto the court from the north, each with a mosaic floor and painted walls, showing several layers of successive decoration (frequently imitating marble). The abstract mosaics in the central room have a surround of theatrical masks: in the subsidiary room to east is a famous depiction of Dionysus, wearing Oriental garb and seated on a panther. The details show even the whiskers of the animal.

A similar design is found in the **House of the Dolphins (42)**, just to the northeast, named after its magnificent central mosaic. Concentric rings of elegant wave, key and griffin-head designs surround an emblema which has survived only scantily: pairs of stylised dolphins, ridden by small figures with divine emblems, fill the corners. The mosaic bears a signature by the artist, Asklipiades of Arados, a town in Phoenicia.

MOUNT KYNTHOS, THE TERRACE OF THE FOREIGN DIVINITIES & THE INOPOS VALLEY

East of the House of the Dolphins is the abrupt rise of Mt Kýnthos. An ancient stone path, partly stepped, leads up to the east before turning south to the summit. To the right of the pathway is a curious shrine known as the **Antron** or Cave of Heracles. It is in the form of a grotto with an entrance and a pitched roof formed by huge granite slabs, placed against one another in pairs. The massive blocks of the boundary wall in front are engaged with the bedrock. A Hellenistic shrine to Heracles, it is deliberately built to look primitive and ancient. In front is the marble base of an altar, also Hellenistic.

In the corner of the first sharp turn in the stepped pathway is a sanctuary attributed by the Athenians to Agatha Tyche (Good Fortune) **(43)**, which later served as a **Philadelpheion**, dedicated to the cult of Arsinoë, sister and wife of Ptolemy II Philadelphus, deified after her death in 270 BC. From here the **summit of Mt Kýnthos** (112m), sacred to Apollo and Artemis, is easily reached.

The site has yielded remains of the 3rd millennium BC, but was abandoned for long periods and became an important sanctuary only in 281–267 BC, when the existing buildings were built and a rectangular peribolos constructed. On the flattened summit stood the **Sanctuary of Kynthian Zeus and Athena**, with niches for votive offerings, statue bases, and a dedicatory mosaic. A hundred metres to the southeast, on the south summit, are the remains of a small **Sanctuary to Zeus Hypsistos**. To the east, on a barely accessible terrace, has been excavated the 5th-century BC **Sanctuary of Artemis Locheia**. On the way down the north side are the ruins of over a dozen other tiny sanctuaries dedicated to unknown and Oriental deities. A large protruding rock, 100m north of the summit, bears the 5th-century BC inscription 'the boundary of Leto'.

The Heraion

North of the bottom of the path is an area dense with the ruins of superimposed buildings and temples. In earliest times this area was dedicated to Hera, whose anger forced Leto to Delos. The venerable 6th-century BC **Temple of Hera (44)** is immediately to the north, beyond a broken altar, and consists of a south-facing entrance with two standing columns, and a fine marble east wall which rises almost imperceptibly in the centre. The interior floor is missing, revealing the base of a preceding late Geometric temple.

The Terrace of the Foreign Deities

To the north and west opens a large area known as the Terrace of the Foreign Deities, testimony to the cosmopolitan nature of Delos in the last period of its mercantile prosperity during late Hellenistic and Roman times. The Heraion became surrounded by the sanctuaries of new, imported divinities: Egyptian Serapis to the south and west, and Syrian divinities to the north. The popularity of Serapis derived from the fact that he was believed to have the powers of healing and of prophecy.

The **Serapeion (45)** is an extensive complex which must have grown rapidly during the course of the 2nd century BC. Numerous inscriptions testify to Athenian patronage in its construction. It comprised two colonnaded courts, several temples to Serapis, Isis and Anubis, altars, inscriptions and ex-votos, its haphazard growth indicated by the disorganised and unplanned appearance. The long trapezoidal court below the polygonal retaining wall of the Heraion is divided lengthways by a sacred avenue, Egyptian-style, lined with altars and crouching sphinxes, leading to a small temple. The narrow north end of this court abuts another paved area, bounded on the south and (partly) west by an Ionic portico and surrounded by small temples and sacred rooms. The two most conspicuous temples are, to the north, a Temple of Serapis from the first half of the 2nd century BC; and to the east, on a higher level, a Temple of Isis with a pedimented façade (reassembled). Against its back wall is a statue of the goddess. Lower down in front of the temple is an incense altar.

To the north lies the grander **Sanctuary of the Syrian Gods (46)**, Hadad and Atargatis, whose cult was introduced in the early 2nd century BC. Its beginnings would have been small and private, but by the end of the century it was made 'official' under the aegis of an Athenian high priest. In the process, Atargatis became identified with Aphrodite and the more extreme orgiastic rites of the cult were abandoned. The original entrance to the sanctuary was by the stepped street (visible) rising up to the terrace from the west. The sanctuary was arranged around a central terrace, flanked to the west by a portico. In an exedra just left of its centre is an area of pavement with a mosaic inscription commemorating the benefaction of an Athenian named Phormion. Opposite is the sanctuary's small theatre (accommodating 400–500 spectators), where sacred rites were performed, protected from view by walls and an internal portico on three sides.

The area of the Ínopos

The stepped path descending to the west leads down to a large rock-cut public cistern, the **Ínopos Reservoir (47)**. It collected the variable waters of the Ínopos torrent, which drained from a source on the slope of Mt Kýnthos and flowed intermittently down to the Sacred Lake and the Bay of Skardaná. A small terrace lined with benches overlooked the cistern from the north.

On the opposite side, south of the reservoir, are the ruins of the **Samothrakeion (48)**, dedicated to the Cabeiri (Kabeiroi; *see p. 532*), built on two terraces. On the upper level stood a 4th-century BC Doric temple. On the lower level were a circular shrine of the 2nd century BC for offerings to the Chthonic divinities, and a monument to Mithridates Eupator, King of Pontus (120–63 BC), with two Ionic columns and a frieze of medallions depicting his generals and allies.

A street runs between the Ínopos Reservoir and a row of shops to the east: between two of the shops is an alley, with a bench carved with dedicatory inscriptions to Serapis, Isis and Anubis. At the end of the alley a staircase leads to the ruins of **Serapeion B**, marked by several small 'horned' altars. The small temple is placed in the northwest corner of the court, facing south. The main street continues, bearing left in front of the House of the Inopos (*see below*). On the left beyond the reservoir and the Shrine of the Nymphs to its west is **Serapeion A (49)**, the oldest and most intimate sanctuary of Serapis on the island. Its temple stood facing west in a court, between two small porticoes; under its naos is a rectangular crypt, reached by a staircase and supplied with water by a conduit. Opposite the temple is a meeting room with marble benches with carved dedication to the Egyptians gods. On the surface of the bench on the west side has been carved a 12-by-12 chequerboard for playing games.

Three fine houses

In this area are three of the finer Delian houses: to the north of Serapeion A is a house with a simple, perfectly preserved mosaic floor, on which stands a single column. To the east, behind a beautiful marble street façade, is the **House of the Inopos (50)**, built around a central court with a peristyle on two sides. There are eleven large, un-finished, monolithic marble columns which lie where they were found, in an adjacent room. Further downhill to the east the pathway passes the **House of Hermes (51)**, an elaborate, four-storey dwelling of the late 2nd century BC, partially restored. The house takes its name from a number of herms found on the site. The entrance is by a narrow hallway; immediately to left are the latrines; at the end of the hall on the left is the bathroom proper with a terracotta bathtub still in place. The Doric peristyle court surrounds a marble impluvium. In the opposite (north) wall a wide marble doorway leads into the main reception room with two subsidiary rooms. On the east side of the court a small dining-room still preserves a painted plaster decoration, imitating marble plaques. Steps lead up to the upper floor.

Further to the west is a small late 4th-century BC **Sanctuary of Aphrodite (52)**, con-sisting of a temple surrounded by a number of ancillary buildings. Beyond this point, the path returns either to the museum or to the embarkation mole.

SOUTH OF THE HARBOUR

Along the shore to the south of the Sacred Harbour, a series of **magazines** or ware-houses have their backs to the Theatre Quarter. They would have opened onto a quay bordering one of the five basins of the Commercial Harbour. All have substantial thresholds for the fixing and locking of gates; one has a well-preserved peristyle court. Further south is the line of the city wall running down to the sea, followed by a second group of magazines. The blocks of buildings which follow are divided by streets run-ning parallel to the sea or at right angles to it; each has a central court surrounded by large structures used as bonded warehouses. A typical example is the **Magazine of the Columns (53)**. A hundred metres further south are the remains of a shoreside sanctu-ary of the Dioskouroi from the 6th century BC.

Approximately 800m beyond, following an indistinct path, is the Bay of Phourni; on the promontory to its north are the ruins of a Sanctuary of Asclepius. It consists of three buildings. The northernmost is a prostyle Doric temple with four columns; beyond is a large hall, probably an abaton or infirmary; and finally the propylaia to the sanctuary, paved in white marble.

RHENEIA

Less than 1km west of Delos stretches the lower half of Rheneia (pron: *Rínia; map p. 49*). The Rematiáris islets lie in the channel between. The archaeological interest on Rheneia lies mostly in its northern part, joined to the lower portion by an isthmus less than 100m across. The ancient settlement was around the bay of Aghía Triáda on the west coast. On the north side of the bay are remains of a **Sanctuary of Heracles** from the 2nd century BC. An impressive and curious rectangular building in the sanctuary has a deep, semicircular tank with a water spout in the form of a shell, and a delightful floor mosaic depicting swimming dolphins.

Of greater significance is the extensive **necropolis** on the east coast, opposite Delos. This was in effect the cemetery of Delos in the centuries following the prohibition of death and burial on the island after 426 BC. The purification involved the exhumation of all previous graves on Delos and their transferral to a prepared purification pit, located below the church of Aghía Kyriakí on the eastern shore. Its contents, with pottery from the 9th–5th centuries BC, are on Mykonos (*see p. 88*).

The area further south along the coast continued to be used as the **cemetery** for Delos after 426 BC. A large number of tombs, altars, sarcophagi, and several hundred carved stelai and inscriptions have been unearthed. In the midst is an underground two-level complex of loculi, entered by a staircase and central corridor.

On the northernmost tip of the island is the base of an ancient monument.

PRACTICAL INFORMATION

GETTING AROUND

Delos can only be reached from Mykonos (journey time 30mins). Boats run every morning (weather permitting) except Mon, from 9am onwards, from the old harbour of Mykonos (south mole), returning regularly until 3pm, when the site closes. Rheneia, also a restricted archaeological area, can only be visited by private arrangement with a caïque service in Mykonos.

WHERE TO STAY & EAT

Not on Delos. As a protected archaeological zone, the island has no commercial accommodation, nor catering.

FURTHER READING

The French site guide is very good. The 6th-century BC Homeric *Hymn to Apollo* describes much of the myth surrounding the island. See Jules Cashford, *The Homeric Hymns* (Penguin Classics).

MYKONOS

Mykonos is a curious phenomenon. Nobody could have predicted, a century ago, that this waterless and windswept island, known for its harshness since antiquity, would become home to almost 10,000 people, with twice as many guests in addition during the summer, famed for its nightlife, its gay life, its beaches and its international cuisine. It must be said that the frenzy of the '70s and '80s is largely over, and Mykonos has now settled into being a well-ordered, up-market tourist destination. Out of season it can be a delight, and few could be blind to the beauty of the Chora's curving harbour and the houses stacked behind, as seen from the sea on arrival. Mykonos is certainly never boring: for the student of humanity there is ample scope for reflection. With the fading of every riotous Saturday night into the dawn of a new Sunday, as the tables are finally being cleared at some of the more colourful of the island's bars around the church of Aghía Kyriakí, the silver-haired septuagenarian ladies, some with their wind-eroded husbands, are already gathering for a liturgy at the church in the cool of the morning. It is an encounter of two worlds, with nothing at all in common. But somehow both continue undisturbed.

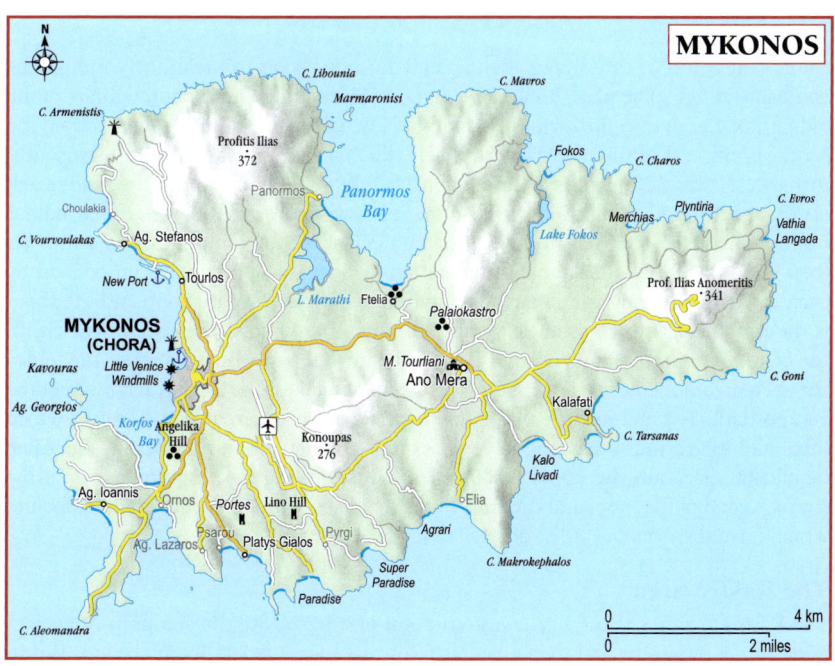

HISTORY OF MYKONOS

Underneath Mykonos, according to myth, lie buried the last of the giants who contested the Olympian gods and were finally destroyed by the rocks hurled by Heracles: the landscape is indeed granitic and boulder-strewn. Despite its infertility, man settled on Mykonos in the 5th millennium BC. There was some continuity through the Early and Middle Cycladic periods, and the recent discovery of a rich Mycenaean tomb near Chora attests a significant Late Bronze Age presence. After the Persian Wars the island became an Athenian colony. Strabo (*Geog. X, 5.9*) noted that baldness was prevalent on the island so that bald men were sometimes called 'Mykoniots'.

In medieval times, Mykonos was ruled by Venice. In 1537 the Turkish corsair Kheir ed-Din Barbarossa took the island and it remained an Ottoman possession for almost 300 years. In 1822, during the struggle for Greek Independence, the islanders repelled a Turkish attack under the leadership of the heroine Mando Mavrogenous. The island was united with the new Greek state in 1830, after which the traditional skills of the islanders as mariners led Mykonos to prominence as a merchant-naval centre until the advent of the new generation of steamships. The boom in tourism beginning in the 1970s meant that the town tripled in size in the space of a little over two decades.

MYKONOS CHORA

Chora's labyrinth of tiny streets, deliberately tortuous so as to break the wind, seems confusing at first. The plan, however, is not complicated: the main thoroughfare of the old part of Chora is in the form of a horseshoe, which begins (as Matogiánni) from the southeastern end of the main waterfront by the taxi stand, makes a deep loop south, turns west after 300m, passes the church of Ághios Geórgios, and then heads back north (as Mitropóleos and Georgoúli) to the southwest corner of the waterfront, not far from the Dimarcheíon. This route passes the main shops and churches, and within its loop it embraces the oldest core of habitation—an area which remains untouched by even the fiercest wind. In the narrow strip between the west of the loop and the shore is the waterfront known as Little Venice; at its southern end is the rise crowned with the famous windmills; at its northern end is the low mound which was once the fort of the ancient and medieval town, whose principal remnant is the beautiful church of the Paraportianí. The architecture of the town speaks of the different social groups which inhabited the various areas; the lower-class houses clustered in the narrow alleys just behind the harbour, the upper middle-class houses in the more spacious area at the southern end of the loop, and the ship-owner's houses with high ceilings and balconies which form the front at Little Venice.

The Kastro area

The Kastro area lies at the northwestern point of town. Once the acropolis of ancient Mykonos, a Byzantine and then a Venetian fortress succeeded it. Today the area is dot-

MYKONOS CHORA

TOURLOS, NEW PORT

Archaeological
Museum   Taxis

Delos

MYKONOS
PORT

Ag. Anna
Beach

N

Folklore
Museum   Dimarcheion

PL.
MAVROGENOUS

L. BONI

Paraportiani
Church   **Kastro** PL.
AG. MONIS

KAMBANI

PASALIADOU

EV.
TRIFONOS

Ag. Kyriaki

AG. ANARGYRON   SOTIROS   AKTI   AG.
KYRIAKIS

POSEIDONOS   **Ano
Myli**   Windmill

**Little
Venice**   GEORGOULI   GERASIMOU   DILOU   MATOGIANNI   ZOUGANELI   AG. SARANDA   AG. GEORGIOU

KAISONI   PL.
MELETO-
POULOU

KALOGERA   Windmill

Cathedral   **Tria
Pigadia**   Lena's House,
Maritime
Mus.   LITOUS

AG. IOANNOU

ANO MERA

MITROPOLEOS   Ag. Georgios   DYNAMEION
FOURNAKION

Catholic
Cathedral   ENOPLON

Windmills   XENIAS   BASOULA   AG. EFTHYMIOU   ARTAKINOU
TITANON

**Kato Myli
Hill**   K. MYLON

XENIAS   ARTEMIOU   N. BERTOU   Belvedere

Cemetery

Bus St.

AG. IOANNOU

0   250 yards

0   250 metres

AIRPORT

ted with churches, which have survived where the fortress itself has disappeared. Most famous is the church of the **Panaghía Paraportianí**, an iconic building of Cycladic architecture. Strictly speaking, the chapel of the Panaghía Paraportianí is the small oratory under the main dome; it is built on top of an earlier (15th-century) church dedicated to the Ághii Anárgyri. Attached on the south side is a church of Aghía Anastasía; to the northwest clings another, to the Holy Saviour (Ághios Sózon), with a third, Ághios Efstáthios, on the east. The result is a highly evocative profile, different from every angle.

In the floor of the small church directly to the south, **Aghía Soteíra tou Kástrou**, is the grave of Manolis Mermelechas, one of the most famous pirates of the Cyclades, who died of cholera on Mykonos in 1854. Some time around 1830, Mermelechas renounced his life of pillage and became a bakery owner, living on Mykonos as an ordinary citizen until his death.

The often windswept **northern quay** (Aktí Kambáni) is also the town's main promenade. A fish-market takes place here in the early morning, regularly attended by the island's tame pelican, Petros.

From the promenade to Káto Mýli and Little Venice

Though Mykonos has no tradition of wall-painting in its churches, there is a great variety of painted and carved wooden iconostases and other church furniture. Southwest of the promenade, set back in a square, is a group of Chora's most important churches, including the highly decorated Orthodox Cathedral of the **Panaghía Pigaditiótissa**, with its ornate wooden throne of 1769, whimsically carved with hidden faces. A broad flight of steps leads from the southwest corner of the square up to Káto Mýli and the low hill crowned by seven **windmills**. Five have been restored and now form part of the well-displayed open-air Museum of Agriculture.

Looking north from the hill of Káto Mýli, the heterogeneous assemblage of façades of the ship-owners' houses in **Little Venice** stretches attractively below. First-floor verandas, supported on beams above the spray of breaking waves, allowed the owners to watch for the arrival of their vessels as they rounded the tip of Rheneia.

The Tría Pigádia area

Inland to the east of Káto Mýli is the area known as Tría Pigádia, 'three wells', which were once the town's only freshwater source. Beside the church of Ághios Geórgios is the beautifully presented **Museum of Lena's House** (*open April–Oct 6–9; until 8 on Sun; free*). Lena Skorvanou died in the early 1970s. Her father was a wood-merchant, and in a manner typical of the merchant classes at the turn of the 20th century, he studied in Paris and his son (Lena's brother) in Alexandria—something which explains the provenance of many of the items exhibited. The bedroom roofs are made in traditional Cycladic fashion: woven with reeds, covered with a layer of seaweed, and bound in a 'cement' made with sand and crushed sea-shells, which sealed it and created a terrace above. This retained warmth in winter and cool in summer. The garden and main reception room of Lena's house are now occupied by the **Aegean Maritime Museum** (*open Easter–Oct daily 10.30–1 & 7–9.30*), which is remarkable for its collection of model ships and ship designs. The original lantern of the Armenistís Lighthouse from northwest Mykonos—the largest of its time in the Aegean (1890)—is exhibited in the garden.

The Archaeological Museum

At the eastern end of the promenade is the small **Plateía Mandoús Mavrogénous** (now the main taxi rank), named after Mando Mavrogenous, a heroine of the Greek independence movement whose bust stands at its centre. In 1822 she led the successful repulse of a Turkish attack on Mykonos.

Detail of the 7th-century BC pithamphora in Mykonos' archaeological museum.

North from the square towards the ferry port (now referred to as the 'old port'), the street skirts the sandy beach of Aghía Ánna: on the rise at its northern end is the **Mykonos Archaeological Museum** (*open daily except Mon, 8.30–3*), purpose-built in 1905 to house the finds from the purification bothros on the island of Rheneia. In 426 BC, following instructions from the Delphic Oracle, the island of Delos was purified for a second time (*see p. 65*): all the bones and grave-offerings were exhumed, transported to Rheneia, and buried in a new bothros, which covered an area of nearly 500m square. When excavated in 1898–1900, it yielded a uniquely complete range of ancient pottery dating from the 9th century BC to 426 BC.

The museum's most prominent exhibit is not from Rheneia but was found in the Chora of Mykonos: the magnificent, 140-cm high, 7th-century BC funerary urn or pithamphora with relief decoration (c. 675 BC) may possibly have been used for a child of noble birth. Around the neck is a wheeled Trojan Horse with carefully depicted soldiers inside, visible through 'windows'. The lower registers return again and again to scenes of Greek warriors wresting young children from resisting and imploring Trojan women. The repeated insistence on such a scene is puzzling.

The vase collection is of extraordinary richness and variety. Particularly fine is the 5th-century BC Attic nuptial lebes by the Syriskos Painter, with its exquisitely depicted dancing figures.

The room to far left (Room IV) contains grave stelae. Two of these, showing disconsolate mariners seated on the rocks with their boats drawn up in front of them, commemorate sailors lost at sea. Note also the block of marble (beside the door to the courtyard) with two pairs of footprints cut into its surface, perhaps of a father and son: this was a not uncommon form of votive dedication made before or after undertaking a long journey.

AROUND THE ISLAND

Fteliá, Palaiókastro and Áno Merá

The north coast of Mykonos is deeply indented by Pánormos Bay. At its southern extremity at **Fteliá**, a low ridge marks the site of the earliest settlement on the island, dating from the 5th millennium BC. The foundations of houses, excavated since the 1980s, are visible. Finds suggest a very different ecology on Neolithic Mykonos: the island was probably forested, and rich in flora and fauna.

On a conical hill overlooking Pánormos Bay from the east is **Palaiókastro**. From a distance the enceinte of medieval walls can be seen at the crown of the hill, with the church of Aghía Triáda at the summit. The 6th-century BC explorer Scylax of Caryanda refers to Mykonos as '*dipolis*', i.e. possessing two cities; if it did (though research on the subject has been inconclusive), then this would presumably have been the acropolis of the island's second city. The medieval remains here are from a Venetian fortress.

Áno Merá, in the centre of the island, lies in one of the few areas of relative fertility on Mykonos, and must always have been an important inland refuge during periods of piracy. Today it is a somewhat dispersed market village with a welcome air of normality. Its most celebrated monument is the Tourlianí Monastery, with an elaborately carved and painted iconostasis. An inscription over the 'royal doors' dates the work to 1776. The gilding and delicate colour are well preserved, enhancing the finely-wrought figures of the Evangelists in the architrave above; note, in particular, St John the Evangelist with the All-seeing Eye of the Almighty. The monastery was founded by monks from Paros in 1542; it was sacked by pirates in 1612, and then rebuilt in its present form in 1767. The marble cladding on the bell-tower dates from the 1930s. For Mykoniots it is perhaps the most important religious focus on the island.

Angeliká and Linó

In 1991, the largest **Mycenaean tholos tomb** in the Cyclades, from the late 15th century BC, was found on the hill of Angeliká about 1.5km south of Chora (*120m after the Ornós junction of the Chora ring-road, on the crown of the hill to right/west. Access is through the Hotel Tharroë of Mykonos, with their permission*). The corbelled dome, c. 5.5m in diameter, rises directly from the ground and is approached by a wide dromos (1.8m), spanned by a single lintel block. An exquisite necklace with papyrus flowers and shells in solid gold, three rock-crystal seal-stones and a quantity of painted pottery were found in the grave, suggesting that it was the burial for someone of considerable importance.

Close together a little further south are the remains of two **Hellenistic towers**. The first is at Pórtes, which marks the hill above Platýs Gialós, and whose lintel is visible against the skyline to the east as the road descends (*reached by taking the narrow concrete road east at the summit, just before the road makes its final descent*). Three monolithic granite blocks form the standing doorway, with the holes for the door fixtures visible. On the hill of Linó, 300m to the east, stands the base of a much grander tower (*1.2km south of the junction of the Aghía Ánna road with the airport road. Shortly after a sharp double turn, the base of the tower stands ahead, on a rocky eminence to the west*). Dating from the early 4th century, it is beautifully constructed of massive granite blocks, perfectly cut and interlocked. To the south are the remains of a rectangular structure of the same period. The complex may have been a small garrison post.

PRACTICAL INFORMATION

GETTING AROUND

Regular flights from Athens serve Mykonos. The airport is 2.5km from Chora. There are also ferry connections from Piraeus (on average three times daily in summer) and Rafína (between 5 and 9 times daily in summer), less frequent in winter. The fastest times are 2hrs from Rafína and 4hrs from Piraeus. The town has two separate ports; it is important to be sure which one you need. There are an average of three connections daily to Syros and Paros, and two to Naxos, during the summer. The caïques for Delos (daily except Mon; journey time 30mins) leave from the west mole of the old harbour.

WHERE TO STAY

Unless you have your own boat, you need to stay on Mykonos to visit Delos and give yourself enough time there. In high season it's busy and noisy; out of season it is extremely pleasant. The hotels suggested below are convenient and central, and out of season should be reasonably peaceful. Mykonos has a staggering quantity of hotels. For those who want to be in the heart of Chora, **Zorzis** is a small boutique hotel, open year-round (rare in Mykonos) with characterfully furnished rooms and friendly management (*Kalogerá 30; T: 22890 22167; www.zorzishotel.com*). Opposite, and similar in style, is the French-owned **Chez Maria** (*T: 22890 27565*), with a restaurant below. Since the 1950s the **Leto Hotel** has provided spaciousness and full services, in its own gardens right beside the museum: it is best patronised outside high season, during which it can become noisy at night (*T: 22890 22207; www.letohotel.com*). Of the luxury hotels, **Cavo Tagoo** has the most interesting architecture (*T: 22890 23692, www.cavotagoo.gr*). Delightful, attentive family management and unpretentiousness have always characterised the **Rhenia Hotel** in Toúrlos: it is set back on the hill above the new port away from noise, 2km from the town centre (*T: 22890 22300, www.rhenia-bungalows.com*.

WHERE TO EAT

The only simple Mykoniot fish taverna left in Chora is **Kounelas**, which serves good seafood in a tiny walled garden (just off the wa-

terfront, two alleys east of the Dimarcheíon). For imaginative Japanese and Pacific fusion cuisine, **Nobu of Mykonos** at the Belvedere Hotel in the Róchari area of Chora is highly prized. **Casa di Giorgio** (in the open *plateía* behind the Catholic Cathedral) has a wide variety of genuine Italian dishes. For a pleasing vantage point from which to watch the sun set, it is hard to do better than the balcony of the **Veranda Bar** in Little Venice.

Elsewhere on the island, traditional fare and environment can be found at **To Koutouki tou Limniou** in Ághios Stéfanos, north of Chora. Some of the island's best fresh fish is prepared by **Markos' Taverna** at Divoúnia, in the east of the island below Kalaváti.

BEACHES

The sandy coves in the south of the island are very popular, and boast serried ranks of raffia umbrellas and sunbeds. There are nudist beaches here too: the names (Paradise, Super Paradise) are something of a giveaway. In the north the beaches are quieter: Fókos and Pánormos are more popular with families. The beach of Ághios Ioánnis in the southwest featured in the film *Shirley Valentine*.

FURTHER READING

James Theodore Bent's description of the μοιρολογίσται of Mykonos (the versifying professional mourners at funerals) is one of the best chapters of his work *The Cyclades, or Life among the Insular Greeks* (1885), reissued 2002 by Archaeopress, Oxford in the '3rd Guides' series, and in an abridged version by Anagnosis as *Island-Hopping in the Cyclades*.

TINOS

Tinos is largely untouched by foreign tourism but it is the most important destination for Greek religious pilgrimage. It is also a living island: there is a sense of activity here, a restless energy, felt in the incessant flow of pilgrims coming to visit one of Greece's holiest icons, but also in the ubiquitous terraces on the hillsides, arising from the toil of centuries of cultivation. It is felt, too, in the beautiful dovecotes dotting every corner of the island, reflecting a spirit of architectural playfulness; and in the marble, lovingly carved and used at every possible opportunity.

HISTORY OF TINOS

In antiquity the island was called Ophiousa ('abounding in snakes'); the name Tinos may derive from a Phoenician word meaning a serpent. A celebrated temple was dedicated to Poseidon, who was credited with sending storks to eradicate the snakes.

Tinos was settled in prehistoric times and flourished in the Middle Bronze Age; a small tholos tomb in the north of the island is evidence of a later Mycenaean presence. Around 950 BC the island was settled by Ionians. The main settlement on the island from the 7th century BC was Xóbourgo. In 480 BC the islanders were forced to serve in the Persian fleet against Greece, but their trireme defected to the Greeks before the Battle of Salamis, providing crucial information about Persian intentions. In the 4th century BC, the city was relocated from Xóbourgo to the site of the present town of Tinos. At the same time the sanctuary of Poseidon and Amphitrite was founded nearby.

In the wake of the capture of Constantinople in the Fourth Crusade in 1204, Tinos was assigned to the Latin Emperor; the island was taken by Marco Sanudo, nephew of the aged Venetian doge, Enrico Dandolo, and given by him to Andrea and Geremia Ghisi to rule as vassals. In 1390 Tinos, together with Mykonos, was bequeathed to the state of Venice. In 1407 it was awarded to Giovanni Querini, lord of the island of Astypálaia, but after his fall from favour it was ruled by a rector appointed by the Serene Republic. The island remained Venetian until 1715, the longest held of all Venice's possessions in the Aegean. As a consequence, it has the largest Roman Catholic population in the Cyclades, with its own bishop, convents, schools and churches.

After no less than 11 unsuccessful attempts, the Turks eventually captured the island in 1715, granting it a number of privileges. The raising of the flag of independence at Pýrgos in March 1821, however, provoked Turkish reprisals. In this highly charged atmosphere, a miraculous icon of the Virgin was unearthed in 1823. The cult of the icon has since made Tinos a place of national pilgrimage, not only at the major feasts of the Annunciation (25th March) and the Dormition and Assumption (15th August), but throughout the year. On the very day of the Feast of the Assumption, in 1940, a Greek cruiser, the *Helle*, was torpedoed by an Italian submarine in the port of Tinos, on the eve of the outbreak of war between Greece and Italy. During the German occupa-

TINOS

Andros

N

D

C

B

A

1

2

3

C. Livada

Livada Bay

C. Selinos

Drakonisi
I Kolymbithra Bay

Straits of Disvato

C. Steno
Disvato

C. Axenos

Plantiis
Panormou Bay
Rochares

Profitis Ilias
400

Koumelas
Mali
Marlas
Mamados
Ag. Thekla

Ormos
Panormou
Kyra Xeni
Pyrgos
Platia
Venardados
Ormos
Istemion
Apokofos

Katapoliani
Isternia

Kardiani
Ormos
Kardianis

Kolymbithra
Kato Kleisma
Aetofolia
Kalados
Kaloni
Komi
Ormos

Skalados
Krokos
Smardakito
Perastra
Monastria
Tarambados
Chatzirados
Ag. Romanos

Agapi
Skavochori
Volax
Loutra
Koumaros
Kambos
Xynara
Xobürgo
Sanctuary of Poseidon
and Amphitrite
Kionia
Klikados
M. Kechrovouni
Mountados

Livada

Mt Tsiknias
727
Myrsini
Stenı
Falatados
Mesi
Zados
Kato
Tripotamos
Sperados

Kardamados
Dio Chora
Triandaros
Berdemiaros
Stavros

Kechrovouni

Ag. Varvara
Ag. Phokas
Vryo Kastro

Lychnaftia
Fero Chorio
Ag. Ioannis Porto
Izbuli
Ag. Sostis
C. Ourio

Evangelistria
Chora
(Tinos)

5 km
2,5 miles
0
0

tion, there was heavy loss of life, especially in the north of the island. Over the last two centuries Tinos has suffered considerable emigration; but the population, estimated at 25,000 in the mid-19th century, has now stabilised at about 8,000.

TINOS CHORA & ENVIRONS

Modern Tinos (*map p. 92, C3*) is a busy, functional centre, grouped around the island's only reasonable harbour, on the site of the ancient Hellenistic city of Tenos. Much re-built in recent years, it lacks traditional character, but there is still plenty to see.

The old town and port

What is left of the old quarter lies directly inland of the port to the northeast, where two large churches encapsulate an important aspect of the island: within a stone's throw of each other are the **Orthodox church of the Malamaténia** and the **Roman Catholic church of St Nicholas**, symbolising the co-existence of the two communi-ties. In the main street west of the two churches stands a late Ottoman fountain, made by a local marble workshop.

The main harbour mole bears a simple **memorial** to a defining event of modern Greek and Tiniot history: the destruction by an Italian submarine torpedo of the naval cruiser *Helle*, or Ήλλη, on 15th August 1940 (*see History, above*). On the promontory protecting the harbour to the south is a monument to the islanders who lost their lives in the Second World War (with good views of the town and Xóbourgo). The impressive building on the east side of the port now houses the Tinos Cultural Centre, a library and resource-cum-exhibition centre.

The Panaghía Evangelístria

A broad boulevard leads uphill from the port to the Italianate church of the Panaghía Evangelístria (the Virgin of the Annunciation), which dominates the town from above. The matting on the right is for those who wish to make the ascent on their knees: this is one of the most important pilgrimage shrines in Greece. The quality of the Byzantine chant here is particularly high, especially on Sundays or feast days.

THE MIRACULOUS ICON OF TINOS

In July 1822, a nun by the name of Pelagia at the Convent of Kechrovoúni (*see p. 95*) said she had been visited, twice in a dream and once in a vision, by the Virgin Mary, who had revealed to her the whereabouts of a miraculous icon, buried in the ground just outside the city of Tinos. In the autumn, excavations uncovered the ruins of a Byzantine church. On 30th January 1823 the icon was found, and work began on the construction of the present church, completed in 1831.

Two monumental entrances lead into a paved court. The church has two levels: the upper church houses the icon and hosts large public ceremonies; below is the Sanctuary of the Évresi (discovery) of the icon.

Inside the **upper church**, the icon is to the left in an ornate frame, protected in silver sheathing and so encrusted in ornamentation that the actual painting is virtually invisible. It is surrounded by silver ex-voto pendants: these depict anything from fighter-jets, cots, houses and boats, through to forks and even maps of Cyprus. The massive iconostasis incorporates a fine selection of plaques in various Aegean polychrome marbles. All around the gallery of the courtyard are inscriptions and graffiti carved by visitors.

The **Sanctuary of the Évresi** below is divided into three parallel chapels, corresponding to the three apses above. In the central chapel are the remains of the Byzantine church where the icon was found. The north chapel (left) contains a spring which appeared at the time of the discovery, faced with a marble front showing the Virgin Mary as the Fount of Life. The church also contains part of the torpedo which destroyed the *Helle*.

Towards the exit from the courtyard, a room to the right contains a **picture gallery**, with a miscellany of gifts as well as 19th-century works by Tiniot and other artists, including a study of an old woman writing by Nikolaos Gyzis, a native of Tinos and one of Greece's greatest academic painters.

The Archaeological Museum

Halfway down the main boulevard, on the right, is the island's archaeological museum (*open 8.30–3; closed Mon*). The small museum consists of three rooms and a courtyard: a fourth room (left of the entrance) is the curator's office; it is worth asking to see inside, as it contains examples of beautiful carved window casements of the 18th and 19th centuries, some decorated with marine motifs.

The three main rooms exhibit finds from the Archaic Sanctuary of Demeter below Xóbourgo, including magnificent 7th-century BC relief pithoi and an intriguing 1st-century BC sundial, as well as pottery and sculpture from the Hellenistic town and cemetery of Tinos. The courtyard contains sculpture and architectural members from the Sanctuary of Poseidon and Amphitrite at Kiónia (*see opposite*).

THE ENVIRONS OF CHORA

The construction of the new ring-road brought to light (just north of the Evangelístria) stretches of the walls and a bastion of the 4th-century BC town, and an ancient cemetery and the foundations of an ancient round tower (east of the Evangelístria).

Two and a half kilometres east of Chora, the coast road passes a conspicuous conical promontory to the seaward side: this is **Vrýo Kástro** (*map p. 92, C3–D3*), the site of Tinos' earliest prehistoric settlement (3rd millennium BC). Ascent is easy and the views are good, but there is otherwise little for the visitor to see.

The Sanctuary of Poseidon and Amphitrite

Three kilometres west of Chora, the coast road passes the 4th-century BC Sanctuary of Poseidon and Amphitrite at Kiónia (*map p. 92, C3; open 8.30–3; closed Mon*). At first sight, the remains appear uninteresting, but with a bit of imagination they can come to life. To the left on entering lies the podium of the temple. Nothing of the superstructure is standing, although some column drums in grey marble at the western end have been erected where they fell. To the south (between temple and sea) is the base of another small temple or shrine, with ample signs of where the bronze dowels and staples, which held the marble pieces together, have been lifted and removed.

Further behind, in the southwest corner, are the remains of Roman baths; the red, waterproofed plaster of one of the chambers is still well preserved. They were supplied with water from a spring (now dry) and nymphaeum in the northwest corner. In its centre is a semicircular stone bench, originally flanked by columns supporting a roof above. On either side were two rectangular basins of water, constantly filled by a jet of water channelled through two grooves in the marble above. Behind, it is possible to see how the water was led from the main spring, down a covered channel on the left (west) side, into the narrow retaining tanks behind the exedra, from where it flowed into the two open lower tanks.

In the opposite corner, at the back, is a semicircular honorific or sacred monument. It was once crowned with a ring of statuary (the foot-fixtures in one of the blocks are still visible). The much-eroded inscription behind mentions near its centre '....[Posei].. don kai Amphitriti'. Visible at the far southeast corner, is the end of a long stoa. The large area between the stoa and the temple was an open court paved in marble.

THE EAST OF THE ISLAND

Tinos is well organised for walkers; and a network of (partially) signposted paths and mule-tracks criss-crosses the island. A useful publication, available in bookshops in Chora, is *A Travelogue of Tinos*, which describes recommended walks across the island.

The southeast of the island and the Kechrovoúni Convent

The road due east from Chora leads towards Ághios Ioánnis Pórto with its sandy beaches. A kilometre after the pretty church of Aghía Varvára, the **Hellenistic tower** of Movolo is visible in a field below and to the right.

From Aghía Varvára itself, a road to leads north towards the villages of the interior, Triandáros and the beautiful **Dío Choriá**. Two kilometres west of Dío Choriá, the road passes the thriving **convent of Kechrovoúni** (*map p. 92, C3; closed 1–4.30*), dedicated to the Dormition of the Virgin, where in July 1822 Sister (Saint) Pelagia had her dreams and vision of the Virgin (*see p. 93*). The nunnery resembles a fortified Cycladic village: a labyrinth of tiny alleys and houses. The foundation is of the 12th century, though what is visible today mostly dates to the 18th century and after. The oldest part of the complex is the tiny chapel of the Zoödóchos Pigí, just before and to the left of the entrance to the main katholikon. The katholikon has a particularly ornate iconostasis. Most moving are Sister Pelagia's tiny quarters (above and to the right of the katholikon), in their holy simplicity: a living room, a tiny kitchen with a stove and a few pots, and a bedroom with minuscule bed and stone pillow. The views from Kechrovoúni (when it is not in the clouds) are excellent.

To the north, beyond the convent, the road drops down a little into the interior of the island. All around is an intricate patchwork of terracing. There is a grandeur and an openness to the landscape. To the east rises **Mt Tsikniás** (727m), rocky and barren, where at least one mythological tradition sited the abode of Aeolus, god of the winds. Its arid slopes are home to the rare and endemic yellow *Alyssum tenium*.

Below the mountain lies **Stení** (*map p. 92, D3*), another beautiful village, its main street running beneath arches. There are plane trees, gardens and springs, and a small folklore museum (*open mornings in July and Aug only*) containing the typical objects and furniture of a Tiniot house over the last 200 years.

The castle of Xóbourgo

Almost 2km west of Stení, a track leads (left) up to the Jesuit pilgrimage church of the Sacred Heart (Iéri Kardiá), and towards the dramatic Venetian castle of Xóbourgo on the summit above it. Xóbourgo, or properly Exóbourgo, means the 'settlement outside', referring to the fact that the area outside of the castle and around the summit of the hill was densely inhabited during the Middle Ages. Of the town itself, two fine vaulted cisterns (fed by a spring and still in use) survive, where the concrete track joins the asphalt road, as do the massive ruins of a monumental gate just below the church. The Venetian fortress is up a steep, stony path from the church. The first construction was probably from the 13th century and expanded later. The outer enceinte, beautifully constructed, still stands in part, in spite of the Turkish dismantling of the fortress in 1715. At the summit, two bastions dominate and control the final switchback of the ascent, through an outer and then an inner gate. The views from the top are wonderful.

From the Sacred Heart church, a path below leads down to the north, between stone walls, to the delightful village of **Koumáros** (*map p. 92, C2*).

Ancient Tenos

South from the Sacred Heart (*see above*) a path leads down, skirting the south side of Xóbourgo hill. After 10–15mins, you come to the scant but interesting **remains of ancient Tenos** (*map p. 92, C2–C3*), on the lower acropolis of the Geometric, Archaic and Classical periods. The descending path first passes a row of foundations of 6th-century BC buildings on the left; then a section of massive, polygonal Archaic walling of a defensive enceinte defining the lower extent of the acropolis. It continues to the right of the path towards the west and north, rising steeply up the mountain. Along it, a recent excavation has revealed some earlier (Geometric) wall foundations and a rectangular hearth, partly under the Archaic walls. Further west, more walls have been identified as a Sanctuary of Demeter (finds in Tinos museum). Above it, once again well within the enceinte, are more foundations, with storage pithoi still in place.

THE NORTH OF THE ISLAND

Voláx

The tiny village of Voláx (*map p. 92, C2*) stands in a strange lunar landscape of black granite boulders. The village itself, a picturesque settlement, grew up here because of the spring just below. Perhaps a little too pretty for its own good today, it is nonetheless an unforgettable assemblage of varied stone houses and flowering gardens, where the traditional skill of basket-weaving still flourishes. There is also a pleasant taverna.

The valley of Voláx is unique. No other landscape in the Greek islands is similar to this strange and circumscribed area, where either a volcanic eruption or meteorite fall, many millions of years ago, littered the ground with these black boulders.

Just before Skaládos, the landscape returns to normal, and the road descends, at Krókos, into the broad valley that divides the north of the island into two. Here the elaborate **dovecotes** (*see box overleaf*), which have been evident sporadically up until now, become much more numerous.

Sklavochóri and Aetofoliá

Sklavochóri (*map p. 92, C2*) was the birthplace of Nikolaos Gyzis (*see p. 94*). West of here the northward road levels out in a broad and fertile alluvial valley, which runs to the sea at **Kolymbíthra**. There are a couple of beaches here, beautiful and peaceful, but with little shade. From the junction at Kómi, a road takes you via Káto Kleísma to **Aetofoliá** ('Eagle's Nest'; *map p. 92, C2*), a village rich in springs, which rise at the upper end of the main street. The street soon becomes a mule-path as it heads out of the village, and leads to a charming stone bridge in the gorge and then up to the wild plateau above. The newly-built asphalt road rises by a different route to the same point. The Aetofoliá–Istérnia road continues through a wild and rocky landscape, with wide views of the sea.

ISTERNIA, PYRGOS & THE WEST

The village of **Istérnia** (*map p. 92, B2*) has the most panoramic site of any village on the island. Like nearby Pýrgos, this is a village which has lived on the quarrying, cutting and carving of marble, in a region that has done so since antiquity, every element of construction and decoration, from houses to bus shelters bearing witness to that fact. Past Istérnia, a right branch, overlooked by a saddle crowned by ruined windmills, leads to Katapolianí and the 18th-century monastery of the Panaghía Katapolianí.

Pýrgos and the far west

Pýrgos (formerly Pánormos; *map p. 92, B2*) is the largest village on Tinos, lying above the island's only natural deep anchorage. Village life centres on the enchanting *plateía*, with its cafés and tavernas grouped around a 150 year-old plane tree and facing a fine fountain. North and west of the square are a couple of small museums and an exhibition space (*open daily 11.30–2 & 6–8*) which celebrate the Tiniot sculptor Giannoulis

Chalepas, acclaimed as one of the foremost modern Greek sculptors. Pýrgos is also the birthplace of one of the most important Greek painters of the late 19th century, Nikephoros Lytras. Nikolaos and Periklis Lytras, also painters, were his sons. Their works are sometimes exhibited in a colonnaded building in the main street.

THE DOVECOTES OF TINOS

Hundreds of dovecotes stand in the valleys of Tinos, each one different, and each an outburst of architectural fantasy whose decorative value far exceeds any functional need. The intensive breeding of doves may have been introduced by the Venetians in the 13th century, but the first evidence we have of the dovecote as an architectural entity is only from 500 years later. It seems that dovecotes became a kind of status symbol, that neighbours competed with one another in the building of more elaborate ones.

On Tinos, where almost every acre of land was given over to cultivation, there was no pasture for animals and meat was scarce. An average-sized dovecote with a hundred pairs could provide nearly 200kg of meat annually. The birds' droppings were also a valuable fertiliser. The dovecotes are never far from fresh water and they face away from the north wind. They often have more than one floor, and could also be used for storage. The most important element was the lattice of openings at the top, and the external shelves on the sunny sides for the birds to bask on. The openings were created in fine, geometric patterns with small slates mounted in various shapes, creating purely decorative patterns.

From Pýrgos a road leads west to the village of **Marlás** (*map p. 92, B1*), with wide views of the sea. East of Marlás, after 2km, the asphalt road ends at the church of Aghía Thékla and, just below, the small monastery of Kyrá Xéni. Between these two (beside the road above the car park) are the remains of a carefully fashioned **Mycenaean tholos tomb** of the 14th century BC. Only half of the small dome survives.

PRACTICAL INFORMATION

GETTING AROUND

Tinos is reached from the Attic port of Rafína twice daily by regular (3½ hrs) and high-speed (1½ hrs) ferries. Boats call at Tinos Chora. There is no airport.

WHERE TO STAY

Most of the island's hotels are in and around Tinos Chora; good rooms for rent in private houses can also be found in Pýrgos, and in the villages all over the island. Simple, reasonably priced, hospitable and well-appointed, overlooking the harbour yet far enough away to be peaceful, is the **Voreades Hotel** (*open March–Nov; T: 22830 23845; www. voreades.gr*).

WHERE TO EAT

Chora has no shortage of tavernas, but none particularly stands out: for good local food it is best to eat in the villages. **Ta Lefkes** at Triandáros (*map p. 92, D3*) is a good place to sample the piquant, local Tiniot sausage and fresh and mild myzithra cheese. *Marathotiganita* is a very delicious local dish served in many village tavernas: a kind of vegetable fritter, flavoured with dried and fresh fennel. Surprisingly, given the number of dovecotes, it is not easy to find pigeon on the menu, though the **taverna at Loutrá** (*map p. 92, C2*) does commonly serve it.

ANDROS

The second largest island in the Cyclades, Andros strikes the visitor as quiet, reserved, clean and prosperous. The wealth derived from its shipping tradition has permitted the islanders to eschew mass tourism, preserving the natural beauty of the island, which is nonetheless hospitable. Important archaeological sites and a remarkable museum of modern Greek art add to its attractions.

HISTORY OF ANDROS

The island takes its name from the legendary Andreus, a general of Rhadamanthys of Crete, though alternative names include Epagris, Nonagria and the poetic Hydrousa ('well-watered'; Andros does indeed have a lot of water and most of it is good). There is evidence of prehistoric habitation from the early 3rd millennium onwards. Andros was colonised by Ionians around 900 BC. In the 7th century BC the city of Andros was established and flourished at the site now called Palaiópolis; the city founded three colonies in Chalcidice. Andros joined the Persian fleet of Xerxes at Salamis in 480 BC. In 450 BC the island became subject to Athens; and in the 3rd century BC to Macedon. In 199 BC, the Romans captured it, handing it over to Attalus I of Pergamon: the island then passed back to Rome in the will of Attalus III in 133 BC, together with the rest of his kingdom, and became part of the Roman province of Asia.

There were raids at the hands of Arabs (8th century), Venetians (12th century), Genoese (15th century), Turks (15th and 16th centuries), and of pirates throughout the whole period. In the early 9th century, the scholar and logician Leo the Mathematician studied on Andros. The island appeared prosperous and well-populated according to the accounts of 12th-century travellers, who noted its silk production and trade. In 1207 Marco Sanudo took the island and gave it to the Dandolo family as a hereditary fief under Venice. In 1566 it passed to the Turks, but enjoyed a degree of autonomy under Ottoman rule, allowing it to become a commercial centre with its own merchant fleet.

The island became part of the newly constituted Greek state in 1833. Andriot shipowners invested considerably in steam shipping in the early 20th century. In 1927, 79 steamships were registered in Chora. The island's present wealth is the legacy of these activities.

ANDROS CHORA

The setting of Andros Chora (*map p. 101, C3*) is best appreciated from the roads above it to the north and south: It stretches out, along a needle-like promontory jutting into a wide bay. The old whitewashed town (Káto Kástro) occupies the headland, with the 13th-century Venetian fort at its northeastern extremity; the 19th- and 20th-century

ANDROS

0 —————— 5 km
0 —————— 2,5 miles

Tinos

town (Áno Kástro) is inland and behind. The settlement of Chora dates from the early 13th century AD, when people moved here from the old capital on the west coast (Palaiópolis; *see p. 105*).

Chora's striking and dignified Neoclassical buildings reflect its shipping-based 19th- and early 20th-century prosperity. Odós Embiríkou, the main artery of Chora, lined by fine buildings, is named after one of the island's principal shipping families, the Embirikos. The street ends in Plateía Kaïri, lined with cafés and centered on an Ottoman fountain (1818), surmounted by a Byzantine door-finial. It dates from 1818, just three years before the end of the Turkish occupation.

The Archaeological Museum

The museum, on Plateía Kaïri (*open 8.30–3; closed Mon*), is arranged on two floors. On the upper floor are finds mainly from the Geometric settlement at Zagorá (*see p. 107*), giving a sense of life in the so-called 'Dark Age' (9th and 8th centuries BC), including a pot bearing one of the earliest Greek inscriptions.

Finds from Palaiópolis (ancient Andros), the island's principal settlement from the 7th century BC to the 7th century AD, are on the ground floor. These include a fine Archaic kouros and a remarkably well-preserved Roman copy of the *Hermes* of Praxiteles. Faint traces of the original colouring are still visible in places.

The Goulandris Museum of Contemporary Art

The museum (*open June–Sept 10–2 & 6–8 daily except Tues; May and Oct 10–2 Sat, Sun and Mon only*) is in two buildings below the Archaeological Museum to the north: to the left of the stairs is a permanent collection of sculptures by Michalis Tombros, who was of Andriot extraction, as well as works by modern Greek painters. The building to the right of the steps houses a library and a changing exhibition of contemporary Greek art.

Around the Kastro

East of Plateía Kaïri, the street continues through an arched gateway, originally the outer entrance to the Venetian Kastro. The streets beyond are narrower, but most of the buildings are of the 19th century. In a tiny courtyard off the second street to the left is the Catholic church of Ághios Andréas, dating in its present form from 1749.

Back along the main artery of Káto Kástro is the church of Ághios Geórgios, which contains many fine ex-votos of boats. Many of the houses here have arched, upper-storey loggias. The street then finishes in Plateía Ríva at the town's northeastern extremity, dominated by a large bronze statue of the *Unknown Sailor* (Michalis Tombros, 1957). Looking onto the square is the Maritime Museum (*open July and Aug 10–1*).

The town ends here, but on a rocky outcrop separated by a narrow channel are the remains of the Venetian Kastro. From the early 1200s, this citadel protected the small harbour to the north from piracy. In the 14th century it was adapted as the residence of the Sanudo and Dandolo overlords. The core of the main defensive tower still stands to a considerable height, but the walls are mostly gone. A beautiful, steeply-arched bridge still remains, connecting the islet to the promontory.

CENTRAL ANDROS

The Mesariá Valley (*map p. 101, C3*) is a landscape of unspoiled villages, springs and fertile gardens: it also contains a number of interesting and ancient churches. Distances are small, making the area a pleasure to walk in.

Churches of the Mesariá villages

The village of **Mesariá** has a large church of Ághios Nikólaos, restored in the 19th century, with fine marble decorations (18th century) around the west doors; the south doorway is surrounded by a 12th-century marble frame from an earlier church. Across the road is the tiny church of the Taxiárchis Michaïl; its west door has an intricate marble surround of the 12th century. The masonry is also very fine.

The 13th-century church of the Taxiárches at **Ypsiloú** has a Greek-cross plan and a cupola on two columns and two piers. Further west, the village of **Ménites** has many finely decorated springs. The earliest and best preserved of these middle Byzantine churches is at the western extremity of the valley, at **Melída** (*map p. 101, B3*). Again dedicated to the Taxiárchis Michaïl, it dates from the 11th century and its octagonal cupola drum and the faceted apses have beautiful cloisonné masonry. The northeast corner contains an ancient inscribed marble block.

Steniés

The road north from Chora leads to Steniés (*map p. 101, C2*), a beautiful village with a good cross-section of Andriot architecture. The streets are without traffic; the sound is only of running water, gushing from a spring by a central washing area, shaded by a building above. There are many stately Neoclassical mansions with gardens of cypress, lemon and fruit trees. The luminous interior of the **Metropolitan church of Ághios Geórgios** contains some unusual, academic murals of the 1930s by Kostantinos Mavropoulos. A quarter of a kilometre west of the village is the ruined **Bísti (Mouvelá) Tower**, a 17th-century house fortified against pirates. To the east, on the coast, is the unspoilt **pebble beach of Giália**.

Apíkia and the Pithára Valley

From Steniés, the road rises towards **Apíkia** (*map p. 101, C2*): as it crosses the stream on the last bend before the village, steps to the left lead up to the **chapel of Ághios Nikólaos**, part-church, part-cave, carved out of the cliff—very probably the christianising of a pagan shrine to Pan. The **Sáriza spring** rises in Apíkia; its water gushes from a marble lion's mouth just above the Pigi Sariza Hotel in the village. The water is famous, is bottled and marketed in Greece, and is believed to have notable therapeutic qualities. It has a delicate mineral flavour and is worth any journey made here to taste it.

From Apíkia, just before the spring, a footpath leads west up the scenic **Pithára Valley**, which follows a mountain stream with waterfalls and shaded pools, rich in interest for the bird and butterfly lover. A kilometre and a half above Apíkia, the road first passes the abandoned 18th-century monastery of Aghía Eiríni, high up on the hillside, and then the **monastery of Ághios Nikólaos**, 2km further (*1.5km down the signed track to the right*). This is a living and working monastery of great prosperity. The katholikon, founded in 1560 and completely restored in 1757–60, is in a curious masonry of grey-white Andriot marble and yellow Skyros sandstone. The narthex contains remains of frescoes. Witnessing the monastery's continuing vitality, numerous ex-votos hang from the silver candelabra.

THE NORTH OF THE ISLAND

Batsí, Andros' principal tourist centre (*map p. 101, A2*), is a pleasant town built up around a small cove and harbour, with shops, tavernas, cafés and hotels. Three kilometres south of Batsí, the coast road passes the seaward **plateau of Ypsilí**. This site (*closed at the time of writing*) has revealed a Geometric settlement of the 9th and 8th centuries BC, similar to that at Zagorá (*see p. 107*). The wall of the acropolis is clearly visible. To its south are foundations of dwellings. Within the wall are the stone foundations of an early 6th-century BC temple of megaron plan with stone benches and tables inside.

The Zoödóchos Pigí and the tower of Ághios Pétros
On an inland eminence almost due north of Batsí is the **Convent of the Zoödóchos Pigí**, also known as Aghías (*2km north of Batsí on the coast road, a sign points to 'Της Αγίας', reached after a climb of 3.4km; closed 1–4.30*), a vast fortress-like building in a bleak setting, occupied by just two nuns. Though founded before 1400, the present buildings are mostly from the 18th–19th centuries. The katholikon has a fine templon screen.

Three and a half kilometres north, on the southern edge of Gávrio, a road inland followed immediately by a turning to the south, leads to the **Hellenistic tower of Ághios Pétros** (*visible from the road; a track leads 200m across the hillside to it; access is not easy*). This is one of the best preserved ancient Greek cylindrical towers in the Aegean (probably 4th century BC). Such towers were numerous in the Cyclades, but their function remains unclear. Possibilities include signalling, refuge, garrisons and storage. The Ághios Pétros tower, made of large limestone blocks, still stands to over 21m. A massive spiral staircase, still partly preserved, communicated between its four (or five) upper storeys, each of which had a large framed window looking toward the sea. Supports for the first wooden floor can be seen 3–3.5m above the top of the lower chamber.

The surrounding area was vital to the agriculture of the island, but also had iron mines. The tower perhaps played a part in the overseeing and protecting of these activities.

Gávrio and the far north
Gávrio (*map p. 101, A2*) is Andros' only active port, with ferries to and from the mainland. Beyond it lie open, windswept uplands. The coast road leads north to the small Venetian **Makrotántalo tower**, a small, ruined Venetian tower which marked the western entrance to the straits between Euboea and Andros.

On the main road north, shortly after **Epáno Fellós**, which has open views and a good spring, is a track to the right for Amólochos. Here, immediately on the right, are two quarries of local marble. Beyond them the road climbs to **Amólochos** (*map p. 101, A2*), whose stone houses and mansions (many now abandoned) bear witness to former wealth, brought by silk production 200 years ago. Today there remain only the magnificent, open views towards one of wildest corners of the Aegean Sea. East of here, on the coast, is the perfect, unvisited sandy **beach of Vitáli**.

PALAIOPOLIS

Five kilometres south of Batsí, the coast road reaches Palaiópolis (*map p. 101, B3*), the ancient city of Andros and political centre of the island from the 7th century BC to the 6th century AD. The siting is splendid and beautiful, but the archaeological remains are meagre, compensated by the informative displays in the museum by the road.

The city was laid out in a theatre-shaped declivity in the western face of the island's highest mountains (Mts Pétalo and Kouvára). Two main gorges with waterfalls cut through the slopes; they are responsible for the silting up of the ancient harbour below and the burying of much of the city's (lower) public areas.

Visiting the site

Exploration of the site is difficult, and it can only be reached on foot: two paths with steps descend to the harbour and beach: one down the southeastern perimeter, the other down the northwestern side. Clearly visible from above is the submerged harbour mole. Behind the north end of the bay, where the mole meets the shore, are the overgrown remains of Roman Baths; on the rocky outcrop which divides the bay to the south, there appears to have been a watchtower. It is not easy to penetrate the interior of the site, but a small excavation in the centre of the first tier of the hill reveals the marble base of a stoa-like building from the agorá. By the northwestern path, nearly two thirds up, are remains of an Early Christian basilica. Most impressive—but hardest to locate and to reach—are the massive late Classical retaining walls, built of huge blocks, which reinforced the terracing of the city where the slope is at its steepest (*down to the right, below where the northwest path levels out, amongst dense olive and cypress groves on the northern edge of the northern gorge, about 80–100m below the level of the modern road*).

The **Palaiópolis Museum** (*open 10–3 except Mon; free*) displays explanatory material and a choice collection of finds, including a small, articulated puppet (no. 43); a 6th-century BC bronze figure of a dressed kouros, a stone carving of Bellerophon and Pegasus (no. 163), a large Classical lion; and an inscription with a partially legible poem spoken by the goddess Isis.

THE SOUTH OF THE ISLAND

Moní Panachrántou and Epáno Kástro

The slopes on the southern side of the Mesariá Valley are crowned by the whitewashed bulk of Moní Panachrántou (*map p. 101, C3; closed 1–4.30; a pleasant 2-hr walk from Chora; also accessible by car*), built like a fortress, with spectacular views. It is said to have been founded by the soldier-emperor of Byzantium, Nicephorus II Phocas, in the second half of the 10th century. Almost everything visible today is from the 17th century, except for the 15th-century **katholikon**, dedicated to the Dormition. The monastery is entered through a succession of courtyards and arched passages, full of trees, plants and the sound of running water. Once home to over 200 monks, it now has only one permanent resident. The katholikon contains fine frescoes, but its main sight is the **templon screen**, revetted in its lower areas with splendid late 16th-century Iznik tiles.

Just below the monastery is an 18th-century chapel (1759) by a dried-up spring, with a large and curiously-fashioned washing area in front. Further down the slope are several abandoned hermitages clinging to the side of the mountain.

Above the monastery the road crosses a watershed and the landscape changes considerably. A high plateau opens to the south with spectacular views to Tinos; three impressive limestone caps, or tors, march in line across a rugged landscape, chequered with miles and miles of the characteristic Andriot walling.

THE FIELD-WALLS OF ANDROS

The hillsides of Andros are covered everywhere by the island's own peculiar and very original kind of dry-stone walling. These walls, which separate areas of pasture and run for miles across the landscape, are characterised by the inclusion of large, roughly triangular flat pieces of schist, fixed vertically in the ground every two metres or so, parallel to the line of the wall, while the rest of the wall is composed of small, narrow stone in-fill. The result is one of great beauty, in particular when the light is low and the vertical slabs reflect the sun. This method of construction is also found in places on Tinos and on other Cycladic islands, but is nowhere as beautiful and plentiful as on Andros.

To the south of the monastery is the Dipótamos Valley, scattered with villages and **water-mills**. An example of these lies just upstream of the junction of the road from Panachrántos with the Chora–Kórthi road, near Éxo Vouní.

From the Éxo Vouní junction it is 1.7km to Kochýlou, where a small road is signposted to the left to 'Παναγία'. This leads up towards the summit of the easternmost of three limestone tors. At the road's end, steps continue up to a recent church. Beyond it are the remains of the Venetian castle and fortifications of **Epáno Kástro** (*map p. 101, C3*), probably built at the end of the 13th century, in a spectacular site used as the island's safest refuge between the abandoning of Palaiópolis in the 7th century and the foundation of the Chora in the 13th. There are clear remains of cisterns left of the path, and remnants of the fortification wall. The views of the island and of the others scattered around are unforgettable.

Around Kórthi

From Kochýlou the road descends to the bay of Órmos (*map p. 101, C3*) through a chain of villages—Stavrós, Episkopeío, Lardiá, Rogó; often referred to collectively as Palaiókastro—all of which have many abandoned traditional houses. The village of **Kórthi**, 2km inland from the bay, has some stone towers and mansions of the 17th and 18th centuries: perhaps the finest example stands amid cypresses and olives in the valley just below **Aïdónia**. Its principal church (west of the main modern church), dedicated to the Forty Martyrs of Sebaste, is of the early 18th century but incorporates elements from an earlier building. Over the outside of the west door (above and to the right) is an unusual and notable marble icon, carved in folkloric style in the early 1730s: below the Almighty in a nimbus are the 40 semi-naked saints, disposed in rows, with their arms crossed in front of them. Such plaques are a particular feature of 18th-century Andros. A little further north in **Áno Kórthi**, east of the village *plateía*, is the 12th-century church of Ághios Nikólaos, next to a ruined Venetian mansion. The village of **Aïpátia** has some beautiful dovecotes.

ZAGORA

At Stavropéda (*map p. 101, B3*), the main road from Chora descends in a V-shape to join the roads from the south of the island. Half a kilometre south of the junction is the isolated church of Aghía Triáda: from here a path leads down to the archaeological site of Zagorá (*access is difficult and takes 50mins each way: a stick is necessary to clear cobwebs and vegetation along the pathway. The path ascends beside the church and branches to the right: after 15mins, at a T-junction, go steeply right, then follow round to the left. The path skirts the slope of the mountain: it is best not to leave it until you see a clear perpendicular track leading straight down to the neck of the headland*).

The site was first excavated in the 1960s by the University of Sydney, its artefacts are now in the museum in Chora (*see p. 102*). Zagorá's heyday was in the Geometric period, between 850 and 700 BC, though habitation began in the 10th century BC. There are not that many significant sites from this period in Greece, hence Zagorá's importance.

The site

From the path, the layout of the site becomes clear: the headland's escarpment provides a natural fortification on the seaward sides, and its neck is cut transversely by the remarkable 9th-century BC fortifications. Foundations of houses and buildings lie within. The site is protected, commands a tiny harbour far below, and offers strategic views of the sea and neighbouring islands, but no source of water is evident today. More recent walling and buildings make the site a little confusing.

The **fortification wall** is best preserved at the southern end. Constructed meticulously of schist rock, it was probably about 2.5m high, and varies in thickness from 2–4m. A gate is visible with the base of a bastion to its north: this took care of the exposed right-hand side of an external attacker. The town appears to have grown organically with no clear plan. **Remains of houses** are mainly concentrated in the centre, though a number of buildings abut the inside of the walls; they may have been used as magazines. The houses, constructed of schist, had baked mud roofs over wooden beams. In the centre, near the highest point, are the **foundations of a temple**: there is a pronaos, and a naos with the base for what was possibly a cult statue visible in the middle. It is much later, Archaic or Classical, probably built over the site of an earlier predecessor, and was maintained after the abandonment of the settlement. It is orientated on a due north–south axis. Nearby is a **complex of houses and rooms**, one with a central hearth and benches around it.

Cape Strofílas

Important evidence of early prehistoric settlements has been found on the promontory of Strofílas (*map p. 101, B3; access restricted*), where one of the largest Neolithic settlements (5th millennium BC) in the Aegean was protected by substantial walls. Excavation has revealed large buildings, and a very early sanctuary comprising a large hall (c. 100m square) with a circular stone construction at its centre. Perhaps the most significant find here is the variety of shallow-carved rock-art of the late 5th and early 4th millennia BC, found on many of the blocks and flagstones and depicting ships, animals and various abstract designs.

PRACTICAL INFORMATION

GETTING AROUND

Two daily ferries from Rafína (2hrs; 1hr by high-speed). Boats dock at Gávrio.

WHERE TO STAY

There are small hotels in Gávrio, Batsí, Chora and at Órmos. In the centre of Chora is the **Archontiko Eleni Hotel** in a restored Neo-classical mansion (*T: 22820 23471*).

WHERE TO EAT

A reasonable variety of good, principally fish and vegetable dishes can also be found at On-onas, a small *mezedopoleíon* right down in the corner of the harbour below the north side of Káto Kástro in Chora. The tiny **Madoula** res-taurant on the front at Nimboreió, just north of Chora, serves fresh, well-prepared dishes. Traditional fare in beautiful surroundings, can be enjoyed at the taverna of **Tassos**, just beside the Sáriza spring at Apíkia. Two good rural restaurants deserve are the panoramic **Taverna Bozaki** in Ypsiloú, and Taverna Kossis on a wild hillside north of Epáno Fellós. Andros is famous for its spicy sausages, and for an omelette-like dish called *froutália*. Its almond biscuits are called *amygdalotá*.

FURTHER READING

Aegean Days by J. Irving Manatt (originally published 1913) is an interesting period piece with a sensitive evocation (in Part I) of Andros at the turn of the last century.

PAROS

Paros has more than one claim to fame. It is the home of the 7th-century BC poet Archilochus, whom the ancients viewed as almost as great as Homer himself. More visibly, it is the source of some of the world's finest marble, of which many of antiquity's greatest sculptures were made. It is also home to the Ekatontapyliani, one of the most important Byzantine churches in Greece. But Paros wears its greatness lightly. Though only small, it has three beautiful towns, Parikiá, Náoussa and Léfkes, all of quite different and contrasting characters. On the island, it is possible to eat well, visit remarkable monuments and swim from some of the most attractive beaches in the Cyclades.

HISTORY OF PAROS

Paros and its outlying islands attracted prehistoric settlers. A Neolithic village thrived on the islet of Sáliagos in the 5th millennium BC, and important Early Bronze Age settlements and cemeteries existed throughout Paros, already trading with Crete, other islands and the mainland. An important settlement at Koukounariés dates from the last years of the Mycenaean period; after its destruction in the 12th century BC, the site was re-inhabited, and it prospered during the Geometric era. The island was colonised by Ionians, and in the 7th century BC established its own colony on Thasos. Thasos brought her mother-city great wealth, and Paros enjoyed a golden age of influence and creativity in the early 6th century BC, at which time its famous marble also began to be quarried.

In 490 BC, Paros supported the invading Persian fleet. Miltiades, Athenian victor at Marathon, lost his life in a failed retaliatory attack. Paros did not contribute to the defeat of Xerxes at Salamis in 480 BC, and afterwards became subject to Athens. During the Peloponnesian War it tried to shake off Athenian dominion, failed, and was assessed to pay the highest tribute of the Delian League. Independent after 403 BC, it later joined the Second Athenian League (in 377 BC), and came under Macedonian influence after 357 BC. Agoracritus in the 5th and Skopas in the 4th century BC were famous sculptors from Paros. From 100 BC, Paros was part of the Roman province of Asia. In AD 326 St Helen, mother of Constantine the Great,visited the island.

A base for Saracens and pirates during the 8th and 9th centuries, the island became poorer and dramatically less populated. Its fortunes revived in 1207, when it was brought by Marco Sanudo into the Duchy of Naxos; in 1260 the Kastro was built in Parikiá. In 1537 Kheir ed-Din Barbarossa conquered Paros, which remained under Turkish dominion, with an administrative centre at Léfkes, for almost 300 years. Piracy once again flourished. During the Russo-Turkish War of 1768–74, Náoussa became the naval base for the Russian Aegean fleet. Paros was reunited with the fledgling Greek state in 1832, at which time it became the home of the heroine of Greek Independence, Mando Mavrogenous (*see p. 84*).

PAROS & ANTIPAROS

Paros

Antiparos

Despotiko

Viokastro
Filizi
Alyki Bay
Viglakia
Langéri
Ag. Ioánnis
Alyki
Naoussa Bay
Palaeopyrgos
Ambelas
C. Damoulis
Naoussa
Istérnio
C. Antikephalos
C. Korakas
Mt Antiképhalos
C. Kratsi
Molos
Molos Bay
Mt Kephalos
Piso Livadi
Ag. Antónios
Kolymbithres
Ag. Andreas
Marmara
Koukounariés
Protoria
Prodromos
Marpissa
Kamares
M. Longovardas
Kostos
C. Choni
Makronisi
Kalami
Ag. Charalambos
261
Profitis Ilias
Eilitas
Marathi
Ancient quarries
Lefkes
Dryonisi
Dryos Bay
C. Pyrgos
Délion
Tris Ekklisiés
Ag. Minas
Voúnia
Ag. Ioánnis
Kaparoú
Dryos
Krios
Ekatontapyliani
PARIKIA
Vounia
Aspro Chorio
Glyfa
Glyfa Bay
C. Xinos
Cave of Archilochus
Ag. Phokas
Parikia Bay
Kakapetra
Mt Ag. Pantes
Aneratsa
Kamari
Koukoumavlés
Christos tou Dásou
Agéria
Petaloudes
Kampos
Skorpios Museum
Faranges Bay
Portes
Ag. Efini
Sotires
Ghisidia
Alyki
Alyki Bay
Voutakos
C. Mavros Kanos
Panteronisi
Ag. Spyridon
Salangos
Pounda
Tourlos
Straits of Antiparos
C. Makria Miti
Tigani
Preza
Glaropouda
Kambos
Karouaros
Dipla
Antiparos
Soros
Livadi Bay
Cave of Antiparos
Ag. Georgios
Monastiria Bay
C. Trachilos
Tsimintiri
Mandra

5 km

2,5 miles

N

PARIKIA

The island's lovely capital of Parikiá, built over the city of ancient Paros, spreads on the east side of a wide bay. Ancient Paros was a rich city and modern Parikiá also has an air of prosperity. Two main streets traverse the length of the town: running north–south is the street known as Agorá. Its northern extension, Grávari, turns east from below the Kastro and leads to the island's most important monument at the edge of the old town, the 6th-century church of the Panaghía Ekatontapylianí.

THE EKATONTAPYLIANI CHURCH

This is the oldest and the most historically important church in the Aegean islands (*open daily 8–1 & 4–9*). Built over a 4th-century predecessor, it has been a place of Christian worship for nearly 1,700 years, withstanding the sack of Paros by Kheir ed-Din Barbarossa in 1537, as well as several earthquakes, notably that of 1773.

The church, dedicated to the Dormition of the Virgin, has two names, both first recorded in the 16th century. 'Katapolianí' refers to the site of the church as 'outside the city'; and 'Ekatontapylianí' is a poetic reference to the church possessing '100 gates'.

HISTORY OF THE BUILDING

According to tradition, St Helen, mother of the emperor Constantine the Great, put in at Paros during a storm on her way to Jerusalem in 326–27, and vowed to build a church to the Virgin in gratitude for a safe onward journey. Helen died in 328, but her wishes were fulfilled after her death, as a basilica church with a large atrium was built north of an earlier baptistery c. AD 330. In the 6th century, under the emperor Justinian, the church was rebuilt, now with a vaulted roof and dome. Tradition claims that one of the two architects Justinian had employed for Haghia Sophia in Constantinople, probably Isidorus of Miletus, was sent to Paros to superintend the new building, which was executed by a pupil of his, Ignatius.

The main church

A triple-arched entrance, echoed by triple-arched windows above, leads into the **narthex (A)**, a spacious, transverse portico supported by ancient architrave beams, filled at ground level with 7th-century marble panels.

The **naos (B)** is a centrally domed cross of unequal arms, c. 40m in length and 25m in width. The dome, vaults and floor were rebuilt in the 1960s. In front of the eastern piers of the dome, a couple of modern glass panels in the floor reveal two columns from the buildings of the ancient gymnasium beneath.

The **iconostasis** is a composition of different elements: the screen includes an ancient frieze; the columns, in different marbles and carved in heavy relief with vines, are also ancient pieces with 7th-century carving; the rest dates from the 17th century. The icons, many covered with protective silver revetment, were the gift of the of the Mavrogenis family in the 18th century. The only uncovered icon is the beautiful *Dormition of the Virgin* (**1**) to the right, a fine Cretan work of the 17th century. Against the northwest pier is a venerable icon of the *Virgin Orans* (**2**), dated to c. 1200.

The **women's gallery**, or gynaikaion, runs around the interior at the upper level. Only a few of its closure panels are original; most are modern replacements. It is entered by the flight of steps outside the church in the southwest corner (**3**), and provides the best views of the interior and of the area of the sanctuary behind the templon screen.

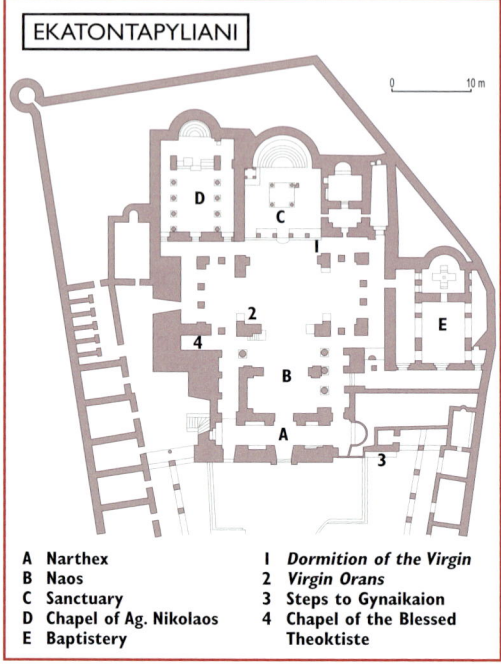

EKATONTAPYLIANI

A   Narthex
B   Naos
C   Sanctuary
D   Chapel of Ag. Niklaos
E   Baptistery

1   *Dormition of the Virgin*
2   *Virgin Orans*
3   Steps to Gynaikaion
4   Chapel of the Blessed Theoktiste

The **sanctuary (C)** is spacious and contains a synthronon with seven rows of seats, below a central episcopal throne flanked by two lesser seats, and centres on an altar covered by a magnificent domed ciborium. Beneath the altar table is an aghiasma, a natural pool of sacred water. The paintings on the wall above date from the early 17th century: they illustrate the stanzas of the Akathist Hymn to the Virgin, a sacred hymn to the Mother of God which is always recited standing up (*a-kathisis* = 'without a chair'). The surface of the paintings has been regularly chipped in preparation for the application of another layer of plaster and painting on top.

In a recess of the north wall is the small **chapel of the Blessed Theoktiste (4)**, a 9th-century hermit and patron saint of Paros, built around her tomb in the floor.

The Chapel of Ághios Nikólaos

The chapel of Ághios Nikólaos (**D**), originally of the 4th century (when it must have had a different dedication, as St Nicholas' cult became common much later), has an air of great antiquity, imparted by its reused ancient Doric columns. Its 6th-century dome has been renovated more recently. In the sanctuary are a small synthronon and throne, and vestiges of opus sectile floor. At the east end of the north wall are remains of 7th–8th-century murals of St Elizabeth and her son, St John the Baptist. The painting of *Christ and the Apostles* in the conch of the apse is from a thousand years later.

The baptistery

The beautiful baptistery **(E)**, contiguous with the main church and connected by a door into its south side, is probably the oldest element of the complex, one of the oldest surviving baptisteries in Christendom. Baptisteries, as places of symbolic death and rebirth, were frequently built on or near the site of a martyrdom: this was a way of celebrating the death of a martyr by acknowledging his or her entry into a new life beyond death, as well as appealing for the martyr's intercession on behalf of the neophytes subsequently baptised on the spot. This baptistery may have come into being, shortly after Constantine's Edict of Tolerance in 313, in order to commemorate the martyrdom of an unknown figure on this site, in the ancient city's gymnasium. The original 4th-century structure was an apsidal basilica; it was given its dome and vaulted roof in the 6th century. Its three door frames are constructed of ancient marble spolia, as is the cruciform font for baptism by immersion. Small areas of the 6th-century mosaic floor are visible north of the west door, beside the north door into the main church, and southwest of the font. The only surviving area of wall-painting, depicting St George and an angel, dates from the 12th century.

The courtyard

The courtyard in front of the main church, filled with flowering trees and cypresses, occupies the area of the porticoed atrium of the first structure. Today the monastic buildings which surround it are all from the 17th century. Mando Mavrogenous, heroine of the War of Independence (*see p. 84*), is buried here. The **monumental gate** (1678) in the courtyard's north wing was once the doorway of the church. The columns framing the door stand on marble bases sculpted into grotesque, pot-bellied, moustachioed figures. In the southwest corner of the courtyard is a small **ecclesiastical museum** (*open as church*), containing a good collection of icons, mostly from the 17th and 18th centuries, though of particular note is a fine 16th-century *Crucifixion* and painted sections of the 15th-century sacristy doors, depicting St Peter, St Paul and the Annunciation.

THE ARCHAEOLOGICAL MUSEUM

East of the Ekatontapylianí, a row of late Hellenistic and Roman sarcophagi marks the entrance to the archaeological museum (*open daily except Mon, 8.30–3.30*). The collection is small, but with some exceptionally fine pieces of ancient sculpture, mostly of Parian marble.

Courtyard: In the centre is a 4th-century BC floor mosaic found beneath the Ekatontapylianí, depicting the Labours of Heracles. South of the court is a row of unusual Archaic sarcophagi shaped in human form. Ahead, under the portico, stands the twice-lifesize cult statue of Artemis from the temple at the Delion (*see p. 118*), reassembled from over 40 fragments. At the left end of the portico is an elegant late 6th-century BC Ionic capital with a 4th-century BC dedicatory inscription to the Parian poet Archilochus (*see p. 118*).

Room 1 (left) contains prehistoric and early material. The earliest piece is a Neolithic figurine of the 4th millennium BC known as the *Fat Lady of Saliago*. Opposite is a very fine 8th-century BC amphora decorated with a battle scene. Also of particular interest (left wall) is a remarkably early grave stele of the 7th century BC, depicting a seated woman on a throne. In the rear partition is part of the Parian Chronicle (the greater part is in the Ashmolean Museum in Oxford), a marble inscription of 264–263 BC with a list of historical events. Two beautiful fragments of Archaic korai are at the centre of the room.

Room 2 (small room in middle) exhibits objects from excavations on the island of Despotikó, including an early 7th-century BC terracotta figurine of a female deity and the heads of three Archaic kouroi, as well as many bronze votives.

Room 3 (right) is dedicated to Archaic and Classical marble sculpture. Of particular importance are the mid-6th-century BC Gorgon (first bay), the lower portion of a relief (c. 500 BC) of a standing female figure wearing a pleated chiton (on right in doorway to second bay), and the statue of an enthroned goddess of the same date. Behind the latter is a marble relief, also of the same date, of the poet Archilochus reclining on a dining-couch, faced by his wife and surrounded by his emblems as both a warrior and a poet. A mid-5th century marble disc, painted with the figure of a discus-thrower, is a rare specimen of ancient painting.

CHURCHES & STREETS OF PARIKIA

The area between the Ekatontapylianí and the Kastro, traversed by Grávari, is an attractive network of streets with mostly **Cycladic houses** of two floors, often with trellised courtyards and wooden balconies on the upper floor, which extend over the street in places, creating small covered passageways. The external corners of buildings are frequently rounded so as to facilitate the passage of donkeys and mules. Along the main thoroughfares are some prominent Neoclassical houses built by prosperous merchant families. A number of these can be seen towards the western end of Grávari. A good example is the pedimented early 20th-century **Dimitrakopoulos Mansion** (south side), with a walled court to one side, a central balcony in wrought-iron supported on carved marble volutes, and a coloured trabeation.

The majority of the churches in the lower part of Paros date from the 17th century: they mostly do not have wall-painting, but have carved wooden iconostases, paved marble floors, and, in some cases, the traditional Cycladic raftered ceiling of reed wattle covered with a layer of seaweed and bound and sealed in a cement made with sand and crushed sea-shells. Of the many examples, two stand out. To the north side of Grávari is the **Panaghía Septemvrianí** (1592), with a fine marble door frame and a marble iconostasis. Two ancient Doric capitals are incorporated into the corners between the narthex and the naos, a third constitutes the altar. Fifty metres further west and one block to the south, on Karávia, is the church of the **Eisódia tis Theotókou** (1645), with wall-paintings of the 18th century.

At the point where Grávari and Agorá streets meet is a substantial **arcaded municipal building**, probably from the late 16th century. To either side of the arcade are two crudely carved reliefs of grotesque figures, a man (right) and a woman (left), apparently holding their stomachs. Opposite is a carved marble fountain (1777), one of three donated by Nikolaos Mavrogenis (*see box below*), who built the aqueduct that fed them. From the fountain, a street leads uphill to the Kastro.

THE MAVROGENIS FAMILY

The Mavrogenis were a Phanariot family, Greeks from Constantinople who had lived in the area of Phanari (today's Fener) on the Golden Horn. When the city was captured by the Turks in 1453, a part of the family left for the Peloponnese, from where they moved to Paros in 1715. They were educated and wealthy people; Petros Mavrogenis served as combined British and Austrian consul in the Cyclades and he sent his son Nicholas (b. 1738) to study in Constantinople with relatives who were dragomans, translator-envoys for Ottoman affairs in the pay of the sultan. Nicholas followed a similar career, and as a brilliant linguist and a favourite of the grand vizier Yusuf Pasha, he rose fast in the hierarchy and was eventually honoured with the title of Prince of Wallachia (Romania). He appears to have run a wayward and extravagant court in Bucharest: his horse was given a bedroom next to his own. But Mavrogenis had many redeeming features, insisting, for example that the peasantry should be able to make their appeals to him in person. His legislation helped both the Jewish and Orthodox communities, and he did much to help and protect his native Cyclades. On Paros, the aqueduct and marble fountains of Parikiá, as well as the lavishly cased icons, are the most visible testimony; but he also restored churches, built schools and upgraded the port facilities.

At first successful in his military campaigns, Mavrogenis ultimately failed the Ottoman cause when the Habsburg army invaded Wallachia in July 1789. A second defeat in 1790 cost him his life: he was killed on the sultan's orders and his head was sent to Istanbul. Thomas Hope, who knew Mavrogenis personally, included aspects of him in his remarkable novel *Anastasius*, which took London by storm when it appeared in 1819. It is an irony that the grand-daughter of this prince of the Ottoman Empire should have been Mando Mavrogenous (*see p. 84*), the heroine of the Greek revolution against Turkish rule. Mando died on Paros in 1840 and is buried in the courtyard of the Ekatontapylianí.

THE KASTRO

From the 6th century BC onwards, the northern side of the hill of Kastro was the site of a sanctuary of Athena. It included an imposingly large temple built in the 520s BC.

Due to erosion, the western two thirds of the **temple** have disappeared. Only parts of the eastern end remain, in and under a church. The temple was an Ionic-style building with two six-column porticoes at either end. Visible outside the church is part of its platform, built of gneiss slabs. Inside the **church of Ághios Konstantínos** (*entered through the adjacent church of the Evangelístria to the south*), several courses of the lateral walls of the temple's cella, in white marble blocks, can be seen constituting the lower part of the north wall. The adjoining 18th-century **church of the Evangelístria** has a low arcaded porch on its southern side, supported by Early Christian window elements from the basilica at Tris Ekklisíes (*see opposite*). In the street which curves northwards from the church, ancient spolia are so abundant that column drums are used as tables in the porches of houses.

On the left side of this street rise the walls of the **Venetian castle**, built c. 1260. The western half of the castle has eroded into the sea; best preserved is the northeast corner. It is constructed from a breathtaking amount of spolia, hundreds of marble blocks, architraves and columns obtained by demolishing temples and other ancient structures. They include 5-m long elements of the temple's marble portal (comparable to the Portára on Naxos; *see p. 134*). Visible from the south, high up at the top of the northeast bastion, is a round 4th-century BC tower-like structure or tholos, originally dedicated to Hestia: its shape served as a ready-made apse for the church of Christós, built around it inside the bastion, but now partially removed.

ENVIRONS OF PARIKIA

At the southern end of the promenade, the coast road rises towards a windmill and makes a detour round the small 17th-century **chapel of Aghía Ánna** (*key in house opposite Dimarcheíon, 50m to south*), which is almost entirely constructed from ancient blocks of Parian marble. Two hundred metres further west, just beyond where the coast road rejoins the ring-road, a scarp rising to the left (south) marks the scant remains of two ancient sanctuaries. Above the road is a 4th-century BC **sanctuary of Asclepius**. It centred on a Doric abaton, projecting perpendicularly from a stoa along the base of the scarp. There are rectangular marble-lined pools, by a spring, against the rock. Of the **sanctuary of Apollo Piathos** above it, only a terrace wall and some foundations survive, marked by a chapel.

East of Parikiá

At the junctions and on the ring-road to the east of Parikiá is a plethora of brown signs indicating minor archaeological sites. The most significant are the following:

Archaic ceramic workshop (*just west of the ring-road, two blocks in, and to the south of the main car park, underneath the extension of an apartment building to the left of the street*): The workshop (Classical to Hellenistic) comprises two large kilns, several smaller kilns, and two lined tanks for preparing clay. Potsherds from the site indicate that the workshop was in use through the Classical and

Hellenistic periods. Two hundred metres to the north, a sculpture workshop, with unfinished sculptures, has also been uncovered.

Hellenistic/Roman house (*underneath the Pensione Evangelitsa, northwest of the main car park on the west side of the ring-road: access down steps into basement*): Both the steps to the original upper floor and the imposing marble door-posts and threshold can be seen; a small earthenware pot is set into the window shelf. The house dates from the 2nd century BC.

Hellenistic houses and the walls of the ancient city (*east of the ring-road, from the junction just south of the Archaeological Museum*): The foundations of several Hellenistic residential blocks have been uncovered immediately east of the road: several floor mosaics are visible. Further up the road, above the modern cemetery, is a section of the Archaic walls, including the door-jambs of a gateway.

The Ághios Pantéléimon area (*behind the building across the main road and adjacent gully, from the upper, eastern tip of the pine-grove beside the Ekatontapyliani*): This large area, part cemetery, part sanctuary, has yielded a number of important pieces of sculpture, now in the Archaeological Museum. The most visible remains are of a stepped, circular Archaic funerary monument in white marble, which bears incisions for a dedicatory column or statue. Clearly visible on its first and second steps are several antique graffiti incised into the marble, including names, the image of a house, a phallic symbol, and many footprints.

The ancient cemeteries (*beside the Post Office, just in from the waterfront, 200m east of the church of Ághios Nikólaos*): This is one of the richest cemeteries so far excavated in the Cyclades, in use from the 8th century BC until the late Roman period. It was organised with walls dividing it into plots according to family or clan. Many different kinds of burial practice are represented: there are 8th-century polyandria, or stone-lined compartments for multiple burials, containing cremated ashes in amphorae; early cist graves for inhumations; graves made of ceramic tiles; Hellenistic marble urns with marble lids for ashes; and, most visible of all, Roman-era sarcophagi with lids designed as pitched roofs and sides decorated with funeral banquet scenes. Several marble grave stelae can be seen. The tallest was a boundary marker for the Geometric cemetery. Finds are displayed in a small exhibition space.

Tris Ekklisíes (*1.5km east of Parikiá, beside the road to Náoussa*): At the site known as Tris Ekklisíes are foundations of a large 6th-century Early Christian basilica, three-aisled with apse, as well as those of an apsidal chapel obtruding from the south wall. The paving of the sanctuary in Parian marble is very fine, and there are numerous marble columns, panels, capitals and templon elements, mostly taken from pagan buildings. Many bear Hellenistic inscriptions, and several show the incised imprints of feet. There is a marked number of these intriguing symbols on Paros, which elsewhere are more frequently found in sanctuaries of Isis and Serapis, as votive gifts or records of the presence of devotees. The inscribed plaques, now in the museum, referring to the building of a heroön to Archilochus, were found near here.

Archilochus

The soldier-poet Archilochus lived in the mid-7th century BC, more than a century after Homer. His subjects are human rather than heroic: he is the author of the earliest love lyrics in Greek and he is often seen as the father of satire.

Archilochus was possibly the illegitimate son of an aristocratic Parian family, and accompanied his father, Telesicles, on the mission to colonise Thasos, where he lived for some time afterwards. Though an effective soldier, in one battle against a Thracian tribe he threw away his shield and fled the field: he commemorates his action without shame, relating the incident with ironic humour in a way that heralds the coming of age of a new Greek humanism. After returning to Paros, he was killed around 652 BC in a battle against Naxos near the Elytas river, by a certain Calondas. The Delphic Oracle cursed Calondas for having slain a favourite, both of Apollo and of the Muses. Archilochus' greatness was never in doubt throughout antiquity, hence the elaborate heroön here on Paros, where his cult could be perpetuated. The monument was said to be the haunt of hornets and wasps.

North of Parikiá

On the panoramic summit of a rocky spur, 3.5km by road north of Parikiá, are the remains of the 5th-century BC sanctuary of Apollo and Artemis, known also just as the **Delion** (its view takes in the sacred island of Delos). In the southwest corner of a square peribolos is the temple, which features a fine marble threshold and a deep recess beneath the floor-level of the interior, probably a treasury for votive gifts; its cult statue was the colossal figure of Artemis in the Parikiá museum portico. East of the temple is an altar, and further south are remains of a porticoed structure with marble benches, perhaps a feasting room.

From the same road a left turn lead to **Kriós** (*map p. 110, C1*). There, near the shore, is a curious building, probably of late Roman or Early Christian date, still standing to a height of 6m and over 20m long, with an apse at the eastern end. Its function is a mystery, but storage has been proposed.

Beyond Kriós, the road finishes at the headland by the church of Ághios Phokás (5km). On the west side of the promontory are several caves; the one furthest south is dubbed the **Cave of Archilochus**.

NAOUSSA & THE NORTH OF THE ISLAND

The route from Parikiá northeast to Náoussa passes several places of interest. At 3km, after Tris Ekklisíes, the **hill of Profítis Ilías** (261m), site of several ancient cults, rises to the west of the road. The summit is best reached from the western side of the hill (*left turn at 3.5km, round north side of hill*) up a track passing a picturesque abandoned

View towards the summit of Mt Profítis Ilías, sacred to Zeus in antiquity.

monastery. The chapel of Profítis Ilías sits on the summit, which was previously, according to an inscription, a cult place of Zeus Hypat[i]os ('the Highest'). Down the spur to the southwest, at a point overlooking the port below, is a plateau with a raised knob of rock about 3m by 1m, perhaps an altar of Aphrodite or of Eileithyia. Further west by the edge of the spur is a cave with votive niches; nearby the faint outlines of feet are incised on a rock.

Longovárda Monastery and the Mycenaean acropolis

East of the main road (*map p. 110, C1*) stands the monastery of Longovárda (*open to male visitors only, 9.30–12*), founded in 1638 and rebuilt on a larger scale in 1675. The upper areas (pendentives, drum and cupola) are the original 17th-century work, while large areas lower down were repainted in the 19th century. Of particular note are two small icons executed by two brothers who were monks, Hierotheus and Methodius, painter and wood-carver respectively, in the late 19th century. The right-hand icon is meticulously and minutely carved with scenes of the life of Christ, a piece of rare and extraordinary skill.

The road descends to the bay of Náoussa, dotted with small islets. There was an important Neolithic cemetery here, but more visible is the **Mycenaean acropolis** on the hill of Koukounariés, immediately west of the bay (*2km to the west of the main road,* *shortly before it enters Náoussa: ascent to the hill is from the southwest side*). A lower enceinte of fortification walls in large polygonal blocks can be seen in places. Just short of the summit a wall of large blocks encloses a flat area, traversed by the foundations of interconnected buildings of varying size. The store-rooms just inside the main wall contained bronze weaponry and other finds, all buried in ash, indicating destruction by force, within the 12th century, not long after the citadel had been built. It remained inhabited after the destruction, until its abandonment in the 7th century BC. Fifty metres southeast of the summit are the remains of dwellings and the base of a temple from the Geometric period.

NAOUSSA

Náoussa (*map p. 110, D1*) is a beautiful series of contiguous harbours, backed by an attractive late medieval town. The moles of the central harbour were first constructed in the early 16th century, with a small Venetian tower at the end. This now constitutes the heart of a small castle built around it in the next century. During the Russo-Turkish War of 1768–74, Náoussa Bay was the Aegean base for the Russian Navy. Today the intimate inner harbour is home to a colourful fleet of fishing caïques.

Woven into the tight Cycladic fabric of the old town are several 17th- and 18th-century churches, many with open-latticework marble belfries. The most interesting is the **church of Ághios Ioánnis Theológos** (1629), in the centre of the original settlement. A small narthex gives onto a wide, domed interior with idiosyncratic wall-paintings (1784). The north wall is dominated by a *Last Judgement*. In the apse is the customary cosmic hierarchy, in which the Word descends from the Almighty, passes through Christ, and down to a painted ciborium behind the real altar. A particularly beautiful 17th-century icon of St John the Evangelist is to the right of the templon doors.

The former Monastery of Ághios Athanásios is now a small **museum of Byzantine art** (*open Easter–mid-Oct daily except Mon, 9–3*). Its displays include the 12th- and 13th-century wall-paintings salvaged from the rural church of Protoría.

Palaiópyrgos

Two kilometres east of Náoussa is the base of a cylindrical Hellenistic tower (*map p. 110, D1: reached by two successive first-left branches off the main road after it turns south to Márpissa*). Known as Palaiópyrgos, the tower, perhaps part of an ancient farmstead, stands to almost 2m in height. To the north is the promontory of Viglákia. A prehistoric settlement, surrounded by a wall, is visible on the islet of Oikonómou west of it.

LEFKES & THE CENTRE OF THE ISLAND

The ancient marble quarries

The source of Paros' famous marble lies 5km due east of Parikiá along the road to Léfkes, in a valley cutting south from the eastern end of Maráthi (*map p. 110, C2*).

There is much evidence of 19th-century quarrying, including the shell of a large factory, from shortly after the reopening of the quarries in 1844, for the specific aim of providing marble for the tomb of Napoleon at Les Invalides.

Three hundred metres south of the road, on the eastern slope, opposite two ruined 19th-century industrial buildings, are the entrances to the principal tunnels of the ancient quarries, active since the early Archaic period (*torch and sturdy footwear necessary*). The two tunnels descend over 100m into the hillside and communicate at their farthest point by a cross-tunnel. A series of smaller chambers and tunnels radiates from the extremity of the northern tunnel. Small debris left to accumulate on the floor facilitated the movement of cut blocks over the sloping surface. The gradient was dictated by the purity of the vein of marble.

Since its neighbour was worked in the 19th century, the southern tunnel (on the right) is more interesting, but also more difficult to descend. The fine regular striations left by ancient picks and chisels are visible in the roof and along the walls. To the left inside the entrance, carved into the rockface behind a protruding boulder, is a mid-4th-century BC relief and inscription dedicated to the nymphs, protectresses of these artificial 'caves'. The eroded scene depicts nymphs, satyrs, sileni, and other figures whose identity is unclear, as is the three-word inscription. Further down the tunnel, on the right, are regularly-spaced pillars of rock left to support to the roof. At various points there are 18th-century or later graffiti. At the bottom of the two tunnels the space opens out: the greatest quantity of marble was extracted from here.

Further quarries are located 200m further up on the west side the valley. On the hill to the west of the quarries is the heavily fortified and buttressed 17th-century monastery of Ághios Minás. A missing fragment of the relief of the nymphs in the quarries below is immured into the solid banister of its steps.

Kóstos and Léfkes

The attractive villages of **Kóstos** (*map p. 110, C2*) and Léfkes grew rapidly in the 16th century as the population began to concentrate here, fleeing from the coastal scourge of piracy. **Léfkes**, the more picturesque, was the capital of the island under Turkish rule, until 1832. It was designed as a walled kastro-type settlement within a ring of houses forming an enceinte which now defines the centre of the village. The churches often contain spolia or have fine 17th-century carved portals, such as that of Aghía Paraskeví, the village's oldest church, originally a 15th-century foundation. There are some fine Neoclassical houses.

In the protected valley between Léfkes and Kóstos, among centuries-old olive groves, the modern road passes a Byzantine bridge at a point 500m north of Lefkés: this lies on an ancient route which joined the west coast at Parikiá with the east coast at Márpissa. The stone-paved segment from Léfkes east to Pródromos (*see below*) can be easily followed on foot (*40mins*). Another pleasant walk is to the monastery of **Ághios Ioánnis Kaparoú**, immersed in vegetation, which is fed by a spring in the deep valley directly below the summit of Mt Ághii Pándes, 2.5km southwest of Léfkes.

AROUND MARPISSA & KEPHALOS HILL

The east coast of the island is dominated by two conical peaks, Képhalos and Anti-képhalos, like two gateposts framing the sweep of Molos Bay.

Pródromos and Mármara

Like Léfkes, **Pródromos** (*map p. 110, D2*) is built as a small medieval kastro, with a web of typically Cycladic streets within. The centre can only be reached through one of a series of gates or small tunnels, the eastern one crowned by a belfry, shared by the two 17th-century chapels to either side. Just 500m east of Pródromos is the village of **Mármara** ('marbles'), so named for the quantities of reused marble from some large pagan sanctuary. There are column drums built into the houses and the walls of both the central churches, Ághios Savvás and the Panaghía Septemvrianí. The doorstep of the latter is made from an ancient boundary marker, which bears the inscription 'HO-PΟΣ ΤΟ ΙΕΡΟ', 'boundary of the sanctuary'. The village well-house, a little way to the north, is ringed by a series of massive column drums, given a concave upper surface so as to act as basins.

On the lane running due south between Mármara and Márpissa is the small fortified **monastery of the Pantocrator**. Tightly fitted into the interior space are the domed katholikon and the abandoned cells.

Fragment of Parian marble column outside a village house

PARIAN MARBLE

No marble in antiquity found greater favour with sculptors than the Parian: it is the white marble *par excellence*; its crystalline structure finer than that of Naxian marble, its colour warmer than the whiter stone of Carrara. The quarries on Paros produce more than one kind of marble: the most valued was referred to as lychnites, from λυχνία, a lamp, probably due to its translucence. It is lychnites which was extracted at Maráthi. It could be obtained only in smaller blocks, large enough for most sculpture, but not in the quantities or dimensions necessary for construction. Sometimes even a statue in lychnites would have to be made of two pieces: this is the case with the *Venus de Milo*, which is joined at the upper rim of the garment. In Roman times, only the head of a statue might be executed in Parian marble.

The physical characteristics of Parian marble were significant. The transparency was particularly important because most ancient sculpture of the Archaic and Classical periods was coloured with encaustic (wax-based) paints, which penetrated the marble and increased its potential translucence almost two-fold. The regular, fine-grained, crystalline consistency of the marble was also important, allowing its surface to be polished with emery to an extraordinary smoothness. Much of the tactile and formal appeal of the Early Cycladic figurines is owed to this quality.

With a natural monopoly on the finest material, Parian sculptors were swift to exercise a monopoly on its crafting, giving rise to important schools of sculpture on the island. The greatest works of Archaic Athens and at Delphi were in Parian marble. Praxiteles' *Hermes*, the *Venus de Milo*, the *Winged Victory of Samothrace* and the *Nike* of Paionios are all of Parian lychnites.

The monastery of Ághios António

From the cemetery of Márpissa, a track leads up to the monastery of Ághios António on the summit of Képhalos Hill (*map p. 110, D2; open 9–1 & 5–8 July and Aug; otherwise the key needs to be obtained from the papás in Pródromos*). The present 16th-century monastery buildings are built on the ruins of a 14th-century Frankish church, which stood at the heart of a 14th–16th-century fortification. Three enceintes originally girded the hill, but are now difficult to perceive in places: the first is passed through by the road, low down on the hill; the second is crossed just below two ruined 15th-century churches on the southeast side; the third protected the crown of the hill. The last lord of the island, Bernardo Sagredo, held out in this castle against Kheir ed-Din Barbarossa for four days in 1537: he returned to Venice after the island fell to the Turks.

The monastery itself and its courtyard contain many ancient capitals, columns and other architectural elements, probably from an Archaic and Classical sanctuary. The katholikon has a three-aisled, inscribed-cross plan, with two domes. The interior still has 17th-century wall-paintings and a pulpit which is supported by a slender marble column standing on an upturned Ionic capital of Archaic design.

THE WEST & SOUTH THE ISLAND

The southern part of Paros was widely populated in the 3rd and 2nd millennia BC, but played less of a role in later times. Its coast, rich in sandy beaches, is easily reached by a direct route from Parikiá, passing some curiosities.

The convent of **Christós tou Dásou** (*map p. 110, C2; open to women only, 10–1*) contains the tomb Ághios Arsénios (1800–77), one of the island's patron saints. A kilometre further is the Valley of the Butterflies or **Petaloúdes**, above the village of Psychopianá, where an abundant spring feeds dense groves of pomegranate, olive, cypress, fig, rose, prunus and citrus trees, once part of the Mavrogenis estate. The stone mansion is visible in the valley. Prominent on the hillside to the south is a ruined **medieval tower**. Every June the butterflies, Jersey Tiger moths (*see p. 289*), return to mate.

From Poúnda, a car ferry crosses to Antíparos. East of the airfield is the idiosyncratic **Skorpios Folklore Museum** (*map p. 110, C3*), devoted to models of everything Cycladic. At 11km, the road reaches the attractive fishing harbour and sandy bay of Alykí.

ANTÍPAROS & DESPOTIKO

One of the oldest organised settlements in the Cyclades is on the low **islet of Sáliagos**, just off Antíparos (*map p. 110, B2*). The islet is visible in the strait (behind the islet of Revmatonísi), 1km to the north of the ferry route between Paros and Antíparos. Like its neighbours, it was originally a rise on a continuum of land between Paros and Antíparos. Probably in the 2nd millennium BC, a massive seismic movement caused the land to sink by 10m–12m, making Antíparos a separate island.

The Neolithic settlement on Sáliagos was inhabited by a community of sheep-farmers and fishermen in the late 5th–4th millennium BC. Stone foundations of buildings, obsidian arrow-heads, stone implements and pottery were found. The famous seated, cross-legged 'fat lady' figurine in Paros Museum was found here.

Northern Antíparos

The north of the island is mostly agricultural, with a central valley of cultivable land, the **Kambos**, 3km south of Chora. The **town of Antíparos** itself, behind the attractive waterfront, was built in the 15th century in an unprotected position. It relied on its quadrant of walls, formed by the high, reinforced exterior of the circuit of dwellings, which opened towards the interior. The single gate is still visible. Ahead of the gate, a flight of steps leads to a raised area (now a cistern), originally the base of a tower.

The area outside the Kastro is all of later date. The principal church of Ághios Nikólaos was begun in 1645. The town continued to be prey to pirate raids: As late as 1790 it was sacked and left with a markedly reduced population.

Southern Antíparos

The south of the island is more mountainous and has remains of 19th-century mines.

The **Cave of Antíparos** (*map p. 110, B3; open daily for tours 10.45–3.45; in winter reduced hours without tours*), 8.5km from Chora, has been known and admired since antiquity. Descending steeply to a depth of over 100m, the space is articulated in chambers of increasing size, festooned with a remarkable density of stalactites and stalagmites. The large stalagmite by the entrance is said to be 45 million years old and is the largest known in Europe. The quantity of names, dates, inscriptions and graffiti carved into the rock, and going back many centuries, is impressive. The names of Byron, Joseph Pitton de Tournefort, King Otto of Greece, and countless other visitors (mostly French and German) of the 18th and 19th centuries are well preserved along with others, often in beautiful calligraphy. The path enters through an area called the antechamber, and then descends steeply in a succession of staircases. At the bottom a branch leads right into the 'Royal Hall', and left into the 'Cathedral': it is at the extremity of the latter path that most of the interest and the names are to be found. Ahead of where the path stops is the 'altar'. It is inscribed at its base: 'HIC IPSE CHRISTUS EJUS NATALIE DIE MEDIA CELEBRATO, MDCLXXIII', recording how on Christmas Day 1673 a candlelight Mass was celebrated in the cave, organised by the French Ambassador to the Sublime Porte, Charles Olier, Marquis of Nointel.

Continuing further south, a branch to the left leads to the southern tip of the island. By continuing west at the junction, you descend to Ághios Geórgios, with good views across the water to Despotikó (boats to the island can also be hired here; *see overleaf*).

DESPOTIKO

The remains that are being revealed by current excavations at the site of Mándra (*map p. 110, A3*) are among the most remarkable in the Cyclades and well worth the trouble involved in getting to see them. The site, undisturbed by any later building, on an uninhabited island, between the sea and the hills behind, is wild and beautiful.

No temple has yet been found, but the presence of potsherds bearing the name 'ΑΠΟΛΛ' would indicate that the sanctuary was dedicated to Apollo. They enclose a rectangular area, at the centre of which is a semicircular base and to one side an altar of Hestia. The most interesting building, Building A, lies just behind at the southwestern edge of the excavated area. It is constructed in fine, well-preserved Archaic masonry of Parian marble. It has several rooms, and a portion of its north façade has a colonnade of eight Doric pillars (south end): the marks left by their bases are visible. To the south is a Classical rectangular paved building marked by a large stone bathtub, a system of drains and circular stone rings for supporting water receptacles. This appears to have been a spacious and well-designed bathroom or washing area.

The small early 7th-century BC painted clay figurine of a female divinity, now in the museum in Paros (*see p. 114*), was found in Building A. Rich deposits of votive objects of Eastern Aegean, Rhodian, Cypriot and Egyptian origin have been unearthed, including bronzes and ivories. Two lower portions of 6th-century BC kouroi were found, reused later as door jambs. A great number of architectural elements from an Archaic Doric temple have been reused in later walls. This suggests that the late 6th-century Archaic temple was destroyed and its fragments used to build a subsequent version. The site appears to have functioned continuously from the 7th century BC into Roman times.

PRACTICAL INFORMATION

GETTING AROUND

To Paros, there are two 35-min flights from Athens. The airport is 10.5km from Parikiá. There are generally two daily car-ferry connections (4½ hrs) from Piraeus in summer, fewer in winter. In late June–late Sept there are also up to four fast daily services (minimum 3hrs), divided equally between Piraeus and Rafína.

The car ferry from Poúnda (7km south of Parikiá) to Antíparos makes the 15-min crossing 23 times a day from 7am till midnight, at half-hourly intervals in the morning and hourly intervals in the afternoon and evening.

Boats to Despotikó must be arranged with the owner of the taverna just above the jetty at Ághios Geórgios. His boat makes the journey in 10mins: he will pick you up again at a pre-arranged time.

WHERE TO STAY

Antíparos
Hotel Artemis (*T: 22840 61469, www.artemis-antiparos.com*) on the north of the bay, is simple and welcoming. For visiting Despotikó, **Oliaros Studios** at Ághios Geórgios, at the south end of the island, is a delightful alternative (*T: 22840 25304/5, www.oliaros.gr*).
Paros
For simplicity and unpretentious comfort, the intimate, family-run **Hotel Dina** in the heart of Parikiá is inexpensive, comfortable and quiet (*T: 22840 21325; www.hoteldina.com*). On the edge of Náoussa, **Yades Studios**

provide tasteful accommodation with helpful management (*T: 22840 51072; www.yades.gr*).

WHERE TO EAT

Antíparos
Locals eat at the *mezedopoleîon* **Tsipouradiko** by the harbour, which has fresh seafood.
Paros
Levantis ■, on Agorá street in Parikiá, is one of the best places to eat in the Cyclades, for food that is refined and yet still Greek. More expensive and with a refined menu is **Daphni** on Grávari. Amongst the myriad eateries around the harbour of Náoussa, the simplest of all, **Mouragio**, has the best and freshest fish. **Le Sud** is also good for more varied and sophisticated cuisine.

FURTHER READING

Thomas Hope's *Anastasius, or Memoirs of a Greek*, first published in 1819, is partly based on Nikolaos Mavrogenis and his world and times; the book caused a sensation when it first came out. It was reissued in 2001 by Elibron Classics. *Paros and Antiparos: History, Monuments and Museums* by Yannos Kourayos (Athens 2004) is a superb guide to the islands' antiquities.

James Theodore Bent's *The Cyclades, or Life among the Insular Greeks* (1885), reissued 2002 by Archaeopress, Oxford, contains descriptions of the earliest excavations of prehistoric Cycladic remains on Antíparos.

NAXOS

Largest of all the Cyclades and with the highest mountains, Naxos is also the central island, around which they all cluster. For millennia, it has been the most important island of the group, its fertile interior permitting it to fall back on itself when necessary. Its history, archaeology and monuments put it amongst the three or four artistically richest islands in the Aegean. Its highly varied landscapes are enhanced by the unique wealth of Byzantine churches dotted among the trees, dating from the 6th–16th centuries, and mostly decorated with paintings of great quality and unforgettable presence. Its ancient remains include the Portára gate by Naxos harbour, and the unforgettable unfinished 6th-century BC statues, lying in their rock-cradles in the hills.

HISTORY OF NAXOS

In myth, Zeus is associated with the island through its former name, Dia. His son Dionysus was born on the island and remained its patron throughout antiquity. The island is best known as the place where Theseus deserted Ariadne, on their journey from Crete to Athens. Dionysus found her, fell in love with her, and had a number of children by her.

First settled in the Neolithic, Naxos played a leading role in Cycladic culture throughout the Bronze Age. Its most vigorous and continuous Bronze Age settlement was Grotta, in virtually the same location as the modern city, which remained the island's main trading centre throughout Mycenaean times and continued into historical times. In the 8th century BC Naxos founded a colony in Sicily (the modern Giardini-Naxos), and one on Amorgós (Arkesine).

Because of the wealth brought by the fertile interior and its seams of fine marble and emery, Naxos was able to dominate the Ionian group of islands and their sacred centre at Delos. The 6th century BC saw a remarkable flourish of marble-sculpting and building, in which Naxos, together with Samos, led the Greek world in innovative technique and designs, as witnessed by the grand Naxian monuments on the island itself, and at Delphi and Delos. In 536 BC a civil war resulted in the overthrow of the landowning class and the rise of a tyrant, Lydgamis. An aristocrat but a champion of the lower classes, he was overthrown in 524 BC. After a brief oligarchy, democracy was established. In 506 BC the island successfully withstood a four-month siege by Aristagoras, tyrant of Miletus. At the end of the century the island was at the peak of its power and influence, fielding a large army and a sizeable fleet.

Naxos' golden age ended with the Persian Wars. The island was devastated by the Persians in 490 BC. It nonetheless sent four ships to join the Greek fleet at Salamis in 480 BC, and fought at the Battle of Plataea. In 479 BC it joined the Delian League, but recalling its own former power, it attempted to secede in 473–472 BC. The Athenians put down the revolt, subjugated the island, settled 1,000 cleruchs, and imposed a heavy tribute. Naxos never again regained its former status. In 377 BC, in the straits

NAXOS

between Paros and Naxos, the Athenians routed a fleet from Sparta, with whom Naxos was then allied, and the island was forced once again to capitulate to Athens. In 338 BC the island came under Macedonian rule, then Ptolemaic rule. From 41 BC, it was governed by Rome, and used as a place of exile.

Saracen raids in the 7th century AD forced the abandonment of coastal settlements, but the interior remained unscathed. The surprising number of important churches of the 6th–9th centuries indicates a quality of life not known elsewhere in the Cyclades at the time. The history of Byzantine Naxos remains hazy. In 1207, after the Fourth Crusade, the island was taken by the nephew of Doge Enrico Dandolo, Marco Sanudo, who established the Venetian Duchy of the Archipelago. The extraordinary renaissance of church-building in the 13th century is testimony to the prosperity and security this brought. His descendants, and the succeeding dynasty of the Crispi, ruled over Naxos and the Cyclades for 360 years. In 1537, Kheir ed-Din Barbarossa attacked the island, but failed to take it; in 1566 it fell to the forces of Sultan Selim II. An Ottoman governor was installed, but the island was never settled by the Turks. Between 1770 and 1774, Naxos was occupied by the Russians, during the first Russo-Turkish War. Much of the island's population was lukewarm in enthusiasm for Greek Independence, expelling the Greek representatives from the island in 1824. In 1832 Naxos became part of the Greek state. Italian forces occupied the island in from 1941 to 1944.

THE CHORA OF NAXOS

Arrival by boat in the port of Naxos (*map p. 128, A2*) offers an immediate view of the long history of the city, ranging from the 6th-century BC Portára by the sea to the late medieval castle on the hill ahead. The expansion of the city in recent decades has led to many archaeological discoveries. The shape of the harbour has been altered over time: prostrate columns and blocks of marble breaking the surface north of the modern mole are what remain of its 13th-century predecessor, which was built of ancient spolia.

The waterfront is rather commercialised today, but inland from it a more traditional atmosphere prevails in a network of narrow, stepped alleyways around the base of the kastro hill. Many of the churches and some houses have door frames composed of reused ancient blocks. A short climb from the southeastern end of the small *plateía* extending back from the shore, an alleyway passes the Pórta tou Gialoú, a gateway entirely constructed of ancient blocks.

The old town divides into two appreciably different areas; the Venetian Kastro on the hill above; and the Greek Bourgo around its circumference, stretching as far as the north shore, at which point it becomes the area of Grotta.

KASTRO

The Kastro occupies the roughly circular summit of the Prehistoric, Classical and Byzantine acropolis. The main entrance is in the northwest corner, below the most substantial remaining segment of the 13th-century Venetian fortifications, which includes many spolia. Projecting to the north is its only remaining tower, known both as **Sanudo's Tower** and as the Tower of the Crispi. Inside it is a small exhibition of Early Christian and Byzantine sculpture.

Marco Sanudo (d. 1227)

It is not known how old Marco Sanudo was when he joined his nonagenarian uncle, Enrico Dandolo, Doge of Venice, in the expedition against Constantinople in 1204. But he was well positioned and had the courage, charm and shrewdness to take full advantage of the opportunities arising from the capture of Constantinople. When the city fell, the partition agreement between the conquerors assigned the Cyclades, Sporades and Dodecanese, as well as the Ionian islands in the Adriatic, to Venice, which delegated the role of overlord of the Cyclades to Marco Sanudo. The only island to resist him was Naxos, as it was currently held by a group of Genoese mercenaries. In 1207, Sanudo landed on the island and burnt his boats so that there could be no turning back. Five weeks later he had taken the stronghold of Apaliros Castle from the Genoese, and the island, indeed the whole western Aegean, was his domain. He proclaimed himself Duke of Naxos—with allegiance primarily to the Latin Emperor in Constantinople rather to than Venice—was later recognised as Duke of the Archipelago (an Italian corruption of the Greek Αιγαίο Πέλαγος, 'Aegean sea') and built his capital on the acropolis of Naxos. Keeping the islands closest to Naxos for himself, he 'leased' others as fiefs to his companions in arms.

Courageous and fortunate in adventure, he was tolerant and intelligent in the exercise of power, attracting loyalty from those below. Ambition, or perhaps mere injudiciousness, however, led him into to two failed enterprises: first an attempt in 1212 to seize Crete for himself from its Venetian governor; and then, in 1213, to attack the exiled Byzantine emperor, Theodore Lascaris, in Nicaea. But what is interesting and instructive about Sanudo's character is how he emerged from these escapades: the Venetian Republic apparently bore him no serious resentment for his disloyalty; and from the emperor Theodore he won back not just his freedom, but the hand of Theodore's sister in marriage. Sanudo raised his son, Angelo, to be bilingual, making him a prominent example of cultural and religious tolerance, which became a model for the peaceful coexistence of Orthodoxy and Catholicism, Greek and Italian. Sanudo died in 1227.

On the fine Gothic main gate into the Kastro, the **Trani Porta**, a vertical incision on the right-hand marble post marks the standard Venetian measure or 'yard' for the pricing of cloth (82cm). Inside the gate, on the right, is the **house of the Della Rocca-Barozzi family** (*open daily 10–2.30 & 4.30–9*). The Della Rocca, originally Burgundian (de la Roche), styled themselves dukes of Athens from 1207 to 1308; the Venetian Barozzi

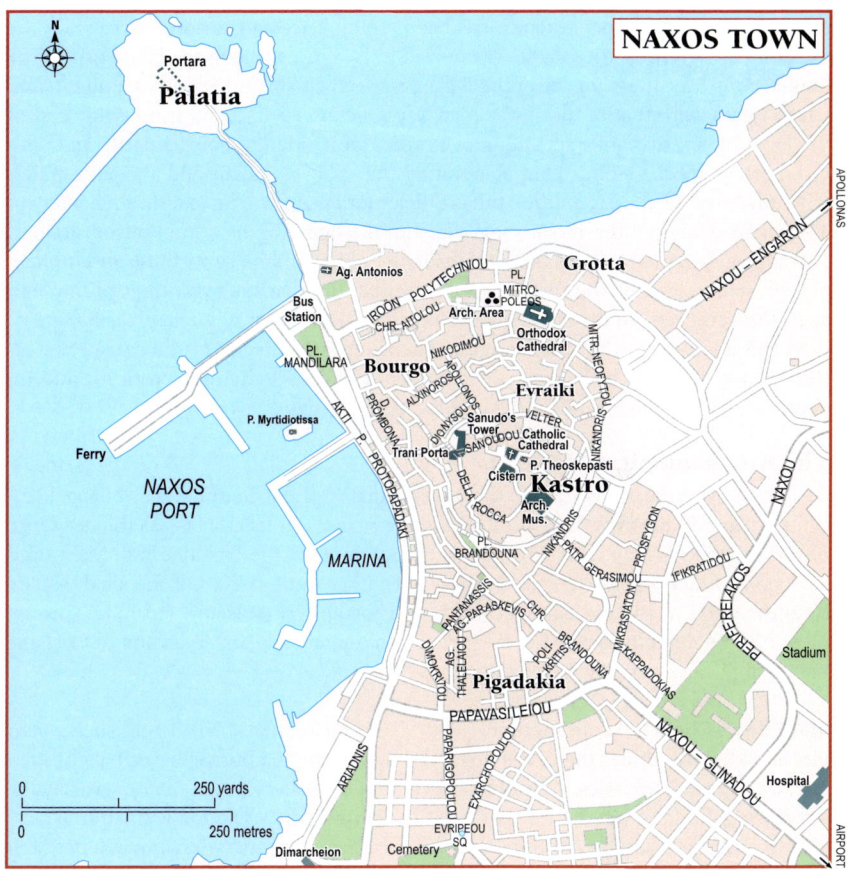

NAXOS TOWN

Portara
Palatia

Ag. Antonios
Bus Station
Grotta
PL. MITRO-POLEOS
Arch. Area
Orthodox Cathedral
PL. MANDILARA
Bourgo
Evraiki
P. Myrtidiotissa
Sanudo's Tower
Catholic Cathedral
Ferry
Trani Porta
P. Theoskepasti
Cistern
Kastro
NAXOS PORT
Arch. Mus.
MARINA
PL. BRANDOUNA
Pigadakia
PAPAVASILEIOU
Stadium
Hospital
Dimarcheion
EVRIPEOU SQ.
Cemetery

APOLLONAS
NAXOU – ENGARON
MITR. NEOPYTOU SIGKINOU
NAXOU
NIKANDROS PATR. GERASIMOU
PROSFYGON
IFIKRATIDOU
PERI. EREIZAKOS
NAXOU – GLINADOU
AIRPORT

0 — 250 yards
0 — 250 metres

family was given the lordship of Santorini by Sanudo in 1207. The building has continuously remained in the possession of the intermarried families: it was their city residence. The rooms are pleasingly proportioned and luminous for a fortified dwelling. Within the substantial thickness of the walls on the west side is a minuscule escape route, communicating with adjacent buildings.

The Catholic cathedral and Panaghía Theosképasti

Both south along the curve of Della Rocca street and up Sanoúdou to the north is the aristocratic **Venetian quarter**, with many stately residences; some with the family coats of arms carved in stone above the entrance. Its focus is the Roman Catholic **Cathedral of the Presentation of the Virgin** at the summit (*open daily 10–1.30, and during services*). This curious, hybrid building was probably adapted in the 13th century from a Byzantine predecessor. It is a basilica with a central dome over an inscribed cross, with no apse. The structure has been rebuilt once and restored twice over the intervening centuries: the façade was re-clad in Naxiot marble in the last century. The escutcheons over the door are of the della Craspere, Crispi and Sanudo families (from left to right), with that of the (?)Venetian Republic inserted second from right. East of the crossing are two antique columns. On the north side the floor is partly laid with elaborate memorial stones commemorating the dead of Italian and French families who inhabited the Kastro in the 16th–18th centuries. Above the altar is a magnificent 13th-century icon of the *Virgin and Child* with the figure of the donor, bishop John of Nicomedia, below. The rear side bears the figure of St John the Baptist (*ask the attendant to turn the icon*). Along the east wall are a number of interesting paintings of the 18th and 19th centuries. In the south aisle is a delicate 17th-century *Virgin of the Rosary*.

In the small church of the **Panaghía Theosképasti**, directly to the east of the cathedral, are two fine 14th-century icons: the Panaghía Hodighítria, with a powerful *Crucifixion* on its reverse, and a damaged icon of St Anastasia.

The Archaeological Museum

To the south of the cathedral are the lower remains of the central tower of the 13th-century Sanudo Fortress, now used as a water cistern. To its east stands the residence of the Catholic bishop, and beyond it, the buildings of the Ursuline monastery and its school, which functioned from the 17th century until 1970. Off the small square by these buildings is the entrance to the Archaeological Museum (*open daily except Mon, 8.30–3*). Its importance lies particularly in the magnificent collection of Cycladic marble figurines and objects.

Main floor: The small collection of Neolithic finds includes the oldest gold artefact from the Cyclades, a small strip of beaten gold, found in the Cave of Zas. The Cycladic artefacts dating from the late 4th and 3rd millennia BC are made of polished local marble. The marble bowls and offering platters are of simple dignity, as are the Cycladic figurines (showcases in first room), varying in size and shape, though most are females of the Spedos type (*see p. 651*), with highly stylised faces. Of particular beauty are several seated female figures, on stools or high-backed 'thrones'.

Subsequent rooms exhibit finds from the Mycenaean burial sites on Naxos, in-cluding a series of small gold sheets with framed and embossed figures of children (middle gallery). Also of note is a small 12th-century BC hydria with an unusual scene of fishermen drawing in a net with fish. The fine collection of Geometric vases comes from cemeteries on Naxos and Donoúsa.

Mezzanine and upper floors: The collection of Archaic exhibits includes a fine 6th-century BC kouros head from Grotta. At the edge of the outside terrace are two unfinished Archaic kouroi. Among the Hellenistic and Roman exhibits (final room, upper floor) is a large collection of beautiful Roman glass.

The museum adjoins the **former Ursuline School**, down the alley to the left. Founded in 1670 with a charter approved by both the pope and the Ottoman sultan, and open to Catholic and Orthodox students alike, it became one of the foremost schools of the Aegean. The novelist Nikos Kazantzakis studied here as a boy in 1896.

BOURGO & GROTTA

The oldest surviving church in Bourgo, the **Profítis Ilías** (?13th century), is one block in from the waterfront at the level of the Emborikí Trápeza (Commercial Bank). Inside are two beautiful 15th-century icons by Angelos of Crete. At the northern extremity of the waterfront, before the causeway to the Portára, is the church of **Ághios Antónios** (St Antony the Hermit; 1452).

The principal thoroughfare—at times scarcely wide enough for two people to pass—which runs east from the waterfront, often under the upper floors of buildings, is **Nikodímou**, named after the island's patron saint (Nicodemus; 1749–1809), whose house can still be seen (third doorway on the left after the Taverna Vassilis) beyond the sharp turn east in the street.

Nikodímou eventually joins Plateía Mitropóleos, dotted with 18th-century churches which surround the **Orthodox cathedral** of the Zoödóchos Pigí, built in 1786. The interior is dominated by an 18th-century marble iconostasis. The dome rests on ancient columns.

At the western side of the square are stones and architectural fragments from the Hellenistic and Roman agorá of Naxos, which lay under the eastern end of this area, stretching as far as the Bay of Grotta.

Grotta

The Bay of Grotta was the site of the **Bronze Age city of Naxos**, revealed by archaeologists in piecemeal fashion amidst today's habitations. The sea level is higher today than in antiquity; much of the prehistoric and later structures now lies underwater. At the neck of the causeway to Palátia, to the east side, just before the first buildings, can be seen a segment of ancient street communicating between the ancient north and south shores.

The area of Grotta has a complex history and represents an important cradle of Cycladic civilisation. The **Mitrópolis Archaeological Area** (*open daily except Mon, 8.30–3; free*), entered opposite the church of Ághios Nikólaos, is an exemplary display of what are complex archaeological finds. The various areas and strata visibly recount a history ranging from the Neolithic (4th millennium) through the Cycladic Early Bronze Age (3rd and 2nd millennia) and the time of the Mycenaean city (later 2nd millennium) to the Geometric period (9th and 8th centuries BC) and beyond. The unusual construction of the Mycenaean walls, mud brick around a stone core, can clearly be seen. There are ceramic workshops from the same period; in one the work-bench and drying shelves are clearly visible. Higher up, above these levels, can be seen Classical doorways and a Roman oven. There is also evidence of a hermax, a pile of stones left by visitors as they exited from a cemetery.

PALATIA

Palátia, a small islet joined to the main island by a causeway, is known for the famous **Portára**, the largest Archaic Greek monolithic doorway still surviving, and the most conspicuous ruin on Naxos: its silhouette dominates views from the island and the sea alike. The Portára is the only standing element remaining from a temple, built c. 530 BC under the tyrant Lygdamis and subsequently left uncompleted. It expresses the prosperity, confidence and technical mastery of Naxos at that time, marking its harbour entrance with what would have been the grandest temple in the Cyclades. Later, the temple was occupied by a 6th-century Christian basilica with an inscribed apse. The Venetians used the remains of the temple as a quarry for the walls of the Kastro. The temple may have been intended for Dionysus, or more likely Apollo. The size of the doorway gives an idea of the monumental structure it was meant to be part of, now thought to have been planned as a full peripteral temple. Local mythology holds that it was on this tiny islet that the sleeping Ariadne woke to see her faithless lover's ship disappear over the horizon to Athens, and grieved until she was found by Dionysus.

Aerial view of the Portára, fronting temple ruins of the 6th century BC.

ARIADNE ON NAXOS

Ariadne was the daughter of King Minos of Crete and his wife Pasiphaë. When Theseus, prince and pre-eminent hero of Athens, came to Knossos in Crete as part of a human tribute of Athenian youths and virgins which was sent each year to King Minos as expiation for the death of his son Androgeus in Attica, Ariadne glimpsed him and fell in love with him. She provided him with a ball of wool to help him escape again from the Labyrinth once he had slain the Minotaur: as she did so, she asked Theseus to promise that he would marry her in return and take her with him when he escaped, so that she would avoid the wrath of her father. Theseus agreed.

Theseus achieved his mission and escaped successfully from the Labyrinth. He and Ariadne fled north: their first stop was Naxos. While Ariadne slept, Theseus set sail for Athens and abandoned her: she awoke to find him gone. Dionysus, finding Ariadne grieving and seeing her beauty, fell in love with her. He presented her with a gold wreath set with precious stones; later this was placed in the heavens as the constellation of Corona Borealis. Ariadne bore Dionysus a number of children, and in antiquity festivals celebrated her story: a mourning festival which recalled her sleep, abandonment and grief; and a subsequent festival which celebrated her awakening, marriage and new lease of life.

The story, as Plutarch recognised (*Theseus, 20*), had many versions, and there were many explanations of Theseus' behaviour. Homer implies that Ariadne was already married to Dionysus when she followed Theseus from Crete, and that she was killed on Dia by Artemis at the request of Dionysus. Anacreon and Apollonius of Rhodes say that she bore Dionysus sons: Anacreon says one, Apollonius four, Hyginus six. Diodorus Siculus and Pausanias claim that Theseus left Ariadne because the gods commanded him to, since Fate would not allow him to marry her. Ovid and Hyginus suggest that Theseus was simply a cad. Plutarch mentions that in some accounts Ariadne came to Cyprus (not Naxos), already pregnant by Theseus, who abandoned her there. In any case, he adds, the Naxiots themselves claimed that there were two different Ariadnes, one for Dionysus and another for Theseus. The story of Ariadne and Theseus encapsulates the ambivalent view that Naxos had of Athens. History had taught Naxos not to trust the city or its people.

Clearly visible on the ground are the two parallel lines of meticulously cut and interlocked blocks of foundations for the walls of the cella (measuring c. 37m by 15.5m by 12m high). The outlines of the antae and the distyle pronaos beside the portal, and of the opisthodomos (also distyle) at the opposite end, are both discernible. All is of exquisite marble and excellently finished. Many of the blocks still possess 'knobs' on their surface, left uncut so as to provide a 'handle' to help with lifting and transporting. These would have been removed and smoothed before completion.

The temple has a somewhat unusual northwest–southeast orientation, perhaps to align with the Kastro hill, although no ancient significance of this is known. In spite of meticulous engineering and cutting of the principal blocks, the running ridges carefully carved on the outer faces of the portal do not continue or correspond from one block to the next, leaving an awkward transition from the horizontal to the verticals.

The configuration of the site is made harder to read by the fact that an Early Christian church (removed in the 19th century) was created within the temple cella in the 6th century. A west entrance was cut directly through the middle of the threshold block of the temple portal.

CENTRAL NAXOS

Around Melanés

East of Naxos Chora, at the junction for Melanés, is the 13th-century church of **Ághios Isídoros** (*map p. 128, A2*), a barrel-vaulted structure with blind arcades in the interior. It is decorated extensively with 14th-century paintings. Two kilometres northwest of here (by immediate left branch) beyond the village of Angídia, north of the road, is the site of the Early Christian Basilica of **Ághios Stéfanos Frarón**, within which a later 11th-century church was built.

In **Melanés** itself is the church of Ághios Geórgios Melánon (*map p. 128, B2; key with the papás*). There are several layers of painting: some fragmentary, graffiti-like designs dating from pre-Iconoclastic times; other aniconic designs; and later 12th- and 13th-century ones, including a fine *Pantocrator*. The church is adjoined by a chapel on the north side, converted from an ancient cistern.

At **Kalamítsia**, 2km south of Melanés by unpaved track, are the atmospheric ruins of the 18th-century palatial mansion of Parátrechos. East of Melanés is the village of **Kourounochóri**, with the turreted and machicolated early Venetian Mavrogenis/Della Rocca Tower. Such 'towers' were the fortified rural manors of important Venetian families of the 14th and 15th centuries.

FLERIO & MYLI

Just beyond Kourounochóri, the road descends to Fleriό (*map p. 128, B2*) and the site of the two unfinished marble kouroi, among the most fascinating remains in the Cyclades, as well as a recently uncovered ancient sanctuary.

The first kouros

A path leads left from where the road ends along a torrent-bed, and then cuts alongside a citrus orchard to the right: just above it, in a small walled enclosure, lies the first kouros, a breathtaking sight. The massive supine figure, 5.8m long, is, beneath the dark patination of its surface, in pure white marble. It lies in the place where the uncut block was initially detached from the bedrock, as is clear from the chiselled stria-

One of the abandoned, unfinished kouroi of Naxos, at Flerió.

tions around. After the piece had been given an approximate form as a kouros, it was moved through 90° from the position in which it was originally roughed out. Then it was abandoned and left unfinished, probably because a fault in the marble at the shins (structurally its weakest point) caused the stone to fracture.

The second kouros

From the first kouros a path leads to a small cottage where refreshments are served. Not far beyond, a path leads diagonally up the hillside to the second kouros, which lies exposed on the hillside. It is of similar dimensions, and though more eroded, was in a slightly more advanced state of completion. The front of the face has sheered off and both legs are broken at the knees. Fragments of the feet and shins lie in the area.

THE UNFINISHED KOUROI OF NAXOS

There are three unfinished gigantic kouroi on Naxos: two at the site of Flerió, and one at Apóllonas (*see p. 149*). The latter is of an apparently bearded male figure, probably Dionysus: begun c. 550 BC, and, at 10.7m long, it is the largest of the three. It lies in its quarry in the bedrock close to the sea, and has been known for a long time. The Flerió kouroi are probably slightly earlier, and have come to light only recently.

The kouroi clearly demonstrate that the sculptors travelled to where the stone was, at least for preliminary work. This left the problem of transportation. It is just possible that this was not necessary at Flerió because the pieces were intended for the sanctuary which has recently been uncovered some 50–100m to the north. Most probably, however, they were intended for export.

The partly finished piece had to be brought down to the sea, a risky and difficult operation: the marble can easily get chipped or broken. As there is no sufficiently navigable stream here, there seems to be no alternative to a 'runway', in parts made of loose marble chips, in other parts of packed earth. Sledges, carts, ropes and a great deal of man- and animal-power would have been necessary to propel and to brake the movement. No evidence of such a piste is visible today, although they are known from quarries elsewhere in Greece (*see p. 622*).

What exactly the kouroi stand for is the subject of debate. The several dozen surviving examples include grave markers and votive statues; some represent divinities, others heroes, some perhaps ordinary mortals or even living athletes; few have attributes of any kind to help define them better. What they all have in common is youth and nudity. The kouroi were unchanging incarnations of beauty, hence the apparent frequency with which they are associated with Apollo. The main Flerió kouros could equally be an anonymous hero, or an image of Apollo. The beard of the kouros at Apóllonas, however, precludes Apollo, and the sculpture is generally thought to have been an image of Dionysus.

Sanctuary of the Chthonic Deities

The most recent discovery in the area of Flerió is the Sanctuary to the Chthonic Deities on the hillside beside where the asphalt road ends. The sanctuary has an interesting and unusual circular configuration of buildings.

The first cult buildings date from the 8th century BC. In the 7th century BC the site was rearranged and a new marble temple built. It was characterised by a monolithic door frame (threshold visible). An earthquake in the 6th century damaged it, but the temple and surrounding buildings, amongst them a hestiatorion, were repaired. The survival, throughout all this, of a sacred hearth for burnt offerings suggests that the divinity worshipped was chthonic, perhaps a fertility divinity or the giants Otos and Ephialtes, who perished on Naxos and were honoured as protectors of quarrymen.

Mýli

The area of Flerió and Mýli, the straggling village along the valley side to its north (*map p. 128, B2*), is remarkably rich in springs, as the name (meaning 'mills') implies. They fed a 5th-century BC aqueduct (supplying the city of Naxos) in the form mostly of a built channel, almost 11km in length. At an early point of its course, a tunnel was excavated. The entrance to the tunnel, refaced in stone in Roman times, can be seen by following the delightful stone-paved path, well worth walking in its own right, which begins by running parallel, and just below, the asphalt road and then runs north round the right-hand side of the valley.

THE PANAGHIA DROSIANI

The road east from Mýli climbs up into an eerie landscape of modern quarries and then descends to Moní (*map p. 128, B2*). The village takes its name from the monastery of the Panaghía Drosianí by the road, 1km below (*generally open from 8–1 & 4–8; offering to the custodian appreciated*), one of the most important Byzantine sites in the Cyclades.

This is a church, or rather complex of chapels, going back to the late 6th or early 7th century, is all that remains of a monastery whose buildings once surrounded it. It is a classic example of chapels or churches 'agglutinating'. The original core of the church is the decorated tri-conch at the eastern end, perhaps built as a sepulchre-church for a holy person. A first additional chapel was tucked at an uncomfortable 45° angle to the axis of the main church against the northwest corner of the tri-conch. Later two further chapels were built on to the west. An aisle was then added, joining them all together.

Exterior view of the Panaghía Drosianí.

Because of their antiquity, the paintings at the Drosianí are of considerable importance. The 6th–7th-century scene of the *Ascension* (a common funerary subject) in the east conch is attended by Apostles whose faces betray late Roman and Early Christian origins. The dome is decorated (same period) with an almost unique subject matter: two busts of Christ, one youthful and beardless holding the Gospel, the other holding a scroll as the Lawgiver: one the human, incarnate Jesus; the other, the Eternal Saviour. The inscription between the two reads: 'For the salvation of Andreas and his wife and their children'. In the north conch, the face of the *Panaghia Nikopoia* (the Virgin as 'Bringer of Victory') is compelling in its intensity. She is framed by Sts Cosmas and Damian. The carved marble templon screen (restored) is probably contemporary with the building.

Of the tiny funerary chapels on the north side, that to the east is decorated with a *Panaghia Platyera*. The central chapel, the only one to have neither dome nor window, has grave loculi to left and right.

THE POTAMIA VALLEY

The valley of Potamiá is the confluence of several springs. Its upper reach is a sequence of burgeoning orchards, mills and plane trees. The valley begins at **Káto Potamiá**, 7.5km southeast of Chora (*map p. 128, B2*). The church of Ághios Geórgios, with large areas of 13th-century painting, lies just north of the road. South of the same point, a road descends, crosses the watercourse, and continues south as a rough track for a further 2km, as far as the ruined church of **Ághios Mámas**, or Panaghía Theosképasti. Built in the 10th century, this was among the largest and most important churches on the island. The church is of an elegant, spacious, domed, cross-in-square design and incorporates ancient spolia. The belfry and double-vaulted narthex were added in the 13th or 14th century.

The road continues among lush scenery via Mési Potamiá to **Áno Potamiá**, a village which straggles almost 2km downstream from the main spring.

Epáno Kástro and Tsikkalareió

As the road climbs from Áno Potamiá, the rocky height of **Epáno Kástro** (*map p. 128, B2*) comes into view to the east (left). The castle can be approached from this side along a path signed from the road, or else from Tsikkalareió, 5km further on (*45mins' climb by either route*). The 13th-century Venetian castle was built on the site of a prehistoric fortification. A small stretch of late Classical walls in isodomic masonry is visible below the summit. The castle had two enceintes: the horseshoe-shaped barbican with artillery emplacements (suggesting a later, 16th-century date) belonged to the outer ring; the curtain-wall higher up was the inner enceinte, reinforced by three rectangular and three semicircular towers, and enclosing cisterns and living quarters. On the surrounding slopes are several barrel-vaulted churches.

Below Epáno Kastro to the southeast, about halfway between the castle and Tsikkalareió, lies an important and unusual **cemetery of the Geometric period** (9th–8th centuries BC; *the tombs are to the south of the footpath to/from Tsikkalareió, reached by a path beside a stone wall which runs south and crosses a small rocky ridge through a defile before descending to the cemetery*). The cemetery appears to be a collection of monumental family tombs on a plateau. The site is dominated by a 2.5-m menhir. The burial tumuli (diameter up to 12m), marked by circles of orthostats, are highly unusual for the period.

In the village of **Tsikkalareió** is the church of Ághios Stéfanos, with remains of 13th-century painting. Uphill, c. 500m to the northeast, is the ?7th-century basilica church of the **Taxiárchis Ráchis** at Monikía, a curious, domeless, three-aisled basilica now in ruinous condition, also with vestiges of early paintings.

BYZANTINE ARCHITECTURE & WALL-PAINTING

At first sight, Byzantine painting can seem much of a muchness. For eyes used to the tradition of the Western Renaissance, with its emphasis on individuality and naturalism, it can appear fossilised and repetitive. Yet within its constrictions it has character, modulation and range; and it is worth acquiring an eye for this.

First, there are chronological differences: the earliest paintings on Naxos, of the 6th and 7th centuries, show the characteristics of late Roman painting: 'sculpted' robes (i.e. painted with a sense of depth and texture), arresting gazes and a sense of vigour. In the 8th and 9th centuries, the Byzantine world was riven by Iconoclastic debate: in 730, Emperor Leo III decreed the destruction of all sacred images in human form. Earlier paintings were plastered over with abstract decorative designs. The end of the Iconoclastic period (843) brought a renewed flourishing of religious art, which emerged as graceful, colourful and with a just balance of space and figure. This lasted beyond the 13th century. With the passing of this renewed energy, and the decline of Byzantium in the 15th century, Byzantine art became more formal and stylised: a flatness pervades; the faces become more distant and elegiac. The 16th and 17th centuries are characterised by an emphasis on narrative content, and a *horror vacui* sets in: every space is filled with detail.

There are distinct personalities at work in the churches of Naxos throughout its history. Drawing on their respective period as well as expressing their own character, they all strive to depict the same world view. The Byzantine church is typically a circle on a square. The circle, with no beginning or end, symbolises the eternal cosmos. The four sides of the square symbolise the earthly world of four elements, four seasons, four cardinal points. Architecturally this is expressed as a dome over a square or rectangular floorplan (heaven over earth). The interior decoration was subsequently planned to match this symbolism: the dome depicts the heavenly panoply, while the lower walls figure the earthly life of Christ and of the saints who dwelt in the world. Shown in the pendentives between these two areas are the Evangelists, the 'communicators' who bridged the gap between the two.

CHALKI & ITS CHURCHES

Located in a fertile valley where citron and olive are cultivated, Chalkí (*map p. 128, B2*) was the capital of the island until 1925. Both the town itself and its surrounding villages display a variety of domestic architecture, from 17th-century Venetian towers to the dignified Neoclassical town houses of the early 20th century. Above all, this is one of the richest areas in Greece for painted, rural Byzantine churches.

At the heart of Chalkí is one of the island's most important churches, the **Protóthronos**, with early paintings (*generally closed except for liturgies in the early morning and evening: the papás, however, is frequently to be seen in the village and will open the church*). The exterior does not betray its antiquity, which goes back to the 6th century. In the 9th century, its original three-aisled form was modified by the addition of a central dome and crossing; in the 11th century a vaulted narthex was added to the west. For much of its early history the church was the seat of the Orthodox bishop of Naxos, hence its name ('first seat'). In the apse of the sanctuary is a synthronon and marble episcopal throne. This is flanked by processions of apostles painted in the 6th or 7th century, which exhibit the characteristic vigour of Early Christian work in their beautifully 'sculpted' robes: in the same phase, the dark-skinned face of St Isidore of Chios was painted on the left jamb of the left-hand window above the throne. The Deësis in the conch above is painted in a very different visual language: the robe and the stylised hair of Christ date from the 13th century, the last phase of painting in the church. Some fragments of 9th-century aniconic decoration have also been revealed on the north crossing vault by the apse. Two other periods of painting are represented, the finest being the work of a particularly graceful painter of the 11th century, who executed the *Annunciation* and *Presentation in the Temple* in the south vault below the dome. Beneath the latter, less fine, is the huddled mass of the *Forty Martyrs of Sebaste*. The dramatic Christ, ringed by saints and archangels in the cupola, is by yet another, slightly later 11th-century hand. The paintings in the northwest parecclesion (off the narthex) are also probably by the same artist.

The double church of the **Panaghía Theosképasti and Ághios Spyridón** (by the High School) consists of two contiguous single-aisled churches. The conches of the twin apses of the south aisle have 13th-century paintings of the *Pantocrator* (north) and the *Panaghia Nikopoia* (south).

North of Chalkí

The simple 11th-century domed church of **Ághios Geórgios Diasorítis** (*signed on a footpath 1km northwest of Chalkí. Generally open 10–2.30 with custodian in summer. Otherwise opening to be arranged with Ephorate; see p. 154*) stands in an olive grove on the edge of the village. Almost its entire original painting programme is intact. A master's hand is visible in the dignified and beautifully executed figures in the apse: a youthful Archangel Gabriel to the left, and an even more youthful and innocent St George (centre), flanked by his mother, St Polychronia, and his father, Gerontius. By the same artist are the angels framing the *Ascension* in the central vault. A quite different hand produced the scenes in the upper corners, such as the Archangel Michael appearing to Joshua (northeast corner, north wall) and the busts of saints on the eastern piers.

The tiny, cruciform, 10th-century **Panaghía Damniótissa** (*800m northeast of Chalkí, west of the road to the Drosianí. Generally open 10–2.30 with custodian in summer. Otherwise opening to be arranged with Ephorate; see p. 154*) has the ruined remains of a (later) narthex to the west. There are paintings in the apse and on other surfaces. Of interest is the expressive, stylised modelling of the faces and the elongated eyes.

The **Basilica of Ághios Isídoros** (*1.5km north of Chalkí by a track 600m west of the main junction in the village centre. Unlocked*) is a large 6th- or 7th-century ruined basilica with three aisles and a single apse. The stone barrel vaults are from the 10th–11th century, as is the narthex. The walls are punctuated with cross-shaped brick decorations.

Vourvouriá, Akadími and Keramí

In the church of **Ághios Konstantínos** (*400m due south of Vourvouriá, map p. 128, B3*), substantial painting remains in the apse of a Virgin of the Blachernae type, above beautifully depicted saints below, dated to 1311 by an inscription in the conch.

Ághios Panteléimon (*500m due south of Akadími*) is a 13th-century church with paintings of the same date, best preserved in the apse and conch, in a highly individualistic style. Note the especially fine Deësis, with a powerful, central Christ figure.

In **Ághios Ioánnis Theológos Keramioú** (*200m east of the main road passing through Keramí, to the north of the village centre; open 10–2.30*) the surviving 13th-century paintings are fragmentary but of high quality. Behind the altar, a Holy Table is painted in the apse, covered with a decorated cloth and a paten bearing the words, 'Take, eat: this is my Body'. The church is of the domed square mausoleum type; the vaulted bay to the west and its belfry were added later. **Ághii Apóstoli** (*250m south of the main road through Keramí, to the west of the village centre. Locked, but most interesting outside*) is an ?11th-century church, with slight remains of 12th- and 13th-century paintings, built on an inscribed-cross plan with a dome supported by free-standing piers. The domed narthex to the west, together with the tall drum of the main dome, creates an exterior profile full of interest. Unusually, a small, domed oratory is incorporated on the upper level above the narthex. The south side is beautifully articulated with a blind arcade with 'pendentive' designs between the arches made with phialostomia: small, hollow, square or cross-shaped elements in terracotta.

The *pýrgi*

There are at least four important fortified manors or *pýrgi* still to be seen in these villages. These structures, though built with a robust, four-square design and bearing crenellations and machicolations, were not primarily for defensive purposes, but expressed the power and status of the rich families who controlled the productive lands around them. Their design is similar in principle: a ground floor of vaulted undercrofts for the storage of produce, often furnished with cisterns; a *piano nobile* above—often accessible by a wooden drawbridge—with a *salone* running the width of the building, with rooms off to the side; an upper area for sleeping rooms; and a flat, crenellated roof for defence and for the collection of water, stored in the cisterns below. The **Barozzi-Grazia Tower** (1742) is in the centre of Chalkí (northeast of the Protóthronos). The **Markopolitis Tower** in Akadími, and the **Kalavros Tower** in Keramí, built around 1770, both belonged to the Politis family, prominent in the struggles of the Greek community, first against the Italians, then against the Turks. The oldest *pýrgos* here is the **Barozzi Tower** in Filóti (*map p. 128, B3*), built in 1650.

WESTERN NAXOS

The western part of Naxos has a concentration of very fine painted churches and several 17th-century towers. The sweeping bays of the coast are interrupted by the rocky knob of Mikrí Vígla (*map p. 128, A3*), which projects into the sea at one of the most exposed points. Excavations on and around the summit have revealed a Middle Bronze Age (2nd millennium BC) settlement. In spring, the marshy areas behind the coast provide an important stopping point for a variety of migratory birds. Especially pleasant are the long sandy beaches of Aghía Ánna and Ághios Geórgios. At ´Yria are the remains of a sanctuary of Dionysus.

THE SANCTUARY OF DIONYSUS AT YRIA

The island of Naxos was sacred to Dionysus, and this spot in the well-watered plain of the Parátrechos river was his main place of cult from at least the 8th century BC (*map p. 128, A2; open daily except Mon, 8.30–3; free*). At its zenith in the 6th century BC it consisted of a walled rectangular precinct (c. 100m by 50m) with a marble temple, an altar, a propylon, several hestiatoria and other ancillary buildings.

HISTORY OF THE SITE

Through the 9th and 8th centuries BC there was a small, flat-roofed, mud-brick shrine and a central sacrificial pit, built over the site of a Mycenaean open-air sanctuary. Around 730 BC this was refashioned, in larger size (c. 11m by 16.5m), with stone walls. Wooden posts on marble bases in the interior supported a wooden ceiling. Fifty years later (680 BC) this was modified again, with the addition of a four-columned porch on the front. A more uncluttered interior was created with only two rows of wooden columns, which flanked the central sacrificial pit. Around 580 BC the much grander temple visible today was constructed on the same site, but at a substantially larger scale (28.4m by 14m). The walls were of granite, but the roof tiles, the south wall and the four-column porch were built in white marble. The interior columns (c. 8m) were also in marble; they framed the central view towards a large chryselephantine statue of Dionysus in the rear chamber.

The Ionic capitals surmounting the columns were fully developed in design and very finely cut. A representative example is exhibited on top of a concrete stand. To the west of the temple is a marble well-shaft and the base of a propylon which would have formed a monumental entrance into the sanctuary from the city. It is possible that the gigantic Archaic statue of Dionysus, lying unfinished in its quarry at Apóllonas at the northern tip of the island (*see p. 149*), was intended for this sanctuary.

PLAKA, GALANADO & SANGRI

Due south of 'Yria, and accessible from the road from Vívlos to Pláka (on a hillside to the north, 1.5km west of Vívlos) is the **Hellenistic Tower of Pláka** (*map p. 128, A3*). The building is about 11m square and of equivalent height, constructed in immaculate isodomic granite masonry. It probably represents a fortified rural building, surveying and protecting the productive valley of Pláka below. Across the road in the valley lies the church of **Ághios Matthaíos**, built on the site of an Early Christian basilica, from which vestiges of mosaic floor, architectural fragments and a baptismal font survive *in situ*. Three kilometres south of Vívlos is the church of **Ághios Ioánnis Theológos Kaknádou**, with 13th-century paintings of distinctive style and chromatic range.

Galanadó

On the southern edge of Galanadó (5km southeast of Chora; *map p. 128, A2*) is the ruined 17th-century Bellonia Tower. Adjacent to it is the double church of Ághios Geórgios and Ághios Ioánnis. The two barrel-vaulted elements are joined by two vaulted passages and bear separate dedications, perhaps originally to accommodate Orthodox and Roman Catholic congregations side by side.

Around Sangrí

Amidst undulating country, with good views of the mountains, are the scattered communities of Káto and Áno Sangrí (*map p. 128, B3*), with two important churches nearby. **Ághios Artémios** (*1.5km east of Káto Sangrí; visible in the valley from the Chalkí–Sangrí road, c. 1.5km north of the Bazaios Tower and 3km south of Chalkí. Opening to be arranged with Ephorate; see p. 154*) is an ancient, single-aisled, domed church of moving simplicity which preserves bands of aniconic decoration in the vault of the sanctuary dating from the 9th century, and imitating marble revetments and ceramic tiles. In the border of the area of spiral volutes is an inscription in red: 'Remember, O Lord, thy servant, Ikonomos, whose name thou knowest. Amen.' It should be noted that everything is hand-drawn, with no stencils or mechanical aids.

   Ághios Nikólaos (*signed south from the eastern end of Áno Sangrí; open in summer Mon–Fri 10–2.30; otherwise opening to be arranged with Ephorate; see p. 154*) has well-preserved areas of painting from 1270 in the interior. Striking use is made of azurite and (?)cinnebar: in places, finer details have been added *a secco* with a pasty lead-white. In two of the pendentives, the Evangelists are represented by their symbols. In the middle of the north wall, lower layers of two earlier phases are visible, depicting the Virgin and Child. Fine scenes of the *Nativity* and of the *Baptism of Christ*, in which a merman symbolises the River Jordan, decorate the sanctuary vault.

The churches around the Bazaios Tower

Due east of Áno Sangrí is the **Bazaios Tower** (*map p. 128, B3*), a former monastery of 1671. It is a useful landmark and point of reference for a further wealth of important churches in the area. Above and to the east is the abandoned **monastery at Kalorítissa** (7th–14th centuries; *partially hidden, but visible, high up on the west slope of the hill of Profítis Ilías above the Bazaios Tower; 30-min climb; outer area unlocked*). In a spacious cave behind the domed refectory building is the church of the Nativity. The centre of interest is in the apse and conch (closed off by a grille): above the synthronon and to either side of the episcopal throne are two framed panels of the apostles, believed to date from the 7th century, before the iconoclastic debate. In better condition is the beautiful 10th-century *Virgin and Child Enthroned*, framed by two symmetrical figures of the Baptist and Isaiah. The other fresco fragments are mostly later.

   Ághios Ioánnis Theológos Avlonítsas, a high, domed church visible from a distance, lies in the fields southwest of the Bazaios Tower. There are good 11th–13th-century paintings both in the church and in the adjoining chapel of St John the Baptist.

   The **Panaghía Arkouliótissa** (*west of the Chalkí–Aghiasós road, 300m south of the Bazaios Tower, opposite the track leading to the Spiliótissa*) is a small church of an unmodified inscribed-cross plan, with a high cupola drum. There are remains of high-quality 11th-century paintings.

THE TEMPLE OF DEMETER & ENVIRONS

In the area of Lathrínos is the church of **Ághios Ioánnis Theológos Adisaroú** (*map p. 128, B3; c. 1km east of the Temple of Demeter site, in a field, 100m to the east of the Chalkí–Aghiasós road. Opening to be arranged with Ephorate; see p. 154*), a 9th-century church, decorated with aniconic paintings from the period of the iconoclastic debate. The domed chapel is of extreme simplicity and the paintings patchy, but of remarkable beauty. The principal influence is a clear memory of Roman inlaid stonework, best seen in the variety of designs in the conch and apse at the east end.

   A hundred metres to the west of the Chalkí–Aghiasós road are the two adjoining chapels of **Ághii Geórgios and Nikólaos Lathrínou** on the site of an Early Christian basilica. Some interesting 13th-century painting remains.

The Archaic Temple of Demeter

The Temple of Demeter at Gýroulas (*map p. 128, B3; accessible from the Chalkí–Aghiasós road or from Áno Sangrí*) has been partially reconstructed and there is a small on-site museum (*open daily except Mon, 8.30–3*). On a small eminence, it provides a visual centre to the surrounding valley. The importance of the site lies in what it has revealed about how cult and architecture developed together. It shows how flexible and varied Greek temple design can be.

Cult at the location goes back at least to the 8th century BC, as indicated by interconnected, shallow offering pits excavated in front of the later temple. Around 530 BC, during the rule of Lygdamis, a temple to Demeter was erected here. Its type is that of a thesmophorion, a place of cult of the chthonic divinities. It was constructed entirely in marble: even the beams and tiles of the roof were made of stone, then a highly modern feature. It had a south-facing portico or pronaos, with five columns in antis. Two large, framed doorways led into the enclosed interior. Its pitched marble roof was supported inside by a transverse row of columns; their heights varied with the slopes of the roof. To the west, a magnificent example of one of the marble beams of the pronaos is preserved.

With the arrival of Christianity, the temple was converted into a church: this happened in two phases and involved reconfiguring the building to accommodate the different orientation required by a Christian place of worship. The portico to the south was filled up between the columns to create a lateral narthex. A doorway was made in the west wall; then, in the 6th century, an apse was created to the east.

The small museum displays the decorative architectural elements and smaller finds from the site.

Apalíros Castle

Looking from the Temple of Demeter, the southeast horizon is dominated by the oldest of the surviving medieval fortresses on Naxos, **Apalíros Castle** (*map p. 128, B3; a track leading east from a point 2km south of the Bazaios Tower, just beyond the turn for the Temple of Demeter, passes over a torrent bed, through a settlement, and ends: a 45-min climb southeast from here takes you to the castle*). More than a point of surveillance and defence, this was a refuge to which the population and their livestock could retreat in times of threat. The enceinte is large (c. 300m by 80m), and the remains of cisterns, houses and churches suggest that there was a permanent living community here.

The castle was begun in the 8th century as protection against the first Arab raids. It became the main stronghold of Byzantine Naxos. The sea is visible, but the site itself is a safe distance from it; it dominated the main areas of agricultural production in the south of the island. When Marco Sanudo came to Naxos in 1207, he landed to the south of here, burned his ships and took five weeks to capture this stronghold from a group of Genoese freebooters who were holding it. Afterwards he built his own castle in Chora, and left this one unaltered, so that it still presents the image of an Early Byzantine fortress. The walls and the fine semicircular bastion have remained in good condition at the northwest corner, the castle's most vulnerable point. There are over 30 vaulted cisterns amongst the ruins of the houses in the interior. Towards the eastern edge are the remains of the 8th-century church of Ághios Geórgios.

In a remote and beautiful valley, 2km as the crow flies to the east of the castle, is the church of Ághios Geórgios at **Káto Marathós** (*map p. 128, B3; a track leads east towards the south side of Apalíros Castle, ending after 2km below the southwestern ascent; a path skirts south round the hill for a further 3km and climbs the valley eastwards up to Ághios Geórgios. Allow 3hrs return*). This is an idiosyncratic church in a dramatic mountain setting. It comprises a main domed aisle (with unusual intersecting vaults), an adjoining barrel-vaulted chapel to the south, and a domed narthex to the west. The church's late 13th-century paintings, of considerable accomplishment, are preserved.

Around Aghiasós

In a flat valley near the coast lies Aghiasós (*map p. 128, B4*). Two 13th-century painted churches can be visited in the low hills to the east: the curiously formed **Panaghía at Archáto** (*map p. 128, B3*); and the remarkable church of the **Panaghía Gialloús** (*map p. 128, B4*), which lies substantially inland from the shore to the south. It is a small mausoleum-type church with very distinctive paintings. One of several inscriptions (which are all votive entreaties of individuals, or of husbands and wives) is dated to the year 6796 since the Creation, i.e. 1288–89. The church was originally a small, domed square: the extension to the west is of later date.

The coastal track south along the coast to the tip of the island, ends at the tiny Byzantine church of **Ághios Sózon Kalantoú**, built into the rocks in gratitude for the safe rescue of sailors from a shipwreck.

NORTHERN NAXOS

Two kilometres out of Chora to the north, the road makes a sharp turn around a creek. Above the bend is the whitewashed chapel of **Ághios Ioánnis Pródromos**. The interior has small areas of 15th-century painting in the apse; the beautiful and expressive face of Christ on the Cross in the niche of the apse, and the saint to the right, are of particular note. Directly below, but now almost completely obscured by oleander bushes, are remains of the Ottoman fountain-house of Ismail Hasan Aga (1759).

After 4km a track leads to the left, and winds to the **Ypsilí Tower** (*map p. 128, A2*), the largest of the fortified manor-monasteries on the island, built at the beginning of the 17th century by the Cocco family. After a further 2km along the main road beyond the Ypsilí turn, the turn left through Galíni towards the beach passes (on the right) the 9th-century church of the Koímisis tis Theotókou or **Panaghía Attaliótissa**, a beautifully-proportioned building with a cross-in-square plan, forming three aisles and apses. Some 14th-century painting of considerable sophistication survives, as well as fragments of a carved marble throne or ambo from the original foundation on the site. To the left of the entrance gate, an ancient frieze with triglyphs is built into the perimeter wall.

Skepóni, Myrísis and Aghiá

After Engarés the coastline becomes steeper, more barren and much less populated. As the road comes to a reservoir, a track heads into the steep interior of the Kóronos massif, to **Skepóni** (*map p. 128, B2*; to its south is the ruined church of Ághios Geórgios, with remains of 13th- and 14th-century painting) and remote and scenic **Myrísis** (*map p. 128, B1*), a good centre for exploring the north of the island on foot: the route from Myrísis to Koronída (Komiáki) is particularly rewarding.

Before the northern tip of the island, the main road passes the striking crenellated **Tower of Aghiá** (*map p. 128, B1*), built in 1717, standing impressively over 200m above the shore. A stepped path to the east leads down to the picturesque monastery of Aghiá, founded in the 12th century and rebuilt in the 17th century.

Apóllonas

Beyond the deserted northern tip of the island, the road drops down to sea-level at Apóllonas (*map p. 128, C1*), set between two small coves. The gigantic, abandoned **kouros of Apóllonas** lies in its quarry just above and to the west of the main road, 500m south of the harbour. This massive figure, 10.7m in height, and probably representing the god Dionysus, would, had it been completed, have been the largest monolithic sculpture of Classical antiquity. Its dimensions and boldness still astonish.

The work is believed to have been begun c. 550 BC. Its upper surface is covered with the marks of a very large bronze point, used perpendicularly to the surface. Around the supine figure, the bedrock bears the parallel striations left from the 'cleaning' of the surface after the outline of the statue had been delineated. A perfectly cylindrical hole in the scarp beside the feet served as a capstan-hole for winching out debris. The projecting arms and hands have broken and eroded with time, but the eyes, nose, beard and pectorals are all still emerging into definition.

It is possible that the figure was destined for the sanctuary of Dionysus at ´Yria (*see p. 144*), which would have presented considerable difficulties of transportation; the figure's weight is estimated at 130 tons. The beginning of the stone ramp which had to be cut down to the shore is just visible to the right of the steps.

Bearded kouros of Apóllonas, thought to represent Dionysus (mid-6th century BC).

Above Apóllonas on the sharp summit (355m) to the southeast of the village, are the remains of the most inaccessible of the island's Venetian fortresses, **Kalógeros Castle** (*accessible by path from the main road, above a hairpin bend 5km south of Apóllonas, at the turning for Mési*), built on the site of earlier Byzantine and prehistoric fortifications.

Síphones and Liónas

The domestic architecture of the villages along the island's northern ridge of mountains reveals a prosperity underpinned historically by emery mining and agriculture, in particular the production of wine.

The tortuous and panoramic road north towards Apóllonas reaches an exposed watershed at Stavrós (*map p. 128, C2*), with magnificent views. Branch roads lead west to the village of **Keramotí**, set on a spur in a deep declivity, hidden from sight, and the deserted settlement of **Síphones**, above which is the double church of Ághios Ioánnis and Ághios Geórgios (*visible below the road to the west before reaching Síphones*). This is a complex of two intercommunicating 11th-century churches, one of which is domed. Both have fragments of 13th–14th-century painting; there are vigorous figures of an archangel and a hierarch to either side of the conch in the north church.

Just before the village of Kóronos, two roads branch to the east within 500m of one another. The first branch (signed) passes the pilgrimage place of the miraculous icon of the **Panaghía Argokiliótissa**. The original 18th-century church is of a curiously long, low rectangular form, designed to accommodate crowds on pilgrimage days. A large modern church is under construction just above. The second branch (also signed) leads into the heart of the emery mining area, and ends at the small coastal settlement of **Liónas** (*map p. 128, C2*), which survives although the mines are now virtually closed. The road descends through a steep and arid landscape, transformed by the human quest for the mineral that has been pursued here for millennia. Emery is one of the hardest naturally occurring rocks on the planet. It is also the material with which Naxian marble was polished since the Bronze Age and throughout Classical antiquity, as were metal tools and weapons throughout the ages. It was the most valuable and unique of the island's exports: until the development of synthetic abrasives in the last century, Naxos alone supplied it to the Western markets. It can still be collected on the surface, in impure form. To the right of the road, tunnels can be seen perforating the hillside. Several abandoned mining structures are visible. Until the advent of modern mining technology in the 20th century, emery had to be extracted from the rock by fire-setting, a procedure that entailed heating rocks and then causing them to crack by dousing them with cold water. The need for fuel led to the deforestation of this part of the island.

EASTERN NAXOS

Apeíranthos

Apeíranthos (*map p. 128, C2*), the principal jumping-off point for exploring the unpopulated east of Naxos, is a very different world from Chora, and even from the rural interior of the island. High up, steep and often cloud-strafed, the forbidding settlement of marble houses and marble streets is cut off from the rest of the island by the central ridge of mountains which runs directly behind the village. It is said that the village was founded by Cretans in the 10th century. Because it clings to a marble scarp, it has no natural centre, but spreads to either side of its central street, starting at the 18th-century church of the Panaghía Apeiranthítissa. From above, the two 17th-century *pýrgi* of the Zevgoli and Bardanis families dominate the village.

There are the four small museums, the Geology Museum, Natural History Museum, Folklore Museum and **Archaeology Museum** (*officially open summer only, 9–3 except Mon*), which exhibits Cycladic artefacts from the 3rd millennium BC. Most remarkable are the rough-hewn limestone slabs, their smoothest faces decorated with pecked and chipped designs, depicting human figures husbanding horned animals, men apparently standing in a boat, and other designs. They come from the excavations of what may have been an open-air shrine on the island's east coast, south of Kanáki, at Korfí t'Ar024onioú.

Aghía Kyriakí Kalonís

The area around Apeíranthos has a number of fine early Byzantine churches. The most notable is the atmospheric Aghía Kyriakí Kalonís, with an array of rare 9th-century aniconic wall-paintings. The church lies camouflaged (though not out of sight) against the stony hillside in the deep valley to the northeast of the village (*a footpath, c. 4.5km, descends from the main road almost opposite the small Natural History Museum and takes at least one hour each way. Unlocked*). The designs of greatest interest are in the lower apse where a dozen fantastic birds—perhaps symbolising the Apostles, who would normally be depicted here—as well as palm trees and fish, fill the space. The remainder of the decoration, which patchily covers the surfaces of the sanctuary, is predominantly patterned or marbled.

South of Apeíranthos

In the cultivated valley to the south of Apeíranthos (east of the main road) are the adjacent, painted churches of Ághios Pachómios and Ághios Geórgios (*on arriving in Apeíranthos from the south, take the concrete road to right, immediately on entering habitation*). The smaller church, **Ághios Geórgios**, dating from the ?11th century, is now in poor condition, and has only vestiges of painting; the masonry templon screen in the interior is—unusually—a structural element partially supporting the dome. **Ághios Pachómios**, of the 13th century, preserves fine paintings, however. The *Transfiguration* (south) and *Crucifixion* (north), as well as the images of the Archangel Michael and St John (northwest pendentive) are noteworthy, as are the angels in the dome.

THE EASTERN COAST

NB: There are no petrol facilities in this deserted southeastern extremity of the island.
As you descend through the hills from Apeíranthos to the coast, the overhead cableway

from the emery mines can be seen to the north. This ambitious project was necessary because the only harbour deep enough to receive cargo ships was **Moutsoúna** (*map p. 128, C2*). Parts of the loading station remain by the shore. Moutsoúna is a tranquil fishing harbour nowadays. To the north stretches the lovely beach of Azalás.

In the foothills of the interior there are many isolated Byzantine churches, most of them in a state of ruin. Just visible from the road at **Ligarídia**, 2km south of Moutsoúna, is the unusual, flat-roofed church of Profítis Ilías Vlacháki, with 13th-century paintings inside (*a track leads west, inland, for 1.5km, from which a footpath climbs up to the south: access difficult*). The church appears to be built on the site of a prehistoric fort.

The most dramatic and beautiful of all Naxos' prehistoric sites, however, is above the sheltered bay of **Pánormos** (*map p. 128, C4*). The hill to the west of the bay forms a natural acropolis: on its crown, an Early Cycladic citadel of the 3rd millennium BC has been excavated. The paved entrance running due east–west, flanked by stone benches to either side and leading to a gateway made of larger blocks, is well-preserved and clearly visible, while inside is a tight-knit web of building foundations and alleyways. The defensive walls here may have been added at the end of the Early Bronze Age.

The Christós Photodóti

Four kilometres south of Apeíranthos, just before the main road to Chora begins to descend to Filóti, a sharp turning to the east climbs over the ridge to Danakós and the monastery of Christós Photodóti, 'Giver of Light' (*left branch after 1km*), the best preserved of the island's tower-monasteries, although in this case the monastery and church existed long before they were encased in a *pýrgos* in the 16th century. The approach to the panoramic site is through an area scattered with magnificent oak trees.

The monastery has its origins in an Early Christian basilica, altered in the 16th century to produce a square, inscribed-cross plan, with a dome supported on columns and a narthex to the west. The synthronon and walls of the original structure survive. The addition of the high square fortress around it, with massive buttresses, permitted the creation of an upper level for a refectory and cells, through which the cupola of the katholikon protrudes.

Mount Zas and the Zas Cave

The road for the Cave of Zas (*map p. 128, B3*) finishes at the springs of Ariés. From here, it is a steep 25-min climb up a torrent bed to the cave, which lies to the left just above another spring. The combination of water and protection which the cave affords has appealed since earliest times; the cave was a place of habitation and burial in the Neolithic (5th–4th millennia BC) and continued to be frequented in the Bronze Age.

From the cave, the summit of Zas (999m), the highest peak of the Cyclades, can be reached in a further 45mins on a very steep approach. The longer path from the north, leaving from the road to Danakós, close by the church of Aghía Marína, is easier (*90mins*). Zas, its name cognate with Zeus, to whom it was sacred, is the best area for glimpsing the colony of griffon vultures inhabiting this mountain ridge.

The Tower of Cheímaros and the south coast

The well-watered **valley of Ariés** is populated with ancient oak trees. There are Byzantine churches scattered amongst the trees and fields. Of greatest interest is the **Panaghía Arión**, a delightful ruined 11th-century church (*east of road, 1.7km after initial junction at Filóti; path doubles back to church in middle of field*). Thirteenth-century paintings survive on the outside of the west wall, formerly enclosed by a domed narthex.

After crossing a panoramic watershed, on what is perhaps the island's most scenic road, the Hellenistic **Tower of Cheímaros** (*map p. 128, C3*), standing to a height of over 15m, appears on a ridge with sweeping views. The circular tower is built of courses of rectangular masonry, shaped perfectly to the curve of the building, suggesting a late 4th-century BC date. To the right of the door (inside), it is clear to see that the tower was constructed with both an inner and outer shell. The tower was the centre of a large agricultural complex, of which extensive remains are visible to its west and southeast: querns, oil-press stones, sedimentation, filtration and settling tanks, etc. can all be seen.

Two early Byzantine churches, on the foundations of an Early Christian basilica, have been built into a corner of the enceinte to the east of the tower.

PRACTICAL INFORMATION

GETTING AROUND

Naxos has on average two or three car ferries per day to Piraeus, and one or two to Rafína; the journey time typically varies between 4¼ and 5½ hrs. Nearly all services stop at Paros en route. There are daily connections to Ios and Santorini in summer, either by ferry or hydrofoil (twice weekly in winter). The *Express Skopelitis* leaves Naxos for the Lesser Cyclades, weather permitting. There is one daily return flight from Athens to Naxos; small aircraft only. The airport is 3½ km from Chora.

WHERE TO STAY

For its size and importance, Naxos is poorly provided with good accommodation. The most charming is the **Chateau Zevgoli**, in the heart of Bourgo, although the rooms are small and overdecorated (*T: 22850 25201*). The owner, Mrs Despina Kitini, also has a couple of spacious studio rooms up in the Kastro. She can be found at the useful Naxos Information Center, which she manages, opposite the main ferry quay. **Karabatsi Studios** at Aghía Ánna offer friendly family hospitality of utter simplicity, at a short distance from Chora (*T: 22850 26440; www.dinanaxos.com*). Of the resort hotels, **Lianos Village** at Ághios Prokópios, also near Chora, is comfortable and unpretentious (*T: 22850 26366; www. lianosvillage.com*).

WHERE TO EAT

Of the myriad tavernas on the harbour-front at Chora, the freshest fish and seafood is to be had at the minuscule **To Steki tou Valetta**, where excellent octopus and wine are served. Of quite different character—elegant and with some carefully designed dishes—is **Elli's** restaurant in the Grotta area of Chora. For beachside eating, just outside Chora, **Paradiso** at Aghía Ánna has good food, served at tables under trees on the sands.

One of the best of all fish restaurants outside Chora is **Michalakos** at Moutsoúna. For its setting by springs in the village of Áno Potamiá, the **Taverna Pigi** is a joy. **Katsalis**, under the plane trees in Filóti, is also to be recommended. And for making a picnic from the best Naxiot wine and produce, the **Tziblakis cheese shop** on the main street, Papavasileíou, in Chora is excellent.

ACCESS TO CHURCHES

Opening arrangements can be a problem as many churches are kept locked. A good proportion of the most important have relatively easy access, although advertised opening times are not adhered to outside the tourist season; some have particular hours; some may require tracking down the local priest in the nearest village to obtain the key. For some of the most important, opening needs to be arranged through the Byzantine Antiquities Ephorate in Chora, located in the Sanudo/Crispi Tower in Kastro (*T: 22850 22225*).

FURTHER READING

J. Theodore Bent, *The Cyclades, or Life Among the Insular Greeks* (1885), reissued 2002 by Archaeopress, Oxford in the '3rd Guides' series and also in an abridged version by Anagnosis: *Island-Hopping in the Cyclades*; Giorgios Mastoropoulos, Νάξος. Τό ἄλλο κάλλος/ *Naxos:Byzantine Monuments*, Athens, 1996, an excellent documentation of Byzantine Naxos.

IOS

Ios (*pron: Íos*), one of the largest Cycladic islands, was for long one of the least populated. The construction of roads and a boom in tourism in recent years have altered
that, inevitably compromising to some degree the island's solitary beauty and grandeur
and sweeping away its traditional structures. Its picturesque *chora* and fine beaches
have attracted a sometimes dissonant type of tourism, but beyond the main resorts the
island has retained much of its character. With its surprising variation of landscape, Ios
can be unexpectedly delightful in the quieter months.

HISTORY OF IOS

Ios was densely settled in the Bronze Age, had Phoenician and Mycenaean contacts from before the 12th century BC, and was, according to ancient tradition, settled by Ionians in the 10th century, though virtually no Geometric remains are yet known. A tenacious tradition maintains that Homer was shipwrecked, died and buried on the island. By the 6th century BC, Ios was a small city-state. Like its Ionian-settled neighbours to the north, it was a member of the Delian League, and under Macedonian rule from 338 BC. After 220 BC it was allied with Rhodes. Remnants of Roman infrastructure suggest that Ios was a trading centre at the time.

With the demise of Roman power, Órmos became a base for piracy and the population moved into the fortified sites of the interior. Ios was one of the original islands constituting Sanudo's Duchy of Naxos in the aftermath of the Fourth Crusade. It was briefly recaptured for Byzantium in 1278–79, but was again under Venetian control by 1296, as a fief of the Schiavi family, who held the island until it passed by marriage first to the Crispi family at the end of the 14th century, and then to the Pisani family, who held onto it until Kheir ed-Din Barbarossa captured it for the Ottoman sultan in 1537. In the first Russo-Turkish War of 1770–74, Ios was occupied by Russian forces along with the other Cyclades. Ios contributed 24 ships and crews to the cause of the Greek War of Independence in 1821 and was united with the liberated Greek state in 1829. The island was much visited by the poet Odysseas Elytis, and was latterly home to the painter Yiannis Gaitis.

ORMOS BAY, SKARKOS & IOS CHORA

Ios had no mineral, and only meagre agricultural, wealth: its two assets in earlier times were its plentiful timber and the sheltered bay of Órmos, site of its port, Gialós. It is one of the most attractive and protected inlets in the Cyclades, lined with beaches and framed by hills. On its east side is the 17th-century church of **Aghía Eiríni**, one of the island's grandest buildings, with two striking domes and belfries. The oldest church in the area, **Ághios Geórgios** (13th or 14th century), lies in an open area about 250m inland, to the right of the road to Chora. In front are the pillars of a former narthex. The dome covers the entire area of its square floorplan. From the bend in the road just beyond, the old *kalderími* leads from the port up to Chora (*15mins on foot*).

Skárkos

One of the most interesting prehistoric sites in the Cyclades lies at Skárkos, a little over 1km inland of the main beach of Órmos, on the slopes a low hill to the northeast side of the valley. Its meticulously constructed buildings and streets are remarkably well preserved (*no official opening times, as excavations continue. The site is reached by taking either one of the rough stone tracks heading north from opposite the filling station behind Gialós; 2.5km by road*).

Aerial view of the landscape of Ios.

The densely-built urban settlement on the northwest side of the hill dates from the mid-3rd millennium BC (Early Cycladic II). The carefully built stone walls of its houses stand 2–3m high and bear remarkable refinements: in places there is a protruding string course; there are well-placed threshold blocks; and at some points the thickness of the wall accommodates storage recesses. Flights of stairs led to upper floors. The network of narrow streets and alleys, connecting small 'squares', suggests a notable degree of organisation.

The remarkable finds, mostly in the museum in Chora, include large clay storage vases with moulded decorations, cooking vessels, and seals. Imported materials indicate commercial links with Crete, the islands, the Greek mainland and Asia Minor.

IOS CHORA

Shortly before reaching Chora from Gialós, the base of the ancient city's 6th-century BC **fortification walls** is visible beside the main road, left of where the *kalderími* crosses its course. They originally encircled the whole hill above, suggesting that Archaic Ios was a sizeable community. Today's Chora climbs attractively up to the rocky peak of the old acropolis, covering the site of the ancient city. An exedra and other vestiges of Hellenistic and Roman buildings are visible just beside the Neoclassical Dimarcheíon (to the south of the road), which also houses a small **archaeological museum** (*open daily except Mon, 8.30–3; free*). The centrepiece of the collection is the rich and varied material from the prehistoric site of Skárkos (*see above*), including figurines, metal tools and large pithoi, used for both storage and burial. There are also some fine Archaic stone stelae.

The churches of Chora

The most important churches of Chora are at the bottom of the acropolis hill. Almost opposite the Dimarcheíon is **Aghía Aikateríni**, a compact 17th-century church, incorporating several column fragments in its cupola drum. Just east of Aghía Aikateríni is the ruined 14th- or 15th-century Frangokklisía ('Latin Church'). Its name implies that it was used by the island's small Catholic community at one point; after this it appears that the church was left unadopted and abandoned. Immediately north of Aghía Aikateríni is the long, low structure of the much earlier (possibly 14th-century) church of **Ághios Ioánnis Pródromos**, with a raised crossed barrel vault, and, abutting it to the north, the island's cathedral of the Evangelismós (1930).

Above the Evangelismós church, the heart of the old *chora* is bisected east–west by the main commercial road, which links two small squares. Beside the upper square, the **double church of Ághios Andréas and Aghía Kyriakí** incorporates ancient spolia in its interior. At the top of the habitation, from the church of the Panaghía Kremniótissa, a path leads up through rocks towards the summit; the penultimate church, **Ághios Geórgios**, just below the top, has part of a marble tablet, densely engraved with early 4th-century decrees, built into the south corner of its façade. The **summit**, now occupied by a chapel of Ághios Nikólaos, was the principal lookout of the ancient acropolis. At the end of the 14th century, the Venetian overlord Marco Crispo built a fortified enclosure here; little of it now remains to be seen beyond short breaks of wall.

Mylopótas

Less than a kilometre south (on foot) from the southeastern corner of Chora is the bay of Mylopótas. This and Manganári Bay in the south of the island lie at the heart of the island's fame as a pleasure resort, and in the 1960s and '70s were places of pilgrimage for a whole generation of hippies, nudists and hedonists.

On the promontory north of the bay, visible from the road as it climbs back to Chora, are two villas, set amongst vegetation, built by the painter Yiannis Gaitis. The creation of the Gaitis-Simosi Museum is in progress here.

EPANO KAMBOS & THE NORTH

The road north from Chora descends into the valley of **Epáno Kámbos**, the agricultural heart of Ios. In its midst are the remains of a Hellenistic farmstead (*coming from Chora, take the first track to the left at the last right-hand bend before the road levels into the valley floor. Fork right after 100m. Where the track ends, a walled path leads on towards a small church to the left, which marks the ruins of the ancient building*). It must have been a substantial farm building, combining storage and dwelling in one. The doorway on the southwest side tapers to the top, suggesting that it was originally corbelled.

The 'Tomb of Homer'

From the northern end of the Epáno Kámbos valley, a new road winds through the rough and uninhabited terrain of the northern tip of the island where, on the northernmost promontory, are the remains of the watchtower of **Psarópyrgos**, the so-called 'Tomb of Homer'. The site has been considerably altered: the masonry of the walls here is not that of a Hellenistic watchtower but of a much later construction; nevertheless, it incorporates some blocks of dressed marble from the door frame of a substantial ancient building. Three of these have been reassembled in recent times as a makeshift shrine for Homer's supposed resting place.

THE EAST OF THE ISLAND

The east coast of the island is wild and exposed, but the remains of foundations and a surface aqueduct from the Roman period, in the coastal area between Aghía Theodóti and Psáthi, suggest that it was more inhabited in antiquity.

Aghía Theodóti and Pýrgos Monastery

The church of **Aghía Theodóti**, set above the wide bay of that name, 5.5km east of the road junction above Epáno Kámbos, is an unusual piece of 16th-century architecture, preceded by a shallow, transverse narthex, and crowned by two successive large domes.

Between Aghía Theodóti and Psáthi, the road climbs high into the mountainous interior. At 12.5km from Chora, just before the road begins to descend again, a detour of 4.5km leads right (south) to the 16th-century **Monastery of Pýrgos**, dedicated to Ághios Ioánnis Pródromos, built on a panoramic ledge just below the highest summit of the island. The fortified quadrangle of monastic buildings is now ruined, but the church, a free-cross design with semi-domes on the lateral arms, stands.

Psáthi

Descending to the coast at Psáthi, the main road passes the ruins of the **Venetian castle of Palaiókastro** (c. 1500), visible on the summit ahead before the road turns sharply east (*15mins by path and steps*). An enceinte of walls encloses an irregular space on the edge of a precipitous drop. The site overlooks an important maritime route. Remains of a cistern and of several buildings survive within, as does the 17th-century church of the Panaghía Palaiokastrítissa.

The road ends at **Psáthi**, a remote bay. An Ionic temple to Poseidon Phytalmios ('the Nourisher') stood here, on the site now occupied by the church of Ághios Nikólaos, also known locally as the Panaghía tou Porí (*not far in from the coast, 400m southeast of the village; marked by a palm tree*). The high podium built of eroded schists is visible below the north side of the church.

The **beach** of Psáthi, together with the others along the island's central eastern coast, is a breeding ground for the Mediterranean sea turtle.

THE SOUTH OF THE ISLAND

The southern extremity of the island is quite different from the centre and north. From Chora, it is either 25km, metalled all the way, on the road via Epáno Kámbos, towards Psáthi, branching south at the junction at 10.5km; or 18km, partially unmade, via Mylopótas. On the south side of the island's central massif the scenery suddenly changes from long scrubby slopes to a strange boulder-strewn landscape produced by a combination of volcanic activity and constant wind erosion. Hidden in an oasis of scattered trees in its midst is the **monastery of Ághios Ioánnis Pródromos of Kálamos**. Never was a dedication to the Baptist more appropriate than in this desert landscape, which here unexpectedly yields water. Before the monastery was founded at the turn of the 19th century, the site must originally have been occupied by a hermitage, reminiscent in setting of the those of the early Desert Fathers. Below the monastery, there is a sandy beach.

PRACTICAL INFORMATION

GETTING AROUND

Ios has no airport. There is one or more daily connections to Piraeus by regular ferry (8–10hrs) or high-speed (4½ hrs). Ios is also a terminus of a route from Santorini and Anáphi via Síkinos and Folégandros, offering connections with these lesser islands five times weekly. In the summer there are fast hydrofoil links almost daily with Santorini and Naxos.

WHERE TO STAY

The **Liostasi Spa Hotel** (*T: 22860 92140, www.liostasi.gr*), situated panoramically between the port and Chora, is modern, welcoming, comfortable and with a wide range of services. At the north end of Órmos Bay are **Petra Villas**, attractively appointed studios, in relative quiet and seclusion, close to the water (*T: 22860 91409*).

WHERE TO EAT

It is not always easy to find simple, genuine Greek cuisine on Ios. In Chora and Gialós it can be found at **Taverna Susanna** in Plateía Limanioú beside the port, and at the small **Koutouki tou Saïni**, near the Epáno Piátsa at the eastern end of the old part of Chora. For good fresh fish, vegetable dishes and salads, the **Taverna Alonistra** at Psáthi on the east coast is reliable and pleasant.

SANTORINI

Santorini (officially Thera; *pron: Thíra*) is one of the most unusual and memorable places in all Greece. The entire island is a caldera, forming a huge circular bay, its beetling cliffs standing witness to an event that shook the Aegean, one of the most violent volcanic eruptions in human history. It buried the flourishing city of Akrotiri, providing posterity with a superbly-preserved Bronze Age site, its streets, squares and houses still standing as they did 3,700 years ago.

The views from the caldera rim, crowned by the towns of Chora and Oía, are unforgettable, and this beauty has made Santorini one of the most popular destinations in the Aegean. But the press of humanity cannot diminish the island's interest or drown out the extraordinary magic of the light, especially before sunset, when the vast bowl of cliffs and islands fills with it, reflected from the water.

For a glimpse of what Santorini was like before, visit the islet of Therasía, which still offers an untouched Theran landscape.

HISTORY OF SANTORINI

There is evidence at Akrotiri for a 5th-millennium BC Neolithic settlement. In the Early Bronze Age (3rd millennium), Akrotiri appears to have been the principal centre, growing by the Middle Bronze Age into a great and cosmopolitan port on the trading routes between Crete, the islands, the mainland and Cyprus. The city was damaged by earthquakes and rebuilt several times, before it was finally destroyed by a massive volcanic eruption in the late 17th century BC, burying all human settlement (an event fancifully connected by some with the Platonic legend of Atlantis). The island was subsequently uninhabited for several centuries.

According to ancient tradition, the island was originally called Strongyle ('round') and later referred to as Kalliste ('most beautiful'). In tradition it was colonised by the Phoenicians, led by Cadmus. In the 9th or 8th century BC, ancient Thera, a Dorian colony from Laconia, was established. It was one of the first Aegean centres to adapt the Phoenician alphabet for writing in Greek. Around 630 BC it was forced by a protracted drought to found its own colony, Cyrene, on the north coast of Africa.

Together with Milos, Thera avoided alliance with Athens in the 5th century BC, remaining in the sphere of Spartan influence. After 375 BC, however, it was absorbed with the other Cycladic islands into the Second Athenian League. In Hellenistic times, the island's strategic position was particularly valued by the Ptolemies, who used Thera as a major naval base, maintained until the death of Ptolemy VI Philometor in 145 BC.

Not much is known about the island's history in later antiquity. In Early Christian times it had a bishop. In the early 12th century the Byzantine emperor Alexius I Comnenus founded the church of the Panaghía Episkopí. After Marco Sanudo took the Cyclades in 1207 (*see p. 130*), he ceded Santorini and Therasía to one of his followers, Giacomo Barozzi, whose descendants ruled the island from a capital at Skáros until 1335, when the island returned to the Sanudo family. The Sanudo possessions passed to the Crispi in 1397, and Santorini was ceded as a marriage dowry to Domenico Pisani, Duke of Crete, in 1480. The island came under Turkish dominion in 1566.

In 1821 Santorini's fleet contributed considerably to the Greek War of Independence; in 1832 the island officially became part of the Greek state. A strong earthquake in July 1956 damaged or destroyed well over half the structures on the island.

In September 2005, a part of the newly-constructed roof over the archaeological site at Akrotiri collapsed, killing a British tourist and injuring others: the site closed for more than four years.

Santorini: view of the caldera with the town of Firá (Chora)
strung out along the clifftop.

Nomenclature

The island is referred to today with equal frequency as Thera (also written Thira) and Santorini. Its ancient name is Thera; the name Santorini (or 'Santa Irene') was given currency by the Venetians in the 13th century. Thira (Θήρα) has recently been re-adopted as the official name, though Santorini has been used in this text, as it is still more familiar to English speakers. The name of the main town, Firá, is also now officially Thira. On the island, it is referred to as Chora, a usage followed in the text below.

THE VOLCANIC CALDERA & THE BRONZE AGE ERUPTION

The caldera of Santorini, a vast flooded volcanic crater, covers an area of c. 85km square. Surrounded by a broken, roughly elliptical rim, its western part is formed by the island of Therasía and the steep rock of Aspronísi. The sea is up to 400m deep within it, and the surrounding cliffs tower up to 300m above the water, giving the caldera a total depth of over 700m. In its centre, two land masses of upthrust magma have appeared since the 3rd century BC, the islets of Palaiá and Néa Kaméni. This whole desolate and beautiful scene is the result of a long volcanic history: the caldera was already ancient by the time of the Bronze Age eruption. Its cliff-faces, with their various coloured strata, present a clear section through the geological history of the island.

The volcanic eruption

The Middle Bronze Age eruption of Thera was one of the largest volcanic explosions in human history. Volcanic events of its scale have only been explicitly described twice (Krakatoa and Mt Tambora). The eruption is estimated to have been audible as far away as modern Iraq or France. The contact between magma and seawater also resulted in a massive steam explosion.

In the initial phase, the island was cauterised by pyroclastic flows, streams of super-heated air. During the eruption, up to 100 cubic kilometres of rock, reduced to ashes, were expelled. The heavier components fell on Santorini, forming the white layer of tephra (pumice) visible on the cliffs, up to 60m thick and covering nearly the entire island. Lighter ash was blown over much of the Aegean. In a second phase, a plume of 35km in height rose into the stratosphere and the volcano continued to expel great boulders, many of which are strewn over the island.

The large-scale results of the eruption far outpaced the immediate effects caused by the obliteration of human activity in the island, whose population appears to have evacuated in advance of the event, perhaps warned by preceding tremors. Tidal surges and tsunamis between 35m and 150m high affected much of the Aegean, with devastating effects especially on the northern coast of Crete, which would also have suffered from ashen rain, devastating its agriculture. Tephra from the eruption is found in Bronze Age sites all over the Aegean, sometimes forming substantial layers. The dust blown into the atmosphere had an appreciable cooling effect on the global climate for several years, as reported in Chinese chronicles.

Dating the Bronze Age eruption

Although the idea that the Santorini eruption was responsible for the end of Minoan civilisation in Crete has long been disproved, it remains one of the few specific events known to have occurred in prehistoric Europe, making its date an important chronological benchmark, especially for the Aegean. The study of the site's pottery and of Egyptian imports, in comparison with material from elsewhere in the East Mediterranean, has suggested a date not long before 1500 BC, which was accepted by many scholars.

Recent research has called for a radical adjustment of this estimate, however. Various scientific methodologies, including the study of northern European tree rings and of Arctic ice cores from Greenland, have tended to suggest various considerably earlier dates, in the 17th century BC. In recent years, Danish geologists have located two olive trees, buried alive in ashes during the eruption, in the caldera's cliff face. Calibrated dates from their tree rings date the eruption to 1609 +/- 9 BC.

Atlantis: the eruption in myth?

Scholars and pseudo-scholars have long tried to create a connection between the Santorini eruption and the tale of Atlantis, recounted twice by Plato at the turn of the 4th century BC. It refers to an ideal proto-civilisation, Atlantis, ruling much of the southeastern Mediterranean and eventually disappearing into the depths of the sea 'in a single day and night', after violent earthquakes and floods. The particular fate of Atlantis as described by Plato, as well as his emphasis on its prosperity and sphere of influence, might suggest that it reflects a memory of the Bronze Age civilisation of the Aegean and the catastrophe of Thera. Critics argue that flood myths and lost island stories are a global phenomenon and that the Atlantis story may simply be a metaphor invented by Plato, which would explain its virtual absence from all other ancient literature.

Subsequent activity

Strabo describes an eruption, probably in 197–196 BC, in which the island of Palaiá Kaméni, then called Hiera, first appeared from under the sea. In AD 46, another islet appeared and vanished. AD 726 saw another eruption, creating the northeastern lobe of Palaiá Kaméni. In 1570 the south coast of Santorini, with the port of Eleusis, collapsed beneath the sea. Mikrá Kaméni appeared in 1573, Néa Kaméni in 1707–11. In 1866 a protracted eruption lasted for two years; an island, named Aphroessa, appeared in 1868 and then disappeared again. The eruptions of 1925–26 joined Mikrá and Néa Kaméni into a single landmass. There were further eruptions in 1939–40 and 1950, leading up to the 1956 earthquake.

CHORA & THE KAMENI ISLETS

Firá or Chora stretches to either side of a main, cobbled alley which follows ridge of the caldera from south to north. To the west are the older parts of the town, cut into the volcanic deposit on ledges overlooking the caldera below from a height of 230m. The southern end of the settlement is dominated by the church of the Panaghía Ypapantís, the Metropolis or Orthodox cathedral of Santorini, rebuilt after its predecessor was destroyed in the earthquake of 1956. The attractive churches down the slope to the west—the (originally 15th-century) Ághios Minás to the south, the 17th-century Ághios Ioánnis Theológos in the cliff directly below, and the 19th-century Aghía Eiríni further to the north—all had to be rebuilt at that time. There are also several examples of older traditional houses on the panoramic west slope. They are cut back into the soft deposit of tephra, their rooms excavated into the cliff-side and always roofed with a vaulted ceiling for safety. External ovens in the small yard in front of the entrance were a frequent feature, and the interior, protected from the wind, was heated by braziers.

The Museum of Prehistoric Thera

At the south end of Chora, the Museum of Prehistoric Thera (*open daily except Mon, 8–7.30*) occupies the new building just below the cathedral. It is an exceptional collection of material from prehistoric Akrotiri. The Theran paintings are primarily sacred narratives, but they are also remarkable compositions of nature. Though not the only examples of Aegean Bronze Age painting, they are the most complete and beautiful, and they possess, by virtue of the conditions in which they were found, a clearer architectural context than the others, helping us to understand their meaning.

Right-hand wing: The first cases display finds from the early settlements at Akrotiri. The fine Middle Cycladic pottery includes 'nipple jars' with exquisite decoration of swallows. There is also a model of the site as excavated so far. Most remarkable are examples of domestic items, among them wooden furniture from the Bronze Age town, reconstituted by injecting plaster into the hollows left by the decayed objects embedded in the solidified ashes.

Rear wing: Objects include three storage pithoi, lead weights and measures, and a large collection of seal-stones. In the second bay is a beautiful ceramic tripod-altar with designs of dolphins. The corner is occupied by a reconstruc-

tion of a room from the House of the Ladies, with wall-paintings including the famous scene of bare-breasted ladies and papyrus plants. The female figures are dressed in fine clothes and wear makeup and jewellery.

Left-hand wing: The display begins with a magnificent array of Theran pottery of the 17th century BC, with its unflagging repertoire of both abstract and floral motifs, swallows and marine animals, followed by a selection of imported objects from mainland Greece, Crete, Egypt and the Middle East, among them a beautiful Egyptian ostrich-egg rhyton.

In the final corner (to left of the entrance) the painted frieze of the Blue Monkeys from Building B has been re-

The 17th-century BC 'Blue Monkey' fresco from Building Beta at Akrotiri.

constructed from dozens of fragments. The last showcase contains the only object of precious metal to have been found so far at Akrotiri, a gold ibex.

The Old Archaeological Museum

A short climb up the main pedestrian street, is the (Old) Archaeology Museum of Thera (*open daily except Mon, 8.30–3*). Although there are some prehistoric finds on show, the collection principally exhibits objects of the historic periods from around the island.

The main gallery displays early historic material, including many large, slip-painted burial amphorae, with painted designs from the Late Geometric period (8th and 7th centuries BC). The centrepiece of the collection of cemetery artefacts is the late 7th-century BC clay figurine of a mourning woman of Daidalic style (immediately left on entering). In the second gallery (to the right) is a display of Archaic and Classical pottery imported from Attica, as well as local Hellenistic sculpture.

The northern part of Chora

Beyond the museum to the left is the terminus of the cablecar, which descends to the old port in 3mins. Further along is a large 19th-century Neoclassical mansion, housing the **Petros Nomikos Centre**. The complex of former wine cellars in the rock behind now houses an exhibition entitled Theran Wall-paintings in Photographic Reproduction (*open daily 10–9*), covering all the paintings so far discovered at Akrotiri. The path continues beyond the building to **Firostefáni** (literally the 'Crown of Firá'), the attractive and panoramic northern extremity of Chora.

One block north from the Old Archaeology Museum, in the Venetian quarter of Chora, the 18th-century Ghisi Mansion houses the **Historical Museum** (*open May–Oct daily 10.30–1 & 5– 8; 10.30– 4.30 on Sun*), with prints and engravings of Santorini from the 17th–19th centuries and an interesting collection of photographs of the island's buildings before and after the 1956 earthquake. Immediately to the west is the Roman Catholic Cathedral of the Immaculate Conception (1823). Close by are the Dominican Convent of the Rosary and the Catholic bishop's residence.

The old port and the volcano on the Kaméni islands

A zigzag of 600 steps descends from the bottom edge of Káto Firá (west from the main crossing of alleys at the centre of Chora) down to the old port, 230m below. Donkeys and mules carry people up and down, preserving a long-standing tradition. When the cablecar opened, it was agreed that a portion of every ticket sold would be given as a subsidy to the muleteers, so that the tradition could be maintained.

From the quay, excursion trips leave for the 'volcano' and the Kaméni islands in the centre of the caldera. The islands are magma domes, pushed up in successive eruptions to a height of 130m above the water. **Palaiá Kaméni** first appeared in the early 2nd century BC. From the (usual) point of disembarkation on the north side of **Néa Kaméni**, a path leads to the summit above the central crater of the volcano, which emits a strong and stinging sulphurous vapour. Nothing lives or grows on the island. From the summit, the cooled magma flows of the last major eruptions can be distinguished: the 1707–11 deposits to the northwest, the main 1925–28 deposits to the east, and the massive areas of the 1866–70 deposits to the south. On the surface to the west the superimposed lava flows of 1925–28 can be seen. Most excursion boats to Kaméni offer the unusual opportunity to swim above an **undersea hot spring**.

IMEROVIGLI TO OIA

Although a separate community, **Imerovígli** is almost a continuation of Firá. At 320m, it occupies the highest point of the caldera, with commanding views. Its two principal religious buildings, the 17th-century convent of Ághios Nikólaos to the south and the church of the Panaghía 'Maltesa' on the main square, were both restored or rebuilt after the earthquake of 1956. A stepped footpath leads west to the eroded rock-stack of Skáros, site of the 13th-century Venetian fortress and capital of the island. In the 18th century, it was abandoned due to erosion. The ruined walls of a few buildings and the stepped street are all that remain. The road from Imerovígli to Oía follows the ridge.

Oía

Picturesque Oía (*pron: Ee-a*) commands the northern entry into the caldera. It was the island's principal commercial centre up until the Second World War. Quieter and more photogenic than Firá, its varied forms and the colours of houses—some still derelict from the 1956 earthquake—flow along the summit of the ridge in a succession of shapes, interspersed with the irregular flights of steps that link them. The houses are constructed in rough volcanic rocks and thickly plastered to give a neat and uniform surface. At the highest level there are several Neoclassical captains' houses. In one of the finest of these, towards the western end of town, is the **Nautical Museum** (*open daily except Tues, 10–3*), containing a number of fine carved ship's figureheads and various maritime memorabilia. On the point at the western extremity of the town is the 15th-century **Venetian Kastro**. At the opposite, eastern extremity, is the separate community of **Finikiá**, with the small 13th-century rock-cut church of Ághios Geórgios.

Below Oía, accessible either by road or by two flights of steps, is the harbour of Ammoúdi. Boats depart from here twice daily to Therasía (*see p. 179*).

CHORA TO ANCIENT THERA

The road east from Chora towards the airport descends to **Mesariá**, whose landmarks are its grand, early Neoclassical mansions built by late 19th-century entrepreneurs and merchants. The Argyros Mansion, built by a successful wine-merchant in 1888, can be visited (*open May–Oct; T: 22860 31669*).

At the traditional settlement of **Vóthonas**, a short way to the south, is a wine museum, created in the underground caves of a winery. The right branch at the main junction between Mesariá and the airport leads towards the resort of **Kamári**, with its beaches of black sand, and ancient Thera (*see overleaf*).

The Panaghía Episkopí

At Episkopí Goniás, a right branch leads 1km up to the church of the Panaghía Episkopí, the most interesting and important church on the island. The existing church was founded in 1115 by Alexius I Comnenus. The small domed inscribed-cross design is built over the sanctuary of a larger Early Christian basilica; the apse and synthronon of the earlier building are maintained in the 12th-century structure. The church is entered through a barrel-vaulted narthex; two openings lead into the naos, which is compact and high. In its centre two columns supporting the dome are probably still *in situ* from the early basilica. The column to the north stands on an ancient altar as its base, and has an unusual, Early Christian, Doric-style capital; that to the south has an altar with carved garlands and bucrania incorporated just below the capital. The side aisles have ancient columns.

The majority of the 12th-century wall-paintings are on the south side. On the south wall of the south bay is the *Dormition of the Virgin*; to left (east wall) is a *Virgin* of the Blachernae type, with a strikingly young and princely Christ; to the right is the *Resur-*

rection. In the arch over the passage into the south bay the subject is *Salome with the Head of the Baptist* and *Herod Enthroned*. There are less well-preserved murals on the north side, and figures of apostles in the conch of the sanctuary. In the southwest corner of the naos is the famous 12th-century processional icon of the *Virgin Glykophilousa*.

The most unusual element of the interior is the decoration of the marble templon screen. The spaces between the decorative patterns have been filled with a paste made from earth-pigments and wax. The surface has then been polished, giving an effect of great richness and beauty.

ANCIENT THERA

The siting of ancient Thera (*open daily except Mon, 8.30–3; plan overleaf*) is one of the most audacious in the Aegean. It occupies the exposed, eastern spur of Mt Profítis Ilías, known as Mesá Vounó. To the west rises the island's highest summit; on all other sides the terrain drops over 300m to the sea. It is the only location on Santorini where foundations can be sunk into limestone rather than volcanic pumice. The remains of the city are interesting and varied: it was the only large settlement on the island in early historic times. Access on foot is arduous: either by an unrelenting, 30-min climb up a switchback road from Kamári (on the north side) or by a rough track from Períssa (south side; *no buses; taxis will, somewhat reluctantly, take visitors to the top of the road*). The paths converge on a narrow saddle between the summit of Profítis Ilías and the ancient acropolis to the east.

HISTORY OF THERA

The city was founded around the 9th or 8th century BC by Dorians from Laconia, under a Spartan leader Theras, taking advantage of a strategic location with harbours both to north and south. The principal harbour was the settlement of ancient Oia (modern Kamari) to the north. The settlement of Eleusis to the south, at the harbour of modern Vlycháda, seems to be a Hellenistic foundation. The finds from the Geometric and Archaic cemeteries of the city show that Thera knew considerable prosperity early on. Thera, as was typical of Dorian settlements, was conservative in its art and external relations. It only became a truly cosmopolitan centre in Hellenistic times under the rule of the Ptolemies. Excavations on the site continue.

The approach to the site

The extensive **cemeteries** are located along the saddle joining Mesá Vounó to the main mountain. By the path from Kamári, recesses and platforms cut into the rock are remainders of Hellenistic tombs; then in the last few switchbacks before the ridge, the bases and steps various slightly earlier funerary buildings are visible to either side of the ancient road to the city. On the Períssa side, just below the site fence, are more monument bases.

On the way to the remains of the city is the double-naved church of **Ághios Sté-fanos**, (perhaps 9th-century), built virtually entirely of ancient spolia, within the remains of a 5th-century Early Christian basilica, dedicated to the Archangel Michael.

Fifty metres beyond Ághios Stéfanos is the Temenos or **Shrine of Artemidorus of Perge (1)**, who was admiral of the Ptolemaic fleet in the late 4th century BC. Little remains of the superstructure of this grand monument, intended equally to honour a group of gods and to promote his own glory. The carved symbols of the principal divinities are clearly visible in the rockface behind: the dolphin of Poseidon, the lion of Apollo and the eagle of Zeus. Artemidorus, as sailor and admiral, had his own image carved in numismatic profile and positioned above the dolphin of Poseidon.

The agorá

After a final rise (steps), the path drops down into the **agorá (2)**. Unusually, the area is drawn out along the ridge of the mountain. The bases of shops are seen to the seaward side (east), while the residential area climbs up above, to the right. The streets of the area are endowed with a network of covered drains.

The 1st-century AD **Royal Stoa (3)**, with a central spine of columns, was the city's principal civic and judicial building. It would have exhibited decrees inscribed on stelae similar to those built into the back wall.

Houses and sanctuaries on the western slope

It is well worth taking a detour, climbing up between the north end of the stoa, and the adjacent small Hellenistic **Temple of Dionysus (4)** to explore part of the residential quarter beyond. At the top of the steps, a path dog-legs to the right across a space occupied by a **gymnasium (5)** to an imposingly large residence with a clearly visible entrance atrium. Due to its size and position, this is sometimes called the **Governor's Residence (6)**. To the left, from the top of the steps above the Temple of Dionysus, the street descends through some of the best-preserved **residential buildings (7)** on the site, often built over cisterns. One house contains its well-preserved latrine; some have mosaics, and many preserve remains of red plaster on the base of their interior walls. Beyond, the path drops down, past the **Sanctuary of the Egyptian Gods (8)**, a rock shelf cut with a multitude of niches and ledges, to the **Temple of Pythian Apollo (9)**, converted in the 6th century into an apsidal church. At this point an immense view opens out over the south coast.

Sanctuaries on the southeast spur

From the agorá, the street south beyond the Royal Stoa narrows, passing a municipal cistern. East of it is the small panoramic 3rd-century BC **theatre (10)**, remodelled in Roman times with an enlarged skene. From here, the Sacred Way leads downhill to the southeast, between finely built walls of houses, to a panoramic promontory with the sacred centre of the Archaic city, the sanctuary of the Dorian cult of Apollo Karneios.

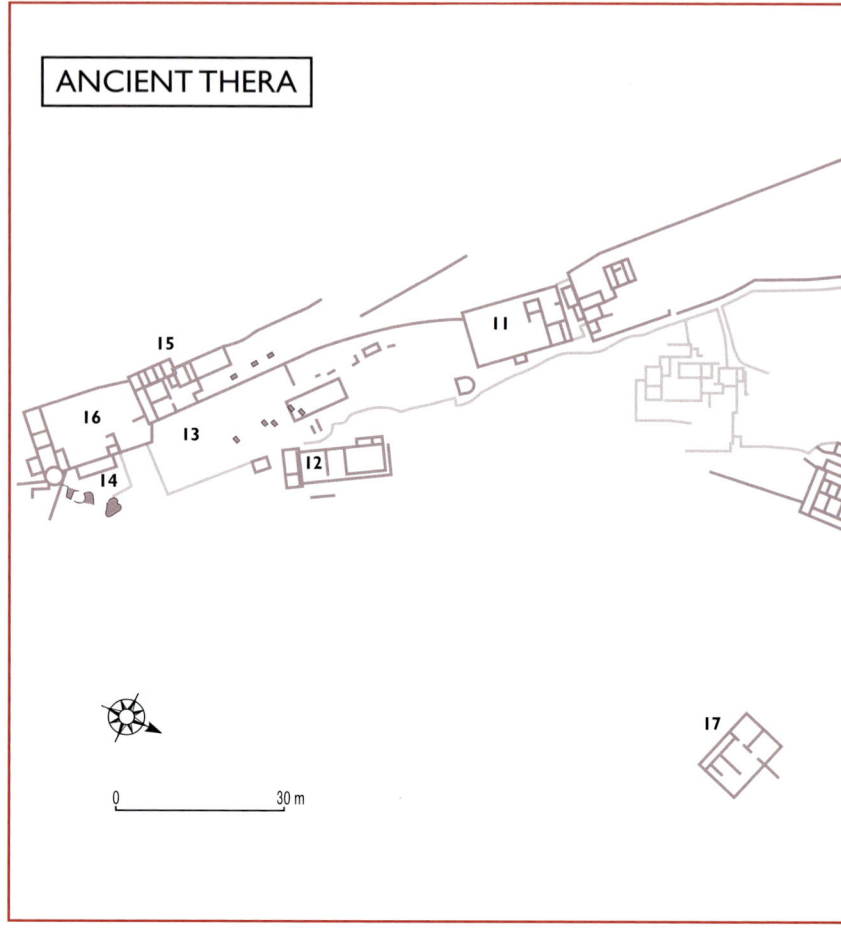

ANCIENT THERA

0   30 m

It spreads over a series of terraces, part cut into the rock, part constructed on massive retaining walls.

The sanctuary area is overlooked from the northwest by the base of a **temple dedicated to Ptolemy III (11)**, from which the layout can be observed: the humped ridge stretches ahead, with the rectangular base of the Temple of Apollo Karneios **(12)** to the left side, and the larger rectangular Terrace of the Epheboi **(13)** to the right.

The base of the **Temple of Apollo Karneios** is cut into the rock of the hillside, on a roughly east–west axis. The temple proper is preceded by a pronaos, a courtyard and further rooms, occupying a space of c. 32m by 10m in total. The rock-cut threshold and door-post slots are at the southeast corner. The temple is preceded by a court, with

1	**Shrine of Artemidorus of Perge**	**10**	**Theatre**
2	**Agora**	**11**	**Temple of Ptolemy III**
3	**Royal Stoa**	**12**	**Temple of Apollo Karneios**
4	**Temple of Dionysus**	**13**	**Terrace of the Epheboi**
5	**Gymnasium**	**14**	**Grotto of Hermes and Heracles**
6	**Governor's residence**	**15**	**Roman baths**
7	**Residential buildings**	**16**	**Gymnasium of the Epheboi**
8	**Sanctuary of the Egyptian Gods**	**17**	**Heroön**
9	**Temple of Pythian Apollo**		

a large roofed cistern below at the northeast side. On the right is possibly a priest's residence, on the left, the front of the temple. Two intact doorways lead from the side of the naos through the southwest wall into small rooms, perhaps treasuries.

The **Terrace of the Epheboi**, also referred to as the Square of the Gymnopaidiai, is the long rectangular platform to the south of the temple across the ridge of rock, built out over massive retaining walls of the 6th century BC, with later repairs. This exposed area is where the *gymnopaidiai*, ritual dances and displays, were performed in honour of Apollo by youths (epheboi) passing from boyhood to manhood, during the Karneia festival, which took place in the heat of August. The performances, which also included martial exercises, were held from at least as early as the 7th century BC. The rocks between the temple and the terrace, where the male spectators sat, are covered with a wealth of scratched inscriptions and graffiti ranging in date from the 7th century BC to later Classical and Hellenistic times. Amongst them are some of the earliest examples of the Greek alphabet in the Aegean. The inscriptions, some of them quite long, are written all over the rocks: they record names and erotic appreciations of the boys who performed here, in cases recounting what appear to be homoerotic sexual feats (e.g. 'here, Krimon was ****ed, by the son of Bathycles'. There are drawings of heads, abstract patterns, and engraved outlines of feet. The presiding divinities of the boys as they reached adulthood were Hermes (for mental faculties and quickness of the wits) and Hercules (for bodily strength and development): on a level below the south corner of the terrace is a deep cave, the sacred **grotto of Hermes and Heracles (14)**. Here, too, there are inscriptions all around. The doorway to the left (west) of the cave leads into the remains of **Roman baths (15)**. The rock-cut esplanade in front of the cave constituted the heart of the **Gymnasium of the Epheboi (16)**, a structure added in Hellenistic times.

About 150m to the north of the Temple of Apollo Karneios is the base of a Hellenistic **heroön (17)**, with a modern chapel built into it.

THE SOUTH OF THE ISLAND

Pýrgos

A road leads directly south from Chora towards Megalochóri (*see below*). As it begins to climb, the silhouette of Pýrgos can be seen to the southeast against the slopes of Mt Profítis Ilías. The village is built in the classic manner of a Cycladic fortified settlement, with a ring of houses forming the outer defensive enceinte, surrounding a central **hilltop fortress**. At the summit is the 17th-century church of the Eisódia tis Theotókou. The restored church of Aghía Triáda houses a small **icon collection** (*open daily 10–4, from Orthodox Easter–Oct*) from the 16th–19th centuries, including works by the Skordilis workshop on Milos.

Below the summit of the mountain, reached by road south from Pýrgos, is the **monastery of Profítis Ilías**, founded in 1711 and extensively restored after 1956. The monastery was home to an important 'secret school' in the first half of the 19th century, keeping alive the Greek language, religion and culture during the last years of Turkish occupation.

Megalochóri

As the road south from Chora crosses the ridge above the modern harbour, the south of the island spreads out below: a patchwork of fields, stippled with green dots against a pale background. These are the **vineyards of Santorini**, nourished by its volcanic earth and unique in their method of cultivation: each green dot is an individual vine, which is not trained on cordons or stakes but is instead wound round and round upon itself, and kept as low as possible to the ground so as to remain undamaged by the strong winds. Santorini has produced wine on a large scale since the 16th century.

Five kilometres from Chora the road reaches **Megalochóri**, the centre of the island's wine production, after which it turns east and heads for the south coast at Períssa.

Emboreió

To the left-hand side of the road, level with the village boundary sign of Emboreió, is the curious chapel of **Ághios Nikólaos Marmarítis**, in effect an exceptionally well-preserved shrine or temple of the 3rd century BC, dedicated, according to an inscription still *in situ*, to the goddess Basileia (*key held in the adjacent house*). It may have functioned also as a family tomb. The beautifully cut and laid limestone slabs of the walls have been partially cemented, but otherwise the building is a whole, ancient structure, complete with its marble roof supported by the original stone beams. The dimensions are diminutive (4.2m by 3.6m), with a dignified door frame in the south wall and a small aedicule or niche on the inside of the north wall, framed by carved Ionic pilasters and a Doric entablature and pediment. The dedicatory inscription is engraved below. Basíleia is a curious divinity, whose cult is associated with that of the mother goddess.

Visible on the hill to the east are the ruins of a 16th-century **Venetian *pýrgos***.

Emboreió (sometimes Nimboreió) is the largest and most attractive of the island's inland villages. As often on Santorini, many of the oldest parts are built half underground. In the midst of its tight tissue of passageways and streets are occasional sunken areas with a cluster of grotto-entrances and troglodyte dwellings. At the centre is a fortified kastro, arranged around the church of the Panaghía. The architecture of Emboreió is unusual and attractive; in contrast to the simple forms of the houses, the churches—especially the porticoes and belfries of the church of Christós and of the Panaghía—have an almost baroque insistence on trefoil and multifoil forms.

Períssa and Vlychada

The main road ends at the resort of **Períssa**, with its famous black sands. Scattered across the modern settlement near the foot of the mountain are excavations with remains of Hellenistic and Roman houses. Behind the southeast corner of the dominating church of the Tímios Stavrós is the well-preserved base of a marble funerary monument of the 1st century AD in the form of a circular tower. Between the church and the cliff are the ruins of the Early Christian basilica of Aghía Eiríni, after which the island took its name. It was probably founded in the 5th century, enlarged in the 6th century, abandoned, and then re-roofed in an improvised fashion in the 13th century.

The coastal road leads southwest to Perívolos and the harbour at **Vlycháda**. The latter may occupy the site of Eleusis, the southern port of Hellenistic Thera. An earthquake in 1570 radically altered this coastline. As a result, the exact location of Eleusis is unclear, although its cemetery has left many remains probably of the 1st and 2nd centuries BC, visible in the cliff to the north of the road between Perívolos and Vlycháda. Beginning at **Perívolos**, there is a series of rock-cut tombs, generally with steps below and pediments above. The track which hugs the foot of the bluff leads to an isolated house, opposite which are several stepped platforms and sarcophagi. To the west, a path leads up through fallen masonry towards a large monumental tomb with a chamber beneath.

THE FAR WEST

From the junction on the main road between Megalochóri and Emboreió, a west branch leads to the village of Akrotíri and the western extremity of the main island. The panoramic hill of Akrotíri is the site of the island's fourth **Venetian kastro** (14th century). The form of the ensemble survives well; a ring of houses and quasi-bastions encircles the summit, originally crowned by the main tower, which was modified to accommodate the modern church. The enceinte is entered by a tunnel above the church of Ághios Geórgios: inside, there is a network of ruined buildings.

A road leads south to the Bronze Age site. Fifteen minutes' walk west of prehistoric Akrotíri is the so-called 'Red Beach' (**Kókkini Paraliá**).

THE PREHISTORIC SITE OF AKROTIRI

NB: Access to the excavations at Akrotiri was closed by the Greek Public Prosecutor after a part of the metal roofing covering the archaeological site collapsed in September 2005, killing a tourist. Several dates, now passed, have been announced for the reopening. Repair works began, after lengthy legal proceedings, in 2010, but it is not clear when the site will reopen. The following description is of Akrotiri as it was at the time it closed.

Prehistoric Akrotiri is among the most important archaeological sites in the world: the streets and houses of a Bronze Age city were buried under fine ash expelled by the 17th-century BC eruption, which later solidified, preserving the structures. Finds and wall-paintings from the site are on display in the Museum of Prehistoric Thera in Chora and the National Archaeological Museum in Athens. The site gives a vivid picture of a prosperous, highly organised and apparently peaceful trading settlement. It is not known whether the town had fortifications or buildings exclusively used for cult, as none have been found so far.

HISTORY OF THE SETTLEMENT

The site was inhabited from the Late Neolithic (5th millennium BC), grew through the early 3rd millennium BC (Early Cycladic period), and became a flourishing settlement in the Middle Cycladic period, probably in the context of trade, especially with Crete. It has been suggested that Akrotiri was a Minoan colony at that time, but its pottery and architecture are clearly Cycladic in origin, though subject to a strong Minoan influence. Several times in its history the town was damaged by earthquakes; on each occasion the ruins were levelled and new buildings placed above, following the same urban plan. It appears that before the 17th-century BC eruption the population had had sufficient warning to leave, taking their valuables and livestock with them.

A Bronze Age staircase in Xeste 3 at Akrotiri.

The excavations

The site was first noticed in the 19th century; but brief French (1867 and 1870) and German (1899) excavations did not reveal its full importance. In 1967, the Greek archaeologist Spyridon Marinatos began large-scale excavations. Since his death in an on-site accident in 1974, they have continued at a slower pace. Several thousand tons of volcanic ash and pumice have so far been removed from an area of about 2 hectares. Less than five per cent of the site has been excavated.

The architecture and paintings

The state of preservation of the buildings is remarkable: many stand to two floors, some to three. Many of the houses were built of loose stone with a mud and straw mortar, with large wooden frames for windows and doors, and sometimes reinforced with cut stone blocks at the corners and around the frames. The wooden elements have not survived, but their imprints were filled with cement plaster during excavation to ensure the buildings' stability. In some places, buttresses have been added for the same purpose. A number of large, possibly public, edifices were constructed entirely or partially in ashlar masonry of regularly cut blocks (e.g. Xeste 3 and 4). Staircases are generally in stone, sometimes in wood. The roofs were flat and insulated with reeds and branches packed and sealed with earth and crushed shells, similar to traditional Cycladic houses today. In some cases, floors were paved with schist slabs. The lowest floors were cool and used for storage, or as workshops: rows of pithoi were commonly

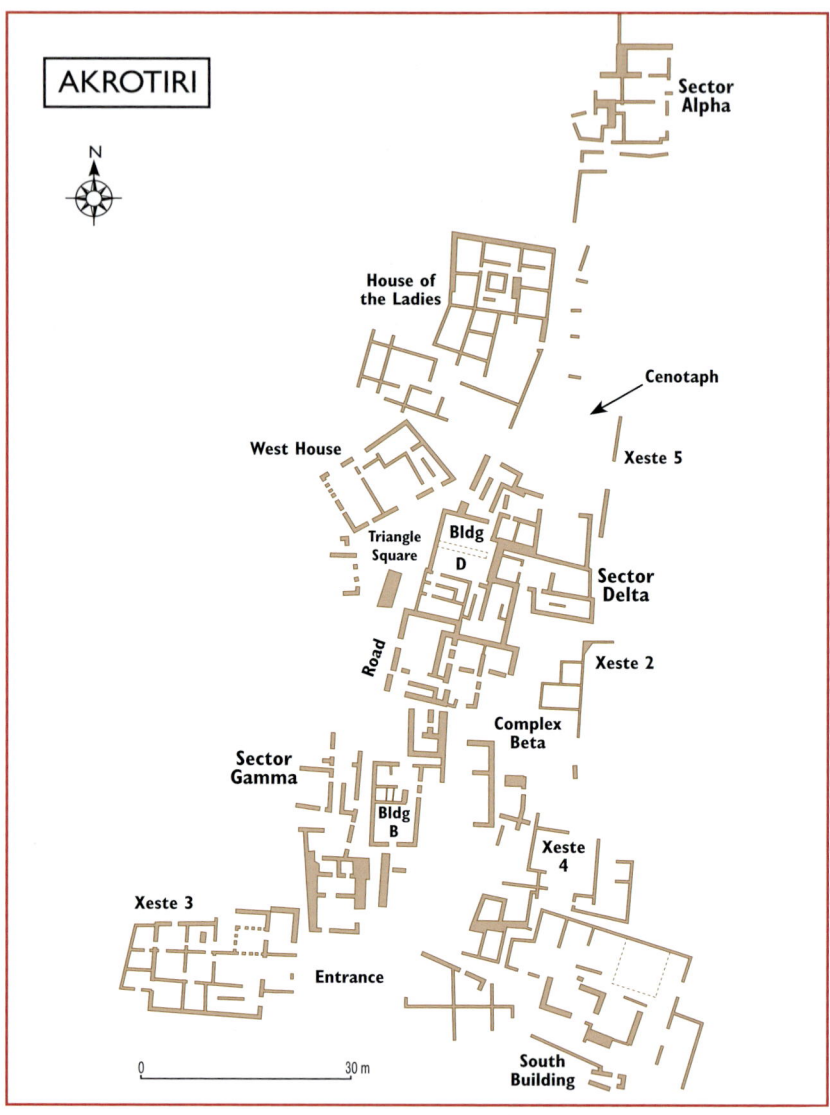

found at semi-basement level. The upper floor was for reception rooms; their walls were coated with a fine plaster, often painted. They frequently contained looms, suggesting that they were predominantly women's quarters. Toilets with a bench-seat, connected by down-pipes to a communal drain that ran under the street, are found, for example, in Room 4 of the West House. Many houses possessed large windows.

Tour of the site

The excavated area, running along a north–south axis, is entered from the south, through an open space between two large building complexes. **Xeste 3**, to the left, was a two-storey dwelling with 14 rooms per floor, constructed in ashlar masonry. The rooms near the path were decorated with paintings of girls gathering crocus (saffron), and may have been used for cult. **Xeste 4**, to the right, is an extensive three-storey building. The small alley to the north passes the two-storey **Building B** (left): its decorations included the famous images of antelopes and boxing children (now in Athens) and the 'Blue Monkeys', on display in Chora (*see picture on p. 167*). In **Building D**, further north to the left, the large door and window frames, and storage areas with pithoi, can be seen. The clay pipes connecting houses to the drainage system beneath the pathway can be seen at certain points. On the right is a horned altar of Minoan type. The street climbs further, past a flight of partially collapsed stone steps to the left. A small stone 'cenotaph' (left) marked the area of a 3rd-millennium BC cemetery under the settlement. Further north and slightly to the left, at the summit, is the so-called **House of the Ladies** (paintings in Chora). At the northern extremity of the site is the Building of the Pithoi, where a concentration of variously decorated, standing storage jars were found in a room with a large, low window perhaps used for dispensing the produce.

The permitted route leads round to the west (left) and down a narrow alley into the small **Triangle Square**, dominated to north by the most important building excavated so far, the **West House**. Behind the large central window on the upper floor was a flight of ceremonial rooms, decorated with important paintings, including boys bearing strings of fish, marine and river landscapes and the 'miniature fresco' depicting a marine landscape with ships. The imposing **west façade of Building D** forms the east side of the little *plateía*. From a small room on its far side came the colourful 'Landscape with Lilies and Swallows' (Archaeological Museum, Athens). The house had a grand entrance with a roofed porch.

THERASIA

Notwithstanding its proximity (2km) to one of the most popular tourist destinations in Europe, Therasía remains quiet and untouched. The island's port is at **Ríva**, below the mid-19th-century church of Aghía Eiríni. A 30-min walk leads to the gentler west slope of the island, with the pleasant hamlets of Potamós and Agriliá. In the latter, the church of the Panaghía ton Eisódion (1887) has a strikingly colourful façade.

Manólas (*40mins on foot from Ríva*), the island's clifftop *chora*, preserves much of its original patchwork of troglodyte houses. Most of its churches were rebuilt after 1956. A steep descent leads to **Kórfos**, the island's old harbour. South of Manólas the ridge-top track leads to the monastery of the **Koímisis tis Theotókou**, panoramically sited on the southernmost point of the island. In the southwest corner of the island are the now abandoned **Alafoúzos pozzolana quarries**, whose pumice was used in the preparation of impermeable cement for the construction of the Suez Canal.

PRACTICAL INFORMATION

GETTING AROUND

There are several daily flights from Athens and Thessaloníki, as well as scheduled flights from abroad. The airport is 4.5km from Chora (taxis available). The ferry port (Athiniós) is 7.5km from Chora. There are generally 2 or 3 daily connections from Piraeus (9hrs by car ferry, 5hrs by high-speed), usually via Paros and/or Naxos. There are frequent links to Anáphi, Folégandros, Síkinos and Ios; less often in winter. There are direct links to Milos twice weekly throughout the year.

Boats for Therasía leave from Ammoúdi (12km from Chora) twice daily. Sometimes the boat route includes Kórfos harbour, directly below Manólas.

WHERE TO STAY

Kavalari Hotel (*T: 22860 22347; www.kavalari.com*) is one of the older hotels on Santorini, centrally placed, with magnificent views, created from traditional houses cut into the lava at the top of the cliff. It is simple, friendly and unpretentious, but there is no lift, and the rooms are reached down precipitous steps. More readily accessible is the **Theoxenia** (*T: 22860 22740; www.theoxenia.net*), panoramic and very pleasant, with good breakfast served in the rooms. The island's oldest hotel, the **Atlantis** (*T: 22860 22111, www.atlantishotel.gr*) is practical, welcoming and superbly sited; it is one of the few hotels open year-round. The **Aressana** (*T: 22860 22860, www.aressana.gr*), opposite the Atlantis, is also comfortable and convenient. On one of the highest points of the cliff, with views directly over the caldera, **Anteliz Apartments** (*T: 22860 28842, www.anteliz.gr*) is modern and attractive, with spacious rooms and a pool.

For boutique chic, **Homeric Poems** (*T: 22860 24661/3, www.homericpoems.gr*) offers a luxurious and rarefied atmosphere.

Oía has the most delightful place to stay on the island, **Chelidonia Villas** ■ (*T: 22860 71827; www.chelidonia.com*), simple, tasteful and friendly.

WHERE TO EAT

Many of Santorini's restaurants serve indifferent and overpriced tourist fare, but there are a few good places. **Ta Delphinia** in the bay of Akrotiri is a family-run fish taverna which serves its own local wine, and the famous Santorinian *fava* and *tomatokeftédes*. The **Taverna Aktaion** (often known as Roussos) at the beginning of Firostefáni serves local food, including a good *prasópita*, a pie made with mixed greens and leeks. **Selene** at the southern extremity of Chora offers a beautiful view in addition to some interesting dishes, more elaborate but still based on Greek ingredients. **Franco's Bar** is a historic institution: one of the first bars of the 1970s on Santorini, it still serves (expensive but well-prepared) cocktails to the accompaniment of Classical music, with views of the most dramatic sunsets in Europe.

FURTHER READING

Nanno Marinatos in *Art and Religion in Thera: Reconstructing a Bronze Age Society* (Athens, 1984) suggests explanations of the paintings from Akrotiri, as does the beautifully-illustrated *The Wall Paintings of Thera* (Athens, 1992) by Christos Doumas, current head of excavations at Akrotiri. Walter Friedrich's *Fire in the Sea, the Santorini Volcano: Natural History and the Legend of Atlantis* (Cambridge 1999) gives a good account of the island's volcanic history.

ANAPHI

Tiny, remote, arid, and hardly touched by tourism, Anáphi (*map p. 49*) is an island of surprises, with unblemished beaches and a richness of ancient remains, including the well-preserved site of a sanctuary to Apollo.

HISTORY OF ANAPHI

According to tradition, the name Anáphi (cognate with the Greek word αναφαίνειν, 'to make apparent') derives from the moment when Apollo revealed the island to Jason and his fellow Argonauts in a flash of lightning during a storm which threatened their lives, thereby offering them a safe haven.

Like Thera, ancient Anaphe was a Dorian colony of the 9th or 8th century BC. The island seems to have been prosperous in the 4th century BC, when it minted its own coins.

In Venetian times the island was known as Nanfio. It was given by Marco Sanudo to Leonardo Foscolo in 1207. After 1269 it came under Byzantine rule, but reverted to Venetian control in 1307. In 1480 it passed as marriage dowry to Domenico Pisani, whose family held it until it was sacked by Kheir ed-Din Barbarossa in the winter of 1537–38. From 1540 Anáphi was formalised as an Ottoman possession and remained so until the Greek War of Independence, apart from a brief interval in 1770–74, when it was under Russian control. During the Russian occupation, many of the island's antiquities were removed to St Petersburg. In 1821, Anáphi contributed two boats to the cause of Greek Independence and in 1832 the island was assumed into the Greek state.

So many islanders emigrated to Athens during the 19th century that the picturesque quarter of Pláka below the Acropolis is still called Anafiótika. During the military dictatorships of the 20th century, Anáphi was used as a detention centre for political exiles.

Anáphi Chora

The tranquil *chora* of Anáphi clusters high above the landing jetty at Ághios Nikólaos, around the remains of the 15th-century Venetian kastro, of which only meagre remains survive. The settlement winds in a crescent towards a small *plateía* at the western end.

The village's appearance is characterised by half-cylindrical vaults over traditional single-room dwellings, alternating with round ovens close to the house entrances. On the east slope of the kastro, directly behind the Koinótita (Municipality) building is the temporary seat of the Archaeological Collection (*for access ask in the Municipality offices*), with a fine collection of headless Roman funerary statues.

Kastélli Hill

The principal interest of the island lies to the east of Chora, accessible by a road which follows the coast at a short distance inland through a treeless rocky landscape. At about 4km from Chora, the road begins to traverse the southern slope of the hill of Kastélli.

The summit to the north, now crowned with the remains of a Venetian fortification, was the acropolis of ancient Anaphe, which had a port to the south, by the bay of Katalymátsa. The stone cairns near the shore were raised by local mariners who traditionally added a stone when departing for a journey. There are many Classical spolia in the area.

As the road momentarily climbs inland, a footpath leads left up the slope towards the summit of Kastélli and to the interesting church of the Panaghía sto Dokári (*10mins*), whose north side is buttressed by an ancient retaining wall. Beside the church is a beautifully decorated Roman sarcophagus. The footpath continues to the Venetian fortress and from there goes on to the church of Ághios Mámas, where there are further ruins of late Hellenistic and Roman tombs. From there a path continues east, following the line of the Sacred Way that joined the ancient city to the Sanctuary of Apollo; parts of its paved surface are visible.

The Sanctuary of Apollo

The great rock promontory of Kálamos, joined to Anáphi by a neck of land, rises sheer from the sea almost half a kilometre upwards into the air. In spring its summit is often circled with clouds: when they part, the tiny silhouette of the church of the Panaghía Kalamiótissa can be seen against the sky, suspended above the precipice. At the foot of the mountain is the sanctuary of Apollo Anaphaios (or Aigletes, from a word meaning 'burst of light'), supposed to have been founded by Jason. There are impressive remains of the temple and its sacred precinct, mostly Hellenistic and standing to a considerable height; many of the marble blocks bear inscriptions.

To the right is a well-preserved stretch of 4th-century BC wall rising over 3m high: this is the west wall of the main temple naos. To either side of the entrance are two blocks carved with Hellenistic inscriptions. The katholikon is modern but built on ancient foundations. Extending to the east and north of the monastery enclosure are the walls of the sanctuary platform.

From the monastery, it is a 75-min climb by a precipitous path up to the summit of the rock (460m). Low down on its north slope is the Drakospiliá, a large cave with stalactite formations. In a rock eyrie a short distance to the west of the summit sits the 18th-century church of the Panaghía Páno Kalamiótissa, with impressive views, though on a windy day the location is exceptionally blustery. It may occupy the site of a pagan shrine.

West of Chora

The dry landscape west of Chora contains many traditional *katoikies*, or rural farmsteads, now mostly abandoned. These generally consist of a small dwelling, baking-oven, animal pens and a storage barn grouped beside a threshing floor. After Kaméni Langáda (2.5km from Chora), the road rises sharply to a curve where it levels out with wide views: due south, above the coast, is a long, low *katoikía*, about 25mins on foot from the road. This is Pyrgí, its main body formed by the massive base of a Hellenistic farmhouse.

PRACTICAL INFORMATION

GETTING AROUND

Anáphi is at the end of ferry routes from Piraeus four times a week. Three times per week, it is linked to Santorini. There are no taxis on the island. Water taxis from the harbour in summer will take you to the eastern beaches of Katsoúni, Flamouroú, Roúkounas and Prassiés.

WHERE TO STAY

There are not many rooms on Anáphi. The most comfortable option is **Villa Apollon**, overlooking Kleisídi Bay near the harbour (*T: 22860 61348; www.apollonvilla.gr*). **Ta Plagia** in Chora offers pleasant self-catering studios (*T: 22860 61308; www.taplagia.gr*). A complete list of rooms for rent in Chora can be found on www.anafi.gr.

WHERE TO EAT

To Steki in Chora is lively and welcoming. **Liotrivi Café** is perhaps slightly better for fish.

FURTHER READING

J. Theodore Bent's description of his visit to Anáphi in 1883 is one of the most succinct and informative chapters in his *The Cyclades, or Life among the Insular Greeks* (1885: reissued 2002 by Archaeopress, Oxford in the '3rd Guides' series. 'There exists no island so remote in its solitude as Anaphi,' he wrote. 'It is a mere speck in the waves, in the direction of Rhodes or Crete, where no one ever goes, and where the 1,000 inhabitants of the one village thereon are as isolated as if they dwelt in an archipelago in the Pacific.'

AMORGOS

Few islands combine as succinctly so much history and such memorable scenery as Amorgós; and fewer do it with such disarming simplicity. Modern development has remained respectful of the island's dignified grandeur. Amorgós offers ample opportunity for walking. The famous monastery of the Panaghía Chozoviótissa, clinging to its sheer cliff above the sea, is one the most unforgettable sights in the Aegean.

HISTORY OF AMORGOS

Amorgós was first settled in the late 5th millennium BC. The 3rd millennium BC marks the island's first apogee, when it was an important centre of Cycladic culture and produced the idiosyncratic Dokathismata-style figurines. In the 2nd millennium BC there was a Mycenaean presence. During the 10th century BC Ionian settlers arrived, founding the three cities of historic times: Arkesine, colonised by Naxos, then Minoa by Samos and Aigiale by Miletus. The island joined the 5th-century Delian League, and participated in the Second Athenian League in 357 BC. Later the island was a possession of Macedonia, then of the Ptolemies, and finally, from the end of the 3rd century BC, of Rhodes. After 133 BC, the three cities were assumed into the Roman province of Asia. Amorgós was often a place of exile in the Roman period.

There is evidence of scattered Early Christian communities, but the increasing frequency of pirate raids pushed habitation into the central uplands. The site of Chora began to be settled in the 9th century. In this period, refugee monks arrived from Palestine with the icon from Choziba. This was followed by the founding of the Chozoviótissa Monastery, allegedly in 1088. In 1207 Amorgós was taken by Geremia and Andrea Ghisi, on behalf of Marco Sanudo's Duchy of Naxos. It subsequently changed hands many times. Formally re-assigned to Venice by treaty in 1303 and governed by the Barozzi family, it was finally sold piecemeal to Giovanni Querini, Lord of Astypálaia, who held the island until its seizure by the Turkish corsair Kheir ed-Din Barbarossa in 1537. In 1540 it became a Turkish possession under a Turkish governor, but by the 18th century the island was self-governing. The island was always a prey to piracy, culminating in one particularly fierce attack in 1797 by Maniot pirates. In 1835 the island became part of the new Kingdom of Greece.

CENTRAL AMORGOS

The commonest point of arrival on Amorgós is **Katápola** (*map p. 185, B2*), located in a bay that cuts deeply into the north coast, forming one of the two principal harbours in an island whose shores are dominated by sheer cliffs. The bay was developed during Roman times as the harbour for the ancient city of Minoa to the south: it was the lower

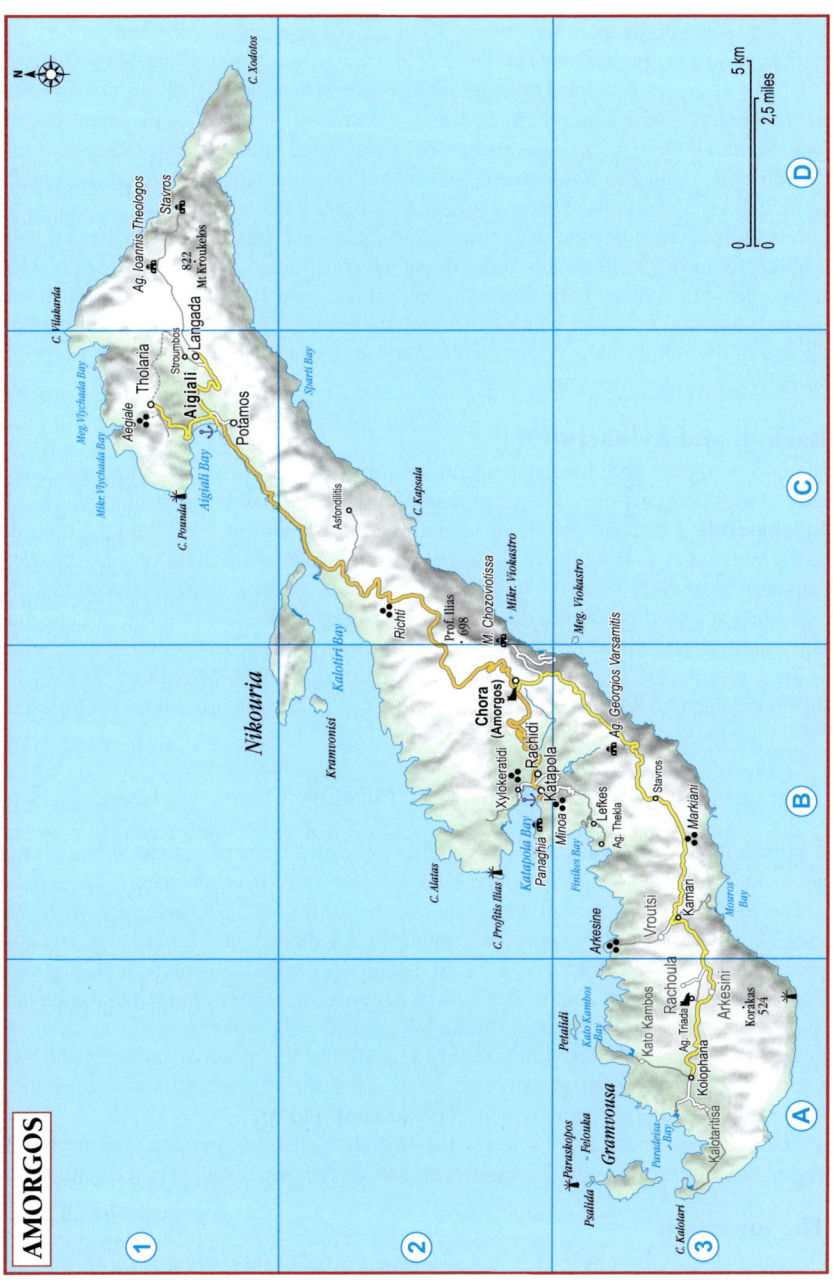

AMORGOS

city (*kato polis*) of the main settlement. There are the remains of three 2nd-century AD Roman tombs at the western extremity of the waterfront, beyond where the houses end. The largest was a small, private mausoleum of temple-like design. To its east, in the garden of the adjacent guest-house, are two small grave-loculi. Many pieces from Roman buildings and monuments are incorporated in the attractive 18th-century church of the Panaghía Katapolianí, 50m inland from the small square on the waterfront. The church will have been rebuilt several times in its history.

A track leads west beyond the Roman tombs, along the south side of the bay for half a kilometre to the small chapel of the Panaghía, constructed almost entirely of blocks from a 4th–5th-century Early Christian predecessor, which in turn used blocks from pagan buildings. A further half kilometre along the track is the late medieval double church of the Ághii Anárgyri. On the bluff above it, overlooking the bay, are traces of an Early Cycladic settlement.

Rachídi and Xylokeratídi

Almost contiguous with Katápola, inland from the east end of the bay, is **Rachídi**, built attractively along a ridge. The third community in the bay is the fishing village of **Xylokeratídi**. A stepped path leads up and inland through the village: on the hillside to the west (after passing the St George Varsamitis Hotel to the right) is a Mycenaean cemetery. Most of the tombs (13th and 12th centuries BC), have eroded, but two remain with the excavated chamber and a clear-cut dromos to the east. On the hill beyond is the 9th-century church of the Evangelismós, one of the oldest on the island, with vestiges of aniconic painting in its interior (*returning from the Mycenaean cemetery to the stone kalderími, keeping left, the path climbs the ridge between two gullies. The church is hidden low in the western gully, 20mins on foot*).

ANCIENT MINOA

A branch road south of Rachídi leads to the impressive ruins of ancient Minoa (3km; *also reached in 30mins by footpath from Katápola. Site always open and mostly unfenced*).

The north slope of the hill was settled in the 10th century BC and grew with the influx of colonisers from Samos; the summit was fortified as an acropolis. The city appears to have reached its apogee in the 4th century BC, when many of the buildings visible today were constructed. Under Roman domination, greater importance was given to the port, which was connected to the hill by walls. The upper city was abandoned in the 4th century AD. Though it is clearly a possibility, the toponym 'Minoa' (which is not unique in the Aegean) does not necessarily indicate a Cretan Minoan connection. It probably refers to a legendary hero-founder named Minos.

There are two main areas: a lower site (mostly Hellenistic remains) on the south slope, and an upper site (with scattered Archaic and earlier remains) at the summit.

The lower site

On approaching the lower area, the well-constructed walls—some for fortification,

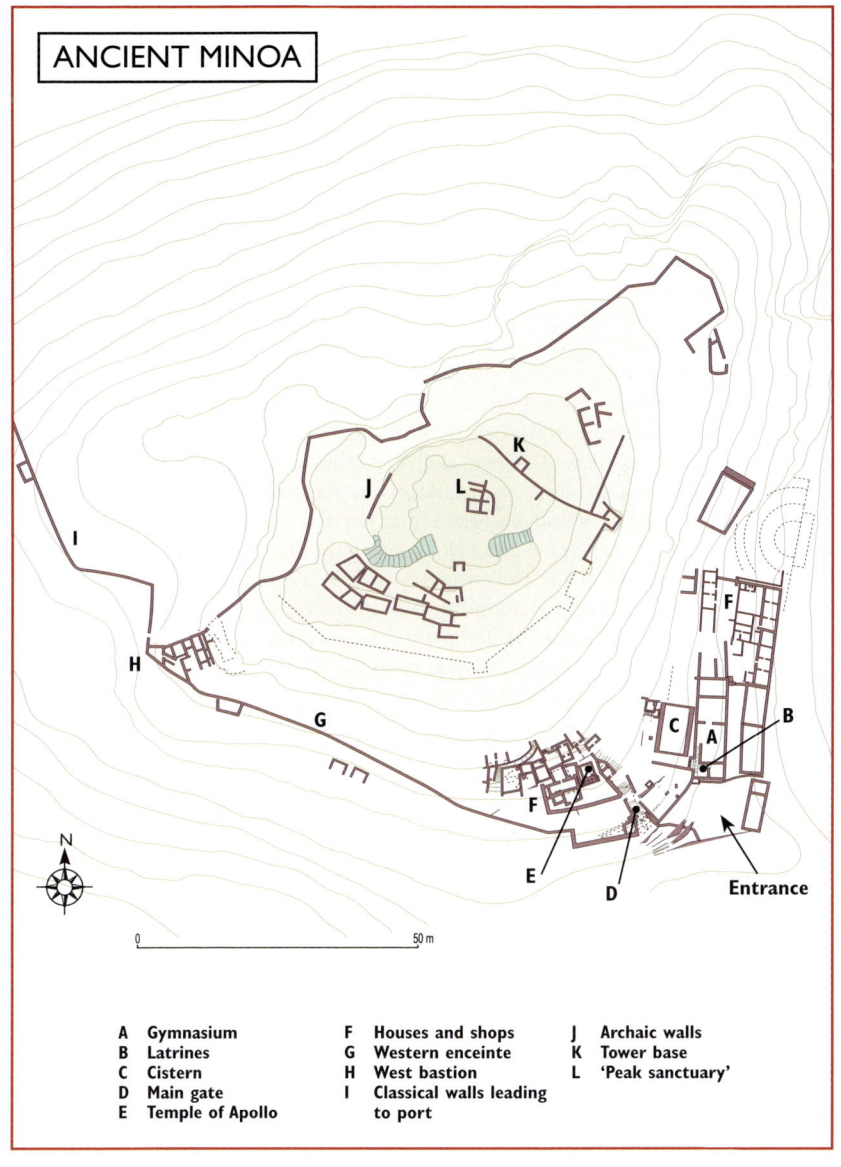

ANCIENT MINOA

A	Gymnasium	F	Houses and shops	J	Archaic walls
B	Latrines	G	Western enceinte	K	Tower base
C	Cistern	H	West bastion	L	'Peak sanctuary'
D	Main gate	I	Classical walls leading		
E	Temple of Apollo		to port		

some for retaining terraces, some for both—make an immediate impact. Viewed from the entrance you see, ahead and to the right, the terracing wall which supported the late 4th-century BC **gymnasium (A)**, constructed in massive, interlocking masonry blocks. On its left side what looks like a postern gate at the head of a narrow channel is in fact the drainage for the **latrines (B)**, which occupy the small wing made from massive stone blocks at the gymnasium's western end. The space still preserves its roof, and the limestone benches cut with individual seats over a drainage channel are unusually well preserved inside. On the hillside directly above rise large walls in a rough stone-rubble bound in mortar; these defined a vaulted **water cistern (C)** of considerable size, which was constructed under Roman dominion in the 2nd century AD. The accumulated water must have supplied the gymnasium and its thermae, and provided drainage water for the latrines directly below. In later times, this vast ruined structure, which was always visible above ground, was referred to as 'Palatía', the imagined palace of Minos, the legendary founder.

Ahead and to the left as you enter is the city's **main gate (D)** in a trapezoid-shaped recess, with bastion walls to either side; to the left of the approach is a votive pedestal; to the right, a drainage channel for rainwater, cut both inside and outside the main threshold. The threshold itself is a single block, shaped and cut to accommodate the doors and their posts. Above the gate, slightly to the left (west), is a small **temple to Apollo (E)**, which faces south from a platform of three marble steps. A fragment of the lower portion of the cult statue has been set up in the centre of the naos.

Both to the left of the temple and below and to the right of the gymnasium, many **houses and shops (F)** of the Hellenistic town have been cleared, many with wells or cisterns still visible. Further around the hill to the west, the remains of the houses have not been cleared, but the line of the **western enceinte** is visible below them **(G)**, becoming clearer as it approaches the **west bastion (H)**. Beyond the bastion, an arm of the walls, added in Classical times **(I)**, continues steeply down the slope to the port below. Climbing up towards the summit from this point leads to a rocky slope where low stretches of the **Archaic walls** (8th or 7th century BC) survive **(J)**, especially on the east and southeast sides. The base of a **tower (K)** can be made out at the northeastern end.

The upper site

The **'peak sanctuary' (L)** is characterised by a rock summit (225m), under which is a deep natural cavern, entered by a small opening. There are traces of activity from the Neolithic (4th millennium BC). The sanctuary continued to be used in Hellenistic times and later, by that time sacred to Dionysus. The entrance to the sanctuary through the Archaic peribolos was rebuilt in Hellenistic times; similarly, the sacred building or 'temple' at the summit was adapted over time. But its form, a small temple orientated east–west, with an inner sanctum or naos, and a forecourt to the east, follows the earliest 8th-century BC plan. Ledges for the placing of offerings are visible. Below the sanctuary area to the southwest, part of the settlement of the Archaic period has been uncovered.

Léfkes and Aghía Thékla

The track to the southwest from the church of the Stavrós, below the archaeological site, continues into an area of considerable beauty, with the two simple hamlets of Léfkes and Aghía Thékla (*map p. 185, B3; 30 and 45mins respectively on foot*).

CHORA

Chora (*map p. 185, B2*) lies on a plateau, invisible from the port, below the watershed to the precipitous eastern side of the island. The town was founded during the 9th century AD, when the bay of Katápola was no longer safe. The original habitation clustered around the prong of rock which formed the community's fortress. It is crowned by the 13th-century **Kastro**, consisting of a tower (south end), a cistern, and a tight enceinte of walls (*access is by steep rock-cut steps, through the church of Ághios Geórgios on the north side. Key either at the Loza bar or at the Kallisti patisserie*). Immediately below on the south face, and partially overhung by the rock into which it is built, is the 10th- or 11th-century chapel of the Kyrá [E]Leoúsa.

The heart of Chora

The main body of Chora extends along two parallel, winding thoroughfares between the open square at the western entrance in the Káto Geitoniá (Lower Town) and the delightful Plateáki, in the Apáno Geitoniá (Upper Town). Fifty metres to the west of Plateáki, along the principal artery, a 17th-century town house known as the Gavras Mansion houses the island's **Archaeological Museum** (*in high season generally open daily except Mon, 8.30–3; otherwise by appointment with the custodian, Georgios Vlavianos, T: 6973 396861*). Many key finds from Amorgós are now on display in the museums of Syros and Athens, but the small collection, ranging from prehistory to the Roman period, has some points of interest, including a Roman marble standard for liquid measures (courtyard).

Many of the buildings and churches in the same street, and around Plateía Lóza to the north, incorporate ancient anthemia and marble stelae with carved funerary reliefs. A short distance northeast of the Plateáki, beside an area of ruined houses, to the right of the path, is the entrance into the **medieval cistern**: it is a vaulted chamber, part-excavated, part-constructed, holding water to this day. Across ruined buildings beyond stands the whitewashed complex of the monastery of Christós Photodótis, a dependency of the Chozoviótissa Monastery.

THE MONASTERY OF THE CHOZOVIOTISSA

A half-hour walk by the road south of Chora, which rises to the watershed and then drops dramatically down the eastern side above the sea, leads to the monastery of the Panaghía Chozoviótissa (*map p. 185, C2; open daily 8.30–1 & 4–sunset*). Hanging 260m above the sea on an almost vertical cliff-face, the monastery is one of the most extraordinary sights in the Aegean. Its walls would not have been whitewashed originally, rendering them invisible from a distance.

The buildings are in part cut from the rock, in part constructed onto it. Two massive buttresses on the front façade were added in the 20th century. Le Corbusier paid a visit in the 1930s, and the monastery is said to have had a major influence on his work.

HISTORY OF THE MONASTERY

Oral tradition maintains that the monastery received a charter from the Byzantine emperor Alexius I Comnenus in 1088, as a sister foundation to the Monastery of St John on Patmos. Today the two are not bound by any special links. All written documentation dates from the 17th century or later, but nevertheless reinforces that tradition. The first monastic presence in small caves on this cliff-face was probably during the 9th century, when monks fleeing from Arab incursions into Palestine sought refuge here, bringing a Holy icon of the Virgin, originally, it is said, from the monastery in Choziba near Jericho. Between the 9th and 11th centuries the community must have expanded rapidly, resulting in the granting of lands and rights and the construction of the main monastery buildings. The structure underwent considerable restoration in the late 15th century, and has undergone small alterations since that time. In the 18th century there were 100 monks; the narrow terraces below the buildings were cultivated and used for pasture. Today there are three monks left.

Above the low, narrow, marble-framed entranceway, a blind arch is surrounded with 13th- or 14th-century phialostomia (decorative terracottas). Immediately inside, op-posite the water-stoup, the fine 19th-century strong-box contains spare clothing for visitors. Steps lead up through the rock to the upper level of the sacristy and to the narrow vaulted space of the katholikon, hugging the precipice (its north side is cut from the natural rock). The original **icon of the *Virgin of Choziba*** is on the south wall, darkened and covered with silver revetment. It is believed to date from the early 9th century. The icons on the iconostasis are all of the 17th century or later.

The **sacristy** contains 23 parchment codices from the 10th–19th centuries. Only a few are exhibited at any time: they usually include exquisitely illuminated Byzantine evangelistaries of the 11th and 13th centuries. Some plate and fine 18th-century liturgical embroideries are also on show.

A footpath east from the monastery (not for the faint-hearted) leads to the ruined hermitage church of **Ághios Ioánnis Chrysóstomos**, with areas of 18th-century wall-painting (*reached in 35mins by the lower branch from the junction encountered after 20mins*); and the rock-hewn chapel of the **Panaghía Theosképasti** (*55mins by the upper branch*).

SOUTHWESTERN AMORGOS

From Chora the road to the south closely follows the spine of the island, with magnificent views alternating to either side. After 4km, the 17th-century **monastery of Ághios Geórgios Varsamítis** is signed to the right (*map p. 185, B3*). At the south end of its narthex is an aghiasma or sacred pool. Small areas of the interior are covered with 17th- and 18th-century wall-paintings (there are images of St John the Baptist and the Virgin and Child on the north pillar of the vault). A curiosity of the church is a number of graffiti of fish in the pavement around the north door.

Further west, the main road climbs onto a saddle, on the western edge of which is the complex of **churches of the Stavrós** (*map p. 185, B3*), with four barrel-vaulted units side by side, namely a symmetrical 12th-century church with two side-aisles, and a separate parallel chapel to Ághios Nikítas, added later to the south. The paving of the main church appears to be from an ancient structure. The area marked the boundary between the territories of Arkesine and Minoa, and a rock bearing the incised word 'ΟΡΟΣ', 'boundary', has been found in the fields beyond the sharp west turn in the road, 300m after Stavrós.

The most significant Early Cycladic settlement on Amorgós, known as **Markianí** (inhabited perhaps from 2800–2000 BC), occupies the rock outcrop and summit just to the left (south) of the road 2km further on. To the north and south sides of the outcrop the foundation walls of dwellings are visible, and the outline of a fortification wall with semicircular bastions can be traced in stretches.

Ancient Arkesine

The northward branch of the asphalt road from Kamári ends after 1km at the village of Vroútsi, from which it is a steep, 30-min descent on foot to the site of ancient Arkesine (*map p. 185, B3*).

Founded in the 8th century BC by settlers from Naxos, Arkesine occupies an exposed promontory. From the path, the best preserved stretch of fortification wall can be seen below and to the right of the acropolis rock, in large isodomic masonry, with later walling on top. Further elements of the bastions and fortifications lie further round the steep, eastern side of the promontory, best seen from the summit above. The acropolis is now occupied by remains of a fortified medieval kastro. The site awaits excavation.

The ancient tower at Aghía Triáda

On the fertile Káto Meriá plateau, 700m north of the modern settlement of Arkesíni, is a 4th-century BC Hellenistic tower at Aghía Triáda (*map p. 185, A3*). Large and well-preserved, it is one of the most signal monuments of its type in the Aegean.

The complex, perhaps a fortified refuge for a rural community, has overall a T-shaped plan: a large, multifunctional rectangular block (25.3m by 11.4m) in front, with a strongly fortified tower (7m by 7m) protruding from the centre of one of the long sides. It is built in precise but varied Hellenistic masonry. The walls have two faces, lined with an inner shell of smaller stones. The front rectangular area is articulated into several divisions, and must have had two floors, as the steps on the south side indicate. A number of the threshold-blocks are single monoliths measuring up to 2.8m, and bear the pivot-holes for doors.

The tower block, surviving to a height of over 5m, is entered through an impressive door frame, with the holes for the bolt-bar visible in the jambs. The lower level of the tower is filled solid, except for the space inside the door, where steps would have led up to the main level; any intruder would be caught vulnerably in the bottom of a stair-well. The tiny apertures on the upper level are shaped as embrasures—an early example of the use of the feature.

The western extremity of the island

From Arkesini the road descends west to Kolophána (*map p. 185, A3*): to the right, below the road (400m before the village) is a small, white, flat-roofed structure amidst ruined buildings. This is the remarkable church of the **Panaghía tou Polití**, once a small temple, now a chapel with three ancient columns and capitals (two Doric, one Ionic) supporting a roof of ancient stone rafters. All around lie other fragments, including part of a stone olive-press.

West of Kolophána, the road ends at the delightful bay of **Paradeísa**. Remains of an Early Christian chapel stand by the north side of the cove.

The track north from Kolophána leads to **Káto Kámbos Bay** (*map p. 185, A3*), the only protected inlet at this end of the island. The chapel of Ághios Ioánnis Theológos at the eastern side of the inlet is built into the east end of an Early Christian basilica. The small 1950s church on the waterfront to the west includes a section of ancient frieze with triglyphs in its front wall.

NORTHEASTERN AMORGOS

Until the construction of the road from Chora to Aigiáli in the 1980s, the two parts of the island functioned as separate entities, linked only by water. From Chora the road describes a wide loop around the hill of Profítis Ilías. Beyond it, before a sharp right bend, the church of Ághios Ioánnis Pródromos at Ríchti is visible below the road to the left (*map p. 185, C2*). Above it stand the ruins of a **Hellenistic tower**, almost 9m in diameter, one of a chain of towers surveying the sea-routes along the north coast.

Two kilometres further on, a branch road (right) leads up a narrow gorge to the semi-abandoned settlement of **Asfondilítis**, overlooking the sea in solitary isolation.

Aigiáli

The attractive harbour town of **Aigiáli** (*map p. 185, C1*), abbreviated to Giáli, is located by an ample and protected bay, surrounded by one of the loveliest landscapes in the Cyclades and ringed with majestic mountains. The long sandy beach here should not be missed. The coast and harbour show signs of Roman presence: marble fragments are scattered in the village; the pedestal of a votive statue stands in the small *plateía* to the east; and the remains of walls are visible a short distance before the north end of the beach.

Ancient Aegiale lay high above this area to the north, near the village of **Tholária**, a village of great charm and tranquillity, with stacked streets, covered walkways, and wide views both to west and to north (*map p. 185, C1; take the first street uphill from below the outer plateía of Tholária, then immediately left; path leads off right towards the hill-top; 15mins*). Magnificent views extend in all directions. The site is unexcavated; visible remains include cuttings in the rocky summit of the ridge and stretches of fortification walls to the north and east.

Around Langáda

The steep mountain slopes on the south side of Aigiáli Bay, with their frequent springs, have given rise to several villages of well-preserved architectural unity: **Potamós** (Ano and Káto) to the west, and **Langáda** to the east (*map p. 185, C1*), overlooking the area from high on a slope of rocks, cactus and small oak. All these villages grew up in the early Middle Ages as part of the general retreat to safety away from the shores and the piracy that infested the coasts. The **rock church of Aghía Triáda**, which sits on a ledge in the cliff to the south (right) of the road just before arriving in Langáda, may have first been used as a hiding place during attack from pirates. The rock pinnacles in the gorge below Langáda to the north also provided a different kind of refuge; the half-deserted *borgo* of **Stroúmbos** must first have been built as such. The gorge around it provides a microclimate in which varieties of acacia, arbutus, broom and olive crowd the rocks and the elusive Ruppell's warbler may be seen. The area is of great beauty.

The monastery of Ághios Ioánnis Theológos

From the northeastern extremity of Langáda, a footpath leads towards the eastern end of the island. After 15mins the paved path continues to the left towards the domed 15th-century church of Ághios Ioánnis Pródromos and the later Panaghía Epanochorianí; the stepped path to the right climbs steeply for another hour to the **monastery of Ághios Ioánnis Theológos** (*map p. 185, D1*), a 14th-century monastery on a small plateau.

The katholikon is heavily buttressed on the south side, and the dome and roof have been rebuilt in recent restorations. The interior (*key under stone by door*) is unexpectedly spacious, with three aisles and a wide apse, furnished with a synthronon and a central abbot's seat. In the conch are fragments of 13th- or 14th-century wall-paintings of considerable quality. The altars in all three apses are composed of ancient capitals and fragments.

Not far beyond the monastery, the land drops precipitously to the sea over 300m below. The whole northern coast and eastern promontory of the island is an unrelenting wall of cliffs, which, directly to the south of here, reach their culmination below the peak of the island, Mt Kroúkelos. A path which crosses the plateau and rises up the slope of Kroúkelos opposite the monastery, leads to the remote **church of the Stavrós** (*75–90mins beyond; map p. 185, D1*), with immense views.

PRACTICAL INFORMATION

GETTING AROUND

Amorgós is reached by ferry from Piraeus (7–8hrs or more), with several stops en route, always including either Naxos or Paros, daily in summer, 5 times weekly in winter, alternating between the ports of Katápola and Aigiáli. It is important to establish which of the two is the port of arrival/departure. Aigiáli is connected with Astypálaia three times per week. Another route links Katápola with the Lesser Cyclades and Naxos daily in summer.

WHERE TO STAY

In the medium price-range are the **Emprostiada Traditional Guest House** in a new building of traditional design in the heart of Chora (*T: 22850 71013, www.amorgos-studios. amorgos.net*) and the more conventional **Hotel Vigla** (*T: 22850 73288, www.vigla-hotel. amorgos.net*) in Tholária, above Aigiáli. Offering simpler facilities are the **Pension Amorgos** on the harbour-front of Katápola (*same number as Emprostiada above*). In Langáda, **Artemis Rooms** (*T: 22850 73226; www.amorgos-studios.amorgos.net*) is open all year; the same owners also rent rooms on the beach near Aigiáli. Highly recommended for visits based around walking, riding, historic sightseeing, botanising and bird-watching are **Special Interest Holidays** ■, who offer an excellent range of activities and places to stay (*T: 6939 820828, or www.special-interest-holidays.com*).

WHERE TO EAT

Some of the best food is to be found in the island's small rural villages: the taverna **Giorgalinis** in Vroútsi, **Marouso** in Arkesíni (Chorió), or **Sandouraki** in Tholária. **To Limani** at Aigiáli serves some of the best seasonal and traditional Greek fare on the island. More rarefied, but offering some interesting *mezédes*, is **To Chyma** in the heart of Chora.

FURTHER READING

Lila Marangou, *The Monastery of the Panaghia Khozoviotissa*, Athens 2005.

THE LESSER CYCLADES

The lake-like waters of this group of small islands (*map pp. 49 and 128*), shielded from the north winds by the great bulk of Naxos, attracted much human activity in the Bronze Age and are beginning to do so again. Some of the islands—Donoúsa and Herakleia—are havens of tranquillity; others—Schinoúsa and Páno Kouphonísi—are developing fast, with visitors attracted by their sandy beaches. All of them offer a simplicity and intimacy which contrasts markedly with the larger surrounding islands.

HISTORY OF THE LESSER CYCLADES

Human settlement has come and gone in these islands, and our knowledge of their history is consequently patchy. Until the first excavations in the late 19th century, there was no awareness of the extraordinary human activity here in the 3rd millennium BC and its importance for subsequent history. Some of the earliest lessons in the shaping of marble and the managing of sea-vessels must have been learnt here. It has even been suggested that the island of Keros was a central, sacred island—a sort of proto-Delos—in the Early Bronze Age. The importance of these small Cycladic centres diminishes in the Middle and Late Bronze Age, as power shifted first to Crete and then to Mycenaean Greece. During the Geometric period two relatively short-lived settlements on Donoúsa and Káto Kouphonísi flourished, followed by a veritable Dark Age. Apart from an entry for Keros—ancient Keria—in Athenian tribute lists of 425 BC and the presence of Hellenistic forts on Herakleia and Schinoúsa, little is known about their fate. The Romans had installations on them, but used them mostly as places of exile. An Early Christian presence is evident on Schinoúsa, but the islands were too vulnerable to piracy and raiders for it to have had any continuity under Byzantine rule, which appears largely to have ignored the area. The archipelago became a base for pirates preying on the shipping routes. In the 18th century Schinoúsa and Herakleia belonged to the Chozoviótissa monastery on Amorgós; the other islands were used as seasonal pasture by the inhabitants of Amorgós, except for Donoúsa which had a permanent population. In 1832 the islands were incorporated into the Greek state together with Naxos. At the end of the 19th and in the early 20th century, Donoúsa had a growing population who worked the iron-ore mines. These closed in 1938 at the outbreak of war. In 1941 the islands were occupied by the Italians and finally liberated from subsequent German occupation in 1944. Electricity was only brought to the archipelago in the 1980s.

HERAKLEIA

Herakleia (*pron: Iraklía*) is the largest of the Lesser Cyclades, a continuation above water of the chain of mountains running from Naxos to Ios. It is the quietest and most beautiful of the islands in the group, with attractive beaches and mountain walks. There are two villages: Ághios Geórgios (the port) and Panaghiá (the *chora*).

Ághios Geórgios

Ághios Geórgios is a deep, sheltered port with a small settlement and two main churches, Ághios Geórgios in the centre and the Taxiárchis at the southwest end. A 15-min walk south leads to the beautiful sandy **bay of Livádi**, dominated by the hill of Kastro, the remains of habitation clearly visible on its ridge. Built over the remains of a prehistoric fortification (still forming the lowest course of the wall that can be seen from the bay, running across the summit), it was inhabited until 1930. At the south end of the ridge, a quantity of large, rectangular blocks from a 4th-century BC Hellenistic structure were reused in later masonry.

About 700m inland, the road to Panaghiá cuts across the old, paved mule-path at a sharp bend; 800m west on it (level with the first olive tree to the left of a scattered grove, and 100m before a T-junction), on exposed, flat-surfaced rocks in the middle of the track, are two **prehistoric petroglyphs**, in the forms of incised concentric rings.

Panaghiá

The metalled road ends at **Panaghiá** (*45mins on foot from Ághios Geórgios*). The main street is punctuated by the church of the Panaghía and Ághios Nektários. From the southern end of the village, the path to the **Cave of Ághios Ioánnis Pródromos** leads down into the valley to the west, before rising steeply to round the panoramic shoulder of Mt Pápas (*the walk is tough and there are no springs. Allow 90mins each way, and bring a powerful torch for the cave interior*). There are two caves, set back in a deep cleft in the hillside. The entrance to the cave of Ághios Ioánnis, to the right, is marked by a hanging bell. Entry is through a small hole on hands and knees, but the cave opens out immediately into a series of vast interconnecting chambers. Beyond the modern sanctuary in the foreground, a clear path to the left side leads past stalactites and stalagmites into the depths of the cave.

SCHINOUSA

Schinoúsa is gentle, with low rolling hills and a deeply indented coastline but little vegetation. In spite of sacrifices made to tourism, Schinoúsa produces some of the best fresh, local wines and cheeses in the Cyclades.

Chora

The road from the attractive harbour of Mersíni up to the **Chora** in the centre of the island (*15mins on foot*) is bordered by rock scarps shot through with openings, perhaps originally burial places, but more recently used as hiding places from pirates. The Chora straggles to either side of an axial street. In the area immediately around its church, a quadrangle of houses marks the outline of the former kastro.

The island's fortified point was always the **hill of Profítis Ilías**, 1km to the south by the left-hand branch of the road south from Chora. The southwest shoulder of the hill has the remains of prehistoric fortifications, with the plan of a rectangular bastion visible, and vestiges survive of the base of the wall along the north side. Below the hill to the southeast are the ruins of a substantial late medieval *pýrgos*.

Tsigoúri Bay, 500m west of Chora, has a wide beach of grey sand.

KOUPHONISIA & KEROS

Kouphonísia

The former character of **Páno Kouphonísi** (*map p. 128*), a remote but busy fishing community, has been transformed by intensive tourist and building development, which is felt all the more pressingly since the island is small and has no other particular features except beaches and beautiful views.

Something of the original nature of the *chora*, built over the remains of a Hellenistic and Roman settlement, can still be felt in its winding main street. Its focus is the church of Ághios Geórgios, with some early Christian spolia in the courtyard. The former port at Loutrá, just west of the *chora*, retains an active boatyard and has a quieter atmosphere. An Early Cycladic cemetery, being rapidly eroded by the sea, was excavated on the western side of the inlet.

Across the water at a distance of less than a kilometre is **Káto Kouphonísi**, uninhabited and with a more varied shoreline and relief. It is famed for its beaches.

Keros

Across the water from Kouphonísi is the is-land of Keros (*visits only with permit from the Greek Archaeological Service*), uninhabited and used mostly for goat-pasturing and bee-keep-ing. The island's fame rests on its integral role in the world of Early Cycladic culture and on the extraordinary quantity of finds of marble figurines and objects, made above all at the island's western extremity at Kávos, and at Daskalió, which though an islet now, was a rocky promontory of the main island in the Early Bronze Age. Keros was the site of an im-portant Early Cycladic ritual centre; recent ex-cavations have revealed an immense deposit of broken marble figurines. Many figurines

Figure of a seated lyre-player, a figurine of the Early Bronze Age Keros-Syros Culture.

looted from there in the 20th century now adorn museums in Athens and, presumably, private collections elsewhere.

DONOUSA

Donoúsa lies separated from the other Lesser Cyclades, in an isolated position 15km from the east coast of Naxos. It is a mountainous island, delightful and peaceful to visit, with a number of fine sandy bays around its shores. The island has three good springs, and early in the year it is remarkably green.

Exploring Donoúsa

The **Chora**, properly called Stavrós, centres around a sheltered bay and beach with a well-watered *kámbos* area behind. The belfry of its eponymous church (1902) incorporates an antique capital and column; its interior is decorated with Byzantine paintings of some quality from the same period.

From the road which circles round Chora to the north, tracks lead up to the former **iron-ore mines** in the centre of the island. To the east, the main surfaced road passes below the church of the Panaghía and then rises above Kedros Bay, one of the island's most attractive beaches (*steps down to the sands*). The main road continues to climb to **Messariá**, a settlement of a few stone houses: from the bend below the village, a track leads downhill towards the important fortified Geometric site of **Vathý Limenári**, which flourished in the 9th and 8th centuries BC. The site is difficult to locate: a promontory crowned by a defunct windmill is clearly visible; the next shoulder to the east has a half-deserted house on its saddle: the site extends to the east of this building.

Climbing higher, the road reaches **Mersíni**, a panoramic village of dry-stone houses. The road ends at **Kalotarítissa**, a tiny village set behind a jetty and a beautiful configuration of bays, with the island of Skoulonísi lying just offshore.

PRACTICAL INFORMATION

GETTING AROUND

For such small islands, the ferry services are frequent. The mainstay of communications is the daily ferry, which leaves Katápola on Amorgós daily in the morning, and plies the route to Naxos, via Páno Kouphonísi, Schinoúsa, and Herakleia; returning down the same line from Naxos. Three days per week the route also includes Donoúsa. A similar route is connected with Piraeus three times a week. Donoúsa has one weekly service to Piraeus (7hrs), and three weekly connections to Naxos and Amorgós.

Excursion boats go to Káto Kouphonísi in the summer, principally to the island's beaches and a seasonal taverna.

WHERE TO STAY

Donoúsa

The island has limited accommodation, the best is represented by the rooms (and adjoining taverna) of **To Iliovasilema** (*T: 22850 51570*), to the east of the harbour.

Herakleia

There is a wide selection of simple rooms on the island: prettiest of all are **Sunset Rooms**, at the top of the village of Ághios Geórgios (*T: 22850 71569; kovmaria@yahoo.gr*); the same owner keeps **Angelos Rooms** (*same numbers*) closer to the centre. Slightly more polished in facilities is **Anna's Place** (*T: 22850 74234*), also in Ághios Geórgios.

Páno Kouphonísi

Of the many good, rent-room possibilities on the island, **Anna's Rooms** (*T: 22850 71061*) are new and welcoming, situated in the quieter area of Loutrá.

Schinoúsa

In Chora, **Christina's Apartments** provide self-catering comfort (*T: 22850 71922, or in Athens, 210 993 1111*).

WHERE TO EAT

Donoúsa

Taverna Tzi-Tzi is memorable for its magnificent, panoramic position above the springs at Mersíni, 3km east of the port at Stavrós.

Herakleia

To Steki, the taverna-cum-bakery in Panaghiá, serves the best home-cooking. In Ághios Geórgios, **To Pefko** has good fare and an attractive position.

Páno Kouphonísi

Lefteris has a pleasing setting, set back from the Megáli Ámmos beach; and **Kapetan Nikolas** (Loutrá) is good for fresh fish and seafood.

Schinoúsa

The taverna **I Vengiera** ■ serves, early in the year, its own tangy myzithra cheese. It has excellent local amber-coloured, sea-salty wine on request. This is a good place to sample the island's famous *fava* (split peas).

FURTHER READING

For a sense of the animated academic debate surrounding Early Cycladic figurines, see Colin Renfrew, *The Cycladic Spirit: Masterpieces from the Nicholas Goulandris Collection*, New York, 1991; Pat Getz-Gentle, *Personal Styles in Early Cycladic Sculpture*, University of Wisconsin Press 2001; Cyprian Broodbank, *An Island Archaeology of the Early Cyclades*, Cambridge, 2002.

KEA

Often overlooked, perhaps due to its proximity to the mainland, the small island of Kea (also known as Keos or Tzia) has recently attracted a rash of coastal development. Nonetheless, it has much to offer. An unspoilt interior abounding in traditional architecture and diverse flora—especially the Valonia oaks of the uplands—makes for rewarding walks. Its archaeological riches include important prehistoric sites and no less than four Classical cities, among them Ioúlis with its remarkable stone lion, and Karthaía, one of the most evocative ancient sites in the Aegean.

HISTORY OF KEA

According to myth, Kea, once called Hydrousa on account of its richness of water, became dry and infertile after the nymphs inhabiting it were driven away by a wild lion; the inhabitants sought the aid of Aristaeus, son of Apollo and Cyrene, who came to the island with a band of fellow Phthians, built an altar of invocation to Zeus Ikmaios, the 'Bringer of Rain', and another to Seirios, divinity of the dog-star (Sirius) whose rising before dawn was believed by the ancients to bring on the scorching heat of midsummer. The cool Aetesian winds blew for 40 days as a result, restoring the fertility of the island.

Settled since the Late Neolithic, Kea had an important Bronze Age centre at Aghía Eiríni, receiving strong influence from Minoan Crete. The island received Ionian settlers during the 10th century, and by the 7th century BC, the four cities of the Kean Tetrapolis, Koresia, Ioulis, Poiëessa, and Karthaia, had been founded. In the 6th and 5th centuries BC, Keos was a wealthy island, expressed in extensive building programmes. The island had a flourishing cultural life: the poets Simonides (?556–?470) and Bacchylides (c. 550–431), Prodicus (friend of Socrates), the physician Erasistratus (c. 315–c. 240) and the 3rd-century BC philosopher Ariston were Keans. Having contributed four ships to the Greek victory at Salamis, Kea joined the Delian League. Its attempted secession from the Second Athenian League in c. 363 BC was suppressed by Athens, which had an interest in controlling the island's production of miltos, a red pigment widely used in the Greek world. In the 3rd century BC, a naval base of operations was created at Koresia under Ptolemy II and the city was renamed Arsinoë. After the Battle of Philippi in 42 BC, Keos was bequeathed by the Athenians to Mark Antony. The main cities on the Roman island were Ioulis and Karthaia. Ioulis became the capital under Byzantine rule and has remained so since.

Kea's medieval history is complicated and unclear: after the Fourth Crusade in 1204, it appears to have been divided between Pietro Giustiniani and Domenico Michiel, with the Ghisi (lords of Tinos and Mykonos) and Pisani families also holding fiefs on the island. Kea briefly returned to Byzantine rule in 1278, but was won back by the Ghisi in 1296. During the campaigns of Kheir ed-Din Barbarossa in 1537–39, Kea was given temporarily to Duke Giovanni IV Crispo by the sultan in exchange for Naxos, but from 1566 it was effectively under Turkish control. The strategic importance of the island's natural harbour of Ághios Nikólaos attracted pirates in the 17th and 18th centuries; the Russians during the Russo-Turkish War of 1787–92—when a Greek in Russian service, Lambros Katsonis, operated a Graeco-Russian flotilla to harass the Ottoman navy from here—and later a variety of European commercial powers. Keos received many refugees from Chios after the 1822 massacre; their arrival coincided with the outbreak of an epidemic: many left again to settle on Syros. In effect independent from the beginning of the uprising, Kea officially became part of the new Kingdom of Greece in 1835.

KORISIA & THE NORTH OF THE ISLAND

The point of arrival on Kea is the bay of Ághios Nikólaos, one of the most sheltered and hidden harbours in the Cyclades and a vital refuge: the waters to the north, exposed to the winds funnelled through the Kavo Doro straits between Euboea and Andros, are notoriously unpredictable. The port of Livádi is on the western shore; the undistinguished settlement of Korisía stretches inland from the south shore.

Ancient Koresia

The headland above the port was the site of the ancient city of Koresia. The headland has two distinct rises, crowned in antiquity with two acropoleis; the Archaic acropolis on the lower hill to the north was originally walled and possessed four, still traceable, bastions; and a 5th-century extension, which included the higher hill to the south, its summit fringed by rock scarps. Reached by a path (*from the road, first right, to Marádes and Xýla Bay*) to the fringe, near a small whitewashed shrine, is the base of an ancient temple, perhaps dedicated to Apollo. The temple was orientated north–south, with massive threshold blocks bearing holes for the bolting mechanism of the doors: the inner threshold is a single monolith, c. 2.5m across. The line of the fortification walls can best be seen on the seaward side of the hill. Directly below the whitewashed shrine, in the north face of the rock scarp, are many niches and cuts into the natural rock. The town itself lay on the eastern slope of the northern hill, between the modern summit church of Ághios Savvás and the harbour. Foundations are visible on the surface. In the mid-2nd century BC, Koresia was annexed to Ioulis, functioning as its port.

AGHIA EIRINI

The shore road east of Korisía leads to the attractive harbours of Gialiskári and Vourkári. On a coastal promontory 500m beyond Vourkári is the prehistoric city of Aghía Eiríni, one of the most important centres of Cycladic culture, in a strategic position between the Attic mainland and the Cyclades (*no opening times, but entirely visible from the perimeter fence*). Its fascinating finds are on display in the museum in Chora.

HISTORY OF AGHIA EIRINI

Settlement on the site was established between 3000 and 2700 BC (in the area north of the present church), but most of the structures now visible were built from 1900 BC onwards, after a period of abandonment. A period of expansion and prosperity seems to have been ended by an earthquake c. 1450 BC. Some of the ruins were cleared, and the buildings and temple adapted and reused in the 12th and 11th centuries BC, and the site continued into Archaic and Classical times as a place of the cult of Dionysus.

The site

The site is a striking example of early, well-organised urban forms, featuring narrow streets with drainage channels beneath a paved surface; carefully built walls with stone door frames. Three structures are particularly conspicuous: the rectangular corner bastion and fortification wall in the northeast corner of the area, dating from c. 1700 BC. Immediately east of the church is the largest single structure uncovered, Building A, seat of the local ruler and the community's administration. The building had three levels: a basement divided into storage areas and workshops clearly visible today, a main floor with reception rooms, and an upper level with painted walls. The lower level appears to have included metal and stone workshops, as well as stores of imported Minoan, Mycenaean and island pottery. Along building A's northeast side was the main cult centre, the temple building recognisable by its long rectangular form divided into chambers. Its origins go back to the 1800s BC, but its present form and structure are from c. 1600 BC. At the seaward end it had an enclosed court with stone benches on the sides and a later rectangular hearth in the centre; a doorway leads into a middle chamber, which in turn leads into an inner sanctum at the western end. In the interior, the shattered pieces of terracotta female figures were found: they were probably damaged in an earthquake around 1450 BC. The fragments were found and venerated afterwards by later inhabitants. Cemeteries of rock-cut tombs were to the west and the east, outside the fortification wall.

THE KEPHALA PENINSULA & THE FAR NORTH

Beyond Aghía Eiríni the coast road passes a late 19th-century **coaling-station** for steamships, and ends at a narrow isthmus with a small monument to Lambros Katsonis (1752–1804; *see History, p. 201*). A path leads to the lighthouse on the promontory. Marble blocks at the west corner of its platform suggest that it may be built on an ancient site.

There is a **Late Neolithic settlement** (founded c. 3300 BC and abandoned after little more than a century) on the peninsula of Képhala, the northwesterly extremity of the island (*reached by taking the track uphill and inland from the coast road at Aghía Eiríni, bearing right over the hill to the promontory*). Important finds have come from its cemetery of about 40 small circular graves, at the foot of the south-facing slope of the head of the peninsula, as it joins the isthmus.

The main road heads inland towards pleasant **Otziás**, situated by a deep bay on the north coast. In antiquity, miltos (*see History, p. 200*), a natural red iron oxide used widely in antiquity for colouring and dyeing, as well as for caulking ships, was exploited in this area. The tunnels used for the mining of the ochre can be seen in hillsides around Kálamos, east of here, in the area still referred to as Trypospiliés ('hole-caves'), 2–3km south.

East of Otziás, the panoramic road along the north coast ends at the **monastery of the Panaghía Kastrianí**, with buildings mostly from 1912.

CHORA (IOULIS) & ENVIRONS

The road to Chora from Korisía gives the first intimation of the very particular land-scape of the island. The valleys are almost immediately deep and steep, the volumes of their hillsides based on interleaving convex and conical forms, constantly folding against one another in compressed space. Every slope is scored with the parallel stria-tions of the immense and centuries-old human labour of terracing. By Cycladic stan-dards the terraces have a good cover of vegetation: almonds, olives and vines.

Leaving Korisía to the south, the road enters a characteristic landscape of deep ter-raced valleys. A branch to the right leads to the **spring of Fléa**, south of which the delightful valley of Mylopótamos has a series of almost a dozen water-mills, some still with their funnel-like tower through which the channelled water fell with sufficient force to turn the (usually) horizontally-mounted wheel.

THE TOWN OF IOULIS

The *chora* officially keeps the name of its pagan predecessor, Ioúlis (or Ioulída, in the demotic form), but is generally referred to as Chora. Ioúlis was noted in antiquity for its convention of obliging citizens of advanced age to commit suicide by drinking hemlock.

The town is entered through a passage under buildings; such *stegádi* are a common feature of the architecture. The street to the left out of the tiny square beyond leads up to the **acropolis** of the ancient city, where a Temple of Apollo once stood. Up

View of Ioúlis (Ioulída).

steps beyond the church of Ághios Charálambos is a stretch of Archaic fortification or retaining wall in large rectangular blocks, on top of which rises the smaller, irregular masonry of the **Venetian Kastro** (1210), mostly demolished in 1865. Only the long, arched gate-house remains. The interior of the Kastro, occupied by modern structures, offers a good view of the superb amphitheatre of whitewashed houses densely packed on the slope opposite.

The Archaeological Museum

A short distance up the main street to the right of the entrance is the Archaeological Museum, a collection of great quality, especially the remarkable finds from Aghía Eiríni (*open daily except Mon, 8.30–3*). These include marble figurines and vessels, as well as the unique statues of female figures with broad skirts, narrow waists and bare breasts, as well as painted pottery. The first floor displays Archaic to Roman material, including decorative sculpture from the early 5th-century BC Temple of Athena at Karthaía, with drill-holes and perforations indicating where the figures were embellished with affixed additions in gilded bronze.

Beyond the museum the main street climbs into the upper part of Chora. Below the buildings to the left (north) of the street are stretches of 6th-century BC defensive walls, best seen from the lower terrace of the café before the Neoclassical Dimarcheíon. The traditional settlement stretches uphill from here.

The Lion of Ioúlis

A 15-min walk from the upper (east) end of the village along an ancient, paved *kalderímī* circling the valley to the north and passing the cemetery, leads to the early Archaic *Lion of Ioúlis*, the largest and one of the earliest pieces of Greek monumental sculpture, a recumbent lion, about 6.4m long, carved from the living rock. Its style suggests a date between c. 620 and 580 BC. Its function and meaning are unclear, but suggestions include a grave-marker, or a memento of the mythical lion (*see History, p. 200*).

POIËESSA & THE SOUTHWEST

The central uplands

West of Chora (1.2km from the parking area), the main road splits into a branch to the east eventually leading to the south coast, and one to the west. Between them lies an upland area of great natural beauty, known for its plant life. A multitude of abandoned terrace walls stands witness to the island's dense inhabitation in antiquity and in the 18th–19th centuries, as do *stávli*, rectangular stone byres. The dwellings are low and flat-roofed, as are the rural churches, of similar design and often distinguished only by a raised belfry: some, such as the **Panaghía Loutrianí**, in a wild setting 2km east of Sklavonikólas; or Panaghía and Ághios Nikólaos at **Vatoúdi**, south of Aghía Marína, are of considerable antiquity and incorporate ancient spolia and vestiges of painting.

The Tower of Aghía Marína

Several ancient towers of the late Classical or Hellenistic periods are to be found in the area. They were used variously for the storage of produce, as protection of fertile areas, and to control frontiers. The easiest to find and most impressive is the Tower of Aghía Marína (*1km west of the main road*). Used as a monastic building since the 16th century, it partly collapsed in an earthquake in 1853. Two corners still stand to a height of 19m, making it the tallest surviving square tower. It overlooked an important road crossing and borders between Poiëessa, Koresia and Ioulis. The method of construction would suggest a date at the end of 5th century BC. The masonry varies, with the corners constructed more regularly than the rest. Towards the top there were two string courses. The interior appears to have been divided into four or five floors in antiquity; the wooden projections at the top are recent. The adjacent monastery church dates from the early 19th century.

The Bay of Písses

The Kremmídi valley, which cuts into the centre of the island from the settlement of **Skiadás**, is of magnificent natural beauty and tranquillity. On the coast, the wide Bay of Písses (Poisses; Ποἰσσες) extends above the commanding **site of ancient Poiëessa**. The acropolis occupied the plateau between the church of the Panaghía Sotíra at the western end of the hill overlooking the sea, and the low summit to its east. The rectangle of walls that descend the slope below follow the lines of the ancient perimeter walls on the east and west sides; the horizontal line of wall joining them is recent. The ancient walls would have descended to the small harbour in the south corner of the bay. Few visible surface remains on the acropolis are reached by the path which climbs up to the Panaghía Sotíra from the road. A fragment of a statue in Parian marble stands outside the church. A mass of rubble shows where the city extended towards the southeast; an *alóni*, or threshing-floor, has been built into the semicircular perimeter of one of the towers. Poiëessa, founded in the 6th century BC, was always relatively small; by the 4th century BC it had lost its independence to Karthaia, but remained inhabited.

Beyond the bay, the road travels along a shore of rocks, sandy coves and magnificent sunsets, to the attractive inlet of **Kambí**. On the hill high above the village is the church of Ághios Geórgios, with an altar-table on an unusual ancient capital with palmettes.

KARTHAIA & THE EAST OF THE ISLAND

The eastern road from Ioúlis climbs up beneath a ridge crowned by ruined windmills. At a sharp turn after 2km, the medieval hilltop church of **Aghía Ánna** comes into view. It is the katholikon of a defunct monastery and has late wall-paintings in the sanctuary and central apse. The altars in the apses are made of ancient spolia.

Less than 2km further south along the road, another defunct monastery, the **Episkopí**, is on the left. There is a remarkable toadstool-shaped rock formation around its north sides. The monastic buildings have medieval origins, but the church was renovated in the 19th century. Spolia include a fine Doric capital in front of the west entrance of the church and the block from an ancient olive-press in the tower.

From the main asphalt road, c. 80m back, northwest of the turning to Episkopí, an attractive stretch of ancient *kalderími* heads uphill to the south. The paved and stepped road, maintained since antiquity, forms part of a network of ancient ways linking the cities of the Tetrapolis and their water sources. Their exploration is one of the greatest joys of walking on Kea. A map of the signed routes is available from the Dimarcheíon in Chora. The *kalderími* passes close by the summit of Profítis Ilías where Aristaeus instituted the cult of Zeus Ikmaios (*see History, p. 200*). The Royal oak or Valonia oak, grows in abundance here, as elsewhere in Kea's uplands.

South from Elliniká

Elliniká, reached by the main road after the Episkopí turn, was the site of a rural community in antiquity, as indicated by many ancient spolia built into its churches and the village spring-house. From the centre, a track leads 1.8km west to the **monastery of Ághios Panteléimon** with a 16th-century church and memorable views. A short distance to the north, a path leads the apse of a ruined 13th-century church, once part of a monastery of St John the Baptist, with surviving wall-paintings and a schist throne.

Two kilometres further along the main road a track (right) leads to a modern church erected below a hermitic **cave of Ághios Timothéos**. A fluted pagan column fragment supports an improvised altar beneath the rock overhang.

Further south along the main road is the attractive 13th-century church of the **Ághii Apóstoli**, of inscribed-cross design with a dome. Although renovated inside, several fragmentary areas of wall-painting are visible. The large-eyed faces in the southwest corner, under the arches and on the pillars, are probably 13th-century, as is the painting in the apse: Christ, with scroll and finger raised. Stylistically different and of later date (16th century) are the *Pantocrator*, the Evangelists in the pendentives and the *Nativity* in the north transept. The altar is a fluted column-fragment. A good example of the typical Kean *stávlos* stands in the field above the east end of the church.

Káto Meriá preserves many traditional Kean structures. Further south, at the scattered settlement of **Stavroudáki**, the road divides. On the left branch, leading down towards the sea and Karthaía, just above where the cement track becomes a stone *kalderími*, is the circular base of a Hellenistic Tower. Outside the village to the west there are many typical *stegádia* and *stávli*, deep, single-room schist buildings with corbelled sides supporting monolithic roofs.

ANCIENT KARTHAIA

From Stavroudáki a paved path (*1hr*) leads down the deep Vathypótamos valley, passing a spring and following a torrent bed to the coast. Only reachable on foot, the site of Karthaía, on and around a natural ridge (Áspri Vígla) jutting into a bay, has preserved its romantic atmosphere.

HISTORY OF KARTHAIA

The site was first settled in the 8th century BC and evolved by the 6th century into a flourishing centre. Saracen incursions in the 7th century AD caused its desertion. Karthaia was probably the most powerful of the four cities of the Kean Tetrapolis. In 1811 the Danish antiquarian Peter Oluf Brönsted examined the site in one of the earliest documented excavations of its age. Its central feature is the ridge-top sacred acropolis, surrounded by a fortification wall with six or more gates.

The site

The massive 6th-century BC **retaining walls** appear above and to the left of the path as it reaches the shore. They are part of the adaptation of a projecting ridge into an acropolis, comprising two sacred terraces with temples. At the seaward extremity, on a terrace overlooking the bay, was the **Temple of Apollo** (c. 530 BC), with a tetrastyle portico and plain outer walls. It faced northeast with its back to the sea, and stood just clear of the rockface above it. The three limestone steps of the pronaos bear the impressions of the portico pillars; behind is the threshold of the naos. To the side of the space in front of the temple, a low limestone ledge below the rockface bears perforations for votive stelae.

Between this platform and the higher platform further inland obtrudes a steep outcrop of rock, with remains of masonry on top. Just below the second (southern) terrace, the rock has been cut to form steps and the supporting wall of the temple terrace, where polygonal blocks interlock with Archaic meticulousness. This was part of the entrance into the sanctuary: a propylon stood directly above on this corner of the terrace. The terrace is shaped like a V, its arms embracing the steep hill which rises towards the church of the Panaghía Myrtiodótissa. On the right arm (east) is the base of the so-called **Temple of Athena** (c. 500 BC), built on a ledge with a steep rockface along the west. It was a peripteral Doric temple—perhaps the earliest of its kind in the Cyclades—with six by eleven columns: the bases along the west side are well preserved; others are currently being replicated. A variety of materials was used: grey limestone for the stylobate, poros (originally stuccoed) for columns, and marble for the naos walls. The roof was tiled in Parian marble. The temple's impressive sculptural decorations are in the Chora museum. Their theme was a battle between Greeks and Amazons.

On the west arm of the terrace is another sacred building of temple-like design, **Building D** (still being excavated). Only the steps that led up to it are visible. Descending to the valley once again, the city's **theatre** is traceable, low down on the southwest slope of Áspri Vígla. It has been filled with alluvial deposits, but some of the seats survive and a vaulted tunnel is visible to the south. On the opposite (northeastern) slope of the hill, cisterns, retaining walls, and fragments of architrave with triglyphs and other decorations, can be seen, representing municipal buildings.

The principal harbour lay to the northeast side, as is evidenced by cuts in the rock at the end of the beach. The small islet offshore was joined to the foot of the acropolis projection by a **harbour mole** (still partially visible). The islet itself shows rock-cuttings from port installations.

GYAROS & MAKRONISOS

The uninhabited islands of Gyáros and Makrónisos (*map p. 49*) share a history as places of exile, most notably during the last century. In 1946, at the outbreak of civil war in Greece, Makrónisos became the principal prison camp for 'enemies of the state', chiefly communist activists or sympathisers. One of the best-known inmates was the musician Mikis Theodorakis, who composed some of his First Symphony here. The camp was used again during the period of the military junta from 1967–74.

On the sea-bed between Makrónisos and Kea lies the wreck of the *Britannic*, which sank in less than an hour after apparently hitting a mine in November 1916. Larger than her sister-ship the *Titanic*, she had been refitted as a hospital ship for the Gallipoli campaign and was on her way to Lemnos for active relief service.

PRACTICAL INFORMATION

GETTING AROUND

Daily ferries to Kea (75mins) operate from Lávrion, with a daily morning service and an afternoon one four times a week. Ferries for Kythnos, Syros and the main Cycladic destinations call at Kea on average two times weekly.

Access to Makrónisos and Gyáros is not restricted, but you need your own boat.

WHERE TO STAY

Charming, simple hotels are lacking on Kea; in the upper categories accommodation tends to be a bit pretentious. The best option at the upper end of the scale is the 4-star **Porto Kea Suites** (*T: 22880 22870/1, www.portokea-suites. com*); and in the middle category the **Hotel Brillante Zoë** (*T: 22880 22685; www.hotelbrillante.gr*). Both have pleasant management and

are in the port town of Korisía. For studios to rent, the **Oasis Hotel** (*T: 22880 21295*), on the road from Korisía to Gialiskári, is clean and comfortable.

WHERE TO EAT

Two of the best places to eat on Kea are in Vourkári: the popular **Aristos**, on the seafront, and **Strophi tou Mimi**, where the road turns inland for Otziás. **Lagoudera**, on the quay in Korisía, has a good variety of *mezédes*.

FURTHER READING

The Praise Singer by Mary Renault is a historical novel about the lyric poet Simonides of Keos. On the Makrónisos internment camp, see Yannis Hamilakis, *The Nation and its Ruins*, Oxford 2008.

KYTHNOS

In spite of being the second closest Cycladic island to Athens, Kythnos remains one of the least developed. The island has little tourist infrastructure; its particular qualities are its unpretentious and traditional island life and its beautiful and panoramic landscape. A special treat are the many fine 17th-century icons in its churches.

HISTORY OF KYTHNOS

Kythnos was first settled exceptionally early, in the Mesolithic (9th millennium BC). Its metal ore deposits gave it an important role in the development of metallurgy during the 3rd millennium BC.

According to Herodotus, Kythnos was originally settled by Dryopes; later Ionian settlers arrived on the island. The ancient city of Kythnos appears to have been continuously inhabited from the 10th century BC to the 7th century AD. Kythnos supplied two ships to the Greek fleet at Salamis, later joining the Delian League and becoming a tributary to Athens.

Due to increasing piracy in the 6th–7th centuries, the ancient city was abandoned in favour of the impregnable site of Kastro tis Oriás. This remained the capital during the periods of Byzantine and Latin rule, when the island was known as Thermia. In 1207 the island came under the rule of the Venetian overlord of Naxos, Marco Sanudo, nephew of Doge Enrico Dandolo, and became one of the eleven islands of the Duchy of the Archipelago. In 1336 Niccolò Sanudo gave the barony of Kythnos to the Gozzadini family of Bologna, who hung onto the island for some time after the capitulation of the larger members of the archipelago to the Turks, to whom it finally fell in 1617.

In 1823 the population was decimated by plague. The island became a place of exile for political prisoners under the rule of Greece's first king. From the mid-19th century until after the Second World War, iron ores were industrially exploited on Kythnos.

THE NORTH OF THE ISLAND

Mérichas to the site of ancient Kythnos

The small port of **Mérichas**, where all ferries arrive (*map p. 211, B3*), is attractively set but has little else to offer. The road north from it follows the coast, turning inland on a ridge above the bay of Episkopí, from where a walled pathway leads northwest to the hilly promontory of Vryókastro (or Rigókastro), the site of **ancient Kythnos**. The ancient city stretched between and below the two northernmost of three summits; its harbour was to the southwest. The archaeological remains are of considerable interest.

At the southern limit of the city a Hellenistic fort topped the second and highest summit. Its entrance threshold and door-jambs are visible in the north, but little else

N

Ⓐ   Ⓑ   Ⓒ

① ② ③ ④

C. Kephalos

Kastro tis Orias

Sarandos Bay

Thermal springs
Loutra
Loutra Bay
Ag. Eirini
Livadaki Bay

357

327

C. Katakolo

Kolona Bay

Apokrisi
Chora
(Kythnos)

Apokrisi Bay
Kythnos
C. Vryokastro

Episkopi Bay
Episkopi

Merichas Bay

Ag. Stefanos
Ag. Ioannis
C. Ag. Ioannis

Martinakia
Merichas

Dryopida
Aousa
Ag. Stefanos Bay
C. Tzoulis

Zogaki
Katafyki Cave

C. Aspri Pounda
Lefkes

Liotrivi
Lefkes Bay

Flambouria Bay
Flambouria

Kalo Livadi

Mavrianou Bay

Kanala
P. Stratilatissa
P. Kanala

Kanala Bay

Stifo Bay
Skylos

C. Mavri Pounda
Skylos Bay

Gaidouromandra

Gaidouromandra Bay

Ag. Dimitrios Bay
Ag. Dimitrios

C. Ag. Dimitrios

0   4 km
0   2 miles

KYTHNOS

remains. From here a curtain of Late Archaic polygonal fortification walls ran along the ridge. In the vicinity are examples of substantial terracing and construction in similar polygonal style, above a level area with rectilinear Hellenistic foundations, underpinned to the west by two massive protrusions of terracing in Hellenistic isodomic masonry, on which may have stood two temples. On the third (northern) peak, the remains of a sanctuary have been uncovered. Inside the corner of an impressively constructed retaining wall (the sanctuary's peribolos) is a rectangular altar, and further to the north, the podium of a temple of the 7th century BC. The temple has a small rectangular adyton running transversely across its east end: rich votive offerings were found here. Remains of the cisterns and aqueduct of the city are visible lower down the hill.

A road with wide and beautiful views leads east to the coast at Apókrisi Bay (also written Apókrousi; with taverna) and the long **sandy beach of Kolóna** (*map p. 211, A2*).

Kythnos Chora

Kythnos Chora (*map p. 211, B2*) has been the administrative capital of the island since 1864. Situated in the fertile centre, the town grew up in the early 1600s as the population transferred from remote Kastro tis Oriás on the northwest coast. The town features many elegant 17th-century churches. At the western extremity of the town's main thoroughfare, the **church of the Sotirás** has—in common with several other churches—icons of great quality by the Skordilis brothers, late 17th-century Cretan-Venetian icon-painters. Further east is the **church of the Taxiárchis**, its central vault supported by an ancient antique column. **Ághios Savvás**, to its east, was used jointly as a place of Orthodox and Catholic worship. The oldest church in Chora, **Aghía Triáda**, much further east, is a broad domed structure of c. 12th-century origin, modernised later, with a fine 17th-century wooden iconostasis. Almost in the centre of the town, a ruined church known as the Katholikon houses a small repository of **archaeological finds**.

Loutrá and Kastro

On the east coast, 5km north of Chora, is the island's main thermal station of **Loutrá** (*map p. 211, B2*). The only large building is the Hydro (1836), covering two hot springs. The original arcaded structure was added to clumsily in the 1970s.

A rough track heads north from Loutrá to the northern extremity of the island; after 2km a branch leads steeply up to the west to a plateau where it divides. The north branch finishes at the attractive medieval church of Ághios Geórgios (modernised). The west branch climbs over a rise and then drops down towards the spectacular site of the medieval capital, **Kastro tis Oriás** (also Kastro tou Kataképhalou), main focus of the island from the 7th to the 16th centuries AD. It occupies a rocky point with steep drops on three sides and wide views across to Kea. The entrance is across a narrow col and through a low gate in an outer enceinte of walls. Visible above a rockface to the right is the church of the Panaghía Eleoúsa, which incorporates Early Byzantine elements. Above lies the dense medieval settlement, with houses, cisterns and various walls. At the northwestern end of the area a partially collapsed barrel-vaulted church preserves some murals in its apse and especially the vault, with a faded 15th-century *Virgin in Majesty*.

THE SOUTH OF THE ISLAND

Lying some 5km east of Mérichas, Dryopis, or **Dryopída** (*map p. 211, B3*), has the tight-knit feel of an island *chora*. It spreads over two adjacent hillsides: a steep older quarter to the north and the main part of the town to the south, with narrow streets and small squares grouped around a shallow hollow of orange and lemon trees, which functions as the orchard and kitchen-garden, or *kámbos*, of the community. To the south is the **Katafýki Cave**, largest of many in the schist slopes. Its shape has been altered by iron prospecting.

South from Dryopída the road climbs to a summit crowned by ruined windmills, then continues along a ridge with views of the Cyclades, Attica and the Peloponnese. A left branch leads to **Kanála** on the east coast (*map p. 211, B3*), where the church of the Panaghía Kanála, on a promontory, contains a fine 17th-century icon of the Virgin by the Skordilis brothers. There are many sheltered sandy coves in this south part of the island (often unshaded).

Back on the main road, the finely proportioned 17th-century domed church of the **Panaghía Stratilátissa** is visible on a ridge (*map p. 211, B3*). A right turn leads to **Flamboúria** on the west coast (*map p. 211, B3*). The waterside church of Panaghía Flambouriará has an attractive 17th-century icon of the Virgin and Child in a water-tub, out of which gushes the Water of Life.

PRACTICAL INFORMATION

GETTING AROUND

There is a daily service by car ferry from Piraeus (4hrs); twice weekly from Lávrion.

WHERE TO STAY

The best solution are the rooms or studios offered in the two principal villages. **Filoxenia Studios** in Chora are comfortable and attractively furnished (*T: 22810 31644, www. filoxenia-kithnos.gr; open all year*). Close to the beach and hot springs at Loutrá are the **Porto Klaras** apartments and studios (*T: 22810 31355; open Easter–Oct*).

WHERE TO EAT

Good home cooking with local ingredients (especially the island's cheeses, such as the piquant *kopanistí*) can be had at **Araxavoli**, by the harbour at Loutrá. **Gialos**, on the front at Mérichas, is welcoming and has the standard offering, but well-prepared. Though unpromising from outside, the very simple **Taverna Pelegra**, close to the church in Dryopída, provides local wine, home-made cheese (*trímma*, a soft, slightly fermented feta cheese), and fresh local meats. Towards sunset the **taverna above Apókrisi Bay** is a memorable spot to eat.

SERIPHOS

L arge and relatively empty, Sériphos is the most mountainous of the Western Cyclades. Its history and landscape have been marked by the extraction of iron. Sériphos has beautiful bays for swimming, and offers excellent walking opportunities. What stays in the memory longest, however, is the image of the island's dramatic *chora*, clustered around its peak far above the harbour like an efflorescence of white crystals, and arranged around one of the most delightful town squares in the Cyclades.

HISTORY OF SERIPHOS

In myth, Sériphos is the island where Danaë and her infant son Perseus were washed ashore and saved, after her father, King Acrisius of Argos, fearing an oracle predicting his death by a grandson's hand, had thrown them into the sea locked in chest.

In the west of the island itself are settlements from the Early Cycladic period, with evidence of ore-mining and metallurgic activity. The first historic settlers were Aeolians from Thessaly. In the 6th century BC the city of Sériphos, today's Chora, became pros-

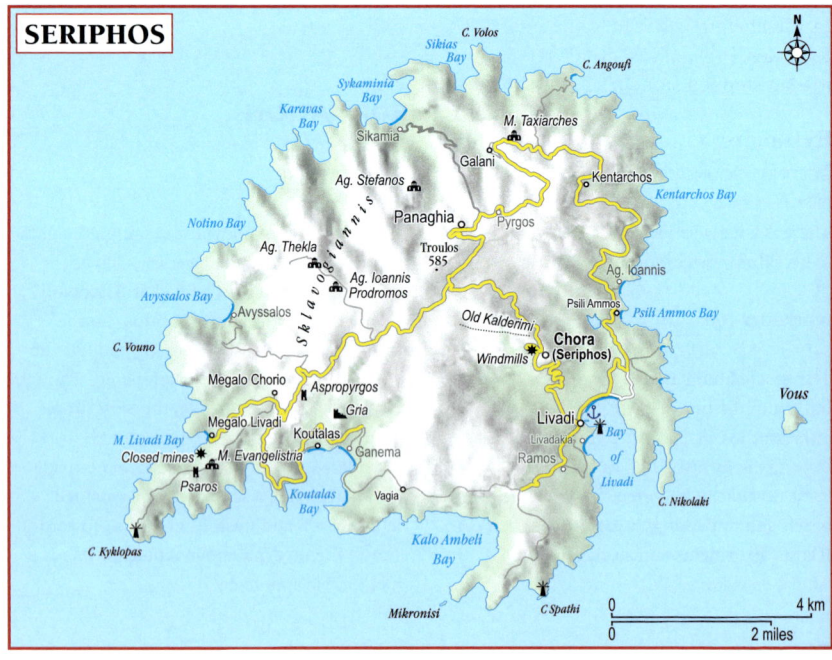

perous through its mining activity, and issued its own coinage. The island became a Roman possession in 146 BC. The mines continued to be exploited and the island was used as a place of exile.

After the capture of Constantinople in 1204, ownership of the island passed into the hands of the Venetian Ghisi and Giustiniani families, although it returned to Byzantine rule between 1276 and 1296. Back in Venetian possession, several names appear as prominent in the late 14th century: Ermolao Minotto, who reopened the mines to commercial activity, and Nicolò Adoldo, a ruthless adventurer supported by Cretan mercenaries, who effectively pillaged the island in 1393. In 1537 Kheir ed-Din Barbarossa captured the island for the Ottoman Empire.

In 1829 Sériphos joined the Greek state. The iron mines reopened on an industrial scale in 1867. Deteriorating safety and poor employment conditions led to a protracted strike in 1916, one of the first and bloodiest in the history of Greece's labour movement. The mines closed in 1963. The island now lives from a moderate seasonal tourism.

LIVADI & CHORA

The modern port of Livádi, the focus of all the island's communications, is set on the western side of a deep bay just below a fertile plain.

The view of Chora, which occupies the north and south slopes of a sharp volcanic cap at a height of 250m to the north of Livádi Bay, is one of the most picturesque in the Cyclades. It is a pleasant 50-min climb on foot. From the first sharp bend in the main road, a stepped stone path leads directly up, repeatedly crossing the road.

Exploring Chora

The original settlement of **ancient Seriphos** appears to have been the only city on the island in antiquity. Due to uninterrupted occupation on the same site, virtually nothing remains to be seen. There are vestiges of Roman walls and mosaic on the southeast slope of the hill, and ancient fragments and stelae are built into houses in the upper part of the village, as well as in the medieval walls near the summit. The **Kastro** occupies what was the acropolis of the ancient town; all that remain are stretches of the 13th-century walls along the north and south sides, built by the Venetian Pietro Giustiniani. The churches which crown the summit—Christós sto Kastro, Aghía Varvára and Ághios Ioánnis Theológos—were all built or restored in the late 19th or early 20th century.

Below the Kastro and to the west is the delightful **main square**, with the white and blue 18th-century church of Ághios Athanásios, in white and blue, and the Neoclassical Dimarcheíon (1907), in yellow and red. Steps lead down from the square to the west, past the former village fountain, to the main road, beside which is the small **Archaeological Collection** (*open June–Oct daily except Mon, 8.30–3; otherwise by arrangement with the custodian, who can be contacted through the Dimarcheíon*). The collection comprises fragments of Hellenistic and Roman statuary from the Kastro and some Neolithic obsidian tools from the islet of Seriphópoula, off Sériphos to the northeast.

West of Chora, clearly visible in the narrow fold of the mountain below, are the old **wash-houses** of the town, a wide-arched loggia in front of the cistern block.

Leaving from beside the windmills above Chora and cutting clearly from right to left across the rocky face of the mountain, can be seen the line of the old *kalderími* joining Chora with Megálo Chorió and Panaghía.

THE SOUTH OF THE ISLAND

The barren and dramatic south coast has a chain of coves and sandy bays, and is the area most exploited for iron. From Livadákia, a road climbs south to Vagiá and the **bay of Koutalás**. The slopes and rocks on its east and west sides are perforated with mining tunnels. Iron and copper ore were mined here from antiquity until the last century. On a summit to the north of the inlet are the meagre remnants of the **Castle of Griá** ('the old lady'), evidence that the bay—then known as Porto Catena—was a centre of habitation and mining activity under Venetian domination.

Further west beyond Koutalás Bay extends the **Akrotíri peninsula**, the area of the most intensive mining. Three hundred metres north of the main road junction above Koutalás, a track leads southwest to the grimly rebuilt monastery of the Evangelístria Akrotirianí, 400m beyond which stands the Hellenistic **watchtower of Psarós**, to the left of the track, with an imposing rectangular base of unusually large schist blocks. The threshold block on the south side has indentations for door fittings. The tower was well sited to monitor movement of the mining activity and transport in the bay below.

Káto Chora, with its flat roofs, steps picked out with whitewash, and painted church.

Megálo Chorió

Megálo Chorió is a scattered community of a few houses to the right of the main road as it descends to the bay of Megálo Livádi. The epithet *megálo* ('large') in these names is a reference to their former size as, respectively, the settlement for the miners and principal loading port during the heyday of the mining period. **Megálo Livádi** is dominated by the Neoclassical 1880s Spiliazeza Mine Company headquarters. The abandoned industrial structures give the not unattractive bay a sombre atmosphere, compounded by the small monument at the north end of the shore which commemorates the 1916 protest (*see History, p. 215*), during which four miners and two gendarmes were killed.

South of Megálo Chorió a northward road passes the conspicuous late 5th-century BC **Asprópyrgos** ('White Tower'), its brilliant white stone surprising in a landscape of dark rock. The marble was quarried nearby. The cylindrical tower survives to over 4.5m on the east side, and preserves part of its finely constructed door frame on the south. The masonry shows some refinements, such as an almost imperceptible, progressive enlargement of the diameter of the two lowest courses.

The road continues to climb into the island's empty centre. A left turn leads north to the upland plateau of Sklavogiánnis, dotted with dovecotes. After 1.5km you come to the isolated 14th-century domed, cross-in-square church of **Ághios Ioánnis Pródromos**, with wall-paintings of the 17th century. Almost 2km further on, the panoramic summit church of **Aghía Thékla** is built over the base of an ancient tower.

THE NORTH OF THE ISLAND

The route to the north of the island from Livádi passes Chora and climbs for 8km, offering excellent views before descending to the village of **Panaghía**, named after the interesting 10th-century church at its centre (*key kept in the shop northeast of the church*). The two marble columns before the door suggest that the church had a different plan originally, and may have extended—perhaps with a portico—further west: two further, identical columns support arches inside. The wall-paintings, perhaps 13th-century, include a *Resurrection* on the north wall of the crossing. In the central apse is the marble throne and synthronon, suggesting that this may have been the seat of a bishop.

A pleasant walk leads from Panaghía to the 11th-century chapel of **Ághios Stéfanos** (*reached by the upper of two paths leading west from the village; after 15mins the church can be seen on a small rock outcrop below the path*).

The landscape around Panaghía bears the marks of centuries of meticulous cultivation: small stone dovecotes, threshing-floors, isolated rural habitations, ubiquitous terracing and abandoned villages. To the east, past the steeply sloping village of Galaní, is the whitewashed bulk of the 15th-century **monastery of the Taxiárches** (*generally closed, but the one surviving monk, Makarios, opens the monastery early in the morning and towards sunset every day*). A flight of stone steps now leads up to a low doorway, originally accessible by a wooden ladder: above it is an improvised machicolation. This and the fortress-like exterior were necessary precautions against pirate attack in such an isolated position. Most of the buildings are of the 17th or 18th centuries, as are the wall-paintings in the katholikon, including a graphic reminder of the torments of Hell. Most attractive is the wooden iconostasis, with beautiful icons by the 17th-century Cretan painter Immanouil Skordilis.

East of the monastery, the road turns south to **Kéntarchos**, or Kallítsos, with remains of a 1st-century AD vaulted Roman tomb, believed to be that of a centurion. Out to sea is the sharp outline of the islet of Seriphópoula, crowned by the base of a Hellenistic lookout tower.

Beyond Kéntarchos the road continues to the bay of **Psilí Ámmos** and its popular beach, and then back to Livádi; the last stretch, with its views of Chora, is especially scenic.

PRACTICAL INFORMATION

GETTING AROUND

There is a daily car ferry (4½ hrs) from Piraeus, supplemented in summer by a second, faster one (2½ hrs). Nearly all services continue to Siphnos and Milos.

WHERE TO STAY

The island's selection of accommodation is plentiful but unremarkable. More comfortable than most are the well-equipped **Studios Niovi**, overlooking the bay of Livádi from the east side (*open Easter–Oct; T: 22810 52564, www.studiosniovi.gr*). The **Hotel Naias** in the port is open all year (*T: 22810 51749*). Currently there are few options available in the more picturesque setting of Chora: a modern and comfortable solution on the edge of Chora is **Anatoli Studios** (*T: 22810 51510*).

WHERE TO EAT

Taverna Marditsa by the beach at Megálo Livádi produces some of the best and simplest home cooking on the island. One of the joys of Sériphos is its excellent amber-coloured wine: this can be sampled together with *mezédes* at the **Café Stou Stratou** in the picturesque *plateía* at Chora.

WALKING

Kalderímia are plentiful on Sériphos and make exploring the island on foot a pleasure. There are three principal routes leading out from Chora; one due north to Kéntarchos (2hrs) and the monastery of the Taxiárches (under 3hrs); one west to the area of Megálo Chorió and the Asprópyrgos (3hrs); and one south to Livádi (40–50mins). In some stretches they coincide with new roads.

SIPHNOS

Siphnos, famed in Classical antiquity for the wealth produced by its gold and silver mines, also prospered from sea commerce in the late medieval and early modern periods. The mementoes of that wealth—the marble-clad ancient fortifications and fascinating system of stone towers, the defensive Venetian kastro, and the mansions and churches of the last three centuries—along with its mixture of cultivated and wild landscapes, make Siphnos a delight to the eye. Small and less well known than many of its neighbours, Siphnos has a varied appeal which amply rewards a visit.

HISTORY OF SIPHNOS

There is some evidence that the gold and silver deposits of Siphnos were worked in prehistory. The island had Early and Late Bronze Age (Mycenaean) settlements, continuing throughout the Geometric period. In the Archaic period its precious metals brought Siphnos pre-eminent wealth, as attested by the rich treasury built by the Siphnians at Delphi in 526 BC. The lodes were soon exhausted, however, and the island's fall from prosperity was famous in antiquity. The fame of the island's riches attracted envy: Herodotus recounts that a detachment of disaffected Samian soldiers landed on the island c. 524 BC and extorted the hefty sum of a hundred talents from the citizens. Siphnos participated in the battles of Salamis and Plataea against the Persians in 480 and 479 BC, and the island was assessed to pay a substantial tribute within the Delian League. In the 5th and 4th centuries alone over 40 fortified towers were built here. In 153 BC, the island was attacked and devastated by forces from Crete.

After the capture of Constantinople by the Latins, the island was taken in 1207 by Doge Dandolo's nephew, Marco Sanudo, and incorporated into his Duchy of the Archipelago. It was recovered briefly for Byzantium in 1279, but was then annexed in 1307 by Gianuli da Corogna, a Knight Hospitaller of St John from what is now La Coruña in Spain. Da Corogna left the Hospitallers and governed the island as his personal domain. In the 15th century the title passed to the Bolognese Gozzadini family, who held the island, together with Kythnos, until 1617 when it finally fell to the Turks. In 1646 Siphnos gained important privileges from the Ottoman sultan, Ibrahim, leading to the rebuilding of many of its churches. Siphnos was liberated from Turkish rule in April 1821 and joined the Greek state.

KAMARES TO KASTRO

Kamáres, the attractive port of arrival on the west coast, takes its name from the 'chambers' of ancient mines in the cliffs by the sea. It is the centre of the island's ceramic industry. Siphnian pottery was praised in antiquity; today's workshops produce

a simple and unsophisticated ware, often with unusual forms, traditionally unglazed, but now with a number of decorations derived from Byzantine traditions.

From the well-protected bay with its lovely beach, a road climbs steadily to the more densely inhabited plateau of eastern Siphnos. Almost exactly 4km up the road from the harbour is the beautiful wayside **church of the Ághii Anárgyri**, built over a sacred spring reached down some steps through from the west corner of the church. Visible directly across the valley to the northeast is the silhouetted profile of the **Kambanarió ancient tower** (early 5th century BC). Of the many ancient towers of Siphnos (*see box opposite*), this is unusual for its decorated doorway.

THE ANCIENT TOWERS OF SIPHNOS

There are the remains of more ancient towers—55 of them—on Siphnos than on any other Aegean island. One quarter of those known so far in the Aegean are here. The island with the next largest concentration, Thasos (33 towers), was also known for mining precious metals in antiquity; thus fortified towers probably played an important role, in an age before bank vaults, in guarding the mines and in temporarily storing the valuable ore until it was coined, bartered or shipped elsewhere. It seems that the construction of the Siphnian towers began soon after the extortion of 100 talents from the islanders by Samian adventurers in c. 524 BC, and that during the 5th century a network of intercommunicating watchtowers around the island was designed to provide an early-warning system in case of attack. While this accounts for about 20 towers, the remaining 30 are harder to explain, especially as the mines were in decline. Perhaps some served as places of refuge in case of pirate raids.

The towers are round (a shape convenient for defence), and often had two or more floors; some had water cisterns in their base; all had well-designed doorways to accommodate robust doors with bolts. A great range of refinements in execution and material adds to their fascination. When they survive to an appreciable height, the towers are majestic, and they appeal through the simple beauty of their craftsmanship.

Further beyond Kamáres, the road rises to a T-junction (Stavrí). To the right and behind is Apollonía, merging into Exámbela to the south; to the left is Áno Petáli, merging with Artemónas to the north. Together they form a continuous settlement along the central ridge. Ancient Siphnos was at the site of Kastro below; another ancient settlement, Apollonia, must have been somewhere beneath today's Apollonía.

Apollonía

Apollonía has been the island capital since 1836. A small **museum of folklore** (*open daily in high season*) is in the small Plateía Iróōn just before the centre. It has a heterogeneous collection of island memorabilia: agricultural tools and weaponry, traditional unglazed pottery, textiles, embroideries, but especially traditional Siphnian women's costumes.

Above the square, the serpentine street which climbs to the south constitutes the heart of the town, lined with elegant 18th-century houses and a succession of interesting churches, nearly all of which are entered from the south side—a Siphnian peculiarity. A beautiful example is the first church on the left, the **church of the Nativity of Christ** from 1587, with its flat schist roof. Further up on the opposite side is the early 18th-century **church of the Tímios Stavrós**, and just beyond it, the **church of the Taxiárchis** (1650), its exterior embellished with coloured faïence dishes (north) and an

Iznik tile high up on the south side. Further up on the left is the 18th-century **church of Ághios Athanásios**, its vault supported on a central column. The two shallow apses opposite it belong to **Ághios Sostís**, the most interesting of them all, a late 16th-century building restored in 1768 by a Venetian patron who has left his coat of arms above the carved marble doorway. The interior has 18th-century wall-paintings. From this point, the street is dominated by the **church of Ághios Spyridón**, founded in 1700 and rebuilt in 1897. It possesses a beautiful 18th-century icon of the life of St Spyridon (right side).

Ano Petáli and Artemónas

From near to the junction of Stavrí, heading north into **Áno Petáli**, a narrow pedestrian street leads uphill towards a modern church of Ághios Ioánnis. The first church on the right, a 16th-century building restored in 1767, is dedicated to the Panaghía Ouranóphora ('Bearer of the Heavens') and to Ághios Geórgios, with a decorative entrance façade. The wide and luminous interior is decorated with 18th-century wall-paintings.

Artemónas, its centre pedestrianised, is best explored from its *plateía* by the church of Ághios Konstantínos (1km north of the junction in Apollonía). The area was favoured by the richer ship-owners and captains of Siphnos; there are a number of 19th-century houses, gardens, and a succession of graceful squares descending the hill, creating an ensemble of great beauty. The church of Ághios Konstantínos to the southeast of the *plateía* presents a typically Cycladic form. It is a three-aisled structure, massively buttressed on the north side, with a belfry and an erratic external staircase rising to the roof in the northwest corner. From the western end of the *plateía*, a marble-paved street climbs to the right, passing between two of the island's grandest Neoclassical residences. Further on is the church of the Panaghía of Ámmos (1788). At the centre of habitation is the church of the Dormition of the Virgin, known as the Panaghía Kóchi ('Virgin of the Niche'). The church has a curious design, broader than it is high.

KASTRO

From below Áno Petáli, a road descends past pretty **Káto Petáli**, and down a ravine scattered with chapels, water mills and a number of beautiful dovecotes. Below lies **Kastro**, on the summit of a promontory above the coast. This is the site of ancient Siphnos. The tiny harbour of Serália to the south retains the form given it in medieval times. The small church on the waterfront contains ancient column-fragments in its porch and a doorstep made from an ancient stele.

The approach road to Kastro cuts through the enceinte of 4th-century BC Hellenistic walls of schist slabs. This was a later, outer enceinte; the inner Archaic walls are visible higher up on the seaward side, and constructed in a quite different manner. The habitation of Kastro is concentrated within the elliptical form given it by the perimeter of the medieval fortified area, reusing ancient fortifications to the east and adding new ones to the west. The exterior aspect has since been altered by the addition of external balconies and windows. There were only five entrances. In the interior, living space is maximised by unusual, split-level public spaces and passageways beneath bridges connecting higher areas. Ancient spolia are used in many buildings, particularly in churches.

Major monuments of Kastro

Making a roughly anti-clockwise tour of the hill, the main monuments are as follows: the first important church encountered is that of the **Koímisis tis Theotókou** (1593). A large pagan altar stands in the sanctuary. Along the north wall are the icons from the former (17th-century) iconostasis. Set down below the street, and surmounted by a typical four-square belfry, is the double-aisled church of **Ághii Dimítrios and Aikateríni** (1653). Just above its north side is a truncated Hellenistic or Roman sarcophagus.

Beyond the church of the Taxiárchis, a narrow entrance leads up into the **inner enceinte**. Beyond the late 16th-century church of Ághios Nikólaos is the long **main street** of Kastro. In the open space in front of the church of Ághios Ioánnis, the limited space is ingeniously used: the square is raised up above storage areas beneath, forming to one side a sunken pathway under bridges, giving access into the houses opposite. To the sides of the winding street ahead, before and after the museum, are two more marble sarcophagi, both of later Roman date. Further fragments are strewn along the street as far as the church of the Panaghía Theosképasti (1631).

Further northwest, before the churches of Christós tou Kástrou and the Aghía Triáda, large sections of the **acropolis walls** (510–500 BC) come into view. Their building materials are of particular interest, reflecting the wealth of the ancient city: layers of white marble, on pink marble, on grey schist. They were altered substantially when the Venetian fortress walls were built on top, but the lowest courses remain largely untouched.

The summit of the hill is marked by the **church of the Panaghía Eleoúsa**, restored in 1635, with a number of beautiful icons in its interior. It probably stands on the site of a temple of Artemis. The pathway which runs around the exterior of Kastro on the north side offers good views of the ancient walls.

The Archaeological Museum

To the right-hand side of the main street, on the upper floor of a building, is the island's archaeological museum, awaiting enlargement and reorganisation (*open 8.30–3, daily except Mon; free*). The finest objects on display are a lugged Early Cycladic marble vase and a beautiful 6th-century BC head of a kouros in Parian marble.

NORTHERN SIPHNOS

North from the *plateía* at Artemónas, a single road heads into the empty north of the island. After 2.4km, a track left leads uphill to Ághios Ioánnis and the 18th-century **monastery of the Panaghía Mánganas**, a mixture of dignified elegance and rustic simplicity.

At Katavátos, a stone pathway heads north to the monastery church of **Ághios Sostís**, in a landscape of unforgiving rock above the shore (*allow over 1hr each way*). There were ancient silver mines around and above this promontory. The most visible evidence is on its southeast side. In the tunnels the marks of the pick and chisel can still be seen as well as the niches for lamps. The hollows roughly excavated in the rocks are evidence of on-site smelting. A few of the shafts are close to water-level, which has given rise to the tradition related by Pausanias that Apollo flooded the mines of Siphnos in retribution when the Siphnian tribute to Delphi ceased to be paid as fully as before.

Ághios Nikítas and Profítis Ilías Troulakíou

On the top of the long ridge of mountain west of Ághios Sostís, appositely called Selládi ('saddle'), are the remains of an ancient fortress-acropolis, marked today by the church of **Ághios Nikítas** (*a small, easily-missed sign indicates the path up from the main road, from a point just west of the church of Ághios Ioánnis at Chóni. Allow at least 50mins each way*). Ághios Nikítas, one of two such sites here, guards the northern and eastern approaches to the island; Profítis Ilías (*see below*) those from the west. Both sites are marked by a dense quantity of fallen limestone masonry. Neither was an acropolis in the sense of a large, habitable place of refuge, but rather a fortified complex of buildings for the security of the land and operations around. The humble church of Ághios Nikítas, constructed from bits of ancient masonry, sits at the southeast corner of an easily discernible rectangular terrace in ancient, probably Archaic, masonry. Finds from Mycenaean times suggest a considerably earlier presence here.

A similar, but less well-defined, Archaic fortification lies to the southwest, on the summit of **Profítis Ilías Troulakíou** (450m), overlooking the bay of Kamáres from the edge of a precipice (*a track leads south by the bend below Trouláki and climbs for 600m, after which a 20-min climb to the right leads through dwarf pines to the summit*). Before reaching the church, the path climbs through a remarkable quantity of fallen masonry. Viewed from above, the outline of two quadrilateral corner towers can be made out. The line of the wall on the east side is visible: this and the north were the only sides that needed fortification, as natural scarps protected the south and west. The ruins of a later, Hellenistic, defensive structure in ashlar masonry perch on the vertiginous slope below.

The far north

Beyond Trouláki (which has a pleasant taverna) lies the northern point of the island, overlooked by no less than six **ancient towers**, none now surviving to more than a few courses of masonry. Their density underscores the importance of protecting the harbours at Vourlídia and Cherónisos. Exposed on the summit of the promontory to the north of Cherónisos (*15mins on foot*) is the small hermitage monastery of Ághios Geórgios. Slightly to the east, at the highest point, is the circular outline of the island's northernmost ancient watchtower, standing only to two courses of masonry between rocks, sea and sky. **Cherónisos** is still a centre of pottery-making.

SOUTHWEST SIPHNOS

From Apollonía it is possible to climb to the **monastery of Profítis Ilías** on the island's highest summit (682m) in a little over 90mins (*a well-made path leaves from the south loop of Apollonía's ring-road, 200m north of the junction for Vathý*). The mid-17th-century structure, built like a fortress, surrounds a large, domed katholikon, its walls rising from the highest rock outcrop on the island. To the west along the ridge and down the northwest slope of the mountain were a number of the island's **ancient mines**; over a dozen **ancient watchtowers** are on the seaward slopes.

AGHIOS ANDREAS

The road for Vathý, branching off southwards from the south loop of the Apollonía ring-road, passes below the hill of Ághios Andréas; the 19th-century church of Ághios Andréas is visible on its summit (*800m from the junction, a footpath is signed from the road; the site is a 20-min climb up the east side of the hill*). On the summit, to the west of the church, is a Mycenaean citadel, overlooking the whole cultivable plateau. Much of its interest lies in the variety of fortifications. The site, abandoned in the 12th century BC, was re-inhabited in the 8th century BC, and continued to be so through to Hellenistic times.

AGHIOS ANDREAS

A Outer walls
B Southwest entrance
C Inner walls
D Bastions
E Street
F Mycenaean houses
G Geometric buildings
H ?Place of cult

Ag. Andreas Church

N

0   20 m

The site

The site is best viewed from below the south side of the impressive ring of 12th-century BC **outer walls (A)**, which would have been surmounted by a mud-brick superstructure supported by vertical posts, the indentations for which are visible. The limestone was quarried from immediately in front of the walls. The main entrance through the walls was in the southeast corner, but it is more instructive at first to enter by the subsidiary entrance to the southwest **(B)**. Inside, it becomes clear that the walls in fact consist of a double ring, the one seen from outside, and an older ring with bastions immediately inside it. The **inner walls (C)** date from the 13th century BC and are constructed with the characteristic Cyclopean boulders of that period. Rectangular stonework dating from the Classical Age directly ahead indicates later use. The space between the Mycenaean walls originally constituted a defensive ditch. Nine square **bastions (D)** strengthened the inner enceinte; the one in the northwest corner, at the most vulnerable point, was enlarged in the second phase and protrudes from the outer walls.

Inside the south entrance is a **street (E)** with houses to either side, some with built hearths (to right), others with large beautiful threshold blocks mostly from the Archaic and Classical periods. The remains of **Mycenaean houses (F)** have been uncovered in the middle of the west side, just inside the walls; to the north, again just inside the walls, are the remains of **Geometric buildings (G)** of the 8th century BC. At the highest, northeast corner are foundations of large buildings, perhaps a **place of cult (H)**. Just the south of this, below the modern custodian's hut, is a large water cistern, part cut from the rock, part constructed.

Vathý

South of Ághios Andréas, past springs at the church of the Taxiárchis Mersínis, the road leads southwest across the interior of the island, until it descends in a couple of panoramic sweeps to the **bay of Vathý**, a deep, naturally protected, elliptical cove, with a long and gently sloping sandy beach, framed by hills and headlands. The small fishing village, grouped around the attractive, twin-domed church of the Taxiárchis, built on the edge of the shore, was until recently only accessible by boat. It has inevitably been transformed by the building of the asphalt road, and now boasts a luxury hotel and a rising number of holiday homes, but it remains nonetheless a tranquil place of scenic beauty.

SOUTHEAST SIPHNOS

Exámbela, almost contiguous with Apollonía, has some fine Neoclassical buildings. At the southern extremity of the village, near the church of Ághios Dimítrios, is one of the island's best-preserved ancient towers, known as the Mávros Pýrgos, 'Black Tower', because of the dark green schist used. It is a 5th-century BC structure, large in diameter (c. 11m), and standing to a height of nearly 6m, with 16 surviving courses of varying width, as well as areas of interlocking polygonal masonry. Its refinements include a protruding base, bevelled joints in the lower courses changing to flush joints above; and an arched entrance.

Moní Vrysianís and Fáros

Beyond Exámbela to the right beyond the bridge over a torrent is the 17th-century **monastery of the Panaghía Vrysianís**. As its name ('of the fountain') implies, it was founded beside one of the island's strongest springs. The katholikon, dedicated to the Nativity of the Virgin, is of classic 17th-century inscribed-cross form. The refectory, kitchens and two floors of cells surround it, in a tight, fortified space: there is a small exhibition room of ecclesiastical objects and manuscripts. The delight of the building is its long entranceway, a deep, finely-proportioned gallery whose length is rhythmically broken by a series of graceful tapered arches which spring from semi-embedded columns and capitals. The ceiling is raftered with cypress and the floor laid with pale flagstones. It is an architectural space of great beauty and dignity.

After the Moní Vrysianís, by the electricity-generating station, a left turn descends to the coast at the small fishing village of **Fáros**. To the south of Fáros is the sandy, tamarisk-shaded **bay of Fasoloú**, which is ideal for swimming.

The White Tower and Platýs Gialós

South of the Panaghía Vrysianís is another monastery, the 19th-century **Panghía tou Vounoú** (*open daily in summer, 11–2*), with ancient columns in the katholikon. Beyond it, a track leads from the road to the island's earliest and most magnificent ancient tower, the **Áspros Pýrgos** (also Asprópyrgos, or 'White Tower'). This was a multi-purpose tower and has many interesting features still visible *in situ*.

The tower overlooks ancient (?)gold and silver mines immediately to the south and east, as well as the area's coasts and harbours. It has an uninterrupted sight-line to the acropolis of Ághios Andréas. Its diameter exceeds 13m. The material and method of construction, with large, regular and trapezoidal blocks, suggest a date c. 500 BC. The white marble, making the tower useful as a landmark, may be from Paros. The tower's special features include an inner lining in smaller stone, a corbelled staircase, and a substantial cistern beneath the floor. A carefully crafted stone olive-press block suggests an agricultural use, perhaps in a later phase. The inner walls, subdividing the interior into three areas, may also be later. Of particular note is the doorway on the southeast, cut and shaped for the fitting and locking of the door: it has two large, protruding, vertical stone rings on the inside to hold a transom for blocking the door.

Just above the White Tower, a branch road to the east leads to the shore, with good views of the picturesque 17th-century monastery of the **Panaghía Chrysopigí**, on a tongue of rock protruding from the shore. North of it is the delightful sand beach of Apokoftó (with taverna).

The main road ends at the long strand of **Platýs Gialós**, the island's most developed tourist resort. Beyond are scenic walks south to the tip of the island.

Visible from the road to Platýs Gialós is the uninhabited **island of Kitrianí** (*excur-*

sions sometimes offered from Kamáres in summer). Its beautiful domed Byzantine chapel of the Panaghía Kitrianí, or Kyprianí, may date from as early as the 11th century

PRACTICAL INFORMATION

GETTING AROUND

There is a (morning) car ferry (5½ hrs) from Piraeus, daily in summer, five times a week in winter, supplemented by two evening services per week. In summer only, an average of two high-speed services make the journey from Piraeus in just under 3hrs.

WHERE TO STAY

Siphnos has a wide range of types of accommodation: international luxury class, represented by the **Elies Resort** at Vathý (*T: 22840 34000, www.eliesresorts.com*); boutique hotels, represented by **Patriarca**, in the heart of Apollonía (*T: 22840 32400, www.patriarca.gr*); the pleasant and unpretentious **Petali Hotel**, in the Áno Petáli quarter of Apollonía (*T: 22840 33024, www.hotelpetali.gr*); and the convenient and inexpensive **Morpheas Apartments**, by the beach at Kamáres, with free WiFi and helpful owners (*T: 22840 33615, www.morpheas.gr*). A pleasing solution combining aspects of all of the above is **Bellavista**

Windmill, just to the east of Artemónas, overlooking Kastro in the distance: it offers a variety of studio rooms and mini-apartments, terraces, a pool and a friendly welcome.

WHERE TO EAT

The family taverna **To Kyma**, at Trouláki by the road to Cherónisos, is one of the most delightful and unpretentious places to eat in the Western Cyclades, both for its stunning sunset view and simple home cooking. Perhaps the best selection of local, traditional dishes is to be had at **Liotrivi** by the entrance into Artemónas. For imaginative 'fusion' fare, **Nerantzi**, on the Apollonía–Exámbela road, is a pleasant and interesting alternative.

FURTHER READING

Siphnos: Ancient Towers B.C., by Norman Ashton (Athens, 1991) is a good study and definitive descriptive catalogue of the island's 55 ancient towers.

MILOS

The character of Milos is determined by its volcanic origins: the whole island is arranged around a flooded crater; there are numerous hot springs; and much of the landscape consists of strangely shaped and coloured rocks. Many of its volcanic minerals have been mined here since antiquity, among them obsidian, first exported from Milos in the Stone Age. The island's ancient archaeology is of great importance, with one of the richest Bronze Age settlements in the Aegean at Phylakopí on the north coast, and the remains of the ancient city of Melos overlooking the entrance to the island's magnificent central caldera-bay. In the area of Melos' Hellenistic gymnasium was unearthed what was to become one of the most famous statues of antiquity, the *Venus de Milo*. Milos also boasts the most extensive Early Christian catacombs in Greece. Milos is famous for the beauty and number of its beaches, and many of its volcanic coastal rock formations offer opportunities to swim.

HISTORY OF MILOS

Obsidian from Milos appears on mainland sites as early as 20,000 years ago, but in those Palaeolithic times the island probably only received occasional human visits to collect the precious material. By the Neolithic, in the 6th millennium BC, more regular settlement and seaborne trade are first attested. Early Bronze Age cemeteries show that Milos was widely and quite densely populated at that time. From 2200 BC, habitation concentrates at Phylakopí on the north coast, which became an important trading centre with Minoan, and later Mycenaean, connections, but was abandoned in the 11th century BC.

Both Herodotus and Thucydides say that the early historic settlers were Dorians from Laconia, who arrived between 1000 and 900 BC. Their city was at Trypití, above Klíma, where cemeteries of the 9th and 8th centuries BC show considerable wealth. Milos was one of only three islands that declined to pay homage to the Persian king Darius, and in 480 BC it contributed two ships to the Greek fleet at Salamis. Like Thera, another Laconian colony, the island stayed out of the Delian League. The island remained independent and neutral until the Peloponnesian War, when it leaned towards Sparta, with whom it had obvious cultural and historical links. After a failed attempt to take the island in 426 BC, Athens determined to coerce it into submission, sending an embassy in 416 BC, whose proposals and threats are vividly recorded by Thucydides in the 'Melian Dialogue'. The Melians declined to submit, were besieged by Athens shortly afterwards, and forced to surrender: the men were executed, the women and children enslaved, and the island colonised by 500 Athenian cleruchs. In 405 BC, the Spartans expelled the cleruchs and resettled the island with what remained of its former inhabitants.

After the Battle of Chaironeia in 338 BC, the island was under Macedonian rule. Subsequently under Roman dominion, it regained stability and considerable prosperity from trading its minerals. Milos flourished in the Early Christian period, being

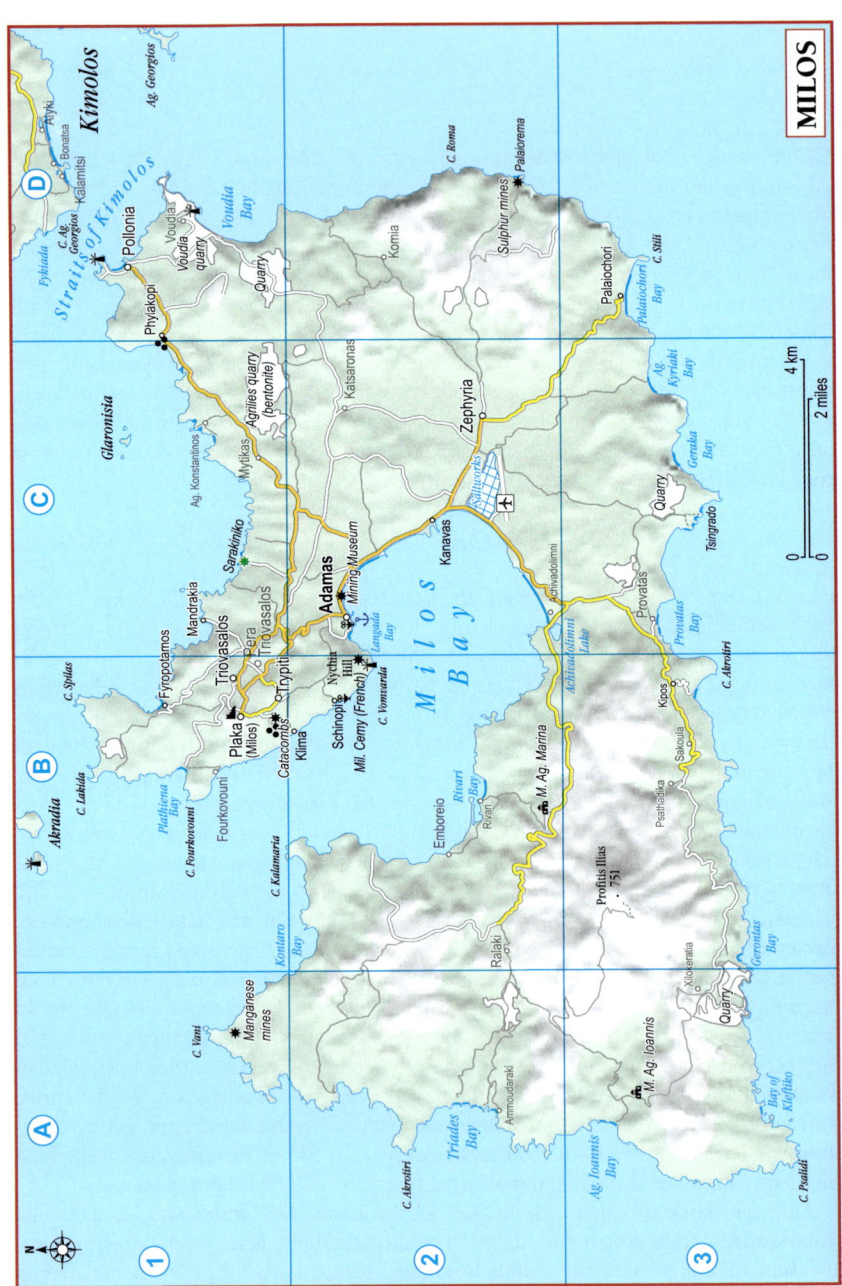

MILOS

represented by its own bishop at the Council of Nicaea in 325. The city was eventually destroyed by a succession of earthquakes in the 6th and 7th centuries, after which the island may have been briefly abandoned.

In 1207 Milos was incorporated into the Duchy of Naxos by Marco Sanudo. A pro-Byzantium revolt against Latin rule in 1261 was quickly put down by Marco Sanudo II. In 1316 the island was raided by a Catalan fleet. Otherwise, the island remained under direct or indirect Venetian control until it came under Turkish rule in 1566. There followed a brief and curious period of independence from 1675 to 1678, when a local corsair, Ioannis (or Georgios) Kapsis, was acclaimed as King of Milos—an act of defiance which earned him capture and execution in Istanbul.

In 1767 the islanders abandoned their capital of Zephyría, either because of a malaria outbreak or because an increase in volcanic activity had caused the escape of noxious gases. They resettled at today's Pláka and Trypití. During the Russo-Turkish War of 1771–74, the island was taken by the Russian forces of Count Orlov. After making an important contribution in the War of Greek Independence in 1821, Milos joined the Greek state in 1830.

In 1862 the sulphur mines at Palaiórema opened, followed in 1890 by the manganese mines at Cape Váni; in 1899 industrial exploitation of kaolin deposits began; in 1934 quarries of baryte opened, in 1952 of bentonite, in 1957 of perlite and in 1984 of pozzolana. Only the first two have since ceased production.

ADAMAS & ENVIRONS

Adámas (also called Adámata), the modern harbour of Milos (*map p. 230, C2*), was founded in the 19th century by Cretan refugees. It is located on the northeast of Milos Bay, one of the largest and safest harbours in the Aegean. Nearly completely enclosed, with a narrow exit to the north, the bay is a flooded volcanic caldera.

Exploring Adámas

The church of **Aghía Triáda**, a short distance from the waterfront, also functions as an ecclesiastical museum. The church dates to the 13th or 14th century and is of unusual shape: triple-aisled, with a central, transverse-vaulted elevation instead of a dome. Byzantine spolia are on display in the courtyard outside; the interior holds mostly Cretan icons, chiefly of the 17th century, showing a fusion with Venetian elements: the works of Antonios and Immanouil Skordilis, who created a workshop on Milos, are the most notable. Earlier icons include an exquisite 14th-century *Deposition*.

The large church further up the hill, dedicated to the **Koímisis and Ághios Charálambos** (1870), contains icons and a beautiful iconostasis taken from the churches of Chora (Zephyría) when it was abandoned as the island's capital in the 1770s.

Opposite a point about 50m west of the embarkation mole, a doorway in the natural wall of rock gives access to the **Lákkos thermal springs** (*open July–Oct daily except Sun, 7–11am*). The waters are mentioned by Hippocrates as a place where patients from as far away as Athens came for the cure of dermatological conditions. Other hot waters rise among the rocks and in the water close to the tiny inlet of **Schinopí**, 2km west of Adámas along the shore. The walk there rounds the small promontory of Vomvárda, with a French Military Cemetery and monument to soldiers of the Crimean War. Beyond, the path enters an area of vulcanological interest: just offshore is the 50m thick **lava apron** on the sea-bed known as the Bombarda Submarine Dome. The path itself passes a shallow pool active with bubbling gas and a brightly coloured gash or vent in the cliff above, referred to locally as the 'volcano'. It is on the hill above this point that the island's principal obsidian deposits are to be found.

Nýchia Hill

The hill of Nýchia can be approached by track either from the northwestern corner of Adámas, behind Langáda Bay, or south from Trypití and Pláka. Halfway between Adámas and Trypití, on top of the hill, a rough track leads off to the southwest. Just below the highest point, the ground is covered with small pieces of black, shiny obsidian. After about 200m, there are areas of *débitage*, or scrap heaps, from Neolithic workshops; in other areas, there are blocks of larger dimensions.

OBSIDIAN

Obsidian is a natural volcanic glass, formed by the rapid cooling of molten rock. Milos is not the only source of the material in the Aegean, but it is the richest and its obsidian is the purest. The Milos deposits are also the most accessible: mining is not required, the material, which occurs in pieces of up to a metre, can simply be picked off the ground.

Before the advent of metal, obsidian provided the best material for sharp cutting tools. It was already being brought from Milos to the mainland in early prehistory (*see History, p. 229*) and became an important traded commodity around the Aegean in the Neolithic and Bronze Ages.

The interesting Mining Museum of Milos, on the shore road 1km east of Adámas (*open daily in summer 9–2 & 6–9; late Sept–late June open mornings only Tues–Sat*), focuses on the geology of the island and the history of mining on it.

PLAKA

The main road north from Adámas leads to the contiguous settlements of Trypití, Pláka and Triovásalos (*map p. 230, B1*). Immediately before the road begins to wind steeply upwards, an unmade road to the right leads to a house, after 70m, where there are the **medicinal hot springs**. Their temperature—85°C—might explain their name, 'Bánia tou Chárou', which means the 'Baths of Death'. Inside, the proprietress prepares a tub in which the hot sulphurous water is mixed with cool water to a tolerable temperature.

The main road climbs onto a plateau and after 4km reaches the **centre of Pláka** (*map p. 230, B1*), officially called Milos, the island's capital since 1767 (*see History, p. 231*). The town is simple and unaffected, with a network of delightful streets and wide views, a few fine stone houses of the 19th century, and some Neoclassical buildings on the perimeter. Many of the houses on the western side of Pláka, with good views over the entrance to the harbour, were built by the boat-pilots for whom Milos was renowned.

The Archaeological Museum

The Milos Archaeological Museum stands above the main square, in a fine Neoclassical building with wide views from its portico (*open 8.30–3.30, daily except Mon*). The small collection is unusually rich, with emphasis on finds from Phylakopí (*see p. 236*).

Room 1 displays early prehistoric finds, including **obsidian tools** and pottery. Room II focuses on the Bronze Age, with displays including an Early Cycladic house model, and much pottery from Phylakopí, among it the mid-14th century BC cult figure known as the *Lady of Phylakopi*, as well as many rhyta in the shape of animals. Room III is dedicated to historical periods, and displays chiefly sculpture, with several interesting 6th-century BC **inscriptions** in the 21-letter **Melian (Doric) alphabet**, different from the usual Greek letters in some respects. Room IV displays later pottery.

The Folklore Museum and Church of the Rosary

Plaka's small well-displayed **Folklore Museum** (*open 10–2 daily in July and Aug*) is at the western edge of the habitation near the church of the **Panaghía Korfiátissa** (1910), which has a fine carved, painted and gilded 18th-century epitaphios in a case on the north side of the entrance. Just to its north is the older Roman Catholic **Church of the Rosary**, referred to as the Katholikí (1823). By the entrance is the canopied, monumental grave of the wife of Louis Brest, the French vice-consul to Milos who removed the *Venus de Milo* to Paris (*see overleaf*). It was Brest who had the church built.

The Kastro

Overlooking Pláka from the north side are the remains of the 13th-century Venetian kastro, enlarged and modified in the 16th century. It incorporates ancient masonry, suggesting that the summit may have been fortified. The path up from Pláka passes a number of scattered churches and houses, old and recent; a number of the older, abandoned houses still preserve carved door frames in local perlite stone, while the churches re-use ancient spolia. The largest is the 14th-century domed Panaghía Thalassítra, restored in the 17th century. The view from the summit encompasses the whole island.

THE CATACOMBS & ANCIENT MELOS

Trypití, the southern extension of Pláka, winds attractively along a ridge overlooking the entrance into Milos Bay. Its name, meaning 'perforated', refers to the extensive network of Early Christian catacombs just to the southwest (*signposted; generally open 8.30–1, daily except Mon; T: 6978 323050*). They are primarily from the 3rd and 4th centuries AD, but the central burial may be earlier. There are five main tunnels, totalling 185m; but only the main one can currently be visited.

These are the most extensive catacombs known in Greece. The large 'sarcophagus' of rock in the centre of the main tunnel probably represents the original burial and the initial nucleus of the complex. The tunnels are cut from a soft, volcanic tufa. The size of the loculi is uniform, their borders often picked out in red; there are inscriptions (scarcely visible) and later graffiti. Areas of the walls, in particular in the arcosolia, show evidence of having been rendered with plaster and painted with abstract designs. Individual catacomb burials, of which there are over 120 here, were originally lit by oil lamps. The original entrance would have been much smaller and could be closed with a stone. By the time the catacombs were studied in the 1840s, they had already been robbed.

Ancient Melos

The ancient city spread around the hill of Profítis Ilías. The remains can be explored by returning up the hill as far as the first sharp bend and taking the track to the left before it. Immediately after turning off the paved road, you are confronted by an impressive **circular bastion** and a stretch of ancient **fortification wall**. The walls are of Archaic or Classical polygonal masonry; the tower, in isodomic masonry, is a Hellenistic addition, designed to strengthen the East Gate, which stood across the path ahead. In the valley to the left was the **stadium**, marked by a long stretch of retaining wall in polygonal masonry (5th century BC) on its south side (*best seen from below*). A **gymnasium** stood above it, immediately below the path to the left. It was here that the *Venus de Milo*, now in the Louvre (copy in Pláka museum) was unearthed in 1820 at the insistence of a young French military officer, Olivier Voutier: the exact spot inside the gymnasium is marked.

The best preserved remains are those of the ancient **theatre**, reached by continuing 200m further along the path. Dating from after the 2nd century BC, it is set in a deep natural cavity, shaped and faced with Parian marble, looking south across the bay. Only the retaining walls at either extremity of the cavea needed to be built up: they are constructed in isodomic masonry of andesite blocks. The corners of the entrance are faced in contrasting white Parian marble. The semicircular orchestra is well below the level of the first of the eight remaining rows of marble seats in the cavea, indicating its use for entertainment spectacles typical of Roman taste. The skene is now in ruins: its fragments in the orchestra indicate an elaborate structure.

Turning back from the theatre to the East Gate, shortly before the point where the *Venus de Milo* was found, a track back to the left leads to a small plateau above the theatre. In the centre of the area, between column stumps, is a small, cruciform **Early Christian baptismal pool**, with some marble revetment still in place. Nothing remains of the baptistery or the basilica to which it must have belonged. It is generally believed that this open, raised area was occupied in antiquity by the city's agorá, where the famous 'Melian Dialogue' related by Thucydides took place (*see History, p. 229*).

Continuing further round to the right (north), the land drops slightly into a dip. In its centre, a rectangle of collapsed stone, with isodomic walls protruding at points, marks the podium of a substantial **Hellenistic temple**.

THE VENUS DE MILO

The Venus—or Aphrodite—of Milos was found accidentally in April 1820 by a local farmer: he was observed by chance by a young ensign, Olivier Voutier, from a French warship which had made a stop at Milos, and who had decided to spend the day with some comrades trying to dig up something of interest among the ruins of the ancient city. Voutier says that he encouraged and cajoled the farmer to continue digging until the whole statue had been unearthed in three principal pieces. It is possible that the sculpture had narrowly escaped being consigned to a furnace for making mortar in the early Byzantine period. Miraculously the piece still possessed—though partially fractured—its original head. Voutier brought the French vice-consul, Louis Brest, to see the statue, but was prevented from taking it away by the captain of his ship, who would not load it. The French ambassador in Constantinople was eventually prevailed upon to purchase the piece for France, and in the following year (1821) it travelled to Toulon and then to Paris, and was presented to the king. In the same year, Voutier resigned from the French navy and joined Greek insurgents, under the command of Alexander Ypsilantis, in the nascent Greek War of Independence.

A fragment of a statue-base found nearby, almost certainly belonging to the sculpture, carried the signature of the artist, a certain '[Alex]andros of Antioch on the Meander': this base was later conveniently lost, perhaps in order to allow full scope to those who wished to believe the Venus might be a work of the golden ages of Pheidias or of Praxiteles. Although consciously Classical in style, both the method of carving and the complex spiral of the design, which is made to seem effortlessly natural, date the piece to the late 2nd century BC. The Venus may originally have stood in a niche, gathering her falling drapery with her right hand and holding an apple in her left. Others have imagined her admiring her own reflection in a polished shield of Ares. A larger than life-size Poseidon holding a trident, now in the Archaeological Museum in Athens and dating from exactly the same period, was found lower down the hill at Klíma in 1877.

Klíma, Triovásalos and the north coast harbour

From the southeastern end of Trypití, a road leads steeply down to the waterside at **Klíma** (*map p. 230, B2*), also reached by a path from below the ancient theatre. This half-hidden haven at the entrance to the bay of Milos functioned as the ancient port. Today it is a picturesque front of boat-houses of all colours, with balconied upper floors.

The wind-eroded kaolin peaks of Sarakíniko Bay.

To the east of Pláka and Trypití, virtually contiguous with them, are **Triovásalos** and Péra Triovásalos. The road northwest leads to **Fyropótamos**, 2.5km along, a small harbour set below white perlite and kaolinite cliffs, creating an effect of white shot through with pink, mauve, magenta and orange. Similar colour effects can be seen at **Mandrákia**, slightly to the east; but perhaps the most bizarre landscape of all is at **Sarakíniko Bay** (*map p. 230, C1*), 4km east of Triovásalos, where the earth is of purest white kaolin, allowing virtually no vegetation to gain any purchase, leaving the smooth slopes open to be eroded by wind and water.

PHYLAKOPI & THE EAST OF THE ISLAND

At the head of a shallow, fertile valley, the extensive ruins of **Phylakopí** stand on a coastal bluff (*see below*). Beyond it, the main road descends to **Pollónia** (*map p. 230, D1*), an attractive harbour and embarkation point for ferry-crossings to Kímolos, which fills the horizon ahead. By arrangement, it is possible to make an excursion to the uninhabited island of Polýaigos and its splendid beaches (*see p. 243*).

PHYLAKOPI

The site of Phylakopí (*map p. 230, C1–D1*) was first examined by the British School in 1896–99, then again in 1911, and in 1974–77. The remains of three successive Bronze Age cities were discovered. In the 2nd millennium BC, this was one of the most important centres in the Aegean, based on the trade of obsidian. Its importance today lies in what it has revealed of the organisation of Bronze Age cities and, above all, of their cult.

HISTORY OF PHYLAKOPI

The first organised settlement with its cemetery, Phylakopi I, dates from 2300–2000 BC. The succeeding centuries show a rapid enlargement of trading links, leading to the development of Phylakopi II (2000–1600 BC), the first real 'city' here, characterised by a refinement of pottery technology as well as increasing imports from Crete and mainland Greece. Phylakopi II appears to have had no fortifications; around 1600 BC it was destroyed by fire, probably in an attack. It was rebuilt with sturdy fortification walls which vary between 3m and 6m in thickness. This is Phylakopi III (1600–1400 BC): a city on a plan of parallel streets and rectangular dwellings, some decorated with wall-paintings. The city was again destroyed c. 1400 BC, perhaps by Mycenaean expansion into the area. Phylakopi IV (1400–1100 BC) represents the final phase. The fortifications were enlarged and reinforced, and a notable Mycenaean influence, seen both in the pottery and in the architecture, replaces the earlier Minoan influence. There is evidence of commercial links throughout and beyond the Aegean. The city was finally abandoned at the end of the 12th century BC, at the time of the collapse of Mycenaean civilisation.

Context and setting

Rainfall was higher than at present in the Bronze Age and would therefore have made the area to the south of Phylakopí substantially more fertile: sea levels were also higher, making the harbours of the town deeper and more manageable. The sea, in fact, may have penetrated and encircled the town more on the east side, increasing its defensibility. This is important because the choice of site is otherwise hard to explain: it is far from the two main obsidian deposits on the island and stands on a coast exposed to the prevailing north winds, making outwards navigation from the harbour much more difficult in certain seasons. The port was of primary importance since the city existed and grew on trade, mostly exporting obsidian and clays. The first settlers, in the mid-3rd millennium BC, had commercial contacts with other centres of the Keros-Syros Culture.

The site

Marine erosion has carried away about half the site. Entering from the south, the imposing scale of the **walls**, of two faces constructed in multicoloured stone blocks with a rubble fill between, stretch well-preserved to the left. Several bastions are visible. Close to the wall on the right is the **Mycenaean shrine**. It evolved through the 14th and 13th centuries BC, consisting of two wings separated by a paved court with a stone bench and standing stone. This is where the *Lady of Phylakopi* was discovered (*see p. 233*).

On site it is often difficult to pick out the rectangular street plan of the settlement; clearly visible on the ground, however, is the plan of the Mycenaean-inspired **megaron**, which lies near the edge of the site to the northeast, recognisable by its massive threshold-block. To the side and in the interior are other massive construction elements, possibly door jambs. The most unusual architectural elements at Phylakopí are natural hexagonal basalt columns from the Glaronísia islets a short distance out to sea.

ZEPHYRÍA & THE EAST

At **Kánavas**, 3.5km south of Adámas along the shore road, directly opposite the electricity generating station, geothermic springs rise on the beach and under the water. Immediately beyond, a left branch leads inland to **Zephyría**.

Zephyría

Zephyría (*map p. 230, C2*), sometimes still called Chora, was the island's capital until 1776. In 1700, it had 5,000 inhabitants and 17 churches; today it is a quiet, underpopulated village centred around the attractive **double church of the Panaghía Portianí and Ághios Charálambos** (rebuilt in the 17th century), with a pleasing configuration of long, low vaults, octagonal drums and cupolas, emphatically pedimented windows, simple marble door frames and the low arches of the medieval *porta* to the west. The paintings are recent, except for areas of 17th-century work on the south wall. The icons of *St John* and of the *Virgin and Child* are fine examples of 17th-century local work.

Palaiochóri and Palaiórema

Southeast from Zephyría the road continues to the south coast at **Palaiochóri** (*map p. 230, D3*), a beachside settlement backed by low cliffs. There is a fumarole with visibly escaping steam to the right-hand side as the road descends; others are concentrated around the far end of the second bay to the west.

A road signed 'Θεορύχεια' leaves Zephyría to the east, leading to the sulphur mines at **Palaiórema** (*map p. 230, D2*), used in antiquity and more recently. Unpaved roads off it lead through a mostly deserted landscape with the occasional chapel or village. Set between multicoloured cliffs below the sulphur mines is a beautiful sandy cove.

THE WEST OF THE ISLAND

The western half of Milos is rugged, mountainous and largely deserted. It is reached by the coast road from Adámas, which passes the airport and reaches a junction near the **lake of Achivadolímni** (*map p. 230, C2*). Further west, a road to the right leads to the 17th-century monastery of **Aghía Marína** (*map p. 230, B2*), in a panoramic position overlooking at the bay of Milos. Rivári Bay, just beyond the monastery, has beautiful places to swim. Further beyond, unpaved roads lead to various mines, and the northwestern point of the island at **Cape Váni** (*map p. 230, A1*).

Kípos and the far west

The southern turn from Achivadolímni leads to **Kípos** (*map p. 230, B3*), with the church of the Panaghía tou Kípou, built in 1911 on the site of a 5th-century Early Christian basilica, remains of which can be seen to its south. Propped against the west wall of the interior are the marble slabs of the Early Byzantine sanctuary screen, which are reused pagan sarcophagus slabs. The greatest surprise lies in the apse of the church, where the tiny 5th-century cruciform baptismal pool has been preserved.

Further west, the (unpaved) road leads along the south coast with views of a mesmerising succession of white promontories behind and the extraordinary spires of volcanic earth off the coast in the bay of Kleftikó ahead. It leads to the remote and solitary **monastery of Ághios Ioánnis Theológos** (*map p. 230, A3*) on the wild slopes of Mt Profítis Ilías and above a bay of the same name. It is a 16th-century foundation, but has been enlarged and renovated in recent times.

PRACTICAL INFORMATION

GETTING AROUND

There are two 40-min flights from Athens to Milos daily. The airport is 4.5km from Adámas. A daily car ferry (8hrs) leaves from Piraeus each morning, supplemented in summer by high-speed connections (4½ hrs). There are three weekly connections with Santorini. Between Pollónia (northeast Milos) and Kímolos, there are 5–6 ferry crossings (25mins) per day.

WHERE TO STAY

In Adámas, **Giannis Apartments** are pleasant and quiet (*T: 22870 22204; www.giannisapartments.gr*). Among the alleyways of Pláka are **Archondoula Studios** (*T: 22870 23820*) and **Betty's Studios** (*T: 22870 21538*), both with good views. At Pollónia, the **Kostantakis Farm** offers comfortable studios, as well as wine and other produce (*T: 22870 41357; www.kostantakis.gr*). The most unusual solution of all is in the converted **Marketos Windmill** on the ridge at Trypití (*T: 22870 22147*).

WHERE TO EAT

To Petrino in Zephyría is a trustworthy place for simple Greek cooking. The **Mezedopoleion Phokas** in Pláka, and **Zygos** in Adámas are also reliable. For good fish, there is **Pelagos**, the easternmost taverna on the beach at Palaiochóri. The speciality of the tavernas here is a succulent lamb dish, slow-cooked in terracotta vessels on the geothermically heated sand of the beach outside.

FURTHER READING

An Island Polity, the Archaeology of Exploitation in Melos, ed. Colin Renfrew and Malcolm Wagstaff, Cambridge 1982. *Disarmed: The Story of the Venus de Milo*, by Gregory Curtis, Vintage Press, 2004. The Australian geologist Ian Plimer, famous for his sceptical view of anthropogenic global warming, has written *Milos Geologic History*, KOAN Publishing House, Athens, 2000. Thucydides' *Peloponnesian War* (*V, 84–116*) is relevant to Milos.

KIMOLOS

Kímolos is a delightful island: peaceful, unpretentious and full of striking land-scapes. It forms part of the Aegean Volcanic Arc, which sweeps from the Argo-Saronic islands through Santorini to Nísyros and Kos, as is evident in the strange colours and shapes of its rocks. Its wildlife is interesting too: the waters between Kímolos and Polýaigos to the east are home to an estimated 20–30 Mediterranean monk seals (*see p. 588*), and schools of dolphin are frequently seen. The extraction of 'Cymolian Earth' brought the arid and infertile island wealth in antiquity. Still quarried today, the mines have left their mark, in the form of white gashes on the island's easternmost point.

HISTORY OF KIMOLOS

A violin-shaped, marble figurine, showing traces of colour, which was found on Kímolos and dates from the 3rd millennium BC, indicates that there may have been a settled Early Cycladic presence on the island. Later there was a small Mycenaean trading-post in the southwest of the island, at the point where the subsequent historical city was

to grow up. The island was afterwards occupied by Doric-speaking Greeks. Like its neighbour Milos, Kímolos did not at first join the Delian League, but may have done so after the subjugation of Milos by Athens in 416–415 BC, when Kímolos enjoyed some independence for the first time. By the end of the 3rd century BC, the island was under the control of the Macedonian kings.

After antiquity, Kímolos may have been deserted for a long time, as there is no historical reference to it until the 1207, when it was one of the islands taken by Marco Sanudo and incorporated in his new Duchy of Naxos (*see p. 130*). In the 14th century, along with the other Sanudo possessions, it passed to the Crispi family, and then to the Bolognese Gozzadini family, feudal lords of Siphnos, Kythnos, Folégandros and Síkinos. The Gozzadini managed to hold on to their islands, in the guise of Turkish tributaries, for longer than any other Christian overlord in the archipelago. During their rule, they resettled a large portion of the population of Kímolos in fortified towns on the island of Antíparos. In 1617 the Turks took over direct management of the island. Kímolos joined the Greek state in 1829.

CHORIO

Boats dock in the bay of Psáthi, a protected cove below the main settlement at Chorió, which towers on a ridge above it, behind it the silhouette of Palaiókastro, the island's highest point and its former acropolis in times of danger (*see overleaf*). A short walk of less than a kilometre up the hill ahead leads to Chorió, created in the 15th century as a moderately fortified or protected **kastro**.

Chorió consists of a rectangle of houses facing inwards: their once blank external walls form the exterior of the enclosure, their windows and doors all face inside. The interior (in ruins) is entered through one of two surviving arched entrances to the south and to the northeast, originally barred with gates. At the centre is the double-aisled church of Christós, which may predate the kastro. Along the north side are the best-preserved houses, some with particularly fine window and door frames opening onto upper-floor balconies. It appears that the town was burnt during a pirate raid in 1638.

North of the kastro is the unexpectedly grand 16th–17th-century church of **Ághios Ioánnis Chrysóstomos**. The unplastered exterior displays the varied colours of Kimolian stone at their best. The church was originally a cross-in-square surmounted by an octagonal drum and cupola, with a later extension to the west. The doorway and window in the south wall are especially fine.

The kastro is surrounded on all sides by other **churches** of interest. West of it are the two parallel 18th-century churches of the Panaghía Oikonómou and the Sotíras (to the north), with the earlier, 17th-century church of the Taxiárchis to their south. The island's largest church is the bulky 19th-century Eisódia tis Panaghías to the east of the kastro: opposite its west front, a building is being prepared to house the island's small archaeological collection.

EXPLORING THE ISLAND

Ancient Kimolos

The road west from Psáthi passes through an area of strikingly-coloured volcanic earth. Beyond Alykí it becomes a track and drops down to the western shore of the island at Dékas and Mavrospília bays, separated by a small, eroding promontory of pumice: in antiquity this joined the islet of Ághios Andréas, or Daskalió, to the main island. This was the **site of ancient Kimolos**, now referred to as Elliniká. Due to subsidence and erosion, the main site lies underwater between the promontory and the islet, leaving only the area of the cemeteries on shore. The remarkable Geometric-period finds (9th and 8th centuries BC) excavated in the area will eventually be displayed in Chorió.

North of Chorió: the quarries

A road heads north from Chorió along the east coast of the island. After 3.5km, it circumvents a steep valley, with the narrow **inlet of Ághios Minás** below; the landscape here bears the traces of quarrying of the local honey-coloured stone, much used in 19th-century Athens.

The road continues as a track to **Prasá**. On the south side of its bay, opposite the islet of Prasónisi, there are **hot springs**.

Beyond Prasá are cliffs and terraces of pure white which lend a turquoise colour to the water below. The headland to the northeast has been cut away and its stone exported from the island for well over 2,000 years: it is one of the main European sources of fuller's earth, antiquity's Cymolian Earth, a hydrous silicate of aluminium, now called cimolite (pron: *simmolite*). This white powder, created by the decomposition of granitic rocks, is a kind of kaolin or china clay. Since antiquity, it has been used for treating skin problems and irritations. It was also used in textile production. The quarries are still active today.

A walk to Palaiókastro

From just north of the Ághios Minás inlet, a track branches left (west) into the central hills of the island. The track is driveable for about 5km, but also rewarding to walk. Four kilometres (*1hr on foot*) from the junction,where two tracks join from the right on a narrow saddle, the route continues to the left. After 1.3 km (*15mins*), it reaches another saddle with views of the sea to the west of the island, on the right side. From here a footpath branches to the right and curves round, first heading west then north onto the ridge of Palaiókastro. After 15mins it splits once again: left (west) for a bizarre mushroom-shaped rock (Skiádi; *15mins*); and right (north) for Palaiókastro (*30mins*).

At Palaiókastro, the island's summit, there are remains from two different periods: stretches of large Cyclopean boulders probably mark a defensive acropolis of the Archaic period; while above them are medieval walls and other structures, including several cisterns. The views take in much of the Cycladic archipelago.

POLYAIGOS

The uninhabited island of Polýaigos lies off Kímolos to the southeast (*map p. 240*). Though it lacks fresh water, its possession was contested in the 4th century BC by Kímolos and Milos, probably because it offered valuable extra pastureland (its name means 'many goats'). Because of the lack of water, it has only known seasonal human habitation throughout history. Today it is a bird and nature reserve, and a favoured habitat of the Mediterranean monk seal. Visits to the island and its exceptional beaches can be arranged privately from Pollónia on Milos (*Warwick Tours, T: 22870 41234*).

PRACTICAL INFORMATION

GETTING AROUND

Kímolos is easily reached from Milos, which is amply connected by air and ferry to the mainland and other islands. There are 5–6 ferry crossings daily from Pollónia on Milos (25mins). From Piraeus, there are two morning (6½ hrs) and one afternoon (7hrs) ferries per week, supplemented by a high-speed service in summer (4½ hrs). All these services continue to Milos (south) and to Siphnos and Sériphos (north).

WHERE TO STAY

Only basic rooms are available on Kímolos. **Sardis Rooms** at Alykí is pleasantly set near the island's south-facing beach; the rooms are simple, and there is a taverna run by the owners (*T: 22870 51458*). Nearer to habitation, **Villa Maria**, on the road between the harbour and Chorió (*T: 22870 51392, www. hellasislands.gr/kimolos/villa-maria*), is an inexpensive and welcoming alternative.

WHERE TO EAT

Taverna Panorama, at the heart of Chorió, is busy and serves a delicious local wine to accompany its simple home cooking. A couple of the shops in Chorió sell the island's excellent goats' cheeses.

FOLEGANDROS

Folégandros (*map p. 49*) is a delightful island, with dramatic cliffs on all sides except the east, attractive beaches and a number of interesting walks along stone-paved mule-paths. Contrasting pleasantly with the beautiful *chora* are the widely dispersed settlements of Áno Meriá in the west, where an unaffected rural life continues.

HISTORY OF FOLEGANDROS

The first evidence of human settlement on Folégandros dates to the 3rd millennium BC and continues through the Middle and Late Bronze Age (1st millennium BC). In the Early Iron Age, the island was colonised by Dorians, but later received much Ionian influence, developing an Ionian dialect in Hellenistic times. Most of the visible ancient remains date from the Hellenistic and Roman periods.

The island was incorporated into the Duchy of Naxos by Marco Sanudo in 1207, and passed to the Bolognese overlords of Kythnos, the Gozzadini family, in 1336. Although Buondelmonti in his *Liber Insularum* described Folégandros as virtually uninhabited when he visited c. 1417, the island appears to have been re-settled from Crete in the 16th century. The Ottomans took complete possession of the island from descendants of the Gozzadini in 1617. In 1715 it suffered a punitive Turkish raid, leaving it once again depopulated. Between 1770 and 1774 it came under Russian rule, along with the other Cyclades. In 1828 it joined the newly independent Greek state. In 1918, 1926, 1936 and again in the 1960s, the island was used as a place of political exile.

FOLEGANDROS CHORA

The *chora* of Folégandros, one of the best preserved and most dramatically sited in the Aegean, divides into two areas: Kastro, semi-fortified and medieval, to the north, and the 17th-century settlement contiguous with it to the south.

Plateía Poúnda and Plateía Doúnavi

All transport stops at or before Plateía Poúnda, with a Neoclassical school building (1908) and an impressive view. Beyond it to the southwest is Plateía Doúnavi ('Danube'), the main centre of Chora and the first of a loose-knit series of squares, its south side bounded by the island's principal church of Ághios Nikólaos. The north side of the square is constituted by the south wall of Kastro (*see below*), which has two entrances: the wider, stepped Loggia to the west, and the narrower Parapórti, which leads out of Plateía Doúnavi at the eastern end of the wall.

Plateía Doúnavi runs south into Plateía Kontaríni, dominated by the façade of the 17th-century church of Ághios Antónios (restored in 1709), with a fine marble door frame, carved by a local artist: there is more such folk art in the painted pillars which flank the screen in the interior.

The Kastro

The Kastro is a medieval settlement in which the houses face inwards and their outside walls form the fortified enceinte. To the north, the rock precipice forms an effective natural defence; the houses had no lime plaster in earlier times, and were indistinguishable from the rock when seen from a distance. Begun in the 13th century, it could accommodate almost 200 families. Where the buildings cross the tiny alleyways, the passages are roofed with cypress and schist blocks; the characteristic wooden balconies and parallel flights of steps have survived unaltered. Projecting on an outcrop at the western extremity of Kastro, with an unforgettable view, is the church of the Panaghía Pantanássa, built by a Cretan immigrant shortly before the end of the 17th century: he appears, kneeling, in the predella of the painting on the south sanctuary-door of the screen.

The church of the Panaghía

To the left of the school overlooking Plateía Poúnda, a street leads into the stepped path which winds up to the church of the Panaghía. As you approach the first bend, a Roman marble bust of a robed male figure has been mounted above an arch in the modern cemetery wall. This area was the heart of the settlement of ancient Folégandros. Outside the church of the Panaghía, ancient fragments include a statue base preserving the tips of the bronze feet of a (probably Roman) statue. Above, embedded in the lower south wall of the bell-tower, is the robed torso of a Roman funerary statue. The church itself dates from c. 1820, incorporating elements from a 17th-century predecessor.

Palaiókastro and Chrysospiliá

The summit above the church of the Panaghía, known as Palaiókastro, functioned successively as the acropolis of ancient Folégandros, and as a fortress in Byzantine and Venetian times. Only the amorphous ruins of mostly later medieval walls and some ancient foundations remain to be seen, but there are fine views. Far down the east slope, at a height of only 20m above the water, is the deep cave of Chrysospiliá, accessible only by water and in exceptionally calm weather (*it is best visited in summer as part of a round-island boat-tour*). By the entrance are three Roman cisterns. The cave appears to have been a place of cult in Hellenistic and Roman times. In several places further in, the walls are covered with clearly readable ancient names and inscriptions predominantly from the 4th century BC, some written in iron oxide pigment, others etched into an applied plaster. The inscriptions are often of an erotic nature; some have interpreted this as relating to a phallic cult prompted by the stalactites in the interior.

AROUND THE ISLAND

The only port, **Karavostásis** (3km), has always been the island's only point of contact with the outside world. Due south of Chora (*40mins on foot*) is the unassuming late 16th-century **monastery-church of Ághios Nikólaos** (1.5km west of Petoúsis). The two contiguous chapels constitute most of the rectangular complex, leaving some space for cells, with stalls for animals and a threshing-floor.

A quarter of a kilometre west of Chora, the road drops into a short dip: to the south, just above the road, is the church of **Ághios Geórgios**, incorporating an ancient grave stele of a caped rider above its door. The **beach of Angáli**, in Vathý Bay, about 3km west of Chora, is one of the most sheltered from the summer winds.

The west of the island consists of the largely agricultural area of **Áno Meriá**, where grain is still harvested by hand and the fields ploughed with animals. The traditional type of house is a miniature independent complex, with storage areas, a living space, cistern, bread oven, chicken coop, livestock shelters and threshing floor, all closely packed around a central space to minimise the impact of the wind. Some idea of its furnishings can be had from the small **Folklore Museum**, to the south of the main road (*generally open 5–10pm in July and Aug. Otherwise, T: 22860 41370*).

At the western end of Áno Meriá is the 15th-century church of **Ághios Ioánnis Pródromos**, with patches of 17th-century wall-painting. Further west, the main road (now a track) ends at the church of the Zoödóchos Pigí, below an outcrop of rock crowned by a medieval watchtower. From this eminence, **Cape Kastéllos**, the northernmost point of the island, can be seen (*best approached via Ághios Geórgios Bay, which is reached in 40mins by a stone mule-path, branching off to the north of the main track, from a point c. 500m before the church of the Zoödóchos Pigí*).

PRACTICAL INFORMATION

GETTING AROUND

Direct connections to Athens run twice weekly from Piraeus, and once a week from Lávrion. In summer there are frequent connections to Ios and Santorini, daily by hydrofoil or by regular ferry five times weekly, on a route between Santorini and Ios, via Folégandros and Síkinos.

WHERE TO STAY

The **Kastro Hotel** ■ in the heart of old Kastro is small and characterful, with raftered rooms, traditional furniture and beautiful views (*open April–Oct; T: 22860 41230, www. hotel-castro.com*). **Anemomylos Studios** (*T: 22860 41309*) and **Artemis Rooms** (*T: 22860 41313*), both at the beginning of the road up to the church of the Panaghía, are simple, pleasant and panoramic.

WHERE TO EAT

Taverna Mimis in Áno Meriá, 4km from Chora, is a traditional taverna with a number of local dishes, such as rabbit with *matsáta*, a homemade pasta. The tavernas in Chora aim more for tourists, though **Spitiko** serves good home-made dishes.

SIKINOS

Síkinos is a tranquil island with a wild mountainous landscape, ideal for walking. There are interesting rural churches, alarmingly perpendicular ancient settlements and one of the best-preserved Roman monuments in the Aegean. Excellent local wine is still produced from the island's remaining vineyards.

HISTORY OF SIKINOS

According to legend, Hypsipyle saved her father, Thoas, son of Dionysus and Ariadne, from the massacre of all the males on the island of Lemnos (*see p. 527*) by putting him in a wooden chest and throwing him into the sea. The chest came ashore at Síkinos, which at that time was called Oinoe ('rich in wine'). Thoas and the nymph Neïda had a child named Sikinos, after whom the island was renamed.

The island was colonised by mainland Dorians, but received much Ionian influence from its neighbours. The first historical mention of Síkinos is a comment made by Solon that he would 'rather be someone from Síkinos than fail in his duty to Athens'— implying that to come from Síkinos was something akin to living in utter oblivion. In

425 BC, the island was assessed to pay the lowest yearly tribute of any island to the Athenian League. Not much is known of its history in later antiquity.

Along with its neighbours, Síkinos became part of the Latin Duchy of Naxos in 1207 under Marco Sanudo, but was briefly re-taken for Byzantium in 1276. It eventually came under Ottoman control in 1566. In 1828, it was incorporated into the Greek state. The island was occupied by Italian forces from 1941–43. Electricity arrived in 1974.

ALOPRONIA, KASTRO & CHORIO

The harbour of **Aloprónia**, or Áno Prónoia, on the east coast, is the only partially sheltered approach on Síkinos; even so, southern winds can leave the island inaccessible for days on end. The inlet's hinterland is watered by one of the island's very few springs. High up to the west overlooking the valley are two of the oldest churches on the island, from the 14th century. The **Panaghía Sykiá** is a 30-min walk up a steep track leading northwest from the main road, just north of the port. Patches of attractive, if unsophisticated, wall-painting survive in its interior, including the *Presentation of the Virgin* on the north side. Visible on the next hill to the south is **Ághios Nikólaos**, which also contains fragmentary wall-painting. It can only be approached by a long sweep west around the head of the ravine (*40mins*). Along the coast are a couple of secluded coves, accessible on foot: Ághios Nikólaos (*45mins northeast*) and Ághios Panteléimon (*90mins southwest*).

Kastro

The road from the port rises steeply to the island's main settlement, along a ridge overlooking the 300-m cliffs of the north coast. It divides into two settlements: Chora or Chorió on the slope to the southwest, and Kastro to the east.

Entering Kastro from the saddle (i.e. from the southwest), a low, tunnel-like entrance, the **Parapórti**, leads into a square, the central area of the medieval fortified unit, built during the second half of the 15th century. The blank rear walls of the houses formed the exterior enceinte, while their façades faced onto the central area. At its centre is the 18th-century church of the Stavrós, also known as the Panaghía Pantanássa. The upper floors of the surrounding buildings have features of noble residences: marble door and window frames carved with vine motifs or embellished with rectangular grooves and cornices. In the southwest corner, above the community offices, is a small **Byzantine Museum** (*open July–mid-Sept 10–1*) with icons from the 17th century and after.

Chorió and the Zoödóchos Pigí

To the southwest of Kastro lies **Chorió**, blending into an area of ruined houses further up the hill to the east. It is separated from Kastro by the main road and the long Neoclassical school building (1900s). Although Chorió, with its steep and narrow alleys, dates from substantially earlier, the main church in its lower area is of the 17th century. The only Byzantine church is the 14th-century Ághios Stéfanos outside the village (*10mins on foot to the south*). There is a small Folklore Museum in Chorió.

Clearly visible from Chorió is the winding path leading up the mountain east of Kastro, past the small chapel of the Panaghía Pantochará, dedicated to the memory of the poet Odysseas Elytis (d. 1996), to the Monastery of the **Zoödóchos Pigí** (*access only regularly possible at around 6 to 6.30pm every day, when a lady from the village opens up the katholikon to service the oil-lamps*). The fortress-like structure provided a last refuge for the islanders when attacked. It was abandoned in 1834.

Just outside Chorió and Kastro, to the north of the road as it heads west, is the 14th-or 15th-century **church of the Metamorphosis**, among pine and almond trees beside a turreted, cliffside Neoclassical house. The church was restored in the 17th century.

EPISKOPI & ANCIENT SIKINOS

The road west from Chorió clings to the slope of Mt Troúllos, following the route of the old *kalderími* nearby, with good views to neighbouring islands. It ends a short distance from the solitary **church of the Episkopí**. This is one of the most unusual buildings in the Cyclades: a well-preserved 2nd- or 3rd-century AD Roman construction, subsequently adapted as a church, set in an unblemished landscape of natural grandeur. Visible ahead to the south is the peak of Aghía Marína, the acropolis of ancient Síkinos.

The path leads to the rear of the building, by the protruding apse of the church. As far up as the distinctive cornice, the masonry is ancient Roman. Above this, surrounding the 17th-century dome, is rough masonry added later to act as a fortification. The south-east corner shows the beginning of a pediment, indicating that the Roman structure had the form of a pedimented temple. The two columns flanking the entrance at rakish angles indicate it had the design of a distyle in antis temple. The spaces between have been filled with rough masonry. In front of the entrance is a deep **rock-cut cistern**, roofed with large stone slabs. Another lies just north. Large pieces of the dentillated cornice are built into the improvised wall opposite the entrance. It seems unlikely that the building was actually a temple. It is built in an area which appears to have been a cemetery (*see below*). It was probably a temple-like heroön or mausoleum to an important individual.

The building may have been converted into a church in late antiquity. The belfry, drum and dome were added in the 17th century, when the height of the main vault was also altered. The church has recently been deconsecrated.

In addition to the vestigial remains of monastic outbuildings, two **14th-century chapels** have survived to the north of the church: Aghía Ánna, beside the church's north wall, with remains of wall-paintings; and Ághios Geórgios, further up the hill, with better-preserved paintings. A quarter of a kilometre southwest of the Episkopí is a **deconsecrated barrel-vaulted chapel**: below its southeast corner, an outcrop of rock has been neatly cut into three steps and a square recess for the pedestal of a funerary monument.

Ancient Síkinos

A 30-min walk to the southwest towards the peak of **Aghía Marína** reaches the site of ancient Síkinos. The habitation occupied a triangular area bounded by a fortress at the summit of Aghía Marína (where a chapel now stands); a shoulder to the northeast of it, where there are remains of fortifications; and another shoulder to the east where there is a platform for a public or sacred building on the ridge looking down to the shore. In the concavity between these three points are the remains of retaining walls and a fortified enceinte. The site is steep and drops straight into the gorge below. On the slope can be seen two lime-kilns, now abandoned, for reducing marble to mortar: this may explain why there is little marble left on the site. From the well-head by the gorge, paths, lead to the remote southwestern extremity of the island

THE NORTHEAST OF THE ISLAND

East of Kastro a road has been driven across to the coast. Continuing northwards from the point where the new road branches downhill to the east (1km east of Kastro), a track follows the ridge for a further 1.5km to the chapel of **Profítis Ilías**. From here, a path leads east to Cape Málta at the eastern extremity of the island: the south face of its promontory is occupied by the archaeological **site of Palaiókastro**. There was an Early Bronze Age (3rd millennium BC) settlement here, but most visible are the remains of ancient and Byzantine habitation across the precipitous slope, even steeper and more exposed than ancient Síkinos (*the walk is a minimum 2.5-hr round trip from Profítis Ilías. The path is clear at first: then, by following the highest contours, it passes the chapel of Aghía Triáda, and thence descends to the narrow neck of the promontory*).

On the low rise in the path beyond the first dip after leaving Profítis Ilías, two rocks with smooth faces have curious carved 19th-century graffiti of two ships.

PRACTICAL INFORMATION

GETTING AROUND

Twice a week there are direct connections from Piraeus, and once a week from Lávrion. Otherwise you need to change in Ios or Santorini, from where there are services five times weekly in summer.

WHERE TO STAY

The most comfortable hotel on Síkinos, **Hotel Porto Sikinos**, is in Aloprónia (*T: 22860 51220; www.portosikinos.gr*). In Chorió, simple rooms with marvellous sunset views can be found at the **Iliovasilema** (*T: 22860 51173; www.sikinos-sunset.gr*). Attached to it is a good patisserie run by the same family.

WHERE TO EAT

Klimatari, just north of the main church of Kastro, has simple Greek fare, local cheese at certain periods, and delicious Sikiniot wine.

THE DODECANESE

The Dodecanese islands extend in an arc from Kastellórizo in the southeast to Patmos and Agathonísi in the north. Although most of the islands in this archipelago closely hug the Turkish coastline, a few (including Kárpathos, Kasos and Astypálaia) stretch out in the opposite direction, into the deeper waters of the Aegean, thus giving the Dodecanese a rather unwieldy geographic aspect. There are slightly over 150 islands altogether, most of them mere specks of uninhabited rock: the name Dodecanese, meaning 'Twelve-islands' in Greek, derives from the medieval and modern focus on the twelve largest islands.

The islands' proximity to the Turkish coastline (and the lack of a mutually agreed maritime border) has led to occasional diplomatic and military incidents, but the situation is now generally calm and ferry links between the larger islands and their corresponding Turkish ports are regular, efficient and easily negotiated.

Although the islands are not closely clustered together, and differ widely from one another in terms of geology, fertility, fresh water provision and population density, anyone who visits more than a handful will soon appreciate that they in fact share quite a number of cultural similarities. Most of these can be traced back to their shared experiences under the Knights of St John, the Ottomans and the Italians. The clearest examples of this are undoubtedly architectural, and include the powerful Knights' castles, the 18th-century Neoclassical merchants' mansions, and the Italian colonial buildings that are scattered liberally through the islands in a way that is not seen elsewhere. Another interesting (and easily overlooked) example of their shared culture is their musical tradition, which is one of the most lively and varied in Greece, and was collectively and purposefully nurtured in the face of external (particularly Italian) displeasure.

Important prehistoric finds have been discovered on several of the islands, and they seem to have been quite closely connected to the heartlands of the Minoan and Mycenaean civilisations. Later tradition states that the northern Dodecanese (as far south as Kálymnos) were settled by Ionian Greeks at the beginning of the 1st millennium BC, while the remaining islands were settled by Dorians from the northeastern Peloponnese; but it is only with the arrival of written records that anything can be meaningfully said about their history.

All of the inhabited Dodecanese islands gained something from their position astride the major ancient trade route from the Black Sea to the Eastern Mediterranean, but two islands in particular, Rhodes and Kos, combined size with good agricultural productivity and safe anchorages, and became important local powers. The smaller islands were often squeezed between these two (and some of the mainland cities or large islands from other neighbouring groups) and were not always able to stay independent and follow their own course in local affairs.

Rhodes, the largest island in the group (and the modern capital of the Dodecanese prefecture), was by far the most powerful and successful, to the extent that it was able to construct a small empire from the surrounding islands and adjacent mainland during the Late Classical and Hellenistic periods, and won fame as a scourge of pirates, an ally of Rome and the home of a flourishing sculptural tradition—including, of course, the Colossus of Rhodes, one of the original Seven Wonders of the World.

Kos also engaged in some expansionism, absorbing neighbouring Kálymnos in the Hellenistic period, but its principal claim to fame was its renowned healing centre and

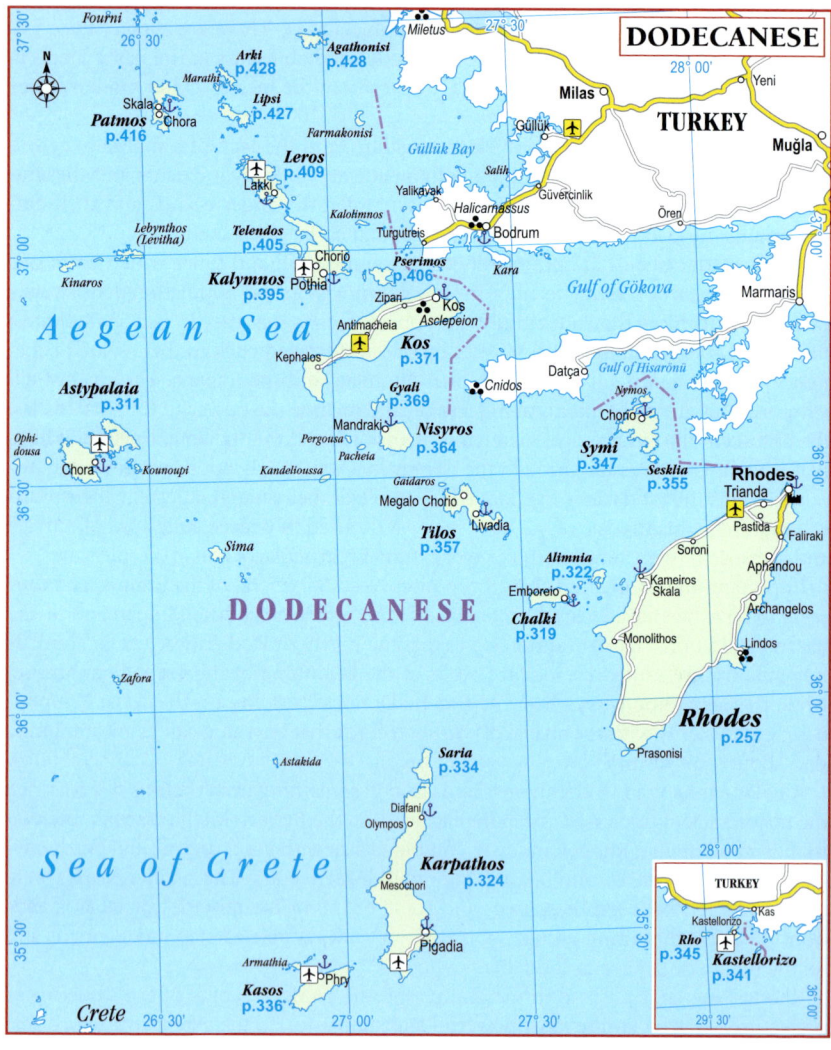

temple site, the Asclepeion, a magnet for health tourism in the ancient world, and one of the major archaeological sites of the Dodecanese today.

Although both of these islands experienced some loss of power when the Romans brought the Dodecanese under their direct control, this loss of sovereignty—and the centuries of peace that ensued—led to a thriving culture that has left extensive archaeological traces throughout the islands. This peace came to an end when the Arab raids and invasions began in the 7th century AD, and things remained volatile until the islands were brought under the control of the Ottoman Empire in the 16th century. The most important moment in the intervening centuries was the arrival of the Knights of St John (*see p. 259*). In the Dodecanese, the Knights constructed fortifications throughout the islands to check the advance of the Turks and keep open the sea lanes towards the Holy Land. In this they succeeded for over two centuries, until the armies of Suleiman the Magnificent took Rhodes in 1522–23.

Once in control, the Ottomans proved to be relatively benign overlords, and many of the islands received beneficial tax concessions in return for specific services, which eventually led to the creation of a wealthy merchant class. This state of affairs ended with the stirrings of Greek independence, and the islands paid a heavy price for their early and enthusiastic espousal of this new cause as, although the struggle eventually resulted in freedom for part of mainland Greece, the Dodecanese islands were not to join the Greek state until 1947. In fact, it was the Italians who freed the Dodecanese islands from Ottoman rule, but they did so in order to impose a regime of their own, invading in 1912 in order to sever seaborne connections between the Ottoman heartland and its far-flung province of Libya, which the Italians were set on conquering. This opportunistic conquest was eventually formalised: Italian possession of the Dodecanese was internationally recognised in 1923, and Italy set about organising the islands as an integral part of its empire. A programme of Italianisation was instituted, which caused much bitterness and led to a rebellious resurgence of traditional Greek culture. Axis defeat in the Second World War finally paved the way for unification, and the Dodecanese island prefecture was formed from the islands of the ex-Italian territories in the Aegean.

The Italian interlude has left an interesting architectural legacy, best seen on Rhodes itself, on Kos and on Leros. These buildings alone would make the Dodecanese islands worth visiting, but they are in fact only a small part of a rich offering which ranges from major ancient Greek sanctuaries such as Lindos on Rhodes and the Asclepeion on Kos to the Monastery of St John on Patmos (where the Saint received his vision of the Apocalypse) and the medieval streets of the old town of Rhodes. None of the islands lacks some site of archaeological or cultural interest, often located in areas of great natural beauty, such as the volcanic landscape of Nísyros or the wild mountains of Kárpathos, and their wildlife is equally fascinating: Tilos has recently established itself as a hunting-free zone, and the quantity and diversity of wildlife has soared as a result.

M.M.

ART & ARCHITECTURE IN THE DODECANESE

Ancient sculpture

The foundation in 408/7 BC of the city of Rhodes brought an influx of famous artists. Lysippus of Sicyon, the sculptor attached to the court of Alexander the Great, produced his famous four-horse Chariot of the Sun in Rhodes; under his influence a school of sculpture was founded, which flourished for three centuries and which is mentioned by Pliny (*Nat. Hist., XXXIV*). Leaders of the school, whose artists worked mainly in bronze, included Chares of Lindos, creator of the Colossus of Rhodes. These were followed by a host of other artists, both native and immigrant, of whom little is known save their names, many of which appear on statue bases on the Lindos acropolis.

The loss of independence to Rome did not halt artistic activity. One sculptor made a colossal statue, 12m high, dedicated to the Roman people, and placed it in the Temple of Athena Polias and Zeus Polieus on the acropolis of Rhodes. There followed Boïthos of Chalcedon, and Apollonius and Tauriscus of Tralles, who are said to have made the magnificent marble group known as the *Farnese Bull*, now in Naples. Perhaps best known of all is another marble group, the *Laocoön*, found in Rome in 1506: it was produced in the 1st century BC by the Rhodian sculptors Agesander, Polydorus and Athenodorus.

The legacy of the Knights of St John

With the arrival of the Knights, the art of Rhodes and its territory becomes westernised. The Grand Masters, most of whom came from France or Spain, naturally favoured the style of their native countries, and French and Catalan Gothic predominated. Two periods can be distinguished: from 1309–1480 and from 1480–1522. In the earlier period the Knights depended on local masons, who were unfamiliar with the Gothic style, and the work can sometimes appear heavy and maladroit, with intrusive Byzantine elements. In the second period, under the aegis of Pierre d'Aubusson (1476–1503), one of the most eminent of the Grand Masters, the hand of Western craftsmen can be discerned. The Gothic forms are more harmonious, the execution surer, and the decoration naturalistic or cleverly stylised. Towards the end of this period a few classicising, Renaissance motifs were introduced. These included marble cornices to doors and windows, elaborate escutcheons, and inscriptions carved in Latin characters.

A legacy of the Ottomans

Ottoman motifs and ideas permeate the decorative arts of the islands, and nowhere more than in what is called 'Rhodian' or 'Lindos Ware'. The exquisite ceramic production of the Turkish workshops of Iznik first came to the island with the Ottoman masters in the 16th century. By the 17th century, a range of new motifs began to supplement the traditional floral designs, amongst them images of fully-rigged ships. These became popular with Greek traders and mariners, who decorated their houses with large displays of such ceramics. Even though most of this production still came from Iznik itself, local imitations and variants were produced, in particular at Lindos.

Italian colonial architecture

The Dodecanese islands, under the sway of an Italy with imperial ambitions, saw an extraordinary architectural flowering in the 1920s. The impetus for this was an artistic master plan which sought to give a unifying architectural stamp to the Mediterranean and African territories which Italy occupied. At first they created a new, Mediterranean, Rationalist architecture which, by incorporating different elements of local traditions—Roman, Crusader, Ottoman, Greek, Islamic—was intended to give visible expression of the extent and diversity of Italy's new empire. This gave rise to the period's greatest and most imaginative buildings. After 1936, with the declaration of the Fascist imperium, architecture had to bend to the demands for monumentality. Some of the earlier buildings were even purged of their decorative elements.

These two phases correspond to the periods in office of the two longest-serving Italian governors of the Dodecanese, both of whom were actively interested in architecture, but who held opposing views: Mario Lago (1924–1936) and Cesare Maria de

The Nomarcheía in Rhodes Town, an example of the Italian colonial architecture of Florestano di Fausto. Note the so-called submerged arcade with its very short columns.

Vecchi (1936–1941), who had formerly been Mussolini's Minister for Education. It was Mario Lago who was responsible for the creation of Porto Lago on Leros, for the rebuilding of Kos after the earthquake of 1933, for promoting archaeological excavations on Rhodes and Kos, and for the commissioning of a comprehensive new master plan for the expansion of the city of Rhodes outside the walls, which was entrusted to the architect Florestano di Fausto. Against the theatrical backdrop of the city of the Knights, with all its associations of Latin dominance, a new Foro Italico of commercial and administrative buildings was to be spaciously laid out along the shore.

The architecture of Florestano di Fausto was highly eclectic, often called Integrationist because of its aspiration to combine local traditions with a new Rationalist approach. It grafted decorative elements from a variety of origins—Moorish domes, Venetian tracery, Gothic arches, and the clear, cuboid volumes of Aegean indigenous building—onto the framework of simple geometric forms favoured by Rationalism. It alternates between a military, Crusader purity and Oriental luxury. Its most characteristic and courageous feature is the submerged arcade, a broad, generally Gothic arch or series of arches, supported on very low, stunted columns, which give the impression of having sunk into the ground. The effect is not unpleasing, and accentuates breadth and horizontality over the soaring height customarily associated with the Gothic arch. An example is the port-side arcade of the old Rhodes Administration Building of 1927 (now the Nomarcheía; *map p. 281, E2*). The other architects who worked in this period, such as Rodolfo Petracco and Pietro Lombardi, created buildings in a similar, if slightly purer, architectural language. Lombardi's design for the baths at Kallithéa (*see p. 293*) is perhaps the most unified masterpiece of the whole movement.

With Armando Bernabiti in the 1930s, there is a transition to a new generation: purer, undecorated and in every way more minimal and more consonant with the politics of de Vecchi. The simplicity is already recognisable in his early aquarium building (1934; *map p. 281, F2*); his later creations—the Puccini Theatre, the Rhodes Town Hall (formerly the Fascist Administration Building) and the Church of St Francis—all tend toward the military in spirit. It was in this later period that a number of di Fausto's works, such as his once extravagant Albergo delle Rose, were purged of their decorative details and arabesques. The contrast between the earlier and later styles is well seen in the planned town of Lakkí on Leros (*see p. 410*).

RHODES

osmopolitan, spacious, immensely varied, and blessed with a fullness of vegetation and a radiance of light, the island of Rhodes has always been a proud world of its own. Roman statesmen and emperors travelled here to imbibe the island's art and culture, and intellectuals came to study with its scientists, thinkers and orators.

The island has a long and important history. One of its most fascinating episodes is the creation of the city of Rhodes itself. It is a testimony to the pragmatism of the ancient Rhodians that three thriving and competing cities in different parts of the island—Lindos, Ialysós and Kameíros—should have taken the decision in 408/7 BC to renounce their independence and combine to found a new city which was to be called, like the island, Rhodes. The result was the emergence of one of the richest cities of the later Greek world, praised by Strabo and Pliny for its beauty and wealth of art.

Over a thousand years later, the island's character was once again transformed, this time by the arrival of an international group of aristocratic warriors, the Knights Hospitallers of St John, who turned the island into a chivalric kingdom in the sea. At the beginning of the last century, the Italians arrived, and turned Rhodes into a regional capital of their empire, with a new centre created in a memorable, eclectic kind of architecture.

As a consequence, of all the cities in Greece, Rhodes is second only to Athens in the wealth of its monuments. Naturally enough, it is one of the most visited places in the country. But the island does not live solely on its past; it supports a vital commercial and cultural life which makes it a pleasure to visit both in and out of season.

HISTORY OF RHODES

In antiquity the island had many names, including Aithrea, Ophiousa (from its snakes) and Telchinia. The name Rhodes is of uncertain etymology: it is probably not derived (as so often stated) from the Greek word for rose, *rhodon*. A more likely root is the Phoenician *erod*: 'snake'.

From antiquity to the coming of the Knights

Neolithic remains have been found at various cave sites, and Ialysós and Triánda in particular have produced important Bronze Age finds. In that period, the island was influenced first by Minoan and then by Mycenaean culture. Homer mentions three cities in Rhodes: Lindos, Ialysos and Kameiros (*Iliad II, 656*). These three cities, with Kos, Cnidos, and Halicarnassus, formed the Dorian Hexapolis, in the southwest corner of Asia Minor. They attained great prosperity, establishing trade routes throughout the Mediterranean and founding colonies in the neighbouring islands and on the coasts of Asia Minor and Europe. Contacts with Egypt are important from earliest times: in the 7th century BC Rhodes participated in the founding of the enclave of Naucratis in Egypt, and mercenaries from Rhodes fought for the pharaohs on several occasions. In

RHODES

408/7 the three cities united to found the new city of Rhodes, which they populated with their own citizens.

In the wars that followed the death of Alexander the Great, the Rhodians allied themselves closely with Ptolemy I, who assisted them in 305–304 BC when their city was besieged by Demetrius Poliorcetes. When Demetrius was compelled to raise the siege, it is said that he was so impressed by the defenders' valour that he left them his artillery, from the sale of which they defrayed the cost of the Colossus, a votive bronze statue, over 30m high, of the island's patron divinity, Helios the sun god.

Soon afterwards Rhodes reached the zenith of her prosperity. Her port became the centre of trade between Italy, Greece and Macedonia, and Asia and Africa. She became the first naval power in the Aegean. Rhodian law, the earliest code of marine law, was universally esteemed: Augustus adopted it as a model and its provisions are still quoted today. With a population of 60–80,000, the city was lavishly adorned and entered an artistic golden age. Even as late as the 1st century AD, when the city had been despoiled of most of its treasures, Pliny claimed that it had no fewer than 2,000 statues, many of them colossal. The orator Aeschines (c. 397–c. 322 BC) founded a school of rhetoric at Rhodes, which was later attended by famous Romans, including Cato, Cicero, Julius Caesar and Lucretius.

Rhodian fortunes now rose and fell in tandem with its favour in Rome, until the city sided with Julius Caesar during the civil wars that ended the Republic, and suffered in consequence at the hands of Cassius, who plundered the city in 43 BC and destroyed or captured the Rhodian fleet. During the reign of Vespasian (AD 70–79), Rhodes was finally incorporated into the Roman Empire as part of the Province of Asia.

In Byzantine times, Rhodes was an important frontier post against Arab expansion. From 654 it was frequently pillaged and for a time occupied by the Saracens. During the Crusades, Christian ships used its ports as a stopping-place. During the Fourth Crusade, which established the Latin empire of Constantinople, the Greek governor of Rhodes, Leo Gavalas, declared the independence of the island. Later, in the mid-13th century, the Genoese obtained partial control of it, and in 1306 it received the Knights of St John of Jerusalem as refugees. Those refugees soon became the island's masters.

Rhodes under the Knights of St John

The Knights of the Hospital of St John of Jerusalem, often just referred to as the Knights of Rhodes and later (after 1530) as the Knights of Malta, were originally Hospitallers united in a charitable brotherhood founded for the protection of pilgrims and the care in hospital of the poor and sick. The Order originated c. 1048 in a hospital which merchants of Amalfi had built in Jerusalem for pilgrims to the Holy Sepulchre. Their first rector, Gerard, formed them into a strictly constituted religious body subject to the jurisdiction of the Patriarch of Jerusalem. The Order soon became predominantly military and the Hospitallers were sworn to defend the Holy Sepulchre to the last drop of their blood and to make war on infidels wherever encountered. In 1191, after Saladin had captured Jerusalem, they retired to Acre. Bitter rivalry arose between them and the Knights Templar, and the Hospitallers were driven out of Acre in 1291. They went first to Cyprus and later, in 1306, they fled from Cyprus to Rhodes. Having in vain demanded the fief of Rhodes from the Byzantine emperor, they took it by force in 1309.

The brethren were divided into three classes: knights (*milites*), chaplains (*cappelani*), and serving brothers or fighting squires (*servientes armorum*), who followed the knights into action. In the 12th century the Order was divided into seven Langues or 'Tongues': Provence, Auvergne, France, Italy, Spain (later, in 1461, subdivided into Aragon and Castile), England and Germany. Each 'Tongue' had a bailiff, and its own headquarters or Auberge. The bailiffs, under the presidency of the Grand Master, elected for life by the Knights, formed the chapter of the Order. The modern British Order of St John of Jerusalem, founded in 1827, may be regarded as a revival of the Tongue of England.

Having conquered Rhodes, the Knights built a powerful fleet to protect the island's trade. For two centuries they defied the Turks. They took part in the capture and later in the defence of Smyrna, and withstood two great sieges: in 1444 by the sultan of Egypt and in 1480 by Mehmet II, the conqueror of Byzantium. At last, in June 1522, Sultan Suleiman the Magnificent attacked Rhodes with a force said to have numbered 100,000 men. The Knights and their supporters mustered fewer than 2,000. In December they capitulated, on honourable terms. On 1st January 1523, the Grand Master, Villiers de l'Isle-Adam, with 180 surviving brethren, left the island. They retired first to Crete, and after over six years of uncertainty and peregrination, to Malta in 1530.

The Ottoman occupation and modern times

For nearly four hundred years (from 1523 until 1912) Rhodes was a provincial administrative capital of the Ottoman Empire. All churches in the city were converted into mosques and a number of Islamic religious complexes were erected. The Greeks were ousted from within the walls of the Old Town, which remained inhabited only by the Turkish masters and by the Jews (in the eastern corner). The Greek population had to resettle in the outlying areas; many were to emigrate over the subsequent centuries, especially to Egypt. Those who remained enjoyed a period of relative prosperity and stability in the 18th and 19th centuries.

In 1912, during their war with Turkey, the Italians captured Rhodes after a short siege, though their possession of the island was not recognised by international treaty until 1924. The 1920s saw an ambitious programme of building and improvement in infrastructure, but the Italians' intentions became less benign in the late 1930s, led by Fascist policy from Rome. In the latter part of the Second World War the Germans took over from the Italians. In 1945 the island was freed by British and Greek commandos, and in 1947 officially became part of the Greek state.

RHODES TOWN

NB: Churches and their saints have been given Latinate names where they relate to foundations or examples principally of the Hospitaller period. In some cases, however, Greek names have been kept for those saints who are more familiar through the Orthodox tradition.

The walls of the Old Town

A one-hour tour of the top of the walls, from the Grand Master's Palace to the Gate of St John (Koskinoú Gate), is available on Tues and Sat at 3pm: tickets 15mins before, at the palace gate. Otherwise, the pathway through the entire length of the moat from Plateía Rimini round to the Acandia Gate is open day and night, and constitutes a uniquely instructive and evocative walk.

The primary importance of the site of Rhodes Town was its group of natural harbours, positioned strategically on one of the Mediterranean's most important sea routes. In antiquity, the city of Rhodes had such a large population that it was able to use the summit to the west of the city (Mt Smith; *map p. 281, D1*) as an acropolis, and the city's habitation amply filled the space between it and the port. As the population declined after the fall of the Roman Empire, this arrangement became less practicable: the hill was too far from the port, and so an area was fortified closer to the harbours. Arab chroniclers of the late 7th century refer to such a fortress, and archaeology has shown that it existed in the area under and to the south of the Grand Master's Palace. This Byzantine fortress, to which the whole population would retreat in times of danger, covered the roughly rectangular area later called the Collachium; it was bounded to the south by the ashlar ramparts visible in stretches along Theophilískou and Agesándrou streets (*map p. 262, C2*), where some of the regularly spaced towers are still recognisable. To the south of this fortress area, and at a later date (probably in the 11th or 12th century), more walls were added to enclose a lower residential and commercial town. These stretched as far south as Omírou (*map p. 262, C3*), and were bounded to the west by the approximate line of Ippodámou (*map p. 262, B3*); to the east they are still clearly visible in excavations near to Pythagóra and below ground level to the north of the Mosque of Ibrahim Pasha. These walls were substantial enough to resist the siege by the Knights of St John for over two years when they arrived in Rhodes in 1306. Until the city fell to them in August 1309, the Knights were based at Philérimos, 10km to the southwest (*see p. 287*).

The walls under the Knights

The Byzantine fortifications belonged to a world of warfare which found itself suddenly outmoded by the arrival of gunpowder and cannon in the 15th century. The Knights embarked on a project to re-equip the city and harbours of Rhodes for the new realities of war. The result is what we see today, one of the most impressive and best-preserved fortified settlements in Europe.

The new enceinte of walls now measured nearly 4km in length. In 1465, the Order divided this into eight sectors, each designated to a different Tongue, who assumed responsibility for the defence and maintenance of their sector. The harbour fortifications were assigned to Castile; then came the landward sectors of Italy, Provence, England, Aragon, Auvergne, Germany and France, whose remit encompassed the Master's Palace.

The current appearance of the fortifications is the result of two principal periods of construction: the first dates from the 14th and early 15th centuries, before the unsuccessful Turkish siege of 1480 and the earthquake of the following year left them in ruins; the second from between 1481 and the second Turkish siege of 1522. During

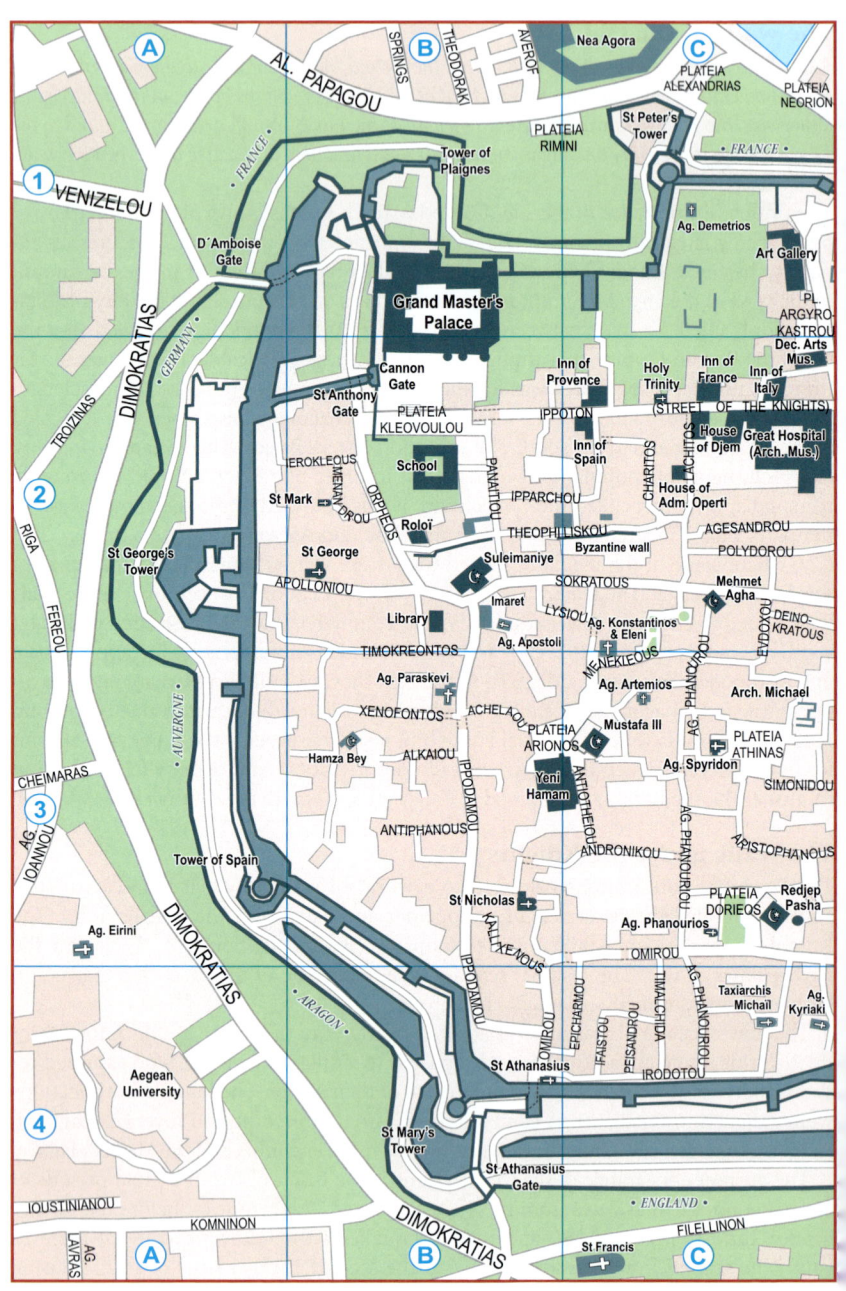

RHODES OLD TOWN

N

0   150 yards
0   150 metres

COMMERCIAL HARBOUR

Liberty Gate
Gate of St Paul
De Naillac Tower
PLATEIA SIMIS
Arsenal Gate
Temple of Aphrodite
AKTI SACHTOURI
St Mary of the Castle
De Melay Ho.
Arnaldo Gate
CASTLE
Inn of England
APELLOU
PROTOGENOUS
AIOLOU
LERMIOU
PL. EVDIMOU
Shadirvan Mosque
Marine Gate
MILTIADOU
ELPIPIDOU
PLATEIA IPPOKRATOUS
Castellania
AKTI SACHTOURI
PLATONOS
DIMOKRITOU
THEMISTOKLEOUS
ARISTOTELOUS
K. RODIOU
Gate of the Virgin
Hospice of St Catherine
PL. PEISIDOROU
St Panteleimon
PL. AG. PANTELEIMONOS
AISCHYLOU
SOPHOKLEOUS
PYTHAGORA
LYSIPPOU
MINOÖS
EVRAION MARTYRON
PL. CALLE ANCHA
DOSIADOU
PINDAROU
BYZANTIOU
St Mary of the Burgh
THISEOS
ALHADEF
Ibrahim Pasha
Byzantine wall
PLATEIA SOPHOKLEOUS
DIMOSTHENOUS
PERIKLEOUS
SYMMIOU
Synagogue
PHEIDIOU
GAVALA
PL. DIONYSOS
Acandia Gate
PLATEIA MELINA MERCOURI
SOPHOKLEOUS
KONTI
PLATEIA KONTI
Byzantine tower
PRAXITELOUS
LEONDONTOS
KLEOVOULINIS
Holy Trinity
PLATEIA L. RODIOU
St Catherine
IKAROU
TAVRISKOU
TLIPOLEMOU
PL. KIMONOS
Del Carretto Bastion
ITALY
PROMITHEOS
DIONYSIOU
KISTINIOU
ITALY
VYRONOS
OMIROU
ARISTEIDOU
Ag. Theodoroi
PYTHAGORA
KLEISTHENOUS
KIMONOS
ARCH. EFTHYMIOU
PL. EIRINIS
NAFSIKAS
EKATONOS
NIKIOU
Ag. Marina
PROVENCE
Gate of St John (Koskinou Gate)
VYRONOS
CODRINGTONOU
XANTHOU
TH. KOLOKOTRONI

Tower of the Windmills
Windmills
St Catherine's Gate
CASTLE

the whole of the second period, the threat of attack was so constant that the walls could never be taken down and fully rebuilt to more modern specifications, but had to be modified piecemeal instead. One of the particular characteristics of the fortifications of Rhodes is the changing design from one sector to the next, reflecting the different siege-experience of the nationalities entrusted with their construction.

On the harbour front, the defences consisted of a curtain wall with a parapet and three forward fortresses to protect the harbour entrance: first, the Tower of Grand Master de Naillac (1396–1421) on the north mole of the Commercial Harbour; and later the Tower of the Windmills to the east and the Tower of St Nicholas to the north of Mandráki Harbour, built under Grand Master Zacosta (1461–67). A chain closed the entrance to the Commercial Harbour, and sunken rock debris was used to fill and close the narrow entrance to the boatyards of Mandráki.

In the end, it was not any deficiency in the design of these defences but the treachery of individuals and exhaustion of manpower that delivered the city to the forces of Suleiman the Magnificent in 1522. The city was, for its time, uniquely well-designed for warfare not by stealth, but by intimidation. Though later Ottoman repairs to the walls (and Italian restorations) were extensive, hardly any alterations were made to their design.

ENTRANCE TO THE COLLACHIUM:
THE D'AMBOISE GATE

There is no better way to enter the walled, medieval town of the Knights of St John than through the magnificent **d'Amboise Gate** (1512; *map p. 262, A1*), directly below the Grand Master's Palace. Forbidding to the stranger and reassuring to the inhabitant, it is the finest of the landward entrances to the city. About 200 paces separate the outer approach from the fourth and final inner gate, a distance that was originally punctuated by three drawbridges, a double-bend within the thickness of the first bastion, an independent advance wall, and three dry moats: most of the gates consisted of double sets of doors. This gives not only an immediate measure of the sophistication and complexity of the city's defences, but also of the perceived magnitude of the Turkish threat in the 16th century, and the position Rhodes occupied as the crucial Mediterranean outpost of the Christian West. These fortifications were also the hub of a further 20 fortresses all over the island and of an extensive network of defences on the other islands, from Kastellórizo to Leros.

The **outer doorway** of the d'Amboise Gate, set between two forbidding semicircular bastions, is surmounted by a marble relief bearing its date of completion (1512) below the armorial bearings of its builder, Grand Master Emery d'Amboise (1503–12). A wide vaulted passage leads through the outer walls and bastion, crosses a second bridge and turns onto a shaded, free-standing advance rampart, with moats to either side, towered over by the west face of the Grand Master's Palace to the left. The last of the four sets of gates is the **Gate of St Anthony**. To the right of it as you approach, steps lead down into an enclosed area littered with stone cannon balls. It was against the force of these sculpted missiles that the walls had to resist: some of them measure more than 50cm in diameter and weigh upwards of 160kg. Opposite the foot of the steps, in the far corner, is a **postern gate** in the form of a vaulted tunnel, which leads into the outer moat underneath the second enceinte of walls. The exterior entrance to this was originally protected from view by a wall which has since been demolished but whose foundations are visible. The passage enabled the defenders to make surprise sallies against the enemy and to clear debris from the moat which might be used by attackers to fill it. The three shafts which pierce the ceiling of the tunnel could be used both for supplying munitions and for attacking intruders if the passageway fell into the hands of the enemy.

The churches of St Mark and St George

The gate of St Anthony leads into Orphéos, a lively thoroughfare which cuts through one of the most interesting and varied corners of the city. It is bordered to the right by shops and to the left by the line of the Byzantine walls. Ahead lie a number of important Ottoman monuments, and to the right is a collection of buildings and excavations which vividly encapsulates the layered density of the city. To reach them, take the second narrow entrance to the right, which leads into a loop formed by Ierokléous and Menándrou. A few metres down Menándrou on the right is the 14th-century **church of St Mark** (*map p. 262, B2*). The Holy Icon of Philérimos was placed here for a period during the siege of 1522, and survived unscathed when the western projection of the church was destroyed in the bombardment. When the Turks later came to convert the damaged church into a mosque, tombs were discovered in the floor. In order not to disturb these burials, the floor was re-filled and a low arch constructed over the area to support the wall above, obviating the need to dig foundations. This is visible low down in the west wall. The church has unequal arms which meet at a vaulted crossing with no cupola. A mihrab niche is still preserved, and there are vestigial remains of wall-paintings.

Just beyond are some of the surviving monastic buildings of the late 14th-century **monastery of St George**. The church itself is the most elegant and sophisticated of the 14th-century churches of Rhodes. Though similar in plan to the rural church of Ághios Nikólaos Foundouklí (*see p. 304*), St George's balanced proportions, graceful lines and fine stonework suggest an architect of considerable pedigree. The interior, though plain, gives an impression of space in excess of its actual size because of the absence of supporting columns. The mouths of earthenware jugs immured in the corners enhanced the acoustics for chant. The church is preceded by a narthex, probably added in the 15th century, and entered from the external courtyard through a door surrounded by a stone cornice carved with a running vine motif. Excavations immediately to the east and northeast have brought to light the paving of a Hellenistic street, as well as the foundations of an Early Christian basilica, a large area of whose fine polychrome marble floor in opus sectile is visible.

Ottoman monuments near the Suleimaniye Mosque

At the end of Orphéos is the late 18th-century **Hafez Ahmed Agha Library** (*map p. 262, B2; open Mon–Sat 9.30–4; free*), set in a walled courtyard of citrus trees and surrounded by *chochlákia* paving. Founded in 1793 as an act of beneficence by one of the sultan's equerries, it was intended for public use and may once have contained as many as 2,000 Arabic, Persian and Ottoman texts. The rectangular building is divided into two domed, luminous chambers. A number of Ottoman stone inscriptions have been collected at the west side.

Directly opposite the library is the handsome **Suleimaniye Mosque**, a faithful early 19th-century re-build of the mosque which Suleiman the Magnificent purportedly ordered to be constructed on the site of the Church of the Holy Apostles after his victorious entry into the city in 1523. On the corner opposite (southeast) is the mosque's imaret (now a café), built around a tranquil courtyard where a few ancient architectural fragments and Ottoman cannon balls have been collected.

Raised up on a surviving 7th-century bastion of the original Byzantine walls to the northwest of the Suleimaniye Mosque is the Clock Tower or **Roloï**, whose eclectic architectural mix has been widely, and perhaps undeservedly, vilified (*open 9–5; until 1am in June, July and Aug*). It was erected by Ahmet Fetih Pasha in 1857. From below it Theophilískou (*map p. 262, B2–C2*), lined attractively with overhanging wooden balconies, stretches due east along the line of the Byzantine walls: the regularly projecting towers (approximately every 25–30m) can still be discerned, often with medieval houses erected on top of them.

Panaitioú returns north, heading into an area devastated by the explosion of a gunpowder cache ignited by lightning in November 1856. Since there was, early on, a shortage of ammunition for the Knights during the siege of 1522, it remains a mystery why this cache was still here, unused, in the vaults of their principal **church of St John**, which was completely destroyed in the blast. Recent excavations have begun to reveal its foundations: its nave lay under where the Neoclassical Turkish school building now stands (*map p. 262, B2*), and its transepts were where the street now runs. The church was founded in 1309–10 and was probably completed by 1325. It contained the sepulchres of the Masters of the Order.

The church was once joined to the Grand Master's Palace by an arched loggia. In 1937 a replica was built by the Italians on the column-bases remaining from the destroyed 15th-century structure, and it now crowns the rise of the Street of the Knights.

THE GRAND MASTER'S PALACE

Open winter daily except Mon, 8.30–3; June–Sept open Tues–Sun 8–8, Mon 12.30–8. Ticket includes access to the exhibitions, open on alternate days.

The exterior of the Grand Master's Palace, with the crisp crenellations and round towers erected by the Italians between 1937 and 1940, is faithful to the general proportions and exterior appearance of what we know of the castle built by the Knights. The interior has been substantially modified and the spaces which saw so much medieval history are gone. Nonetheless, the palace contains many important treasures and two interesting permanent exhibitions, as well as the ghost of a particular period in recent Western history.

HISTORY OF THE BUILDING

The palace stands on the natural hill that formed the acropolis by the Byzantine city. Some of the foundation walls of the Byzantine citadel were uncovered in the basement of the present building in 1988. The construction of a new fortress, of rectangular plan, was begun by the Knights not long after their arrival, probably in the period of Grand Master de Villeneuve (1319–46), and was completed by the end of the century. In peacetime it was the residence of the Master and the assembly place of the Order's councils; in war, it was designed to accommodate the citizenry and to resist a siege, thanks to its strength and extensive underground storage areas. It was little used by the Turkish victors after 1522, except as a prison. The building fell into decay, was damaged in an earthquake in 1851, and then reduced to ground-floor level by the gunpowder explosion of 1856 (*see opposite*).

Restoration was not a priority during the first 20 years of Italian occupation. On the accession to the governorship of Mussolini's close advisor, Cesare Maria de Vecchi, in 1936, the idea first appeared of making it into an appropriate residence for a visit from the *Duce* or the King. With considerable haste and the extensive use of reinforced concrete clad in masonry, the building was re-erected between 1937 and 1940, with an interior redesigned in a manner suitable for modern occupation and in a spirit appropriate to the political aspirations of Rome in the 1930s. Neither Mussolini nor Vittorio Emanuele ever visited, and the work was not long completed when Italy was forced to relinquish the Dodecanese.

Entrance, court and ground floor

The imposing **South Gate** communicates between the military parade ground in front of the castle and its interior court. The chilling bareness of the **interior courtyard** has little architectural relief: the insensitively 'finished' statues of Roman dignitaries on the opposite side, which were brought in 1937 from the ancient odeion in Kos, are the sole figurative elements. A dozen large circular grain-stores had been sunk into the original floor; the marble 'well-heads' which mark three of them were added by the Italians.

The lower floor of the north wing houses the well-displayed permanent exhibition entitled **Ancient Rhodes: 2400 Years** (*open Wed, Fri, Sun*), which covers the history of the city along thematic lines. In the southwest corner is the second exhibition, **Rhodes from the Fourth Century until the Turkish Conquest (1522)** (*open Tues, Thur, Sat*), which displays manuscripts and illustrated books, icons, finely decorated ceramics and objects of trade and ritual.

Upper floor state rooms

The state rooms of the *piano nobile*, though spacious, high and luminous, have the curiously lifeless solemnity that totalitarian regimes always impart to their public spaces. Even the naturally joyous mosaics in the floors seem subdued. There are nearly two dozen panels of **inlaid ancient mosaic**, some from buildings on Rhodes and others brought from Kos, from late Hellenistic and Roman houses and Early Christian basilicas which came to light in Italian excavations after the 1933 earthquake. Some rooms also contain interesting furniture and sculpture, including a **cast of the *Laocoön***, the most famous and representative work of Rhodian Hellenistic sculpture (the original is in the Vatican Collection in Rome).

THE STREET OF THE KNIGHTS

Ippotón, the 'Street of the Knights' (*map p. 262, B2–C2*), leads steeply downhill, following the line of one of the main east–west streets of the ancient city. Photographs from the beginning of the last century show the street overhung by wooden Ottoman balconies, and with a teeming street-life which contrasts markedly with today's rather museified air. The street has seen much damage and much rebuilding, yet it has retained its original dimensions and the colour of its stone, and remains one of the completest and most homogeneous medieval streets in the Mediterranean. It stretches between the two most important poles of the Order of the Knights: the Grand Master's Palace and former church of St John at the top of the street, embodying the higher spiritual ideals of the Order, and the Hospital at the bottom, representing the Order's commitment to the worldly sufferings of the sick and poor. In between are the national representations and conventual residences of the Knights. The lower floor of these is normally a service courtyard surrounded by vaulted storage areas and stables, from which broad, open steps lead to high-ceilinged living and reception rooms above.

The upper part of the street

The oldest and best-preserved of the Knights' *auberges* is the **Inn of the Tongue of Spain** (*entrances both from Ippotón and Ippárchou*). The main entrance is distinguished by the Aragonese design of its arch, with characteristically wide voussoirs. This is one of the few façades in which elements have survived from before the siege of 1480; the original mid-15th-century masonry on the ground floor differs noticeably from that above. Steps lead up to the large hall, which though re-roofed and restored, still preserves its airy proportions and some of the original patterned floor. Opposite is the **Inn of the Tongue of Provence** (1518), with a decorated portal surmounted by four coats of arms set in a cross-shaped niche. A little downhill to the east, a plethora of panels with carved escutcheons (the arms of England appear repeatedly) mark the residence of the Prior of the Church (now the Italian Consulate) and the adjacent domed **Chapel of the Holy Trinity**. The sculpture of the *Madonna and Child* beneath a canopy on the corner is of the same period and has remarkably survived *in situ*.

The lower part of the street

Lower down, the north side of the street is dominated by the imposing front of the **Inn of the Tongue of France**, the west end of which is bounded by a small alleyway leading north to the **House of Djem**, entered through a white marble door frame (1512) carved with acanthus capitals and small rosettes. The house takes its name from the Ottoman prince who was lodged here during the summer of 1482.

> ### Djem, son of the Conqueror
> In the austere world of the Order of St John, the exotic figure of the Turkish prince Djem sounds an anomalous note. In 1481, Mehmet II, conqueror of Byzantium, died and his succession was contested between his two sons, Djem and his elder brother. The brother took the throne as Bayezit II. Thwarted in his bid for power, Djem turned to the Knights of St John and negotiated political asylum in their hands, promising perpetual peace between the Ottoman Empire and Christendom if the Knights helped him overthrow his brother. Grand Master d'Aubusson welcomed the possibility, and the prince was received with great ceremony in Rhodes. When emissaries from Istanbul arrived to sue for his return, Djem was moved to France. D'Aubusson exploited the situation adeptly, securing a yearly allowance of 45,000 ducats to keep the prince under permanent guard in the castle of Bourganeuf in the Auvergne, where each day he bathed, versified, and drank spiced wine in spite of Koranic proscriptions. His poems are beautifully rendered in English by Elias Gibb, in *Ottoman Poems*, published in London in 1882. Djem was too valuable a hostage, however, to survive for long: Pope Innocent VIII demanded his presence in Rome for a planned crusade in 1489. His successor, Alexander VI Borgia, imprisoned him. Charles VIII of France took him back from the pope in 1494. The following year Djem died, at the age of 35, in Capua, north of Naples, supposedly poisoned. He was later buried in Bursa.

On Láchitos, across from the House of Djem, is the **House of Admiral Costanzo Operti** (right), one of the few surviving examples of a bourgeois, civil residence from the period of the Knights. The core of the house dates from 1517; but there have been numerous additions and modifications since. Opposite the Inn of France is the **Mansion of Diomed de Villaragut**, built around a courtyard of cypress trees, with a 19th-century Ottoman fountain at its centre. The central gate is surmounted, as in the Inn of Spain, by an arch with wide voussoirs in the Aragonese manner. Villaragut was victualler to the Grand Master and Captain of the Tongue of Aragon from 1497 to 1504. The building suffered war damage in the last century; at the time of writing its eastern wing was being adapted to host the Archaeological Museum's prehistoric collection.

The two buildings which flank the lower end of street are the **Inn of the Tongue of Italy** of 1519 (much restored; now the offices of the Archaeological Department) and the **Hospital of the Knights** (*see below*), whose subsidiary entrance on the south side is framed by a portal of unexpected grandeur in the finest Gothic style. The main entrance faces the narrow opening of the Arnaldo Gate, due east across the attractive museum square. The entrance to the gate on the inside is flanked by two buildings: to the south is the **Inn of the Tongue of England**, originally erected in 1482, rebuilt in the 19th century and repaired by the British in 1949. Opposite, to the north, is the open portico of the **House of Guy de Melay**, restored by Armando Bernabiti in 1930.

The Hospital of the Knights and the Archaeological Museum

This was the Knights' second, or 'Great Hospital', built 80 years after its mid-14th-century predecessor on the west side of Plateía Argyrokástrou. The carved inscription above the main entrance refers to the founding of a new Xenodocheío (travellers' lodgings) by Grand Master Antonio Fluviá (1421–37), who endowed it with a gift of 10,000 florins. It was badly damaged in the siege of 1480, and was only finally in service towards the end of the same decade. Although tending to the sick was a primary mission of the Knights, their title of Hospitallers also referred to the hospitality and protection they were obliged to give to pilgrims travelling to and from the Holy Land. Only a part of this building, therefore, functioned as an infirmary, the rest being given over to lodgings for people and horses—hence the appearance it has of a caravanserai, with stables and storage space below and sleeping quarters above.

THE TREATMENT OF PATIENTS

The Hospitaller of the Order was by tradition the head of the Tongue of France. He appointed one of the Knights for a period of two years as the Infirmarer, whose job it was to supervise the doctors, surgeons, apothecaries and nurses. Patients did not pay for treatment, but were obliged to abide by the rules of the hospital, which hung on a chain in the main hall. These enforced tranquillity and quiet, and obliged every patient to be confessed on admission and to draw up a will, to abstain from gambling and to read only material of a religious nature. As elsewhere in the medieval world, physicians (superior in status) and surgeons (considered more as artesans) worked independently. When amputation was necessary, the hospital provided a certificate attesting that the intervention was as the result of injury and not a punishment for crimes. Patients were allowed a personal servant; they were allotted an individual bed and cubicle, and ate from silver plate, for what were considered reasons of hygiene. They were visited twice daily by the physicians on duty, as well as by the Infirmarer in person.

The building is conceived with customary military simplicity. The proceeds from renting out the row of seven independent magazines to either side of the entrance helped defray the expenses of the hospital and its work. The **interior courtyard**, substantially restored between 1913 and 1918 and again in 1949 after war damage, has a monastic chastity to it. The surfaces are unadorned except for some minimal attention to the capitals from which the ribs and vaults spring. This starkness is in contrast to the effect of the beautiful **infirmary ward** that occupies the entire length of the east side on the upper level. It should be imagined furnished with its 32 beds, canopied with fine brocade. The focus of the room was the exedra in the centre of the east wall, framed by a wide arch decorated with flamboyant tracery; here, below the high windows, stood the altar where Mass was celebrated daily. To both sides, small doorways lead into windowless cubicles, which probably served to provide a measure of privacy for the more intimate operations and examinations (men and women patients were not segregated).

A number of the Grand Masters' funerary monuments and escutcheons, salvaged from the Church of St John (*see p. 266*) have been collected here: at the north end are the arms of Juan Fernández de Heredia (1377–96), with bronze lettering and dark stone inlay, and an antique sarcophagus reworked as the tomb of Pierre de Corneillan (1353–55); at the southeast corner are the royal arms of England (c. 1400) in grey Lardos marble. The coats of arms (originally coloured) around the capitals of the seven central pillars are those of the Order and of Grand Master Pierre d'Aubusson (1476–1503), under whom the building was completed and who was himself successfully healed of seemingly fatal wounds received during the siege of 1480. To the south, the infirmary communicates with the pharmacy, refectory, kitchens and other service areas. These contain parts of the archaeological collection.

The Archaeological Museum

This is an important, though uneven collection (*open daily except Mon, 8–3; June–Sept 8–7*), with plenty of grave-goods, pottery and votive offerings but little of the great sculpture of the Rhodian School that was of such renown in later antiquity. The courtyard contains poorly-labelled mosaics and inscriptions. A staircase leads to an upper floor largely given over to sculpture (Rooms II–VI) and funerary and votive offerings from Kameíros and Ialysós. The most impressive sculptural piece is undoubtedly the mid-2nd-century BC *Aphrodite*, related in design to Praxiteles' famous *Aphrodite of Cnidos*. Immortalised by Lawrence Durrell as the 'Marine Venus', she was recovered from the sea north of the harbour of Rhodes, and may originally have stood in the Temple of Aphrodite by the Com-

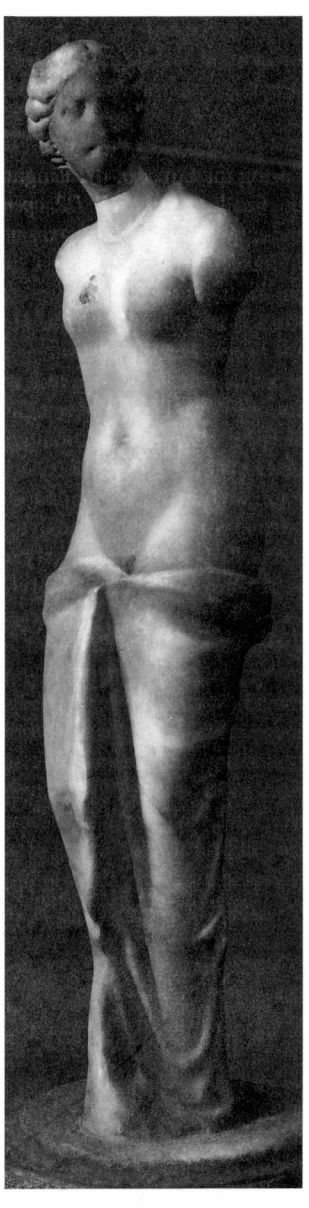

The 'Marine Venus', a 2nd-century BC statue of Aphrodite.

mercial Harbour. Her features have an impressionistic soft focus, the result of erosion by seawater, which has imparted to the stone a translucence akin to the original effect of ganosis, the waxing and polishing of marble statuary practised by the ancient Greeks.

The church of St Mary of the Castle

Facing the Street of the Knights from its lower end is the grand church of St Mary of the Castle (*map p. 263, D2; open daily except Mon, 8.30–3*). The façade is militarily bare, though its central corniced panel was probably decorated in the 15th century with a mural of the Virgin Mary as Protectress of the Castle, flanked by saints and knights of the Order. It was first built in the 11th century as the Panaghía tou Kástrou, the Greek Orthodox Cathedral of Rhodes, on a cross-in-square plan. Within the first decade of the Knights' arrival, its damaged and probably unfinished structure was almost entirely rebuilt as the Roman Catholic Cathedral of St Mary. The interior was transformed and the barrel vaults were given Gothic verticality by the ribs of cross-vaults and the inclusion of a clerestory of pointed windows. The interior is luminous and airy: stained glass, visible as late as 1826, originally modified its light. After 1522, a minaret, mihrab and porch with three cupolas (west front) were added, and the building was used for Islamic worship. The church also contains some Byzantine wall-paintings brought here for safety from the monastery of St Michael at Thári and some late 14th-century paintings salvaged from the tiny, dilapidated church of Ághios Zacharías on Chálki.

Around Plateía Argyrokástrou

Plateía Argyrokástrou (*map p. 262, C1*) houses the Historical Institute and Library of the Dodecanese and the delightful **Museum of Decorative Arts** (*open daily except Mon, 8.30–3*). The objects come from a wide variety of the islands and are exhibited in decorative arrangements loosely inspired by the interiors which they once adorned. Further on is the (Old) **Municipal Art Gallery** (*open daily except Sun, 8–2*), which hosts rotating displays of works by Rhodian artists and contains the Noel Rees Collection of prints and maps of Rhodes and the Dodecanese.

In the open area in front of the gallery are the remains of a 3rd-century BC **Temple of Aphrodite**, uncovered by Italian archaeologists in 1922. The temple—as was customary with shrines to Aphrodite, who was a patron divinity of sailors—occupied a prime location between the commercial and military ports. A clear reading of the site is hindered by the fact that different elements from the temple and the surrounding area have been stored and erected on top of the foundations without respect to the building's original design.

Of the three gates in this area, the main Liberty Gate is a modern breach in the walls created for motor traffic by the Italians in 1924. To its east is the **Gate of St Paul**, erected in the mid-15th century under Jacques de Milly, which was the main communication between the two harbours. To the south, and giving onto the Commercial Harbour, is the **Arsenal Gate**, whose broad, low form was originally designed to permit boats to slip from a boatyard into the water. It was sealed up before the 1480 siege and only opened again under Turkish dominion.

THE CENTRE OF THE OLD TOWN

This area of the medieval city is a labyrinth of tiny, crooked streets. Two itineraries are outlined below: the first begins at the Marine Gate (*map p. 263, D2*); the second at the Mehmet Agha Mosque (*map p. 262, C2*).

From the Marine Gate to the Mehmet Agha Mosque

The **Marine Gate** was the entrance to the city through which all visitors first passed, having disembarked in the Commercial Harbour. Above it are the eroded statues of the Virgin (protectress of the city), St John the Baptist (protector of the Knights) and perhaps St Peter. The gate leads immediately into the liveliest area of the old town. One block west (up Aiólou) is an area of excavation where the foundations of the east wall of the Byzantine fortifications can be seen below the ruins of a Turkish hamam. The hamam was part of the complex of the **Shadirvan Mosque** (10m south on Aristoménous), whose bold octagonal form and imposing height dominate the surrounding skyline.

The main street leads directly left into Plateía Ippokrátous, the heart of the commercial area of the old town. The building which dominates the square to the east is the **Castellania**, whose principal floor, built over an open loggia below, is approached by a flight of external steps rising to a terrace offering a good panorama over the lower part of the city. The building, constructed in 1507, housed the city's penal and commercial courts in the days of the Knights. Under the Turks, the upper floor became a prayer hall and the lower portico a fish-market: today it is home to the municipal library.

Pythagóra runs from the south of the square, following the line of one of the arteries of ancient Rhodes' Hippodamian plan. The second street west leads you into the plane-shaded square in front of the **Ibrahim Pasha Djami** (*map p. 263, D3*), founded in 1531 and now the principal mosque of the city's Muslim community. The minaret was re-erected on its original base by the Italians in 1928.

As Pythagóra continues south, it passes underneath the abandoned **Hadji Halil Mansion**, built between 1880 and 1890 in an elegant, Neoclassical style. Its tower, directly over the street, with its pedimented façade of triple round-arched windows, is a city landmark. A gently curving external wooden staircase leads to the upper floor. To the east is a large area of citrus orchard, thronged with bird life. With gardens to both sides of the street, this was one of the old town's most gracious dwellings in the last years of the Ottoman occupation.

Just beyond the Hadji Halil Mansion, in the excavated area of Plateía Kónti, the outer Byzantine walls emerge into view. Directly to the south, a medieval windmill stands on top of the remains of the southeast corner tower. Below it, on the south side, is a row of three Ottoman water-fountains. The windmill is private property, but another one, 100m to the west, can be visited. To get there, go west up Omírou. In a loop to the south is Aristeídou, which brings you to the **windmill**, whose parapet, reached by the spiral staircase inside, offers a comprehensive view over the old town.

A gateway on the north side of Omírou leads through into the open area of Plateía Doriéos, shaded by mature ficus trees and dominated to the east by the most beautiful and architecturally interesting of the many mosques in the city, the **Redjep Pasha Dja-mi** (1588; *map p. 262, C3*), beautifully proportioned and with fine external decoration. The decorations of the interior include 16th-century Iznik tile panels bearing Koranic verses in fine calligraphy. Above the door is the dedicatory inscription of Redjep Pasha, expressing the wish that the space 'may inspire an uplifting of the spirit'. The octagonal shadirvan (ritual fountain) to the west has survived in good condition. To the east side, overgrown with vegetation, is the türbe of Redjep Pasha. Its windows have the inter-locking voussoirs typical of high Ottoman architecture.

The western exit of Plateía Doriéos leads into one of the best-preserved arteries of the medieval town, Aghíou Phanourioú. Its length is punctuated by bracing buttresses between the buildings to each side, giving them support in time of earthquakes. To the south is the 13th-century church of **Ághios Phanoúrios**, important before the arrival of the Knights and still one of the most frequented churches of the city today. Beyond an unenticing metal and glass vestibule, the old church lies at a considerably lower level, its numinous, domed interior entirely decorated with three successive layers of wall-paint-ings (13th, early 14th and 15th centuries) in severely deteriorating condition. The most legible area (dated by inscription to 1335–36) is the niche on the right as you enter, showing donors and their wives presenting the church to Christ, in a garden of pome-granate trees. The ghostly forms of the Archangel Michael in the north transept and of the *Pantocrator* in the dome are visible, but many of the other scenes are unreadable.

Another church which predates the arrival of the Knights, the 13th-century **Ághios Spyridón**, lies 200m to the north, down the narrow alley opposite the Marco Polo Hotel. It is of an inscribed-cross plan, surmounted by a low cupola, pleasingly decorated with a slightly uneven blind arcade. Plateía Athinás opens out to the east. It is bisected by the impressive ruins of the 14th-century **basilica of the Archangel Michael**, perhaps built by the Greek community as a new cathedral after the Panaghía tou Kástrou (whose form it closely resembles) had been appropriated by the Knights. On the north side excava-tions reveal the foundations of a large Early Christian basilica of the 6th century (part of the curve of the main apse protrudes at the lowest level). This was destroyed perhaps as early as the 8th century; a small Byzantine church was then built over its south aisle, which survived until the larger 14th-century church was built to replace it.

The northern extension of Aghíou Phanourioú ends below one of the city's most visible mosques, whose windows and wide wooden eaves overlook the street at a con-spicuously different angle from everything else: this is the recently restored **Mehmet Agha Mosque** (*see below*).

From the Mehmet Agha Mosque to the Gate of St John

The **Mehmet Agha Mosque** (*map p. 262, C2*) was built in two separate phases between 1820 and 1875. The prayer hall was raised above a ground floor of arcaded shops, the rent from which contributed to the upkeep and charitable work of the mosque. The (restored) minaret, which here takes the form of a central, canopied wooden tower above the main door, is of a design common in Syria and the Levant, and shows the eclecticism of Ottoman architecture in this twilight period. The three water fountains below, surmounted by marble plaques inscribed in Osmanli and dated 1291 (1874/5 in the Western calendar), are contemporary with the mosque.

A few metres to the west, Sokrátous meets Menekléous. Menekléous winds through a succession of small squares lined with restaurants and cafés, opening at its summit into Plateía Ariónos, in front of the bulky form of the **Mosque of Mustafa III** (1765). The building has lost its minaret, the porch which shaded the main door, and the canopy over its finely carved fountain in front. But some of its decoration still survives: an ornate inscription over the door (bearing the sultan's dedication), and the mimbar, the mihrab and the wooden gallery inside the spacious prayer hall. Opposite the mosque are the buildings of the **Yeni Hamam**, restored and functioning as municipal baths (*map p. 262, B3; open daily except Sun, 10–5; Sat 8–5*). The earliest complex on the site was first built as a men's baths either under Suleiman the Magnificent or his successor, Selim II, between 1558 and 1568; in 1765 it was enlarged by Mustafa III with the addition of the women's baths. Together they constitute one of the finest examples of an Ottoman hamam outside the three royal cities of Istanbul, Bursa and Edirne.

From Plateía Ariónos, Acheláou leads north to Ippodámou. Follow it south until you see the narrow entrance of Androníkou on your left (signed to the 'Traditional Theatre'). It leads east to the entrance of the 15th-century monastic complex of **St Nicholas** (*map p. 262, B3*). The attractively walled and landscaped compound is entered through an ornate doorway, bordered by a carved rope design and surmounted by a framed niche, now lacking its dedicatory mural.

At the southern extremity of Ippodámou, in the corner to the left, are the remains of buildings from the **Roman agorá**. The area is still too small to see clearly the context of what has been uncovered. It is a sunken area, paved and backed by an immaculately constructed stretch of limestone wall in isodomic blocks with beautifully hand-worked surfaces. One block with an inscription in Greek is visible in the centre of the second row, and the column bases of a stoa form a line below. The circular base of a much later windmill stands at a higher level. This is the only part yet uncovered of an agorá complex which must have stretched for a considerable distance to both east and west.

Beyond the point where Ippodámou rejoins Omírou is the **St Athanasius Gate** of the Tongue of Aragon (*map p. 262, B4*). In 1401 Grand Master d'Aubusson ordered that this gate be sealed, and in September 1522 it was briefly re-opened for a sortie: by this time parts of the walls in this sector had been reduced to rubble by Turkish mining and artillery fire. It appears that Suleiman the Magnificent first entered the city by this gate, giving orders immediately afterwards that it be walled up so that nobody else might pass through it again. It was only reopened in 1922.

As you stand on the bridge, the inner walls of the sector of the Tongue of England stretch to the east, towards the Gate of St John (*see below*).

THE EAST OF THE OLD TOWN

The Gate of St John

At the Gate of St John, also called the Koskinoú Gate (*map p. 263, D4*), a high bridge leads across to the outer entrance. To either side diagonal lines in the masonry show where the tower was heightened and consolidated before 1522, and several blocked circular ports (originally cannon emplacements) can be seen in the parapet to the eastern side. The top of the parapet slopes outward to deflect missiles. The outer gate leads into an independent bastion, whose crescent plan completely shields the square Tower of St John at its centre. This is reached across a second, exposed bridge (now stone, but originally a wooden drawbridge) leading to a second gate, with the chapel of St John the Baptist to the left. The gate leads into a crowded area of popular houses and workshops. Opposite are the steps which are the exit of the tour of the walls.

Holy Trinity and St Catherine's

Plateía L. Rodíou is dominated to the west by the striking silhouette of the 15th-century **church of the Holy Trinity** (Aghía Triáda; *map p. 263, E3–E4*), which rises above an area of fragrant jasmine, bougainvillea and hibiscus (*officially open daily except Mon, 12.30–2.30*). The building probably began as the katholikon of a monastic complex, and though humble in proportions it was once outstandingly decorated: the large, ornate insets of Latin-cross form to either side of the north doorway were once filled with ornamental ceramic tiles; the exquisite wooden doors are now preserved in the exhibition 'Rhodes from the Fourth Century until the Turkish Conquest' in the Grand Master's Palace. The interior floor is laid with coloured marbles and the walls are decorated with interesting paintings.

The square around the church has suffered war damage; on the east side, however, a house of some importance, with 16th-century corniced windows, has survived. To its south is the 14th-century **church of St Catherine**, whose Turkish name, Ilk Mihrab, meaning 'First Mihrab', suggests that this was the first place of Christian worship to be turned to Muslim use. Though small and architecturally unprepossessing, it is magnificently decorated with paintings by 14th- and 15th-century artists of considerable accomplishment.

The eastern extremity of the old town

The Acandia Gate of the Tongue of Italy (*map p. 263, F3*) is protected to the south by the Del Carretto Bastion. This was always one of the more vulnerable points of the city's enceinte because it is here that the moat levels out towards the coast. Suleiman directed his most insistent artillery and cannon fire against this gate.

A short distance south along Kisthiníou, on the left, is a **commemorative fountain** dedicated by the International Jewish Community in 1913 to General Giovanni Ameglio, who took Rhodes for the Italians in May 1912, entering the city through the Jewish Quarter. He became the island's first commander and promoted largely respectful relations between the authorities and the Jewish community, which then numbered nearly 5,000 people.

The streets ends in front of the 15th-century church of **St Panteleimon** (*map p. 263, F2*), whose interior has been lavishly redecorated with modern Byzantine paintings of considerable merit, executed on linen. Behind the church, against the eastern extremity of the walls, are the scant excavated remains of a large, Gothic church, dedicated by Pierre d'Aubusson to 'Our Lady of Victory'. The church's life was short and poignant: built after the 1480 siege in thanks to the Virgin, it was destroyed in the siege of 1522; its ruins suffered a final destruction in the last war.

The Hospice of St Catherine and the Virgin of the Burgh

Straddling the line of the Hellenistic harbour walls is the predominantly 15th-century **Hospice of St Catherine** (*map p. 263, E2*), founded in 1392 by Fra' Domenico d'Alemagna to accommodate Italian pilgrims travelling to and from the Holy Land.

Pindárou returns west towards the commercial area, passing alongside the substantial remains of **St Mary of the Burgh**, roofless apart from a southwest chapel and the three Gothic apses, which still stand with long lancet windows and ribbed vaults. For most of the last century the site was bisected by the course of Alhádef street: the street has since been closed and the church nave is now a theatrical setting for children to play among the column bases and for swallows to nest under the arches. Built according to a Western Gothic design just after the middle of the 14th century, it slightly postdates its sister-church of St Mary of the Castle, from whom its epithet distinguishes it: the 'Castle' was the area of the Knights, while the 'Burgh', to the east, was the area of the commoners and merchants.

The synagogue

Pindárou leads into what was known to the Jewish community as the Calle Ancha ('Broad Street'), the heart of the *Judería*, renamed the Square of the Jewish Martyrs in memory of those who died in the Holocaust. It is a pleasant space, surrounded by balconied buildings, and occupies the area of a medieval square named after another victim of persecution, St Sebastian. A modern fountain decorated with seahorses stands in its centre. Both of the two narrow streets running south from Calle Ancha (Byzantíou and Symmíou) lead into the heart of Jewish Rhodes. On the right-hand side of Byzantíou, a doorway with a Hebrew inscription gives onto the roofless ruin of what was once the **Kahal Midrash** synagogue. During the last war, this area was the worst affected by British air raids, just as it had been the area most damaged in the sieges of 1480 and 1522. Only about 40 Jews now remain on Rhodes, and only one of the four synagogues and three oratories that once served the community survives: the **Kahal Kadosh Shalom** (or 'Congregation of Peace') at no. 8 Symmíou. Built between 1575 and 1577, it is also the oldest surviving synagogue in Greece (*open daily except Sat, 10.30–3*). The layout is typical of Sephardic synagogues, with the tevah in the centre of the room facing the canonical direction of Jerusalem. The floor is attractively paved in Rhodian *chochlákia* work with an abstract design, and bears the date 5601 (1840). The walls were originally decorated with murals of the Ten Commandments: these have been partially—and a little clumsily—repainted on the left-hand wall. The collection box is a fluted pagan altar-stand. To the east side of the building is a courtyard where a water-fountain has been recently uncovered, bearing a Hebrew inscription with the date 5338 (1577), the same year as the completion of the synagogue.

THE JEWISH COMMUNITY OF RHODES

Jews were present on Rhodes from the 3rd or 2nd century BC, and in the 12th century AD there was a community of over 500. Their co-existence with the Knights of St John was peaceful and constructive until in 1502 when, in the wake of the Spanish expulsion of Jews, Grand Master Pierre d'Aubusson, under pressure from the Church, imposed either exile or forced conversion on the Rhodian community. Most took advantage of the 40-day period of grace and left for Salonica, Ferrara, Constantinople and other destinations with large Jewish populations. Suleiman the Magnificent, on taking the city, did more than rescind this proscription: he encouraged the repatriation of Jews to Rhodes, sanctioned a measure of administrative autonomy for them, and accorded several privileges to the community. This attracted many Jews to the city, but the result was that the balance of the community changed: there were now more Sephardim than Greek-speaking Romaniot Jews, and they brought with them a Judaeo-Spanish language, known as Ladino, that was widely used right into the 20th century. Italian occupation after 1912 initially brought no particular problems, but from the mid-1930s restrictions increased and autonomy was reduced, until the Fascist laws finally enshrined the elimination of Jewry as an article of faith. The inevitable consequences of the island coming under Nazi German control in 1943 are dispassionately recounted in the small display in the rooms adjoining the synagogue. In July 1944, almost 1,600 Jews, those who had not had the opportunity or the foresight to flee, were rounded up, shipped to Athens, and thence ultimately to Auschwitz. Only 30 men and perhaps 120 women survived.

THE NEW TOWN & AREAS OUTSIDE THE WALLS

The Aquarium

The Aquarium at the northern tip of the town (*map p. 281, F2*) is one of the most pure and memorable buildings of the later period of the Italian occupation (1934; Armando Bernabiti). The plain façade is relieved only by the blue and white reliefs of sea creatures around the doorway. The paving of the approach is lined with ceramic medallions sporting the symbols of the various Dodecanese islands.

The building houses the interesting Marine Aquarium and Hydrobiological Institute (*open daily 9–8.30; Nov–March 9–4.30*). The collection, which is mostly laid out below sea-level, consists of an artificial labyrinthine grotto of seawater tanks containing a wide variety of local marine life, fish, crustaceans and reptiles (turtles). The upper floor has a number of unusual preserved specimens and some interesting marine exhibits visible through microscopes. The remarkable display of an ancient monk seal burial, dating from the 1st century BC, is unique in what it tells us of ancient attitudes to animals:

the seal's remains, together with small grave gifts and the remains of humans and of a dog (also given funerary honours), were found ritually buried in a family inhumation which came to light during excavations in the area of the Commercial Harbour in 1999.

The Museum of Modern Greek Art

The elongated elliptical square directly to the south of the Aquarium was part of the New Urban Plan drawn up in 1926. In a large building on the eastern side of the square is the Museum of Modern Greek Art, which incorporates the collection of the former Art Gallery of Rhodes (*map p. 281, F2; open Tues–Sat 8–2; also 5–8pm on Fri*).

The collection is well displayed over two floors: the first floor dedicated to masters of 19th- and 20th-century Greek art and the upper floor to contemporary painting in Greece. The first shows the constant tension within early modern Greek painting between those who worked within a European (predominantly French-influenced) academic tradition, and the voice of a Greek 'folk' tradition, often of a consciously naïf character. Several of the most prominent artists of the age, including Alekos Fassianos and Yiannis Gaïtis, are represented on the upper floor.

The Grand' Albergo delle Rose and Ottoman Cemetery

South from the Aquarium is the large building of the **Grand'Albergo delle Rose** (Florestano di Fausto; *map p. 281, F2*), which today also incorporates the city's Casino. Just beyond the southern exit is the tiny **Villa Cleobolus**, where Lawrence Durrell lived from May 1945 until April 1947 and composed the greater part of his *Reflections on a Marine Venus*. 'It is difficult to convey the extraordinary silence of this garden', he wrote, referring to the dense vegetation in the picturesque **Ottoman Cemetery**, a corner of which the minuscule villa occupies. The large area of the cemetery, shaded with eucalyptus trees, which today encompasses several domed mausolea and a multitude of inscribed tombstones, was occupied in the 15th century by a cemetery of the Knights and a walled garden belonging to the Grand Master. The entrance is at the eastern extremity, through a doorway on the west side of Plateía Koundouriótou. A passage between two fine Ottoman houses in a perilous state of repair leads into a pebble-paved courtyard where the Turkish guardian and his family still live. The 19th-century mosque (left), with its ornate minaret in Egyptian style, still functions; it is built on the site of the former Hospitaller Church of St Anthony. The **türbe** to the right contains the green-draped sarcophagus of a 16th-century corsair, Murat Reis, who became admiral under Suleiman the Magnificent and played an important role in the elimination of piracy from Ottoman waters. He died in 1609 and his tomb is respectfully maintained as a place of cult.

Plateía Koundouriótou and the cathedral

Plateía Koundouriótou (*map p. 281, F3*) is a rich assemblage of some of the most interesting architecture of the Italian period. On the landward side, the low cemetery wall (punctuated by a fine, carved Ottoman fountain, 10m to the north of the cemetery entrance) joins the **Naval Administration Building** (1925) to the south; to the north is the **Rhodes Garrison Building** (1926). Opposite (north side of the square) is the

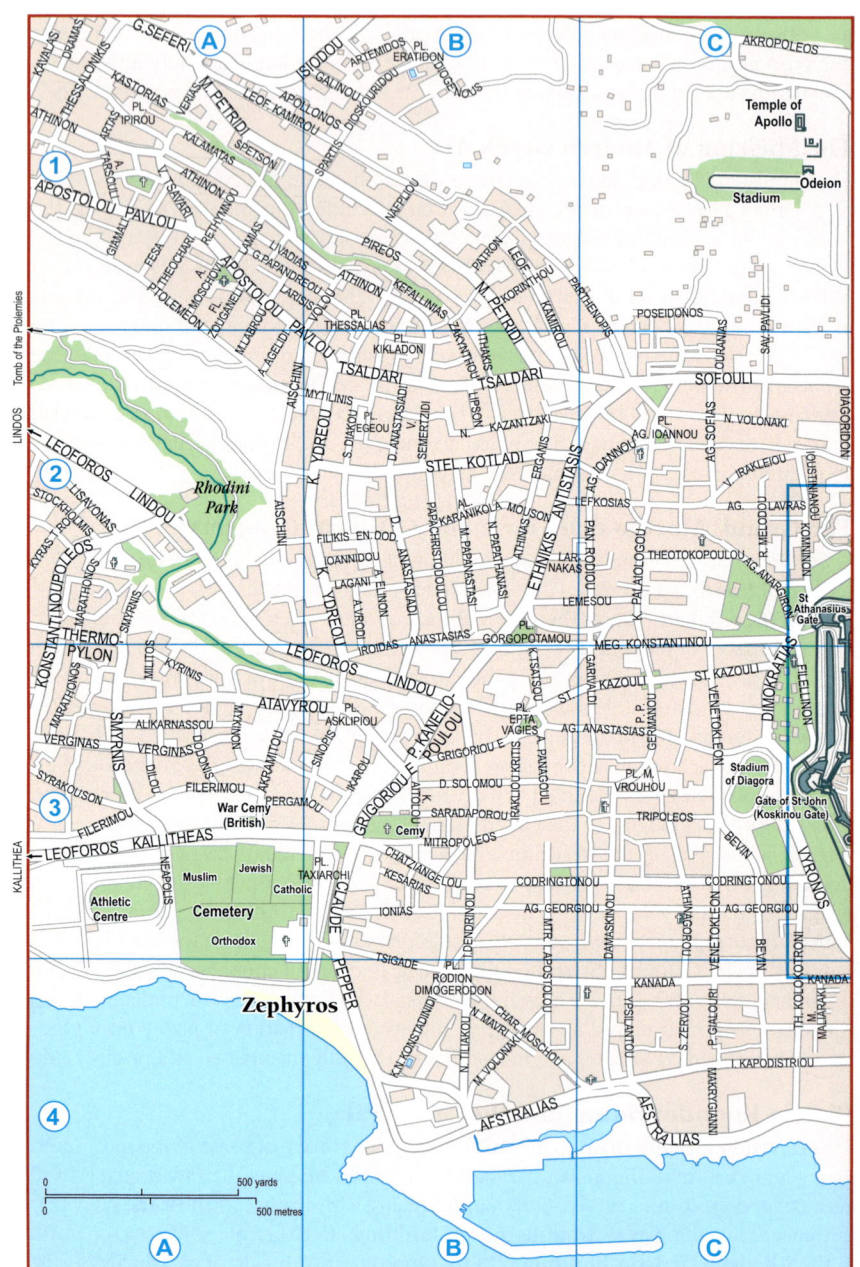

AIRPORT, IALYSOS

D E F

N

1

DIAGORIDON

Temple of
Zeus and Athena

Mt
Smith

Nymphaea

AKROPOLEOS

VOREIOU IPIROU

ENOPLON DYNAMEION

CHEIMARAS

PINDOU

PAPALOUKA

VOREIOU IPIROU

METAXA

AKTI KANARI

APODIMON

THEO

AMERIKIS

PL. ARCH.
CHRISANTHOU

AKTI

ORFANIDOU

KENNEDY

SOFOULI

PAVLOU
MELA

PINDOU

ERYTH. STAVROU

ENZELOU

G.
LEODOUS

G. GRIVA

OKTOVRIOU

KATHOPOULI

IONOS DRAGOUMI

KILIS

MANDILARA

N. G. GRIVA

AKTI

MIAOULI

KALYMNOU

Aquarium

AG. IOANNOU

CHEIMARAS

NAVARINOU

RIGA FEREOU

VROXINAS

DIMOKRATIAS

ALEX. DIAKOU

ENZELOU

28

MANDILARA

IROON POLYTECHNIOU

AKADIMIAS

SERRMOUI

PL.
ENIDRIOU

KO

KASOU

G. CHARITOS

Modern
Art
KO Mus.

2

Aegean
University

St George's
Tower

D. Amboise
Gate

ORFEOS

MAKARIOU

AL PAPAGOU

AMERIKIS

PL.
KIPROU

MARTIOU

25

MARTIOU

EFSTATHIOU

ZORGIOU PAPANIKOLAOU

PL.
SAVIA

Delle Rose
(Casino)

Ottoman
Cemy

Theatre

PL.
ELEFTHERIAS

PL.
KOUNDOU-
RIOTOU

2

IPPODAMOU

Suleimaniye

OMIROU

PL.
KLAVRIO-
NOS

Grand Master's
Palace

MAKARIOU

Dimarcheion

Nomarcheia

AG.
PHANOURIOU

PL.
DORIEOS
ATHINAS

OMIROU

SOKRATOUS

IPPOTON

PL.
RIMINIS

Nea Agora

Cathedral

SOPHOK-
LEOUS

PYTHAGORA

IPPOK-
RATOUS

ALEXANDRIAS

Great
Hospital

St Mary
of the Castle

Arnaldo
Gate

Liberty
Gate

PL.
NEORION

AKTI BOUBOULINAS

MANDRAKI
HARBOUR

Tower of
St Nicholas

ARISTOTELOUS

Marine Gate

Arsenal
Gate

Gate of
St Paul

Windmills

3

PL.
EVRAION
MARTYRON

LI RODIOU

SACHTOURI

LYNX

COMMERCIAL
HARBOUR

De Naillac
Tower

Del
Carretto
Bastion

St Mary
of the Burgh

Gate of the Virgin

St Catherine's Gate

Tower
of the Windmills

Acandia
Gate

KISTHINIOU

MILHOS

PL.
MELINA
MERCOURI

pp.262–263

AUSTRALIAS

ACANDIA
BAY

4

D E

RHODES TOWN

large pantheon-like dome of the **Elli Building** (1935), formerly the La Ronda Sea Baths complex (*under restoration at the time of writing*). Towards the shore is Rodolfo Petracco's **former Navy Club** of 1929 (now the Lido building), with an extravagantly Oriental silhouette and entrance decorated with relief mouldings of marine creatures and an anchor. Closing off the square to the south is the most ornate of the four façades of the **Rhodes Administration Building** (Florestano di Fausto; 1926–27; now the Nomarcheía; *see p. 256*). At its southern end, it is linked by means of an open Flag Court to the offices of the Metropolitan of Rhodes, which in turn is contiguous with the city's cathedral. The court is a wide-arched space, framing open views of the harbour and enclosing a ceremonial flag-pole mounted inside a well-preserved 2nd-century AD Roman altar. The two ecclesiastical buildings, the offices of the Metropolitan (former Archbishopric) and the Cathedral of St John (now the Metropolitan Church of the Annunciation), strike a rather dour note by comparison. The **cathedral**, by Florestano di Fausto, was created as a faithful recreation of the Hospitaller church of St John, which once stood across from the Grand Master's Palace (*see p. 266*). Its exterior was originally spare and its interior undecorated. When it became an Orthodox place of worship after 1947, a complete cycle of wall-paintings was commissioned for it from the painter Photis Kontoglou. The cycle includes the scenes of the lives of Christ and the Virgin according to the 24 verses of the Akathist Hymn.

A pleasant walk along the harbour-front to the south passes the Post Office, Court House, the Bank of Greece and the **Néa Agorá** (Florestano di Fausto; 1925–26; *map p. 281, E3*). It is entered through a gateway facing the port. At the centre of the leafy and spacious interior is the raised fish-market kiosk, with the original scagliola counters and water-fountain under a cupola.

Mandráki Harbour

Mandráki (*map p. 281, E3*), the more northerly of the city's two natural harbours, was the military port of the ancient city. In the Middle Ages it was the principal shipyard. The long mole which forms its eastern side (crowned with three ruined 17th-century **windmills**) is the result of a continuous enlargement of the original 4th-century BC harbour walls. At its tip, the strategically important **Fortress of St Nicholas** (*closed at the time of writing*) was built in the mid-1460s. It constituted the only forward bastion of the city's defences to the north, vital for the protection of the two harbours. The crenellated circular tower in the centre, together with the lower, south-facing, additional stirrup-tower, constitute the 15th-century core; the elliptical enceinte of walls was added as part of the early 16th-century re-fortification: the whole was repaired and modified in Ottoman times.

The entrance to the harbour is marked by two columns supporting **bronze statues of a stag and a doe**, symbols of the City of Rhodes. It is here that folk tradition holds that the Colossus of Rhodes once stood, although it appears more likely that it was the largest of a group of smaller statues erected either in the southwest corner of the harbour, where the Néa Agorá now stands, or else slightly further to the southwest, on the natural rise now occupied by the Grand Master's Palace.

THE COLOSSUS OF RHODES

It was common practice in the ancient world to dedicate a statue from the captured booty of a victorious campaign. Thus the proceeds from the sale of the
armaments left behind when Demetrius Poliorcetes abandoned his siege in 304–
303 BC was put to the making of a bronze statue of Helios, the patron god of
the island. Chares of Lindos, a student of Lysippus, one of the greatest bronze-
sculptors of antiquity, was given the commission for the work, a task which is
said to have led him to bankruptcy and suicide.

The hollow statue, cast in many sections, stood to a height of around 32m and
took twelve years to complete. Gilded sun-rays burst from around its head, and,
according to some versions, it held a flaming torch in one raised arm, which functioned as a beacon to mariners. In 227 BC, less than 60 years after its completion,
an earthquake sundered it. An oracular pronouncement apparently forbade the
citizens to re-erect it. It still lay felled almost 250 years later, in the time of Strabo
and Pliny, 'still a marvel as it lies on the ground', according to the latter, who says
that it was hardly possible for a man to join arms around the thumb.

The statue's bronze was eventually sold as scrap metal in the Levant by Jewish
traders in the 7th century AD. Because the writer known as Pseudo-Philo of Byzantium included the Colossus in his Seven Wonders of the World, the vanished work
excited great curiosity in medieval times, and was recreated in the popular imagination—impressively but improbably—bestriding the entrance to the harbour.

ANCIENT RHODES: OUTSIDE THE CITY CENTRE

The ancient city of Rhodes, according to Strabo (*Geog. XIV, 2.9*), had been laid out on a plan drawn up by the 'architect of the Piraeus', namely Hippodamus of Miletus. It occupied a terrain which was neither steep nor confined by problematic geography, nor previously inhabited to any significant degree. Because the territory was ample, the city was spaciously planned. Its original core stretched in a wide, sloping band west from the Commercial Harbour and Acandia Bay to the summit of the acropolis (today's Mt Smith), which was crowned with large temples. As the city grew in wealth and population, it expanded both northwards and to the southeast, into the area occupied today by Zéphyros. It measured approximately 3km from the northern limit to the southeast walls. The 4th-century southern walls run east along a course which cuts diagonally through the blocks south of today's Konstantínou Palaiológou and Garíváldi streets, across Plateía Eptá Vaghiés, and then follows Grigoríou E and Claude Pepper and descends to the shore along the north side of the main modern cemetery (*map p. 280, C2–B3*). The ancient cemeteries extended beyond this line to the south.

There are many points where elements of the ancient break through the fabric of the modern. The most significant are mentioned below in two groups: in the area between the new town and the ancient acropolis (Mt Smith); and in the areas further to the south and east, which were occupied predominantly by the ancient cemeteries.

Between the new town and the acropolis

The storage rooms of a Hellenistic house give a rare picture of the service areas and cellars of a 4th-century BC dwelling (*entered to the left side of the large Tourism School on Troizínas, across from the d'Amboise Gate. The site is at the far side of the car parking area, and currently lies underneath a school building; map p. 281, D2*). Steps lead down to the ancient floor-level, where there are two areas of polychrome floor decoration, suggesting a well-to-do residence. Beside this and below are several deep chambers cut into the bedrock that were used for storing grain and other perishables. The easternmost chamber has small steps leading into it and grooves for sliding a wooden retaining door; there are wedge-shaped shafts at various points used for filling the chambers. At the opposite end is a deep cylindrical well with foot-holes to each side.

On the slopes of the acropolis

The **Early Christian basilica** beneath the buildings at the intersection of Cheimáras and Pávlou Melá (*map p. 281, D2*), about halfway up the acropolis hill, is the most extensive and important Palaeochristian complex uncovered in the city. The site is unattractively overhung with apartment buildings, which rise on concrete piles from the excavations, but the area uncovered and the quality of the mosaic floor (visible from Pávlou Melá), make it worth seeking out. One block further west, along the edge of Sofoúli, are the foundations of street-facing **Hellenistic houses**. The streets in this area closely follow the ancient Hippodamian grid. Nearby to either side of Enóplon Dynámeon (*map p. 281, D1*) are the excavations of a so-called '**Palatial Building**' and **Hellenistic House**.

The area of olive and oak trees stretching to the west of Diagorídon and up to the crown of the hill is an archaeological park (*map p. 280, C1; always open*) comprising the ancient stadium, an odeion and the Temple of Pythian Apollo, most of which was first uncovered by Italian archaeologists between 1919 and 1929. According to the notions of the time, what was uncovered was also considerably restored, in a manner that has deadened its antique appeal. The ground level of the 2nd-century BC **stadium** has risen, leaving the first row of seats partly sunken: a gentle swelling curve in the two long sides can be detected. At the points where steps descend through the seating, small slots can be seen in the row of seats with back-rests, for fixing wooden retaining panels or doors. Beyond its north end is a small building referred to as a theatre, which has been mostly reconstructed (apart from the orchestra and three of the seats, which are original). Although too small for a theatre proper, this probably functioned as an **odeion**.

From the odeion, steps lead up an impressive work of terracing. The Italian restorers have intervened heavily, but the well-designed stepping of some of the lower areas and the rustication of the ancient blocks clearly distinguish the antique work from the new. At the top, the ground levels out onto the terrace of the twin sanctuary of Apollo Pythios and his sister Artemis, whose temple stood below, a little to the north. The columns of one corner of the 4th-century BC **Temple of Apollo** were re-built by the Italian archaeologists to indicate the height of the building: it was a hexastyle Doric temple, orientated due east.

Mount Smith

Along the ridge of Mt Smith (which takes its name from Admiral Sir William Sidney Smith, who lodged in a house on the hill in 1799 and 1800 during his campaigns against the French Navy in the Napoleonic Wars) are the few scattered remains of the acropolis of ancient Rhodes. At the highest point (111m), to the northern end, were sited the two **temples of Zeus Polieus and of Athena Polias**, dominating the skyline from every direction. Virtually nothing remains except for a few scattered column-drums. To the east and a little below, extensive cutting of the rock and stretches of walling give an intimation of the flight of terraces which led to them. These mark the edge of an interesting area of underground nymphaea.

These **sanctuaries of the nymphs**, which sink deeply down from ground level at the northern end of Mt Smith, just east of the summit, probably began life as cisterns. A good place to begin is the hidden hermitage or grotto of Ághios Nikólaos, where the pagan cult of the nymphs seems to live on in a Christian guise (just below the east side of Voreíou Ipírou; *map p. 281, D1*). Across the road is a series of interconnected chambers with arched niches below ground level, with rock-cut steps leading down into them. The complex is entered down a long, rock-cut sloping dromos from the east.

The ancient cemeteries and walls

Ancient cemeteries lay outside inhabited areas. Rhodes was a large city with a wealthy population, and the area given over to burials extends for nearly 3km to the south and southeast. A lot of it can be seen by following the line of the main north–south artery of Sofoúli and Tsaldári (southeast of the acropolis hill; *map pp. 281, D1–280, B2*). At the large junction with Ethnikís Antístasis is a small funerary area with some mosaic remains and small *oikia* for inhumation. By following Parthenópis west for 700m from this junction, you come to the **Monument of the Shield**, a Hellenistic tomb with an emblematic carved shield over the door. The tomb extends in a long wall which must imitate the street façades of city houses of the period: to the right side the front is carved with the appearance of wooden doors. All this provided a quasi-theatrical backdrop to any ceremony of remembrance for the dead. To the north of here is the area supposed by some archaeologists to be the site of the theatre of the ancient city.

Tsaldári ends where Konstantínou Ydréou cuts across it to the east. To the south stretches Rhodíni Park, purported site of Rhodes' ancient school of rhetoric. Seven hundred metres of track southwest through the park brings you to the so-called **Tomb of the Ptolemies** or Ptolemaion (*beyond map p. 280, A2*), an important Hellenistic funerary monument with a pedimented doorway and stuccoed façade. This is in effect an outcrop of natural rock fashioned into a 30-m square rectangle, which has been dressed on the north side with a row of carved, engaged pilasters which have been plastered and were once coloured, and which stand as if on a stepped crepis. As with the Monument of the Shield, this may give us a picture of how the street-front of a well-to-do residence would have appeared. In the interior is a transverse entrance chamber that leads into the main burial chamber with niches for the deposition of bodies. Below the façade are other, humbler burial loculi in the ground. The whole block shows evidence of having been faced on its other sides. The tomb's name has no historical foundation and the ascription in local folklore to the ruling royal family of Egypt, with whom Rhodes had very close connections, is no more than a reference to the fact that this is one of the biggest tomb complexes in the area.

The route out of the city to Aghía Marína and Kallithéa down Codringtónou (named after Admiral Sir Edward Codrington, hero of both the Battle of Trafalgar and of the Battle of Navarino in the Greek War of Independence), crosses the best-preserved stretch of the **ancient city walls**, re-built after the siege of Demetrius Poliorcetes in 304–303 BC. Areas of foundations and towers stretch to left and right.

On the west side of Leofóros Kallithéas are several more fine necropoleis cut into the rock. Decorated marble altars still stand in front of some of the sarcophagus chambers.

NORTHWEST RHODES & KAMEIROS

Excavations near the coast at the wide **bay of Triánda** (*map p. 258, C1*) have uncovered an extensive and important prehistoric settlement, established in the 16th century BC by the Minoans to facilitate trade between Crete and Asia, and later superseded by a larger Mycenaean settlement. A 30-cm layer of volcanic ash from Thera was found in one of the lowest levels. Further back, towards the base of the hill to the south, a wealth of burial finds have come to light, from Mycenaean down to Classical times. The finds are exhibited both in the Archaeological Museum of Rhodes and in the British Museum.

The **village of Triánda** occupies the site of the commercial area of ancient Ialysós, a prosperous independent Dorian city, and one of the three major ancient settlements of the island, whose acropolis was on the summit of Mt Philérimos, behind and to the south. It was famous in antiquity for the Diagoridai, a family of oligarchs who also produced a number of Olympic victors.

THE ACROPOLIS OF IALYSOS

A winding road (*signed*) climbs up from Triánda through dense pine woods to the panoramic acropolis of ancient Ialysós, on the flat limestone summit of Mt Philérimos (267m). In spite of its importance in antiquity, there are fewer ancient remains to see here than at either Lindos or Kameíros; a monastery stands here now.

The Temple of Athena and monastery

On entering the enclosure (*open April–Oct 8.30–7.30; 8.30–2.30 in winter; closed Mon*), the remains of the 3rd-century BC **Temple of Athena Ialysia** are visible directly in front of the monastery buildings. The stylobate is preserved, perfectly orientated to the cardinal points, and nearby are the drums of fluted columns, some of which retain vestiges of coloured stucco. In the 6th century AD, an Early Christian basilica with three aisles was built over the temple. The existing **monastery church** to the north is dedicated to the Virgin of Philérimos (or Filermo) and was heavily rebuilt by the Italians in 1931. The plan is highly unusual, with three separate chapels inside, reached through a vaulted vestibule.

THE VIRGIN OF PHILERIMOS

The monastery's treasure was the priceless icon of the Virgin of Philérimos, which was brought from Jerusalem in the 13th century and was believed to have been painted by St Luke. At times of great danger it was transferred to Rhodes to give the city divine protection. The icon was one of the only possessions the Knights took with them when they sailed away from Rhodes in January 1523 after the second Turkish siege. It was then kept in the Co-Cathedral of St John in Valletta. Later, when Malta was surrendered to the French in 1798, the ill-starred Grand Master, Ferdinand von Hompesch, sent the icon to Tsar Paul of Russia; after the Bolshevik Revolution it left Russia, finding its way to Yugoslavia, where it subsequently disappeared. There are claims that it is now in Montenegro.

On the outside of the church (east side) is an unusually high stone pulpit, looking onto the monastery's tranquil cloister; beyond this is the former abbot's residence. The most unspoiled medieval survival is the tiny underground **chapel of Ághios Geórgios Chostós** (the epithet refers to his 'penetrating' lance), below the level of the temple (*reached by turning left at the entrance to the site*). It was probably the crypt or funerary chapel of a church which once stood above. Its interior is covered in wall-paintings which, though in poor condition, are still legible.

The fortress and water-fountain

The hilltop to the east of the monastery bears the traces of much history. At the northeast extremity are the remains of a Byzantine fortress incorporating fragments of ancient building material; this fell to the Knights of St John in 1306, was enlarged by them and, in turn, was captured by Suleiman the Magnificent in 1522. The sultan planned his siege of Rhodes from a camp on this vantage point.

The treasure of the site (*closed at the time of writing*) is the ancient **spring and colonnaded water-fountain**, deep down the southern side of the acropolis, amidst a stand of plane trees. Steps descend steeply 50m from the southern extremity of the archaeological enclosure to the elegant Hellenistic structure, which dates from the mid-4th century BC and was reassembled in 1926 by Italian archaeologists. The colonnade is about 9m long with the fountain tanks behind, faced in marble with decorative lions' heads both on the rear wall, just above water-level, and on the front: only one of these was perforated and functioned as a spout. One of the antae bears a scarcely legible inscription with regulations for the use of the fountain.

THE COASTAL ROUTE TO KAMEIROS

Although considerably built up in the last few decades, the main coastal area southwest of Triánda still preserves a number of beautiful **Neoclassical villas**, some along the main road itself. Usually marked by venerable pine trees in their gardens (or in a couple of cases by immense ficus trees), these elegant constructions date from a period of relative prosperity between 1890 and 1920. **Kremastí**, the next village after Triánda, is a lively centre, clustered around a small castle (just inland of the main road), whose base is a 15th-century fortress built by the Knights and reworked in later epochs. The village is noted for its nine-day festival for the Assumption of the Virgin (14th–23rd August), which combines religious ceremonies, athletics, craft displays, music and dance.

Beyond Kremastí a road leaves to the left, connecting the airport with the east coast and the southern suburbs of Rhodes Town. After six kilometres, on the right, just south of the village of Pastída, is the **Rhodes Bee Museum** (*map p. 258, C1; open Mon–Sat 8.30–3*) with a shop and live apiary displays. The coast road continues southwest past the airport. Near the turning for Theológos, the Hellenistic **Sanctuary of Erythimian Apollo** is signed to the left (500m), but little actually remains to be seen of the temple.

Inland, approximately 5km beyond the village of Theológos is **Petaloúdes**, the 'Valley of the Butterflies'—too renowned, perhaps, for the good of the insects themselves (*open with ticket 8.30–6 July–Sept; unrestricted and free at other times of year*). This is a densely wooded valley, coursed with streams and criss-crossed by wooden walkways and bridges aimed at containing visitor access to the spectacle of the large numbers of a single species of colourful moth which congregate here during the summer months.

PETALOUDES

The moths of the Valley of the Butterflies, of the species *Callimorpha quadripunctaria* (the second epithet referring to the pattern of a Roman IV on the upper wing) are generally referred to as Jersey Tiger moths in English. They come here in large numbers, drawn by the humidity and the presence of the *Styrax officinalis* and *Liquidambar orientalis* trees, whose sweet-smelling resin attracts them. The moths are present in the greatest numbers from July–Sept, after which they leave to lay their eggs elsewhere. The next generation will return the following year. When at rest the moths appear grey, but whey they fly, they reveal the brilliant orange of their lower wings. Tourists anxious to see this have for decades disturbed them with clapping and noises, which has caused a marked decline in numbers. Controls including CCTV, as well as strenuous appeals for silence, have helped to stem the decline.

A turn to the south after Soroní leads to the wooded rural chapel and curative spring of **Ághios Sýllas**. The final chapter of Lawrence Durrell's *Reflections on a Marine Venus* is dedicated to the ritual athletic, eating, dancing and drinking celebrations that occur here on the saint's feast day (29th–30th July), a rich example of the continuity from pagan to modern in the rural Greek world.

ANCIENT KAMEIROS

A turning in from the shore opposite Cape Minás leads up through olives and pines to the tranquil and beautiful site of ancient Kameíros (*map p. 258, B2; open Tues–Sat,*

April–Oct 8–7.30; winter 8.30–2.30). Undisturbed by overbuilding in later epochs, and remarkably well preserved, few other places in the Greek islands give a more complete and unfragmented picture of the layout of a small ancient centre. Much of the site is still to be uncovered. No theatre has yet been located, nor—remarkably—any fortification walls. Cemeteries have been extensively explored on the lateral slopes, and the magnificent finds which they have yielded are in the museum in Rhodes.

HISTORY OF KAMEIROS

Named after a grandson of Helios and the nymph Rhode, Kameíros was the smallest of the three original Dorian settlements on the island. Its economy was primarily agricultural, and the need to store and transport its surplus produce of oil and wine was the stimulus for a vigorous local ceramic industry. It possessed a shallow and rather exposed harbour, Mylantia, on the coast below: but it may also have used the more protected port 13km further south along the coast at modern-day Kameíros Skála. This inconvenient state of affairs may have contributed to its willingness to participate in the creation of the new city of Rhodes in 407/8 BC, which had superb ports and a commanding position for trade. Kameíros was devastated by an earthquake in 226 BC, and this means that much of what is standing above ground dates from the rebuilding which followed that disaster. One of the most interesting features is the city's system of storage and distribution of water, effected by a network of large underground conduits.

The site: lower area

The site entrance takes you into what was the **agorá (A)**. This space was bounded by sacred buildings and by the fountain complex and public meeting-space to the southeast, against the central slope of the hill. To the right on entering is a **distyle temple (1)** that was probably dedicated to Pythian Apollo. Several different coloured materials have been used in its base: a yellow threshold step on the front (south) side and a course of local marble at the lowest level; originally this would have provided greater contrast, since the upper areas of sandstone would have been plastered. Inside, the base for the cult statue is

visible, with a sunken treasury for offerings behind and two bases for votive offerings to either side of the entrance of the naos. By the northwest corner of the temple is a large 3rd-century BC **shrine (2)**, with a statue base in its interior. Further to the west, at the edge of the excavated area, are the remains of a **Roman house (3)**, with an interior room with apse (possibly a small nymphaeum) still preserving some brightly coloured plaster.

The **Fountain Square (B)** is the open rectangular area to your right. It is surrounded by the bases for votive statues, many of them with beautiful, clear in-

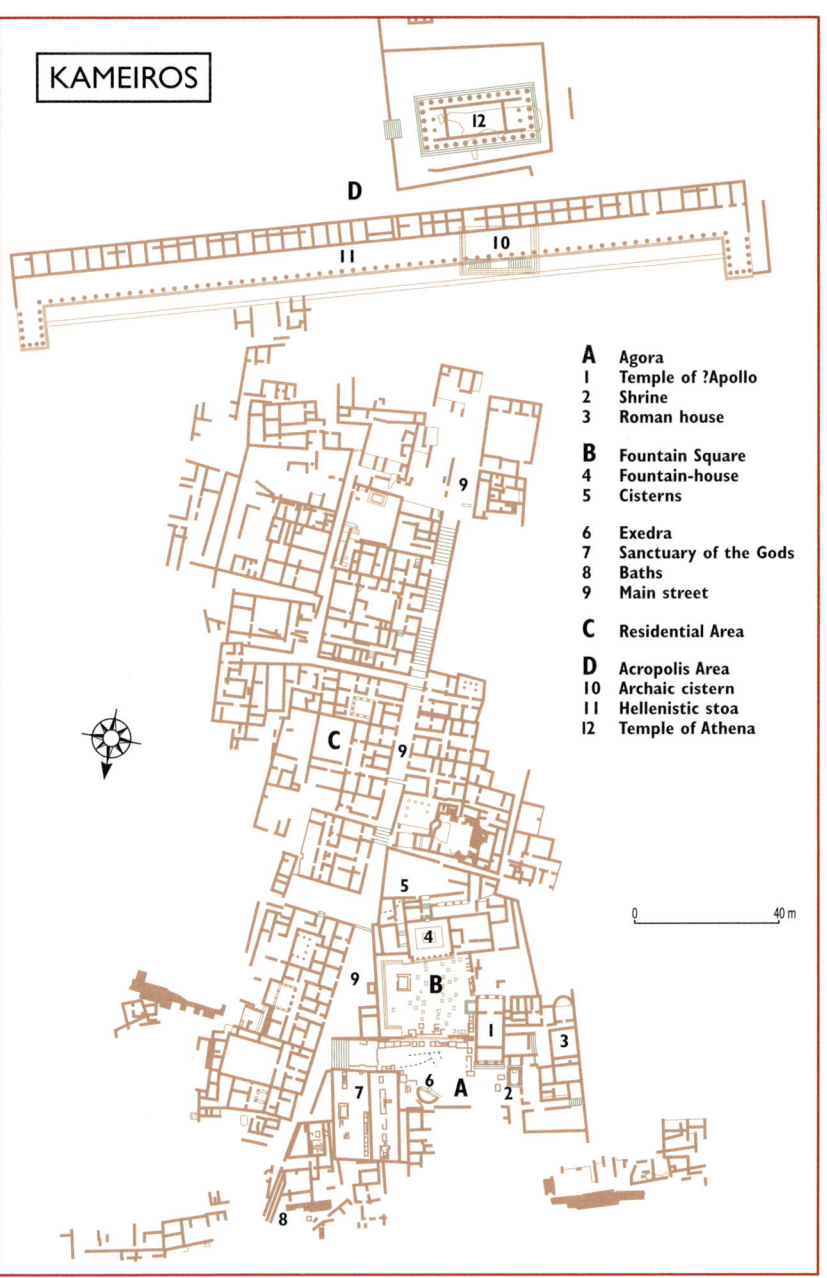

KAMEIROS

D

11   10

9

A Agora
1 Temple of ?Apollo
2 Shrine
3 Roman house

B Fountain Square
4 Fountain-house
5 Cisterns

6 Exedra
7 Sanctuary of the Gods
8 Baths
9 Main street

C Residential Area

D Acropolis Area
10 Archaic cistern
11 Hellenistic stoa
12 Temple of Athena

C   9

5

4

9   B

1

3

7   6   A   2

8

0   40 m

scriptions. A number have been moved and lined up along the eastern edge of the area. On the north (seaward) side are two curiosities: densely inscribed stones of grey marble sculpted in a plastic and amorphous manner, as if to simulate gnarled wood. The forms are too incomplete and the inscriptions too eroded to permit any certain identification of what these unusual items signified. The **fountain-house** proper **(4)** lies to the south, with a row of erected columns in front with incisions to hold in place cross-pieces from floor to waist level. A large trapezoid-shaped area of **cisterns (5)** lay below the high, dressed-stone wall to the south.

Leaving this area to the north, towards the sea, you pass through what was once a long enclosure wall with engaged columns. At an angle, to the right, is an **exedra (6)**, with an altar or statue-base centrally placed in front. Behind this is a terraced area referred to as the **Sanctuary of the Gods (7)**, containing parallel rows of altars to the various divinities whose names are inscribed on the front. Directly behind this sanctuary, in the northeast corner of the site, is the later **bath complex (8)**, with evidence of hypocaust and plastered walls for impermeability. From here the fine spectacle of the stepped **main street (9)** opens out, running uphill to the south with houses and shops to the left.

Middle area

The large **residential area (C)**, still only partially excavated, is a pleasure to explore. The houses were constructed around an open peristyle, with a single, central entrance onto the street: the columns supporting the roof of the peri-style have been re-erected in a couple of instances. The rooms off of the courtyards were small and the spaces between houses narrow. Just before the steps begin, an iron grille covers the main street's drain.

Upper area

At the top of the street the broad **acropolis area (D)** opens out. The first thing to locate at this level is the oldest element, a huge **Archaic cistern** (6th century BC) **(10)** carefully plastered and with two well-preserved flights of steps leading down into it. After 226 BC, a **Hellenistic stoa (11)** of remarkable dimensions (over 200m in length) was constructed to crown the whole width of the summit of the town. Such a stoa would have consisted of a colonnade in front, a wall of shop- or office entrances set back under the colonnade, and a rear supporting wall. The front colonnade was built up on the wall which bisects the cistern and which extends further to east and west; the middle wall (i.e. the front wall of the shops/offices) runs just behind the cistern; and the base of the rear wall is visible below the line of trees behind, divided into room units. The coolness of this shady building, with its wide north-facing panorama over the city and the surrounding islands, must have made it an enviable place to do business. The view to the south is also magnificent; this would have been enjoyed by the sanctuary of the other great building which occupied this summit, the **Temple of Athena Kameiras (12)**. The visible remains here of a base and enclosure wall are from the last temple on the site, built after 226 BC to replace the earlier, Classical Doric temple that had been shaken down.

KAMEIROS SKALA & KASTELLOS

The coastline to the immediate south of Kameíros is largely uninhabited. Just before the headland of Cape Kopriá is the quiet harbour of **Kameíros Skála** (*map p. 258, A2*), with two passable fish tavernas. On the south escarpment, almost behind the Taverna Loukas, are the remains of a Lycian tomb. Most of its carved elements (pilasters etc) have eroded, but the forms of the pediment and the architrave, cut in to the rockface, are clear. The warm rock here seems particularly favoured by the 'Rhodes dragons' or agama lizards. These have more the appearance of iguanas and can grow to about 35cm in length: they are a principally African and west Asian species (*Agama stellio*). It is possible that they were brought to a number of the islands in the Aegean as part of the cult of Apollo, with whom they are associated.

The castle of Kritinía, often just referred to as **Kástellos**, is the largest of the Knights' fortresses along the island's west coast. From its cliff-side position, high above emerald water (130m), it dominates the western passage and the channel of Chálki and has fine views beyond to Tilos, Symi and Nísyros. The walls on the landward side are well-preserved with three imposing towers, one rectangular, one polygonal and one circular. The village of **Kritinía** itself (*map p. 258, A2*) is attractively sited in a panoramic hollow of the hills above, around a plane-shaded *plateía* with a small fountain. The folklore museum above the village by the main road has a wide variety of local kinds of earthenware and pottery, urns and storage pithoi.

THE NORTHEAST

The east coast of the island is sheltered from the prevailing winds, punctuated by majestic headlands, and has a more intimate feel than the flatter western shoreline. The greatest concentration of tourist infrastructure and large hotels is to be found here.

Kallithéa

Thermal springs rise close to the shore at Kallithéa (*map p. 258, C1*): these were known in antiquity and their therapeutic qualities were allegedly recognised by Hippocrates. Their average temperature is only 19°C, and the water is indicated for drinking more than for bathing. The buildings of the thermal spa, designed by Pietro Lombardi in 1927, add charm to an otherwise ordinary stretch of coast. In the way in which they sympathetically relate to the landscape and create pleasing, semi-covered spaces, they represent what is best and most imaginative in Italian colonial architecture in the islands. The Italian occupying forces landed here in May 1912. The decision to conse-crate the spot with a grandiose spa was aimed principally at encouraging holidaymak-ers to the island. Lombardi created an unusual complex of low circular buildings and radiating hemicycles which combines many references both local and foreign; there are memories of the Gothic portals of the Knights, the open stoas of ancient Greece, and the *chochlákia* pebble pavements of the Dodecanese, mixed with orientalising, quasi-Moorish touches and embellished with palms. Once again, the keynote form is the unusually wide and low arch, springing from short quarter-columns, whose effect is greatly to accentuate breadth and lateral space. A complete restoration project was begun in 2003.

After Kallithéa the road descends into the long **bay of Faliráki**, the often strident tourist epicentre of the island. Below the headland at the far southern end of the bay is the church of **Profítis Amós**, a 17th-century single-aisle church with a pebble floor and vestiges of its original paintings on the walls and on the masonry templon screen.

AROUND APHANDOU BAY

Beyond the headland of Cape Ladikó, the bay of Aphándou opens out. Halfway along it, and midway between the main road and the parallel road along the shoreline, is the interesting **church of the Panaghía Katholikí**. The tiny, 16th-century cruciform church is huddled into the remains of an Early Christian basilica, whose opus alexan-drinum floor in polychrome marble can still be seen outside the west door. Just to the left of the door is a clerical throne, constructed from heterogeneous marble elements taken from the early church. On the north exterior some of the masonry and two Rho-dian marble columns from the Early Christian basilica are embedded in the wall, and other remains of Early Christian buildings can be seen further to the east. Inside, the floor is pebbled and the walls are covered with lively, but damaged, paintings. On the south wall, above a row of tormented figures in Hell (predominantly women), bound by serpents and licked by flames, is the figure of St Michael dispensing justice; to the left of him are several interesting 18th-century votive graffiti of sailing ships, scratched into the plaster by grateful sailors.

Churches in the Psínthos area

Inland of Aphándou is the quiet rural centre of Psínthos (*map p. 258, C2*): in its vicinity are two early churches, delightful for their simplicity, antiquity and setting. Both are reached by taking the road to the left (signed to Archípolis) on entering the village. Less than 2km from the junction and just to the left of the road, is the minuscule 13th-century church of **Moní Aghías Triádas** (*key on nail to left of door*). The wall-paintings, which cover every surface, are possibly contemporary with the building, though now much obscured by candle soot and with repainted faces in places; on the south wall is a deësis with a finely painted St John the Baptist. On the west wall to the left of the door, the donor, between two rose trees, presents the church to the Saviour. Further down the same road is the **church of the Parmeniótissa** (*reached by turning left at the*

Fountain hall with Moorish arches at Kallithéa, built by the Italians in 1927.

only eucalyptus tree after 2km–600m of asphalt and 1.4km of track; the church is hidden from view on a small rise about 100m from the road). This is another tiny, isolated building in un-rendered stone. Although the 15th-century paintings are generally not in good condition, one area in the apse (above and to the right) shows the careful quality of the draughtsmanship. There are scenes of the life and Passion of Christ, and a fine St Cosmas on the south wall.

Kolýmbia, Eptá Pighés and Tsambíkas

At the south end of Aphándou Bay is the settlement of **Kolýmbia**. Originally named San Benedetto, it was created as a model agricultural village by the Italians in the 1930s for settling colonists. Inland of Kolýmbia, a turning (right) off the main road leads west up a shallow valley to **Eptá Pighés** (*map p. 258, C2*) where, in a ravine of pines and plane trees, the confluence of seven year-round springs feeds a small lake used for irrigation. The place is a peaceful retreat from the summer heat and is frequented by picnickers and peacocks.

After the Eptá Pighés junction, the road rises with Mt Tsambíka to the left. A left turning leads up to the hermitage of **Panaghía Tsambíka Kyrá** on its summit. The Virgin of Tsambíka is especially the protectress of women in pregnancy, and of problems related to conceiving and bearing children. Inside the chapel, the whitewash has been spared at one point to reveal the fine, bearded head of a saint, in a style contemporary with the hermitage's foundation in the 16th century. The views are magnificent.

Archángelos

Archángelos (*map p. 258, C2*) is the principal settlement between Rhodes and Lindos, in a hidden location behind an escarpment so as to avoid the attentions of coastal pirates, and dedicated for yet further protection to the Archangel Michael. The area is rich in a light clay ideal for potting, and for this reason it had a flourishing **ceramic production** from as far back as the 5th century BC. The anonymous account of the building of Haghia Sophia in Constantinople, known as the *Narratio*, alleges that the bricks in its dome were made in Rhodes, and that twelve of them would weigh only as much as one ordinary brick: these would have been Archángelos bricks. The **castle**, built by the Knights of St John in the mid-15th century, dominates the horizon. It is best approached by foot through the town, from where the beautiful, abstract contours of the masses of rock rising up against the well-preserved curtain of walls can best be appreciated. Though impressive from below, the castle is small, occupying a tight triangular space, with a modern chapel and the remains of only a couple of inner buildings at floor level inside the enceinte.

Pheráklos Castle

After Archángelos the road descends into a wide coastal plain. At the foot of the descent, a turning is indicated right, to Pheráklos Castle, visible 2km to the south of the road (*map p. 258, C2*). From its size and magnificence, it is clear that this castle, unlike the fort at Archángelos, was a protective refuge for the local population in times of danger and was designed to endure a siege: the large cisterns inside confirm as much. When the Knights arrived in Rhodes in 1306, a Byzantine castle (which they captured) already existed here; they appear to have rebuilt it entirely for themselves over the next two decades, maintaining the same foundations but reconstructing the walls and cisterns. After settling in Rhodes, the Knights often used the castle as a detention centre for prisoners and errant members of the Order. The enceinte is entered on the southwest side: nearby, the base of a lookout tower is visible at the highest point. A number of deep tunnels were cut into the hill at ground level during the Second World War, for storage and for use as refuges; the entrance to one of these is on the right of the path as you descend.

LINDOS

Lindos (*map p. 258, C3*) has the most impressive archaeological remains, the oldest Byzantine churches, and the finest vernacular buildings on the island: it is a town of architectural beauty in a consummate natural setting. This inevitably means that the flood of visitors in the tiny streets and spaces, from Easter onwards, is daunting: on days when large cruise-ships are in the port of Rhodes, the problem can assume impossible proportions. For a peaceful visit, it is best to go as early in the morning, or as late in the afternoon, as can be reconciled with the opening times of the acropolis (*see below*). The light and shadow are at their best at these times and further enhance the beauty of the setting.

HISTORY OF LINDOS

From a distance, whether approaching by sea or by land, the reason for the founding and for the enduring importance of Lindos is clear: an isolated and panoramic natural acropolis with two splendid bays for ports. These elements compensated for a terrain which offered little scope for agriculture and meant that Lindos, unlike Ialysós and Kameíros, had to live primarily on trade. Of the three ancient Dorian cities it was always the most important and maintained its influence, especially as a religious centre, long after the 5th-century BC synoecism and the creation of the federal state of Rhodes. Lindos also acquired prestige through her early colonies, in particular Gela in Sicily and Phaselis in Lycia (Asia Minor).

Neolithic and Mycenaean occupation of the promontory are attested by archaeology, while the cult of Athena Lindia appears to go back at least to the 10th century BC. Most of what the visitor sees today, however, dates from later rebuilding of the 4th century BC. The site was too important to neglect in later epochs; passing Crusaders and expanding Venetian trade brought Lindos prosperity in the 12th century, further nurtured by the Knights of St John, who fortified the acropolis and stationed a permanent garrison here. The prosperity of many of the families of Lindos is reflected both in the dignified and decorated mansions which are to be found in the narrow streets of the lower town, and in the finely-painted churches.

THE LOWER TOWN

The road from the main junction above the town descends steeply past the cemetery and the chapel of the Phaneroméni on the left, to a *plateía* shaded with mulberry trees: to one side is the town's **ancient water-source**, flowing from an 18th-century marble frontage with a partially abraded inscription in Osmanli script.

On entering the town, the low parish **church of the Panaghía** is almost immediately on the left. Of Latin-cross form with an octagonal drum and cupola, it was restored and enlarged in 1489 by the Grand Master Pierre d'Aubusson, whose coat of arms is clearly visible above the entrance: the original foundation is much earlier, possibly 12th century. The low and broad interior is one of the most completely and homogeneously decorated in the Dodecanese. The complete programme of paintings (restored in 1927) which cover the interior walls, is by Gregory of Symi, signed and dated 1779 in an inscription on the lintel in the north transept. The disposition of the paintings throughout the church follows the classic iconographic topography for a building of this form (*see p. 141*). The *Last Judgement* on the west wall is particularly noteworthy. Visiting the **church museum** (*open daily April–Oct*) gives the opportunity to see the finest and earliest wall-paintings of the complex, over the outside door of the funerary chapel of the north transept. The museum itself contains a fine embroidered epitaphios and a small collection of liturgical objects: in the open-air courtyard are fragments of a Classical frieze.

Lindos has a number of other, smaller Byzantine churches which substantially pre-date the arrival of the Knights. Several of them have the remains of wall-paintings which range in date from the 12th–15th centuries, but whose condition is generally not good. There are also a number of well-preserved private houses that date to the 16th and 17th centuries. The **Papakostantis House** (1626) is the most accessible example, particularly as it now functions as a pleasant café.

THE MANSIONS OF LINDOS

Stone-built, flat-roofed and generally constructed around two or three sides of a paved courtyard, the houses of Lindos nearly always present a monumental doorway to the street: this is typically embellished with a striking stone door frame, often carved in a 'rope' design and surmounted by a lintel or arch decorated with doves, flowers, rosettes or crosses, and sometimes bearing the name of the owners and the date. Windows may be similarly decorated. A peculiarity of some of the houses is a windowed room on the first floor built out across the street. Most of the houses are built over a cistern cut into the rock below the courtyard. Inside, the main reception area generally faces the entrance across the courtyard, while the service rooms are to the side(s). Decorated wooden ceilings were supported by a single wide, pointed arch: the furniture was carved and the floor often paved with intricate designs. Fine coloured ceramics adorn the walls, either 17th-century Iznik work or pieces of Lindos Ware inspired by it (*see p. 254*).

THE ACROPOLIS

Open April–Oct 8–7.30; 8.30–2.30 in winter; closed Mon in winter.
The inhabited settlement was never contiguous with the acropolis, but separated by a clear break of open rock and pine trees. Once through the outer gate there is a shaded terrace punctuated by the mouths of three large, plaster-lined **Byzantine cisterns (a)**: the acropolis had no spring within its walls and depended on water collected in such cisterns; there are many more on the summit.

The approach to the summit
At the first turn in the path, the visitor is faced with an impressive **votive relief of the stern of a ship (b)** with a **dedicatory exedra** to its left, both skilfully carved into the rock. Though contiguous, these are two separate dedications. An inscription on the side of the ship states that the work was 'dedicated to Agesander, son of Mikion, by the people of Lindos', and that it was the work of the Rhodian sculptor Pythocritus. The exedra to the left may be a little earlier; it surrounds a base on which an honorific statue would have stood. Much later, in the 3rd century AD, the long inscription (originally picked out in red) was added by Aglochartus, priest of Athena Lindia.

View of Lindos acropolis, Lindos town and the harbour.

To the left of the present stairs leading up to the acropolis are vestiges of the ancient Sacred Way. Much higher up to the left is a flight of **14th-century steps (c)**, added by the Knights of St John, which originally gave direct access to the **Governor's Residence (d)** by means of a wooden drawbridge. The residence, extensively restored, dates from the period of Grand Master Pierre d'Aubusson (1476–1503), and bears his arms high up on the exterior wall. The building now houses the local archaeological offices.

The vaulted entrance, containing a number of capitals and finely inscribed altars and statue bases, gives onto an inner esplanade covered with many more of the same. This (only a fraction of the total number on the site) gives some indication of the forest of votive statuary in bronze and marble, as well as paintings and other works of art, which would have greeted the pilgrim in ancient times: several ancient writers also mention the works of art and spoils of war that were dedicated here.

The acropolis plateau

The plateau of the acropolis is a roughly triangular area of 8400 square metres, rising to a height of 116m. The layout we see today dates from a Hellenistic building programme begun in the 4th century BC; before that, the **Sacred Way** had led directly across the open area: some part of its paving can be seen (beside the long base of a Hellenistic monument) by turning sharply left and passing through the **Governor's Residence (d)**.

There are three phases of building in the complex, which all followed on from the restoration of the temple after its destruction by fire in 392 BC. From the earliest phase is the **propylaia (e)** enclosing the temple sanctuary at the top, which dates from short-ly after the fire, i.e. the early 4th century. The wide **stoa (f)** on the next level down dates from 300–290 BC. The vaulted **storage areas (g)** below the stoa were the last ele-ments to be added, around 100 BC. These storage vaults support the first terrace of the Hellenistic grand approach to the Temple of Athena. Just in front of the staircase that divides the line of vaults, a block of stone on the ground preserves an ancient mason's sketch of a piece of lifting machinery, scratched on the surface facing away from the steps. At the northern (left) extremity of the area there was once a **Roman prostyle temple (h)**, which faced towards the Temple of Athena.

The temple approach

As well as physically corralling pilgrims and mentally preparing them for the approach to the temple, the wide stoa served as a shaded space where votive gifts, and especially paintings, could be exhibited. It was minimally reconstructed at the beginning of the last century to give some idea of its form. Originally, the Doric colonnade would have run the entire width of the building (87m), but its roof was omitted in the centre to allow a clear view of the next flight of steps up to the main propylaia. This (only visible in foundations now) was in effect two contiguous propylaia: one **symmetrical Doric colonnade (e)** at the top of the flight of stairs, with two slightly projecting wings at either end; and an internal **L-shaped colonnade (e2)** which gave onto the temple. These marked the boundary of the sanctuary; access beyond this point was limited, and the area could be entered only after ritual purification.

The temple

The **Temple of Athena Lindia (i)**, tetrastyle amphiprostyle in design and measuring 22m by 8m, seems small after such a grand approach. It hugs the very edge of the southern precipice: its placing, its size and its form are all faithful to the older Archaic temple that stood here until the fire of 392 BC (traces of its crepidoma can be seen in the bedrock of dark limestone inside the present building). There has been consider-able restoration, but much of the west wall is original; the east wall rises straight out of the rock of the precipice. The stone would originally have been covered with a layer of light-coloured plaster.

The temple has a long history: according to Herodotus (*Histories II, 182*) it was the Danaids in their flight from the sons of Aegyptus who established the cult; according to Diodorus Siculus (*5.58.1*) it was Danaus himself. One of the temple's early donors, the pharaoh Ahmose II, dedicated here a remarkable linen corselet. When the temple was rebuilt after the great fire, the worship of Zeus Polieus was added, and at the same time Athena became identified as Athena Polias. The original Archaic cult statue inside the temple was probably a wooden image of the goddess, seated and wearing a golden diadem. Such was the fame and influence of the *Athena Parthenos* by Pheidias in Ath-ens, however, that this original seated Athena was replaced in the 5th or 4th century

LINDOS: THE ACROPOLIS

a   Byzantine cisterns
b   Ship relief and exedra
c   14th-century stairs
d   Governor's Residence
e   Propylaia
e2 L-shaped colonnade
f   Stoa
g   Storage vaults
h   Roman temple
i   Temple of Athena
j   Aghios Ioannis

0 _____ 40 m

by an image of the goddess standing and armed, as in the Parthenon. It must have been this statue that was transported to Byzantium by Theodosius in the 5th century AD when the temple cult was officially suppressed, and which perished in a fire there later that century.

The entrance to the temple was at the north: on either side of it were two marble plaques inscribed with the chronological lists of the priests of Athena Lindia, running from 406 BC through to AD 47. These precious records were removed in the Middle Ages and used as floor slabs in the church of Ághios Stéfanos (*see below*).

In the narrow area in front of the south entrance are signs of extensive Archaic cutting in the bedrock. The view from the edge looks down on the natural harbour below, where tradition holds that St Paul took refuge from a storm (*see below*).

The pathway descends by steps to the west, passing a deep water-storage pool and continuing towards the massive supporting wall for the western end of the stoa. Above it to the north are the tall ruins of the 13th-century **church of Ághios Ioánnis (j)**.

The theatre, Tetrastoön and Ághios Pávlos

Around the base of the acropolis hill are three important ancient sites. Below the south-west side, and reached by taking a right-hand (south) route through the lower town from the church of the Panaghía, is the **ancient theatre** (4th century BC), whose cavea is cut into the living rock of the slope. Although only the central part is visible today, its design is clear, with a deep diazoma separating the lower 19 rows of seats from the upper seven. It would have had a capacity of almost 2,000.

Next to the theatre are the remaining foundations of a large, almost square building with a peristyle, constructed over a century later. Referred to as the **Tetrastoön**, its exact function is unknown. The fact that no fewer than three churches had been built on the site in later times, and that a number of Christian burials were found here, would suggest that it was used for cult purposes in antiquity, since it was always the habit of early Christian communities to transform places of pagan worship into churches or sacred Christian sites. It was here, in the floor of the **now demolished church of Ághios Stéfanos**, that the inscribed stones with the lists of Athena's priests were found during excavations in the early 1900s, as well as the 'Lindian Chronicle', a list of dedications made to the temple, plus details of three miraculous apparitions of Athena, which was drawn up in 99 BC and is now in the Archaeological Museum in Copenhagen.

From the Terastoön and the theatre, it is a short walk down to the **harbour of Ághios Pávlos**, where St Paul is thought to have landed on Rhodes. In the opposite direction, beyond the limits of the lower town and on the slope approximately 100m north-northeast of the acropolis, is a site referred to as the **Boukopeion**, a 'place for the sacrifice of oxen'. Vestiges of foundations show there to have been a sizeable temple of the Geometric period here (10th century BC).

The Tomb of Archocrates and Tomb of Cleoboulos

In the face of Kraná hill behind the town, due west of the acropolis—and clearly visible from it, just above the upper line of the area of habitation—is a ruined Hellenistic chamber tomb known as the **Tomb of Archocrates**, dating from c. 200 BC (*access is difficult; from the southwest corner of the town*). The tomb is now very decayed, although there is a well-preserved row of four carved altars (bearing the names of the dead) in front of the entrance. These were originally placed on the deep, rock-cut ledge above the entrance, to which access was gained from the hill above.

More distant, and magnificently sited on the extremity of the northern cape of the Great Harbour, is the circular monument known as the **Tomb of Cleoboulos** (*reached by a 30-min walk. From a signed junction halfway down the road from the plateía to the beach, a path leads out onto the headland*). The terrain is rough and rocky but carpeted in season with asphodel and saffron-bearing crocus and punctuated by a few tenacious pomegranate trees. The tomb (9m wide and c. 1.7m high) conspicuously marks the entrance to the natural harbour, above a steep drop into the sea. Its fine masonry and precise construction would suggest a date in the 4th or 3rd century BC—certainly later than Cleoboulos (*see box below*). Tradition alone has connected the building with Lindos' most famous citizen, and it might not be a tomb at all (even though this remains the most probable hypothesis). Its similarity to the base of other Hellenistic towers, and in particular to the lighthouse tower of Akératos on Thasos (*see p. 567*), suggest other possible functions: the tower on Thasos was both a monument to Akeratos and a functioning signal-point.

Cleoboulos and the Seven Sages
A figure of patriarchal wisdom, combining valour, humility and moderation, Cleoboulos of Lindos was considered one of the Seven Sages, revered for their wisdom and first recorded as being seven in number by Plato. The group included, in addition to Cleoboulos, Thales of Miletus, Bias of Priene, Pittacus of Mytilene, Solon of Athens, Chilon of Sparta and Periander of Corinth. Cleoboulos appears to have been an enlightened leader of Lindos in the early decades of the 6th century BC, and presided over the city's period of greatest prestige and prosperity. He was a talented poet, and like many of his generation had travelled to, and felt the influence of, Egypt and her culture. The guiding maxim 'Nothing in excess' is attributed to him.

CENTRAL RHODES

The centre of Rhodes is a relatively wild and wooded landscape, not much visited nor over affected by modern construction. To the west it is dominated by the three mountains of Mt Profítis Ilías (798m), Mt Attávyros (1216m) and Mt Akramýtis (825m), in effect three peaks of the same massif; to the east, deeply folded valleys of pine woods and olives slope down to the coast, their waters draining down wide, seasonal torrents. The mountains are of pure limestone; the eastern valleys often have a pale, sandy alluvial soil and sandstone features creating a wide range of habitats for plants and animals.

AROUND MOUNT PROFITIS ILIAS

The curious, semi-abandoned hilltop village of **Eleoúsa** (*map p. 258, B2*), created by the Italians as the Campochiaro Agricultural Settlement in 1935, at the eastern end of Mt Profítis Ilías, is surrounded by rich agricultural land. By a series of laws of expropriation passed between 1924 and 1929, the Italians transferred the island's agricultural production from the local population to Italian settlers, and brand new settlements were created here and at other points on the island. After the Italians left, the Greeks renamed this village after an attribute of the Virgin, *eleoúsa*, 'compassionate': they returned to the cultivation of the land, abandoning the Italian buildings to the ruin of time. An unreal atmosphere prevails today, in the shade of the now mature umbrella pines and palm trees.

Ághios Nikólaos Foundouklí

Two kilometres west of Eleoúsa, beside a spring, is the church of Ághios Nikólaos Foundouklí (*map p. 258, B2*) beautiful both in itself and for its panoramic and bucolic site. This is a domed 14th-century votive chapel built on a Greek-cross plan which has been extended with apses to give the impression of a quatrefoil. It measures no more than 8m by 8m and is surmounted by an attractively arcaded cupola decorated with knotted pilasters and a belfry above the west door. It preserves, almost complete, the cycle of wall-paintings of its interior, executed perhaps a century or more after the church's construction. The narrative scenes are conceived with clarity and liveliness, and show slight Italian influence. Beside the west door is the dedicatory scene with the donors and their family presenting a model of the church to Christ.

Sálakos and Apóllona

The continuation of the beautifully wooded road to the west (right-hand branch after 1.5km) leads towards the **summit of Mt Profítis Ilías**. Of all the island's mountains, this has perhaps the richest flora. Its mature woods of pine and cypress are favoured by drifts of wild flowers in the clearings.

To the north of the ridge is the attractive village of **Sálakos** (*map p. 258, B2*), where there are abundant springs, two Byzantine churches of the 14th and 15th centuries, and the remains of a fortress. On the south side of the ridge is **Apóllona**, reached by a panoramic descent. There is a small museum in the centre exhibiting domestic artefacts, folk art and a selection of ancient pieces: sarcophagi, and altars decorated with garlands and bucrania.

From Apóllona a long and rural road (*18km, unsurfaced*) leads through densely wooded, uninhabited valleys to Láerma.

AROUND MOUNT ATTAVYROS

Mount Attávyros (1216m) is the island's highest, bulkiest and—in antiquity—most sacred mountain. The ascent to the summit can be made either from the south in a relatively gradual 5–6-hr (return) climb from the village of Ághios Isídoros, or else by road and military track (leading to the NATO installation at the top) from the junction 5km south of the southern exit of Kritiniá, which climbs through the pine forests in the saddle between the two peaks of the mountain and approaches Ághios Ioánnis (the summit) from the southwest. Either way the effort is amply rewarded, if the weather is clear, by the sight of one of the most dramatically-placed sanctuaries in the Aegean. The whole island lies beneath; Crete is visible to the southwest and Asia Minor to the northeast.

The Temple of Zeus Atabyrios

It is said that Althaemenes, son of Catreus, King of Crete, fled to Rhodes after a frightening oracular prediction and settled on the island, founding a temple to Zeus Atabyrios on the only point on the island from which his homeland could clearly be seen. The extensive remains are clearly visible on the ridge 500m to the southeast of the military radar tower. The large rectangular base (c. 15m by 11m) of a structure surrounded by a peribolos occupies the top of the ridge. Below, to the northeast side, is the 20-m base of a stoa or portico in four courses of rusticated ashlar blocks of probably 5th-century workmanship, with what appears to be a water pool at its western end. Elements of other structures fill the space between the two areas. Yet there is no evidence of columns or entablature suggesting a temple. What was here probably partook more of the nature of a large altar, orientated perfectly east–west.

Émbonas and Ághios Isídoros

On the fertile lower slopes of the northern side of the mountain are some of the island's most renowned vines. The sprawling settlement of **Émbonas** (*map p. 258, A2*) is the principal centre for wine production; the C.A.I.R. co-operative is based here, which produces a variety of wines, amongst which is Greece's only *méthode champenoise* wine. Production of a less commercial nature continues on the southern slopes at **Ághios Isídoros** (*map p. 258, A3*), a tranquil village backed by the massif of the mountain and overlooking an ocean of pine-clad hills descending to the sea towards the east.

Moní Thári

In a peaceful setting 4km to the southwest of Láerma is the oldest monastic foundation on the island (and still one of the most active): the monastery of the Archangel Michael 'Tharinos', or Moní Thári (*map p. 258, B3; open continuously until sunset*). The foundation may go back as far as the 9th century. The main katholikon is of the early 12th century and there are wall-paintings in several layers, all of considerable quality. Recently rescued from decline, the monastic community now numbers over 20.

The church is cruciform with two short arms and a long nave, surmounted by an arcaded cupola-drum. The west door is curiously off-centre, perhaps because of the position of the threshold in a pre-existing structure (whose foundations can be seen to the north side of the church). Many periods of painting are represented in the impressive interior: the austere figures of the Church Fathers in the lowest area in the apse are probably contemporary with the construction of the church (12th century); the paintings in the dome, drum, vault and sanctuary walls—the (damaged) *Pantocrator*, the Virgin, St John the Baptist, angels and prophets—are slightly later work of the early 13th century. A later layer of 17th-century paintings which originally covered these was removed and is now displayed in the church of St Mary of the Castle in Rhodes Town (*see p. 272*). An inscription in the prothesis niche, to the left of the sanctuary, dates the paintings of the upper cylinder of the apse to 1506. In the lateral arms of the church the Archangels (south), Sts Demetrius and George (north) and the *Annunciation* (with donor) and *Dormition* (north) are also of the 16th century. The **scenes of the life of Christ along the vault of the nave** (early 18th century) are in many ways the most remarkable: the style of the artist is quite individual and details of costume or background are delicately described as if with a fine pen; the effect is most unusual. The compositions—*Christ and the Woman of Samaria*, the *Angel at the Sepulchre*, the *Storm* *on the Sea of Galilee*—are beautifully balanced and executed by an artist of considerable talent. The finely carved wooden iconostasis is also work of the early 18th century.

Sixteen kilometres of winding, wooded track lead down from Moní Thári to the east coast via the monastery's dependent foundations: the contemporaneous Ághios Geórgios Ínkou and the 19th-century convent of the Panaghía Ypsenís.

AROUND MOUNT AKRAMYTIS

The short stretch of panoramic road between Mt Attávyros and Mt Akramýtis is the most dramatic on the island. Just under 2km before entering **Siána** (a village famous for its aromatic honey and *soúma*, a spirit similar to grappa), a track leads west (right) to **Steliés** (*map p. 258, A3*) and the empty, southern loop of Mt Akramýtis. Although little explored, there is a large area here, designated with the ancient name Kymisala, with widely scattered remains of habitation from the Classical and Hellenistic periods.

The fortress or **castle of Monólithos** (*map p. 258, A3*), from which the nearby village takes its name, is 2km to the southwest towards the coast. In effect this is a fortified, precipitous rock, referred to as the Monópetra, with sheer sides dropping 200m to the valley below and with access from only one point by means of a precarious neck of land. The position commands the approaches to the island from the south. This was primarily a watchtower and signalling post; its interior area is compact and its cisterns sufficient only for a small garrison. Of the two chapels inside, one is in ruins, the other, Ághios Panteléimonas, recently restored. The latest phase of building here is that of the energetic Pierre d'Aubusson. His master plan must have conceived of the whole island as one huge, single fortress.

SOUTHERN RHODES

The southern tip of the island is a spacious and panoramic landscape bordered by long, sandy shores. Its central hills are surrounded by a good circuit road linking the main settlements of Gennádi, Apolakkiá and Kattavía.

Pylónas and Lárdos

West of Lindos is the village of **Pylónas** (*map p. 258, B3*), where the 15th-century church of Ághios Geórgios has paintings on its north interior wall (sadly in deteriorating condition). A right turn off the main road is signed to the **Mycenaean cemetery of Asprópilia**, which was excavated between 1993 and 1996. This consists of six tombs, two with side-chambers cut into the soft sandstone rock, dating from the late Mycenaean period (14th–12th centuries BC). Each is entered by a dromos on the same axis, almost due south.

Shortly after Pylónas is **Lárdos**, an important junction at the crossing of a seasonal river and the main market-town of a large hinterland to the north. It has given its name to the mottled grey marble quarried in the area. After this the road meets the coast.

Asklipeío

At Kiotári, a turning leads 3.5km inland to Asklipeío (*map p. 258, B3*). The village is proud of its bread. Its other treasure is the 11th-century church of the **Koímisis tis Theotókou** in the central square, whose magnificent painted interior is comparable with the church of the Panaghía in Lindos (*see p. 297*) and with Moní Thári (*see p. 305*) for completeness and beauty (*often locked outside times of liturgies; the custodian in the house directly to the south keeps the key*). The long, low interior, which is paved with a *chochlákia* floor, is covered on all sides with wall-paintings of the late 16th century. The whole range of scripture is here, from Genesis to Revelation, disposed around the walls with the meticulous 'universal' logic typical of Byzantine church designs. The *Pantocrator* in the celestial sphere of the dome; the Evangelists, as transmitters of divine wisdom, in the pendentives; the *Virgin and Child* in the apse. Scenes relating to mortality appear in the transepts: the *Apocalypse* and *Dormition* to the south; to the north a dramatically large and solemn Archangel Michael clasping a shrouded human soul in his hand, and the *Massacre of the Innocents*. Along the vault of the nave is the Fall from Grace, related in the scenes from Genesis, after which comes redemption through the life of Christ. All this swirls above us, while standing at our level are the intercessors, St John the Baptist and St George in their own niches to either side of the congregational area, and the others ranged around. Most splendidly dressed of all are Sts Constantine and Helen in the north arm. As we exit to the world outside, images of the *Last Judgement* around the door in the west wall act as a salutary warning.

The plan and development of the church is clear from the vantage point of the small early 15th-century **castle** above: two aisles to north and south were added in the 18th century onto the central nave of the original cruciform church: this original structure may also have evolved in two phases, beginning as a Greek-cross plan, and then being modified into a Latin-cross plan by addition to the west arm. The fortress itself is considerably ruined, but its two cylindrical towers survive.

Váti, Profília and Aghía Eiríni

From Gennádi (*map p. 258, B3*) a road cuts west across the tip of the island to Apolakkiá, passing through **Váti**, a small village with a picturesque main square of stone houses, which lies in the centre of a hilly landscape, ideal for exploration on foot. There are many rural churches in the vicinity, some with wall-paintings, some with ancient marbles as altars, some decorated only in the last few years. The most remarkable is in the village of **Profília**, to the north of the road. Here the 12th-century church of Ághii Michaïl and Geórgios has late 12th-century paintings of the highest quality, in a fresh and vigorous style. The spare lines of the figures, and in particular the compelling faces and eyes of Christ, John the Baptist and the Virgin, are marvellous examples of art of the Comnene age, one of the last periods of Byzantine art before a fossilisation of forms sets in. These are perhaps the finest paintings on the island. By happy coincidence, an excellent rural taverna (*see p. 310*) is opposite the church.

The villages to the west of here are small agricultural centres, set in a verdant and well-watered landscape, with stone houses grouped around a *plateía* and church. Before

Apolakkiá is the site of **Aghía Eiríni** (*map p. 258, A3*), where there are remains of two Early Christian basilicas and a baptistery (*the site is in a field beyond a small grove of olive trees, 100m west of the Arnítha–Ístrio road at a point 30m north of the sign to the monastery of Ághios Ioánnis, as you come from Arnítha*). There are the remains of at least two ?6th-century churches, standing to over 2m high in places. One, to the south of the area, has a double apse; the larger one to the north has its synthronon still visible and the base of the altar and its canopy. There are several columns in fine, local marble within the ruins; just to the west, in the field, are fragments of a large water-stoup or font and other pieces of worked stone. To the north is the floor of a tetraconch baptistery with mosaic floor, featuring abstract patterns and designs with birds. It is difficult to assess how large the site once was; potsherds litter the area for some distance around.

From the east side of Apolakkiá, a track leads off to the north towards a water reservoir and dam. After 3km a left turn leads up a steep slope to the isolated church of **Ághios Geórgios Várdas**, a simple, single-aisled building with paintings dated by donor inscription to 1289–90. Even though their condition is not good, many of the scenes are legible: *Christ's Entry into Jerusalem* (south side) and some of the figures of saints, such as Tryphon and Nikitas (northwest corner), stand out in particular. Their quality is good but they have no great originality: a moment's comparison with those in Profília shows how fossilisation had taken hold in the hundred years that separate these two cycles.

The southern tip of the island

The shallow waters around the southern tip of the island are a habitat of both green and loggerhead turtles, which may still breed in the vicinity of the promontory of **Cape Germatá**, due south of Chochlakás. This was considered one of their last breeding places in the Dodecanese. The dunes and areas of garrigue by the shore in this southeast corner are also rich in bird-life and flowers. King Ferdinand's orchid (*Ophrys regis-fernandii*), known as the 'earwig orchid' because its lip has the form of an earwig's body and head, is endemic to this corner of the Aegean.

West of Chochlakás, beside the main road, is the disused concrete structure of the **church of Ághios Pávlos** (Petracco and Bernabiti, 1936), formerly the Catholic church of the Italian agricultural settlement of San Marco.

Kattavía (*map p. 258, A4*) has the feel of the end of the line: many of its fine houses are abandoned or ruined. Mycenaean tombs have been found in the vicinity of the village, and there is evidence of a Late Bronze Age settlement here on the spur of Ághios Minás. Finds of later Greek and Roman pottery show that occupation continued into historic times. The principal archaeological remains in the area, however, are to be seen at the very extremity of the island 9km to the south across a deserted area now occupied mostly by the army. The track to the right (west), just in front of the isthmus of the islet of Prasonísi, leads to the foot of a sloping promontory, on which are the remains of **ancient Vrouliá**, a Late Geometric–Early Archaic settlement (8th–6th centuries BC).

The peninsula of **Prasonísi** is tethered to the island by a narrow isthmus that defines two sweeping sandy bays, one or other of which takes the force of any wind blowing, creating conditions ideal for surfing. The meagre settlement by the isthmus is mostly given over to this sport in the summer. In the winter there is nobody; and the sunsets and the surf are dramatic.

PRACTICAL INFORMATION

GETTING AROUND

With a total of 6–7 daily flights from Athens to Rhodes, the island is easily accessible at all times of year. There are also local flights to Kastellórizo, Kárpathos and Kasos (almost daily), and to Kos, Leros and Astypálaia (three times weekly). Daily connections go to Thessaloníki and Herakleion. The airport is 15km southwest of Rhodes Town. The port of Rhodes is also the principal hub for the Dodecanese, though the frequency of connections to the lesser islands varies considerably according to season (see entries for individual islands). There are year-round, direct connections by car-ferry to Piraeus (c. 16hrs) every day. Since the port is large and has several harbours, it is important to know which part of it a ferry will leave from. Chálki is served twice weekly from Rhodes Town, and there is a daily service from Kameíros Skála (2hrs; every day in summer, less often in winter). The GNTO office in the New Town (corner of Makaríou and Papágou, T: 22410 44335; *map p. 281, E2*) provides helpful sheets with weekly boat departures, museum opening times, a price-list for taxis and bus times and fares for the whole island.

WHERE TO STAY

The most beautiful and characterful place to stay in the Old Town of Rhodes is the **Hotel Marco Polo** ■ (*open May–late Oct; Aghíou Phanourioú 42, T: 22410 25562; www.marcopolomansion.gr; map p. 262, C3*). Elegant, modern luxury at a higher price, in an enviable location just off the Street of the Knights, is offered by the **Avalon Boutique Hotel** ■ (*T: 22410 31438, www.avalonrhodes.gr*), open all year round. The Old Town also has many small and characterful pensions: worthy of mention are the **Apollo Guesthouse** (*T: 22410 32003, www.apollo-touristhouse.com*) and **Hotel Andreas** (*T: 22410 34156, www.hotelandreas.com*), at 28c and 28d Omírou, overlooking the ancient church of Aghía Kyriakí (*map p. 262, C4*). Both are relatively inexpensive, and occupy interesting buildings; the rooms are comfortable but small. Both close between late Oct and the week before Easter. Also in the heart of the Old Town is the **Hotel Isole** (*Evdóxou 75; T: 22410 20682, www.hotelisole.com; map p. 262, C2*), run by a charming Italian-Dutch couple who speak most European languages. They serve excellent breakfasts and convivial pre-dinner drinks in a restored Ottoman house. Rooms are small but charming.

The New Town has a number of hotels which are open year-round and offer convenience and good service. Comfortable and relatively attractive, without being too big or expensive, is the **Hotel Mediterranean**, opposite the Casino (*Ko 35; T: 22410 24661, www.mediterranean.gr; map p. 281, F2*). Most rooms have good sea views. Exceptionally good value off-season is the **Esperia Hotel**

(*Gríva 7; T: 22410 23941/4; map p. 281, E2*), which is warm, pleasant and functional: the poolside rooms are quietest.

WHERE TO EAT

Rhodes Town
Rhodes offers some of the best and most varied eating possibilities in the Aegean, although in the city itself you will need to explore outside the Old Town to find the best Greek food. In the Old Town, unimaginative and often overpriced tourist fare prevails. However, there are one or two good places: the **Marco Polo** ▪ (*see Where to Stay, above*); **Dinoris** (upper medium price) in a tiny alley across from the entrance to the Archaeological Museum (*map p. 262, C2*), an elegant and traditional taverna of long standing, regularly frequented by locals; **Photis** (*expensive; open all year; on Menekléous; map p. 262, C3*), an elegant and well-established fish restaurant (the quality and presentation of the dishes is high; this compensates for the hauteur of the reception and service).

In the New Town there are many excellent places. The modest-looking **Taverna Chalki** (*inexpensive; Kathopoúli 30, map p. 281, E2–F2*) has fresh, home-cooked food of the best and most traditional simplicity. At lunchtime, **Indigo** ▪ (medium price), inside the Néa Agorá market building (*no.105/6 beside Mandráki harbour; map p. 281, E3*), offers delicious, finely-prepared dishes from the tradition of Greek Asia Minor.

Further afield (but without question worth the short taxi-ride) in Zéphyros, southeast of the city centre, is the **Paragadi** ▪ fish restaurant (*medium expensive; corner of Claude Pepper and Afstralías; reservation recommended; T:* 22410 37775; map p. 280, B4) with an exceptional quality of service and of seafood and fish dishes, prepared in the best and simplest manner. Nearby, open all year, and usually packed with locals, is **To Steki tou Cheila** (*inexpensive; southern end of Codringtónou, on the corner of Chatziangélou and Dendrinoú; p. 280, B3*): the *symiakí* (tiny shrimps) and the wine are both fresh and delicious.

Around the island
Mavrikos in Lindos (*expensive; reservations recommended, T: 22440 31232*) is a fine and justly famous restaurant with a pleasing setting, serving many home-made products. Tiny and panoramic, **To Limeri tou Listi** ▪ ('The Robber's Den') in Profília (*T: 22440 61578; map p. 258, A3*), in the central south of the island, is one of the best places to eat on Rhodes: it has imaginatively and carefully prepared traditional dishes of the highest standard, including a superb *imam bayildi*. Nearby, **Petrino**, in the picturesque *plateía* of Váti (*map p. 258, B3*), is a good country taverna with fresh and unaffected cuisine.

FURTHER READING

Cecil Torr, *Rhodes in Ancient Times* and *Rhodes in Modern Times* (first published by CUP in 1885, both now re-issued by Archaeopress '3rd guides', Oxford); Lawrence Durrell, *Reflections on a Marine Venus* (Faber & Faber, London, 1953); H.J.A. Sire, *The Knights of Malta* (Yale, London & New Haven, 1994); Vassilis Colonas, *Italian Architecture in the Dodecanese Islands, 1912–1943* (Olkos Press, Athens, 2002); Elias Kollias, *The Mediaeval City of Rhodes* (Ministry of Culture, Athens, 1998).

ASTYPALAIA

Astypálaia is a solitary island in many respects, on the distant edge of the Dodeca-nese (to which it belongs administratively) and far from the main heart of the Cyclades to its west (to which it is linked in culture and architecture). Though modest in size, it has a dramatically spacious feel, its seascape always impinging on the interior, which is rich in gorges and streams. Its treasures include of one the most beautiful of all island *choras* and a wealth of fascinating Early Christian mosaics. Rich in natural beauty and unobtrusively flourishing, Astypálaia is one of the most independent and untrammelled corners of the Aegean.

The name Astypálaia (meaning 'Old City') is varyingly pronounced with the empha-sis on virtually any of its five syllables except the first. The generally accepted accentua-tion is on the third syllable, but the islanders themselves seem to favour the accent on the last. During its Venetian occupation the island's name was Stampalia.

HISTORY OF ASTYPALAIA

Astypálaia was settled in the Early Cycladic and Mycenaean periods but apparently played no particularly important role in prehistory. It received Dorian colonists from Mégara and Epidaurus in the Argolid, and its importance increased through Archa-ic and Classical antiquity. The island was also called Ichthyoessa ('rich in fish'). The Classical/Hellenistic city was prosperous and sizeable, with numerous sanctuaries. Throughout most of its history Astypálaia maintained a relative independence and autonomy. In the Roman period this was formalised by a *feodus aequum*, a 'friendly treaty', in 105 BC, by which the Romans could use the island's harbours, not least in their campaigns against piracy, in exchange for respecting its autonomy.

After the demise of the Roman Empire, Astypálaia again became a base for pirates. From the 9th century the island was a bishopric, subject to the Metropolitan of Rhodes. By the 12th century its links were particularly close with Amorgós, since much of the island had been granted to the Chozoviótissa Monastery (*see p. 189*). In 1207 Marco Sanudo, Duke of Naxos, gave the island to Giovanni Querini, in recognition of his help in establishing the Duchy. The island was sacked by the Turks under Umur Pasha in 1334, and probably left abandoned. In 1413, Giovanni IV Querini began to repopulate the island with settlers from Mykonos and Tinos, dubbing his new city Astynea ('New City'). In 1537 Kheir ed-Din Barbarossa captured the island for the Ottoman sultan; its name was altered to Ustrupalia. Except during the Cretan War (1648–68) and the Greek revolutionary uprising of 1821–28, the Turks held Astypálaia until 1912, when it became the first of the Dodecanese to be occupied by the Italians, who used it as the springboard for their operations against Rhodes. Astypálaia was incorporated into the Greek state in 1948, together with the other islands of the Dodecanese. In July 1956 the island suffered an earthquake of 7.5 on the Richter scale.

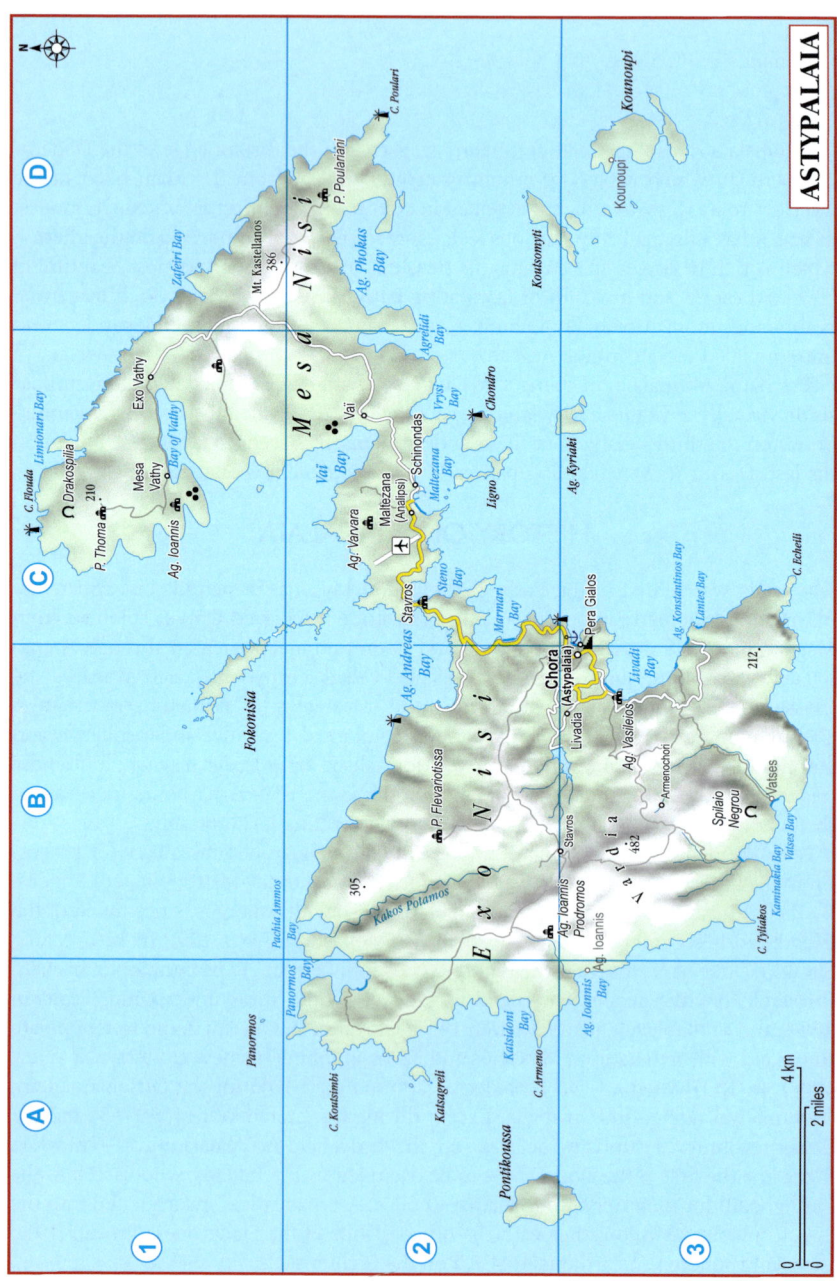

ASTYPALAIA

Cleomedes: the Houdini of Astypálaia
Cleomedes of Astypálaia was a heavyweight pugilist who killed his opponent, Ic-cus of Epidaurus, in a boxing match during the 71st Olympiad of 496 BC and as a result was heavily fined and disqualified. He returned to his native island stricken with rage and grief and in his frenzy, according to Pausanias, he pulled down the local school about its children's ears. In order to escape the wrath of the citizens, who pelted him with stones, he took refuge in the Temple of Athena inside a wooden chest, drawing down the lid. The citizens were unable to open the chest; at last, breaking into it by force, they found no Cleomedes within. Mystified by this escape, they appealed to the Delphic Oracle, who merely responded with the couplet: 'Last of heroes is Cleomedes of Astypálaia; / Honour him with sacrifices as being no longer mortal.' Thereafter, a hero-cult of Cleomedes was instituted on the island.

THE AREA OF CHORA

The Chora of Astypálaia (*map p. 312, B3*) is located on a promontory overlooking the sea, jutting between good harbours and visible from much of the island. The modern town is built on the site of the ancient city: the Venetian kastro stands on the former acropolis and the medieval and modern town over the ancient commercial and residential areas. Only the ancient cemeteries on the outskirts have been systematically excavated. The main cemetery, on the slope opposite Chora to the west, was used from Early Archaic to Roman times. A second cemetery, its excavations still visible directly below the street where the houses of Chora end on the southwestern slope of the Kastro hill, an area known as Kýlindra, appears to have been used exclusively for the burial of new-born infants in pottery urns. Over two thousand such burials have been found, a reminder of the high rate of infant mortality in the ancient world.

Entrance to the old town
The ridge west of the Kastro (where there are two car parks) is punctuated by eight 18th-century windmills. The entrance to the old town is across a pleasant, elongated square lined with cafés and shops. At the far end, the street climbs to the Dimarcheíon and then splits. The right branch passes the low, barrel-vaulted church of Ághios Charálambos, then continues past the chapel of Ághios Spyrídon to an area of predominantly late 18th- and early 19th-century houses, representing the first enlargement of the town outside the Kastro towards the south. After 1830 the spaces between the earliest buildings were filled in with other dwellings, streets were formed, and the area took on its present the appearance.

The **houses of Chora** are closer in style to those of the Cyclades than to those of the Dodecanese. Generally cuboid in form, they have flat roofs surrounded by a ridge with a drain-hole leading to a cistern in the rock below. As on Mykonos, many houses have protruding balconies and steep external steps leading to the upper floor. At ground level were storerooms and work-rooms; on the upper floor the living and sleeping rooms. Simpler dwellings were often just a single rectangular space, called a *monóspito*, ingeniously subdivided with interior wooden structures. Chief of these was the ornate bed-balcony, raised up over an *apokrevátos*, or storage area. The walls were often lined with shelves displaying painted ceramic dishes. Many of the larger houses still possess their fine carved wooden ceilings. Many houses have simple exterior decorations, such as carved window frames.

The Portaïítissa and around the Kastro

At the southeastern end of the old town, on a higher level, enormous cypress trees mark the grand, 18th-century church of the **Panaghía Portaïítissa** (1762). It was founded as a convent of nuns, but now functions as the island's cathedral. The bell-tower (1880) is Neoclassical in design. The episcopal throne and the ornate gilded iconostasis in the interior are both contemporary with the founding of the church.

Above the Portaïítissa to the north looms the partially restored southeast bastion of the Kastro, referred to locally as the **Seraí** (a corruption of seraglio). A pathway leads around the hill. As it regains habitation on the north side of the Kastro, a cluster of chapels and churches on different levels appears below. The principal church is that of the **Megáli Panaghía**, with three other chapels. All incorporate ancient spolia but the chapel of the **Tímios Stavrós**, the uppermost of the three smaller chapels, is almost entirely constructed from large and beautifully finished blocks of ancient marble. The Megáli Panaghía itself, with the small chapel of Ághios Nikólaos along its north side, is originally an 18th-century foundation but was rebuilt in the mid-19th century. Its courtyard has a figurative pebble mosaic (1879).

Directly below the western extremity of the Kastro, southwest of the Megáli Panaghía, the path passes the apses of a series of six contiguous, almost identical, **barrel-vaulted chapels**; in front of their west entrance are a further three. All appear to be built from large blocks of masonry, probably of ancient origin; the third on the left preserves a fragment of ancient entablature with triglyphs on the exterior, and a small area of wall-painting in the interior.

The Kastro

All uphill paths lead ultimately to the entrance into the Kastro on the western side (*no restrictions on access*). The citadel was built by the Venetians between 1413 and 1417, when they resettled the island. The decorated façade of the gatehouse (unhappily reinforced with modern concrete buttresses), with its arches and pediments in low relief, is unusual among the Latin fortresses in the Cyclades. The whole complex is a notable piece of urban design.

Though once inhabited by up to 4,000 people, there is only one entrance. A low, cross-vaulted passage, passing underneath the church of the Panaghía tou Kástrou, leads into the oblong interior, a multitude of dwellings arranged around a central piazza. The space is intimate, and speaks of a leisured life not over obsessed with security, even though in times of emergency the size of the complex served to protect the whole population from pirates. Around the north, west and south sides are the remains of abandoned two- and three-storey houses. Another church, Ághios Geórgios, stands to the east. A group of ancient capitals and pagan and Early Christian fragments has been gathered under its porch. Like the Panaghía tou Kástrou, it was rebuilt in the 19th century, replacing or adapting a church originally designed for the Latin rite. Both churches possess ornately carved iconostases. At several points the carved escutcheons of the Querini family can be seen; a particularly fine example supports a window frame in a house to the north Ághios Geórgios.

Péra Gialós

The shoreline settlement of Péra Gialós or Skála, on the site of the ancient harbour, is linked to Chora by a stepped street. North of the modern church of Ághios Nikólaos is the island's single-roomed **Archaeological Museum** (*open daily except Mon, 8.30–2.30; free*) On the exterior wall hangs an honorific stele with a carved olive crown for an athlete. The small collection includes interesting finds from 14th-century BC Mycenaean graves, examples of Archaic infant burials in urns from Kýlindra, and numerous ancient marble inscriptions, as well as sculpture.

Livádia and Ághios Vasíleios

The asphalt ring-road around Chora descends beyond the windmills, almost immediately passing the whitewashed church of the **Ághii Anárgyri**. To its south and west are extensive remains of floor mosaics from a 5th-century Christian basilica. The road continues into the coastal plain of **Livádia**, its fertility contrasting with the barren slopes all around. The church of Ághios Vasíleios, on a saddle south of the bay (*map p. 312, B3*), is built over an Early Christian basilica, with surviving mosaics. There are many unspoilt beaches around the island, often reached only by tracks or by boat. More easily reached are the bays of Ághios Konstantínos and Lántes, on the road south from Livádia.

EXO NISI

Astypálaia has a curious and memorable shape: two hilly land masses connected by an isthmus, 7km long and only 100m across at its narrowest point. The western part of the island is known as Éxo Nisí. Its landscape is spacious and beautiful, at times even majestic. During migration times, it has a rich birdlife. A circuit of the interior begins from the branch road above the asphalt ring-road, northwest of Chora. (*NB: After 300m the road is unsurfaced for the rest of the loop: fuel or refreshments are not available along it.*)

The Flevariótissa and Ághios Ioánnis

Four and a half kilometres west of Chora, a turning to the right leads to the tranquil 19th-century monastery-church of the **Panaghía Flevariótissa** (*map p. 312, B2*), hidden in a dip. The religious focus was the cave-shrine visible to the left in the interior of the church, outside which are many ancient spolia.

The main track continues southwest to a second junction at Stavrós (*map p. 312, B3*). Here, the northwest (right) branch leads towards Pánormos Bay. Along it, a left-hand branch reaches the remote church of **Ághios Ioánnis Pródromos** (*map p. 312, B2*), above a ravine with a waterfall. The church (15th-century or earlier) is a domed free cross with three aisles, its eastern end built into the rock. The scant remains of a fortified medieval settlement can still be detected on the slope to the northwest, well below the jagged summit. It was destroyed by Kheir ed-Din Barbarossa in 1537. At the shore below is the protected bay of Ághios Ioánnis, reached by a 25-min walk down the path which skirts the southern perimeter of the cultivated area south of the church.

Armenochóri and Vátses

To the south of the junction at Stavrós (*map p. 312, B3*), the track climbs steeply to a saddle, then drops southwards (with deteriorating quality) before turning north across the sheltered plateau of **Armenochóri** (*map p. 312, B3*). The finds from two Mycenaean chamber-tombs in Armenochóri are displayed in the museum in Chora.

After passing the chapel of Ághios Dimítrios on the descent from Armenochóri, a branch track to the south leads down an impressive gorge to the Bay of Vátses (*map p. 312, B3*). On the rocky north slope above the bay is the entrance to the island's largest cave, the so-called **Spílaio Négrou**, named after a pirate who is said to have used it as a lair. There are vestiges of a small chapel in the interior, among the chambers of stalactites and stalagmites. The main road continues, eventually returning to Livádia and Chora.

THE ISTHMUS

North of Chora, a winding coastal road passes several substantial abandoned stone farmsteads. By the church of the Stavrós, the isthmus joining the two parts of the island is only 100m wide: there are good views from here.

Aghía Varvára

Near to the airport is the church of Aghía Varvára (*map p. 312, C2; almost at the entrance to the airport, follow the track bearing right. The church is visible from here, a small cluster of white buildings on the hillside to the southeast, to the left of a windmill. Continue straight after c. 700m, when the track turns sharp left. This branch ends after a further 50m. The church is reached by skirting round the hill, through fields*). The modern chapel occupies a small portion of a large 5th-century basilica, whose fine mosaics extend to all sides of it, as well as inside the chapel itself (covered with whitewash). The succession of marble column-bases dividing the nave from the south aisle survives; the monolithic columns they supported lie nearby. The broad narthex is floored with some of the best-preserved mosaics, featuring vine and chalice designs.

Análipsi

The port of Análipsi (*map p. 312, C2*) is commonly known as Maltezána, a name that originally meant 'Maltese' but which over time came to refer generically to pirates, for whom this bay would have been a useful base. Behind the port, two fields contain the remains of the Roman **Baths of Talaras**, dating from the late 4th century. There are several archaeologists' trenches in the first field; most of what remains is to be seen in the second, further away from the shore, where the charming mosaic floor of the central thermal chamber—the tepidarium—is clearly visible. It depicts the 12 signs of the Zodiac circling a bright-eyed female divinity, representing Fortune or Destiny. To the northwest side are a small, marble-lined fountain pool and two sunken bathing chambers with hydraulic plaster still visible in places. Under the water towards the opposite (western) end of the same bay are further Roman foundations, best seen while swimming.

On the point, around the margin of the next bay to the east from Maltezána, stands a **memorial to Hippolyte Bisson**, a French philhellene who detonated his ship here to avoid its capture by pirates on November 6th 1827, just days after the Battle of Navarino. A hundred and fifty metres along the shore beyond the monument are the badly-eroded remains of a 5th-century **Early Christian basilica**, with magnificent mosaics, including vine and chalice motifs in the nave and dolphins in the narthex.

MESA NISI

The eastern part of the island, Mésa Nisí, is drier and stonier than the west. The unsurfaced road into its interior leaves from Schinóndas (*map p. 312, C2*) and climbs east and then north above the Bay of Vaï. Visible on the hilltop to the north of the bay are the remains of a square **medieval watchtower**. Further east, the long inlet of Agrelídi Bay comes into view. The abandoned and collapsed stone houses and walls behind the bay are remains of a settlement destroyed in the 1956 earthquake.

The southeastern tip of Mésa Nisí is reached along a track through a panoramic landscape that passes below the summit of Mt Kastellános, crowned by the ruins of an Italian military fort (1912), with excellent views. The track ends beside the remote chapel of the **Panaghía Poularianí** (*map p. 312, D2*), its altar a fluted pagan altar-table support.

Around Vathý Bay

The bay of Vathý (*map p. 312, C1*) cuts deep into the island from the west. At the inner extremity is Éxo Vathý ('Outer' Vathý), while at the western end is Mésa Vathý ('Inner' Vathý); their naming reflects the point of view of the sea-borne approach. Approaching by car, you descend into **Éxo Vathý** among examples of traditional rural architecture, or *katoikiá*: square or round stone huts, roofed with mud, wattle and straw, often standing in groups linked by walls that define animal pens and winnowing areas. Sowing and reaping by hand is still the norm in the fields below. To the right the track passes the entrance to the ruined two-aisled medieval church of Ághios Ioánnis Pródromos.

Dominating both the bay and the settlement is the 18th-century monastery-church of Ághios Nikólaos, on the hilltop to the south: its altar is supported by an ancient Corinthian capital.

From Éxo Vathý, the track follows the north shore of the bay as far as **Mésa Vathý**. To the west of the settlement, at the western end of an unexpectedly fertile dip, is the late medieval church of Ághios Ioánnis. On the long promontory to the south, an ancient structure overlooks the narrow entrance of the bay. The main ruin is usually described as **Hellenistic watchtower**, but appears to represent something more substantial (*access is not easy since there is no clear path. Follow the shoreline round from Mésa Vathý to the east as far as possible and cut up to the ruins on the low plateau just before its eastern extremity*). The ruins of a circular medieval tower stand on a substantial rectangular substructure of Hellenistic masonry: a rectangular podium, c. 12m by 20m. On the east side, steps and terraces descend to landing point constructed on the tip of the promontory. On the northeast side are remains of earlier (?prehistoric) walls.

From Mésa Vathý the track continues to a summit above the island's northern tip, crowned by the small, barrel-vaulted chapel of the Panaghía tou Thomá (*map p. 312, C1*). Below it to the northwest, about 50m above the shoreline, is the **Drakospiliá** ('Cave of the Dragon'), with fine chambers of stalagmites and stalactites, where archaeological finds from the Geometric period have been made. It is best approached from the sea.

PRACTICAL INFORMATION

GETTING AROUND

Five flights per week serve Astypálaia's tiny airport, via Kálymnos, and three connect it with Rhodes, via Leros and Kos. There are three ferries a week from Piraeus (8½–10hrs), via Amorgós and either Naxos or Paros. Ferries dock at Ághios Andréas, 7km north of Chora.

WHERE TO STAY

Akti Studios, in the bay below Chora (*T: 22430 61114; www.aktirooms.gr*) offer simple and inexpensive self-catering accommoda-

tion: ask for rooms facing the water. Further west at Livádia are the **Kalderimi Hotel** (*www.kalderimi.gr*) and the **Satinomare** (*T: 6944 183398, www.satinomare.gr*).

WHERE TO EAT

Several of the island's best places are in Péra Gialós. The **Taverna Akti** is particularly good. Nearby, and opposite one another, are **Maistrali** and **Aitherio**, both offering good fish and good value.

In summer, **Linda's** at Kaminákia Bay (*map p. 312, B3*) provides excellent dishes prepared with home-grown vegetables.

CHALKI

The wealth once brought to the tiny island of Chálki by the sponge trade in the 19th century is immediately evident in the gracious sweep of stone houses of Neoclassical inspiration which encircle the harbour. The underwater sponge-beds were the island's principal 'garden', since the harsh and waterless mountains of its interior afford only a few oases for cultivation. Although the island's name appears to refer to copper (Greek: *chalkós*), the extraction and working of metal on the island has left no evidence behind. It is possible that the name instead derives from the Phoenician *karki*, meaning 'shells'. Chálki today is a peaceful retreat, offering uncrowded beaches, scenic walks, and both a dramatic landscape inland and an attractive seascape all around, formed by its outlying islands.

HISTORY OF CHALKI

Neolithic obsidian tools found at Kepháli in the extreme northwest of the island provide the earliest evidence of human settlement, but Chálki only steps into the pages of written texts or inscriptions in the Classical period, first appearing in the fiscal lists of the Delian League, to which the island belonged in the 5th century BC. Thucydides notes that it played an important role as an operations base (411 BC) for the Athenian fleet during the Peloponnesian War, acting against enemy ships in Rhodes. Its subsequent independence was short-lived, and the island became part of the Rhodian State in the late 4th century BC, subject to the deme of Kameíros. Little is known about it beyond Strabo's observation that it possessed a harbour and a temple of Apollo (*Geog. X, 488*), although archaeological finds from Hellenistic tombs attest considerable wealth.

Apart from some scattered and vestigial Early Christian remains, little is known of the island's fortunes up into the medieval period except that the constant danger of pirate raids forced the population to move well inland and re-settle in the protected area of the ancient acropolis (Chorió). After the Fourth Crusade of 1204, the Venetians and Genoese re-fortified this height and, in 1366, Chálki and Alimniá were granted to the Assanti family. The Knights of St John subsequently rebuilt the castle on the acropolis in the mid-15th century, only to lose it in 1522–23 to the Turks, who governed the island up until 1912, when the Italians took control. Italian occupation was further confirmed by the Second Treaty of Lausanne of 1924. After the compulsory imposition of the Italian language, a secret school was set up in a cave, where children were taught in Greek. The Italians surrendered to German forces in 1943. In May 1947 the island was incorporated into the Greek state together with the other islands of the Dodecanese. It saw a steady decline in population throughout the 20th century as families who had worked in the sponge trade left for the United States, moving principally to Tarpon Springs, Florida.

AROUND THE ISLAND

Emboreió
The wide arc of dignified 19th-century stone houses grouped around the island's protected harbour forms a harmonious sweep, punctuated by the municipal clock-tower and the campanile of Ághios Nikólaos. The latter belongs to the principal church of the island, which is surrounded by a fine pebble-mosaic floor (1868). A baptismal font and the tomb of the church's principal benefactor lie in the forecourt to the south. Although the church is originally a 16th-century foundation, it presents itself today as a largely 19th-century re-build and possesses an impressive templon screen inside. The five-tier bell-tower (32m) incorporates pieces of ancient marble from the Temple of Apollo at Pefkiá, two of which form the crown of the arch on the west side. There is a small ecclesiastical museum above the narthex, entered from the outside of the church.

The expatriate community has financed many of the recent public projects of the island, including the Tarpon Springs Boulevard, which leads from Emboreió to the monastery of Ághios Ioánnis.

The beaches on the north coast (Aréta, Ághios Geórgios and Dío Gialí) are best reached by boat from Emboreió.

NORTH TO PEFKIA

As the road crosses the low ridge north of Emboreió, a left branch leads to the ruined church of **Ághios Zacharías**. The church appears to have been built on the site of a pagan temple which, in turn, was succeeded by an Early Christian place of worship: the present building sits in the northeast corner of the foundations of the Early Christian building. Its interior was once finely decorated with 14th-century wall-paintings.

These have been removed to prevent further decay and are now exhibited in the Pan-aghía tou Kástrou in Rhodes.

On the saddle of the mountain to the northeast, just to the west of the summit marked by a triangulation post, are the remains of the Hellenistic **Sanctuary of Apollo at Pefkiá**, possibly the one referred to by Strabo. The temple stood in the lee of the western shoulder of the final summit (*it is best approached by skirting the lower perimeter stone wall of the valley from behind the stand of pine trees. The rough path passes a huge standing rock in the middle of the valley, then rises up past a conspicuous cave entrance towards the saddle. Well in from the ridge, at the right-hand corner, are the overgrown ruins, beside a small stone hut*). Some finely-turned marble columns, bases, drums and other fragments mark the site. A carved stone basin and a deep cistern lie just to the northeast.

WEST TO CHORIO & THE CENTRE OF THE ISLAND

After leaving the houses behind Emboreió, the road passes along the inlet of **Póntamos** (*10mins on foot*), with a taverna and attractive beach. Several 4th-century BC tombs have been excavated here and have yielded a wealth of finds. After Póntamos the modern road climbs to the west and, at the top of the rise (*25mins*), the road levels out: the deserted settlement of Palaió Chorió is to the left, below the castle on the summit; to the right is the **cemetery church of the Sotíros** (Metamorphosis), constructed from a number of re-used ancient blocks and with fragments of Hellenistic funerary monuments visible above the door. Above and behind is a stretch of ancient wall, and there are many large 19th-century stone sarcophagi in the graveyard around the church.

Palaió Chorió

The remains of Palaió Chorió stretch up the mountain slope to the south, punctuated by three whitewashed churches. This was the site of the capital of the island in both Classical antiquity and medieval times, when piracy had made coastal habitation untenable.

The path leads up first to the early 14th-century **church of the Panaghía** (*if locked, the key may be obtained from the taverna at Póntamos*). The interior is a graceful, vaulted chamber with pebble floor, decorated in the apse and on the ceiling with relatively well preserved wall-paintings of the mid-1600s. A path through the gate at the southwest corner of the courtyard leads uphill to another small church, with damaged 15th-century wall-paintings and a fine ancient marble drum as an altar. Remains of the ancient settlement become increasingly apparent as you climb: deep, rock-cut cisterns, often with finely shaped mouths; carved rectangular niches; and two fragments of inscribed architrave.

The **Castle of the Knights of St John** bears the coat of arms of the Order's Grand Master, Pierre d'Aubusson (1476–1503). The entrance leads into a roofless guardroom with cannon embrasures, beyond which a magnificent ancient doorway opens into the oblong area of the ruined interior. The finely castellated north wall of the enceinte, which follows the line of the ancient Hellenistic walls, is particularly well preserved, with its narrow sentry walk, central tower (with latrine beside), and rooms built into the interior face to accommodate inhabitants during periods of siege. The south wall is mostly collapsed and preserves only the bases of two of its towers. A deep cistern (probably of ancient origin) is still visible midway between the north and south walls. The central area is dominated by the roofless church of Ághios Nikólaos and, although exposed to the elements, areas of the original wall-paintings are still visible. To the south the land drops away dramatically to the Tracheiá peninsula below, with its two shallow anchorages at the isthmus. From here there is a magnificent view of the south-west coast of Rhodes with its two prominent castles; this lookout post would have protected the main sea-route to Rhodes from Crete and the west.

The **beach of Gialí** can be reached in a 30-min walk down the track that leaves Chorió to the southwest.

THE WEST OF THE ISLAND

The western half of Chálki is mostly a dramatically rocky limestone plateau. Its beaches are deserted and largely shadeless pebble coves. Although largely uninhabited and uncultivated, it is a mass of wild flowers in the early spring. There is a scattering of isolated chapels and monastery churches, which are now easier of access thanks to the new road: this leads all the way to **Ághios Ioánnis Alárga** (**St John 'the Far'**), which is a 2½-hr walk from the port. Its open courtyard is bounded on two sides by cells and punctuated by a large cypress tree. The main church, with a re-laid floor, is simple and undecorated inside. A hundred metres to its northwest is the church of the **Panaghía Enniamerítissa**, which incorporates material from an Early Christian predecessor. It has extensive, but damaged, 14th-century wall-paintings inside and a founder's in-scription bearing the date 6875 (= years since Creation, i.e. 1375).

The road ends at this point; but a one-hour hike northwest from here to the western extremity of the island leads to the **Kepháli promontory** where, among the ruins of an enceinte of walls and vestiges of an Early Christian basilica, there are the remains of an ancient tower which surveyed the sea-routes towards Kárpathos.

ALIMNIA

The island of Alimniá (also Alimiá; *map p. 252*) lies about 6km northeast of Chálki. The beautiful and protected bay of Ághios Geórgios, where boats arrive, bears out the is-land's ancient name, Eulimnia ('good harbours'). As you enter the bay, to the east is the picturesque church of Ághios Minás, beside which rise the ruins of the military build-ings put up by the Italians during their occupation of the Dodecanese. Ahead, among the trees behind the beach, was the main settlement, clustered around the church of Ághios Geórgios. The tranquil beauty of the bay is at odds with its recent history: dur-ing the Second World War, this deep harbour was used by German occupying forces as a submarine base. The base was attacked in April 1944 by seven British commandos, who were captured, sent to Thessaloníki and executed. The local islanders confessed to having assisted them and were consequently deported. Since the 1960s the island has been uninhabited. In one of the abandoned buildings (formerly a taverna) near the church of Ághios Geórgios, pictures of ships and submarines painted by Italian soldiers can still be seen. The ruins of a 14th-century Hospitaller castle crown the sharp peak to the north. There is no clear path up; ascent takes nearly an hour, and the castle can only be entered—with difficulty—from the east end.

PRACTICAL INFORMATION

GETTING THERE

To Chálki there are daily service in season (slightly less regular off-season) taking 90mins from/to Kameíros Skála on Rhodes, with limited capacity for cars. Larger ferries stop at Chálki three times weekly en route between Rhodes and Kárpathos, Kasos and western Crete. A local water taxi (Alevandros, T: 22460 45251 or 6944 434429) connects Alimniá with Chálki, on request (40mins)

WHERE TO STAY

Lodging is limited on Chálki, although slowly increasing. The **Captain's House** (*T: 22460 45201; captainshouse@ath.forthnet.gr; open generally May–late Oct*) is a charming and hospitable place with garden, set back from Emboreió harbour a little east of the main church. For longer stays, **Villa Praxithea** ▬ (*T: 22410 70172 or 6972 427272; www.villapraxithea. com*) is an elegant house on the waterfront sensitively converted into furnished apartments by the architect-owner.

WHERE TO EAT

On Chálki, a number of tavernas by the port in Emboreió serve fresh, locally-caught fish. **Omonia tou Nouri** on the waterfront also has excellent spit-roasts and vegetable dishes.

KARPATHOS

Kárpathos has the wildest landscape and coastal waters of the Dodecanese and, with an area marginally larger than Kos, it is the biggest island of the group after Rhodes. Its northern half is a steep, sculpted ridge of mountains that drops abruptly to the sea, while the southern tip is an open landscape of soft, eroded sandstone. Between the two lies the moderately fertile area of springs and low hills where the majority of the population is concentrated. Recent history has seen massive emigration, in particular to the Antipodes: half a century later some members of those families are returning to Kárpathos or building properties here. For this reason, a sometimes rootless modernity prevails in Pigádia, the capital, and has spread to some of the nearby villages, scattering the landscape with buildings that appear at once out of place, out of time and out of context. A number of the charming mountain villages, however, such as Óthos, Pylés and Mesochóri, have preserved some of the typical architecture and interiors of the past two centuries. Like Crete, Kárpathos is rich in the variety of its music and dance, which survive in the island's *panigýria*, at Ólympos (15th Aug) and Vrykoúnda (28th–30th Aug), and at Stes (27th–29th July).

HISTORY OF KARPATHOS

Even though Homer calls it 'Krapathos', the island was always known as Kárpathos in antiquity. The medieval name of Scarpanto was revived by the Italians at the beginning of the last century and is still sometimes used: the Turks called it Kerpe. Evidence of a Neolithic presence on Kárpathos as early as the beginning of the 4th millennium BC has been found on the acropolis headland at Pigádia, and by the 2nd millennium BC, the island begins to show the overt influence and presence of Cretan, Minoan culture. Almost a hundred Bronze Age vases have been recovered from tombs, reinforcing the evidence for occupation during this period. Minoan and Mycenaean remains have been found at many sites, both in the Pigádia area and at other points around the island. The island was colonised by Dorian settlers from Argos in the Peloponnese around 1000 BC.

In the 5th century BC, the communities of the island appear in Athenian tribute lists of the Delian League. In the 4th century the island was incorporated into the Rhodian state, and in AD 42 it was annexed by Rome. In the Early Byzantine period, the island was under the archdiocese of Rhodes. In the last decade of the 11th century the Byzantine fleet used the island as a supply base for its campaign to suppress uprisings on Crete. The Byzantine emperor Andronicus II Palaeologus gave the island in fief to the Genoese adventurers and brothers Andrea and Lodovico Moresco, and in 1306 it was acquired by the Cornaro family of Venice. The Knights of Rhodes took over the island in 1315, but held it for only two years before returning it to Andrea Cornaro, under a threat from Venice which amounted to financial extortion. The Cornaro dynasty finally surrendered Kárpathos to the Turks in 1538. In 1823 the island was momentarily lib-

A

C. Paraspori

N

Saria

Argos

Galatia Bay

C. Akrotiri

630
Pachy Vouno

Straits of Saria

Amou

Tristomo

Karpathos

Cape
Vrychounda

Brykous

Orkili
·743

Avlona

B

Avlona

Mt
Koryfi

Olympos

Fises Bay

719
Profitis Ilias

C

Vananda Cove

Diafani

Papa Mina Cove

C. Makria Pounda

1

Nati Bay

Ag. Eirini Bay

Makrys Gialos Bay

Spoa

Mesochori

Ag. Nikolaos

C. Marinaki

Apella Bay

Sokastro

Ag. Georgios

C. Pounda

K. Lefkos

Frangolimionas Bay

Kali Limni
1215

C. Panaghia

Kyra Panaghia

2

Myrtonas

Katodi

Kato
Lastos

Flaskia Gorge

Volada

Aperi

Stes   Othos

Mt Profitis Ilias
499

Achata Valley

C. Tragopidima

Proni Bay

Pyles

Vronti Bay

Ag. Photini

Pigadia Bay

3

Chamali
685

Menetes

Cape Finiki   Finiki

**Pigadia
(Karpathos)**

Ag. Sophia   Arkasa

Arkaseia

Kefalas

Amopi

Lakki

Amorphos Bay

C. Volakas

Diakoftis

C. Ag. Theodoros

Mira

C. Akrotiri

Kastello Bay

Makrygialos Bay

C. Liki

4

Cape Kastello

0   5 km

0   2,5 miles

KARPATHOS

erated during the Greek War of Independence and joined to the fledgling Greek state, before being returned to Turkey in 1830. Five years later, Sultan Mahmud II allowed Kárpathos beneficial financial privileges. Kárpathos was finally united with Greece, together with the other Dodecanese islands, in May 1948.

THE CENTRE & SOUTH OF THE ISLAND

Pigádia

The port of Kárpathos, more commonly known as Pigádia (*map p. 325, C3*), has been the island's capital since 1894, when it succeeded Apéri as the administrative centre. Little traditional architecture remains, but the wide curve of the modern waterfront is not unattractive, especially when alive and illuminated at night. Stretching in an arc between two promontories, the smaller to the west marked by the tower of the Italian colonial administrative buildings, the larger to the east, by two small churches and the cemetery, Pigádia occupies the area of the ancient settlement of Potidaion. Of the four ancient cities generally associated with the island, this was the most important, especially in later Hellenistic and Roman times. The eastern promontory functioned as its fortified acropolis, and appears to have been crowned by a temple to Athena Lindia, known from inscriptions, but of which no trace now remains.

The western wing of the buildings that stand on the rise at the western end of the port houses the island's **archaeological museum**, which in the space of three rooms exhibits a number of remarkable artefacts and introduces the ancient history of the island with great clarity.

Around Pigádia

A kilometre from the centre of Pigádia, along the road north for Apéri, is Plateía Konstantínos Philippídi, just beyond the Miramare Hotel. A left branch at a small grocery shop leads inland and, after less than a kilometre, a flight of steps leads up to a cave in the rockface, whose rectangular entrance has been crafted into the doorway for a small **tomb complex**. It is the best preserved from an area which was used as a necropolis in Hellenistic times.

In the narrow space between the beach and the main road to Apéri, 1.5km north-west of the centre of Pigádia, are the standing remains of the Early Christian basilica of Aghía Photí, or **Aghía Photiní** (*map p. 325, C3*), whose foundation dates from the late 4th or early 5th century AD, although the buildings have probably seen later modification. The large and elegantly decorated marble templon screen, which is formed by two exceptionally large marble plaques fixed and held by carved posts (the left one only recently broken), is most striking. This fine marble-work contrasts with the humility of the simple terracotta-tiled floor and the general roughness of the stonework in the walls. The quantity of ancient spolia incorporated into the basilica suggests that it was originally the site of a pagan temple, possibly that of the Dioscuri referred to elsewhere in inscriptions. This may account for the marked difference in floor level between nave and aisles, but does not shed light on how the intercommunication of these spaces functioned architecturally in Early Christian times.

Apéri and the Acháta valley

After turning inland from the shore of Vrónti Bay, the road climbs swiftly to **Apéri** (*map p. 325, B3*), the seat of the Metropolitan of Kárpathos and Kasos. A stream divides the village, which is set steeply over several slopes with many stepped streets. Although in ruinous condition, the church of the Ághii Theódori above Apéri preserves damaged fragments of early 14th-century wall-paintings (including an uncommon depiction of the Betrayal), now exposed to the elements by the collapse of the church's fabric.

Further east, the road continues steeply down the **valley of Acháta**, hemmed to the south by the stone cliffs of Mt Profítis Ilías, and to the north by rock formations which have formed cavernous apse-like breaches, one of which is partially walled in so as to create an anchorite's dwelling. The road finishes at one of the island's most attractive beaches, a secluded strand of shingle, with clear water and occasional pine and tamarisk trees.

Voláda and Óthos

The route west from the junction 1km above Apéri leads over the watershed to the west coast through some of the island's most interesting traditional villages. Both Voláda and Óthos contain examples of traditional dwellings. The most accessible, the Kárpathos House Museum, is in Óthos (*map p. 325, B3; when closed, the key is kept by an elderly local painter, Michaïl Chapsis, who sells his paintings, in traditional, naïf style, from a shop on the west side of the street in the middle of the village*). The small house displays fine examples of local ceramics, furniture and embroidery, which on Kárpathos acquires a particularly elaborate beauty: there are also examples of the decorated Karpathian lyre and bow, used for accompanying the spontaneous versifications in song for which the island is famous.

ARKASA & THE FAR SOUTH

On the coast west of Pigádia below are the two promontories of Finíki and Arkása (*map p. 325, B3–B4*). On the spit of land which joins the rocky headland of Arkása to the shore is the site of ancient Arkaseia and of an Early Christian basilica.

Ancient Arkaseia and modern Arkása

In spite of the fact that areas of the Early Christian mosaics from Arkása were moved to the museum in Rhodes by the Italians in the 1930s, there is still much to see here. The site includes three buildings of slightly varying periods. The earliest work, perhaps from as early as the turn of the 4th–5th century AD, is the **floor** of a building to the north of the small church of Aghía Sophía (the first part encountered, coming from the end of the track), which may have functioned principally as a baptistery. The later, 6th-century basilica of **Aghía Anastasía** lies under and to the west and south of

Aghía Sophía. This was a large structure (25m long) with a more ambitious design to its floor, extending well beyond the low building which was later erected at an odd angle over the southwest corner of the basilica's floor. The design of the mosaic floor is best preserved inside this building. Beyond this complex and further to the west are what remains of a third building programme, the **Basilica of Eucharistos**, named after a bishop mentioned in its dedicatory inscription, and dating from the end of the 5th century.

Small stretches of **ancient polygonal walling** can be seen on the southeast face of the rock. These are the remains of what was a complete circuit of walls, up to 2m in width, which formed the Mycenaean fortification of the acropolis. Slightly to the right of this (below the modern walls) is more polygonal masonry, different in appearance and dating perhaps from a later enceinte of the early historic period, which belonged to the city referred to by ancient writers as Arkaseia. The rock constitutes a perfect natural acropolis, and appears to have been used with little interruption from the Bronze Age through to medieval times. A path winds steeply up to a shoulder of the headland on the north side, densely covered in potsherds from a wide span of periods: ancient, Byzantine and medieval.

The brightly-coloured houses of the **modern village of Arkása** climb to either side of a torrent bed: the church of the Panaghía Marmariní incorporates in its porch a couple of columns brought from the ancient acropolis. There is also a small local **museum**, which has gathered together ancient and Early Christian fragments displayed alongside various liturgical and domestic items from more recent times.

South of Arkása

The area to the south of the road from Pigádia to Arkása is an open, eroded landscape of sandstone ravines and plateaux, with clear views to Kasos over the often bristling channel between the two islands. The southern extremity of the island is dominated by a parched and flat-topped headland, referred to as **Kastéllo** (*map p. 325, B4*) from the castle built in the 15th century by the Cornaro overlords. The protected bay to its north constituted an obvious roadstead on the prehistoric sea-route from Crete to Asia Minor and Cyprus, and the whole area has yielded evidence of scattered habitation of the 3rd and 2nd millennia BC.

MESOCHORI & ENVIRONS

The narrow, stepped streets of **Mesochóri** (*map p. 325, B2*) are inaccessible to vehicles. At the opposite side from where the road ends, a flat-topped, panoramic bluff at the western edge of the settlement constitutes the village's *plateía*: today it is marked by the three low chapels of Aghía Triáda and the twin 18th-century churches of Ághios Nikólaos (1764) and of the Stavrós (c. 1700), but this natural vantage point was also the site of lookout structures in both ancient and medieval times. At the top of the village, just below where the road ends, is the church of Ághios Ioánnis (1781), with extensive (but blackened) wall-paintings of the 18th century depicting scenes of the life of Christ and a graphic depiction of the fiery jaws of Hell on the west wall. The attractive pebble floor and the iconostasis carved with a vine motif are also from the late 18th century.

Ághios Geórgios

Five and a half kilometres south of Mesochóri down the west coast road is the settlement of Ághios Geórgios (*map p. 325, B2*), which takes its name from the unusual 12th-century church of **Ághios Geórgios tou Lefkoú** (or 'tou Notará'), hidden in a small ravine 150m to the southeast of the village, and just visible from the road to the south of the junction for Lefkós. The design of the church is unlike any other in the Dodecanese: the plan is of a cross-in-square surmounted by a central drum around which are grouped four further small cupolas. There are two parallel west entrances. The interior space is dominated by the square pillars from which the vaults supporting the domes spring. Areas of painting from the turn of the 14th century have been revealed from beneath the predominating whitewash: two particularly fine faces can be seen, of Ághios Dimítrios and of an angel whose expression is full of compassion. The narrative scenes around the walls are harder to read.

On the hill above the church to the south is the base of a **Hellenistic fort** measuring about 9m square: the large blocks of isodomic masonry stand to a height of three courses on one side. A farmer's stone hut has been improvised in the southern corner of the foundations.

Lefkós

The shoreline below Ághios Geórgios at Lefkós—a low, shelving, sandstone promontory with offshore islets—is of a configuration typically favoured by prehistoric and early settlers: Mycenaean rock graves have been found inside the escarpment behind the long, west-facing bay of Frangolimiónas. The landscape is punctuated with small natural caves and man-made tombs and niches. The most curious antiquity here is a **Roman or Hellenistic hypogeum** (*map p. 325, B2*), which appears to have functioned as a large, pillared water cistern (*a sign indicating 'Roman Cistern' branches to the north after 1km of descent from Ághios Geórgios towards Lefkós; after 800m a track, and subsequently a footpath, leads a further 800m to the site in the middle of a scrub-covered plateau*).

The underground chamber is entered by rock-cut steps to the west into a roughly rectangular area. Seven excavated tunnels lead off, three to the north and four to the east. Their purpose was to increase storage capacity without the construction of a further roofed area. A small pedimented aedicule can be seen below the ceiling on the east side. Waterproofing plaster in the tunnels suggests the storage of water, as do the entry steps, which provide easy access whatever the seasonal variation in the water level. There may originally have been a weak spring here, which is now dry.

Káto Lefkós has several fine sandy beaches, dotted with ruins and antiquities. The semicircular apse of a 5th-century basilica projects from the sand into the water at the western end of the first cove. Another basilica of the same period stood 200m inland from the shore at the foot of the low escarpment behind the village, where the low chapel of the Panaghía Gialochorafítissa now stands. The present church is built into the apse of the basilica, the blocks of which can be seen outside at the southeast corner. The interior of the chapel also contains Early Christian and ancient fragments. The hillside behind is dotted with traces of ancient and medieval walls and rock graves. Remains of a medieval vaulted structure, now mostly submerged in sand, can be seen on the isthmus of land that links the rocks to the shore in Poúnda Bay, west of the village, while more substantial remains of a Byzantine or mediaeval fortress can be seen on the offshore island of Sókastro.

The Flaskiá Gorge

The road south from the junction at Ághios Geórgios is one of the most panoramic and beautiful on the island: after 8km it drops to the coast and passes the mouth of the Flaskiá Gorge (*map p. 325, B3*). The ascent on foot through the gorge to the plateau at Káto Lástos can be made in about 3hrs; there are springs after one hour and shortly before the end and, though the path is steep, it is shaded with Aleppo pines and enlivened by breaks of oleanders.

THE NORTH OF THE ISLAND

Spóa marks the beginning of the wild north of Kárpathos: it lies at the point where the more varied and inhabited southern half of the island gives way to a narrow and dramatic ridge of largely uninhabited and inhospitable mountains rising steeply on the eastern side and dropping almost sheer to the west. The coasts are rarely much more than 4km apart over the whole area. In the 20km stretch between Spóa and Ólympos, the principal centre of the north, driveable tracks are a recent arrival: their condition is still primitive and it takes a full 40mins by jeep along a wild and scenic route. The sites of the north are still more comfortably reached by boat. Both scheduled ferries and caïques ply the route between Pigádia and Diafáni, the principal harbour of the north.

Spóa and ancient Márathos

Spóa (*map p. 325, B2*) has little to detain the visitor beyond its striking position: its name is perhaps a corruption of *sta póda*, meaning 'at the foot [of the mountains]'. Before the advent of roads, the village's door to the world was the harbour of Ághios Nikólaos, in an east-facing cove 330m below. The remains of a fortress of the Cornaro overlords can be seen at a considerable height on the mountain spur to the south of the harbour, indicating that there was once some strategic importance to the landing and the village far above.

On the north side of the inlet of Ághios Nikólaos (c. 450m from the harbour) a modern, unplastered chapel marks the **site of the deserted settlement of Márathos**, and the ruined Early Christian basilica of the Panaghía Eftavatoúsa. As decoration in its west façade, the chapel incorporates small fragments of coloured mosaic floor of the 5th–6th centuries. Márathos was probably a small settlement in origin, which survived to become a prosperous Christian community until it was abandoned under pressure from Arab and pirate incursions in the 7th century.

From the northern end of Spóa, the main (unsurfaced) route for Ólympos heads north, high above the shore with dramatic views along the eastern coast, through a landscape at times wooded with pines, at others bare and eroded. The land and the villages are given over almost exclusively to goats and goatherds. There is a minimal cultivation of olives and cereals today, but the extensive and meticulous terracing of past centuries is evident on almost every slope.

Ólympos

The first and last impression of this extraordinary village (*map p. 325, B1*) is its setting. It clings to a mountainside above a deep and spacious valley to its east, and a precipitous 300m drop to the sea below to its west. Two forbidding peaks of bald limestone mountain loom behind and in front: Profítis Ilías (719m) to the south and Korýfi (588m) to the north. Against this uncompromising background the colours, decorations and irregular forms of the houses and churches make a brave plea for attention.

Ólympos has remained cut off for so long that it has preserved its tranquillity and individuality better than many places in the Aegean islands. The mountain road from Pigádia, via Spóa, first linked Ólympos with the rest of the island in 1979, and electricity only arrived a year later. Since then the rate of change has been rapid and the village has acquired official status as a tourist attraction, encouraging the fossilisation of its once vital and meaningful traditions. In spite of this, however, some curiosities survive unselfconsciously: many women still wear the goatskin boots, headscarf and colourfully embroidered costume of the village as a matter of course; the unaltered local dialect survives, said to contain elements of the language and pronunciation of the villagers' Dorian forebears; and a few of the houses still use a kind of wooden doorlock and key, said (perhaps tendentiously) to be of the same pattern as those used in Homeric times. It is immediately noticeable that women predominate numerically, and are busy with most of the tasks of shop-keeping, baking, storing firewood, managing the beasts of burden and running the village: it has always been so, and needed to be thus in a society where men were mostly absent at sea for over half the year. This has given rise to the village's ancient system of inheritance by which, as well as the eldest son (called the *kanakáris*) receiving his father's property, the *kanakára*, or eldest daughter, also inherits the entire property and dowry of her mother.

The village dates from the period when the coastal settlements, such as Vrychoúnda, ceased to be viable because of piracy and Saracen incursions in the 7th and 8th centuries. There are churches from the 12th century, if not earlier; some of the 30 windmills may go back as far as the 16th century; most of the dwellings are from the 18th and 19th centuries. The traditional cuboid houses are sometimes brilliantly coloured; balconies, even modern concrete ones, are covered with bright designs—scenes from festivals, monograms, invented heraldic symbols, doves, peacocks and, commonest of all, the double-headed eagle of the Byzantine Orthodox Church. Banisters end in newel posts in the form of sphinxes, and pilasters are surmounted with moulded birds.

Against the bleak backdrop of the rocky mountain-faces, such decoration is a welcome relief.

On entering the village from the west, a couple of the oldest churches are immediately above and to the left: the ruined remains of the 12th-century chapel of Ághios Onoúphrios and the church of **Aghía Triáda**, the latter with an attractive iconostasis and an altar of ancient spolia. Another fine example of the village's decorative painted iconostases is in the late 18th-century church of **Aghía Varvára**, beside the main street to the right. The older houses that line the street are partially cut back into the rock, while the more recent ones are built out over it. The village *plateía*, perched on the watershed of the ridge in front of the main church of the Koímisis tis Theotókou, is a delightful ensemble of buildings in spite of being such a small and narrow space.

Below Ólympos, in the valley to its east, are the two chapels of Aghía Ánna and Ághii Saránda (*these lie down a path below and to the west of the road from Ólympos to Diafáni, shortly north of the junction with the road to Spóa*). Both churches have been restored: the smaller, **Ághii Saránda**, has the remains of a 13th-century *Pantocrator* in its conch; in the larger, **Aghía Ánna**, there are areas of wall-paintings with non-figurative, mostly geometric decorations in red, white and black—a rare example of the survival of aniconic art. The traditions of the Iconoclastic period of the 8th century died out more slowly in the islands, and these decorations probably date from the 10th or 11th century.

DIAFANI & THE NORTHERN TIP OF THE ISLAND

The rugged and scenic northern extremity of Kárpathos is of considerable archaeological interest; there is also unusual flora and fauna in its empty panoramic valleys. Exploration takes time and necessitates staying in Ólympos or Diafáni. The latter is the only place from which a boat to visit the uninhabited island of Saría can be easily arranged, and the same excursion can be designed (weather permitting) to include the sites of ancient Brykous and Trístomo as well—both of these are perhaps best understood when approached from the water. Otherwise they are reached by long, but rewarding, walks. These walks are mostly self-explanatory with the aid of a good map; but a hiking guide (in German) is locally available, and the *Rough Guide to the Dodecanese* by Marc Dubin gives accurate and helpful directions.

Diafáni

Diafáni (*map p. 325, C1*) is the port of disembarkation for the north end of the island, served by long-distance ferries and by local connections to Pigádia. The harbour village provides essential services, and is connected with Ólympos, 8.5km to the west, by a good road which winds through a wooded valley watered seasonally by the run-off from Mt Korýfi. The promontory just to the south of Diafáni, at Kámbi, shows evidence of ancient occupation, and there are the remains of a Byzantine chapel on its southwest flank. A much earlier Mycenaean presence is attested by grave finds (seven vases and a bronze sword) from the slopes behind the village. The coastline is empty and punctuated by small coves and shore-side chapels to both north (Vanánda) and south (Papá Miná). These provide good opportunities for swimming, but are susceptible to wind.

Avlóna

Below the eastern slope of Mt Korýfi is the hamlet of Avlóna (*map p. 325, B1*; mostly occupied only during harvest time). The shallow alluvial soil on the floor of the limestone valley, husbanded into stone-walled fields, provided the grain for Ólympos, just as it probably functioned as the granary for Brykous in antiquity. From the north end of the village, a path (following the line of the ancient road, and latterly with stretches of flagstones and steps) bears left for Vrykoúnda or Vourgoúnda, and descends after an hour to the northwest point of the island at ancient Brykous.

Vrykoúnda

The site of ancient Brykous (*map p. 325, A2 inset*) occupies an exposed tongue of rock projecting into the sea. This was the third of the ancient cities on the island and has one of the wildest settings of any in the Aegean. The promontory projects in a way that gives the site dramatic views down the rugged west coast and into the hemicycle of mountains to the east formed by the tip of Kárpathos and the island of Saría.

Arriving from Avlóna, the final descent to sea-level enters through the area of the ancient cemetery. Beside the route there are a number of **rock-cut tombs** of the Hellenistic period, which take advantage of the numerous limestone outcrops, perforating their faces with funerary chambers, ancillary loculi and doorways, approached sometimes by a short dromos. Some of these rise to two floors of tombs. The west-facing side of one of the most prominent examples is partially cut away into a sarcophagus and decorated above with shields carved in relief; others had carved reliefs with figures, now too eroded to read. Most are in the area to the southeast of the acropolis rock, which rises steeply at the neck of the promontory. The litter of fragments of architectural elements on the lower slopes and sides of the **acropolis** itself shows that it was once fortified and substantially built up: inscriptions speak of the cult of Athena Lindia on its summit. Long stretches of late Classical or Hellenistic rampart walls in isodomic masonry appear at intervals along the east side of the promontory, and the remains of habitations, though considerably overlaid with later building in places, stretch along the top of the headland. Finely-cut statue bases and architectural elements lie strewn amongst the euphorbia, which grows in abundance everywhere.

At the northern extremity of the promontory, steps lead down into a spacious **natural cave** deep within the headland, which provides an almost perfectly insulated refuge from the elements. To the left was the spring which served the settlement in antiquity; it is possible that the sanctuary of the nymphs was here, from which a relief showing Hermes and the nymphs, formerly immured in the forecourt of the church of the Koímisis in Ólympos, once came. The cave is now organised as the shrine of Ághios Ioánnis, whose screen, font and altar are composed of various ancient spolia. This cave comes alive with festivities and dancing for the two-day (and all night) *panigýri* of the feast of St John on 28th–29th August.

Trístomo

From Vrykoúnda, a 1-hr walk following the coast to the east brings you to the inlet of Trístomo (*map p. 325, A1 inset*). The shores are rocky and barren, and the water a vivid emerald colour. Apart from the two whitewashed churches, there is no living community at Trístomo, only a couple of seasonal dwellings and the ruins of Italian army barracks by the shore. From the southern shore of the inlet, a track climbs up past a deserted hamlet to a ridge (*40mins*) with spectacular views over the inlet, the straits and the island of Saría, before cutting through the hills back to Avlóna (*2½ hrs total*), and thence on to Ólympos (*1hr further*).

SARIA

Saría (*map p. 325, A1 inset*) is a small, steep, uninhabited island, separated from the uninhabited northern tip of its larger neighbour by a narrow strait famous for its tidal races. Steps lead down to either side of the strait at the narrowest point, and until recently livestock was ferried across at this point at the beginning of each new season. The animals had to swim the channel, tied to boats which were rowed from one side to the other. The practice probably goes back to ancient times.

The island is only seasonally inhabited by goatherds and bee-keepers; it is built like a natural fortress with sheer cliffs on the southeast side offering no anchorage or shelter. The only refuge is in the northeast corner, where the small bay of **Palatía**, marked by two rock-stacks to the north of the entrance, cuts in from the coast at the foot of a deep valley. Due west, the valley narrows into a gorge between rock cliffs, perforated with countless holes and caves. On the summit to the north side of the gorge is an abandoned settlement, known as **Argos**, inhabited intermittently from prehistoric times right through until the end of the last century.

The finding of a dagger blade, a bronze chisel, various weapons (including a stone axe now in the Fitzwilliam Museum in Cambridge) as well as surface pottery sherds both on the plateau of Argos and at Palatía, suggests that Saría has been inhabited since the late 3rd millennium BC. The first written evidence of ancient Saros is in the tribute lists of the Delian League. Though there are traces of ancient walls at Palatía, the most substantial visible remains, which cover a surprising area and suggest a large community, are from the Early Christian and medieval periods. The curious style of some of the standing buildings on the hillside to the northwest of the bay, with steep vaults and corbelled beehive cupolas that have parallels in the Middle East, has led to the suggestion that the island was used as a settled base by Arab raiders from the 8th–10th centuries.

Just inland of the shore and to the left (south) is the modern chapel of **Aghía Sophía**. The interior is plain, with an altar made from an ancient column fragment and a carved marble plaque with the cross of the Knights of St John immured in the wall above. Outside, many fragments of Early Christian marble—Corinthian-style capitals, pieces of architrave and broken columns—lie around the precinct. Traces of mosaic floor are visible in front of the entrance. The chapel is built over the sanctuary of a 5th-century basilica, whose synthronon can be seen behind the apse. To the south lie the remains of baths.

PRACTICAL INFORMATION

GETTING AROUND

There are flights to Kárpathos from Rhodes (35mins) and non-stop services to and from Athens (75mins) approx. five times weekly. At least one of the flights from Rhodes each day also continues to Kasos. The airport is 13km from the main town. Kárpathos lies on the ferry route between Piraeus and Rhodes, via Crete, which is operated by LANE Ferries (www.lane.gr): this provides at least three services weekly to Kasos, Santorini, Milos and Piraeus to the west, and to Chálki, Rhodes (and once weekly to Kastellórizo) to the east. Once a week there is a service through the northern Dodecanese to Samos and Thessaloníki. LANE ferries stop at both the main port of Pigádia and at Diafáni, and this can sometimes be a convenient way of getting from one end of the island to the other.

Visits to Saría are best arranged through Orphanos Travel in Diafáni (*T: 22450 51289*).

WHERE TO STAY

There are many studios and rooms for rent, but hotels of character have not yet arrived on Kárpathos. The most pleasant is the **Hotel Romantica** (*T: 22450 22461; www.hotelromantica.gr*), 1km west of the port. In the centre of Pigádia is the **Hotel Titania** (*open year-round; T: 22450 22144 or 23307; www.titaniaKárpathos.gr*). Both are simple, clean and inexpensive. In Diafáni, the **Nikos Hotel** (*T: 22450 51289*), operated by the owner of Orphanos Travel, is the best solution; and in Ólympos, the **Hotel Aphrodite** (*T: 22450 51307*) offers simple rooms with fine views.

WHERE TO EAT

Of the many places that line the port at Pigádia, one of the few that has a local, family character is **Anna**, in the corner closest to the Port Authority. The **Ellenikó** restaurant, one block in from the harbour, provides good local dishes but with a rather aloof and disengaged service. Good local wine—very slightly sweet and of the colour of quince jelly—can be had at **Spitakia** in the main street perpendicular to the harbour-front.

KASOS

In spite of a tragic recent history, Kasos today is a friendly and unpretentious island, at last beginning to see a little modest prosperity. Although mostly treeless, it is small and easily walkable. With little agricultural production possible, the island has lived by seafaring and Kasiots historically have been renowned mariners. The older houses date from a prosperous and distinguished past built up by sea-trade; their dilapidation today speaks of mass emigration and a renaissance which has been slow to arrive.

HISTORY OF KASOS

The Phoenician *kas*, meaning 'sea-spray', is probably the origin of the name Kasos: its waters have always been famous for their unpredictability. There are scattered traces of human presence on Kasos itself (the Cave of Ellinokamára) and on Armáthia from the 4th and 3rd millennia BC. The earliest explored settlements show strong Minoan influence and were in the vicinity of Chélatros Bay, the island's only sheltered inlet. These functioned up until c. 1450 BC, after which, with the building of a Mycenaean citadel at Póli, the centre of settlement moved to the north of the island, where it has remained

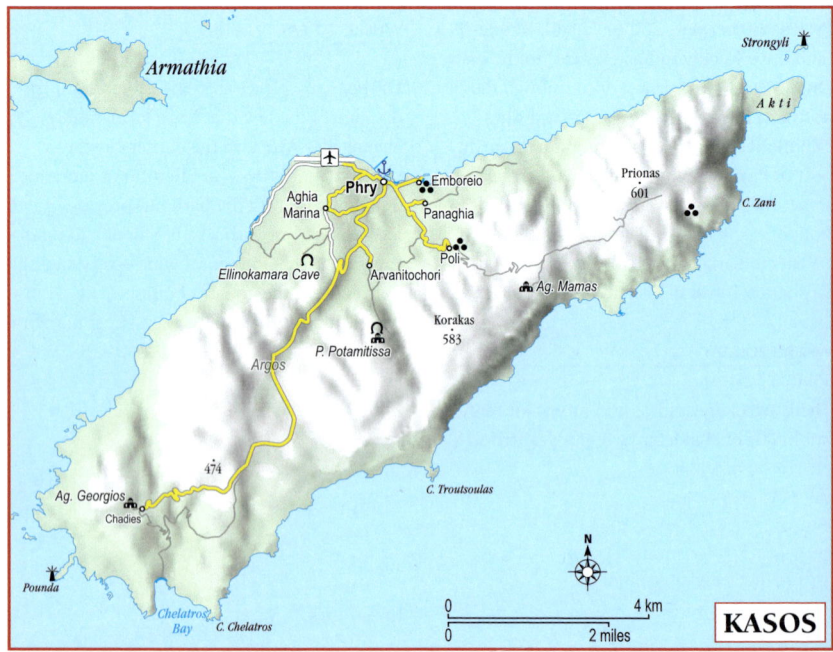

KASOS

until today. Kasos seems to have been independent during the 3rd century BC, but was incorporated into the Rhodian state in the first half of the next century.

With the eradication of Aegean piracy by Rome after 67 BC, the main settlement of the island moved to the coast at today's Emboreió. Here it slowly increased in prosperity, culminating in the building of at least two large Early Christian basilicas and other public buildings. The return of piracy and the threat of Saracen attack meant that settlement retreated inland again. In the Byzantine era the island belonged to the theme of Crete. In 1207 the island was captured by the Venetians, was briefly taken by the Knights of St John in 1311, but then returned to the Venetian overlords—the Cornaro family—in 1315, together with Kárpathos. After the Turks took the island in 1537, Suleiman the Magnificent granted it some self-government in return for the *maktu*, or annual tribute.

Already in the late 17th century the mercantile fleet of Kasos numbered almost 100 ships—a remarkable number for an island with no good natural harbour. By 1820 the number had grown to almost 700, with a population of islanders of more than 9,000. In the feverish atmosphere of the evolving War of Independence, the fleet became a fighting navy and was turned over to the cause of Greek freedom, pursuing raids on the Asia Minor and Levantine coasts. In July 1821, Kasos fought bravely for the liberation of Crete and became a place of refuge for Cretans. These actions provoked the Ottoman sultan to seek the help of the substantial forces of Mohammed Ali, khedive of Egypt, and on 7th June 1824, in a catastrophe never forgotten, the population was massacred and their lands burnt. Men were slaughtered and women and children shipped to Alexandria to be sold into slavery. The island was left abandoned for several years.

By 1830 the few who had escaped and survived returned, and began to rebuild a life on Kasos. Italian occupation in 1912, and the development of steam ships, contributed to the virtual demise of the Kasiot fleet. In 1948, Kasos joined the Greek state together with the other islands of the Dodecanese. Neither the economy nor the island's vegetation has ever recovered from the 1824 catastrophe: the resident population today, just over 1,000, is a tenth of what it was in the heyday of the early 19th century.

EXPLORING KASOS

All settlement on Kasos is located around the centre of the north coast; the south of the island is a wall of blank mountains and cliffs looking onto an expanse of water which stretches uninterrupted to the coast of Africa. The island's half dozen villages circle the edge of the only valley of moderate fertility, watered by the seasonal run-off from the limestone hills to the south. The three villages on the west side (Phry, Aghía Marína and Arvanitochóri) thrive; the three to the east (Emboreió, Panaghía and Póli) have scarcely enough residents to merit being called villages. In all of them there are occasional examples of pedimented, Neoclassical house façades, with pilasters and attractive colours of plaster, and each village centres on a stately church of large dimensions with interiors which are luminous and spacious and characterised by a strong local tradition of painted altar screens. The villages can be visited in a few hours in an easily-walked circuit.

Phry

The ferry landing and tiny airstrip are both within a short distance of the main village of Phry (*pron: Free*), whose name is a local contraction of its proper name, Othrys. The village grew up mostly in the 1830s to accommodate the return of inhabitants to the island after the 1824 disaster. It is an unassuming place with a quiet and business-like dignity: a couple of streets of inconsequential shops, many unoccupied houses, and the old-fashioned **Kafeneion O Mattheios** beside the church, where locals gather. At its heart is the small, workaday **harbour** referred to as 'Bouka', overlooked by a group of newer cafés. Directly above to the east is the fine 19th-century church of Ághios Spyrídonas, the island's patron saint. A short distance to the south, in a 19th-century Kasiot house, is the new **Archaeological Museum**—a tiny but model assemblage of clear and succinct displays relating the history of the island and its antiquities.

Emboreió and Panaghía

Phry elides into **Emboreió**, 600m to its east, with no clear demarcation. Though very exposed to north winds, Emboreió occupies the most sheltered point of the north coast, and was the site of both the ancient harbour and the important shipyards of the 19th-century Kasiot fleet. Several deep rock-cut tombs and burial loculi of the Roman and Early Christian period are visible to the left of the road before arriving in Emboreió. Close to the large mid-19th-century church of the Eisódia tis Panaghías, which dominates the bay to the south, are remains from the 5th or 6th century. The unexcavated remains of a large basilica lie to the southwest of the church; further to the south can be traced a two-room baptistery with a sunken, cylindrical immersion font.

Directly above and to the south of Emboreió is **Panaghía**, whose stone-built sea-captains' houses lend it a gracious air. The late 18th-century church of the Panaghía is the oldest of the large parish churches on the island and has a bell-tower of more sophisticated design than the others. Beneath the stairs leading to the gallery is an undecorated late Hellenistic or Roman lidded sarcophagus, dubbed by island tradition the 'Tomb of Ághios Kasianós'. At the top of the village is an unusual row of six almost identical contiguous chapels, said locally to have been erected in order to exorcise six evil spirits.

Póli, Ághios Mámas and Grámmata

The village of **Póli** stands on the site of ancient Kasos, the *polis* of the island. The attractive and panoramic site served also as capital and main settlement in the Middle Ages. The hillside opposite the church functioned as the acropolis of the ancient city, and a wealth of surface pottery finds (displayed in the museum in Phry) show that the site was perhaps continuously inhabited from the Early Bronze Age to Early Christian times. Visible on the eastern side are the lower courses of a 4th-century fortification wall of roughly squared blocks. It was the lower southern slopes of the hill, and the facing slope to the south, which yielded the 51 inscribed circular grave markers which are unique to Kasos (also in the museum).

From Póli, an unmade road climbs up the wide gorge to the watershed, and then drops down to the isolated **monastery of Ághios Mámas** (*90mins on foot*). Though the monastery buildings are unexceptional, the view and the solitude of the place fully merit the walk.

From the junction at the summit above Ághios Mámas, the track continues for a further 3km towards the eastern extremity of the island and one of the island's most evocative antiquities. The site, referred to locally as **Grámmata** ('Letters') because of the ancient inscriptions there, lies almost due east of where the track ends, on a ledge in the precipitous drop of the east-facing slope of the mountains. It appears to have been an open-air sanctuary to the gods (precise identity unknown) and the nymphs. The sanctuary overlooked, and would have been visible from, the often tempestuous channel below. Preserved on the rock are carved inscriptions invoking and greeting the divinities.

Arvanitochóri and the Panaghía Potamítissa

From below Póli it is possible to cut across west by track to the village of **Arvanitochóri**, which lies to either side of a wide, seasonal torrent bed. It probably takes its name from the Albanian (*Arvanitos* = Albanian) refugees who settled here as early as the 18th century. As at Panaghía, there are a number of fine stone houses of the 19th century, many with walled forecourts or gardens, some in ruins. Behind the main church of Ághios Dimítrios is the fine mausoleum of the Dikakis family; the cemetery beyond has other such mausolea of prosperous Kasiot shipping and trading families in interesting architectural styles.

From the village, a path leads south to the **cave-church of the Panaghía Potamítissa**. After 30mins' walk, some distance after a concrete dam, the cave-entrance is hidden high up in the cliff on the left (east) side, clearly marked by the white painted cross above the chapel's façade. The building itself is new, but the cave, which has a beautiful shape and was once fed by a spring, has long been used as a hermitage.

Aghía Marína and Ellinokamára

A metalled road leads up a rise from the west side of Arvanitochóri to **Aghía Marína**, the most attractive of the island's villages, dotted with chapels and churches and spread around a shallow dip of olive, yew and palm trees. The island's olive mill is here; there are windmills, pleasing views and many houses with flourishing gardens.

It is a 30-min walk south from Aghía Marína to the **Cave of Ellinokamára** (*currently unsigned: take the north circuit road through Aghía Marína, passing a restored windmill, beyond which the road divides. Take the right fork, past the church of Ághios Phanoúrios, and continue straight. The road soon becomes a track between stone walls. Where the right-hand wall ends, take another walled pathway leading uphill, diagonally to the left. Cross over the wall to the right of the ruined, rectangular stone building at the top of the rise, and drop down to find the cave entrance, which looks due north, a little way below*). A natural cave has been meticulously closed by a massive wall of dressed stone blocks laid in parallel courses, with a central doorway leading in. Given the hidden site and its commanding view (from eastern Crete to the coast of Kárpathos), it is possible that the cave was used as a lookout post. However, the carefully-cut steps and platforms in the bedrock before the entrance seem to suggest a cult use.

The interior of the cave is not large (c. 20m by 13m), but interpreting it is complicated by the fact that there has been extensive subsequent adaptation of the space. A stone wall of later construction runs perpendicular to the entrance, and another (less clear) runs parallel to it to the west, dividing the interior into a central dromos and two lateral chambers. Finds within the cave from prehistoric to Byzantine times show a very ancient and continuous use, though there is nothing which shows conclusively that it was a chthonic sanctuary in antiquity.

Chélatros Bay

The road to Chélatros Bay leads through a bare and dramatic landscape, scored by torrent courses. The asphalt ends after 11km from Phry at the monastery of Ághios Geórgios at Chadiés: an immaculate group of white monastery buildings in a landscape of limestone hills, unrelieved by vegetation. The foundation of the monastery is 17th-century, but the buildings and the murals of the katholikon are all of the last few decades. There are no resident monks year-round: the spot is tranquil and looks down to the sea at the bay of Chélatros. It was in the vicinity of this sheltered, south-facing inlet that the first settlements on the island were made: there were no less than four Minoan settlements in the area. In the Late Bronze Age/Mycenaean period, however, the centre of habitation moved to the north coast, where it remained throughout subsequent history, leaving this corner devoid of human presence.

PRACTICAL INFORMATION

GETTING AROUND

There are year-round daily flights from Rhodes via Kárpathos. The airport is a short walk (300m) from Phry. Ferries operated by LANE (www.lane.gr) link Kasos to Piraeus and Rhodes: this provides at least three services weekly to Santorini, Milos and Piraeus to the west, and to Kárpathos, Chálki, Rhodes (and once weekly to Kastellórizo) to the east. Once weekly there is a service north through the northern Dodecanese to Samos. In the summer there is a thrice-weekly caïque from Kasos to Finíki on Kárpathos. The M/S *Athina*, run by Kassos Maritime Tourist Agency, makes summer excursions to the islets of Armáthia and Makrá, with their long, clear beaches.

WHERE TO STAY

The island's only hotel is the **Hotel Anagennisis** in Phry (*T: 22450 41495*; breakfast not provided). Otherwise there are self-catering apartments or rooms, such as **Georgios Vrettos** (*T: 22450 41235*) above the shop opposite the Dimarcheíon. Rooms are also available for rent in most of the villages.

WHERE TO EAT

There is not a lot of choice, but **To Koutouki tis Boukas**, near the church in Phry, is reasonable and serves local fruit-sweets after a meal.

KASTELLORIZO

Seventy-five nautical miles from its nearest neighbour in Greek territory, and equidistant between Alexandria and Athens, this anomalous splinter of Hellenism in the eastern Mediterranean has refused to be forgotten by history. Fought over and occupied by the Knights Hospitallers, the Mamelukes, the Spanish, the Venetians, the Ottoman Turks, the Italians, the French, the Germans and the British, the flag it now flies is finally that of the language it has always spoken. In spite of all this turmoil, Kastellórizo is a charming, sleepy place, with much of interest and beauty to detain the traveller.

HISTORY OF KASTELLORIZO

Kastellórizo's position on the maritime route between the Aegean and the Levantine coast has given the island an importance beyond its meagre size: its port represents one of the few truly sheltered harbours along the Asian coast between Rhodes and Beirut. In antiquity the island was called Megísti ('Greatest'), i.e. the largest of the small archipelago of eleven islets which surround it. The current name derives from the Italian 'Castel Rosso'. Archaeological finds attest Neolithic and Mycenaean habitation. The descendants of Dorian settlers established a fortified town and acropolis on the hill of Palaiókastro, which constitute the principal ancient urban remains. The island was under Rhodian administration by the mid-4th century BC and appears to have prospered on a vigorous trade in wine. In 1306 the island was taken by the Knights of St John; it served as a vital link in their firm grip on the Turkish coast. Over the next 300 years the castle was destroyed and rebuilt several times until the Ottomans finally secured control over it.

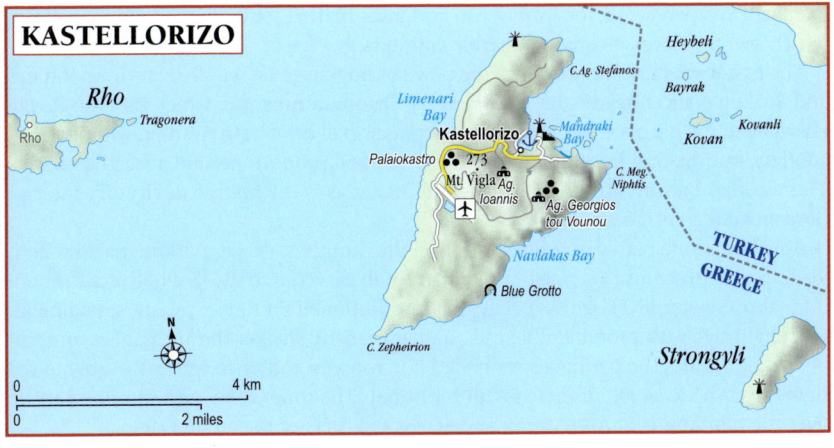

In March 1913 the population took the Ottoman garrison hostage and proclaimed a provisional government; in August of the same year an 'Overseer', supported by a force of gendarmes, was sent by the Greek government from Samos. Only two years later, however, an expeditionary force of the French army, seeking a base from which to prosecute their war in Syria, landed on the island and occupied it. This in turn provoked heavy bombardment from Turkey. The French kept the island until it passed to Italy in 1921. A severe earthquake five years later compounded the accumulated damage to an already declining community.

During the Second World War, the British briefly held the island in 1941, only to lose it again a few days later to an Italian force from Rhodes. In September 1943 the Italians capitulated to the Allies, and the island was again held by the British. Under heavy German bombing in 1944, the Allies evacuated the population to safety in refugee camps in the Gaza Strip. Kastellórizo only came under Greek administration in September 1947, and joined the Greek state in March 1948, together with the other Dodecanese islands. Sixty years of peace, combined with the island's close ties with its emigré communities, especially in northern Australia, have fostered a growing population once again, and at last brought some tranquillity.

KASTELLORIZO TOWN

The harbour and Lycian tomb

The horseshoe sweep of the harbour front is a homogeneous display of colourful two- and three-storey Neoclassical houses, with high ceilings, central balconies and hipped roofs; the façades are often embellished with Ionic pilasters, volutes and pediments. The centre of activity is the small square in the middle of the waterfront called **Plateía Afstralías**, testimony to the strong links which still exist between the island and its diaspora in the Southern Hemisphere (Afstralía = Australia). A few metres to the east is the small arcaded *agorá*, the former fish and meat market, built by the Italians in 1934, which still preserves its original marble counters.

The eastern waterfront leads past the new landing-stage (at which boats from Rhodes and Turkey dock) towards the 17th-century **Ottoman mosque**, which punctuates the entrance to the harbour. Both minaret and prayer-hall have been restored without great subtlety, but the building still preserves its dignified proportions and attractive profile. The wooden balcony in the interior is still intact, as is the marble dedicatory inscription above the entrance.

A narrow stone pathway continues round the promontory. After 300m, narrow steps lead up to a 4th-century BC rock-cut **Lycian tomb** carved into the face of the cliff, about 30m above water-level, with a beautifully proportioned entrance, pilasters, pediment, and architrave with prominent dentils, similar to many all over the ancient Lycian coast of Turkey. Inside, the perimeter is divided horizontally and once vertically (only to the right) to provide small, discrete loculi for burial. The tomb looks east into the sunrise over the mountains of Asia Minor, and across the islets of the archipelago.

The museum and castle area

The **museum** (*open 7–2, closed Mon; free*) is housed in a handsome mansion built around a courtyard. The undoubted highlight of the small collection is a rare (because largely unbroken) collection of 13th-century ceramics that were salvaged from a shipwreck in Afros Bay.

A path leads uphill from the museum toward the castle of the Knights of St John, the core of which dates from early in the Grand Mastership of Juan Fernández de Heredia (1377–96). As his coat of arms showed six golden castles against a red field, it has been suggested that an alternative derivation of the island's name could be a corruption of the Italian Castel Oro ('Golden Castle'). The castle—little bigger than a heavily fortified watchtower—was the stronghold of a larger enceinte (incorporating outer bastions), nearly all of which has now gone. The upper area, from where there are magnificent all-round views, can be entered via a ladder in the east corner. The massive talus or batter, which was clearly added later to support and reinforce the original walls, protects the three landward sides: it incorporates blocks of ancient masonry and may be built upon the foundations of a pre-existing ancient fortification.

The cathedral and Mandráki Bay

Continuing downhill to the area of Choráfia, you reach, on the rise between the harbour and the bay of Mandráki to the east, the broad, low **cathedral**, dedicated to Constantine and his mother Helen, completed in 1835 and now surrounded by a spacious pebbled courtyard. Two monolithic ancient columns lie on its the north side. A short distance to the west is a **statue of Despina Achladiotou**, the 'Lady of Rho' (*see p. 345*). Further west is the **church of Ághios Geórgios Santrapé**, begun in 1906 and named after its benefactor, Loukas Santrapé, a wealthy Kastellorizan cotton merchant in Egypt. The church has remained incomplete since his death. It is built on the site of an Early Christian basilica. East of the church is a small octagonal Ottoman structure (prayer hall), later converted into a chapel and now abandoned.

The Blue Grotto

Boats leave from the main harbour between 8 and 9am, according to demand: return journey time approx. 90mins. Boats do not run if swell prevents entry to the grotto.

Larger, less crowded, and just as impressive as its famous homonym on Capri, Kastellórizo's Blue Grotto makes a captivating expedition, as much for the journey through the archipelago of islets on the way as for the grotto itself. The chromatic effect in the grotto depends on strong sunlight being reflected up from sand at the mouth of the cave, at a sufficient depth for refraction by the water to impart a pervading, translucent blue colour. Its effects are best seen early in the morning when the sun is strong and in the east.

THE INTERIOR OF THE ISLAND

NB: The main points of interest on the island can be explored on foot in a half-day. Before setting off you will need to obtain the keys for the monastery of Ághios Geórgios tou Vounoú from Kyría Nektaría, at the taverna of the same name on the lower east waterfront of the harbour: this is easily done, and no other method of access is possible. A torch will also be useful. It is important to bear in mind that the upper plateau of the island is a military zone. Though the Greek Army is generally relaxed about walkers, it is possible that an exercise may temporarily limit access to some areas. A camera should be used with discretion, and only for photographing places that do not include even small military installations.

Ághios Geórgios tou Vounoú

From the Choráfia area of Kastellórizo town, west of the church of Ághios Geórgios Santrapé, a partly whitewashed zig-zag of steps winds steeply up the mountainside to the crest. This takes 20–30mins and affords marvellous views of the town, the islets and the Turkish coast. At the top, a clear path heads straight inland until the solitary, square block of the **monastery of Ághios Geórgios tou Vounoú** comes into view after 15mins. The church building is in good condition, unlike the 18th-century living areas that surround it. The floor of the nave (except for the inserted central panels) is an Early Christian mosaic of abstract design, possibly from as early as the 6th century. The columns supporting the vault ribs are ancient, with Corinthian capitals. Opposite the entrance, beneath an icon of Ághios Charálambos on the north wall, a narrow hole, covered by a wooden trap-door, leads down six awkward steps through the floor to spring water below and to the minuscule rock-cut **chapel of Ághios Charálambos** (*torch useful since there is no light*). Ághios Charálambos was a healer and protector of the sick; the water in this pool was believed to possess healing qualities, and may also have been used for baptisms.

About 15m northeast of the monastery is a cleft in the bedrock which leads to an **excavated tunnel**, with ancient cuttings in the rock to the right of its entrance. This is one of many similar phenomena in this area, probably a tomb of the 4th or 3rd century BC. The fact that, in 1914, a finely crafted Hellenistic gold wreath (now in the National Archaeological Museum in Athens) was found in this area in just such a context suggests that many of these chambers are in fact tombs, although some may simply be storage chambers, cisterns or animal pens. Just south of the southeast corner of the monastery is an ancient wine-pressing area, cut in the rock.

Ághios Ioánnis and the cyclopean walls

To the south of the monastery is a wide track which leads west, around the ridge to the right and into the next valley, where (just visible to the northeast at the far end of the valley) there are some trees beside the **church of Ághios Ioánnis**. The summit of Mt Vígla (273m) rises above to the west. The church is reached by cutting straight up the west side of the valley: it incorporates a number of ancient blocks and fragments, and to its east is a large rock-cut *patitírion*, or grape-treading area.

A short distance further to the north, overlooking the harbour, is the edge of the mountain, where there is a well-preserved stretch of grey, polygonal **cyclopean walling** visible at the ridge. These walls, which fill a stretch of the mountain edge that had little natural defence, have presented problems of dating: the earliest date suggested is Mycenaean (13th century BC); most scholars now favour the 9th century BC, though some ascribe them to a Hellenistic (4th-century) system of fortifications created to protect the productive interior of the island.

Palaiókastro

The hill of Palaiókastro can be seen from the ridge below Mt Vígla: in the foreground are the two churches of Ághios Geórgios Ftochouláki ('St George of the Needy') and the larger Ághios Panteléimon. Palaiókastro was the acropolis of the island's principal settlement during Classical antiquity. Visible from a distance are several periods of construction. At the lower level is the outer enceinte of walls, probably of the 9th century BC, with three (later) protruding bastions. Above this (in the southeast corner, to the left of the large ilex tree) is the inner enceinte, with the base of a Classical tower in perfectly cut ashlar stonework of the late 5th century. Much more recent are the three churches (from left to right, Ághios Nikólaos, Panaghía Palaiokastrítissa and Ághios Stéfanos), built in the 19th century. Detached, to the west of the hill, is the church of Aghía Paraskeví; to the east, Aghía Marína, both built into ancient foundations.

Palaiókastro is the island's most useful vantage point, with natural protection and all-round vision. The view south has changed radically since the airport runway was created and the large water reservoir dug immediately beyond it. Until recently the island depended on deliveries of water by boat from Rhodes or on its desalination plant at Mandráki. The reservoir is intended to make the island more self-sufficient.

From below the chapel of Aghía Marína, at the northern extremity of the area, a rocky path leads down the mountain towards the port.

THE ISLET OF RHO

The rocky islet of Rho (ancient Rhoge), also called Ághios Geórgios, lies 6km west of Kastellórizo (*map p. 341*). It is home to a large population of goats and a small military station: it can only be visited by arrangement with a local boat-operator, although some summer pleasure cruises from Kastellórizo make a circuit around the island. The impressive remains of a substantial Hellenistic fort and tower (4th century BC) crown the ridge in the middle of the island. In recent history the island had a famous inhabitant, Despina Achladiotou, who lived here for 30 years until her death at the age of 90 in 1982. She became known as the 'Lady of Rho', acquiring national fame by unfailingly raising the Greek flag on the island each morning. She has been commemorated in stories, songs and even on postage stamps.

PRACTICAL INFORMATION

GETTING AROUND

Access to Kastellórizo is always through Rhodes. In the summer, the island is served by frequent flights from Rhodes; in the winter the service is somewhat reduced. In summer two ferry companies make a total of three weekly journeys (4½ hrs) from Rhodes; in winter, only two. The island's harbour is an increasingly popular haven for private boats and yachts. There are informal local connections to Kas on the Turkish mainland in the summer season.

WHERE TO STAY

The **Hotel Megisti** (*T: 22460 49272, or reserve through the booking office in Rhodes, T: 22410 66056*) is the largest and longest-established hotel, comfortable and with a spacious swimming area at the end of the west side of the port. Next door is the **Mediterranean Pension** (*T: 22460 49007*) in a restored mansion. In the centre of the same west harbour-front is the smart **Hotel Kastellorizo** (*T: 22460 49044, www.kastellorizohotel.gr*). There are many rooms and apartments of various di-

mensions available for rent, e.g. **Karnagia Apartments** (*T: 22460 49266*) in the port's southwest corner. In more traditional style is the **Pension Asimina** (*T: 22460 49631*), just behind the fish-market, in an old Kastellórizan house.

WHERE TO EAT

The island's few tavernas serve more or less the same food, i.e. what comes from the markets in Rhodes, supplemented by local catches of fish and seafood. The **Taverna Athena**, in the centre of the waterfront, is popular with visitors and has perhaps the widest selection. Locals tend to patronise **Ipomonis** on the east side of the harbour, near the corner. The small **Taverna Mediterraneo**, just beside the cathedral in Choráfia, offers cooking at its simplest and most authentic, in a very peaceful setting.

FURTHER READING

N.G. Ashton, *Ancient Megiste: The Forgotten Kastellorizo*, Perth, 1995.

SYMI

In return for guaranteeing a supply of sponges to the harem of the Ottoman court, the islanders of Symi (pron: *Sími*) gained a substantial measure of self-government under the long period of Turkish dominion. They were talented sailors and renowned ship-builders, and were also entrusted with making and manning the fast skiffs which carried official mail between the Sublime Porte and the Ottoman fleet. As a result, tiny

Symi prospered remarkably in the 18th and 19th centuries and became in proportion to its population one of the richest ports of the Aegean. Today Symi lives by tourism: in the summer the day-trips from Rhodes can seem to engulf the town, but in the evenings and early mornings, the island regains its tranquillity and charm. A visit to Symi will ideally make time for three things: a leisurely exploration of the harbour and old town; a trip into the mountainous interior; and a boat ride around the deeply indented coast.

HISTORY OF SYMI

Symi's mythological origins are variously and conflictingly told by different writers, but it appears that the island cherished a connection with Glaucus, a fisherman, sailor and boatwright who is said to have helped build Jason's ship, the *Argo*. Born mortal, he later became a deity; he abducted Syme, the daughter of King Ialysos of Rhodes, and brought her to the island, endowing it with her name. The island's first settlers were allegedly from Caria in Asia Minor; later colonists (11th century BC) were from Laconia in the Peloponnese, and subsequently from Rhodes and Cnidos. Thucydides briefly mentions the island in his account of the naval defeat of the Athenians by the Spartans off Cnidos in 411 BC (*see Pontikókastro; p. 351*). For most of its ancient history from 400 BC onwards Symi seems to have been a dominion of Rhodes, and it appears early on to have begun providing Byzantium with fast ships and good sailors, a service they continued for the Knights of St John after they took the island in 1309. Two Ottoman attacks were successfully repelled in 1457 and 1485; but in 1522, perceiving the futility of further resistance, the island negotiated an agreement with the Turks which guaranteed important concessions of self-governance and free trading, in exchange for certain favours. Symi was also permitted to cultivate land on the Turkish mainland. The agreement ushered in a period of stability and prosperity in which sponge-fishing, boat-building and trade all flourished. Schools of Theology and religious painting were established on the island in the 18th century. In 1821 Symi revolted and joined the temporary administration of independent Greece; when it was brought back under Turkish control in 1830 its ancient freedoms were severely curtailed. In 1912 the Italians took possession of the Dodecanese and Symi lost her fertile lands in Asia Minor. Her trade collapsed and her population declined. In May 1945 the German surrender of all the Dodecanese islands was signed on the waterfront at Symi, and in March 1948 Symi joined the Greek state.

THE PORT & OLD TOWN

Every approach to Symi by sea runs beside long stretches of rocky and inhospitable cliff: the island seems virtually uninhabited. Then, all of a sudden, on rounding sharply into a long harbour, a steeply rising theatre of colourful Neoclassical houses comes into view. This is Gialós, the 19th-century harbour area. Beyond its high southern ridge it blends continuously into Chorió, the old town of Symi, high up, airy and hidden from the predatory view of passing pirates. The shops, hotels, cafés, tavernas and offices are below in Gialós; the former acropolis, the museum, most of the churches and the older houses are in Chorió. A broad staircase of some 500 steps, called the Kalí Stráta, or 'Good Street', unites the two.

GIALOS

A pleasantly unreal air is imparted by the symmetry and uniformity of the houses in Gialós. Most date from 1830–1910 and are arranged in a mounting repetition of rectangles and triangles punctuated by pilasters and protruding balconies. The pediments are often characterised by a central circular aperture (many now blocked), which allowed air to pass under the roof, cooling the high-ceilinged rooms below. A typical large mansion would consist of five levels: a rock-cut cistern at the lowest level; cool rooms for storage at ground or lower ground level; the main floor with entrance and symmetrical plan; the upper floor with a central balcony supported on stone volutes and with a wrought-iron railing; and finally the hipped, pedimented roof for ventilation. The colours of the houses are strictly controlled by the municipality, although today synthetic pigments are used (especially custard yellow), different from the tempera washes pigmented with Attic earth and other iron-oxide colours which may still be seen on the abandoned houses in Chorió: their colours are generally darker and richer. A marine blue was more widely used than today, because of its property of averting the evil eye.

Exploring Gialós

The commercial and shopping centre of Gialós is a grid of narrow streets in the area between the end of the harbour and the elegant metropolitan church of **Ághios Ioánnis Pródromos** (1838). The church stands in an area entirely paved with black and white *chochlákia* work. It incorporates several ancient fragments found on the site: an inscription in the northwest corner, a curious, eroded grave stele by the north door, and part of a draped figure high up in the north wall. Note also the impressive ship's mast which has been planted in the forecourt and dedicated here as a votive offering: several other churches in Chorió possess similar trophies. A little way to the north is the open area behind the stone bridge which was, until the Second World War, the island's main boatyard and dry-dock. The dignified and unostentatious Dimarcheíon stands on its north side; at the western end is the **Nautical Museum** (*open daily in summer 11–2.30*) in a more extravagant architectural style. It contains models and memorabilia of the island's maritime history and of its sponge-divers.

A **war memorial** (which copies a famous relief from Lindos in Rhodes) is carved into the rockface along the north harbour quay, and bears the inscription 'Today freedom spoke to me secretly. Cease, Twelve Islands, from being downcast! 8th May 1945'. It commemorates the date when the Germans formally surrendered the Dodecanese to the Allies.

The road along this quay continues into the next inlet of Charáni (dominated by the modern church of the Evangelístria on the hill above) and known also as the Bay of

N.O.S. after the acronym for the Symi Naval Club, which is further along the shore. This is the area of the present-day **boatyards**: in spite of deforestation, which has left the industry without a local source of timber, the yards continue a small-scale production at the hands of a number of dedicated artisans.

Nimboreió

From the boatyards, a scenic track with views of the adjacent islet of Nýmos (ancient Hymos, with vestigial remains of ancient and medieval fortifications and habitation) leads round the headland into the tranquil bay of Nimboreió. In the last century Symiots would often keep a summer house here. Nimboreió, as its name implies, was the ancient *emporeion* (trading centre) of the island: its remains lie at the very northern end of the western shore. An Early Christian basilica stood where three contiguous chapels to the Virgin, Aghía Kára and the Saviour are now; a substantial area of **mosaics** (?4th century) can be seen just to the north of them. An Early Christian church was erected over the basilica in around the 6th century: elements of it are visible in the central chapel (the oldest of the three). About 50m above and to the south of the chapels, where the stand of trees to the left finishes, is a hole in the ground which leads into an underground **vaulted catacomb** (locally called the *Dódeka Spílaia*, 'Twelve Caves') with ten lateral loculi. This may well have been a burial area or possibly the crypt of a now vanished building above, used later as a secret refuge or even as a storage area.

CHORIO

There are several routes up from Gialós to Chorió on foot, but the Kalí Stráta, whose broad steps begin just inland of the southwest corner of the harbour, is the most impressive. It passes the finest Neoclassical mansions—some roofless, some lived-in, a few with gardens and venerable trees. The top of the stairs is the beginning of Áno Chorió, the Upper Town, which occupies a saddle in the slope of Mt Vígla, which drops slowly down to the Bay of Pédi to the east. The fertile slope of this valley was the island's main area of cultivation. The town above spreads around a central eminence topped by the castle (the ancient acropolis). The area immediately around it has small, closely clustered houses, narrow stone alleys, and few open spaces.

The museum

The combined Folklore and Archaeological Museum of Symi (*open April–Oct 8–2.30; closed Mon; 200m from the main Panormítis road at the top of the inhabited area of Chorió; no closer access by taxi*) is high up at the southeastern extremity of the town, and is indicated by a paper-chase of wooden signs through a labyrinth of narrow streets. Housed in two Symiot mansions, the collection is arranged in half a dozen rooms around a shaded courtyard which contains Classical and Early Christian fragments, gravestones and inscriptions. One of the buildings has delightfully painted wooden eaves.

From the edge of the courtyard a stone staircase gives access to the Chatziagápitos Mansion, an imposing, late 18th-century *archontikó* of Italian design. The reception rooms sport faded but delightful murals by local artists, and ornately carved wooden panels, characteristic of the more opulent Symiot interiors.

The castle

Viewed from the south, the **Castle of the Knights of St John** incorporates a bastion in massive but irregular 5th-century BC masonry from the ancient acropolis of Syme, on which once stood a temple to Athena. Abutting it to the left is a semicircular redoubt built by the Knights in 1507. There are two further redoubts which face east and northeast. These are all later additions to the earlier castle of 1407, which remarkably withstood a siege by Mehmet the Conqueror in 1457. On the summit stands the church of the Panaghía tou Kástrou (the 'Greater', so as to distinguish it from the 'Lesser' below). To right and left of the entrance door are Hospitaller escutcheons in stone, taken from the walls of the castle. Inside the church is the renowned and beautiful icon of the Second Coming by the late 16th-century Cretan artist Georgios Klontzas. To one side of the church belfry hangs a bell made from the nose-cone of an enemy bomb. Although from the Hospitallers' point of view the castle was not especially practical for signalling purposes, the panorama from its heights are spectacular, including in its sweep the coast of Asia Minor, Gialós, the bay of Pédi and the ridge in between with its line of windmills which culminates in the Pontikókastro (*see below*).

Below the castle to the east is the church of the **Panaghía Katomeniá**. The modern interior contains a finely carved iconostasis, throne, pulpit and lectern. Further to the northeast is the **Old Pharmacy** building, a memorable piece of Symiot Neoclassical architecture, complete with 19th-century fittings and a makeshift operating room behind.

Pontikókastro

On the ridge of the hill called Nouliá to the northeast of Chorió is a line of more than 15 **windmills** in varying states of decay, which once produced the rough flour used for Symi's famous breads, and for the ship's biscuit which was the staple of the island's mariners. Beyond them and just above is an enigmatic ancient construction known as the **Pontikókastro**. A circular drum of massive, roughly finished ashlar masonry, 17m in diameter and on average about 1.5m high, it dates most probably from somewhere between 550 and 400 BC. In the *Peloponnesian War* (*Book VIII, 42*), Thucydides mentions that the Spartans and their allies, after their naval victory over the Athenians off Cnidos in 411 BC, 'sailed with combined fleet to Syme and there set up a trophy, and anchored again at Cnidos'. It is possible that this circular platform is the base of a victory monument set up to display the spoils of battle.

Pédi Bay and the 'Drakou' archaeological site

The fertile valley behind Pédi Bay descends gently to the sea to the east of Pontikókastro and Chorió. On the lower slope of the steep hills that form the south side of this valley is another archaeological curiosity, referred to by its popular local name, 'Drakou' or 'Dragon's Lair' (*sited halfway up the southern slope of the valley and level with a line about 100m back from the shore. Access by the rough track, signed, leading east from the first hairpin bend after the habitation of Chorió ends on the Panormítis road: 20mins on foot).* There are two things to see here, both ancient: an unidentified, very cleanly constructed edifice in ashlar masonry; and an area of walling, terracing or fortification just beyond (east) and further up the hill. The latter has been modified by medieval and later walls placed on top of it. The former is more remarkable because of the fine cutting and finishing of its limestone. Its location, overlooking virtually the only fertile area of the island, suggests a place for the cult of Demeter, but it is perhaps more likely to have been a secular building relating to the agricultural work of the area.

From Pédi Bay, local boats can be hired to go to the **islet of Aghía Marína**, which lies just off the coast to the north and where there is a tiny monastery beside the water. It is swimming distance from the coast opposite, where there is a small seasonal community which can be reached by foot (*30mins*) from the north side of Pédi Bay.

THE INTERIOR OF THE ISLAND

The island is traversed from north to south by a road that spans the 24km from Gialós to Panormítis. Most sites and points of interest can be explored by small diversions or walks off this main axis. Some of the coastal sites are more easily reached by local boats, and this is indicated where relevant. The route crosses the high plateau of the interior and gives a good sense of the variety of the island's terrain.

WEST TO SKOUMISA BAY

Climbing steeply up from the edge of Chorió, the road passes the town's cemetery at Aghía Marína. At 7km, after reaching a panoramic altitude, a junction is signed (right) to the **Monastery of the Taxiárchis Michaïl Roukouniótis** (4km), whose entrance is marked by a walled enclosure around a spreading cypress tree. Although no longer functioning, it is cared for and kept open by a local custodian. The monastery's foundation is probably 11th century, although the gateway and much of the monastic building which surrounds the katholikon date from an 18th-century rebuilding. The space inside tightly encloses the katholikon, which has two levels: the lower level, almost like a subterranean grotto, has paintings (now very blackened) and a pebble floor; in its tiny domed narthex are original traces of the Four Evangelists in the pendentives. The upper level, rebuilt after a fire in the 14th century, is decorated with murals by the island's best-known painter, Gregory of Symi, in a popular, narrative style (1738). The monastery, which was latterly under Russian protection, possessed from early times an important library; a 12th-century Gospel was rescued from the fire and is now in Rhodes.

Passing below the monastery, along the edge of a military camp, you come to the **monastery of the Anárgyri** (visible just across the valley), decorated similarly with 18th-century wall-paintings. From here, a meandering track (*1hr*) leads west to the secluded **Skoumísa Bay**, where the tiny church and monastery of Ághios Aimilianós sits on an islet joined to the shore by a causeway. This may also be reached by boat from

Gialós (*45mins*). Built in the mid-19th century by the Hadjimachalis family, the monastery is typical of many that were erected by rich families and donated to the Church, whose right it was to choose the dedication; the family would often endow the building for its future maintenance, and would be able to use it for retreat.

SOUTH TO PANORMITIS

The main north–south road continues towards Panormíti, passing a turning for the Panaghía Stýlou (8km). At 11km, a narrow road is signed left to Chamés and Kampiótissa and descends rapidly into an inhospitably rocky landscape. By following this turning you come at the top of the subsequent rise to the 13th-century church of **Ághios Ioánnis Pródromos Tsagriá**, marked by two large ilex trees: its interior has paintings in poor condition. Just beyond and around the corner, on the rise to the right of the road, are clear signs of **ancient construction**, probably the base of what was once an impressively large Hellenistic fortified building.

Ághios Prokópios and Kourkouniótis

Just beyond the Chamés/Kampiótissa junction, the road reaches its summit (12km) and then slowly descends. At 13km, an alluvial dip in the rocky landscape forms a tiny fertile circular plain for cultivation, appropriately called Xerolimniá ('Dry Lake'). Here a track to the right (signed) leads towards the isolated church of **Ághios Prokópios**, with 15th-century wall-paintings, set in a wooded valley full of birdsong.

Returning to the main road, c. 400m beyond the track to Ághios Prokópios, a broad and moderately fertile valley slopes down eastwards into a ring of hills. The remains of a **medieval castle** are visible on the eastern peak; the valley is criss-crossed with walls and terraces which have been constantly rebuilt, but whose material and lines are Byzantine in origin; in the centre of the lower level of the valley a tiny church (now mostly whitewashed inside) still preserves a small, surprisingly beautiful 15th-century painted fragment of the *Madonna and Child Enthroned*. The area is known as **Kourkouniótis**, and by virtue of being both hidden from the sea and more fertile than most of the island, it appears that it was lived in and cultivated from Neolithic times. It is uninhabited now, and most of what is visible today dates from the 11th–17th centuries. The most remarkable remains here are of a large number of **Byzantine stone wine presses**, scattered all over the southern slopes of the valley amongst the cypress and fir trees.

Panormítis

The final stretch of the road to Panormíti descends dramatically down to sea-level again. Below, the almost perfect ellipse of the cove of Panormíti comes into view. At 22km a turning to the east (left) leads down to the pebble **beach of Marathoúnda**, in a peaceful and enclosed bay and creek. Two kilometres beyond the turning, the road ends at the **Monastery of the Taxiárchis Michaïl Panormítis**, whose extensive buildings stretch along the waterfront with the pine-clad hills behind (*open daily 7–2 & 4–8. Appropriate dress required. Simple accommodation, T: 22460 71354, is available in the*

monastery buildings; reservation recommended July–Sept. Direct boat connections to Rhodes in summer). The long 19th–20th-century buildings that overwhelm the small church at their centre are designed to accommodate the large numbers of pilgrims who gather here in summer and for the saint's festival (7th–8th Nov).

The three-tier bell-tower, built in 1905 over the central gate, complete with affixed terracotta eagles and acroteria, gives onto an arcaded courtyard paved with abstract pebble mosaics which surrounds the plain exterior of the katholikon in the centre. The latter was completely rebuilt in 1783 by Anastasis Karnavas from Rhodes, replacing an earlier monastery of which there are records only as far back as 1460, but which may well have been a 5th- or 6th-century foundation. The interior of the katholikon is dark and impressively decorated. It is a single nave, with 'gothic' cross-vaulting in a typical Dodecanesian style, entirely decorated with wall-paintings by the Symiot brothers Nikitas and Mikhaïl Karakostides (inscription over entrance) in 1792. They are in relatively good condition, and best preserved on the north side.

The monastery has two museums (*combined ticket*): an ecclesiastical museum and a folklore museum, as well as a library and picture gallery. Between them these contain a remarkably varied range of ecclesiastical objects, icons, furniture and votive gifts, including—most unusual—numerous bottles containing donations or prayers to St Michael which were launched on the waves in different parts of Greece, and by one route or another have found their way here. There are also memorabilia of the brave and ultimately tragic resistance organised from the monastery during the Second World War, when Allied soldiers were given sanctuary here and a radio transmitter was set up: these acts cost the abbot, Fr Chrysanthos Maroudakis, and two of his local helpers, their lives when they were executed in front of the monastery in February 1944 by German forces. After the war ended, the monastery was virtually abandoned: for the next three decades it was painstakingly rebuilt under the guiding hand of a single monk who, having made a vow to St Michael when the ship in which he and his family were travelling was torpedoed and sunk, devoted the rest of his life and energy to the monastery in gratitude to the Archangel for his miraculous survival.

SESKLIA

This small island, south of the southern tip of Symi (*map p. 347*), belongs to the Monastery of Panormítis. In common with many of Symi's surrounding islands and sheltered bays, there is archaeological evidence of human presence as far back as the late Neolithic (4th millennium BC), and there are also small stretches of ancient wall near the island's summit. Thucydides mentions that it was here that the Athenian fleet, under its general, Charminos, retreated and hid after its unexpected defeat at the hands of Spartan ships off Cnidos in 411 BC (*see p. 348*).

Icon of St Michael, in the Panormítis monastery.

PRACTICAL INFORMATION

GETTING AROUND

The island has no airport, and only three or four ferry services a week from Piraeus (16hrs). Access is easy from Rhodes, however, where there is a selection of fast daily (c. 1hr) services by hydrofoil (*Aigli*) and catamaran (*Dodekanisos Express*), or by regular ferry (*Symi I and II*). These are all managed by ANES (Rhodes, T: 22410 37769; Symi, T: 22460 71444). Once a week the F/B *Kalymnos* runs local routes to Kos, Kálymnos, Astypálaia, Rhodes and Kastellórizo.

WHERE TO STAY

The **Hotel Les Catherinettes** (*T: 22460 72698*) on the north waterfront of the harbour (close to where the ferries dock) is not expensive, but the comfort is basic and the balconied rooms with their painted ceilings can be noisy at night. **Garden Studios** (*T: 22460 72429*), quiet, in a Symiot house surrounded by a garden, are set some way back from the southwest corner of the harbour. Just beyond this, the **Opera House Hotel** is similar in concept but is larger and less inti-mate (*T: 22460 72035*). Both have comfortable studio apartments at moderate prices. More expensive and stylish is the **Hotel Aliki**, in a restored mansion on the south waterfront with a pleasant roof-terrace (*open April–Oct; T: 22460 71655*). Monastic lodging can be arranged at the **Panormítis monastery** (*T: 22460 71354*).

WHERE TO EAT

On the south waterfront of Gialós are two good places of quite different character. **Mythos** serves ambitious variants on traditional Greek dishes, mostly imaginative and successful: both chef and wine-list are acclaimed. Further out along the same waterfront is **Dimitri**, for those seeking a simple, unostentatious *mezedopoleíon*. Similar in style, **Meraklis** (set back from the port near the church of Ághios Ioánnis) has good home-cooked dishes that are less specifically fish-orientated. Finally, near the top of Kalí Stráta, is **Grigoris**, which has good, hearty home-cooked dishes and excellent views over the sea.

TILOS

Tilos is a tranquil island which in the last decade has suddenly distinguished itself by espousing the cause of environmental conservation. The process has not been un-contentious, but populations of small and migratory birds have surged and the raptors they attract have returned. Tourism on Tilos too is less noisy than elsewhere, more independent and more attentive to nature. Wildlife in fact marked the history of the island when in 1971 the fossilised remains of a species of dwarf elephant were discovered, forcing a re-assessment of some of the assumptions of Mediterranean palaeontology.

HISTORY OF TILOS

Tilos' unique pre-human history is discussed below (Charkadió Cave; *see p. 359*). The cave has also yielded evidence of a Late Neolithic human presence, as well as Early Bronze Age artefacts. Tilos was significant enough in the 7th century BC to participate, together with Lindos (which was then a major naval power) in the colonisation of Gela in Sicily. It appears from historical testimony and inscriptions that 'Telos' was an independent, democratic state throughout the 5th and 4th centuries BC. The island is

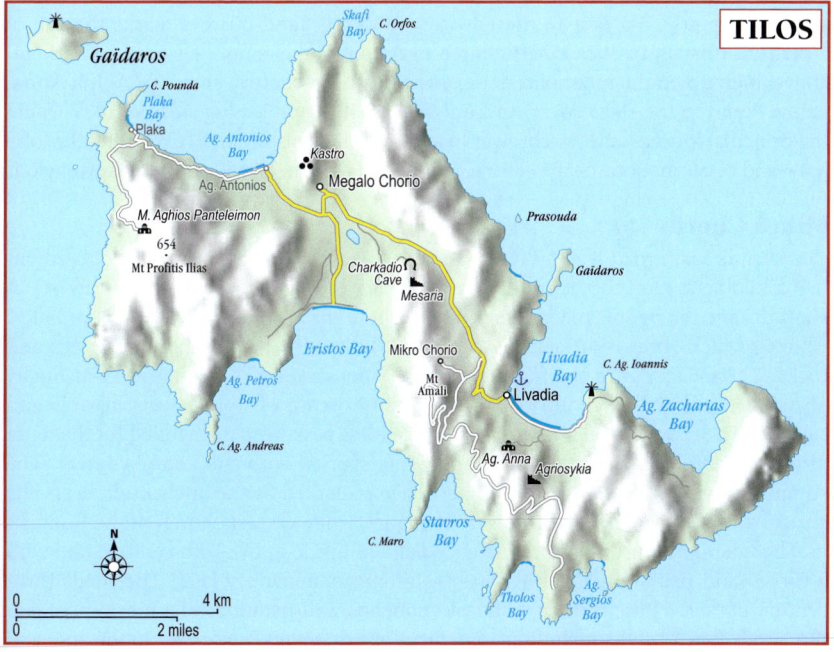

sometimes referred to as Agathousa ('Beneficent'), and Pliny mentions it as a source of perfume (possibly made from oil of marjoram, which grows profusely). The lyric poetess Erinna may have lived on Tilos in the 4th century BC; most of her work is now lost, but her reputation in antiquity was high and she was often compared with Sappho. Tilos lost its independence in the second half of the 3rd century BC and was annexed to the Rhodian state, becoming a part of the deme of Kameiros. In 1204 the island was taken over by the Venetians and in 1309 by the Knights of St John, who leased it to Borello Assanti of Ischia in 1366. Its medieval name was Piskopia or Episkopi ('lookout' or 'surveying point'). The Knights fortified the island with a series of seven castles and fortresses. Its vital importance in the chain of communication between Kos and Rhodes attracted an unsuccessful siege by Mehmet II in 1479. Tilos eventually passed, with Rhodes, under Turkish control in January 1523. The Turks held the island until it came under Italian control in 1912; no significant buildings remain from either period of occupation. In 1948 the island was incorporated into the Greek state together with the other Dodecanese islands.

LIVADIA & MIKRO CHORIO

Livádia, the port of Tilos, is set in the western corner of a wide bay ringed by steep hills. The modern church of Ághios Nikólaos (1973) dominates the waterfront just south of the port. Further to the left (east) a dense stand of trees marks the site of an Early Christian basilica at the church of Ághios Panteléimon. Directly behind and above, high up on the mountain slope, is the tiny 13th-century chapel of **Aghía Ánna**; below it and to the right (west) in front, is Kastéllo, a projecting ridge of rock where the principal fortress and watchtower in ancient times was situated. Crowning the lofty left-hand (eastern) spur of the central mountain is the medieval **castle of Agriosykiá**.

Mikró Chorió

The island's main road leaves Livádia to the west and climbs over a low ridge. About half a kilometre after the hairpin bend, a branch leads back to the left (southwest). A short distance along this road a sign points right to the abandoned settlement of Mikró Chorió, which spreads attractively across the hillside to the north among trees and rocks. The village, once the island's most populous centre of habitation, was finally abandoned only half a century ago. It is a dense weave of stone streets, narrow and stepped. The symmetrical houses (most of the roofs have been dismantled for the reuse of the valuable wooden rafters) are amply interspersed with oak and olive trees. The summit at the northern extremity of the village is marked by the finely built, keep-like structure of the medieval watchtower. The large, whitewashed church of the Koímisis tis Theotókou lies just below, extensively painted inside in the 18th century, and with a carved and painted wooden iconostasis of almost a century later. The small 15th-century church a little further to the east contains wall-paintings of a more spontaneous and colourful style, including a fragment of a dramatic *Pantocrator* in the apse and a clear and beautiful scene of Abraham and Sarah giving hospitality to the trinity of angels at a table decked with victuals.

From the road junction below the village, a network of expensively constructed roads leads to the summit at the OTE telecommunications tower on Mt Amalí, with extensive views over virtually the whole island.

The Charkadió Cave

Three kilometres north of Livádia, the main road cuts through a defile of pozzolana, volcanic dust deposited by an eruption of Nísyros: there is a pure, pale grey pumice in the cuttings beside the road. At 4km a road, signed left to the **Charkadió Cave**, ends after little more than a kilometre at a gate, leading to a small, modern stone theatre. A path leads up to the cave just above, which is normally locked unless excavation is in progress. It is here that important palaeontological finds were made in 1971 by Nikolaos Symeonides of the University of Athens—not only the famous dwarf elephants, but also deer, tortoises and small mammals from as far back as 150,000 years ago. The cave is broad but not particularly deep: it has filled with dust and alluvial soil over the millennia, and it is in this rich sediment that the finds were made.

THE DWARF ELEPHANTS OF TILOS

The species of dwarf elephant found in the Charkadió Cave (*Palaeoloxodon Antiquus Falconeri*) was the last elephant to dwell in Europe, and became extinct only 4,000 years ago. Its ancestors must have come to Tilos during the Quaternary, when a lowering of the sea level effectively joined the island to the mainland. With the subsequent raising of sea levels, the animals found themselves trapped: over many generations they grew smaller to adapt to the much reduced area and quantity of food available to them. Those whose remains were found in the Charkadió Cave were little bigger than a very large dog, standing only about 1.3m tall. The ongoing excavations have uncovered many thousands of pieces of bone, coming from more than 40 dwarf elephants that lived on Tilos between 4,000 and 45,000 years ago, while lower down (at a depth of 8m) were found the bones of deer from approximately 140,000 years ago. Traces of human occupation from the Neolithic to medieval periods have also been found in the cave. The quantity and variety of finds made here make this one of Europe's most significant palaeontological sites.

The finds leave a number of important questions still unanswered. It is not yet established whether the reason for the extinction of these elephants was a climatic change in the Late Quaternary Period, or the result of a major volcanic event. Nor is it clear whether man arrived on the island before, or after, the extinction of the elephants. For this reason we cannot be certain whether the death of the elephants in the cave was a result of natural catastrophe, or whether man was responsible for killing them for food—or at least for transferring their body parts to the cave.

A path leads up above the cave to the medieval **castle of Mesariá**, which crowns the summit above.

MEGALO CHORIO & ENVIRONS

The island's capital, Megálo Chorió, in the northern part of Tilos, is now a small and tranquil village partially occupying the site of the ancient settlement of Telos, at the foot of the castellated peak of the ancient acropolis. The plain below contained the cemeteries of ancient Telos, and traces of them can be found all around. Two kilometres to the south is Éristos Bay, a beautiful, south-facing sandy beach, with further attractive coves accessible on foot to the east.

The church of the Taxiárchis Michaïl

The centre of the village is marked by the church of the Taxiárchis Michaïl, preceded by a courtyard with a traditional island flooring in pebbles, which continues inside the church itself. The very fine wooden iconostasis, pulpit and throne are the work of artists from Smyrna in the 1820s: the tiny carved scenes of the *Annunciation* (left) and *Nativity* (right) beside the central door of the screen are beautifully enhanced by gilding and some paint in primary colours. Note also the red-tinted candles inside the church: it is an island tradition to colour the wax pink with *rouvía*, the extract of the common madder plant (*Rubia tinctorum*), which grows locally and which was used by artists in the Renaissance for the pigment known as rose-madder.

Directly behind the church to the north is a well-preserved stretch of the **southern wall of the ancient city**: judging by the masonry this would appear to be from the early Classical period. There are other stretches of ancient wall and terracing in the village, particularly towards its northeast corner.

The museum

The building across the courtyard from the church houses the Dimarcheíon; on the floor below, and entered from the street on the south side, is the island's tiny Archaeological and Palaeontological Museum (*free entry; opened on request at the Dimarcheíon above, who may also provide a free English-speaking guide*). Here is exhibited a **skeleton of a dwarf elephant** from the Charkadió Cave (recomposed from finds belonging to several different examples). There is also didactic material related both to the cave and to the burial finds from the beach of Ághios Antónios (*see opposite*). There are plans to move the material to a custom-built museum at Charkadió.

The Kastro and acropolis

The medieval kastro and acropolis of ancient Telos are reached by a steep, 40-min climb to the summit of the hill above the village. A path leads up from the upper right-hand corner of Megálo Chorió, beside a large water cistern. The path traverses the hillside diagonally from right to left, passing a number of ancient rock-cut cisterns (to the right) and some stretches of substantial early Classical retaining walls (to the left). As it begins to zig-zag near the summit, it passes through an area dense with ruined medieval houses, chapels and cisterns, before a final stretch of steps which are cut into the living rock and lead up to the gateway.

The core of the monumental gateway incorporates the entrance of the Classical acropolis, little modified by the medieval builders, and with its original 5th-century BC threshold and lintel blocks intact. In antiquity the summit was crowned by a sanctuary dedicated to Zeus and Athena Polias, joint protectors of the city; the flight of marble stairs, to the left on entering, would have led up to their sanctuary, and the slots cut into the right-hand side of the steps may have held votive stelae. Many pieces from the pagan temple(s) have been incorporated into the walls and roof-vaults of the now ruined early medieval church of the Archangel Michael in the centre of the enclosed area, with vestiges of 14th- and 15th-century wall-paintings.

AGHIOS PANTELEIMON & THE WEST

The wide and exposed bay of Ághios Antónios, west of Megálo Chorió, looks directly across to Nísyros. Approximately halfway along the beach, just at the mean water level, a couple of oval rings of stones can be discerned. These are thought to be late antique or early Byzantine graves (from sometime between the 5th and 8th centuries AD), dug at a time when the shoreline would have been further to the north. The human bones and crania found in them had become petrified by a process not fully understood, but perhaps due to some volcanic event. Others explain them as vulcanised bodies from an eruption on Nísyros, which were washed up on the shore here and given some sort of token burial by the perplexed inhabitants.

The monastery of Ághios Pantaléimon

Beyond Ághios Antónios, the road hugs the coast for a couple of kilometres, passing the sheltered and shaded bay of Pláka, after which it turns south and climbs with dramatic views to the west, before ending at the Monastery of Ághios Pantaléimon (*open erratically from 10–2 in winter; until 7 in summer. The key is held by the papás, Fr Manolis Pokias, T: 6946 151019*). This isolated monastery, at its most beautiful towards sunset, stands high above the sea amidst an oasis of lush vegetation and venerable cypress trees. Dedicated to the island's patron saint, the 3rd-century physician and martyr Panteleon of Nicomedia, the monastery sits on the site of both pagan and Early Christian predecessors, built here because of the plentiful freshwater spring. The compact interior is entered through a fortified lookout tower that opens onto a narrow courtyard with a fine early 19th-century *chochlákia* pavement.

There is some confusion about the history of the buildings and the paintings. An inscription carved over the entrance to the katholikon states that it was restored in 1703; the design of the katholikon is consonant with the reputed foundation date of c. 1470, and it has been restored more than once since then, not only in 1703. The

Detail of the 18th-century wall-paintings in the monastery church of Ághios Pantelémon.

elaborate iconostasis is of 1714; but the paintings inside, dated 1776 and attributed to Gregory of Symi, were clearly retouched in a late 19th-century restoration of the whole interior, at the time when the monastery cells around the courtyard were also rebuilt. The only part of the paintings to have remained unchanged as the work of the 18th-century Symiot master is the small panel set into the south wall, showing the founder, the Blessed Jonas of Crete, holding a model of the monastery. The floor is inlaid in places with fine marbles, including a dark red brecciated jasper from Iasos in Asia Minor. Some Early Christian capitals have been re-used in the central arch, and there are pieces of the Byzantine ambo on the north side. The intimate interior constitutes a pleasing stylistic miscellany.

From the monastery, an arduous four-hour walk skirts the slopes of Mt Profítis Ilías and rejoins habitation at Éristos Bay.

PRACTICAL INFORMATION

GETTING AROUND

The municipally owned catamaran *Tilos Star* runs a daily service to Rhodes from June–

mid-Oct: the route also includes (depending on the day of the week) stops at Nísyros and Chálki twice weekly. Three times weekly throughout the year, larger car-ferries ply the route up and down the Dodecanese chain between Patmos and Rhodes, with stops at Leros, Kálymnos, Kos, Nísyros and (less frequently) Symi, and providing three connections per week to Piraeus.

WHERE TO STAY

Lodging is mostly in Livádia. The **Hotel Irini** (*T: 22460 44293; www.tilosholidays.gr*), set back from the shore in a flourishing garden, provides pleasant and comfortable accommodation; its offshoot **Ilidi Rock Studios** (*same numbers*) is an operation with more pretentions, on the hillside above the port. The **Hotel Faros** (*T: 22460 44068*) at the opposite (eastern) end of Livádia Bay, is peaceful and less institutional.

Megálo Chorió offers little accommodation; the most convenient is **Milios Apartments** (*T: 22460 44204*).

WHERE TO EAT

Blue Sky taverna, by the port (it also has pleasant rooms for rent above), looks un-promising but serves good, fresh, locally-caught fish. A variety of simple and genuine Greek dishes can be found at **Sofia's Restaurant**, 300m south from the port along the shore of the bay; its sympathetic host is a Greek with a passion for English football. Good fish and home-made fare is well prepared at **Delfini**, in the bay of Ághios António.

FURTHER READING

The Tilos Park Association, which sustains the environment and wildlife lobby of Tilos, produces a quarterly journal which can be viewed on www.tilos-park.org.gr/journal.htm (NB: website subject to change; if the URL no longer works, just type Tilos Park Journal into your search engine).

WALKING

For all the walks on the island, helpful guidance may be obtained both from a hiking map available in local shops and from local experts, contactable at fulton@otenet.gr.

NISYROS

Nísyros rises from the sea with a low, broken, conical profile: after Santorini, it is the most significant volcano in the Aegean. Relatively stable, yet by no means extinct, it lies at the eastern extremity of the Aegean Volcanic Arc, which sweeps in a broad crescent through Astypálaia, Santorini, Milos and the islands of the Saronic Gulf, and whose periodic activity is the result of pressure caused by the slow collision of the African and Eurasian tectonic plates. The bubbling fumaroles of the different craters in the island's vast central depression are fascinating to both expert and amateur visitors. At any time of year the landscape is colourful, foreboding and unforgettable.

HISTORY OF NISYROS

Greek myth explained the peculiar geology of the island by imagining that Poseidon, while pursing Polyvotis, broke off a fragment of Kos and buried the fuming giant beneath it. This legend didn't discourage habitation though, and Herodotus tells us that the first settlers came from Epidaurus in the Peloponnese. In the early 5th century Nísyros was, together with Kos and Kálymnos, under the control of Queen Artemisia of Halicarnassus; but the five ships that went with her to the Battle of Salamis in 480 BC switched allegiance to the Greek side. In the 4th century BC Nísyros was an autonomous city-state, minting its own coinage (bearing various motifs, most commonly dolphins). In 200 BC the island became part of the Rhodian State, before being incorpo-

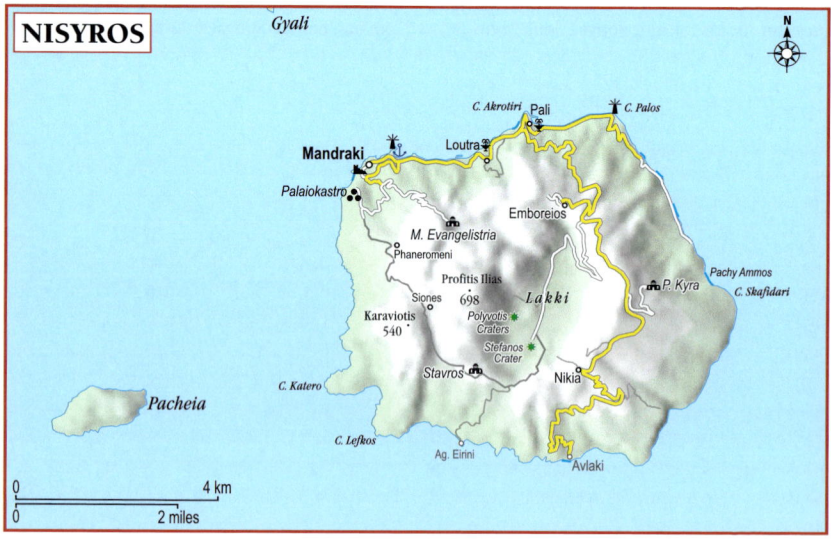

rated successively into the Roman and Byzantine empires. In the 7th century it became subject to the Caliphate of Syria, and in the 11th century was conquered by the Seljuk Turks, before eventually being reunited with the Byzantine state in 1204, and then taken in 1312 by the Knights of St John. Four years later the vassalage of the island (together with Chálki, Alimniá and Tilos) was given to the Assanti family of Ischia in thanks for help they had given to the Order. In 1433 it passed to the Venetian admiral Fantino Querini, the governor of Kos. The island's population was decimated by the attack of Sultan Mehmet II in 1457 during his campaign of subjugation of the Aegean: in 1523 the island came under full Ottoman control, together with Rhodes. Although a self-liberated Nísyros momentarily participated in the Provisional Administration of Greece in 1823, the island remained under Ottoman control until it passed to the Italians in 1912. In common with the other neighbouring islands, it was liberated by Allied forces in 1944 and was incorporated into the Greek state in 1948. Major eruptions of the volcano in 1871, 1873 and 1887, and a strong earthquake in 1953, have repeatedly wrought damage to the buildings and landscape of the island.

MANDRAKI

The port lies a few hundred metres to the east of Mandráki, the island's capital, whose houses spread attractively along the bay as far as the rocky western promontory crowned by the Knights' castle and the whitewashed complex of the Panaghía Spilianí. The main street (right) into the town passes an open-air display of traditional household objects (querns, presses, millstones etc.) made from the local volcanic stone.

After 250m the street divides to either side of the island's only bank. The right branch follows the shoreline and passes the Museum of Archaeology and Folklore (*open in summer only*).

Plateía Ilikioménis and Ághios Ioánnis

The left branch of the road leads towards the centre of Mandráki. Along this route are a number of scattered ancient remains which indicate that this area was close to the heart of the ancient settlement of Nísyros. After a short walk, the street opens into the delightful **Plateía Ilikioménis** ('Square of the Elderly'). It is an intimate and always lively space, shaded year-round by two vast ficus trees, and populated by cafés, tavernas, shops and a municipal library (containing a number of useful books on Nísyros and the nearby islands). Above its south side is the church of **Ághios Ioánnis Pródromos**, a particularly beautiful example of the miscellany of vernacular decoration and architectural design, typical of the best island churches (*if locked, the key is held by the papás, whose office is just by the eastern exit of the plateía*). The church is set low down in an enclosure of stone walls planted with fruit trees, and is preceded by an open, vaulted narthex which contains many ancient and Early Christian stone oddments, some with inscriptions. The building, originally 15th-century, was restored in the mid-19th century; the interior incorporates Byzantine columns, antique capitals, and a fine 18th-century *chochlákia* floor.

North of the Potamítissa

In a narrow passage to the southwest of the Dimarcheíon is the **Panaghía Potamítissa**, a highly decorated late 19th-century construction, which is the town's principal church. Perpendicular to its west end is the original main street of the town, a winding alleyway which climbs slowly towards the south. Immediately north (downhill) from here, and on the left, is the impressive and immaculately constructed talus of the **Castle of the Knights**, rising 30–40m to where an eroded triple escutcheon in white marble is visible. The castle dates from the first Venetian fort built here in 1312, and was enlarged by the Knights in the course of the same century. A gate beneath a belltower leads down into the monastery of the **Panaghía Spilianí**, which has grown up around another sacred spot associated with an anchorite's cave in the rock, and whose origins long predate the castle. Further north, the street passes the small **Church Museum** (collection of liturgical and ecclesiastical objects: *open summer only, 10–3*), and reaches the shore beside the church of **Ághios Nikólaos**, cut into the rock of the cliff, with ancient spolia by its door and in its altar. A footpath leads round below the cliff, over rocks of solidified magma shot through with veins of yellow ferrous oxide, to a bay of volcanic rocks and crystalline water.

Palaiókastro

Turn south (uphill) along the original main street of town and a delightful climb up a stone pathway (starting between some houses just south of Aghía Aikateríni) will bring you through terraces of olives, oak, figs, almonds and flowering cactus to the ruins of Palaiókastro in just under half an hour, passing occasional ancient relics (marble column bases, etc.) along the route. On the plateau, the ponderous fortification walls of the acropolis come into view, unexpectedly massive and well-preserved and standing to a full height of 7m in places. It is strange that a city as apparently insignificant as ancient Nísyros should have felt the need to defend itself with walls of such magnitude. What is visible today, however, does not constitute a complete enceinte, and it is not clear how far the walls may have extended to the north, or what protected the western side other than the natural drop of the land: if there were other extensions of walls of comparable size, their remains have vanished. A 4th-century BC inscription on the wall prohibits the erection of any building in proximity to the exterior surface of the walls. Inside the walls, among the trees, are the remains of the Early Christian basilica of Ághios Ioánnis. A half-buried row of white marble columns from the nave (some with fine crosses carved on them) are being brought to light by excavation, as well as a number of fine Byzantine Corinthian capitals.

AROUND THE ISLAND

Loutrá and Palí

Just over a kilometre east of the port is **Loutrá**, once a flourishing thermal station, as indicated by the partially abandoned spa building along the shore. The spa was first established here in 1872, and today a part of the buildings still functions as a hotel in the summer season. The hotel runs the thermal plant, which consists of clean, individual cabins. There is both hot water (39°C) and a clear, slightly tart cold water for drinking.

The fishing village of **Palí** is dominated to the east by the huge Pantelides Thermal Establishment. In front and to the west, the sea is slightly warmed by existing springs which rise at between 33°–44°C at source. Directly inland of the centre of the Pantelides building, 50m from the shore and a little below ground level, is the charming church of the **Panaghía Thermaní**, a tiny chapel with the remains of a wall-painting in the apse, built into the corner of the remains of ancient Roman thermal baths dating probably from the 3rd century AD. Sediment and earth has now filled up the Roman buildings to the point at which the vaults spring, but the fine brick-ribbing of the vaults themselves is still visible and complete, and there are remains of stucco decoration.

THE VOLCANO AT EMBOREIOS

From the junction above Palí the main road climbs steeply up to Emboreiós and the rim of the volcano.

THE VOLCANO OF NISYROS

The volcano of Nísyros is the most recently active remnant of a large, prehistoric volcanic field (the Kos Caldera), whose boundaries are the approximately circular area defined to the north by the western end of Kos, to the west by the islands of Pyrgoúsa and Pachiá, and to the east by Nísyros itself. The eruption of this whole area 160,000 years ago was the most significant volcanic event in the history of the eastern Mediterranean. The last major magmatic activity of Nísyros happened about 25,000 years ago, and it was then that the summit of the volcano imploded, producing the caldera visible today. In the process, the collapse of tall (15–20km) columns of material ejected from the volcano created the volcanic domes of dacite and pyroclastic deposits which we recognise today as the mountain peaks of the western side—Profítis Ilías, Nýphios, Trapezína etc.

A slowly rising magma chamber currently lies at a depth of 3–4km below Nísyros. Though the volcano has been active many times since the last magmatic eruption, this activity has been in the less drastic form of hydrothermal eruptions. The craters, such as the magnificent Stéphanos, in the southern part of the depression, are therefore only the latest elements in this long chain of activity. Activity has continued into recent history, with hydrothermal eruptions in 1422, and a whole series in 1871–73 (creating the Phlégethron and Polyvótis craters), and again in 1887–88 (Mikrós Polyvótis). The vulcanological monitoring unit Geowarn notes that the temperature of the fumaroles in Stéfanos rose from 98°C in 2000 to 103°C in 2004.

Just before the road ends and the houses of the village begin, to the right-hand side, is a small, doorless stone entrance into the rock which is outlined in white paint. Inside is a minute circular space with a low stone seat. Holes low down on the left and at eye-level to the right function as vents from the volcano sending up hot vapours which are used as a sort of natural, curative sauna.

As a result of emigration and a lack of fresh water, Emboreiós has remained almost abandoned for some time, although its dignified stone houses indicate that it was once prosperous and populous. The sole taverna in the village offers splendid views and (when open) good food.

From below Emboreiós the road continues south into the central **volcanic depression** of the island, a drop of 300m down to the floor of the crater, which lies at about 100m above sea-level. This is a complex area of surprising diversity with its own climatic environment. The north slope, down which the road descends, is rich in vegetation thanks to the artificially warm and protected air; the southern slopes, by contrast, are bare and scarred with volcanic activity and the air is filled with the smell of sulphur. What you see as you descend is the result of two separate periods in geological history: first, the formation 25,000 years ago of the whole wide depression, with the mountains heaped to its west side; and second, the creation only 4,000 years ago of the discrete craters or explosion sinks, visible in the floor at the southern end.

Visiting the volcano

Exploration of the site is neither especially difficult nor dangerous, and affords visions of vapour seams, mud pools, cliffs of kaleidoscopic colour, and the ubiquitous and ephemeral formations of brilliant yellow, feathery sulphur crystals beside the smaller vapour holes. It is easy to descend into the largest crater, Stéfanos (330m across and 27m deep), by a path on the west side. In the centre of the flat floor are breaches and holes in which a pale grey or black viscous water (condensed from vapour as it encounters the cold exterior air) simmers at just under 100°C, while the whole of the lower eastern side is perforated with fumaroles, creating together a perceptible hissing sound. It is here that the greatest quantity of sulphur crystals form. Climbing up the ash-heaps to the northwest of Stéfanos, you reach (furthest south) the Phlégethron crater (also called Aléxandros), whose depth of 30m in proportion to its diameter of 100m makes it seem impressively deep, and the Polyvótis complex of craters. To the right of the summit of the path is the Mikrós Polyvótis, narrow, highly colourful, and with constant and audible activity. The sulphur from this area has been intermittently exploited from early antiquity (Phoenicians) up until the Ottoman occupation, when it was prized as an ingredient in explosives.

Panaghía Kyrá

From the junction east of Emboreiós and just below the north crater rim, the asphalt road continues south. After 1.5km a track leads down right (east) to the 18th-century monastery of Panaghía Kyrá. The setting is delightful, with the finely finished katholikon surrounded by monastery buildings, a bread-oven and an outside *xystos* for eating

Nikiá

Nikiá occupies a spectacular position on the southeastern rim of the volcanic caldera: the odour of sulphur intermittently arrives here on the breeze. Beyond the good taverna at the village entrance, a winding alley between stone houses and *kafeneía* leads to the memorable oval *plateía*, often referred to as the Porta, arranged like a small opera set, with sweeping views out to sea opposite.

Nikiá's greatest gem is the tiny, 15th-century church of Aghía Triáda (*100m downhill south of the village, directly below the cemetery, tucked under some stairs to the right of the pathway. Unlocked*). It is a single-vaulted chapel entirely covered with 15th-century paintings of considerable stylistic sophistication, though in poor condition in places. Scenes of the lives of Mary and of Jesus cover the vault. The technical quality of the depiction of faces, drapery and pose is remarkably fine.

WEST OF MANDRAKI

A short way along the coastal road from the port of Mandráki, a road climbs south at a junction. A left turn, signposted to the **Moní Evangelístria**, climbs up, with good views back towards the town, the castle and the ancient acropolis. This road ends at a large ligustrum tree in front of the 18th-century monastery buildings set low on a hidden plateau with the peak of Profítis Ilías above. Panoramic footpaths due east to Emboreiós (*45mins*), southeast to Nýphios and thence to the floor of the volcanic caldera (*90mins*), and due south to the summit of Profítis Ilías (*60mins each way*), all leave from this point.

Phaneroméni and the monastery of the Stavrós

From the edge of Mandráki, leaving Palaiókastro to your right, an unsurfaced road heads south, at first through a fertile cultivated area and then into successively wilder and rockier landscape. About a kilometre after the Palaiókastro turning, before a sharp bend to the right, is a wooden sign pointing up a track to **Phaneroméni**. A short climb up and to the right leads to a large, abandoned community of stone houses many of which, though small, are still beautifully vaulted. Up to the left (east) of a point one kilometre further along the unmade road, is another abandoned community, **Siónes**.

From here the road climbs into a wilder, more barren landscape. After passing through a defile, wide views open out over the sea to the south. The deserted, white-washed **monastery of the Stavrós** is built on the site of one of the ancient settlements of Nísyros (possibly named Argos); in subsequent centuries an Early Christian basilica and then a medieval castle were all built here. Beyond Stavrós, the road descends into the multicoloured landscape of the volcanic caldera, this time from the south rim.

GYALI

Gyalí, between Nísyros and Kos (*map p. 252*), is the largest of the satellite islands of Nísyros, and one of the most productive quarries of pumice in the world. This pumice is used today in a range of abrasive household cleaning fluids sold all over the world. Recent excavations have brought to light remains of many houses from the period of the Ottoman occupation, and a significant Late Neolithic settlement near the summit of the southwest part of the island. The southern peninsula boasts several of the best beaches to be found in this group of islands, and they are visitable by excursion boat from Mandráki in summer.

PRACTICAL INFORMATION

GETTING AROUND

The only service to run regularly throughout the year is the local M/V *Aghios Kostantinos* from Nísyros to Kardámaina on Kos (60mins). From May–Oct, M/V *Panaghia Spiliani* plies the Kos–Nísyros route 4–5 times weekly (90mins) Both have capacity for about two vehicles. GA car ferries call at Nísyros 3 times (summer) or twice (winter) weekly on the main Dodecanese route, with stops at nearly all the islands between Rhodes and Patmos, and connections with the same frequency to Piraeus. The Tilos catamaran *Sea Star* provides fast connections with Tilos and Rhodes twice weekly from June–mid-Oct.

WHERE TO STAY

Lodging is not plentiful and is mostly in or around Mandráki. The **Hotel Porphyris** (*T: 22420 31376; open May–end Sept*), though simple, is the island's most comfortable and friendly solution, providing breakfast and a pleasant seawater swimming pool. For atmosphere and a taste of times gone by, the **thermal baths at Loutrá** have basic and inexpensive rooms (no private facilities) from mid-June–end Sept (*T: 22420 31011*). Out of season, there is very little choice: the gloomy **Hotel Charitos** (*T: 22420 31322*) at least has heating.

WHERE TO EAT

Kleanthis, by the waterfront in Mandráki, is both welcoming and serves good seafood and many home-made vegetable dishes and salads. Hidden and sheltered from the wind is the **Taverna Nisyros**, in a narrow street (Odós Giannídi) perpendicular to the shoreline in Mandráki, with unexceptional food but a pleasing atmosphere.

The panoramic **Restaurant Andriotis**, just at the entrance to Nikiá, provides the most ambitious variety of food on the island, including well-prepared local goat dishes.

KOS

Kos has a wide and spacious feel: long beaches, clear mountains, open plateaux, and, beyond them all, bright and sweeping views in all directions. Famed from antiquity through to modern times for its gentle fertility and its gardens (which produced a type of lettuce that still bears the island's name—also known as Romaine lettuce, the type used for Caesar salad), its healthy climate was immortalised by the school of Hippocrates, whose teachings were to become the focus and stimulus for one of the most far-reaching revolutions in human thinking and which constitute the foundations of Western medical analysis and practice.

The island has an astonishing variety of remains from all periods, and there is a special beauty in the constant interlacing of ancient ruins and modern streets in the island's capital. The town's skyline is exotically punctuated by minarets left by the Ottoman occupation and giant palm trees left by the Italians. Above and behind everything else rise the protective peaks of the long ridge of Mt Horomedon, the water from whose northern slopes gives life to the broad plains below.

HISTORY OF KOS

Evidence of prehistoric habitation, first observed from Late Neolithic finds in the cave of Asprípetra in the southwestern peninsula, has now emerged from several other points on the island. After Mycenaean occupation, the island was colonised by Dorian settlers from Epidaurus and later belonged to the Dorian Hexapolis (with Halicarnassus, Cnidos and the three early cities on Rhodes). Proximity to the mainland of Asia Minor meant that it was easily subjected to the Lygdamid rulers of Halicarnassus (modern Bodrum) in the 6th century BC; at the Battle of Salamis in 480 BC, Kos fought for Persia under the command of Queen Artemisia of Halicarnassus, later defecting in 478/7 BC to become an ally of Athens. Kos was devastated by an earthquake in 412 BC and, in this vulnerable condition, was twice sacked, first in 411 by Spartan forces and then in 410 by the Athenians. Against this grim backdrop, the 5th century nonetheless saw the flourishing of intellectual activity, following the teachings and founding of the medical school of Hippocrates.

In 366 BC, the island, which had previously been organised in separate cities, united (in similar fashion to the synoecism on Rhodes; *see pp. 257–59*) to form a single city-state with a new capital and port on the site of the modern city of Kos. The fame of its School of Medicine and Sanctuary of Asclepius spread throughout the Greek world. Apart from a brief period subject to King Mausolus of Halicarnassus, and later in 256 BC to Antigonus Gonatas, Kos remained democratic and independent, allied to the dynasty of the Ptolemies and with strong trading links to Egypt. It was the people of Kos who commissioned (c. 364 BC) a statue of Aphrodite from Praxiteles, then the most prestigious sculptor alive: when he presented them with a choice of two, one draped, the

KOS

D

C Ag. Phokas
Ag. Phokas
Cape Louros
Psalidi
Embros Thermi
Bay of Kos
Syketros
482

KOS
Lambi
Platani
Asclepeion
Ag. Dimitros
Zipari
Aspendiou
Lagoudi
Amaniou
Zía
Mt Dikaios
843
Palaio Pylio
Tingaki
Linopolis
Pyli
Salt Lake

Kardamaina

C
Pserimos
Tingaki
Marmari

Kalymnos

Antimacheia
Castle
Halasarna
C. Ag. Nikolaos

Mastichari
Antimacheia
Ag. Ioannis
Forest of Plaka
Polemi
Pelos Gremmos

B

Strongili

Gyali

TURKEY
GREECE
C. Iskandil
Cnidos
C. Deveboynu

5 km
2.5 miles

N

T. Stavros
Neru
Safonidi

Limnionas
Kephalos
Milies
Ag Stefanos
Aghios Stefanos
Kastri
Kamari
Kephalos Bay
Mt Zini
351
P. Palatiani
Kamari
Kephalos Peninsula
Ag. Theologos
Ag. Ioannis
Thymianos
Chilandriou Bay
Aspripetra
Skinos Bay
427
Ag. Mamas
C. Kriketos
C. Ag. Ioannis

A
1
2
3

other nude, they chose the former. Cnidos, the island's constant rival, then snapped up the nude Aphrodite, which soon became one of the most celebrated works of its age.

Kos was loyal to Rome, and under Augustus was incorporated into the province of Asia. A tradition holds that St Paul visited the island in AD 57, and Kos was, early on, the seat of a bishop who was already sufficiently senior by 325 to have participated in the First Council of Nicaea, and thereafter in most subsequent Church councils. The island's medieval name was Lango (perhaps on account of its length) and it was also referred to as Stanchio (supposedly a corruption of 'Στην Κω') by the Italians. After 1204 the island was under Venetian control (except for a brief interlude under the Genoese in 1304) until it was ceded along with Rhodes to the Knights of St John in 1306. It was only after 1337 that the Knights began seriously to fortify the island and assert their presence. Outside its castles, the island was always vulnerable, and it was repeatedly under attack from the Turks—in 1457, 1460 and 1477. Only after the fall of Rhodes in January 1523 did Kos come under Turkish rule: their name for island was Istanköy. After nearly 400 years of Turkish rule, the island was taken in 1912 by the Italians, who began an ambitious project of architectural embellishment as a way of asserting their presence. This was given new urgency by a catastrophic earthquake in 1933. In 1948, Kos was united with the Greek state.

KOS TOWN & ENVIRONS

Kos has been shaken again and again by earthquakes throughout its history, and the city's buildings have been destroyed many times over. The town of Kos is immensely rich in archaeological remains; in fact the last catastrophe of 1933 was responsible for revealing many of the large areas which now remain as open-air archaeological enclosures and which are a memorable feature of the townscape. The chronological landscape of Kos is equally rich and extended, with important remains from ancient and Early Christian times, and from the periods of occupation by the Knights of Rhodes, the Ottomans and the Italians, all in close proximity to one another.

Ancient Kos stretches everywhere underneath the centre of the modern town, and much of it was uncovered by the demolition work done after the 1933 earthquake. Other parts have come to light as building plots have been cleared. All this means that islands of excavation and ancient remains often appear in the midst of streets and residential buildings. As a result, it is often hard to see the complete underlying plan of the ancient town, which was roughly as follows: its central focus was a low acropolis which corresponds to the hill of the Seraglio area and the Plateía Diagóra of today (*map p. 374, A4*). This small, raised area was inhabited from about 1500 BC onwards, through the late Bronze Age and Geometric periods, and formed the nucleus of the Archaic and Classical town, known as Kos Meropis, in the 6th and 5th centuries BC. Then, in 366 BC, Kos Meropis and the other ancient settlements on the island pooled their resources to found the new city. This spread out all around the acropolis hill and completely filled the area between it and the harbour. Two main excavation areas have begun to

KOS TOWN

N

| 0 | | 250 yards |
| 0 | | 250 metres |

Beach

FILINOU
PORFYRIOU
P.P. GERMANOU
ANTIMACHOU
SOKRATOUS
KRITIS
SYKIAS
AMERIKIS
ETHNIKIS ANTISTASEOS
POREYRIOU
KONSTANTINOU KANARI
NEOM. CHRISTOU
THEMISTOKLEOUS
AVEROF
PAMFILON
MANDILARA
NAVARINOU
SPETSON
ALIKARNASSOU
YDRAS
SALAMINAS
THEMISTOKLEOUS
AVEROF
ETHNIKIS ANTISTASEOS
NAVARINOU
SPETSON
AMERKIS
PSARON
K. KANARI
AKTI KOUNDOURIOTOU
VERIOPOULOU
BOUBOULINAS
IEROU LOCHOU
ALIKARNASSOU
PATAKOU
PL. IROON POLYTECHNIOU
MANDILARA
PINDOU
OMIROU
VERIOPOULOU
IROONDOU
KIPROU
Harbour Baths
MEG. ALEXANDROU

PORT OF KOS

Castle of the Knights

AKTI MIAOULI

EL. VENIZELOU
KOUTSOURADI
KLEOVOULOU
THEOFRASTOU
MEG. ALEXANDROU
Ancient Stadium
Roman Houses
Northern Baths
TSALDARI
25 MARTIOU
GALLIA
MAKARIOU
25 MARTIOU
R. FERAIOU
AKTI KOUNDOURIOTOU
Hippocrates' Plane
PL. PLATANOU
Mosque
PL. PLATANOU
DIAKOU
NAFKLIROU
KAZOULI
Archaeological Museum
Deftedar Mosque
PL.
Ancient Agora
Schlegelholz Bastion
PL. PALEOLOGOU
Y. IPERIOU
Gymnasium
NISYRIOU
PL. DIAGORA
KOLOKOTRONI
APELLOU
IFAISTOU
Market
ELEFTHERIAS
Ag. Paraskevi
PL. AG. PARASKEVI
IPPOKRATOUS
XANTHOU
Albergo Gelsomino
Evangelismos
School
KORAI
ASCLEPEION
Baths
PEISANDROU
Bus Station
PEISANDROU
KLEOPATRAS
IOANNIDOU
K. PAVLOU
ELEFTHERIOU VENIZELOU
MITROPOLEOS
AG. NIKOLAOU
KAVAKOPOULOU
VRONOS
Hospital
Bank (Casa Balilla)
ARTEMISIAS
Western Excavations (Acropolis)
GRIGORIOU E
Odeion
Altar of Dionysus
Casa Romana
Central Baths
Ag. Ioannis
MAKRYGIANNI
KORAI
NATHANAIL
IOANNIDOU
G.
KOUROUKLI
THYMIANAKI
FILIMONOS
AMBAVRIS
AGHIOS PHOKAS

reveal its extent: the ancient harbour area and agorá (*map p. 374, C3*) between Plateía Eleftherías and Hippocrates' plane tree, and the Western Excavations immediately below and around the acropolis hill (*map p. 374, A4*). Between them is the museum (*map p. 374, B3*), which houses some of the more important sculptural finds. Around these two main areas, however, are many other smaller sites. To the north is an area which includes less visible remains of a stadium, Roman baths and other miscellaneous buildings (*map p. 374, A3*); to the south of the acropolis hill is the reconstructed odeion and an impressive private residence known as the Casa Romana (*map p. 374, B4*) with more Roman baths next to it and the ancient theatre beyond. Finally, near to these last, is a constellation of smaller archaeological areas which are currently being dug, between the Altar of Dionysus and the agorá.

The Foro Italico area

Exploration of this part of town begins in the shade of the giant ficus trees across the road from the prominent Albergo Gelsomino building on the south promenade (*map p. 374, C4*), 250m south of the castle and port, which today houses the tourist information office. Many of the buildings in the area along the shore to the south of the castle date from the Italian occupation of Kos between 1912 and 1943. Kos was the second administrative centre of the Italian Dodecanese province, and these buildings were meant as showpieces for the new administration as well as to provide a functional base for its operations. Together they constitute what was called the Foro Italico, and they form part of a master plan for the expansion and renewal of the city, drawn up in 1928. The idea was to create a new, pan-Mediterranean architectural vocabulary: clear, rational and based on the simple forms of the architecture of ancient Rome (which the regime was keen to emulate) but at the same time acknowledging the traditions of local architecture, which in Greece meant the whitewashed, geometric forms of vernacular building and the medieval castellations and pointed arches of the structures left by the Knights of Rhodes.

Albergo Gelsomino was originally the official hotel. To its south stand two lower buildings, the former mayor's residence (now the **Kos Cultural Centre**) and the **Italian Club**. Immediately beside you and behind is the (less successful) **Church of the Evangelismós** (formerly the Catholic Cathedral of the Agnus Dei). Inland behind it is the **Kos Boys' School** (Ippokráteio Lýkeio), and one block further up Ippokrátous is the **hospital**. A hundred and fifty metres to the north along the promenade road, just before the Castle and the Avenue of Palms, is the **Kos Administration Building**, originally the seat of the Governorate. Directly behind it is the **Court House** and, at the far end of the Avenue of Palms, overlooking the harbour is the former Governor's Residence (now the **Dimarcheíon**). All these buildings were designed by Florestano di Fausto (*see p. 256*), with the exception of the Albergo Gelsomino, which is by Rodolfo Petracco, and all were erected between 1927 and 1929. Then came the earthquake of 1933, and a new and more ambitions urban plan for the city was required. One of the few buildings in this immediate area from after 1933 is the former **Casa del Balilla**, or Fascist Youth Building (now the Agrotikí Bank), on the corner of Koraï and Artemísias, 100m to the southwest.

The old agorá and harbour quarter

The medieval building on the corner directly to the north of the ficus trees is the **Schlegelholz Bastion** (*map p. 374, C3*), and it marks the southern limit of the medieval Collachium, or walled city, built by the Knights of St John between 1391 and 1396 against the threatened attack of Sultan Yildirim ('Thunderbolt') Beyazit I. The bastion bears the coats of arms of Schlegelholz, Governor of Kos (1391–1412), and of Grand Master Juan Fernández de Heredia (1377–96). The walled city enclosed an area south of the Castle, now occupied by the agorá excavations and the buildings adjoining the southeast corner of the harbour: its southern wall, well-preserved at some points, runs along the northern side of Ippokrátous. A reconstructed eastern gateway, incorporating ancient and medieval spolia, leads in from the shore promenade just north of the bastion, beside the Hospitaller **House of Francesco Sans**. Through the gateway is a deserted area with two small medieval churches, separated by a funerary chapel and a monument to the Thymanakis family, which has an inscribed fragment of ancient cornice as its western step. The small 15th-century church of **Ághios Geórgios** to the south incorporates many ancient fragments, including a broken column protruding perpendicularly on the north side and other decorative pieces and architraves. The church to the north, **Ághios Ioánnis**, of the same period, is similarly constructed using ancient pieces. These churches, now isolated, were once immersed in the dense habitation and narrow streets of the medieval town, which was cleared after the earthquake of 1933. Just beyond Ághios Ioánnis to the north are the remains of early 17th-century **Ottoman baths**, later used as a store and deposit for salt. The bathing chamber is still clearly recognisable, but in bad condition.

The medieval city rose over the remains of the ancient agorá and harbour quarter. The remains were first scientifically explored by Rudolf Herzog in 1900, and then properly cleared and dug by Italian archaeologists after the 1933 earthquake. The Greek Archaeological Service is now pursuing work here. The visible area represents approximately 4–5 percent of the extent of the city in its heyday. The ancient port penetrated substantially further inland than the present one, and the buildings would have stood much closer to the water than they now appear. The best preserved stretch of the **4th-century BC city walls**, built in rusticated, isodomic blocks, is visible heading northwest from the back corner of the site. Immediately within the walls (the area to the left of these walls, between the axial pathway and Ippokrátous) was a dense conurbation of stores, workshops, taverns and bakeries, typical of the activity that would be expected in proximity to the port. The six barrel-vaulted **warehouses** (which stand higher than anything else) have survived destruction because their internal spaces easily served the purpose of churches in later centuries. The logical division of the area into insulae or blocks divided by streets is clear: at important points, such as on the corners of the blocks, the foundations of a bakery or tavern and a food shop are visible, with the base of a brick oven and buried pithoi for storage of foodstuffs. Further west, at the edge of the site, the corner of the agorá square proper is visible, cut across by the modern street and a projection of unexcavated land around the tiny church of **Ághios Konstantínos**. This would have been an extensive, marble-paved space that would have

Roman-era mosaic in the ruins of the agorá.

stretched more than 200m to the south from here. The agorá was badly damaged in the earthquake of AD 142, after which it was rebuilt with a monumental entrance in a style and building technique which was typically Roman: the bulky vaulted arches in opus caementicium, still with vestiges of stucco decoration, which are heaped in ruins just to the north, come from this gateway building which stood at the top of a flight of steps.

The remains on the north side of the axial pathway, i.e. outside the original north wall of the ancient city, are of a predominantly sacred nature. Beginning again at the eastern entrance, and taking the path to the right in the direction of the Mosque of the Loggia (*see below*), the base of a small, 2nd-century BC **Temple of Heracles** (a popular semi-divinity in port areas as the protector of stevedores and manual labourers) comes into view to the left. The temple (7.2m by 4.8m) was orientated north–south. At the extremity of this path (below and in front of the Mosque of the Loggia) are the remains of a very large brick structure at a higher level than the surrounding buildings. This was an **Early Christian basilica**, built in the 5th century AD (perhaps after this area had been levelled by the earthquake of AD 469), consisting of three aisles which appear not to be interconnected and are separated by solid walls. At an obtuse angle across its west end and narthex marches a row of columns which have been re-erected with their acanthus leaf capitals in the position they would have occupied before the basilica was built. They constituted the front colonnade of the late 4th-century BC **Harbour Stoa**, which would have extended another 30 or 40m in both directions. The marble of the columns is cipollino from Euboea; when polished, it would have been of a veined and translucent blue-green colour, reflecting the water of the harbour which it embellished.

To the west of the Temple of Heracles, marked by a raised stone stylobate and erected column fragments, was a 2nd-century BC **Sanctuary of Aphrodite**, another divinity often found in proximity to ports because she was the protectress of sailors. Here the sanctuary comprised two identical temples to different attributes of the goddess: Aphrodite Pandemos (protectress of the city as a whole) and Aphrodite Pontia (protectress of sailors). The twin temples were prostyle, with four columns supporting a pediment, set in the middle of a colonnaded courtyard (62m by 45m), with altars in front of them, and preceded by two axial entrance gates with columns and steps.

Plateía Platánou

The **Ottoman baths** are just behind di Fausto's ex-Governorate Building of 1928. The path behind leads to a square dominated by a venerable plane tree, called **Hippocrates' Plane** (*map p. 374, C3*), under which the philosopher is supposed to have taught. The tree, which has four main branches of varying ages artificially supported at many points, is certainly over 500 years old, but is unlikely to have existed for the 2,450 years required for it to have shaded Hippocrates: it may be the descendant of a sacred tree which has always occupied this site. On the side towards the Castle is a decorated **Ottoman fountain** bearing the date 1200 (= 1780 in the Hejira calendar), whose rear side is part of a carved Hellenistic sarcophagus. On the other side is another Ottoman fountain, this time in the form of a canopied sabil with 14 sides, each with carved cypress-tree motif. Seven truncated ancient columns with late Corinthian capitals support the domed canopy over it. Many beautiful ancient fragments lie around, including pieces with inscriptions and ancient graffiti, altars with bucrania, and columns and fragments in Rhodian and other kinds of marble: the east corner-stone of the fountain platform bears a fragmentary ancient inscription. This fountain was built together with the imposing Mosque of Gazi Hassan Pasha (1786), also known as the **Mosque of the Loggia**, which rises directly behind. The minaret survives, though restored, with carved geometric embellishments: at its foot is an ancient sculptural fragment of a lion skin from a statue of Heracles and a portion of a frieze of a lion and bull fighting.

Fifty metres down Nafklírou and to the right into Diákou, at no. 4, is the former **synagogue**, with dramatic decorative chevrons in its façade. It ceased to function as a place of worship after the deportations of 1944, a mere ten years after it was built as part of the New Urban Plan.

The Castle of the Knights

Where once there was a wooden drawbridge over a moat filled with seawater, a stone bridge now leads from Hippocrates' Plane across the impressive avenue of palm trees to the Castle of the Knights of St John of Rhodes, for whom this was the second most important city fortress of their embattled territory (*open winter 8.30–3; until 8pm in summer; closed Mon*). Its medieval name, Nerantzia Castle, comes from the orange groves which once surrounded it. The outer enceinte is complete, and gives the castle a satisfyingly low and compact profile. Over the south entrance from the bridge is an escutcheon of the quartered arms of the Order with those of its Grand Master, Emery d'Amboise (1503–12). Below it, the builders have intentionally incorporated a Hellenistic frieze of garlands and grimacing theatrical masks; such faces were long believed to ward off evil. The basic development of the site can be seen on entering: in the centre of the area in front is the original rectangular castle of 1450–78. Around it, and separated by a wide fosse on three sides, is a second, more sophisticated enceinte of walls, built almost 50 years later, between 1495 and 1514.

In the open courtyard in front, as well as in the enclosed antiquarium in the south wall, is a seemingly endless quantity of marble objects which come from the ancient buildings of Kos and the Asclepeion. Kos is unusually rich in inscriptions, which greatly help to define its history and topography, and many of them are stored here. There are also dozens of altars with garlands and bucrania, fluted columns, inscribed stelae, fragments of honorific statuary etc.; many more are incorporated in the walls, and the ordinary blocks from which the walls are made mostly come from ancient buildings torn down to provide the stone. It soon becomes clear why so little is left at the ancient sites themselves.

A sloping ramp leads across to the entrance of the inner fortress, marked by a projecting ravelin to the left. The imposing inner gate is roofed with ten horizontal monolithic granite columns. Inside the enclosed area are the foundations of the **Hospitallers' Church**, with the conspicuous well-head of a cistern in the southeast corner.

Around Plateía Eleftherías

The streets leading inland to either side of the Governor's Palace bring you up to Plateía Eleftherías (*map p. 374, B3*), the city's main square, which is marked by the conspicuous minaret of the 18th-century **Deftedar Mosque**. Behind the mosque to the east, and now almost entirely overgrown by bougainvillea, is what was the principal entrance into the medieval walled city of the Knights, the Pórta tou Fórou, whose masonry, doorposts and lintel blocks are still just visible beneath the vegetation. The open space of Plateía Eleftherías is bounded by buildings erected by the Italians as part of the New Urban Plan after the 1933 earthquake: the museum to the north, the **New Market** opposite it to the south, and the **old Fascist Party Headquarters** (now a cinema and theatre) between them to the west. All date from 1934–45.

The collection on display in the **Archaeological Museum** (*open 8.30–3.30; closed Mon*) is, given the richness and variety of ancient and medieval archaeological remains on the island, decidedly limited in scope. It is arranged in three rooms around a central atrium; the pottery collection on the upper floor, which provides important evidence of prehistoric habitation and of the specific Bronze Age, Geometric and Archaic settlements in the city, was closed at the time of writing. The ground-floor rooms contain some beautiful mosaics and sculpture, including a rare votive statue of Hades.

Heading to the acropolis area from the southwest corner of Plateía Eleftherías, Ifaístou, which then becomes Apéllou, leads gently uphill past cafés, shops and an Ottoman wall-fountain. In the corner of Nisyríou (*map p. 374, A4*), behind the summit, is the large 17th-century stone **mansion of Mehmet Pasha**. Its woodwork, attractively painted ceilings and domed hamam have recently been restored and converted into the Anatolia Hamam restaurant and bar.

The Western Excavations

This large open area to the south and west of the original acropolis hill (*map p. 374, A4*), is reached by taking Ifaístou uphill from the southwest corner of the square outside the museum. Although Plateía Diagóra, at the top of the street, occupies the only area which has been uninterruptedly inhabited since the 3rd millennium BC, the excavations below and around the hill display remains from the first five centuries AD only. The alleyway and steps by the minaret, which leave Diagóra to the south, descend to Grigoríou E, where, just to the right, are more steps which lead into the excavated area. The broad paved line of the ancient decumanus, the city's main east–west artery, is immediately visible, running below and parallel to the existing road. Extravagantly broad (10.5m), endowed with wide sidewalks, backed by rows of shops behind, and with a slightly arched surface for drainage, the street's importance attracted many of the finest residences, which provide the principal interest here. These lie just to the south, below the visible remains of the Hellenistic retaining wall on the hill behind. Both of the two houses here preserve areas of painting and floor mosaics in good condition, and yielded much of the sculpture which is now in the museum. To the left, the 2nd-century AD **House of the Europa Mosaic** is a typical wealthy residence built around a spacious colonnaded peristyle, with a four-lobe water fountain, once decorated in coloured marbles, in the centre of its paved court. The unusually complete mosaic of the abduction of Europa is to the left. To the east of the atrium is a curious narrow room with painted walls, a meticulous drainage system, and a series of interconnected decantation pools for liquids. The house adjacent to the east also possesses fine areas of mosaic floor and decorated walls.

Two hundred metres further west is the important junction where the decumanus meets the north–south cardo. Much narrower and hemmed in by the construction of later buildings, its immaculately paved course is nonetheless clear and visible to the north, as it heads into an area of public buildings mostly dedicated to sport and recreation. Terracotta water pipes are visible running down its west side: above, along the same side, are the ruins of large **Roman baths**, parts of which were later converted into an Early Christian church complex after the earthquake of AD 469, creating a complicated superimposition of buildings and uses.

In the 3rd century AD, two important structures which related to the baths flanked them to left and right. The 30-m swimming-pool, with stepped lobes at either end, occupies the area behind a colonnade to the left. Seventeen of the original 81 Doric columns in this colonnade have been re-erected: they formed the support for a roofed area known as the **Xystos Dromos**, where athletic competitions and training could take place during inclement weather. This building was the eastern extremity of a very large **gymnasium**, which extended under the modern buildings to the north and west and included the city's stadium. Flanking the baths to the other side, and bordering on the cardo, is the large, four-square edifice of the **public lavatories** (foricae). Though this building merely served a basic public necessity, it is decked out with Ionic capitals, marble revetment, and abstract and figurative mosaics in the central floor; every functional aspect was carefully designed: the main drainage channel around the perimeter was continually flushed with water, and the two pouring cascades from the high spouts above the basins on the west side cooled and circulated the air, while their welcome sound would have drowned out any less desirable noises.

The northern extremity of the excavations is closed and traversed by the vestibule of a large public building, whose floor is decorated with magnificent mosaics. A running border with scenes of exotic animals and performers surrounds a central panel (left) of Paris in judgment of the three jealous goddesses, framed above and below by other divinities.

The stadium, Harbour Baths and northern sites

Steps and a pathway up the south side of the foricae building, followed by a left turn into Makaríou, lead past the remains of houses of the Roman period on Gallías (*map p. 374, B3*), between Makaríou and Tsaldári, and further north to an area surrounded by apartment blocks, where there are vestiges of other public thermae. Further to the north of here, in a plot between the harbour front and Irodótou, are more thermae, referred to as the **Harbour Baths**, which incorporate much earlier material in their construction. Part of the harbour walls are visible in the north corner of this area. In the declivity which occupies the entirety of two blocks between Megálou Aléxandrou and Tsaldári is the site of the 2nd-century BC **stadium** (*map p. 374, A3*). This was rectangular in shape (180m by 30m) and did not possess the usual curved sphendone at one end. The marble starting block can be seen beside the church of Aghía Ánna at the north end, and some of the stone seating survives at the southern end.

The odeion and Casa Romana area

These two buildings are the most conspicuous standing remains of the ancient town— as well as the most substantially modified and reconstructed by the Italian archaeologists of the 1930s. They are both on Grigoríou E. The main theatre of the ancient city lay to the south of here; this small **odeion** (*map p. 374, A4*), of the 2nd century BC, had a different purpose. It served for small musical gatherings, poetry readings and political meetings. It was always an intimate space; originally roofed, decorated inside with statuary, and embellished with a polychrome marble floor in opus sectile. The original marble seating of the cavea has been extensively restored with modern additions in similar stone. The building had a compact rectangular exterior, and the spacious and well-constructed undercrofts, or tabernae, beneath the seating area were also exploited in a practical use of valuable space in a crowded city centre.

Three hundred metres further east along Grigoríou E is the so-called **Casa Romana** (*map p. 374, B4; open 8am–9.30pm; closed Mon*). This was a splendid city residence, rebuilt in Roman times on the foundations (still visible at the lowest courses of masonry) of an earlier Hellenistic house destroyed in the earthquake of AD 142. At 2400 square metres in area, it occupied a whole city block, and has a spaciousness which makes an abiding impression on the visitor. All of its finer mosaics were removed by the Italians and taken to the newly restored Grand Master's Palace in Rhodes: nonetheless, the few that remain still give a sense of their sophisticated quality. Virtually no interior surface was left undecorated, either by wall-painting or with the much more expensive revetment in precious coloured marbles, of which some dusty vestiges still remain. Everything displayed the owner's wealth, from the moment one entered: on the small platform in the floor opposite the main entrance would have stood the strongbox, containing the gold or coin with which he paid his workers and rewarded his clients. The southern half of the house (left of the entrance) is occupied by an airy peristyle hall, where the columns rise the full height of the building; at it southern end, and looking across it, is the tablinum, the principal reception room. Private baths are adjacent in the southeast corner. In the opposite, northwest corner, beyond the kitchens, is the north-facing triclinium, looking across a fountain in the centre of the peristyle to an elaborate and decorated nymphaeum opposite. Water, and the sound of water, were fundamental to the plan of the house. Few other examples in the Aegean area give a better sense of the sumptuous dwellings of the rich in the late Hellenistic and Roman periods.

The next insula east of the house is occupied by the 3rd-century AD **Central Baths**, the largest of the public thermal complexes, with its hypocaust system well preserved.

One other monument of interest lies close by. Between the odeion and the Casa Romana, Anapávseos leads south to the Catholic Cemetery and Church of the Agnus Dei. Behind the church is the remarkable late 5th- or early 6th-century domed **baptistery of Ághios Ioánnis** (*map p. 374, A4*). This was once attached to a large Early Christian basilica, whose remains now lie under the surrounding cemetery (*interior open only irregularly in the morning at c. 7am, sometimes on Sat evenings, and for funerals*). The building's importance lies in the fact that this is one of only two Early Christian baptisteries in Greece to have survived complete. The floor is now paved with marble slabs: the original baptismal pool in the centre was filled in when the building became a funerary church, possibly as early as the 11th century. Vestiges of 13th- and 14th-century wall-paintings are perceptible in some of the conches. A door in the north side would have communicated with the main basilica church, which once stood in the area now occupied by the cemetery to the north.

The area of the Altar of Dionysus

The base of the **Altar of Dionysus** (*map p. 374, B4*) is visible in a sunken area below the pine trees across Grigoríou E to the northeast of the Casa Romana and Central Baths. It faced due east with a ramp for access from the west, and would have been a low structure of a broad Π shape, with two levels in the interior so as to provide a wide ledge for offerings, surrounded by a flat cornice with a carved relief running in segments just below, depicting an Amazonomachia with Dionysus and his followers. This design and decoration has led to the suggestion that the altar and its temple were gifts from the Attalid rulers of Pergamon in the 2nd century BC, whose own famous altar (now in Berlin) shows structural similarities. A small **Doric temple**, possibly the one dedicated to Dionysus, stood just to the north and east.

KOS TOWN TO THERMA

The main road along the shoreline to the southeast of Kos passes a long, gently curving bay, lined with eucalyptus trees, which has witnessed much of the island's tourist development over the last decade. Shortly after the New Yacht Marina, to the right of the road, can be seen recent excavations (*map p. 372, D1*) which have revealed the outlines of a major **Archaic temple and large altar** of the 6th century BC, and brought to light a wide array of votive offerings: Egyptian scarabs, Corinthian aryballoi, swords and figurines of female deities. Little had previously come to light from this early period on Kos, and these important excavations are helping to fill gaps in the understanding of the continuity of the island's history.

The road continues round the eastern extremity of the island, marked (north) by Cape Loúros and (south) Ághios Phokás. As the road turns south and west, the landscape becomes dramatically more arid along the treeless southern slopes of the Horomedon massif. Wide views of the Cnidos peninsula and Nísyros open out. After Ághios Phokás the asphalt finishes, and a track (beside a refreshments stall) heads steeply down to the shore below, leading (600m) to a narrow strand of shingle between the cliffs and the sea: at its western end, a spring of hot sulphurous water known as **Embrós Thérmi**, or often just Thermá (*map p. 372, D1*) emerges at just under 50°C and flows directly into the sea from under the cliff, mixing to a pleasant temperature with the seawater in an area roughly enclosed by a wide ring of boulders, where further small jets rise underwater. The first severe storms of the autumn bury the spring under sand; it is then dug out once again at the end of each winter. The consequent warmth in the surrounding sea attracts octopus in large numbers. Some of these inevitably find their way onto the tables of the fish taverna that occupies the only building on the shore.

The northeastern slopes of Mount Horomedon

The ridge of Mt Horomedon, with its peak of Díkaios, dominates the eastern half of the island, from which it rises clear to its summit of 843m. The rough track along its ridge offers some of the finest views in the Dodecanese: south to Cnidos, Nísyros and Tilos; east to Bodrum and mainland Turkey; north to Psérimos, Kálymnos and Leros; and west out even as far as distant Amorgós. The labyrinth of tracks that traverses these slopes is best reached by leaving the main town just west of the Casa Romana from Grigoríou E, on the road which heads south alongside the ruined Ottoman aqueduct through the suburb of Ambavrís.

THE ASCLEPEION

At the southwest corner of Kos Town is the large roundabout from which the main east–west road of the island (for the airport and Képhalos) departs: a well-signed, smaller road to the left leads (2.5km) to the Asclepeion (*map p. 372, C1*). The road is bordered with cypresses and probably follows the line of the ancient Sacred Way that linked the Sanctuary of Asclepius with the town and port. Almost immediately on the left is the neglected **Jewish Cemetery**, the sole relic of a community that had been present on the island since antiquity but which vanished with the deportations of 1940–44; further on (on the same side) is the **Muslim Cemetery**, behind a white-washed wall, with turbaned tombstones crowded beneath olive and cypress trees. Most are engraved in Osmanli script, but those post-1926 are in Romanised letters, witness to the continuity of a substantial Turkish community on the island. In fact, in the village of **Platáni** (1km) just beyond, Turkish is still to be heard in the cafés and tavernas, several of which serve good food of Turkish inspiration (*see p. 394*).

At 1.8km from Kos Town the road splits (to the left is the International Hippocratic Foundation). The right branch leads to the ancient Asclepeion (*open daily except Mon, 8.30–3; until 7 in summer*).

HISTORY OF THE ASCLEPEION

The first cult on this hillside was actually of Apollo, who was venerated here in a sacred cypress grove from the end of the 6th century BC. Apollo was father of Asclepius, the part-human, part-divine god or hero of medicine and healing in antiquity; and by virtue of the presence of important curative waters in this area, a parallel cult of Asclepius also took root here early on. Places of cult of Asclepius attracted both those who sought his healing powers, and those who practised them. These practitioners called themselves 'descendants' of Asclepius, and were organised in a closed order or brotherhood. They are often referred to as Asclepeiads. Hippocrates was one such 'descendant'. His wisdom, gathered from experience here and on journeys all over Greece, transformed the practice of medicine. It is important to bear in mind, though, that everything visible today dates from the two centuries after his death in c. 370 BC.

It seems as though the sanctuary was originally conceived as a unified whole, but that it took two centuries to complete. It now occupies a rise of three terraces, the first of which divided the functional and hospital areas of the sanctuary (First Terrace) from the cult areas (Middle Terrace); the third, Upper Terrace, completed a hundred years later in the mid-2nd century BC, was added (in a form reflecting the shape of the lowest terrace) as the sanctuary expanded and began to accumulate greater wealth. Many additions and re-buildings after earthquakes were subsequently made, such as the large Roman thermal complex.

The site was identified by a local antiquary, Iakovos Zaraftis, and excavations were first undertaken between 1902 and 1905, under the Ottoman administration, by the German scholar and archaeologist Rudolf Herzog and later continued by Italian archaeologists during the 1920s and 1930s, during which considerable consolidation and reconstruction work on the terracing and some monuments (Temple of Apollo) was undertaken.

In antiquity the visitor arrived at the monumental entrance of the sanctuary by way of a long avenue, or Sacred Way, from the city, which lay 3km away.

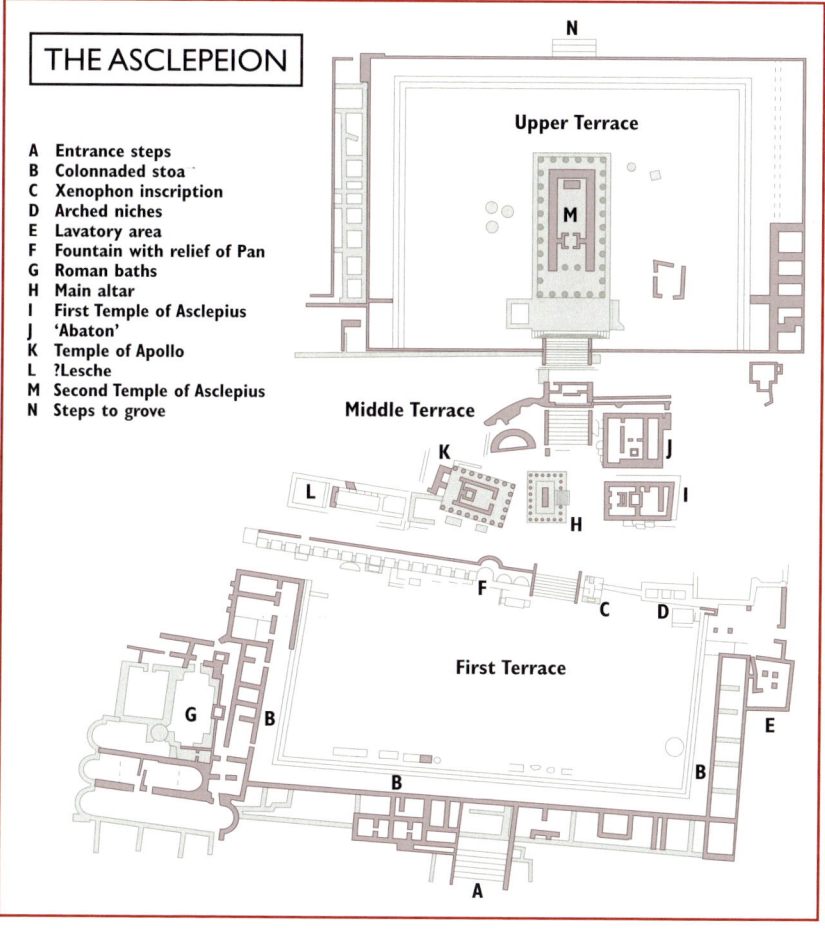

THE ASCLEPEION

A Entrance steps
B Colonnaded stoa
C Xenophon inscription
D Arched niches
E Lavatory area
F Fountain with relief of Pan
G Roman baths
H Main altar
I First Temple of Asclepius
J 'Abaton'
K Temple of Apollo
L ?Lesche
M Second Temple of Asclepius
N Steps to grove

Upper Terrace

Middle Terrace

First Terrace

First Terrace

Originally entered through a tetrastyle pedimented gateway which stood at the initial flight of open **steps (A)**, the First Terrace was an enclosed area bounded on three sides by a continuous colonnaded **stoa (B)**, with its fourth side formed by the retaining wall of the Middle Terrace straight ahead, whose niches would have been peopled with statuary and running fountains of water. The area thus enclosed provided lodging for patients, and constituted the principal workplace of the practitioners, who were neither solely priests nor doctors but a hybrid of the two.

HIPPOCRATES & THE HIPPOCRATIC WRITINGS

Beyond the fact that he existed, little is known for certain about Hippocrates. It is generally held that he was born in Kos around 460 BC and died in Thessaly at an advanced age, some time after 375 BC. Where he travelled in his lifetime, with whom he spoke and studied, and what exactly he may have written, remains largely conjecture. A huge body of literature does, however, bear his name: the so-called Hippocratic Corpus, consisting of about 70 treatises. Much of this was written by his contemporaries and students, some of it added later, and maybe some part of it is by Hippocrates himself. It contains writings that represent three main strands of thinking within ancient Greek medicine: first, the primarily speculative work of the medical theorists; second, the factually descriptive and observational clinical diaries, which typify the medical school of Cnidos, across the water from Kos; and lastly, the works of the circle of Hippocrates and the school of Kos, who based their thinking on meticulous observation but were concerned always to interpret it and understand it in the wider context of the human condition. Hippocrates treated cases of illness in women, or injury of slaves, with a humane and disinterested social impartiality which contrasts with several of the greater thinkers of the next generation, such as Plato and Aristotle. His teaching rid medicine of superstition, false fears, false hopes and false practice. It was heir to the earliest and best impulses of Greek thinking: clarity, universal analysis, and respect for the power of nature; and as such it laid the basis of our modern understanding of the human body. One version or another of his outline of the ethical precepts of the profession, known as the Hippocratic Oath, is still used in most countries in the world to this day at the ceremonial qualification of doctors.

To the right of the central staircase ahead is a niche with a pedestal in white marble, on which stood a statue of Nero as Asclepius. A legible **inscription** below **(C)** refers to the person who dedicated it, [Gaius Stertinius] Xenophon, a 1st-century AD physician from Kos who practiced successfully in the imperial court at Rome and who appears also to have endowed a medical library at this sanctuary. Further to the right are three **arched niches (D)** with thermal water pools at ground level for the therapeutic waters and a rectangular ablutions sink and an area of **lavatories (E)**, added in the 3rd century AD.

To the left of the central stairs is a **fountain (F)** surmounted by an eroded relief of Pan playing the syrinx. The wall all along here has been extensively restored and rebuilt: the two despoiled and headless statues at the far left-hand end of it give little impression of the wall's original effect when peopled with the fine dedicatory sculptures mentioned by Strabo and Pliny. The whole of the terrace's eastern end is dominated by the massive ruins of a later addition, namely the **Roman baths (G)** of the 3rd century AD.

Middle Terrace

A largely restored flight of steps leads to the Middle Terrace, which constituted the sacred focus of the sanctuary. In the centre, at the top of the stairs, are the ruins of the **main altar (H)**, which was enlarged at least twice during its history. The original altar of 350 BC was replaced by a 3rd-century BC structure which would have had a form not dissimilar to the Altar of Dionysus in the town: a stepped platform, with a central offering table open to the skies, surmounted by a colonnade which was broken on the west side to allow access by a ramp of steps. The colonnade may have contained sculptures by the school of Praxiteles. The altar would have been sacred to both Apollo and Asclepius, but an inscription found on the site mentions other lesser divinities also: Helios, Hemera, Hecate and Machaon (son of Asclepius and suitor of Helen). Looking onto the altar from the west was the (first) **Temple of Asclepius (I)**, an Ionic temple, distyle in antis, erected c. 300 BC. The two columns of the portico remain in reassembled fragments: only the right-hand (north) one still stands on its original base. Clearly visible in the interior, to the south side, is a large, stone-built coffer in the floor, referred to as the thesauros, or treasury: its monolithic lid has a hole in the centre for the depositing of offerings to the god. Strabo implies (*Geog. XIV, 2.19*) that a number of great paintings were to be seen in the temple, amongst which he mentions Apelles' *Aphrodite Anadyomene*. It was removed to Rome in the 1st century by Augustus.

Behind the temple is a building generally referred to as the **abaton (J)**, where the sick would have slept in the hope of receiving divine assistance through their dreams. It has, however, also been interpreted as a residence for the priests. In some way its function and existence must be linked to the spring in the far southwest corner, where steps lead down to a pool in a deep cavity beneath the retaining wall of the Upper Terrace.

Across to the east of the altar is the base of the small Roman peripteral **Temple of Apollo (K)**. Of the re-erected columns, only two small fluted fragments are original from the 2nd-century AD building. The rest is all reconstruction. Wholly original, however, are the elaborately decorated fragments of the ornate entablature and ceiling of the temple's peristyle, which lie on the ground to the east. The displaying of important votive gifts to a sanctuary such as this was a visible manifestation of its prestige and importance, and the building whose foundations are visible further east of the Temple of Apollo, also referred to as a **Lesche**, or meeting room **(L)**, probably served this purpose. The hemicycle of niches just to the east of the next flight of stairs may have had the same function of display, and the small, semicircular rostrum in front of it, a related ceremonial function.

Upper Terrace

From the third or Upper Terrace a beautiful view opens out across the city, the islands and the mainland opposite. The form of this terrace mirrored the First: the sides and back were lined by a continuous colonnaded stoa and the fourth side was open to the panoramic view. Once this area was completed, shortly after 200 BC, the sanctuary had a complete, closed form, with two colonnaded terraces reflecting one another across a transverse axis of sacred buildings. In 170–160 BC the new and **Greater Temple to Asclepius (M)** was erected in the centre of this terrace. It was peripteral in design, orientated north–south, and with no apparent altar in front. Only the marble floor and finely cut steps of the platform remain. Anything that remained of the original 32 columns of the Doric colonnade was taken to Kos by the Knights of Rhodes for their Castle and other buildings. Over the temple's pronaos, a small medieval chapel was erected, generally referred to as the Panaghía tou Álsous or Társou. The T-shaped assemblage of ancient and Byzantine spolia to the east side was its altar. The stone sarcophagi visible to the west are evidence of a Christian cemetery on this site.

Steps (N) lead up the hill into the area occupied by the original grove of cypress trees, sacred to Apollo. A little way up and to the left is the platform of another temple, probably also Hellenistic, perfectly orientated on an east–west axis: the base of the walls of the naos can be traced, and the south side of the crepidoma remains well-preserved. Above it, a curious natural limestone ridge traverses the hillside, which shows signs of having been cut by hand at several points: this may have been the peribolos or perimeter line of the sacred grove. The hill levels out further up: the land drops away towards the sea in one direction, and rises to the crenellated peak of Díkaios in the other.

ZIPARI & ASPHENDIOU

Zipári

Six and a half kilometres west of Kos Town along the island's main road is the village of Zipári (*map p. 372, C1*), an important centre of population in Early Christian times, with remains today of two basilicas (*a track leads back and down through fields to the site from 500m before the central junction in Zipári, and just before an Argos filling-station, right*). The most impressive part of the late 5th-century **basilica of Ághios Pávlos** is the square baptistery, which still stands to the original height of the pendentives (c. 7m) which once supported its cupola. The building had a marble floor with sunken font and decorated walls, but the growth of vegetation makes this and the patches of mosaic which adorned the floor hard to see. On the edge of Zipári is a second basilica, referred to as **Kapamás** from the name of the area where it is found (*in the centre of the village, a road south/left leads to the cemetery and turns sharp right past a football pitch: the ruins are in front and below*). The three-aisled plan of the church is clear, with a well-preserved 5th-century baptistery standing to the southeast. In the centre of the circular interior is a cruciform font, with two smaller ones in the two corners of the west side.

Two kilometres west of Zipári, the main island road splits into two carriageways for a short distance, so as to accommodate the ruined arches of a **Roman aqueduct** in the space in between.

The Asphendioú mountain villages

The verdant northern slopes below the peak of Díkaios command wide views of the plains below and out to sea beyond: for this reason they were a safe and practical refuge from piracy yet always remained in proximity to the island's main agricultural areas. The earliest and most important settlement here was Palaió Pylí (*map p. 372, C1*). Much later, in the 18th century, a chain of villages referred to collectively as **Asphendioú**— Ághios Dimítrios, Asómatos, Evangelístria, Ziá, Lagoúdi and Amanioú—grew up further east in more open space, sometimes around the nucleus of a pre-existing church or hermitage. With the sole exception of Ziá, whose picturesqueness has made it a prey to organised tours, these villages of old stone-built houses (many abandoned) are a peaceful and welcome contrast to the pressure of tourism on the coast. They may be reached either by the signed road due south from the centre of Zipári, or by continuing on the paved road west, beyond the Asclepeion.

By the middle of the 19th century, Palaió Pylí had been abandoned and the population had settled at **Pylí** (*map p. 372, C1*), 3km to the northwest, in an area that already had a long history of its own and possessed interesting monuments from antiquity and Byzantine times. Most unusual amongst these is the 3rd-century BC Tomb of Harmylos, uphill from the *plateía* in the southeast corner of the village (signed). This is a moderately rare example of semicircular ancient Greek vaulting, achieved with expertly shaped masonry, and here used to cover a hypogeum with 12 burial loculi. The Greeks very seldom used the arch in their architecture, but understood its design nonetheless. The Ionic monument which once marked this important tomb or Heroön has been dismantled and re-used in the tiny church of the Tímios Stavrós above.

THE WEST OF THE ISLAND

The landscape of the centre of the island is volcanic and flat, a raised plateau of pumice, riven by the gullies of seasonal torrents, forming a long neck or isthmus linking the mountains of the Képhalos peninsula in the west to the Horomedon massif in the east. This is, in effect, the sunken rim of the Kos Caldera, which erupted 160,000 years ago and stretches underwater to the active volcano of Nísyros to the south. It has created a landscape of long bays, splendid beaches and wide views.

Antimácheia

The central road of the island, which runs virtually at sea-level for the first 17km west of Kos Town, rises over 100m onto the volcanic plateau before reaching Antimácheia (*map p. 372, B2*). Before the village is a road to the south beside a military post, signed to 'Kastro', for **Antimácheia Castle** (*unrestricted opening*). This castle was designed to accommodate and protect a large number of people and livestock against a protracted siege. In 1457 it withstood a 20-day siege by Mehmet the Conqueror. Arriving by road from the northwest, it is hard to appreciate that the site of the castle is on the crown of a ridge which drops steeply to the coastal strip: with such natural protection to its south, it needed its strongest defences to the north. The original walls are of the 14th century, erected between 1337 and 1346, shortly after the Knights of St John first arrived on Kos, during the mastership of Hélion de Villeneuve. These have been significantly strengthened by a continuous talus reaching three-quarters of the way up their height as well as by a massive semicircular redoubt protecting the northwest entrance, added in 1494. Below the machicolations above the entrance are the arms of Grand Master Pierre d'Aubusson, who carried out both of these improvements and repaired the walls after the earthquake of 1493.

The interior is bleak, a sea of rubble remains, as of a densely inhabited town: streets, houses, churches, threshing floors and cisterns. The central building, ahead inside the gate, was used by the Turks after 1523 as a mosque: there are the vestiges of a minaret on its southwest corner. The other two buildings within the enceinte which are still integral and roofed are the two churches contemporary with the construction of the castle, built with the sparseness of line and form characteristic of their military founders.

The modern village of **Antimácheia** occupies the site of its ancient predecessor. In its main square is a typical village house, decked out as a small museum of local folklore, and opposite is a restored windmill, one of many that once caught the wind on this long central ridge.

Mastichári

Almost 2km west of the pleasant harbour of Mastichári (*map p. 372, B1*; with a seasonal ferry to Kálymnos) are the remains of the 5th-century **basilica of Ághios Ioánnis**, (*reached in 20mins by a shoreline promenade and path west from the harbour along the coast*). It has extensive and ornate floor mosaics, although most of them have now been covered with gravel for protection: those that are still visible are in the adjoining rooms to the south of the main basilica.

Kardámaina

Kardámaina (*map p. 372, C2*) has both Early Christian and ancient remains. The village and harbour, which provides a year-round ferry service across to Nísyros, have been engulfed by a disproportionate expansion of building and tourist infrastructure along the coast, leaving Kardámaina with little natural appeal beyond its sandy beaches and setting. In the process of this expansion evidence has come to light of no less than three Palaeochristian basilicas in the area: the floorplan of the most accessible of these, the 5th-century **Aghía Theótis**, can be seen 50m northwest of the square beside the port in a block bounded by Kanári and Pátmou streets. It was a three-aisled basilica with narthex and baptistery to its west. The other two lay southwest of Kardámaina, on the site of the **ancient city of Halasarna** (*reached by following the shore less than 1km along the road that crosses the watercourse just west of the centre*). The ancient settlement

Aerial view of the ruins of the 5th-century double basilica of Ághios Stéfanos.

grew up between the shore and the bluff behind (now occupied by a military base), which functioned as its acropolis. The site has only been partially uncovered and is pressed upon by modern construction, but it has already revealed some striking remains. There are several levels: most easily distinguishable by eye are the houses of the Early Christian era, which are built over the sharper, meticulous masonry of the Hellenistic buildings below. In the southwest corner is the lower part of a beautifully constructed 2nd-century BC marble public building (probably not a temple), whose base is constructed in an unusual red stone. North and east of this, a 3rd-century BC temple of Apollo Halasarnas is being unearthed. At the upper level of excavation are the remains of houses, a basilica and a cemetery of the Early Christian era. Traces of the late Hellenistic theatre have been identified on the far side of the acropolis hill; the ruined apse of yet another Early Christian basilica stands in the fields between the Apollon Hotel and the acropolis hill. Although systematic excavations by the University of Athens have only just begun to uncover the extent of the remains, it is clear that the whole area was densely inhabited in antiquity.

The Forest of Pláka and Ághios Stéfanos

The road west of Antimácheia skirts the airport; after 2.5km a paved road leads off right to Pláka. Unexpected and hidden, at the confluence of several eroded folds of the volcanic surface of this part of the island, is a dense and shady forest of pine trees. The continuation of the road through the woods rejoins the main road further west after 2km.

To the south of the road at this point are some of the island's longest and sandiest beaches—Polémi, Psilós Gremmós and Kamíla, different segments, with different characters, of one protracted south-facing shore—as crowded in summer as they are deserted in winter. The sands are backed by dunes and cedar bushes, and the steep escarpment directly behind has meant that they have escaped building. At their western extremity, the road drops from the plateau to the shore beside one of the island's most memorable sights, the sea-girt ruins of the **double basilica of Ághios Stéfanos** (*map p. 372, A3*), with the rocky islet of Kastrí in front (*access to the shore by the small paved road to the right of the entrance of the Club Mediterranée complex*). The site consists of two 5th-century basilicas, of almost equal size, contiguous and sharing a common wall, which have been squeezed transversely onto a rocky outcrop protruding into the sea. Both were probably destroyed and abandoned in the following century. There are many marble remains and areas of mosaic. Both basilicas have a narthex to the west; there is a single baptistery to the northeast, and some other rooms (perhaps a funerary chapel) to the southwest. The sea surrounds them on all sides except the north.

THE KEPHALOS PENINSULA

Almost a separate island, the southwestern peninsula of Kos has its own water sources, its own mountain peaks rising from the sea to 427m, and its own character and history. Evidence of the earliest habitation on the island comes from this promontory, and Strabo mentions a city in this area named Astypalaia which was, he says, the 'ancient (i.e. Archaic period) capital' of the island.

The modern village of **Képhalos** (*map p. 372, A2–A3*) straddles a windswept bluff overlooking the long procession of the island eastwards to the peak of Díkaios. There are also clear sightlines to Kálymnos and Nísyros, and for this reason the Knights of Rhodes built a castle here sometime before 1420 (the year in which it is first mentioned in sources). The ruins of its high walls visible today may represent only a part of a larger complex, the rest of which has been swept away since 1505, when the Knights abandoned the outpost in favour of their larger castles at Antimácheia and Kos. North of Képhalos, a left branch in the road leads into an area of stone-walled houses and cultivated enclosures fed by the springs at Miliés: the main road north continues down to the coast, where it drops steeply to the natural harbour of Limniónas.

Palatía

A kilometre south of Képhalos on the road which heads towards the mountains, and c. 50m to the east of the road, can be seen the profile of the remarkable little church of the **Panaghía Palatianí**, on an eminence with views of the Bay of Képhalos below. This roofless and collapsing church occupies the site of—and is constructed out of the remains of—a Hellenistic temple to Demeter, the podium of the pagan building still clearly visible beneath the southeast corner. Many ancient stones and fragments lie within and around, and the terracing and decorative elements of its sanctuary or neighbouring buildings can be seen below. The temple to Demeter did not stand alone here, but must have been on the edge of the ancient city of Astypalaia, whose overgrown remains, known locally as **Palatía**, lie in the pinewoods further to the west (*continue* *along the road a further 600–700m: 20m before a junction with a water fountain, where the road splits for Ághios Theológos, an unsigned metal gate on the east side of the road leads into the trees).* Just below the road is a small ancient theatre: the bases of the proscenium columns and a couple of rows of marble seats are visible. A few metres further to the west is a small Doric temple, distyle in antis, orientated due east and constructed in the large, clear masonry typical of the late Classical period. The city stretched up behind to the watershed above, which looks out also to the west: the platform of another temple (this time orientated north–south) and column fragments can be seen here, just above the level of the modern road.

The far southwest

Beyond the junction at Palatía, the right fork leads down (4.5km) through a beautiful and undisturbed landscape to the west coast at the church of **Ághios Theológos**. The (main) left branch continues south. A track off to the left after 1800m leads towards the summit of Mt Zíni: on its southern slopes is the **Cave of Asprípetra** (*a path indicated by red, then green marks on the rocks leaves from the middle of the split in the road 600m down the track from the previous junction: 25mins' walk*). The cave is small in proportion to its historic importance. First excavated by Italian archaeologists in 1922, it yielded finds and artefacts from the late Neolithic, Mycenaean and Geometric periods, as well as evidence that Pan and the nymphs were venerated here in Hellenistic and Roman times.

The continuation of the principal road leads into a wild and open landscape, to the monastery of **Ághios Ioánnis Thymianós** and on (a further 5km of track) to the remote church of **Ághios Mámas**. Much of the original 19th-century structure of Ághios Ioánnis has decayed and been replaced by more modest, recent buildings. A spring here feeds a monumental plane tree. There are extensive views to the south and west, and into the sun which sets over the distant island of Astypálaia.

PRACTICAL INFORMATION

GETTING AROUND

Kos has an international airport (23km from Kos Town) with twice-daily connections from Athens and charter arrivals from many destinations in northern Europe. There are also local flights three times weekly to Astypálaia, Leros and Rhodes.

There are daily services by catamaran (*Dodecanese Express*) and four weekly services by car ferry (F/B *Nisos Kalymnos*) plying the route between Rhodes, Kos, Kálymnos, Leros, Patmos (and Samos, ferry only). To Piraeus and Rhodes, Blue Star Ferries run four times weekly, and GA Ferries (who include Nísyros, Tilos and Symi en route) three times weekly. The faster Flying Dolphin services also link Kos with the smaller Dodecanese islands between Samos and Rhodes, and run daily in summer. From Kardámaina there is a daily connection with Nísyros throughout the year, weather permitting.

WHERE TO STAY

Kos suffers from touts who wait at the ferry port and try to lure visitors to their establishments. Some have even been known to lie about the name of their hotel in order to persuade people with a pre-existing booking to go with them. Decline their offers firmly but politely, and head into town to look for a place to stay if you haven't already booked one. Outside the tourist complexes, the most comfortable place is the **Kos Aktis Hotel** ▬ (*T: 22420 47200; www.kosaktis.gr*). Stylish and modern and with a good restaurant, it is conveniently placed near the Castle, and all its rooms have balconies overlooking the shore. The price is moderate to expensive. For the hospitality, friendliness and helpfulness of the owner, the family-run **Hotel Afendoulis** (*T: 22420 25321*), just in from the shore to the south of the centre on Evripídou, is a pleasant, basic, good-value guesthouse.

WHERE TO EAT

In the town centre, for inexpensive and genuine fare, with good fresh, local wine, the small **Taverna Kriti** (just below the steps northwest of the church of Aghía Paraskeví, on Ypsilántou (*map p. 374, B3*) is reliable and convivial. The nearby **Kafeneion Ainaos** in front of the Deftedar Mosque, opposite the Central Market building, makes a proper Greek coffee. **Otto e Mezzo** on Apéllou (*map p. 374, B4*) is good for Italian cuisine.

Many of the most interesting and enjoyable places to eat, however, are a little out of the centre; for a delightful rural, courtyard setting, there is the **Taverna Ambavris** (in Ambavrís, 1km along the road south (left) from just beyond the Casa Romana as you approach it from the centre of town).

At the crossroads in Platáni, along the road to the Asclepeion, **Ali's** is a Turkish restaurant with some good quasi-Turkish dishes, very popular with locals for Sunday lunch. **To Palaio Pyli**, 1km below Palaió Pylí, offers good fish, a hospitable welcome and a good sunset view. With a comparable sunset view, home-grown wine and home-made traditional dishes, the quiet and friendly **Taverna Panórama** ▬ (2.5km up the Asphendioú road from Zipári) in a family house and garden, is highly recommended. If the catch has been good, the best fish on the island is at the isolated **Taverna Thermá** ▬ on the beach above the hot springs at Embrós Thérmi, preceded by a hot plunge in the springs, if desired (NB: It is best not to take a car down to the shore, but to walk the last 10mins to the taverna and back; if at night, a torch helps on the return).

FURTHER READING

Susan Sherwin-White's *Ancient Kos*, a historical study from the Dorian settlement to the imperial period, is an authoritative and detailed study of the island in antiquity. Vassilis Colonas's *Italian Architecture in the Dodecanese Islands* (Olkos Press, Athens, 2002) is good on the buildings and architectural ideas of the Italian occupation. The Hippocratic corpus is selected and translated as *The Medical Works of Hippocrates* by Chadwick and Mann (Oxford, Blackwell). The very short *Walks in Western Kos* by Lance Chilton has well-described itineraries.

KALYMNOS

The bare mountains of Kálymnos frame shallow plains of dense, green fertility, while geological activity has fashioned the waters and mountains of the west of the island into one of the most beautiful and dramatic marine landscapes in the Aegean. By contrast the island's capital, Póthia, has a busy, metropolitan feel. Large for the overall size of the island, and built on the wealth that came from fishing and sponge-trading, it is a

KALYMNOS

pleasant and businesslike port with none of the artificiality that comes of a dependence on tourism. This is an island with a strong sense of identity: a perceptible accent of its own in spoken Greek and a proud perpetuation of Byzantine names and old-fashioned, more poetic, forms of address. There is a number of small museums celebrating this cultural tenacity as well as telling the remarkable story of the island's pre-eminence in the sponge trade.

SPONGES

Roman soldiers carried sponges to hold lightweight liquid refreshment, and Roman civilians used them as a kind of washable lavatory paper; in ancient Greece they were kept for bathing and washing; artists of the Renaissance experimented with them in fresco-painting; the Ottoman sultan's harem ordered them for cosmetic purposes; and potters throughout the ages have used them as an aid in finishing a pot. For millennia, the total world demand for sponges never exceeded the supply guaranteed by the trained bands of sponge-divers who worked in the warm waters of the southeast Aegean, principally on Symi, Chálki, Astypálaia and Kálymnos. Their island waters produced sponges of the very best quality.

The Industrial Revolution changed both the demand and the supply. A rising urban bourgeoisie developed a great appetite for sponges; at the same time, the development of a deep-water diving suit, the *skáfandro*, revolutionised the quantity and whole method of sponge collection. The sponge lost its luxury status and became an industrial commodity. This brought wealth to the islands, but the boom was short-lived: war broke out in 1914; the Italians moved to limit sponge-fishing during their occupation in the 1920s; the first cheap, synthetic sponges appeared around 1930; a bacterial disease hit Mediterranean sponge-beds in 1938; and a gradual awareness grew that the crippling or fatal effects of rapid decompression upon the diver as he rose to the surface in the *skáfandro* had for too long been ignored. The industry collapsed, and those whom it supported emigrated, mostly to Tarpon Springs, Florida, where they plied the only trade they knew, and set up what soon became the largest sponge farms and factories in the world.

HISTORY OF KALYMNOS

The name Kalymna, often taken to refer to the island's several good (*kali-*) harbours (*-limin*), only appears in the 4th century BC; until then, the island is referred to as Kalydna ('beautiful waters'). The island's many caves have yielded evidence for Late Neolithic (4th millennium BC) and Early Bronze Age settlement, with continued use into Mycenaean times. The first settlers in early historic times were from Epidaurus in the Argolid: the main centres of habitation, determined as always by the presence of fresh water, were in the same two valleys as are populated today. After the Battle of Salamis in 480 BC, where the Kalymniots fought for the Persian side (together with Kos) under the command of Queen Artemisia of Halicarnassus, the island turned to Athens and became a member of the Delian League. In the aftermath of the death of Alexander the Great, the southeast Aegean saw considerable turmoil, and it is to this period that many of the fortifications on the island date. In 205–204 BC Kálymnos became linked and subject to Kos by an arrangement of *homopoliteia* (a constitutional joining of cities), and its history thereafter follows that of its larger neighbour.

A flourishing Early Christian community on Kálymnos has left behind the remains of a large number of once richly decorated Palaeochristian churches. Many were destroyed by earthquake in AD 554, and 7th-century Arab invasions subsequently led to abandonment of the coastal settlements. After 1204 Venetian and Genoese overlords ruled the island until it came under the control of the Knights of Rhodes in 1313. They held and fortified Kálymnos until their defeat in Rhodes by Suleiman the Magnificent in 1522–23.

After 1523, the island maintained a considerable degree of autonomy under the Ottoman occupation. This provided the opportunity for the fishing and sponge trades to bring prosperity and, in the 19th-century, urban development also followed. A new capital at Póthia was created and the island's population more than quadrupled between 1821 (5,000) and 1912 (23,000). The Italian occupation after 1912 brought considerable economic and cultural restrictions, and the historically independent spirit of the Kalymniots rebelled against the imposition of the Italian language and the elimination of Greek in schools. Riots were suppressed in 1935, and many islanders were jailed or exiled. The island joined the Greek state together with the other Dodecanese islands in March 1948.

POTHIA & THE SOUTH

Póthia

Póthia is dominated by the huge cross and modern convent of Ághii Pándes, high up on the southwestern mountain (*see below*). The Ottoman and 19th-century commercial quarter of the town lies on the slopes below: a network of narrow streets bordered by balconied stone buildings with pedimented windows and sternly rusticated corners. Across, at the opposite side of the bay, are the old boatyards and chandlers' shops of the area of Lafássi; inland of there, and slightly to the west along the foot of the hills to the north, is the main residential area of stately 19th-century mansions, known as Evangelístria. In between these two poles stretches the waterfront, punctuated at its centre by the low, domed mass of the **Kálymnos Administration Building**, originally built between 1926–28 by Florestano di Fausto (main block) and then significantly enlarged in 1934 by Armando Bernabiti (the part to the east, with its more severe lines and squat cupolas). Contemporary with Bernabiti's addition and in similar style, further to the north, is the market building by Rodolfo Petracco.

The rest of the waterfront is a heterogeneous assemblage of buildings of different periods, including a few well-preserved Neoclassical façades with wrought-iron balconies. One interesting building towards the southern end of the front is the former *anagnostírion* (reading-room) '**Ai Musai**' of 1904: above the Ionic pilasters of its entrance are three bronze panels depicting scenes of Kalymniot life by the local artist Michalis Kokkinos: the interior (now an unpretentious *kafeneíon*) preserves many of the paintings and portrait busts of the original décor.

On the north side of the administration building is a square, bounded to the north by the **church of the Metamorphosis** (1861), with a gilded marble iconostasis by Giannoulis Chalepas (*see p. 98*). On the opposite side is the **Nautical Museum** (*open 10–2 except Mon; free*), with an interesting display on the island's trades and history, and above all on the life and tribulations of the sponge-fishers. Some of what is exhibited here can be complemented by a visit to a functioning sponge factory, of which there are a couple in Póthia (Kálymnos is the only Dodecanese island to preserve a small sponge-fishing fleet). One factory (signed) lies behind the corner at the west end of the waterfront; another is to the left of the road out to Vathýs, at the eastern side of the port.

One of Kálymnos' richest and most successful entrepreneurs, and the first to begin wholesale exportation of sponges, was Nikolaos Vouvalis (1841–1918): in the highly decorated and furnished **Vouvalis Mansion** in the Evanglístira area (*open 10–2 except Mon; free*) you can visit Vouvalis's study, with two small 4th-century BC marble heads on his desk; the dining-room and upstairs drawing-room. Adjacent is the **Archaeological Museum** (*open daily except Mon*), which houses finds from the Temple of Apollo (*see p. 404*) and the magnificent *Lady of Kalymnos*, a larger than life-size bronze statue of a woman wearing a chiton and himation. It was found by a fisherman in 1994.

South of Póthia

The main road to Vlychádia and the southwest of the island climbs up to the **monastery of Ághii Pándes**, often referred to as Ághios Savvás after the monk, later canonised, who spent the last 20 years of his life here. Ághios Savvás (1862–1948) has now become the patron saint of the island. Born in Thrace, he lived for a while on Mount Athos before spending ten years as a hermit in the Jordanian desert. He returned to Greece, later to become a priest on Aegina. He came to Kálymnos in 1927 and lived at Ághii Pándes as a spiritual teacher and ascetic until his death in 1948. The vast monastery—almost an independent city—has expanded far beyond the ascetic aspirations of Savvás.

In the village of **Vothíni**, to the right of the main road and shortly beyond the turning for Ághii Pándes, is a folklore museum and traditional Kalymniot house (*open daily 9–3*). The display is informative and well-presented on sponge-fishing, as well as on marriage and domestic life. Samples of traditional Kalymniot wine (similar to port) are offered. Continuing 2.5km further south, on the shorefront at **Vlychádia**, is another museum, the Valsamidis Museum of the Sea and of Sponge-diving (*open daily 9–6*), created with considerable energy by the local diving master.

Two kilometres southwest of Vothíni is the **Cave of Kephála** (*open daily June–Sept 10–6*), reached by a newly-made track heading west from the monastery of Aghía Aikateríni, just to the west of the village. This is the most accessible of the many caves on the island: the almost 1000 square metres of six interconnected chambers are entered by a narrow passageway and provide an impressive display of stalactites and stalagmites. It is sometimes referred to as the Cave of Zeus: this is more a tribute to its size than a reflection of any cult. Caïques from Póthia also offer a service to the shore below, from which it is a 200-m walk: these trips also allow you to stop on the **islet of Nerá** to see the attractive monastery of the Tímios Stavrós.

THE VALLEY OF VATHYS

The best way to arrive at the Vathýs valley, north of Póthia, is either by boat into its dramatic, fjord-like inlet, or by taking the old flagstone *kalderími*, rebuilt during the Italian occupation, over the hills northeast of Póthia (*it leaves from beside the church of Aghía Triáda, not far above the Vouvalis Mansion*): it is a shadeless but panoramic 2-hr walk that passes in the first 20mins below the vestigial remains of the acropolis (to the east) of the ancient settlement of Pothaia. To explore the Vathýs valley fully, however, it is best to drive: there is a lot to see, and doing it all on foot would take considerable time. As you approach by car, the asphalt road east of Póthia passes along the scarred and barren south coast of the island: there are fine views to Turkey as it turns north; then all of a sudden the valley of Vathýs comes into view, carpeted with intense green vegetation.

Rína

Rína, a corruption of Aghía Eiríni, is a tiny harbour crowded with small fishing boats, perfectly out of sight of the open sea and protected by its long, narrow inlet. In this safe haven, a large Early Christian community flourished from the 4th–7th centuries and populated the north-facing slope to the south of the harbour. Immediately above the water on the south side is the Early Christian **church of the Anástasis**, its original size deducible from the position of the retaining wall to the south. Across the harbour to the north, reached by steps behind the busy boatyard, is **Aghía Eiríni**, where a tiny chapel and a rose garden have been built on the north side of the site of a large, apsidal basilica of the 5th century, with another ruined basilica, of unknown dedication, beyond to the east. A few pieces of rectangular masonry, cut and dressed in typical Hellenistic fashion, suggest the pre-existence here of what was perhaps a fort or watchtower.

At this point you are above and a little to the west of the **Cave of Daskaleió** at the north side of the harbour entrance. This can only be visited by boat, either from Rína or from Póthia. It is the island's largest cave, whose importance lies in the finds attesting Late Neolithic, Minoan and Mycenaean occupation. Immediately inside the cave is a chamber about 25m long, from which another, with stalagmites and stalactites and a cavity full of brackish water, opens out (right) at a lower level.

The central valley

Inland of Rína is a network of lanes between high, whitewashed walls, behind which rise stately stone houses and gardens bursting with pomegranate, citrus trees, olives and vines, punctuated with rose-bushes and cypress. Eight hundred metres from the harbour-front, to the right of the road on the lower slopes of the hill, just above the line of cultivation, are the remains of a remarkable structure known as **Phylakés**. It is constructed of massive rectangular blocks of the local sedimentary stone, creating a chambered structure about 10m by 6m. There is evidence of cutting in the bedrock in the area behind and to the east side, where more huge blocks are visible. The position is good for surveying the surrounding cultivations, and the walls must represent what remains of a heavily fortified farmstead of the late Classical or Hellenistic period. From here, it is possible to cross the fields to the west (via the church of Ághios Panteléimon) to the ruins of the fine, 5th-century **Palaiopanaghiá** (an easier route to it lies along the road and to the right at the junction). There are substantial remains here, both of the buildings' lower walls (occasionally plastered and painted) and of the floor mosaics. The main basilica is a spacious building with three long aisles, once delineated by slender columns. To the north is a large baptistery with a cruciform, marble-clad font sunk into the floor: the base of a ciborium can be seen on its east side. The step in the passage between the baptistery and the north aisle of the main basilica is made of a piece of carved marble templon screen from an earlier building, and suggests that this room was added or rebuilt at a later date.

Half a kilometre to the west is the open square of the village of **Plátanos**, with a café, plane trees and an old water-fountain. A short distance to its northwest is the valley's richest site, the ancient **fortress of Empóla**, which comes into view on top of a low ridge, accessible by a track to the right of the road. The rise is crowned by a long stretch of 4th-century BC walls in isodomic masonry: the southern stretch, which is encountered first, may have been added in a later enlargement to the principal area to the north, which includes the sizeable Hellenistic tower standing a little to the west of the Early Christian church. Tracing the lines of the walls in the surrounding fields gives a sense of the imposing size of the original structure. The 6th-century AD basilica within it, which incorporates both the ancient walls at its east end, and the ancient tower in its narthex to the west, is commensurately grand, endowed with clearly-patterned mosaic floors. The ancient spolia are of particular interest and suggest that there may have been more here in antiquity than just a fortified building (perhaps a temple and/or necropolis). The south aisle of the basilica is today occupied by the 14th-century church of the Taxiárchis Michaïl, whose simple interior preserves beautiful wall-paintings. Some of them (the Pantocrator and Evangelists in the apse) are contemporary with the foundation; others (the fine *Entry into Jerusalem*, *Nativity* and saints) probably date from 200 years later.

The northern valley

A road leads from the western end of Plátanos to Metóchi; from here, a new track to the northeast leads up the mountainside to the fortified 18th-century monastery of the **Panaghía Kyrá Psilí** (*when the track reaches the watershed at the chapel of the Stavrós, a signed footpath to the right leads on up to the church*). The dramatically-sited monastery was a votive gift made by a native of the island who converted to Islam and served as a high official in the Ottoman administration; when a fleet of ships under his management was miraculously rescued from a storm by the intervention of the Virgin, he dedicated and built this monastery on what was probably the site of an earlier hermitage (and of even earlier pagan cult, inside the grottoes where the chapels within the walls now stand). Its hidden and fortified location served as a refuge for the inhabitants of the valley in times of danger.

From Stavrós the pathway to the northeast leads (*45mins*) down to the island's north shore at the wild and solitary **inlet of Pezónda**. Along the ridge to the west of Stavrós, at a point where it projects south over the valley in a natural acropolis, is a site known as **Kastéllas**: the settlement here, marked by large blocks of collapsed masonry, seems to have been continuously used through the Geometric, Archaic and Classical periods. Jewellery, bronze arrow-heads, coins and glass vessels have recently been found here.

CHORIO & THE NORTH OF THE ISLAND

Between 80–90 percent of the island's population lives in the sloping valley between the port of Póthia and Pánormos above the west coast. What were once three or four separate communities have now become an almost continuous band of habitation. The valley is hemmed in by bare limestone slopes to either side, both of which were watched by two sizeable castles.

The castle of Chrysocheriá

To the south of the valley stands the castle of Chrysocheriá (*always open; reached by a track to the right of the road to Vlychádia as it leaves the southwest corner of Póthia*). This was originally a 12th-century Byzantine fortress, taken over by the Knights of Rhodes in the early 1400s and strengthened by them. The prominent escutcheons are of Grand Master Antonio Fluviá (1421–37) and Fantino Querini, Venetian admiral and governor of Kos in the 1440s. The small space enclosed within the walls points to this having always been more of a look-out and signalling station than a refuge for the population during attack: its position splendidly commands the whole of the centre of the island and the port. The 15th-century church of the Metamorphosis (the lower and older of the two churches within the enceinte) is decorated with 16th-century wall-paintings, now in poor condition. Beside its door, a marble block with a clear Hellenistic inscription has been immured.

Chorió

Chorió or Chóra was the island's capital until the mid-19th century, founded on a site safely away from the coast and with good natural fortifications, during the period of instability and piracy that followed from the first Arab incursions of the 8th century. Today it is an unpretentious town, free of tourist paraphernalia. Its narrow streets radiate out from the large, central church of the Panaghía Charitoméni ('the Gentle Virgin') of 1805.

Streets lead eastwards from the church and uphill to the edge of the habitation, from where a steep and exposed climb on a path across the rocks brings you to the castle,

Péra Kástro (*permanently open*), completely encircled by a fine curtain of 15th-century walls with wide crenellations, rising directly from the bare rock. Once again, the Knights of Rhodes will have strengthened pre-existing fortifications, probably in the 15th century—although the presence of the arms of Grand Master del Carretto (1513–21), exhibited prominently on the east walls, suggests that this work may have continued into the next century. The walls rarely exceed a metre in thickness, and the gate here is not built with particular attention to indestructibility: the castle was designed first and foremost as a functioning walled city rather than as a last refuge against siege. Inside and near the entrance are ancient spolia and fragments of marble entablature on the ground, with a massive millstone nearby; other ancient pieces (fluted columns and capitals, etc) are incorporated into the nine small churches on the site, which constitute its greatest interest. To the east side the double church of the Dormition, attached to the church of Ághios Nikólaos, represents an unusual grouping of forms, including a short narthex on the south side. To the west, the churches of the Tímios Stavrós, of Aghía Paraskeví, and of the Metamorphosis, have wall-paintings of the 16th century and incorporate ancient and Early Christian spolia in their fabric. At the top of the enclosure is the greatest concentration of stone houses that have preserved their walls to a reasonable height, mostly built over deep water cisterns underneath. The few larger public buildings are all of a functional, four-square, military design.

At the western extremity of Chorió, on the main road to Pánormos, is the **town cemetery**, its entrance dominated by the 7-m high *Christ Crucified* by the Kalymniot sculptor Michalis Kokkinos.

THE SANCTUARY OF APOLLO

Less than 1km from Chorió along the main road to Pánormos is the site of the island's most important centre of cult in antiquity, the **Sanctuary of Apollo Dalios**, which straddles the site now bisected by the road.

In the Early Christian period, two basilicas were built over the sanctuary, one of which, known as the basilica of **Christ of Jerusalem** (south of the road; *see overleaf*), incorporates a mass of important ancient inscriptions and architectural elements. These were observed by Charles Newton as early as 1854–55; he removed a number of them to the British Museum in London. The site was more systematically uncovered by the Italians in 1937, and ongoing excavations by the Greek archaeological authorities are bringing to light new material each year. Two colossal cult statues of Asclepius and Hygieia, divinities of healing and health, have recently been found.

Tombs from Hellenistic and Roman times, often with precious or informative grave goods, have been found widely in the area of this valley, while on the slopes of the hill opposite the Sanctuary of Apollo to the north, on a rise between two ravines, excavations are revealing the ancient Hellenistic settlement of **Damos** (north of the road), where residential insulae and stepped streets are currently being uncovered.

View of Chorió.

The Temple of Apollo

The base of the temple is visible to the south of the standing apse of the basilica of Christ of Jerusalem, below the line of the subsidiary road. It was probably a 4th-century BC building, even though the cult of Apollo here goes back to the 7th century BC and carried on into Roman times. It would have been a small, tetrastyle Ionic temple; parts of an entablature and fluted columns near the ruined apse almost certainly belonged to it, as did the fragments of a fine cornice with deep dentils on the rear exterior of the apse. The temple was surrounded by a dense grove of sacred bay trees, and there was a small theatre, where competitions of song and music were held. The sanctuary would have been thronged with votive sculptures, especially kouroi, sculptures of young men, mostly nude, as if in the likeness of Apollo himself.

The basilica of Christ of Jerusalem

The huge central apse of the basilica of Christ of Jerusalem is one of the most evocative Early Christian remains in the Greek islands. The seats of the synthronon in the apse are adapted from those of the ancient theatre, and the walls and the floor are composed of inscribed stelae and pieces of entablature, some mounted sideways, some upside down, some religious (e.g. the beautiful inscription mentioning the dedication to Apollo Dalios on the north side), some political (e.g. the public decrees, citizen lists, arbitration texts and dedications of different periods, to the south side), some purely decorative (e.g. the running, tendrilled flower motif on the projections to both sides), all jumbled together with imperious indifference. The church's long nave was flanked by fluted columns separating the space of the aisles to north and south, and roofed with wooden beams and terracotta tiles. Legend holds that the church's foundation goes back to the visit of the emperor Arcadius (395–408) on his way back to Byzantium from Jerusalem: the building's grandeur would certainly suggest a founder of such importance.

A little way (50m) to the east of the apse, across an area of chicken-coops and heaped ancient fragments, are excavations which are revealing the mosaic floors and walls of another late Roman or Palaeochristian building, referred to as both the Basilica of the Evangelístria and Aghía Sophía. The exact form of the building remains uncertain until more of it is excavated: the presence of an unusual semicircular 'apse' in the middle of the south wall suggests that it had no ordinary basilica form.

MYRTIES & THE ISLAND OF TELENDOS

Linária and **Kantoúni**, two contiguous villages with attractive houses and gardens, overlook an intimate west-facing bay with sandy beaches. **Pánormos**, which also has an attractive beach (Platýs Gialós), is a scattered community of houses and gardens on the lower, west-facing slopes of Mt Profítis Ilías, which rises to the island's highest peak (678m) behind. Before the main road begins to descend steeply to the coast at Myrtiés, with striking views across to Télendos, a sign indicates a left turn to the Early Christian basilica of Ághios Ioánnis at **Melitsáchas**: it possibly occupies what was the panoramic site of a temple of Poseidon, and has fine mosaics. From here, the road descends steeply to **Myrtiés**, the harbour both for the regular shuttle-boats to Télendos (*see below*) and for the daily ferry, which sails through the dramatic bay of Arginónda and round the northern point of the island to Xirókambos on Leros.

The coastal strip between Myrtiés and Masoúri and a little beyond is dedicated to seasonal tourism. Seawards, it is dominated by the imposing profile of Télendos across the water; landwards, it is backed by dramatic mountains which, to the north of Masoúri, drop in vertical rockfaces below their summits and are perforated with caves and overhangs. These are a rock-climber's paradise—a sport for which Kálymnos is becoming increasingly well-known.

The deep **bay of Arginónda** constitutes another half-amphitheatre of mountainous rockfaces with many impressive caves, at the head of which, in a rare oasis of green, is the village of Arginónda, at the heart of the island's quietest and least inhabited area. From here, tracks lead southeast over the pass to Metóchi and into the Valley of Vathýs (*see p. 399*).

The island of Télendos

Boats from Myrtiés cross to Télendos every 30mins (*15-min crossing*), and arrive at a peaceful waterfront of cafés, tavernas and supply-shops, undisturbed by motor traffic. It is possible to stay on the island: the walking, swimming and bird-watching are all good, in addition to the quantity of Early Christian remains. Popular tradition holds that Télendos was joined to Kálymnos until an earthquake in AD 554 caused the low land to its east to subside, leaving Télendos a separated island. It is true that the foundations of small buildings may be seen underwater near the harbour, as well as at points along the eastern shore, but gradual land subsidence is the more likely explanation.

The path to the right of the landing-quay turns toward the north and leads to the massive Early Christian **basilica of Ághios Vasíleios**. At 40m long by 25m wide and still standing to a height of nearly 8m in places, this is the largest and best preserved Early Christian structure on the two islands. The large, finely-cut strengthening blocks in the corners appear to have been taken from an earlier pagan construction: other marble blocks, some carved with Byzantine crosses, lie around or have been incorporated as architraves, etc. Between the church and the shore are the remains of a bath-house chamber of the same date, which also incorporates ancient spolia. The surrounding area is covered with the remains of houses and other buildings of the Palaeochristian period.

From here, the path continues along the shore and then climbs over rocks. At the base of a small promontory separating the Bay of Pótha from the next cove to the north (referred to as 'Paradise Bay' by its largely nudist clientèle) are the vestigial remains of another Early Christian church, with foundations partly submerged in the sea. It is from here that a rough and stony path (marked initially by faded, white and blue paint-spots) leads steeply from the shore round to the north side of the island and climbs to the **deserted settlement of Ághios Konstantínos** (*1hr each way*). Spread over a ledge at an altitude of 170m, with a dominating escarpment above rising to a summit of 458m and with sweeping views of the mountains and Bay of Arginónda, the setting here takes its place amongst the most dramatic Byzantine sites in the islands. With the beginning of hostile incursions into the southeast Aegean in the late 7th century AD, the populace sought protection in this inaccessible refuge; the settlement appears to have been abandoned in the 10th century. It was protected on the north side by walls, with a protruding rampart below what must have been a watchtower in the centre. Plastered cisterns, which are all around, formed the foundations of the houses. On a rock outcrop at the eastern extremity is the **church of Ághii Konstantínos and Eléni**, built inside the surviving apse of its predecessor of the 7th century and still preserving patches of the original painting on its ceiling.

THE NORTH OF THE ISLAND

The finest archaeological remains in the far north of Kálymnos are the ruins of the Hellenistic **fortress of Kastrí**, a fortified cleft in the mountainside which commands some of the most stunning views in the area. The site is well camouflaged—almost invisible in fact; it nestles about halfway below the summit of the rockface to the north of the last sharp bend in the road before the settlement of Emboreió begins (*from the house and goat-pens just above the road, a path, vestigially marked with red spots, leads directly up the mountain, first to the right of the torrent-course and then to the left, until the roughly rectangular hewn blocks of the construction come into view below the rockface. The ascent is steep, rocky and takes the full sun*). The site consists of a curtain wall in polygonal masonry linking two small rectangular towers on rocky spurs to either side and sealing off a natural cleft in the rock. Below are rock-cut steps and a doorway hewn through the rock, with the fixtures for the gate cut into its surface. This leads steeply up to the east side and onto a rock ledge, where there is a plastered cistern, again carved from the living rock. The view is magnificent.

Kastrí would have protected and served as an acropolis for the settlement of **Emboreió**, a sleepy, end-of-the-road kind of place today, but once perhaps much more important—certainly if its name, which means 'trading station' is anything to go by. Systematic excavation has not been undertaken, but there are ancient blocks incorporated into walls of buildings and fields in this area, and the ground is often richly scattered with potsherds. The church of Ághios Geórgios is built on the ruins of an Early Christian predecessor, and a few remains of late Roman thermae can be seen by the shore at the east end of the bay. Prominently visible on the hillside above and to the east of Emboreió is a large stone-built barn-like construction, probably dating from the 6th century AD.

PSERIMOS

Psérimos (*map p. 252*) is one of the most tranquil corners of the Dodecanese, with a beautiful coastline and profile and an undisturbed landscape of rocks and herbs and goats, often so silent that every movement of the breeze can be heard. Enjoyment of these qualities is compromised by the fact that every day throughout the summer season, tour boats arrive from Kos. While the tavernas and the main beach get thronged with trippers, however, the rest of the island offers untouched and unvisited bays of great beauty and some historical interest.

Avláki

The tiny settlement of Psérimos, also referred to as Avláki, at the head of a narrow inlet behind a superb beach of gently sloping fine sand, occupies the same area as its ancient predecessor. The most visible point of interest is the 19th-century church of the Panaghía, the interior of which is unexceptional but for its carved, wooden throne and some fine 19th-century icons. The courtyard contains a selection of remarkable ancient and Early Christian spolia, suggesting that the site has a long history. Psérimos has never been thoroughly explored archaeologically, but the traces of four Early Christian churches have been identified.

Uphill to the southeast, at a distance of about 400m from the port, is the chapel of the Taxiárches, overlooking the interior of the island from its solitary position. The church is modern, but built on an Early Christian site. Ten metres northeast of the apse of the chapel, inside a high-walled, open goat-pen, is a (ruined) barrel-vaulted Early Christian tomb. The remains of another are used as a goat byre closer to the chapel's southeast corner: the building is covered over for the animals but, inside it, in addition to the tomb, it is possible to make out the curve of the apse of the 5th-century church.

PRACTICAL INFORMATION

GETTING AROUND

There are flights to Kálymnos from Athens several times a week, often with a stop at Astypálaia. There are daily services by catamaran (*Dodecanese Express*) and four times weekly by car ferry (F/B *Nisos Kálymnos*), plying the route between Kos, Leros, Patmos (and Samos, ferry only). To Piraeus and Rhodes there are daily boats operated by GA Ferries, also making twice-weekly stops at Tilos, Nísyros and Symi on the way to Rhodes. The faster Flying Dolphin services link Kálymnos (Póthia) with the smaller Dodecanese islands between Samos and Rhodes, and run daily in summer. There are also daily services in summer (weather permitting; only intermittently out of season) between Myrtiés and Xirókambos on Leros.

The only regular service to Psérimos is from Kálymnos, from which the *Pegasus* leaves in the morning and returns in the afternoon every day in summer, more intermittently in winter. From Kos there are round-trip tour boats which always include other stops, as well as food and entertainment, in the price. In order to stay on Psérimos for any time, you will need to negotiate a price with separate boats, one to drop, the other to pick up.

WHERE TO STAY

Kálymnos

For character and tranquillity, **Villa Theme-**

lina ▆ is easily the most congenial place to stay in Póthia (*T: 22430 22682 or 23920*). It is a Belle-Epoque family mansion with high-ceilinged rooms (and some newer studio rooms around the swimming pool) in a quiet area close to the museum. The **Hotel Panorama** (*T: 22430 23138 or 22917*) has more straightforward facilities, and a good view of the town. For beachside accommodation in Kantoúni Bay, **Koletti Studios** are in a delightful setting (*T: 22430 47922, or, out of season, 210 692 8909*); and the tiny, shoreside guesthouse **On the Rocks**, facing Kálymnos from on the islet of Télendos (*T: 22430 48260 or 48261*) is perfect for a peaceful retreat.

Psérimos

At the time of writing there were two places to stay: the **Hotel Tripolitis** (*T: 22430 23196*), and **Kalliston Studios** (*T: 22430 24561*), both offering basic accommodation. Booking advisable in high season.

WHERE TO EAT

Kálymnos

In Póthia the **Taverna Pandelis**, in a tiny square directly behind the Olympic Hotel on the waterfront, does not have a wide choice, but what is offered is good. The **Ouzeri Sphoungaras**, in an alley behind the

Emboriki Bank (where Patr. Maxímou meets the promenade) has excellent *mezédes* and is crowded with locals at lunchtime.

Around the island, both **Popy's** at Vathýs and **Akti** in Emboreió are good for fresh fish.

Psérimos

There is not a lot to choose from, but Katerina Xyloura's **Kalikardia** taverna at the east end of the beach has fresh fish, simple dishes and the most friendly service.

BOOKS & MUSIC

Bitter Sea: The real story of Greek Sponge Diving, by Faith Warn (2000); and *The Bellstone: Greek Sponge Divers of the Aegean*, by Michael Kalafatas (2003). Pandelis Ghinis, himself the captain on a sponge-fishing boat, made a famous recording in the 1960s of *Dirlada*, a bawdy sponge divers' song. You can hear it on http://www.all-about.gr/kalymnos-island-Greece/diving/Diving-Heritage/Superstructure/Music-and-Dances/Dirlada-by-PANDELIS-GHINIS.asp.

WALKING & CLIMBING

Information from the Municipal Athletics Organisation's Climbing Information Desk (*T: 22430 59445*) in Masoúri.

LEROS

In spite of a dark reputation in recent history (*see below*), Leros has peace, beauty and a wide variety of interest for its modest size, including the unique 1930s Rationalist planned town of Lakkí, the dramatic castle overlooking virtually the whole island, early rural churches and some interesting museums.

HISTORY OF LEROS

Leros has yielded evidence of prehistoric settlement and trade from the Late Neolithic (4th millennium BC) but not much is known of its Bronze Age. Leros was influenced and settled by people from Miletus, one of the greatest of the Ionian cities in the 6th century BC, and in early historic times it was the southernmost island to be Ionian, whereas Kálymnos, which almost touches it, was Dorian. Athenian tribute lists of 454–453 BC refer to Milesians 'from Leros'. By the 4th century BC, Leros appears as a deme of Miletus. The 6th-century BC philosopher Demodicus, and the Hellenistic mythographer Pherecydes, were both from Leros. The main settlement on the island in antiquity, continuously inhabited from Geometric through to Early Christian times, was in Alínda Bay; the principal religious centre was the Sanctuary of Artemis in Parthéni Bay. Early Christian basilicas were built across the island. A bishop of Leros is first mentioned as present at the Fifth Ecumenical Council of Constantinople in AD 553.

In 1088, against opposition from the islanders, parts of Leros were given by the Byzantine emperor Alexius I Comnenus to Hosios Chistodoulos as revenue for the Monastery of St John on Patmos. Together with Rhodes and Kos, Leros was acquired by the Knights of St John in 1306. In 1319 their garrison was killed by the islanders, who wished to return to the protection of Byzantium, but the Knights forcibly retook it the same year. In 1522 it became a Turkish possession. It was taken briefly by the Venetian admiral Leonardo Foscolo in 1648. Leros generally enjoyed a measure of independence under Ottoman rule; it participated actively in the War of Independence in 1821; in 1830 it briefly had a local Greek governor, but returned to Ottoman rule the same year. In the mid-19th century, emigrants from Leros formed an influential community of intellectuals and businessmen in Egypt, becoming important benefactors of the island.

During the Italian occupation of the Dodecanese (*see p. 255*) Leros was transformed by the avant-garde building projects of the new Porto Lago (Lakkí) area. Fierce fighting in the Second World War culminated in the Battle of Leros in November 1943, when the island was taken by German forces. It joined the Greek state in 1948, together with all the Dodecanese islands. The Italian military buildings were used for confining political prisoners during the period of the Colonels' junta (1967–74), and thereafter as a mental institution. A European Union inquest (1989–95) into maltreatment of patients led to substantial improvements.

LAKKI & THE SOUTH OF THE ISLAND

Set on a large and beautiful natural harbour, today's Órmos Lakkíou (Lakkí Bay), named Porto Lago by the Italians, Lakkí is a new town built between 1934 and 1938, and is unlike anything else in Greece. Taking advantage of the protected harbour, the Italians founded a naval and seaplane station (1923) at Lépida on the south shore of the bay, which quickly became the largest Italian military base in the East Mediterranean. The authorities expropriated land and created the new town of 'Porto Lago', today's Lakkí, in 1934, designed to meet the civilian needs of a military community of about 7,500 people. Its designers were Rodolfo Petracco and Armando Bernabiti, proponents of the Rationalist architectural style favoured by Italian fascism (*see pp. 255–56*). Lakkí constitutes the most coherent and complete example of such planning

and architecture in the Eastern Mediterranean: it is a town of broad streets and open squares, completely unlike most other Greek island towns.

Exploring Lakkí

The street plan is not a regimented grid pattern but a rounded and decentralised design, orientated on the curve of the shoreline and reflected by the varied forms of the buildings. Along and behind the promenade (west to east) are the circular tower of the former **Town Hall**, the long horizontal **Hotel Roma** (now in ruins) and the semicircular projecting foyer of the **Theatre** (all by Bernabiti); and the sharp vertical of the **Clock Tower** beside the low, half-domed circle-in-a-square of the **Food Market** with its airy internal peristyle (both by Petracco). Further east is the curving **Commercial Building** with its unusual decorated façade, and finally the arcaded **Elementary School** by the shore. This is Petracco's design and is the most interesting of the whole complex. The administrative buildings framing the town are more rectilinear; between them are warehouses, barracks, hospital buildings, the **Church of St Francis** (now Ághios Nikólaos) by Bernabiti, and many idiosyncratic private houses built for the non-commissioned officers.

A number of monuments and war memorials punctuate the townscape: those on the waterfront commemorate a defining moment in the Dodecanese campaign of 1943: the sinking by the German Air Force of the Greek destroyer *Vasilissa Olga*, and (on the road south to Lépida) of the British destroyer HMS *Intrepid*, both on 26th September 1943.

WEST OF LAKKI

The road climbing over the rise by the ferry port follows the north shore to **Merikiá** (1.5km from Lakkí), where a cove is backed with naval buildings from the Italian occupation. The valley of hills inland from here is perforated with war-time tunnels and ammunition deposits: one houses a small **war museum** (*generally open daily in summer, 10.30–1.30; T: 22470 22109*), its entrance marked by a fighter jet, with memorabilia relating to the Battle of Leros. Beyond, on the hill to the left, 200m inland, is a ruined late medieval church with a chapel of Ághios Zacharías in the domed crossing. As so often on Leros, the hanging bell is a converted war relic. In a valley still further beyond, after the asphalt ends, is the double church of Ághios Spyridón and Aghía Paraskeví, 14th century with a 1970s porch. The north chapel has paintings of different periods

From beside the hospital in Lakkí, a road signed Fytório and Kamaráki leads inland, into rolling terrain, attractive for walking. Conspicuous on a knoll at the centre of the upland hills is the whitewashed **chapel of Profítis Ilías**, incorporating ancient spolia and with patches of mosaic outside. The track south from here leads to the modern gorge-side **monastery of the Holy Angels** (*open 4.30–7.30*). Behind and above it is the low-domed 14th-century **church of Ághios Pétros**, built into an Early Christian basilica (with views across the water to Patmos).

Drymónas and Kokáli

The road north from Lakkí (signed for Goúrna Bay and the airport) climbs amongst gardens and Neoclassical houses predating the Italian occupation. After less than 1km, on a bend in the road opposite a balconied mansion, is the fine and unusual church of **Ághios Ioánnis Theológos**. The central domed space is flanked by two transverse vaulted aisles, the eastern of which has an apse decorated on the exterior with patterned brickwork. This is the original core of an 11th-century church. In the interior (*under restoration at the time of writing*) it can be seen how that basic church was modified by the Knights of Rhodes in the 14th century to accommodate the Latin liturgy and a different architectural taste by the addition of the side-aisles defining a Western-style nave. Patches of 13th-century painting on the walls of the original structure survive in places. One shows St Mary of Egypt receiving Communion.

Just before the road reaches Goúrna Bay (with a good sandy beach) is the tiny 14th-century church of the **Panaghía Gourlamáta**, hidden from sight amongst olive trees in a fold in the hill (*the church is difficult to locate and is best reached from the opposite direction: i.e. climbing back out of Goúrna Bay and Drymónas towards Lakkí. About 60m after the first sharp bend, a scarcely visible sign points right (west) to the church, through a gap between some houses*). It preserves some original wall-paintings, including a compelling Deësis.

Before the road continues along Goúrna Bay to Kokáli, a sharp left turn leads to **Drymónas** village. At the western end of the road along the waterfront is the tiny 14th-century church of Ághios Geórgios. **Kokáli** is 1km further on. From the western end of the waterfront, a 100-m causeway leads out to the picturesque islet and church of Ághios Isídoros. Under the water, below the southeast corner of the chapel, can be seen the blocks and rectangular plan of the foundations of an ancient building.

Lakkí to Xirókambos

The naval base at **Lépida**, in the southeast corner of Lakkí Bay, was begun by the British and developed after 1923 by the Italians, who established the G. Rosetti Air Base, erecting two large buildings, the long officers' quarters and the more classical administration building to its west. The complex is now part of the Leros National Sanatorium (a mental illness institution) and is out of bounds to visitors.

From the road south of Lépida, the site of **Palaiókastro** is visible on the left, crowning the low ridge between the bays of Lakkí and Xirókambos; it is reached by a steep track from the main road. Its whitewashed church of the Panaghía and enclosure wall are recent, but immediately below and east of the chapel are well-preserved stretches of 4th-century BC wall in isodomic masonry. The extent of it suggests a small fortress, with controlling views of the south coast and good sight-lines to the ancient acropolis above Aghía Marína. There are traces of Early Christian mosaic by the door of the chapel.

The quiet fishing harbour of **Xirókambos** has magnificent views of Kálymnos. From here, it is possible to make the crossing through a beautiful seascape to Myrtiés on Kálymnos by early-morning caïque, returning the same afternoon. Half a kilometre along the east of the inlet, a steep path leads to the shore, where the minuscule chapel of the **Panaghía Kavourádaina** (Virgin 'of the Crab-fisher') marks the spot where an icon was reputedly found by a crab-gatherer. Inside the chapel is a charming recent icon of the Virgin in an aureole in the form of a crab.

AGHIA MARINA & THE NORTH OF THE ISLAND

Aghía Marína, 5.5km due north of Lakkí, is officially the island's second port. It is more varied than Lakkí, and some would say more attractive. It is located below the site of the ancient acropolis, now crowned by the medieval castle (*see below*). Its attractive waterfront stretches between the Italian Customs House and Police Building (both 1934–35) and a windmill at the bay's far western extremity. Today the eastern promontory of Bourtzi is marked by the ruins of a medieval coastal fortress. To the north, its houses line the bay of Alínda (good sandy beach), merging first into Krithóni and then Alínda itself. The heart of the island, its main churches, finest houses, museums and shops, are found in this attractive and varied complex of settlements, together with Plátanos, the administrative capital.

Pandéli and the castle

The attractive south-facing harbour of Pandéli and its mass of white houses are dominated from on high by Pandéli Castle (*open daily 8–1; also 3–7 on Wed, Sat and Sun*). Substantially repaired after damage during the Second World War, it is the principal medieval monument on the island, occupying its most panoramic site, once the acropolis of the ancient settlement of Leros. Some ancient spolia have been incorporated into the fortifications. It is a massive complex consisting of three successive enclosures: the inner two were originally Byzantine (10th–11th centuries), but were substantially reinforced by the Knights of St John in the early 14th century, who also constructed the third, much larger, outer enclosure at this northernmost stronghold of their territory. In the 15th century the population retired within the castle walls at night for protection.

Entrance is by a small gate protected by the massive, projecting southwest bastion. The path leads up to the church of the Panaghía tou Kástrou. Originally an armoury, this was converted into a church in the 17th century to house a miraculous icon. Some Byzantine fragments are incorporated into its fabric: the interior is dominated by a fine carved iconostasis. Attached to the church is a small and well-displayed ecclesiastical museum, with good 18th- and 19th-century icons.

To the south, the gateway to the inner fortifications leads through a barrel-vaulted tunnel; a former chapel within the wall is to the left. The passage emerges into a confined space between the two inner enceintes. Modifications made by the Knights include an unusual projecting corridor from the northeast corner, added to protect the north side of the outer enclosure. Northwest outside the castle entrance, the small church of Aghía Varvára is built over ancient and Early Christian remains.

Plátanos

A stepped path from the castle leads to Plátanos, the island's capital, characterised by many stately Neoclassical houses, often in attractive colours. The finest houses and gardens are in the area of Odós Asklipieíou, on the slope opposite the castle. At the beginning of the street is the church of the Stavrós with, in its south porch, a fine row of columns in Rhodian marble, surmounted by Byzantine capitals.

The road from Plátanos to Aghía Marína passes the **Archaeological Museum** (*open daily except Mon, 8.30–3; free*) in a former school building (1882). The well-labelled display ranges from prehistory to the Middle Ages. Highlights include Hellenistic votive terracotta masks with singularly beautiful detail, a Byzantine mosaic inscription and Byzantine glass.

Alínda

The pleasant shoreline between Aghía Marína, Krithóni and Alínda does not betray its violent history. At the beginning of the sweep of Alínda Bay proper (on the inside of the shoreline road, 50m before the left turn for the road to Parthéni) is the **British and Commonwealth War Cemetery** with memorials to 183 servicemen, most of whom lost their lives during the four-day Battle of Leros (12th–16th November 1943), considered the last British defeat in the Second World War. After the Italian surrender in 1943, Britain had occupied several of the Dodecanese. After being swiftly and violently expelled from Kos and Leros by German troops, British forces evacuated Samos, Ikaría and various smaller islands. The first German landings on Leros were to the northeast of here, and the bay of Alínda itself saw some of the fiercest conflict (a Visitors' Book and information are stowed in the gatepost). There is an exhibition on the battle on the upper floor of the **Bellenis Tower** (1925), behind the coastal road at Alínda. The tower also houses the Folklore Museum (*open May–Sept daily except Mon, 9–12.30 & 2.30–6.30*).

A short distance inland behind Alínda is the church of the **Tesserakónta Mártyres** ('Forty Martyrs'; *first road inland from the shore to the north of the main road signed to Parthéni and the airport*). In front of the door are remains of a mosaic floor from an Early Christian basilica.

THE NORTH OF THE ISLAND

The north coast of the island is partly tranquil, partly busy, with the airport and various industrial and military installations. The landscape of low hills and coastal marshes was once the setting for the island's principal sanctuary, dedicated to the cult of Artemis or, more correctly, of the **Parthenos Iokallis**. The exact location of the temple is not known. It was famous for its sacred guinea-fowl, descended from the sisters of Meleager, whose cries at their brother's killing by the goddess prompted her to turn them into birds.

Ancient remains, once erroneously thought to be those of the Temple of Artemis, can be seen in the centre of the southern side of Parthéni Bay. Here, on the summit of the ridge just to the west of the airstrip (reached by the road west, before the airport) is the platform and base of a square 4th-century BC **Hellenistic tower** (c. 8m by 8m), probably similar in concept to the tower on Lípsi. Other smaller, later buildings have left foundations and square cuts in the rocks to the south. To the north of the tower an early medieval church was constructed almost entirely from its blocks. Two hundred metres further north along the same ridge (*path below, along the east side*) is the early 11th-century church of **Ághios Geórgios**, incorporating Early Christian remains, with a 15th–16th-century wall-painting of *St George and the Dragon*.

The area is full of relics of the Second World War: the peaks are marked with Italian watchtowers; the current barracks at Parthéni are of Italian origin; and the near-circular bay of Plefoúti (1km east of Parthéni) is marked by more military structures, now harmless and elegiac.

The most remarkable monument here is in the tiny **chapel of Aghía Kiourá**, on the isthmus separating Parthéni and Plefoúti bays (1km northeast of Parthéni). The interior is decorated with murals, painted in 1970 by detainees of the Colonels' junta who were exiled to Parthéni.

PRACTICAL INFORMATION

GETTING AROUND

Leros has a small airport (12km from Lakkí), served daily (in summer) from Athens. There is also a flight three times weekly to Astypálaia, Kos and Rhodes. The port at Lakkí is served by ferry from Piraeus four times a week (late at night), by catamaran on the Samos–Rhodes route daily, and by ferry on that route four times a week. The faster hydrofoils along the same route call daily at Aghía Marína (summer only). There are also local services to Lípsi and Patmos from Aghía Marína, and from Xirókambos to Myrtiés on Kálymnos.

WHERE TO STAY

One of the dozen nicest places to stay in all the Greek islands is on Leros, and is highly recommended: the moderately-priced **Hotel Archontikou Angelou** ■ (*T: 22470 22749 or mobile 6944 908182, www.hotel-angelou-leros. com*) in Alínda is a 19th-century Neoclassical mansion set in its own gardens. No TVs in the rooms; they are proud of this. In Xirókambos, the **Villa Maria** studios (*T: 22470 27827*) are very simple, set amongst flowers.

WHERE TO EAT

Some of Leros' best eating places are *meze* tavernas, serving a wide variety of small dishes to be eaten together with ouzo or wine. The **Mezedepoleion Dimitris** has the most imaginative selection: it is signposted from a bend on the main Lakkí–Aghía Marína road above the north end of Vromólithos Bay. **To Koulouki**, beside the shore at Kouloúki Bay southwest of Lakkí, serves hot and cold *mezédes* on a peaceful terrace. For a shoreside setting of great beauty and for good-quality fish, **To Kima**, on the eastern side of Xirókambos Bay, is a reliable taverna. The liveliest experience and best value of all is represented by the small café in the tiny square just in from the shore at **Pandéli**, which produces a remarkable variety of *mezédes*.

BOOKS & FILM

Alistair MacLean's novel *The Guns of Navarone* (1957) is a fictional account inspired in part by the 1943 Battle of Leros. In 1961, it was turned into an Oscar-winning film starring David Niven, Gregory Peck and Anthony Quinn.

PATMOS

Both by reputation and in reality, Patmos is dominated by the great Monastery of St John, founded where the saint received his vision of the Apocalypse. There is much else to the island too, including its beautiful and architecturally interesting *chora*, its scattered hermitages and its deeply indented shoreline. The monastery itself, grandiose and intimate at the same time, is the focus of a three-day celebration of Orthodox Easter, perhaps the most memorable experience of the public sobriety followed by collective exuberance that characterises the most significant religious event in Greece.

HISTORY OF PATMOS

Only scattered evidence of prehistoric settlement has been found on Patmos. In historic times, the island was inhabited by Dorians, and later by Ionian colonists from Miletus. It had only minor importance in the Greek world, although there appears to have been a sizeable city in Hellenistic times and a temple to Artemis Patnia on the summit where the monastery now stands. The island was a small Roman outpost when St John

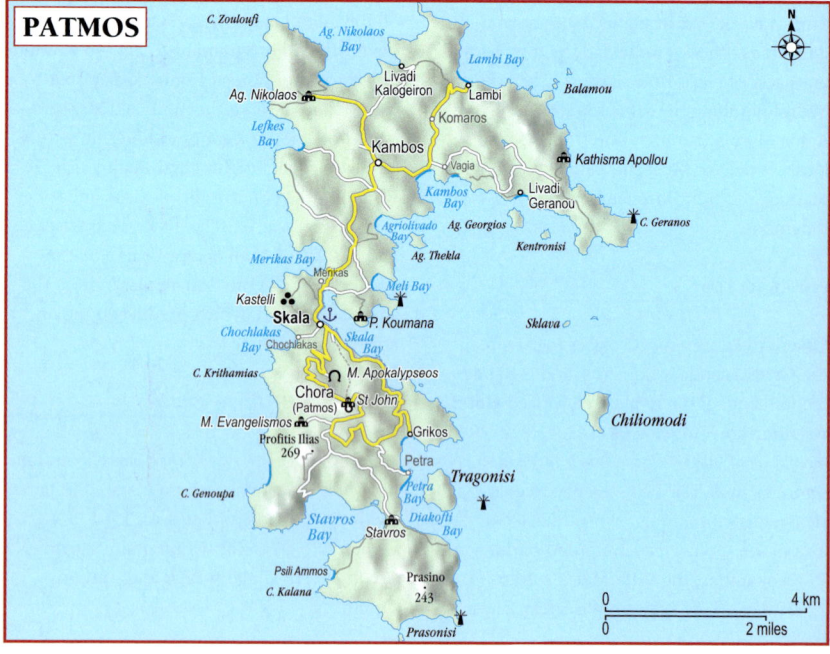

the Divine was exiled here from Ephesus in AD 95, at the end of the reign of Domitian. By his own testimony he received the vision of the Revelation, which is now the last book of the New Testament, during his 18-month sojourn on the island.

After the fall of the Roman Empire, the island, ravaged by Saracen incursions, became depopulated, and remains largely unmentioned until the arrival in 1088 of the Blessed Christodoulos, an abbot from Asia Minor, who had the blessing and support of the Byzantine emperor, Alexius I Comnenus, to establish a monastery on the island in honour of St John. In 1091, Seljuk Turkish attacks forced the monks and the founder to flee: Christodoulos died in Euboea in 1093 (*see p. 604*), but his followers returned to complete the monastery according to his instructions. Under Venetian occupation after 1207, under the protection of Pope Pius II after 1461, and finally under Ottoman dominion after 1523, the monastery's integrity and independence were respected and preserved. Refugees arrived from Constantinople in 1453, and from Candia (Herakleion) on Crete in 1669, enriching and embellishing the island's cultural and architectural heritage, although the year 1659 saw Chora plundered by the Venetian admiral Francesco Morosini. An influential theological school was first established in 1713, and in the course of the 18th and 19th centuries a growing mercantile class brought prosperity to the island and developed the port area of Skála. Emmanouil Xanthos, one of the co-founders in 1814 of the secret Greek Independence Party, or Philikí Etaireía ('Society of Friends'), was from Patmos.

Independence came in 1821, only for Turkish control to be re-imposed in 1830. The Italian occupation after 1912 gave rise to the only instance of coercion to change language and liturgy in the monastery's long history. The island joined the Greek state together with the other Dodecanese islands in 1948. Over the last three decades, Patmos has become increasingly popular with discriminating and independent tourists, and strict rules govern the construction and restoration of buildings, especially in Chora.

PATMOS CHORA

The startling white crystalline appearance of Patmos Chora, clustered around its fortress monastery, dominates much of the surrounding waters. From the port at Skála you can reach Chora either by a winding road (*3km; buses roughly every 2hrs out of season, more frequently in summer*) or by walking (*50mins*) along an old stone-paved *kalderími* which leaves from the southern end of Skála. Halfway up either route are the buildings of the **Patmiada School**, which belongs to the monastery. It is primarily a theological seminary, founded in 1713 and is still functioning today, in postwar buildings. Throughout Greek history it has been a focus of academic and spiritual instruction.

The Convent of the Apocalypse

Below the school is the Moní Apokalýpseos (*open same times as the Monastery of St John; see below; free*). A simple entrance leads into a small complex of churches and cells dating from the last two centuries. Steps lead down to the original part of the complex,

The embattled walls of the Monastery of St John the Divine rise high above the houses of Chora.

where a double church has enclosed the mouth of a shallow cave in the hillside. This is an early 17th-century construction which replaced the 12th-century building erected here some decades after the building of the Monastery of St John. The part which is entered first is the chapel of Aghía Ánna. To the right is the inner portion, the Cave of St John the Divine, which is believed to have been the saint's refuge, the place where he received his vision of the Apocalypse ('Unveiling'), preserved in the Book of Revelation. Tradition holds that the two silver-framed niches to the right of the iconostasis mark the spot where the elderly saint rested his head and placed his hand to raise or support himself. The ledge of rock further to the right was supposedly used by Prochoros, St John's assistant, to support the parchment on which he wrote the words that were dictated to him. Behind the late 16th-century iconostasis, which displays the impressive icon of *St John Receiving the Revelation*, by the Cretan artist Thomas Vathas (1596), are the remains of some 12th-century wall-paintings. One fragment, animated by graceful and symbolic gestures, depicts St John dictating his vision to Prochoros.

THE MONASTERY OF ST JOHN THE DIVINE

Open Mon, Thur, Fri, Sat 8–1.30; Tues, Wed 8–1.30 & 4–6; Sun 8–1 & 4–6. Hours may vary; T: 22470 31223. Free admission to monastery, fee for treasury/museum. NB: The monastery gets thronged in high season; try to visit early or late in the day.

A steep street climbs up through an area of fine stone houses, built mostly by 19th-century ship-owners, to the monastery entrance at the summit of the hill.

HISTORY OF THE MONASTERY

Ancient spolia and inscriptions suggest that the monastery was built over the remains of a temple dedicated to Artemis Patnia, followed by a church of the 4th century AD. Its fortified bulk is eloquent both of the insecurity of the medieval Aegean and of the material and spiritual treasure the walls were designed to protect. From its founding in 1088 (*see p. 417*) it possessed important manuscripts, icons and documents, to which were added a library of valuable incunabula, gold and silver liturgical objects, antiquities and paintings. From its inception, the monastery stood on the border of Christianity with Islam.

By the Fourth Crusade in 1204 the monastery had acquired wealth from its land revenues as well as a certain pan-Christian prestige, and it was left largely independent by the Venetian conquerors of Constantinople; after 1306, the Knights of Rhodes accorded it similar privileges. When Suleiman the Magnificent defeated the Knights in 1522–23, the monastery acknowledged Turkish suzerainty and was again left largely undisturbed. After 1912, the Italian authorities tried to impose language and other restrictions on it, and in 1935 attempted to create a separate Dodecanesian Church, which they hoped eventually to subsume into the Church of Rome. The monastic school continued to function in hiding. Today the monastery preserves an independent status within the Greek state. It is one of the most successful and long-lived monasteries of the Byzantine world.

The walls

The enceinte of almost windowless crenellated walls stands 16m–18m in height, with a single protected entrance in the north. They were part of the 11th-century structure, substantially strengthened in the 17th century by the addition of the impressive scarps on the exterior. The complex was extended in the 16th and 17th centuries to the south; in this period the **ramp of steps (1)** leading up to the north entrance was added, including the projecting terrace supporting the beautifully-proportioned **Chapel of the Holy Apostles (2)**. The unscarped western wing was added in the 20th century.

The courtyard and exonarthex

From the machicolated entrance gate, a steep corridor leads up into a narrow cobbled **courtyard (3)**. Additions to the main church have encroached on it, including the high buttress-arches overhead, belonging to the 1698 addition of the double-storey arched gallery in ashlar to the south, known as the Tzafará, a residential wing for the monks. Immediately to the left is the entrance into the original 11th-century katholikon, preceded by an exonarthex and narthex added in the 12th century. Much of the

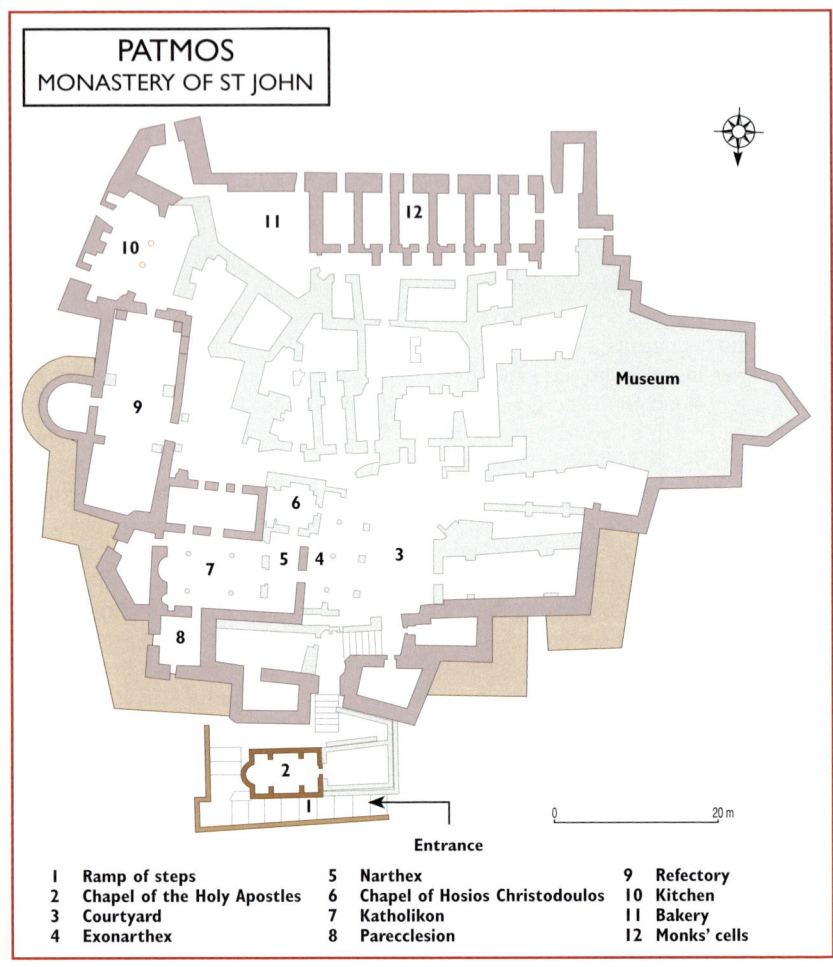

PATMOS
MONASTERY OF ST JOHN

11
12
10
Museum
9
6
5 4
7   3
8

2
1
Entrance

0   20 m

1	Ramp of steps	5	Narthex	9	Refectory
2	Chapel of the Holy Apostles	6	Chapel of Hosios Christodoulos	10	Kitchen
3	Courtyard	7	Katholikon	11	Bakery
4	Exonarthex	8	Parecclesion	12	Monks' cells

four-arched colonnade and balustrade defining the **exonarthex (4)** is composed of ancient and Early Christian spolia, including a balustrade pilaster in red jasper from Iasos on the coast of Asia Minor, opposite Patmos. The narrative wall-paintings, mostly scenes and miracles from the life of St John, date from the 19th century. Decorated stone surrounds frame the beautifully carved 17th-century wooden doors, with an image of the *Annunciation*, giving access to the narthex.

The narthex and katholikon

The narrow **narthex (5)** contains the monastery's large principal icon of St John the Divine, a 15th-century repainting of great beauty over a 12th-century original. The saint's finely-modelled robe and his eyes and brow, of great dignity and compassion, command attention. He holds a book open at the first verses of his Gospel; behind is a small ink-well and pen. The candlesmoke-blackened 16th-century wall-paintings all around are being cleaned, revealing rich colours. The small chamber to the south **(6)** is a **chapel** containing the bones and relics of Hosios Christodoulos, brought back from Euboea by his followers after his death.

The dark and tiny 11th-century **katholikon (7)** is domed on an inscribed-cross plan. It is of a modest design, but very tall. Today an ornate, gilded iconostasis (1820) dominates it, with some minutely carved scenes above the rail. The floor is in polychrome marble inlay. The two icons to either side of the central screen door were donated by Catherine the Great. The beautiful wall-paintings are early 17th-century Cretan works: amongst the finest are the *Pantocrator* in the dome, the *Dormition of the Virgin* (west), and *St John in the Cave of the Apocalypse* (north). Two doors, one in the north wall, the other hidden in the southeast corner, lead into two former treasury rooms.

St John the Divine

St John the Divine, also known as St John the Apostle and St John the Evangelist (he is traditionally recognised as the author of the Fourth Gospel), and designated in Greek as Aghios Ioannis Theologos, was probably exiled to Patmos from Ephesus in c. AD 95 towards the end of the reign of Domitian, which had been marked by a period of zealous repression of Christianity. He must have been already in his eighties; he appears to have returned afterwards to Ephesus (when the proscriptions of Domitian were repealed following his assassination in AD 96), and to have died there around the year 100. It is supposed that he is the same John who was Jesus' 'beloved' disciple, but it is not certain. Patmos was an insignificant island at the time, but with historic links to the city of Ephesus through the shared cult of Artemis. The vision which St John received here and addressed to the 'seven churches of Asia' was a gift of hope that their sufferings were not in vain, that their persecutors (the Roman authorities) would be destroyed, and that all would be turned to good for the chosen faithful.

In iconographic tradition there is a spiritual hierarchy implied in the way the Revelation is depicted. St John is generally placed in a higher position, outside the cave, while Prochoros sits hunched within, mechanically writing. John's head is turned away towards the hand of an invisible Almighty, to whom his right hand gestures in awe, while his other hand opens downwards to his humble servant. In this way, he functions as a conduit for divine wisdom. Other depictions of John typically show him at the foot of the Cross, with the Virgin on the other side; or holding a cup with a serpent in it, a symbol of the poison chalice which the priestess of Artemis at Ephesus enjoined him to drink. His symbol as Evangelist is the eagle.

The doorway in the south wall of the katholikon leads into the **parecclesion (8)**, or Chapel of the Theotókos. As Jesus commanded St John to take care of his mother, her chapel is found beside his. As a result of an earthquake in 1956, the original 12th-century wall-paintings came to light beneath later ones. The *Virgin and Child Enthroned with Archangels* on the east wall is perhaps the finest. Depicted above it is the *Hospitality of Abraham*. On the opposite wall is the damaged but impressive scene of *Christ Healing the Infirm Woman*. The side walls are decorated mostly with figures of saints and patriarchs of Jerusalem (beside the south door). The iconostasis is of the early 17th century. The whole chapel has its original marble floor. By the door to the katholikon is a perforated, upturned Early Christian capital, used as a lid for the cistern underneath.

The refectory area

Next to the parecclesion is the early 12th-century **refectory (9)**, entered from the west. Its form is that laid out by the founder, but it was completed after his death, originally with a simple timber roof, replaced a century later by a stone vault and dome. Running its length are the two original low stone refectory tables, with small individual niches below the counter for each monk to store a bowl and knife. The room was originally painted, with remains visible mostly on the west wall. There are three distinct phases of paintings. The few that remain from c. 1180 are on the flat wall of the blind arch north of the door: the upper portion of four saints can be seen, while above are sections of two scenes, the *Appearance of Christ to the Disciples on Lake Tiberias*, and the *Multiplication of the Loaves*. Subsequently, around 1280, the same scenes were painted on the new surface above. This phase covers the rest of the wall in this northern half of the refectory, and is characterised by dramatic, crowded scenes of stylised figures. A third phase, still late 13th-century, covers the same wall south of the doorway, with Crucifixion and Passion scenes over the door.

Beyond the refectory to the south are the **kitchens (10)** and **bakery (11)**, with ovens at one end and, at the other end, a (purportedly 11th-century) kneading-trough, carved from a single piece of wood. From here a small doorway leads to the **monks' cells** and living quarters **(12)**, along the monastery's south side.

The museum

The Treasury Museum is one of the most interesting ecclesiastical collections in Greece due to the range and importance of items it displays. They are well labelled in English; only a few highlights are mentioned here. On the lower floor, the first section (manuscripts) is dominated by the early 6th-century *Codex Purpureus*, written in gold and silver on purple vellum, and the magnificent Imperial Chrysobull of Alexius I Comnenus, donating title and lands of the monastery: it bears the emperor's signature. The icons, mostly of Cretan or Constantinopolitan workmanship, range from the 12th to the 19th centuries and include a rare 11th-century micro-mosaic icon of St Nicholas and a 16th-century *St John and Prochoros in the Cave of the Apocalypse*, as well a much-damaged *Christ on the Way to Calvary*, believed to be by Domenikos Theotokopoulos, later known as El Greco. There are also liturgical vestments, metalwork and jewellery. The upper floor includes some ancient finds from the island, among them a late 5th-century head of Dionysus in Parian marble and a long 2nd-century AD inscription from the Temple of Artemis referring to Orestes, son of Agamemnon, bringing the cult to Patmos.

Reached from the upper floor of the museum is the roof terrace, with the domed Chapel of the Holy Cross (1598). It affords matchless views.

PATMOS CHORA

Following the wishes of Christodoulos, little was built in the area around the monastery walls. It was after the Sack of Constantinople in 1453 that 'a hundred' refugee families from the capital settled here, creating the neighbourhood of Alótina, to the west of the monastery. The arrival *en masse* of these sophisticated urbanites into the midst of a community of tenant farmers gave rise to a flourishing of vernacular architecture. In 1669, a further 'fifty' families from Crete sought refuge after the Venetian capture of Candia and created the area of Kritiká, east of the monastery. In the early 19th century, the island's successful ship-owners created their own neighbourhood, west of Aportianá, on the steep northern slope below the monastery, overlooking the harbour and their boats. The mansions of the 16th and 17th centuries were once large, free-standing complexes set in their own plots or gardens. With increasing population, the spaces between them were filled with smaller dwellings until the whole area became a contiguous urban web of tiny streets and houses. Characteristic of the whole settlement are the dressed stone corners of the houses and the beautiful window- and door-frames, set off against the plaster. Roofs are flat to catch rainwater, which is channelled into underground cisterns. A balance of openness, ventilation and privacy is achieved by a walled courtyard or *avlí*, often repeated on the upper floor as a roofed veranda, vaulted with arches. As a result of its organic growth, the town has a rambling labyrinthine street plan and few open spaces.

Exploring Patmos Chora

About 150m west of the monastery entrance is the Neoclassical Dimarcheíon (1884): the statue, on the north side of the open Plateía Lótza in front, is of Emmanouil Xanthos (*see p. 417*). To the left of the Dimarcheíon is a house whose window frames bear the date 1589. The street beginning in front of it divides after 50m (with an ancient inscription built into a corner), the rightmost branch leading to the early 17th-century **convent of the Zoödóchos Pigí** (*open 8–12 & 4–7*). The katholikon is dedicated to the Virgin, its parecclesion to St John on the south side. The high-quality 17th- and 18th-century interior features comprise icons, wood carvings and wall-paintings, the latter culminating in a *Presentation of the Virgin* (right of iconostasis) and the *Deposition* on the north wall.

Almost bordering the convent, and entered from the parallel street one block to its west, is the **Archontikó Simandíris** (*open 9–1.30 & 5–7*). Built in 1625, the mansion surprises by the airy spaciousness of its interior, especially the arcaded, upper-floor veranda (views). The present owner is the eighth generation of her family to live here. The areas below function as work and storage rooms, while reception and sleeping areas occupy the upper floor. The pictures, objects and furniture displayed have mostly curiosity value, but they give a vivid picture of middle-class island life over the last 200 years.

Returning uphill to the junction with the inscription, the street to its east leads around the southern side of the town, with the towering fortifications and scarps of the monastery to the left. The large church of the Panaghía Diasózoussa was entirely rebuilt after the earthquake of 1956. In the area around are many small churches of different ages. After the street has climbed and turned towards the north into the heart of the Kritiká area, it opens out into **Plateía Lesvías**, the town's only true *plateía*, bounded by a couple of tavernas and cafés. The north exit leads under buildings and follows the curve of the hill around the monastery towards the north. After 100m, the 18th-century **Nikolaïdis Mansion** (*open Tues–Sun 11–2; free*) is down a street to the right. It houses an exhibition on the history and archaeology of Patmos and examples of painted furniture.

THE SOUTH OF THE ISLAND

A kilometre and a half southwest of Chora is the magnificently sited **Convent of the Evangelismós** (*open daily 9–11.30*). It mostly dates from 1937, but in the southwest corner are the 17th-century hermitage chapel of St Luke and the Church of the Annunciation, with an exquisite 16th-century icon of the *Annunciation* (just left on entering).

In the dramatic volcanic landscape south of Chora, the island narrows to a thin isthmus marked by the church of the Stavrós. The road ends here; but by following the track further south, down the west coast from Stavrós, you climb up and then descend into Patmos' purest sand beach, **Psilí Ámmos**. There is the shade of tamarisk trees, and a taverna which operates in the summer months. From Stavrós, a route (part track, part road) leads north up the east shore towards Grikós. The sweep of the bays of Diakófti and Petra is broken by the conspicuous Kalikatsoú ('cormorant') Rock, attached to the shore by a flat spit of land, and carved with caves, steps and deep channels for water collection by generations of medieval hermits. The road continues to **Grikós**, the island's principal resort, set in a sheltered position looking out onto the natural theatre of the bay, the hills grouped around the small island of Tragonísi, and distant views of Leros beyond. A short distance further north, the road reaches Skála through its quiet, southeastern suburb of Konsoláto, named after the few foreign consulates that opened here in the shipping heyday of the 19th century.

SKALA & THE NORTH OF THE ISLAND

Skála, the port town of Patmos in the centre of the island, is a lively place, built around the island's only deep protected harbour. The harbour itself is ancient, but its development as a centre of habitation dates from c. 1600. The 1930 Customs Building, opposite the main mole, is in the familiar style of the Italian Dodecanese period (*see p. 255*). Similar arcaded architecture stretches inland behind, to the animated *plateía* with the church of Ághios Ioánnis beyond its southeast corner.

Just north of the main harbour mole, as the shoreline road curves left, scant remains of a **Roman wall**, protected by iron railings, are claimed by local tradition to be the remains of a baptismal font used by St John. The only substantial ancient remains on the island are on the hilltop directly above here to the west, at **Kastélli**, where the ruins of a fortified acropolis of the 4th century BC still stand and command splendid views of the island (*the first road turning inland from the south end of the beach curves to the left; then a flight of steps on the right leads to a path along the east side of the hill, leading up to a saddle. From here the previously hidden church of Ághios Konstantínos comes into view on the top of the rise: the acropolis stretches south along the ridge from above the church*). Remains of walls and towers can be seen on the climb up, the best preserved being the north and northeast sections; the northeast tower stands to 3.5m. Within the northwest tower, just above the church of Ághios Konstantínos, a flight of six steps is visible.

Panaghía Koumána

At the north end of the bay of Skála, a right turn leads towards Melí Bay. On a rise, a further right turn winds up to the monastery of the Panaghía Koumána, founded in 1748 by the monastery of St John. There are many such 'Holy Seats' around the island; they are hermitages, often with a small farmstead attached. The church (1780), built against the rock, occupies what was once a hermit's cave. It contains a particularly beautiful icon of the *Virgin and Child*, said to be 12th-century but possibly a little later given its slightly Italianising style.

Kámbos and Lámbi

The main road north from Skála leads to the protected and cultivated valley of Kámbos, dotted with traditional stone houses. Beside the *plateía* in **Áno Kámbos**, a road branches left for Ághios Nikólaos, passing (left) the triple church of the Megáli Panaghía. Its central part, Aghía Triáda, dates from the 12th century, with the two lateral chapels (Panaghía to the south, Ághios Athanásios to the north) added a hundred years later. There is a fine 16th-century icon of the *Dormition* in the south church.

The even older church of **Ághios Nikólaos Évdilos**, said to be the oldest on the island and built in 1087, one year before the Monastery of St John was begun, lies 1.5km further along the road to the west: the simple chapel has been unfortunately repainted in recent times. Hosios Christodoulos laid down in his Rule that the lay community who had helped build the monastery be confined to this remote area, lest their women and children distract monastic life.

Leaving by the same road from Kámbos, a track (right) after 500m is signed to the monastic seat of **Livádi Kalogeíron**, founded in 1700 by monks from Mt Athos. A track from here leads east over the ridge to **Lámbi**, also reached by the north branch of the road from Kámbos Bay. This is a long, north-facing pebble shore whose small stones seem unremarkable at first, but closer inspection reveals them to be small fragments of a rock similar to agate, which when wet reveals variegated patterns of ochre yellow shot through with patches of translucent purple and criss-crossed with striations of white. The mottled effect is extraordinarily beautiful.

Livádi Geranoú

At the north end of Káto Kámbos, a right turn leads through a wild and beautiful coastal landscape towards the bay of Livádi Geranoú. Before the final descent a track rises to the left, crossing a ridge, to the **Káthisma Apolloú**, or 'Apollo's Seat', an attractively-sited monastery named not after the god but after one of its first hermitic occupants. A spring, a church and a small dwelling complex, in a wild and tranquil setting, constitute the hermitage, which is a dependency of the Monastery of St John. On the small promontory below are the remains of a mill and threshing floor.

PRACTICAL INFORMATION

GETTING AROUND

Patmos has no airport but is connected almost daily by sea to Piraeus, Kos and Rhodes. In the summer season there are daily services by catamaran (*Dodecanese Express*) and four times weekly by car ferry on the Dodecanese route between Rhodes and Patmos. Hydrofoils ply the same route daily in summer only, continuing to Samos. Caïques run local services to smaller islands in high season.

WHERE TO STAY

Patmos offers a wide range of accommodation. A comfortable choice is the **Petra Hotel** in Gríkos Bay (*T: 22470 34020; www.petra-hotel-patmos.com*). **Irini Traditional Homes** (*T: 22470 32826, www.traditional.gr*) offers studio-apartments overlooking the main bay. For old-fashioned practicality, **Hotel Skala** (*T: 22470 31343; breakfasts poor*), set back in its own garden, is reliable and convenient for ferries. In old Chora, mainly rooms are available. Two nice, simple choices are those of **Georgia Triandafyllou** (*T: 22470 31963*) and **Marouso Kouna** (*T: 22470 31026*).

WHERE TO EAT

Chiliomodi, 100m inland of Skála harbour, to the left of the road to Chora, has excellent seafood (good sea urchins, shrimps and wine). Also in Skála, **Grigoris**, on the waterfront, looks unpromising but is good for meat. **Lambi**, on the beach of that name, provides only what is available that day and so can be variable, but the place is quiet and the setting beautiful. **Stefanos** or 'Meli', overlooking Melí beach, has good home cooking.

FURTHER READING

A very readable translation of the Rule written by Hosios Christodoulos in 1091, containing his autobiographical introduction, can be found in Dumbarton Oaks: Byzantine Monastic Foundation Documents (www.doaks.org/publications/doaks_online_publications/typ000.html).

The Book of Revelation is essential reading on Patmos, preferably (for the most sonorous language) in the King James Version.

LIPSI, ARKI & MARATHI
& AGATHONISI

These scattered islands, lying between Leros, Patmos, Samos and the coast of Asia Minor, form a seascape of ever-changing beauty. Although they once guarded the important sea-lanes out of Miletus, modern borders have separated them from the mainland, making them remote backwaters, whose principal appeal today is that very fact.

HISTORY OF THE ARCHIPELAGO

Lípsi and its neighbours were settled in the Neolithic, but the islands played virtually no role in ancient history. The notion that Lípsi was Ogygia, home of the nymph Calypso, who delayed Odysseus on his return from Troy, is charming but fanciful. In the Hellenistic period, when these islands were part of Miletus, Lípsi had a small fortified acropolis and a sanctuary of Apollo Lepsios. Julius Caesar was captured by pirates on Pharmakousa (Farmakonísi; now a military zone) in 74 BC.

The subsequent history of the islands is obscure until 1088, the date of the foundation of the Monastery of St John on Patmos: Lípsi became its possession until 1654, and the monastery still has property on the island. In recent centuries the islands have followed the history of the Dodecanese, coming under Turkish rule in 1523, fighting for Greek independence, passing to the Italians in 1912, and joining the Greek state in 1948.

LIPSI

The landscape of Lípsi (*map p. 252*) is punctuated by tiny, steeply-domed chapels in white and blue. Most are modern and not particularly noteworthy, taken singly, but their number and distinctive form are a determining element of the island's appearance.

Lípsi Chora

Lípsi has a pleasant *chora*, clustered around a small hill. Behind the lively and airy promenade, up a flight of steps, are the narrow streets of the old centre and its principal church, **Ághios Ioánnis Theológos**, begun in 1931. It houses (to the right on entering) the miraculous icon of the Panaghía tou Chárou, with the Virgin holding the dead Christ, said to revive a withered lily each year on 23rd–24th August.

On Plateía Xánthou is the curious **Nikephoreion Ecclesiastical Museum** (*open in summer mostly weekdays 9.30–1.30 & 4–8, weekends 10–2; free. If closed, ask in the Dimarcheíon opposite*). The jumbled display in its single room covers the island's history from the Neolithic to the present, including sculpture, documents and costumes.

South of Chora

A road leads south from Chora, past a complex of modern churches, to a headland by the harbour bay, on which stands the church of **Ághios Nikólaos**, possibly on the site of the temple of Apollo Lepsios. An ancient column lies in front of the entrance. To the right of the road, down in a grove of pomegranates and citrus trees, the church of the **Panaghía Kousélios** also includes spolia, as does **Aghía Markélla**, a short way inland.

Beyond Aghía Markélla, as views open out, a path doubles back to the right, leading up to the **acropolis of ancient Lepsia**. Traces of Hellenistic fortification walls are visible and the base of a tower or bastion can be clearly seen. There are good views from the top, including the lovely early 17th-century church of the **Panaghía tou Chárou** (reached by another road), once home to the miraculous icon now held in Chora.

North of Chora

From the western end of the harbour of Lípsi, a road leads via the fertile Kámbos valley towards the north coast. Where the main island road joins from the right, a stony path, marked infrequently with red spots, leads in the opposite direction up the hill to the left. A 25-min walk takes you to the hermitage church of the Stavrós. Further along the road, a left turn leads past a modern hilltop sanctuary to the beautifully sited hermitage of Káto Koímisi. From the shore, a manicured stone path leads up the western slope of the bay to Áno Koímisi (*15mins*), where another hermitage sits on a peaceful and panoramic ledge above the sea. It was occupied until 2000.

ARKI & MARATHI

The name **Arkí** refers to a group of a dozen rocky islets, of which the largest was ancient Arkite. This main island is centred on its placid town, which bears the grand Italian name of Porto Augusta. Visible on the low headland west of the new ferry jetty (port side) are the remains of a 4th-century BC Hellenistic watchtower (*easily reached on foot*).

The hill of Kastro, crowned by the church of the Panaghía Pantanoússa, is reached by a dilapidated stone-paved mule-track leading up to the left of a conspicuous long wall, past ruined traditional houses. Footpaths lead to pleasant beaches in the south, especially Tiganáki, a turquoise lagoon in an inlet of the rocky coast.

Maráthi

With a population of only nine, Maráthi is greener and gentler than its neighbour. On the western hillside above the port, amongst the ruins around a tiny church of Ághios Nikólaos, are the remains of a large Early Christian vaulted barn or cistern, immaculately lined with brick tiles in patterns. Along with Early Christian spolia in front of the church, it suggests the presence of a small, stable community in the 5th and 6th centuries AD.

AGATHONISI

Agathonísi (ancient Tragia) is served by the neat and attractive port of **Ághios Geórgios**. The main road from the harbour leads to the capital, the tiny community of **Megálo Chorió** ('Big Village') at the summit of a ridge. Also from the harbour, a concrete road leads up (800m) to the mostly abandoned **Mikró Chorió** ('Small Village'). The most substantial ancient remains are at the island's eastern end. An hour's walk on a panoramic road from Megálo Chorió leads to the abandoned village of Kathóliko (marked by its church). From the junction above Kathóliko a second clear track continues south beside a deep, sheltered inlet into the eastern promontory of the island, as far as the whitewashed chapel of Ághios Nikólaos on the hillside. Where a fertile strip crosses the saddle of the promontory from southwest to northeast are the grand ruins of an early vaulted structure referred to simply as the **Tholoi**, the 'vaults' or 'domes' of three parallel chambers joined to a fourth at right angles. Date and purpose are unclear; theories include late Roman baths, Early Christian granaries, and a 17th-century Venetian manor house.

On the north coast, a spit of land encloses a natural harbour where, at **Kastráki**, archaeological digs are revealing the presence of a sizeable Hellenistic and Roman port installation and fortified enceinte.

PRACTICAL INFORMATION

GETTING AROUND

Agathonísi is connected by ferry with Lípsi, Patmos and Samos (Pythagóreio), four times a week from April–Oct, less frequently otherwise. To **Lípsi** there are 2–3 ferry connections from Piraeus (10hrs) per week. From April–Oct, Lípsi is connected by car ferry to Pythagóreio on Samos four times per week, and to Kos and the central Dodecanese daily by catamaran. Frequencies reduce off-season **Arkí** is linked by ferry with Samos, Patmos and Lípsi four times a week (April–Oct, less frequent otherwise). **Maráthi** is reached by excursion boats from Lípsi or Patmos during the summer.

WHERE TO STAY & EAT

Agathonísi
Most lodging is at the harbour: **Maria Kamitsis's Rooms**, with a pleasant shaded terrace, is recommended (*T: 22470 29003*). **George's**

Taverna beside the port is good and reliable for fish and salads.
Arkí
Both seafront tarvernas in Arkí, **Trypas** (*T: 22470 32230*) and **Nikolaos** (*T: 22470 32477*) serve good food (and offer rooms).
Lípsi
There are many good, inexpensive studios in Lípsi town. Peaceful and set in gardens are **Studios Anna** (*T: 22470 41126*) and **Kalymnos Studios** (*T: 22470 41102*).
The best fresh fish and simplest Greek dishes are to be had at the inconspicuous **Taverna Theologos** on the western half of the harbour promenade. It is difficult to eat badly on Lípsi: locals tend to favour **Karnagio**, the last taverna at the east end of the second bay of the port. Lípsi is famous for its dark, sweet and strong *mávro krasí* ('black wine').
Maráthi
Pantelis (*T: 22740 32609*) and **Marathi** (*T: 22740 31580*) both have good food and rooms to rent.

THE ISLANDS OF THE
EASTERN AEGEAN

The Eastern Aegean islands divide neatly into two groups: Samos, with Ikaría and Foúrni; and Chios, with Psará and Oinoússes. This division is administrative as well as geographic, as these groups constitute two entire and separate prefectures in the North Aegean peripheral zone (the third being Lesbos, with Lemnos and Ághios Efstrátios). This sense of separation is exacerbated by the divergent attitude that Chios and Samos have taken towards tourism, with Samos wholeheartedly embracing the mass market and Chios resolutely eschewing it. The modern visitor will therefore struggle to find much that the islands have in common with each other. One of the only things is their generally plentiful water supply, which (forest fires aside) has granted them a fertile and well-wooded aspect that is in marked contrast to the Cyclades.

Chios and Samos dominate these islands in terms of population, size, economic might and historical importance. Even though they were members of the same ethnically-based region in the ancient world, Ionia, they did not always see eye-to-eye and experienced quite different fortunes. Excavation has shown that Chios was settled through the Neolithic and Bronze Ages, but nothing of any significance has yet been found on Samos before the 1st millennium BC. Samos became famous in the Archaic and Classical periods for its tyrants and their magnificent constructions; Chios for its intellectuals and artists. The period of Roman rule was kind to both, but disparity returned with the Arab raids in the 7th century, which led to the near abandonment of Samos. Chios recovered and (with the assistance of a Byzantine emperor and his consort) entered an architectural and religious golden age. The Genoese gained control of both islands, and favoured Chios over Samos, but both eventually fell to the Ottomans. The Samians persuaded the Chiots to revolt in support of the Greek War of Independence in 1821, but whereas the Samian fleet was able to repel the Turks on three separate occasions, Chios was not so fortunate and suffered terribly from their reprisals. The islands were finally united with Greece in 1912, together with their outliers. Where the history of the smaller islands is known, it follows the same general lines as that of their large neighbours.

These historical vicissitudes have left a strangely complementary archaeological landscape across the islands, with extensive and evocative ruins of the Archaic, Classical and Roman periods on Samos and Ikaría. These include the Tunnel of Eupalinos on Samos (one of the pre-eminent engineering marvels of the ancient world), the Drákanon tower on Ikaría, and the ancient city of Samos itself, around modern Pythagóreio. The ancient town of Emporeió on Chios is impressive too, though neither as extensive nor as rich in monuments. Byzantine remains, on the other hand, are few and far between on Samos and Ikaría. Chios, however, boasts one of the finest Byzantine monasteries in the Aegean islands, Néa Moní, and a collection of beautiful and unique medieval villages (the Mastic Villages) in the south of the island. One thing that Chios and Samos have in common is first-rate archaeological museums, none of which should be missed (there are two on Samos and one on Chios). The enormous Samos Kouros in the museum in Vathý is particularly impressive.

These archaeological and cultural riches are more than matched by the beautiful landscapes of the islands, all of which offer good walking and hiking. Samos is home to more than 60 species of wild orchid, and Chios is the only place where the mastic tree has been extensively cultivated. While Chios is famous for its spoon sweets (sweet preserves served on a spoon with a cold drink, rather than being used as a spread), Samos produces a fine thyme honey and an excellent sweet wine.   M.M.

CHIOS

Grand and solitary, rich in architecture and flora, but tinged with a note of tragedy that lingers from the events of its long and complex history, Chios is, more than any island in the Aegean, a world in itself. It is separated by wide, open waters from its nearest neighbours: it lies 55 nautical miles from Samos, with whom relations in antiquity were cool, and a comparable distance from Lesbos, with whom its historical links were few. It has acquired over time a proud independence and self-sufficiency.

Unique to the south of Chios are the house-fronts decorated in grey and white geometric designs in sgraffito technique, which constitute such an attractive aspect of Pyrgí and others of the Mastic Villages. Flora, birds and butterflies are abundant and varied on Chios. The island is rich in herbs and honey, and in aromatic samphire, which grows on the seaward cliffs and is a distinctive ingredient in salads.

HISTORY OF CHIOS

According to some claims, the name Chios is of Phoenician origin and means 'mastic'. Excavation has shown that the island was settled through the Neolithic and Bronze Ages, but after the demise of the Mycenaean world, Ionians from Histiaia in Euboea migrated here under the leadership of Amphicles, who is mentioned as the island's first king. The main centres appear to have been where Chios Town now stands, and at the bay of Emporeió, on the island's southeast coast. Because of its origins, Chios was one of the twelve cities united in the Ionic Confederacy, whose common sanctuary was the Panionion on the promontory of Mycale, opposite Samos. These cities soon attained a high degree of civilised prosperity, and the arts and literature throve in them as nowhere else in the Greek world, save Athens. The earliest exponent of this flowering was Homer, who was claimed as a native of Chios; but a lengthy list of Chiot thinkers, artists and authors followed, including the tragic poet Ion, the historian Theopompus and the sophist Theocritus. In the 6th century BC, the island had a celebrated school of sculpture, and Glaucus of Chios (fl. 490 BC) is said to have invented the art of soldering metals.

Thucydides calls Chios the greatest *polis* of Ionia and its citizens among the wealthiest of all Greeks. Chios was the first Greek city to engage in the slave trade, and towards the end of the 5th century BC the Chiots had more domestic slaves than any other Greek state except Sparta. The city came under the control of Persia in 546 BC, and in 499 BC joined the Ionian revolt against Persian domination. The Greek fleet was defeated at the Battle of Lade in 494 BC, despite the valour of the Chiot squadron of 100 ships. Miletus was sacked, and Chios also appears to have suffered some destruction. In 477 BC, after the defeat of the Persian invasions, Chios encouraged Athens to set up the Delian League, and remained a member of it until 412 BC. In this year Chios revolted against Athens, but was defeated. In 333 BC the island was captured by a general of Alexander the Great. In the 1st century BC her famed wealth led to her being pillaged

CHIOS

by the forces of Mithridates, the great enemy of Rome, and it is recorded that the Chiots, when subjugated by him, were delivered up to their own slaves to be carried away captive to Colchis. Chios regained its independence in 86 BC, and this was respected by the Roman emperors until Vespasian incorporated it into the Province of the Islands.

Hereafter the history of the island becomes obscure for a period. A Christian community was established, whose patron saint was Isidore, a 3rd-century Roman military martyr of the reign of Decius. Imperial Byzantine interest in the building of Néa Moní brought an architectural and religious golden age to the island, interrupted by its occupation at the hands of the Turkish emir of Smyrna. It was freed in 1092 by Alexius Comnenus, but was taken by the Venetian doge Vitale Michiel in 1172. The partition of territories of 1204, after the Fourth Crusade, awarded Chios to the Latin emperor in Constantinople, who proved unable to hold it, and the treaty of Nymphaion in 1261 placed it officially under Genoese control for the first time. There followed incursions by Franks, Catalans and Turks, but by the middle of the 14th century, Genoese domination was secure under the aegis of the Giustiniani family, who embarked on an impressive project of fortifying the whole island with castles and towers, and securing, as fortified settlements, the villages that produced the mastic crop. The Genoese remained until 1566, when the Turks, under Piali Pasha, captured the island. Thereafter, until 1821, despite several uprisings, Chios enjoyed a measure of semi-independence. At the beginning of the Greek War of Independence in 1821, the Samians fatally pressed the Chiots to join them in their revolt. In 1822 the Turks inflicted a dreadful and disproportionate punishment: it is said that they massacred over 20,000 islanders and deported or enslaved twice that number. Only the Mastic Villages were spared. Eugène Delacroix immortalised the incident in his famous painting *Le Massacre de Scio*, which was exhibited in the Grand Salon of the Louvre less than two years later.

Chios never fully recovered from the events of 1822. In June of the same year the Greek admiral Konstantinos Kanaris avenged his compatriots by destroying the Turkish flagship with its commander, Kara Ali, aboard. This proved to be a sweet but hollow victory: the city was destroyed and those Chiots who had escaped the massacre had already fled abroad. In 1881, a powerful earthquake killed more than 3,500 islanders and again destroyed a large amount of the city and the island's architectural heritage. In 1912 the island was liberated by the Greek fleet and became part of the Greek state.

CHIOS TOWN & THE KAMPOS AREA

On arrival today, the modern appearance of the harbour-front does no service to what was formerly one of the most elegant and sophisticated towns in the Aegean: the severe earthquake of 1881 destroyed much of the grand architecture, and what has been put up in the last 40 years has been an aesthetic disaster of comparable magnitude.

The town centre
The true heart of the town lies a few blocks inland, around the public gardens (*map*

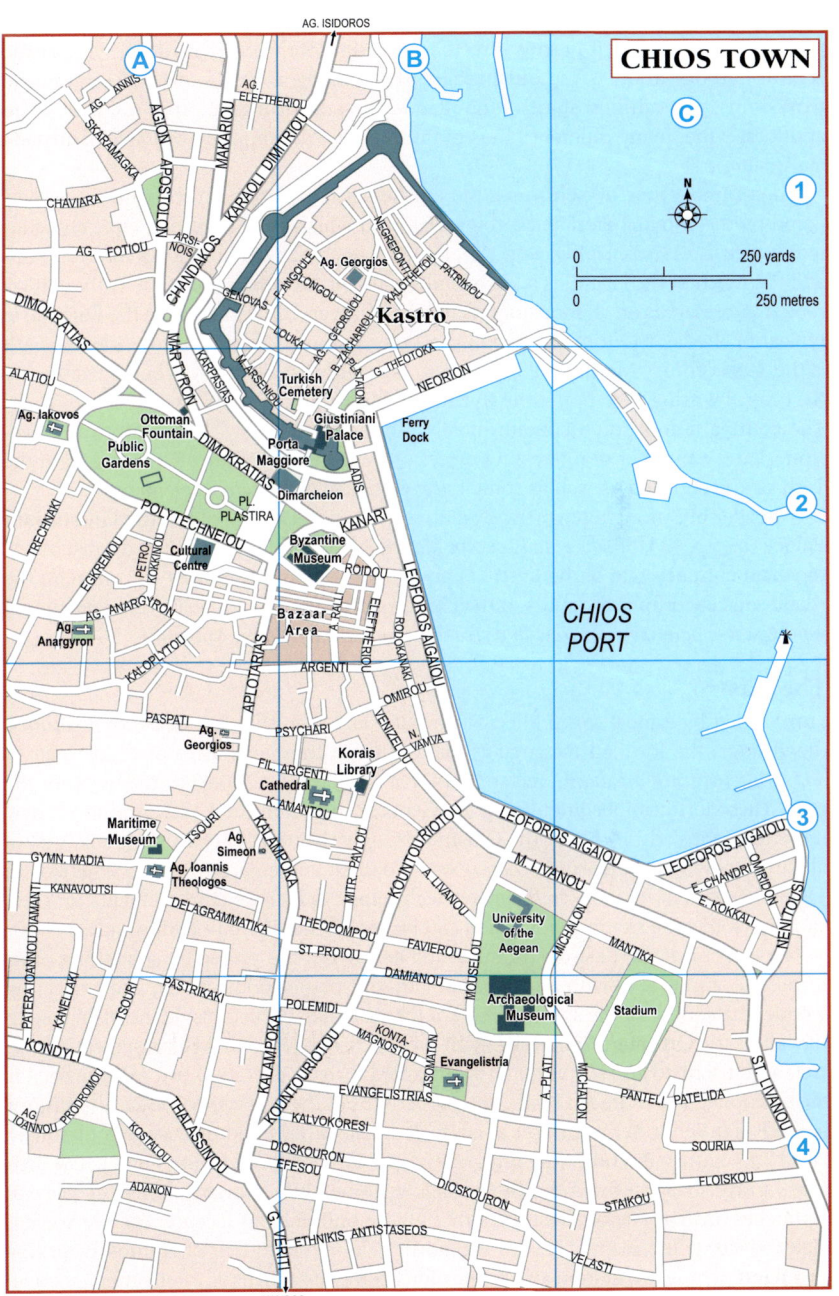

CHIOS TOWN

AG. ISIDOROS

Ⓐ Ⓑ Ⓒ

① ② ③ ④

N

0   250 yards
0   250 metres

CHIOS PORT

Kastro

Ag. Georgios

Turkish Cemetery

Ottoman Fountain

Public Gardens

Ag. Iakovos

Porta Maggiore

Giustiniani Palace

Ferry Dock

Dimarcheion

PL PLASTIRA

Cultural Centre

Byzantine Museum

Bazaar Area

Ag. Anargyron

Koraïs Library

Ag. Georgios

Cathedral

Maritime Museum

Ag. Simeon

GYMN. MADIA

Ag. Ioannis Theologos

University of the Aegean

Archaeological Museum

Stadium

Evangelistria

AG. ANNIS, SKARAMAGKA, CHAVIARA, AG. FOTIOU, DIMOKRATIAS, ALATIOU, AGION APOSTOLON, MAKARIOU, KARAOLI DIMITRIOU, AG. ELEFTHERIOU, CHANDAKOS, ARSI NOISOU, GENOVAS, P. ANGOLOU, NEGREPONTOU, KALOTHETOU, PATRIKIOU, LOUKA, AG. ZACHAIOU, B. ZACHAROU, PLATONOS, G. THEOTOKA, NEORION, G. THEOTOKA, MARTYRON, KARPASIAS, M. MARSENIOU, DIMOKRATIAS, LADIS, KANARI, POLYTECHNEIOU, TECHNAKI, EGKREMOU, PETRO-KOKKINOU, AG. ANARGYRON, ROIDOU, LEOFOROS AIGAIOU, RODOKANAKI, OMIROU, KALOPLYTOU, ARGENTI, APLOTARIAS, PASPATI, PSYCHARI, ELEFTHERIOU, FIL. ARGENTI, N. VAMVA, VENIZELOU, TSOURI, KALAMPOKA, K. AMANTOU, MITR. PAVLOU, KOUNTOURIOTOU, A. LIVANOU, DELAGRAMMATIKA, THEOPOMPOU, FAVIEROU, MOUSELOU, M. LIVANOU, MICHALON, MANTIKA, LEOFOROS AIGAIOU, E. CHANDRI, E. KOKKALI, OMIRON, NENITOUSI, KANAVOUTSI, ST. PROIOU, DAMIANOU, PASTRIKAKI, PATERA IOANNOU DIAMANTI, KANELLAKI, TSOURI, KONDYLI, POLEMIDI, KALAMPOKA, KOUNTOURIOTOU, KONTA-MAGNOSTOU, ASOMATON, A. PLATI, MICHALON, STAKIOU, PANTELI PATELIDA, SOURIA, ST. LIVANOU, FLOISKOU, AG. IOANNOU PRODROMOU, THALASSINOU, KOSTALOU, EVANGELISTRIAS, KALVOKORESI, DIOSKOURON, EFESOU, ADANON, DIOSKOURON, G. VERITI, ETHNIKIS ANTISTASEOS, VELASTI, KAMBOS *p. 435, A2*). The area of narrow streets just to the south of the gardens, west of the central harbour-front, is the **old bazaar**: here, among a wide variety of tradesman's workshops, you can find some of the island's specialities: mastic products, good ouzo and local wine, many different kinds of bread, and wild samphire (*kritamó*; *Crithmum maritimum*).

Odós Dimokratías, which forms the northeastern boundary of the gardens, is bordered by the Dimarcheíon and a row of *kafeneía* which have remained virtually unaltered since the 1950s. Halfway up Dimokratías, where the road branches for Vrontádos and the north of the island, is a free-standing marble **Ottoman fountain**. Although re-roofed, it preserves on all four sides its fine original carved decoration in the florid style typical of the later Ottoman period. The other Ottoman monument beside the park is the 19th-century **Medjediye Mosque** to the southeast, which was being restored at the time of writing to re-house the **Byzantine Museum** (*open daily except Mon, 8.30–1*). The courtyard and porch contain mostly salvaged items (Jewish and Muslim gravestones) and a number of interesting pieces of Genoese Renaissance sculpture from the 14th–16th centuries, as well as some Early Christian architectural elements.

A smaller but more noteworthy Byzantine collection can be seen in the **Giustiniani Palace** (*map p. 435, B2; open daily except Mon, 8.30–3*), along Odós Kennedy, just inside the main entrance gate of the Kastro. This contains some of the finest paintings on the island, detached from the walls of the church of the Panaghía K.rína (*NB: at the time of writing, these paintings were due to be transferred to the Byzantine Museum*).

The Kastro

Surrounded by a moat, once filled with water, and accessible by means of a wooden drawbridge, the fortified rectangular mass of the fortress or Kastro of Chios (*map p. 435, B1*), occupies a roughly rectangular area (c. 600m by 250m) to the north of the port. These fortifications are principally Genoese, begun in the 1320s, and given new impetus in the early 1400s by the Giustiniani; only the northern bastion (the largest of all, and known as the Torrione Zeno) was modified and enlarged by the Venetians in 1694–95, with more modern defensive technology to include emplacements for their cannon (some fine examples of which can be seen in the Byzantine Museum).

The interior of the Kastro, still inhabited and lively, has preserved something of its former Levantine feel, with a number of lath-and-plaster house-fronts and projecting wooden balconies. At the southern end of the main axial street, inside the main gate to the left, is the **Ottoman Cemetery**, with most of its gravestones well preserved and intact, and inscribed and surmounted with carved turbans or fezzes. Towards the back is the sarcophagus of Kara Ali Pasha, the perpetrator of the massacre of 1822 (*see History, p. 434*). A little further north, set at an angle to the other buildings, is the four-square late 18th-century **Bayrakli Mosque**, now deprived of its porch and minaret. The spacious prayer-hall, surmounted by a shallow dome sitting on an interesting play of squinches, is in a state of abandon, although the building has recently been re-roofed. Halfway down the main street on the north side is the church of **Ághios Geórgios Frourioú**, whose orientation and proportions betray its origins as a converted mosque.

The Koraïs Library and Maritime Museum

South of the main square, on Odós Koraï, is the **Koraïs Library and Argentis Folklore Museum**, behind a sober, pedimented façade (*map p. 435, B3; open Mon–Fri 8–2*). The library, founded in the 18th century, is one of the most important in the Aegean. Since the initial bequest of books in 1792 by an influential humanist and Classical scholar from Smyrna, Adamantios Koraïs, the library has attracted the donation of many other collections, most recently the gift of an art and costume collection by Philip Argentis in 1948. The library and reading-rooms are downstairs and the Argentis Museum is on the upper floor. The collection contains much family memorabilia and portraiture, but nonetheless has some evocative and unusual pieces.

Next to the library is the cathedral, and 200m to the west of it, at no. 20 Stefánou Tsourí, is the small **Maritime Museum** (*map p. 435, A3; open daily except Sun, 10–2*), containing pictures, models and photographs of Aegean ships and maritime life, and memorabilia of Admiral Kanaris (*see History, p. 434*). It is housed in a grand early 20th-century mansion of the Pateras family, one of the most important shipping families of Oinoússes and Chios.

Archaeological Museum

Two blocks in from the southwest corner of the harbour are the buildings of the University of the Aegean, which stand behind a garden of palms; next to them is the Archaeological Museum, which should not be missed (*map p. 435, B4; open daily except Mon, 8.30–3*). The collection is laid out on three levels in a custom-designed building of 1970, with six principal rooms or zones and an outside courtyard in which a 2nd-century BC Macedonian-style mausoleum has been reassembled. The richness and idiosyncrasy of Chios clearly emerge in the remarkable variety and unusualness of some of the categories of objects, in particular the rare and moving **Hellenistic grave stelae** with their fluid incised designs. One of the principal themes of this museum is wine-trading, and there is an excellent display of **Chiot amphorae** in Room III, mounted so as to show their chronological development from the heavier, swollen-neck designs of the 6th century BC through the 5th-century BC cylindrical-neck design to the later Hellenistic forms with narrow bodies and long necks, for more efficient storage in the holds of boats. There is also an official liquid-measure standard, in marble. Also in this room are **two engraved letters from Alexander the Great to Chios**. Room VI on the upper floor is dedicated solely to finds from the neighbouring island of Psará.

The basilica of Ághios Isídoros

Just under 2km north of the city, on the road to Vrontádos, is a row of four restored windmills on the edge of the sea; two blocks inland of this point is the concrete church of Aghía Myrópi and Ághios Isídoros, in a small square of the same name. Underneath it are the substantial remains of the Early Christian basilica of the island's patron saint, St Isidore, a Roman legionary from Alexandria who was martyred in Chios in AD 251, in the reign of Decius: the presence of his relics here must have made this the most important Early Christian site on the island. In 1125 his (headless) remains were stolen by the Venetians and later put in a marble sarcophagus in a chapel in St Mark's. The treasure of the site is the large amount of well-preserved 5th–6th-century mosaic flooring in the interior (*the key for the church is kept at no. 38, on the north side of the square, and hangs on the back of the letterbox*).

THE KAMBOS & ENVIRONS

Everything that may disappoint in the architecture of Chios Town is compensated for by the beauty of the Kámbos area. Though a shadow of what it was before the massacre of 1822, the earthquake of 1881, and the encroachment of the airport and city periphery, the area's patrician villas and churches, its wooded gardens and the warmth of the variegated red stone from which everything is built, still combine to make this one of the most atmospheric and architecturally significant suburbs in the Greek world. The area lies 4–5km due south of Chios, in the plain bounded by the city itself to the north, the shoreline to the east, and the village of Thymianá to the south. It is reached either by cutting inland from the coast, after the south end of the airport runway, or by following signs for Neochóri and Thymianá from the centre of town: it is a labyrinth of high-walled streets and water-channels, and deserves leisurely exploration.

HISTORY OF THE KAMBOS

The Kámbos area was the main cultivated area for the city of Chios from antiquity onwards. In the 14th and 15th centuries, the Genoese masters of the island built towers (*pýrgi*) in this area, which functioned as glorified tool-sheds and as residences for farm-managers, built sturdily so as to mark and protect their estates. With the greater security afforded by Ottoman occupation, these *pýrgi* were gradually turned into summer retreats on family estates. The important merchant families, with their combination of wealth from trading in the island's produce and experience, through their travels, of the great city suburbs in Egypt, Italy and the Levantine coast, began to compete in the construction of ever-finer villas and residences, adopting some of the architectural lessons learnt from overseas. The late 18th–early 19th century was the short-lived heyday of this area: not long after, the majority of the owners were rounded up and killed in the 1822 massacre, as an example to others, and many of the houses were abandoned or suffered subsequent destruction in the earthquake of 1881. For these reasons only a portion of the villas remain, some restored (more or less faithfully), and others in a state of ruin.

The design of the villas

The villas functioned both as farmhouses for the family estate and as country residences: hence they are surrounded by low storage buildings and stone barns, and centred on a shaded courtyard around a well from which water was channelled throughout the estate to irrigate the citrus and fruit trees. The sleeping and reception rooms were on the upper floors, illuminated by long windows and opening onto shaded terraces and balconies, from which it was possible to see, and be seen, above the walls. Access to this upper area is generally by a grand stone staircase on the outside of the building; its landings and balustrades are punctuated with carved stone urns. The overall design is prevailingly Italian—distantly reminiscent of suburban villas in Genoa—but the decorative gateways onto the street often have an Ottoman flavour, in their alternating use of two colours of stone in the arches and in the porch-like roofs which cover them.

The Ypapantí Chapel

In the village of Vavíli (*map p. 433, C3*), at the southwestern corner of the Kámbos plain, is one of the island's most unexpected treasures: the minuscule chapel of the Ypapantí (the Purification of the Virgin), whose interior is entirely covered with murals, painted in 1963 by Juliette May Fraser, an artist from Honolulu (*the chapel is c. 200m north of the main village church of Ághios Nikólaos, on Odós May Fraser. The key is kept in the house opposite and slightly further north*). While working in Athens in the early 1960s, she volunteered to paint these murals together with the artist David Asherman, as a gift to the village. The interior is fresh in colour and clear in design. Not unexpectedly, the scenes are a hybrid of Eastern and Western, Byzantine and representational, modern and ancient; perspective comes and goes, the scenes are sometimes (such as the *Presentation of Christ*) in local topography, sometimes in eternal landscapes. The whole is unified by an airiness and overall brilliance of colour, and is executed with such genuine joy that it provides a valuable counterpoint to the island's wealth of early Byzantine art—one of the best examples of which is the Panaghía Krína (*see below*).

The Panaghía Krína

Sophisticated in design and beautifully decorated with blind arches and lively brick patterns on the exterior, and with paintings inside, this is a church close in date and in architectural conception to Néa Moní (*undergoing restoration at the time of writing, it is in a solitary location 2.5km west of Vavíli; map p. 433, C3*). It appears to have been a 12th-century Constantinopolitan commission, donated by two members of the imperial court, though both the reason for its commission and the remote setting remain unclear. From outside, the similarities to Néa Moní are clear: the dynamic profile with a steep drum and cupola over the sanctuary and another, smaller dome over the narthex; the materials and brick patterns (especially the decorated lunette over the narthex entrance); and the long, linear axis preceding the naos through an exonarthex (18th century) and a transverse narthex (12th century). Once inside, the dignified and luminous octagonal naos is even more redolent of the earlier monastery.

Two series of wall-paintings exhibited in Chios (the 14th-century paintings from the cupola, in Palazzo Giustiniani, and the upper layer of 18th-century paintings from the naos, in the Byzantine Museum) were removed to reveal the original 12th-century paintings which now decorate the main area, and whose quality suggests the hand of an artist from Constantinople.

CENTRAL CHIOS & NEA MONI

The main road due west from Chora rises steadily, passing on the right the modern monastery of the Panaghía Voitheía. After 6km the road climbs steeply in switchbacks, with magnificent views opening onto the Turkish mainland: the hillside is dotted with other monasteries, churches and hermitages, which profited from the spiritual and clerical traffic that the presence of Néa Moní attracted. One of these (left turn at 8.8km; *map p. 433, C2*) is the intimate **Monastery of Ághios Márkos**. The Blessed Parthenios, who was the principal force behind the rebuilding of Néa Moní after the earthquake of 1881, is buried here: his hermitic cave-cell (*key from monastery*) is on the hill below, beside a stand of fir trees.

NEA MONI

A little over half a kilometre further along the principal road is a left turn for the 11th-century Néa Moní (*map p. 433, B3*), which for its mosaics and architectural design is one of most significant Byzantine sites in the Greek world (*undergoing extensive restoration at the time of writing; normally open daily 8–1 & 4–7; appropriate dress required*). From the approach road, the beauty of the setting is immediately visible. Today the outbuildings are mostly abandoned shells, although the arcaded aqueduct still brings water from the north into the 11th-century cisterns. The monastery never recovered fully from the two catastrophes of the 19th century: the Turkish destruction of 1822 was visited with particular severity on those who sought refuge here, and the chapel of the **Tímios Stavrós**, immediately to the left of the gate on entering (**A** *on the plan on p. 442*), functions as an ossuary and memorial to those killed here.

The foundation

The name ('New Monastery') is curious; Néa Moní is in fact dedicated to the Assumption of the Virgin, to commemorate the finding of a miraculous icon of the Virgin on the mountainside in the early 11th century, but it has been universally known as the 'New Monastery' ever since it received its endowment from the Byzantine emperor in 1042. The imperial gifts of money, land and materials, as well as the bringing of the architects and artesans who constructed the complex, was the fulfilment of a vow made by Constantine IX Monomachos, when the hermits from here predicted his return from exile in Lesbos to Constantinople to become emperor. His consort and co-founder was the remarkable Empress Zoë, through whom the line of imperial succession passed. A virgin until the age of 50, she subsequently enjoyed three nuptials to successive ruling emperors, the last of whom was Constantine. Building and decoration were both largely completed by 1056.

The katholikon: exterior and design

Viewed both from the east or from the side, the width and height of the drum and cupola of the katholikon (**B** *on the plan overleaf*) dominate the profile of the building inordinately. There are highly stylised proportions in the floorplan of the church, too: for example, the narrow transverse exonarthex is wider than any other part, and the four-square plan of the naos evolves as it rises into eight unequal conches, which subsequently dissolve into the circle of the dome.

This is not stylisation for the sake of stylisation: it is part of a conscious intention on the part of the architects to give spiritual meaning to the progression of the worshipper through the spaces of the church, from the narrow, dark areas of the exonarthex and narthex to the magnificently luminous, high space of the naos. It is this that creates the dramatic effects. In the naos this is further enhanced by the complex vertical passage from square plan to circular cupola, through an octagonal intermediary; this has the practical effect of leaving the central space free of supporting piers, as well as giving a rhythm of alternating narrow and wide conches or niches. In all these ways Néa Moní contrasts interestingly with its near contemporary, the Monastery of St John on Patmos (1088): the church of the latter is a humble structure, modestly decorated and unambitious in design. At Néa Moní, costly mosaics and the full power of architectural sophistication from the imperial capital have been brought to bear.

The interior decoration

The interior is a procession of spaces (*see* **B** *on the plan overleaf*), all of different forms, heights, colours and kinds of decoration: a rectangular atrium next to the belfry, which is entered first, precedes an exonarthex, which precedes a narthex, which precedes the naos, each stage more finely decorated than the previous. Such a succession of spaces at Haghia Sophia in Constantinople was linked to ceremonial demand, related principally to the entry of the Emperor, who symbolically transformed himself from temporal to religious monarch as he progressed from one space to the next: here at Néa Moní, the design is an expression of the imperial interest that lay behind the building's creation.

The display of mosaics begins in the narthex, where they were set off by the low, flickering light of candles and lamps. The cycle here, though fragmentary, is one of the three most important still surviving in Greece (with those at Hosios Loukas near Delphi and Daphni near Athens). They are contemporary with the construction of the building (1040s and '50s) and are executed in a combination of different materials: tesserae of coloured stone and glass paste for the figurative and decorative designs, and tesserae for the background made in the ancient technique of fusing gold leaf in clear glass.

Narthex: The images of the ceiling are principally of saints, martyrs and prophets, grouped protectively around the central presence of the Virgin in the cupola (damaged) (**1**), with the beautifully conceived figures in the pendentives below of her parents, Joachim (**2**) and Anne (**3**), and of Sts Panteleimon (**4**) and Stephen (**5**). To the right are scenes of the *Raising of Lazarus* (**8**) and the

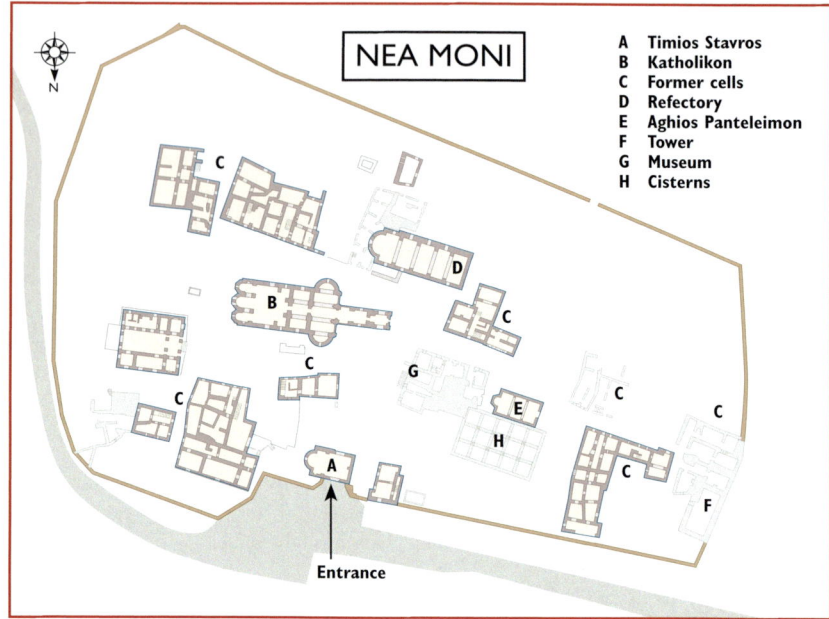

Washing of the Feet **(10)**. In the opposite bay is the *Ascension* **(13)**, witnessed by a magnificent group of robed spectators. **Naos:** The decorative plan here is far more wide-ranging, and the space is very differently illuminated: the Pantocrator and angels of the cupola were lost in the earthquake of 1881, but the important scenes of the conches have mostly survived: the *Baptism* **(17)**, *Crucifixion* **(19)**, and *Harrowing of Hell* **(21)**. The culminating image of the Virgin in the central apse behind the templon has only survived in the lower portions **(26)**, flanked by the archangels Michael **(27)** and Gabriel **(28)**. The weightless shimmer of the mosaics overhead, especially when illuminated in the dark, is balanced by the coloured marbles underfoot and around the walls.

The monastery buildings

Of the surrounding monastery buildings, many of those which originally housed the cells of the monastic community are now in ruins. The original **refectory (D)** survives, restored and re-roofed; it is a long, luminous, apsidal hall, down the centre of which runs the original 11th-century stone refectory table, inlaid with large designs in polychrome marbles. A cobbled street to the west leads past the chapel of **Ághios Panteléimon (E)** (1889) towards the ruined, four-square **tower (F)** that used to house the library. The books and treasury of the monastery mostly disappeared when the monastery was torched during the 1822 massacres; for this reason the small **museum (G)** contains a limited collection of largely 19th-century liturgical items and icons. Behind the museum is an arch, elaborately framed with tiles, which gives onto the magnificent 11th-century **cistern building (H)**, whose deep rectangular form is roofed with 15 vaults supported on marble columns.

Today only one frail and elderly nun, followed in her peregrinations around the buildings by a flock of chickens, doves and cats, still inhabits Néa Moní. Costly and far-reaching restoration work is underway, involving the re-pointing of the brickwork with modern mortar and the renewing of the window frames with machine-cut marble. The new generation of monks or nuns—if there should be one—will inherit a monastery whose interior, once darkened with smoke, will be crisply clean as never before.

Ághii Patéras

Built in the late 19th century, on a scale that dwarfs the size of Néa Moní, is the nearby monastery of the Ághii Patéras, higher up the mountain and 900m to the west (*reached*

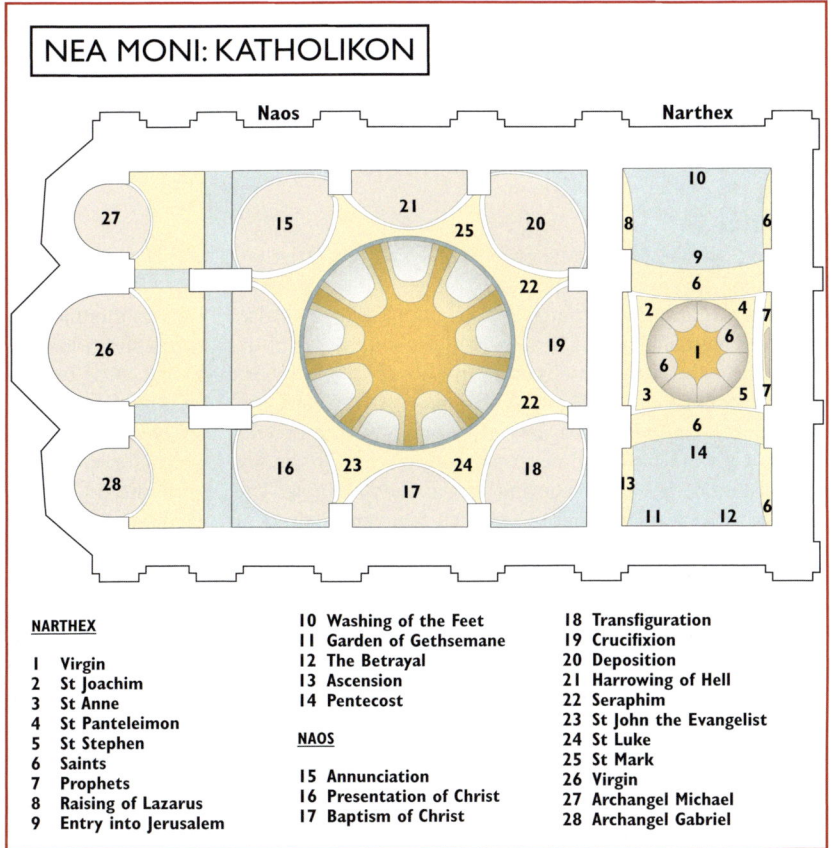

NEA MONI: KATHOLIKON

Naos   Narthex

NARTHEX

1 Virgin
2 St Joachim
3 St Anne
4 St Panteleimon
5 St Stephen
6 Saints
7 Prophets
8 Raising of Lazarus
9 Entry into Jerusalem
10 Washing of the Feet
11 Garden of Gethsemane
12 The Betrayal
13 Ascension
14 Pentecost

NAOS

15 Annunciation
16 Presentation of Christ
17 Baptism of Christ
18 Transfiguration
19 Crucifixion
20 Deposition
21 Harrowing of Hell
22 Seraphim
23 St John the Evangelist
24 St Luke
25 St Mark
26 Virgin
27 Archangel Michael
28 Archangel Gabriel

by a path directly from Néa Moní, or by road, returning to the island's main east–west road from Néa Moní, continuing 1.2km west, and taking a panoramic road left). The large complex of buildings, now home to four monks, has grown up around a hermit's cave, which was first closed by a church in the 17th century.

ANAVATOS & THE CENTRAL WEST COAST

The western slopes of Chios are wild and densely forested with pine. The natural acropolis of Anávatos has a number of advantages which may explain its improbable choice as a place of settlement: apart from formidable natural defences, a deep, sinuous gorge to the west gave direct and quick access to the bay of Elínda, which cuts into the central part of the west coast—the stretch most heavily fortified by the Genoese for protection against piracy. Anávatos and Avgónyma, further south, are also the closest points to Chios Town that survey the western approaches to the island; they were therefore vital links in the defence of Chios as a whole. The wild and dramatic coastline is regularly punctuated by Genoese watchtowers, placed strategically on successive rises or promontories. Those above the bays of Tigáni (*map p. 433, B2*) and Trachíli (*map p. 433, B3*) are well preserved and easily accessible. Another marks the entrance to the bay of Elínda, immediately north of the road junction. This protected and beautiful inlet of turquoise water, with a pebble strand, was the harbour for Anávatos and Avgónyma.

Anávatos

Anávatos (*map p. 433, B2*) is one of the most dramatically-sited villages in the Aegean. It appears to have been a flourishing community at the time of the massacres of 1822, which abruptly terminated its existence and gave rise to the abandonment of the site. The inhabitants, spurred on by a combination of desperation and pride, are said to have thrown themselves over the western cliff rather than yield to capture by their Turkish assailants. The tiers of uninhabited houses, built in un-rendered stone, are perfectly camouflaged against the limestone escarpments; they have the form of towers, with the minimum necessary perforations for windows, which are only rarely embellished with a small relieving arch above the frame. The stepped streets lead up to the fortress at the summit, where a curtain wall encloses an area dominated by the ruins of a double-naved church. This type of design generally arose from the need to celebrate both the Latin and the Orthodox rites, suggesting a mixed community here of Genoese and local Greeks.

Lithí

South of Avgónyma is the protected and sandy bay of Lithí (*map p. 433, B3*), where there is a small harbour, good bathing and several tavernas, well known for their fresh, locally-caught fish. Andreas Syngros, the 19th-century philanthropist and banker, was from this village; the principal artery from Athens to Fáliro and Piraeus, Syngrou Avenue, is named after him, and he was instrumental in financing the completion of the Corinth Canal in 1893.

The ruined village of Anávatos, perched on its crag.

SOUTHERN CHIOS & THE MASTIC VILLAGES

Armólia and Kalamotí

Armólia, 19.5km from Chora on the southern southwest loop road (*map p. 433, B4*), is a centre for the production of decorated ceramics. A kilometre northwest of the village is the 15th-century **Castle of Apolichnés** (*reached by a steep track from the north end of the village*), built by Girolamo Giustiniani in 1446. The fortress, enclosed by double ramparts, was large enough to afford temporary protection to the locals in case of attack. It still preserves its great tower, or keep, and a number of smaller defensive and look-out towers in the walls. To the south of Armólia extends the fertile valley of Kalamotí.

A kilometre southwest of the village of Kalamotí is the solitary church of the **Panaghía Agrelopoúsaina** (*700m south from the southwest corner of the village, then 300m west to the top of the hill*), now deprived of the monastery buildings which must once have surrounded it. The church was a 14th-century dependency of Néa Moní, but the presence of Early Christian spolia nearby and of a fine section of ancient cornice moulding with palmette design, incorporated into the building over the west door, indicate earlier places of worship, possibly on this same panoramic site. The simple vaulted space of the interior is articulated with blind arcades along the lateral walls and with the scant remains of wall-paintings: the best-preserved area of 14th-century paintings is in the domed narthex, where the figures of the donors remain; the name of one, Eirini Mentoni, is legible.

KOMI & EMPOREIO

South of Kalamotí, a fertile agricultural plain extends to the coast at Kómi; this is probably the oldest consistently cultivated area of Chios, which provided food for the island's earliest settlements around the protected harbour of Emporeió at its southern extremity (*map p. 433, B4*). Emporeió harbour is marked by a hill to the west, ideal as an acropolis, and by another, higher mountain (Profítis Ilías) to its north and east. With a source of fresh water directly behind the bay, the site was an obvious choice for settlement.

HISTORY OF EMPOREIO

Excavations at the neck of the west promontory have revealed settlement remains beginning as early as the 5th millennium BC: no less than ten subsequent phases have been distinguished, of which Phase III (late 3rd millennium BC) is the first to have had a strong defensive wall. Mycenaean finds show that settlement continued until the end of the Bronze Age. When the island was re-colonised by Ionians from Histiaia on Euboea, in the 8th century BC, the site they chose was on the slopes of the hill to the east and north, which was to function as their acropolis. Here they constructed the sanctuary and temple of their patron goddess, Athena, while below, by the harbour, a sanctuary to Artemis was established. Between the two stretched the town with its simple residences. The area was populated in Roman times, when a fortress was erected on the summit of the promontory to the west of the harbour, and in Early Christian times, when the temple of Artemis was dismantled and used as a quarry to build an Early Christian basilica, whose baptismal font is still visible today.

The site

The entrance to the archaeological site is on the south slopes of the hill of Profítis Ilías (*open daily, 8.30–7 in summer; 9–1hr before sunset in winter; free*). First excavated and published by John Boardman and the British School between 1951 and 1954, the hillside today is laid out as a slightly sterile archaeological park with concrete walkways and suggested itineraries. The visitor encounters four principal types of architecture: temple, megaron, simple dwelling and storage house.

The focus of the ancient town was the **Temple of Athena**, which sits at the top of the site within a walled acropolis encompassing the summit and the southern shoulder of the hill. In the earliest phase (8th century BC) there was only a rectangular altar here (Altar A). The first temple was built in the 6th century BC, and would have been a flat-roofed, rectangular building with a porch: it enclosed and covered that first altar—the sanctuary's most sacred spot—and housed the cult image. A new external altar (Altar B) was now built for communal cult. Immediately following its destruction in the early

4th century BC, the temple was rebuilt in the form visible today, this time with a pitched roof: a new altar (Altar C) was created in front of the east entrance, but at a curiously skewed angle to the temple building.

From in front of the temple, what remains of the 800m circuit of **acropolis walls** can be seen flanking the ridge to east and west as they rise up to the summit. Almost contiguous with the western wall, and just north of the temple, is the **megaron** of the 8th century BC, a long rectangular hall preceded by a porch supported by wooden columns, whose stone bases can still be seen: this was the official residence of the ruler, and would also have served as a council chamber for the elders. The lowest courses of its perimeter wall are of massive blocks settled amongst pieces of the bedrock; on top of these, the walls are made of smaller stone pieces. They would have been finished with plastered mud brick at the top and covered with a flat roof, supported on a line of three central wooden columns.

Below the walls, on the slopes of the hill, a number of **houses** of great simplicity have been uncovered: mostly single-chambered dwellings with a stone bench along the walls for sleeping, sometimes a semi-interred storage area, and a single threshold giving onto an external courtyard, often shared by more than one such house.

Early Christian remains

Forty or fifty metres up the road that rises to the west of the harbour, a signed track leads (right) into a field below some modern houses, where there are the remains of a late 6th-century **Palaeochristian basilica and baptismal font**. The road continues up over the hill to the southwest of the harbour, and drops down almost immediately to the '**Black Beach**' of Mávra Vólia Bay, where, between the sea and ochre-coloured cliffs behind, an extraordinary volcanic strand of evenly-sized black pebbles stretches for 100m.

THE MASTIC VILLAGES & ANCIENT PHANAI

The hilly landscape of the south of Chios is dominated by the cultivation of mastic trees, and the villages in this area were the centres of production for the gum. Mastic never was nor could be a large-scale industry, but the demand was constant from Byzantine times on, and this part of Chios was the only place in the Mediterranean where the tree could be successfully cultivated and cropped. Byzantium and Italy were the principal markets, later to be superseded by Turkey and the Orient, and most of the villages in this area probably have Byzantine origins. However, it was only under Genoese rule in the 14th and 15th centuries that the villages were properly organised into a community, with special administration and architectural design to protect them from the predations of piracy.

The villages, still referred to generically as the Mastichochória, have certain features in common: they lie inland and are hidden from view from the sea; for protection they are surrounded by walls with towers and gates; and the walls in turn surround a central fortified tower, which formed the ultimate safe refuge for the inhabitants and their precious product in case of attack. The villages have a tight-knit plan of narrow streets and passageways in which the backs of the outer ring of houses is one with the enceinte of walls. The special administrative privileges put in place by the Genoese were confirmed and increased when the Turks took control of the island in the 16th century; so important was the mastic trade and supply to Istanbul, that the Mastic Villages were specifically spared the gruesome Ottoman reprisals of 1822. The Mastic Villages are canonically over 20 in number; four of the finest examples, Pyrgí, Olýmpi, Mestá and Véssa, are described here.

MASTIC

The evergreen mastic tree (*Pistacia lentiscus*) is low, dense and 'sculpted' in form, with dark leathery leaves and a rough, corrugated bark, from which it spontaneously weeps a pale yellow, largely odourless, resin or hardened sap. This 'weeping' can be promoted by making incisions (called 'hurts') in the trunk and branches of the mature tree and by harvesting the resin from June through to September; 'hurting' too young a tree, however, inhibits its growth. The sap coagulates as it drips from the cuts. It is collected, rinsed in barrels, and dried: a second cleaning is done by hand. A mature tree will yield 4.5kg of mastic gum in one season.

Mastic was known in antiquity as a treatment for duodenal ulcer and heartburn. But its most enduring quality has been its power, when masticated (same etymology), to neutralise and scent the breath. This was widely appreciated in the harems of Arabia and Turkey; 18th-century reports suggest that the Ottoman sultan kept half of the annual harvest from Chios for the seraglio in Top Kapi—a quantity equivalent to about 125 tons. The flavour of mastic is initially bitter, but after a few minutes of chewing it softens and releases a light, cedar-like freshness, which remains in the mouth for about 15–20 mins. On Chios its distinctive flavour can be sampled in many ways: principally in the local grape spirit, Masticha, or else in a variety of 'spoon sweets'. Something of a renaissance in the marketing of mastic has occurred in the last decade, and it is now sold as a nostalgically packaged luxury item, both on the island and further afield in Greece.

Pyrgí

The largest and most important of the Mastic Villages, because of its central position, is Pyrgí (*map p. 433, B4*). The village is most memorable for its idiosyncratic grey and white sgraffito decorations on the house façades. Although this is found elsewhere in the villages, nowhere has it reached a comparable complexity and ubiquity.

The town originally had one principal entrance, a gateway on the north side, which is the most appropriate way to approach the town. Ahead is the central *plateía*, grouped around the large, modern church of the Koímisis tis Theotókou. To the south, at the highest point of the town, is the three-storey *pýrgos* or **great tower**, now partially ruined and lower than its original imposing height; it stands at the heart of the town, with an empty *cordon sanitaire* around it that separates it from the dense network of streets beyond. This was the refuge in case of attack, and was originally entered by a wooden bridge which was then removed and pulled inside.

One of the island's loveliest and most important churches, the 14th-century **church of the Ághii Apóstoli**, is entered down an arched alley off the east side of the central square (*open daily except Mon, 8.30–3*). The interior is covered with wall-paintings. As always with late Byzantine painting, the accent is on narrative content and decorative pattern: this is particularly noticeable in the two memorable scenes of the *Ascension* and of the *Harrowing of Hell*, respectively on the south and north walls of the crossing.

Environs of Pyrgí: Dótia and Aghía Marína

The Genoese **Tower of Dótia** (*map p. 433, B4*), 8km south of Pyrgí, constituted the impressive central keep of a fortified settlement smaller than but similar to Pyrgí. Although most is now rubble, the walls and corner bastions of the surrounding settlement are still visible.

Just over 2km west of Pyrgí, along the branch road southwest to Phaná, is the tiny chapel of **Aghía Marína**, to the north of the road. The modern construction is built on ancient foundations and incorporates ancient masonry in its structure: it is probably the site of a small 5th-century sanctuary, related to the presence of the main Sanctuary of Apollo Phanaios further southwest on the coast (*see below*).

Olýmpi

The quiet village of Olýmpi (*map p. 433, B4*), spread low on the floor of a wide valley, was, like Pyrgí, laid out in its present form by the Genoese in the 14th century. There is no access into it from the south and east sides; the main entrance is once again in the north walls, by way of a monumental gateway that preserves its original stone frame. From here the cobbled street leads under a passage decorated with *xysta* to the central square, where the rectangular fortress-tower has survived to a substantial height; even though it is the centre of the settlement, there is deliberately no axial access to it. To the north of the tower are the churches of Aghía Paraskeví and of the Taxiárches, simple, low and roofed with stone schist.

Half a kilometre east of Olýmpi, a road branches south towards the coast, and leads after 5.5km to the **Olýmpi Cave** (*open daily except Mon, in May 11–5; June–Oct 10–8*). Discovered as recently as 1985, this is a small cave between 60m and 70m in depth at certain points, with particularly fine 'filigree' stalactite and stalagmite formations (still actively forming) of a prevailing yellowy-reddish hue. A small, natural entrance lets sunlight in from above. The cave is estimated to be approximately 150 million years old.

Ancient Phanai

Almost parallel to the road to the Olýmpi Cave and slightly to the east, a track leads south to Phaná, the site of ancient Phanai (*map p. 433, A4; also accessible by 5.5km of partially metalled road, directly from Pyrgí*). As the track begins to approach the shore, a spring-house to the left, which incorporates some finely-drafted pieces of Classical masonry, gives an intimation of ancient presence in the area. The archaeological site is 100m further on, beside the modern chapel of Ághios Theódoros (marked on some maps as Aghía Markélla), which is built over the **Temple of Apollo Phanaios**. The apse of Ághios Theódoros preserves a small, carved capital as its altar table. The shoreline has in all probability receded; the pagan temple would have stood on a high, terraced platform directly above the water, from which flights of steps (visible in places) would have given access to the sanctuary. The foundations and the corner of the platform of a 6th-century BC temple can be seen to the northeast of the church. This temple was perhaps destroyed in the aftermath of the unsuccessful Ionian revolt of 494 BC, and rebuilt at least once in the late 5th or early 4th century BC. It is from this period that the beautiful masonry, visible to the south and east of the church by the road, dates. An Early Christian church, the foundations of whose apse are visible to the east of the present church, was constructed here from the stones of the temple.

This was primarily a place of cult, not an inhabited settlement; what is visible at the site gives little sense of the size, importance and longevity of the sanctuary, where finds of the Geometric period attest the worship of Apollo since the 9th century BC.

Mestá and Skouriá

Mestá (*map p. 433, A3*) is linked to Olýmpi by a pleasant, well-signed footpath. In aspect it is perhaps the most medieval of the Mastic Villages, and clearly preserves the pentagonal shape of its original 14th-century plan. The habitation is densely packed and low, and the streets are narrow and labyrinthine. Many of the alleys pass under buildings and through passageways; this system linked each building to the next, creating a network of contiguous roofs which allowed free movement across them in times of attack and danger. Everything revolves around the large central square, dominated by the disproportionate size of the church of the Taxiárches at its centre; it stands on the site of the original Genoese tower, which was demolished when the church was erected in 1868. Beside the doors of the west entrance of the church, a fragment of ancient stone clearly inscribed with a decree has been built into the wall.

The shallow, fertile valley to the west of Mestá, sown with isolated stone churches, provides a pleasant walk among groves of olive and fruit trees down to the shore at Merikoúnda Bay. At the top of the rise, 600m north of Mestá, a track branches left for **Skouriá** (*map p. 433, A3*) and the Livadiou watchtower, which dominates and protects the bay of Mestá and its harbour of Liménas. The 14th-century cylindrical stone tower still preserves some of its crenellations and machicolations at the rim: the only access—a stone-framed window—is a good 7m above ground level.

Véssa

Véssa (*map p. 433, B3*) is in many ways the most attractive and unchanged of the Mastic Villages: the centre is reached at the end of an avenue of eucalyptus. The settlement, hidden from view until the last moment, straddles the fertile floor of a shallow valley between two limestone ridges. The stone houses along its compact grid of narrow streets have many of the elements typical of the 14th-century Genoese master plan for these villages: narrow stone relieving arches above windows and doors, protruding machicolations and turrets, balconies supported on small arches, upper floors which cross the streets creating covered passageways, storage areas on the lower levels, towers, gates and fortifications. Concrete has hardly disturbed the stone and mortar buildings at any point. Many of the fine structures around the attractive *plateía*, though medieval in origin, bear the dates of their reconstruction or renovation, typically in the 1820s and '30s.

THE NORTHWEST OF THE ISLAND

Volissós and Limniá

Thucydides (*VIII, 24*) refers to 'Boliskos', which much be the ancient city on this site (*map p. 433, A2*), although little is to be seen today of an ancient precursor. The town was the home of the Homeridai, a clan that claimed descent from Homer. The acropolis hill is now occupied by a fine Genoese castle; the harbour, **Limniá** (1.5km from the town) still functions, and the watercourses have, until recently, fed a series of **watermills** of varying age, in the stretch between Volissós and Mánagros Bay (*the mills are visitable by taking a pleasant route on foot, signed 'Mánagros', from below the eastern side of Volissós; this is one of the richest areas on the island for wild flowers in spring*).

What distinguishes Volissós from many other Chiot villages is the variety of styles of architecture: in a short distance there are simple Neoclassical residences, Ottoman-style houses with overhanging wooden balconies, and medieval stone houses; the latter increasingly predominate as one climbs up towards the kastro. The **castle** was a key element in the late 14th-century fortification of the island undertaken by the Genoese and, though ruined, has been little modified through time. The tradition that the castle was built by Justinian's general, Belisarius, in the 6th century is almost certainly legend, but the remarkable 11th-century historian and imperial princess, Anna Comnena, mentions Volissós and its castle in her *Alexiad*. What she was referring to was probably demolished by the Genoese builders when they began the construction of the existing fort.

From the harbour of Limniá a road follows the coast west to the bay and monastery of **Aghía Markélla** (*map p. 433, A2*), site of the martyrdom of the young virgin saint of the (?)16th century from Volissós, whose feast day, 22nd July, is the most widely celebrated in the island's religious calendar. A simple cross at the water's edge at the far end of the beach marks the point where she died, reputedly at the hands of her possessed father: two springs of therapeutic water rise at the site, whose high mineral content has coloured the rock a deep red, symbolic of the blood of martyrdom.

The west coast to Ághio Gála

The main road which heads northwest from Volissós winds through a wide, sandstone landscape different in vegetation from elsewhere on the island: the villages, set athwart the ravines of mountain torrents, are open and panoramic, with the curious exception of **Melaniós** (*map p. 433, A1*), which is huddled out of sight in a seemingly subterranean dip at the island's western tip. After this, the road turns into the steep valley of **Ághio Gála**, the site of the earliest human habitation so far discovered on Chios. The village itself is built high up along the ridge of a projecting spur: the rock beneath is perforated with a network of deep caves, entered from the cliff of the gorge above the watercourse below. It is here that human settlers from as early as 6000 BC have left artefacts relating to their habitation or worship. The cult continued here intermittently from the Neolithic Age into historic times and on into the Christian era. Today it is the Christian buildings which are visible: the cave entrance is closed by the 14th-century church of the Panaghía Aghiogaloúsaina ('Virgin of the Sacred Milk'), whose apse and elongated cupola are in the typical style of late medieval Chios (*generally kept locked except in July and Aug. The key can be obtained from the guardian in the village plateía*). The principal interest of the interior is the intricately carved iconostasis, and the one remaining area of painting in the apse, which shows the Virgin with open arms. Around the church are grouped the abandoned hermitage buildings, probably dating from the 17th century. Standing entirely within the cave, reached through the church of the Panaghía, is the contemporaneous chapel of Aghía Ánna, with wall-paintings in deteriorating condition. The cave penetrates for 200m into the rock, through a series of linked chambers with active stalagmite and stalactite formation.

The north coast to Aghiásmata

The route east from Ághio Gála, which winds from ravine to ravine high above the largely deserted north coast, is densely forested and well-watered. In antiquity this area produced Ariousion wine, the most famous wine of the island. A distant descendant of this wine is still to be had in the attractive village of **Kouroúnia** (*map p. 433, A1*). From Aphrodísia, further east, a branch road plunges down into the ravine towards Aghiásmata. The small community of **Kéramos**, at the head of the valley that runs south of Aghiásmata, still preserves some of the ruined mine buildings associated with the extraction of antimony. This is an area generally rich in minerals, and the hot thermal waters which rise by the sea at **Aghiásmata** (the name means 'sacred waters') derive their curative qualities from this. These therapeutic powers have been appreciated and used continuously since Byzantine times, if not before, and are mentioned with approval by visitors and writers from the 17th century on. The springs are at the western edge of the beach, just beyond the abandoned bath house on the shore; the water, which rises at 68°C, is now pumped from a concrete hut over the springs directly back to the hydrotherapy spa, 500m to the south in the floor of the valley (*at the time of writing only open July–Sept*). The cliffs nearby are good for collecting samphire.

THE NORTHEAST OF THE ISLAND

Vrontádos and the Sanctuary of Cybele

The northern stretches of Chios Town blend seamlessly into Vrontádos (*map p. 433, C2*), which ends at the mouth of a ravine: at this site, between mountain, torrent and sea, a Sanctuary to Cybele was established perhaps as early as the 6th century BC. Its remains are known as the **Daskalópetra** or 'Teacher's Stone', sometimes just referred to as 'Homer's Rock' because it was long considered to be the spot where Homer taught his pupils the poet's art. The predominantly Ionic nature of the mixed dialect of Homer's epics has always been taken to suggest the poet's origins in this part of the Greek world, and Chios and Smyrna (modern Izmir) on the mainland opposite have traditionally had the strongest claims to have been his birthplace. What the visitor sees here is an outcrop of limestone whose upper surfaces have been fashioned by hand into a terrace; in the middle of this is a roughly cuboid protrusion of bedrock—originally a throne—on whose sides the very eroded reliefs of lions and (at the four lower corners) lions' claws can just be discerned. The wild setting of the gorge, the overhanging mountains, the torrent and the shore, combine to make this site typical of such ancient sanctuaries. The lion reliefs help to identify the cult as that of Cybele, the great mother goddess of Anatolia. As a mistress of wild nature, she was symbolised by attendant lions. Cybele was widely honoured on Chios, and this may have been one of her principal sanctuaries. Archaeological finds from this area (now in the museum in Chios Town) confirm the identity of the cult: it took place in the open air, and often involved ecstatic states inducing prophetic rapture and insensibility to pain.

Langáda and Kidiánta

The deep inlet and attractive waterfront of **Langáda** (*map p. 433, C2*), with fertile land behind and around, are a welcome sight on this inhospitably rocky coast. Ancient inscriptions and archaeological soundings have shown that a sanctuary of Delphinios Apollo and Delphinia Artemis was located in the north area of the bay (now occupied by a military camp). It was in this bay, following the revolt of Chios against Athens in 412 BC, that the Athenians fortified their position, after the capture of Oinoússes, and remained until 406 BC.

A year-round water-taxi service runs between Langáda and the islands of Oinoússes (four nautical miles to the east). Inland of Langáda, a steep cemented track climbs up through the village of Agrelopó to the deserted settlement of **Kidiánta**, set in a valley to one side of an impressive bare gorge. The village was a stronghold of the islanders' resistance to German occupation during the Second World War. Beyond Kidiánta, the track climbs further onto the bleak rock plateau above, with views across Oinoússes and far into Turkey. On the saddle (c. 2km beyond Kidiánta), dominated by a flat-topped tor to the east, scattered masonry and ancient remains have been located, which are believed to correspond to the site of ancient Koila.

The Kardámyla valley

The valley of Kardámyla (*map p. 433, C1*) is one of the island's most attractive corners, with a long and little-explored history. Apart from the references to 'Koila' and 'Kardamyle' in Herodotus and Thucydides, there is epigraphic evidence of the cult of Zeus Patroös in a forested grove on Mt Pelinnaíon above Áno Kardámyla, as well as of Dionysus Actaeus, Aphrodite Kytheria and Poseidon in other parts of the territory, at places yet to be securely identified. The remains of the 15th-century **Grías Castle** stand on a steep eminence directly to the south. It is a small fortress, consisting of two towers of slightly different form, linked by curtain walls and built over the site of earlier Hellenistic fortifications (*accessible on foot in 45mins from Áno Kardámyla by signed footpaths*). Recent settlement in the area is split between two nuclei: the picturesque hillside village of Áno Kardámyla and **Mármaro** (*map p. 433, C1*), the administrative centre around the coastal inlet to the northeast: the fertile *kámbos* lies between the two, fed by the waters that descend from Pelinnaíon through the upper village into the valley.

Around Mount Pelinnaíon

Northwest of Mármaro is **Nagós** (*map p. 433, C1*), whose name is a corruption of naos, 'temple'. The 4th-century BC remains of the village's namesake were found during excavations (now covered) in the vicinity of the spring, west of the inhabited area.

Kambiá (*map p. 433, B1*) is famous for its production (and festivals) of cherries: to the north, on precipitous rock-stacks in the ravine below, are the ruined Castle of Oria and the precariously perched church of the Panaghía; to the west are hillsides, traced and retraced with stone walls defining an extraordinary variety of shapes across the barren rocky terrain. To the south (2.5km) the watershed is marked by the remains of a medieval watchtower, directly east of the peak of Mt Pelinnaíon, which rises to a craggy 1297m above. The **summit** is best reached by the safer route from Víki, which is marked and takes about 2½ hrs each way; otherwise there is a slightly longer and shadeless route up from Spartoúnda (5km south of Kambiá).

Moní Moundón

The monastery of Ághios Ioánnis Pródromos, known as Moní Moundón (*map p. 433, B2*), lies above the village of Diefchá. The combination of its position with stunning views (especially at sunset), its atmospheric ruined buildings, and its unusual cycles of wall-paintings make this one of the most interesting monasteries in northern Chios (*outer buildings always open; katholikon closed. Key from the custodian in Diefchá; T: 22740 22011*). Originally a late 15th-century foundation, the monastery was enlarged and re-established in 1574, after which it acquired considerable importance, functioning as a monastic retreat and school for the Chiot aristocracy. The present paintings date from 1849, with restorations carried out after the earthquake of 1881. They include many traditional images, treated with the attractive naïveté of folk art: a good example is the *Ladder to Heaven*, in which a huddle of robed monks, encouraged by St Michael, leave the security of the cloister to attempt the precarious ladder that ascends to Paradise, while demons attempt to derail their endeavours.

Mount Aípos, Pityós and Rimókastro

While Mt Pelinnaíon is a grand massif with conspicuous peaks, **Mt Aípos**, to its south (*map p. 433, C2*), is quite different in character: a wide, shadeless, undulating mountain plateau of seemingly waterless rock. In a cleft between the two sits the once remote settlement of **Pityós**. A tenuous local tradition links the village with Homer; until not long ago, visitors were shown the 'house where the poet was born'. The village is dominated by the 13th-century fort, a curious military building shaped like a half-melon, with a curved castellated front to the north and a flat side to the south: the unusual shape is not dictated by the space available but may arise from modifications made when an existing, four-square Byzantine fort was reinforced by the Genoese.

Southwest of here, on the main road towards Chora, a landscape of frightening austerity unfolds. At the summit, a rough track leads north across the rock plateau to **Rimókastro** (*map p. 433, C2*). The main road descends slowly towards the precipitous edge of the plateau of Aípos. It reaches a belvedere 7km short of Chios Chora, with a sudden and magnificent panorama of Vrontádos and Chios far below, and the mountains of Turkey stretching beyond. The descent is dramatic thereafter.

PRACTICAL INFORMATION

GETTING AROUND

Domestic flights go regularly from Athens. There are also connections with Thessaloníki, including a local Eastern Aegean route from Thessaloníki to Rhodes via Lemnos, Mytilene and (once a week only) Samos. The airport is 3km from the centre of Chios Town.

The principal sea route (Piraeus, Chios, Mytilene) is served by Hellenic Seaways, with a daily departure from Piraeus (6½ hrs), continuing to Mytilene and returning to Piraeus overnight. GA Ferries run three times weekly along the route from/to Samos to the south, and Mytilene, Lemnos and Kaválato the north. Smaller boats connect Chios Town with Psará (5 times weekly) and Oinoússes (6 times weekly). Crossings to Turkey (Çesme) run almost daily in summer (Easter–mid-Oct); thereafter much more infrequently.

WHERE TO STAY

A number of the nicest places to stay on Chios are in Kámbos, to the south of the main town, in the elegant stone villas which are so characteristic of the area. Two can be particularly recommended: **Perivoli** ■ (*Odós Argénti; T: 22710 31513, www.perivolihotel.gr*) and **Perleas** ■ (*Odós Vitiádou; T: 22710 32217, www. perleas.gr*). Both offer simple accommodation and attentive hospitality, moderately priced, in elegant villas with gardens. Although signposted, neither is easy to find: if you call ahead, you will be piloted or collected. There is public transport, but a rental car is advised. In the centre of town, at the south end of the port, is the **Hotel Kyma**, in a stone-built mansion looking onto the sea (*T: 22710 44500*). Though old-fashioned and somewhat down at heel (the plumbing is not very good), this is more than compensated for by the friendliness and attentive hospitality of the owners and by the antiquated charm of the building. A different experience is offered by **Spilia Xenonas**, at Kardámyla, above the northeast coast (*T: 22720 22933, www.spilia-chios.gr*). This is a group of small, carefully restored, characteristic stone cottages at the top of the village, with views towards the sea in the distance: a good home-made breakfast is provided. Wooden signposts guide you up to the cottages on steep stone paths through the village; any car will need to be left well below.

WHERE TO EAT

In Chios Town, both **Byzantinio** and **Elliniki Kouzina**, on opposite sides of the junction of Rálli and Roídou between the port and the public gardens (*map p. 435, B2*), are favoured by locals for their inexpensive home cooking and well-prepared food. **Iakovou** (evenings only), on Ághiou Georgíou in the Kastro (*map p. 435, B1*), has more atmosphere, and offers a number of dishes from Asia Minor.

Roussikó in Thymianá (just east of the main church) is a delightful taverna, with fresh, imaginative dishes and good *bourekákia* (lightly fried phyllo pastry rolls). **Lefteris** at Pandoukiós (just south of Langáda on the northeast coast; *map p. 433, C2*), **Tria Adelphia** on Lithí beach (*map p. 433, B3*) and the taverna **Limani Meston** in Liménas (*map p. 433, A3*), all offer excellent fresh fish dishes in pleasant settings by the shore. **Markellos** at Pityós is well known for local meat and vegetable dishes; **Pheragides** offers *mezédes* in the delightful setting of a plane-shaded *plateía* at Kardámyla.

On the cliffs and rocky coasts of the island, samphire (*kritamó*) grows abundantly. It is a distinctive element in salads—always worth asking for, if it has not already been included. The island has a tradition of excellence in Oriental pastries; the quality of the *baklavá* and other sweets made by the **Amandier patisserie** on Livánou (south side of the port in Chios Town) is worthy of any Ottoman pastry-chef.

FURTHER READING

For social history of the important families of Chios and for the events of 1821–22, the following site contains much valuable information: www.christopherlong.co.uk/pub/chiosinfo.html.

FOURNI

Part of an archipelago of several islands (only two of them inhabited), Foúrni (*map p. 430*) is a pleasant and quiet retreat. The island, largely deforested by charcoal burning (its name means 'furnaces'), is covered with wild flowers in spring.

EXPLORING THE ISLAND

Chora

The modern *chora* of Foúrni is pleasingly ringed by hills. Its marble-paved main street, lined with mulberry trees, leads from the port to a charming main square, a corner of which is dominated by a massive, lidless Roman sarcophagus (1st century AD) in local marble, all that remains visible of an ancient settlement here.

Foúrni's points of historical interest are reached by taking the principal road which leaves from the south (surfaced for the first 2km). After 1km, four windmills on a saddle mark the descent on the southern side into Kambí and its bay. At 1.7km there is a junction: the road to the left heads north, to the right it continues south to Ághios Ioánnis Thermastís (6km). Both itineraries are described below.

North to Chrysomiliá

Just over a kilometre beyond the road junction south of Chora is the panoramic **church of Aghía Marína**, with fragments from a Byzantine predecessor gathered beside it. Half a kilometre further, past a modern church on the right, just as the road descends and the view opens, the chapel of Ághios Geórgios is visible on a lower spur to the south-west, the site of the **acropolis of ancient Korsiai** (*reached in 15mins on a rough path*). Its scant remains include ancient graffiti near the chapel.

At 9.6km from Chora, a right turn leads to the eastern shore at **Kamári**, the tiny harbour for crossing to the island monastery of Ághios Minás opposite. To the northwest above the village is the church of Ághios Nikólaos. Columns and carved stones in its precinct suggest an ancient settlement.

The main road continues to the beautifully-sited town of **Chrysomiliá** (14km from Chora), in a ravine high above the shore. The road to the harbour of Kambí (*also reached by caïque from Foúrni*) passes the church of Aghía Triáda, shortly after Chrysomiliá, built on an isodomic marble terrace that may have supported a Hellenistic tower. The waterfront of Kambí has a pebbled strand of limpid water, backed by trees.

South to Ághios Ioánnis Thermastís

At 2.2km south from Foúrni harbour, 600m from the main junction, an unsurfaced road leads downhill to the southeast into the next bay (1km), to the **ancient marble quarry of Petrokopeió**, one of the best-preserved ancient quarries in the Aegean. It produced a white marble much used in Ephesus. At the entrance on the shore below are abandoned pieces awaiting shipment: column drums, capitals, a large sarcophagus (unhollowed), corner elements for an architrave. They are all roughouts; detailed carvings would have been applied at their destination. The beach is composed solely of naturally smoothed and bleached marble pebbles.

The main road continues to the tiny fishing village of **Ághios Ioánnis Thermastís** (6km), at the head of a sheltered bay. A kilometre east of here, across the southern headland, is Vitsiliá Bay, with a secluded shingle beach.

THYMAINA

The island of Thýmaina (*map p. 430*), sparsely inhabited and little visited, takes its name from the abundance of wild thyme, whose scent at times fills the air. Its harbour is particularly sheltered; the tiny settlement is grouped around two parallel churches. There are no tavernas or licensed rooms for rent, only a small food store. The walk up the eastern side of Mt Tsímbes to the hermitage of Ághios Geórgios affords beautiful views.

PRACTICAL INFORMATION

GETTING AROUND

A caïque runs from Foúrni to Ikaría (Ághios Kírykos) in the morning and returns in the afternoon most days in summer, less frequently in winter. Hydrofoils link Foúrni with Ikaría and Samos (Pythagóreio; both 1hr) twice weekly between mid-April and mid-Oct, more frequently in high summer. Throughout the year there is a twice-weekly car ferry to Ikaría and Samos (Karlóvasi and Vathý): it also stops at nearby Thýmaina. There is a twice-weekly ferry to Piraeus.

WHERE TO STAY

A number of the houses have rooms to let. **Maria's Rooms** (*T: 22750 51204*), on the south side of the main street, are pleasantly appointed. **Toula's** (*T: 22750 51332*), on the waterfront, has studios for rent. The nicest place to stay is the **Archipelagos** (*T: 22750 51250, www.archipelagoshotel.gr*).

WHERE TO EAT

Building on the fame of Foúrni's lobster-fishing fleet, the two main restaurants on the waterfront, Nikos' (or more properly **Taverna Remezzo**) and **Miltos'**, are popular with locals and visitors alike. Inland along the main street, **To Koutouki tou Psaradikou** specialises in traditional oven-cooked dishes such as *papoutsáki* (stuffed aubergine) and *briám* (a kind of Greek *ratatouille*). **O Kalokardos**, beside the church of Ághios Nikólaos, is good for local wine and specialises in meat dishes. The **fish taverna at Kamári** is popular in summer; likewise the little taverna **Pilavaki** in Chrysomiliá.

IKARIA

Mountainous Ikaría, at first sight forbidding and windswept, is one of the most idiosyncratic islands of the Aegean, home to much unaffected beauty and a fierce sense of community. Untouched by mass tourism, its immensely varied landscapes, with the older villages literally hidden inland and underground, are highly rewarding.

HISTORY OF IKARIA

Ikaría has been inhabited since Neolithic times. From early in its history it appears to have had several names: Dolichi ('elongated') and Ichtheoussa ('rich in fish'). The modern name Ikaría is more likely to come from the Phoenician word for fish, *ikor*, than from the mythical Icarus, despite the connection of his legend to the island (*see p. 463*). Ikaría is frequently cited in ancient literature, nearly always—other than for the fable of Icarus—for the wildness of its seas or for its famous wine (*see p. 462*). Two small Classical cities, Oenoe and Therma, were separate members of the Delian League. Therma's importance seems to have been superseded by the Hellenistic foundation of Drákanon, at the island's eastern tip. Both cities were further developed in Roman times; Oenoe became the seat of the Byzantine governor.

Christianity was established here relatively early. Under Byzantium, the island, now named Nikaria and frequently used as a place of exile, was linked to the destiny of Samos and Chios, passing together with them under Genoese rule in the 14th and 15th centuries. In 1481 Ikaría was taken by the Knights of Rhodes, falling to the Turks in 1522. Throughout these uncertain centuries the inhabitants learned to hide in the mountains for long periods which became known as the *apháneia*, the 'disappearances'. The people perfected a kind of semi-subterranean architecture, practically invisible from the sea. The remote valley of Langáda became home to an unorthodox and autonomous administration. Although participating in the Independence Revolution of 1821, Ikaría fell back under Turkish rule in 1835. Finally, in 1912, in an almost bloodless insurrection, the inhabitants evicted their Turkish overlords and established their independence. Four months later, Ikaría joined the free Greek state.

In the 20th century the island's population was depleted by emigration to the New World. During the Greek Civil War of 1946–49, and later under the Colonels' junta, Ikaría became a place of exile for political dissidents, who at times outnumbered the islanders. Mikis Theodorakis, the composer and musician, was exiled here in 1947. The island has a reputation for vigorous left-wing politics.

AGHIOS KIRYKOS & THE SOUTH COAST

Ághios Kírykos (*map p. 460, D2*), referred to locally simply as 'Ághios', is a pleasant,

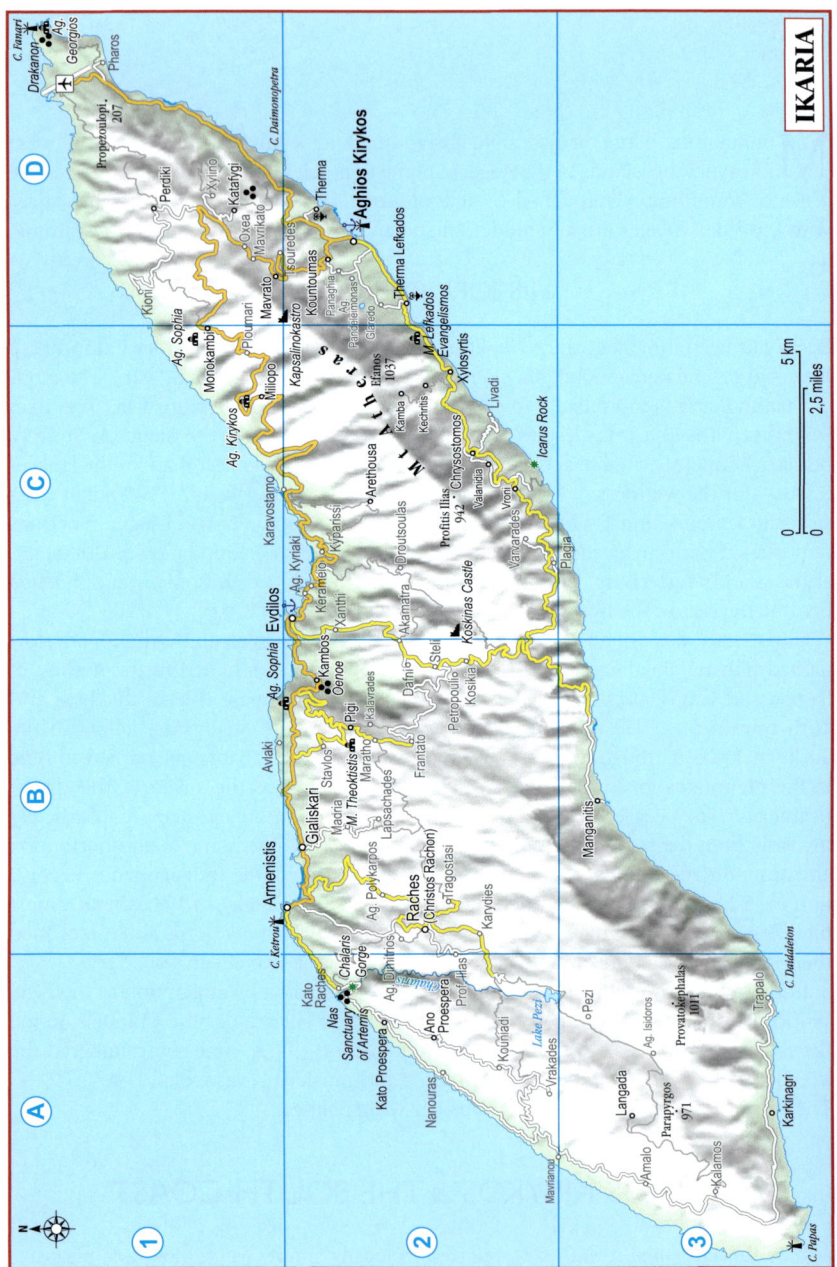

IKARIA

0 5 km
0 2,5 miles

C. Fanari
Drakanon
Ag. Georgos
Pharos
Propezoulopi. 207
Perdiki
Skyiro
C. Daimonopetra
Akatavigi
Oxea
Mavrikato
Kloni
Therma
Aghios Kirykos
Vouretes
Kountoumas
Ag. Sophia
Monokambla
Ag. Kirykos
Milopo
Plouman
Mavrato
Kapsalinokastro
Perianglia
Ag. Pori
Pano Hemonasol
Gialedo
Therma Lefkados
Lefkados
Evangelismos
M. Atheras
Kylosyrtis
Eidanos 1037
Kamba
Kechnfs
Livadi
Karavostamo
Arethousa
Nyparissi
Icarus Rock
Ag. Kyriaki
Kerametio
Xanthi
Droutsoulias
Proftis Ilias 942
Valanda
Vroni
Vanarades
Plaa
Evdilos
Kambos
Oenoe
Pigi
Akamatra
Koskinas Castle
Kosika
Kechnis
Ag. Sophia
Stel
Dafni
Petropodlia
Armenistis
Aviaki
Gialiskari
Madria
Stavlos
M. Theoktistis
Kavradez
Lapsachades
Frantato
Manganitis
Raches
(Christos Rachon)
Ag. Polykarpos
Maratho
Tragostasi
Karydies
C. Ketnia
Chalaris Gorge
Ag. Dimitros
Proftis Ilias
Kato Raches
Nas
Sanctuary of Artemis
Ano Proespera
Kato Proespera
Kouniadi
Vrakades
Lake Pezi
Pezi
Trapalo
Provatokephalas 1011
C. Daidaleion
Nanouras
Mavriano
Amalo
Parapyrgos 971
Langada
Ag. Isidoros
Kalamos
Karkinagri
C. Papas

N

① ② ③
A B C D

business-like port, named after the Eastern Church's youngest martyr (*see p. 464*). The harbour's outer mole is dominated by a seven-metre modern bronze monument to Icarus. What remains of the old town is just inland and west of the port. There is also a small Archaeological Museum (*closed at the time of writing*).

NORTHEAST TO DRAKANON

Thérma

Two kilometres northeast of Ághios Kírykos is the small settlement of **Thérma** (*map p. 460, D2*), at the foot of a gorge. It is a well-frequented thermal spa with several springs containing radium. The principal Apollon Spa is opposite the shore (*open 7–1 & 5–8*). These springs formed the nucleus of an ancient healing resort and Asclepeion. A path leads east along the coast for 400m to **Chalasména Thérma**, the vestiges of a later Roman and early Byzantine thermal establishment with built and rock-cut features (*path from east end of Thérma Bay; through the terrace in front of the Agriolykos Pension, up behind its far side, and on for 10mins until it descends to the shore*).

Drákanon

Beyond the small coastal village of Pháros, 100m before the road ends at the sea, at a poorly-signed turning to the left, a track leads to Drákanon (*map p. 460, D1*). The site is impressive both for its dramatic situation and for the magnificent state of preservation of its **Hellenistic tower**, incorporated into an enceinte of walls. On a defensible site overlooking two harbour inlets, the city guarded the Samos–Foúrni channel to the east. It is known from inscriptions that Drákanon was particularly associated with the cult of Dionysus.

The 4th-century BC tower stands to a height of nearly 30 courses. Its only equal is the tower at Ághios Pétros on Andros (*see p. 104*). It is entered by a beautifully arched doorway facing due east. The interior diameter is c. 6.5m. The fixing holes for two wooden floors are visible. It is integrated into the system of fortifications, which comprise a triangle of walls with two bastions to north and south. The well-preserved south bastion has an intact entrance. Ongoing excavations have revealed buildings and statue bases east of the tower, and some structures within the walls.

A path leads downhill to the east, to the chapel of **Ághios Geórgios**, where a fluted antique altar has been incorporated into the interior wall of the apse.

SOUTH TO THE ICARUS ROCK

Two kilometres south of Ághios Kírykos, a tiny blue and white sign reading 'Hot mineral springs' points the way to **Thermá Lefkádos** (*map p. 460, D2*), where three hot springs rise by the shore and mix with the seawater in a large pool, roughly defined in the sea by a ring of boulders. A further 1.5km west along the coast road is the late 18th-century **monastery of Lefkádos Evangelismós**, with a pleasant katholikon.

Xylosýrtis

The delightful village of Xylosýrtis (*map p. 460, C2*) is overlooked by the highest summit of Mt Athéras, the Pramnos of antiquity. At the western end of the village a fork leads up the mountain. After 2km of climbing, the village of **Kechrítis** comes into view on the right, an abandoned settlement, now ruined, of low stone houses deliberately designed to be almost indistinguishable from the rocky landscape. The road terminates at **Kámba**, 1.5km beyond, at a height of almost 700m above the shore, with fantastic views. The simple, windowless 18th-century church of the Panaghía, constructed in unrendered stone, preserves its original schist roof. Beyond it stretches a network of stone-walled fields bursting with vines. The special climate, altitude, humidity, soil and water on this high ledge favour the cultivation of a rich and excellent grape. In antiquity Ikaría was renowned for its very dark red Pramnian wine, which was famous for its medicinal properties. The vines here stand in a long line of descent from their prized Pramnian ancestors.

PRAMNIAN WINE

It was into a concoction based on cheese, fresh honey and Pramnian wine that Circe poured the potion which was to turn Odysseus' men into swine (*Odyssey X, 635*). In fact Homer mentions the wine more than once, always indicating that it was mixed with grated cheese or barley. Plato, Aristophanes, Hippocrates, Diogenes Laertius and Athenaeus also describe or refer to it. Common to them all is the suggestion that the wine was almost never drunk pure or for refreshment, but instead was used medicinally. What can such a wine have been like? Athenaeus of Naucratis, the connoisseur of all matters of the palate, describes Pramnian wine as 'neither sweet nor dense, but with a sharp and astringent and powerful taste' (*Deipnosophistai I, 15*). The wine was apparently 'black', was endowed with the 'power to assuage anger' and matured when left to stand (Hesychius of Alexandria). Eustathius, in his commentaries on Homer, says it was 'not for quenching thirst, but rather for alleviating satiety'—perhaps somewhat like a modern digestif. Hippocrates and Galen speak of its therapeutic qualities, both as an unction (Hippocrates) and for consumption (Galen). Much later, the French Jesuit missionary Jacques-Paul Babin again described the wine as 'hard', but added that the island had 'the best winter grapes I ever encountered, being round and red, and growing between the rocks in such dangerous places that they are gathered with considerable hazard'. (The same Fr Babin was astonished to note that the islanders of Ikaría rowed their boats naked, explaining that clothes were an impediment to them and wore out too quickly when rowing.)

It is hard to find anything today on Ikaría that corresponds to these descriptions. Interestingly, however, warmed red wine with barley in it is still drunk in winter by the older rural inhabitants, both here and on Samos.

Níkaris rock

Beyond Xylosýrtis, the coast road leads through a fertile landscape to the villages Chrysóstomos, Valanidiá, Vróni, and Plagiá. From Vróni (*map p. 460, C2*), a small trapezoidal rock is visible in the bay just offshore: this is the **rock of Níkaris**, traditionally believed to mark the place where Icarus fell into the sea and drowned on his airborne escape from Crete.

THE LEGEND OF ICARUS

The fullest literary account of the escape of Daedalus and Icarus from the Labyrinth of Crete is Ovid's in the *Metamorphoses* (*VIII, 182ff*). An older version, however, is probably recounted in Pausanias (*Description of Greece, IX,11*), in which Daedalus, whom King Minos of Crete had imprisoned together with his son Icarus in the Labyrinth (designed by Daedalus himself at Minos' command), escapes by a boat rigged with his newly-invented sails, which were able to outrun the oar-powered ships of Minos. Daedalus fared well, but Icarus, who did not properly understand how to control his sails, capsized and drowned near Lebynthos (modern Lévitha, 40km west of Kálymnos). His body was washed by the storm to Ikaría where, in other accounts, it was later found and buried by Heracles. Ovid's version, more romantic and far better known, has the ingenious Daedalus make wings of wax and feathers for the escape. Before embarking, Daedalus advises his son to fly neither too low, where humidity might weigh down the feathers, nor too high, where the sun might melt the wax. Once well out of danger, Icarus ignores the warning, falls into the sea and drowns, leaving Daedalus to bury his body on the island which, as Ovid says, has ever since borne his name. Ovid's account is vivid and moving: its details inspired Brueghel's masterpiece of 1569, *Landscape with the Fall of Icarus*, which in turn inspired W.H. Auden's poem of c. 1932, 'Musée des Beaux Arts, Brussels' (where the picture is still to be seen).

Beyond Plagiá the road branches. The main road takes a dramatically beautiful cliffside route to Évdilos (*see p. 465*). The left branch passes through a tunnel and on to **Manganítis** (*map p. 460, B3*), in an isolated and astonishing landscape of vast granite boulders and Aleppo pines. Manganítis itself is a quiet recreational spot with a couple of good *mezedopoleía*, and a tiny, attractive harbour.

AGHIOS KIRYKOS TO EVDILOS

Inland from Ághios Kírykos

The road north from Ághios Kírykos climbs through various villages, passing several ruined water mills. West of Kountoúmas, a long winding track climbs to the **monument to the victims of the forest fires** of 1993. From Mavráto (*map p. 460, D1*) a path leads steeply west towards the summit of the ridge (*45mins*) to the remains of **Kapsalinókastro**, a 15th-century fortress with ample views. Beyond the agricultural centres of Mavrikáto and Oxéa, a road drops sharply off to the left to Katafýgi on the slopes below. The villages in this area have many stone houses dating from the last 200 years. Due south, a hill rises to a summit of 470m: this was the site of the **Archaic settlement of Kataphydion**, used through and beyond Classical times as the acropolis for Thérma, on the coast below. All that remains is collapsed masonry along the summit, but some remnants of the lower courses of the citadel walls are discernible at the south escarpment of the hill.

A kilometre beyond the Katafýgi turning, the main road reaches a summit with commanding views of Foúrni and Samos. The attractive traditional village of **Perdíki** lies 2km down a branch road to the north. It has a small folklore museum. An unpaved road to the east leads to the coast near the airport. Before dropping to sea level, it descends the hill of Propezoulopí, where a number of possibly prehistoric **menhirs** stand in the adjacent fields.

The main route to Évdilos

The main road to Évdilos leads through a landscape of ravines to **Monokámbi** (*map p. 460, C1*), completely hidden from sight from the sea below. Visible from the road to the north of the village, under a ridge of slanting rock, is the tiny, rock-cut chapel of Aghía Sophía (*access by path and steps from the north end of the village*). After Ploumári the road skirts a wide gorge, beyond which is the rudimentary and ancient church of **Aghía Ioulítta and Ághios Kírykos**. Saints Julitta and Kirykos, from Iconium in Asia Minor (modern Konya), were mother and infant son: Kirykos was killed in Tarsus, during the persecutions of Diocletian, at the age of three, and his mother was later beheaded in 296. The building is hard to date because its roof has been rebuilt and an incongruous column added to support it; but the simple flagstone floor and roughly assembled walls may be of considerable antiquity. There are remains of fortifications, cisterns and habitations on the spur of Gérakas above and to the north. Just beyond, in the next ravine, below the tiny settlement of **Miliopó** (*map p. 460, C1*), are remains of the Early Christian basilica of the Taxiárchis, perhaps the island's earliest surviving place of Christian worship.

From Miliopó, through the area of Karavóstamo and down to the coast at Évdilos, the road weaves repeatedly inland and then back towards the sea, as it skirts ravine after ravine, slowly descending through a terrain that becomes ever more cultivated. The settlements are mostly modern: their predecessors, from the period of the *apháneia* or 'disappearances' (*see History, p. 459*), are all higher up inland. One such settlement is **Arethoúsa** (*map p. 460, C2*), a loose group of scattered villages where life centres around viticulture, the cultivating of fruits (especially apricots and plums) and the production of cheese. Even *kafeneía* are few and far between: but in them can often be found intense and old-style local wines, together with some equally intense and old-style political commentary, and a sense of dress and décor that has remained unchanged for a lifetime.

Évdilos and Koskinás Castle

At the central point of the north coast, **Évdilos** (*map p. 460, C2*), meaning 'Clear' or 'Visible', is the capital of the north of the island. It is a peaceful and attractive port, with an old quarter on the hill to the west directly above the harbour. In antiquity Évdilos was called Histoi. The deep, fertile, protected valley which cuts across to its south was the island's principal granary. It therefore needed protection, provided throughout the Middle Ages by the impressively-sited **Castle of Koskinás** (*the castle is 8.5km due south of Évdilos, to the east of the road which connects it with Plagiá on the south coast. From Akamátra it is reached by an unmetalled road. Alternatively, an equally dramatic approach can be made from the south from the Plagiá road, where 800m after the summit of the ridge, an unsurfaced road leads to the castle in 3.5km*). The castle, its walls relatively well preserved, perches precariously at an altitude of over 700m, and is entered by a small, low gate. The bases of two watchtowers are clearly visible. The construction is originally Byzantine, from the 11th or 12th century, but was partially modified by the Genoese in the 14th century, who probably then rebuilt the large church of Ághios Geórgios Dorganás ('St George of the Shining Spear'), which dominates the summit. Its interior contains a number of ancient spolia: a granite column in its templon screen and a fluted drum which supports the altar. Also visible, in the body of the south and west walls, are a number of immured clay pots: this was a Byzantine habit which enhanced a building's acoustics. The other castles on Ikaría are visible from Koskinás.

THE WEST OF THE ISLAND

Ancient Oenoe

Around the bay and village of Kámbos (*map p. 460, B2*) are the remains of ancient Oenoe, whose name, cognate with the Greek word for wine, is a clue to the source of its wealth and the reason for its fame. The site is a clear choice for an early settlement: a natural acropolis dominating a fertile estuary with a beach and port, through which the wine produced on the valley slopes to the south would have been traded and exported. Prosperity from the wine trade would have made the city an obvious choice of seat for later Roman and Byzantine governors; and it is the evidence of their presence that remains today. Referred to locally as **Palatía**, the ruined complex with conspicuous arched windows, visible on the northeast side of the acropolis hill in the centre of the valley, is the principal remnant of what was probably a Byzantine governor's residence, created out of a variety of earlier Roman buildings (*access is easiest from around the western side of the hill*). Though officially referred to as a Roman odeion, it is more likely to be early Byzantine, perhaps an audience chamber. The summit of the **acropolis** above reveals the base of a fortress tower, but little else of substance beyond the fine views.

Below the summit on the south side is the fine 12th-century church of **Aghía Eiríni**, built over part of the site of a much larger 5th-century basilica, with remains of magnificent mosaics visible north of the entrance to the later church and under the steps to the museum. The 12th-century church has an unusual synthronon at its east end.

Just above the church is the small Archaeological Museum (*open mornings in summer; otherwise no regular hours: the key is kept in the café/shop on the main road just below; free*). It contains finds from Oenoe and elsewhere on the island.

ARMENISTIS & THE FAR WEST

The coast road continues east from Kámbos, by the ancient church at **Aghía Sophía** (1km), towards the island's main tourist centres, Gialiskári and Armenistís, known for their sandy beaches. **Armenistís** (*map p. 460, B1*) has a number of tavernas and the widest variety of good hotels on the island. It is an attractive and still little-developed resort.

West of the Kámbos inlet, a beautiful route southwest reaches the **Theoktístis Monastery** (*map p. 460, B2; open 8–1 & 4–8*). In the small katholikon is a remarkable, near-complete cycle of 17th-century wall-paintings, revealing an unusually sophisticated style. The *Baptism of Christ* in a River Jordan teeming with fish—one particularly large one by his foot—plays on the Christological symbolism of fish (south side of ceiling). Directly behind the exterior east end of the church is a cramped, rock-cut hermit's sleeping cell; another is at the foot of the steps to the south of the monastery area; and the largest—and most dramatically troglodytic of all—at the top of the flight of steps, beneath a projecting granite boulder.

The village of **Pigí** above the monastery has two typical stone-roofed churches side by side.

Ráches and the Chaláris Gorge

Spread across a wide hollow between rugged hills, Ráches ('Ridges') is a collection of several contiguous villages. Its principal centre, **Christós Rachón** (*map p. 460, B2*), is an unexpected pleasure to come upon: lush, peaceful and hidden away, a seemingly endless tissue of tiny houses immersed each in its own garden. Bustling with life, with a tiny centre of stone-paved streets shaded by pergolas or trees and lined with cafés and tavernas, Christós has long been the commercial centre of this part of the island, in particular during the periods of the 'disappearances'.

The area is well-suited for walking (*information and maps available in Christós Rachón, in the photography and stationery shops*). Marked paths traverse the **Chaláris Gorge** and its succession of pools and cascades. It is home to a varied and interesting flora and fauna, with several varieties of cyclamen and wild orchid. The kingfisher is a regular resident, most easily observed in winter when the trees are bare; little egrets are common in the lower reaches. Rare migrants include the black-winged stilt and little bittern.

The Sanctuary of Artemis

Such densely-wooded terrain was, in antiquity, the natural domain of the huntress goddess Artemis. The Chaláris river would at that time have carried much more water and its small estuary would have formed the only viable roadstead for boats on the west side of the island. Above this natural harbour, therefore, the **Sanctuary of Artemis Tauropolos** at Nas grew up (*map p. 460, A2*). Tauropolos means 'drawn by a yoke of bulls' or perhaps 'hunting bulls'; Nas is a corruption of naos, 'temple'. This seemingly remote spot had great importance in antiquity as the first or last harbour on the Asia Minor side of the Aegean for pilgrims on their way to or from the Sanctuary of Apollo on Delos (the birthplace of Artemis). The popularity of the cult of Artemis spread from Asia Minor (principally Ephesus), and this sanctuary, already established by the 7th century BC, would appear to be one of the oldest in the Greek islands.

The site of Nas is tranquil and beautiful, but little of substance remains to be seen: the columns and statuary, which were recorded as being still visible on the site a little over a hundred years ago, were later zealously consigned to the kilns to make mortar for new churches. The site banks up the hill to the south side of the river inlet, now closed by a sandbar. At the lowest level are the remains of some late 1st-century BC wharves and port installations. Further up, there is extensive terracing, which at several points has been rebuilt in later times. Above all of this, and perfectly orientated to the cardinal points, is a podium, about 26m on its longer north–south axis, on which the principal temple may have been erected. Beyond this point, the litter of potsherds on the southern hillside is witness to the extent and density of habitation here. The site, especially towards sunset, has a pure and austere beauty.

The far west

The true fascination of Ikaría is its 'wild west', into whose protected and beautiful fastness the inhabitants retreated from the threat of piracy and invasion. Here can be found the strange troglodyte dwellings—half natural granite boulder, half stone-built house—which were used during these periods of retreat, in the 15th–18th centuries, which have come to be known as the 'disappearances'. Beyond Nas is **Káto Proespéra** (*map p. 460, A2*). A side road to Áno Proespéra passes many 'invisible' dwellings, some over 500 years old, often hidden behind massive granite boulders.

The area is served by a network of dirt roads passing through beautiful unspoilt terrain and allowing glimpses of other 'hidden' villages, including formerly self-governed **Langáda** (*map p. 460, A3*). The wide and beautiful upland valley here is completely cut off and invisible from the sea, hence its choice as the principal retreat during the disappearances. Langáda became a self-governing community, the seat of the islanders' self-appointed council: the abandoned municipal buildings are still to be seen at the northeastern end of the valley. Some sense of Langáda's importance as a capital is given by the impressive church of the Panaghítsa, at the base of the valley amidst a grove of immense and ancient plane trees. The village hosts the island's greatest *panigýri* for the Feast of the Virgin (14–16 Aug).

At **Karkinágri** (*map p. 460, A3*), on a narrow and fertile coastal plain, only a few old stone houses remain from the time when the village was an isolated fishing port; it is now a place of summer resort, with a couple of good tavernas and a sprinkling of modern houses and gardens hemmed between the mountains, the sea and the midday sun. A caïque service runs between Karkinágri and Ághios Kírykos three times a week in good weather (*typically Mon, Wed and Fri*). The journey along the wild and precipitous south coast leaves a vivid impression of the island's geography.

PRACTICAL INFORMATION

GETTING AROUND

The small airport, 11km from Ághios Kírykos (shuttle bus), is served by daily flights from Athens. Ferries from Piraeus to Samos serve the island's two ports: Évdilos almost daily (5hrs, summer only; otherwise 8–9hrs) and Ághios Kírykos less frequently. Fast hydrofoil links (1hr) from Pythagóreio on Samos run four times weekly in summer, twice weekly in April–May and Sept–Oct. Various local caïque services are available in Ághios Kírykos.

WHERE TO STAY

The **Agriolykos Pension** at Thérma (*T: 22750 22433 or 22383, www.island-ikaria.com/hotels/ agriolykos.asp*) is very quiet, set in a delightful garden of tamarisks at the top of a flight of steps above the north end of the bay. Rooms are small and simple, but have air conditioning (NB: access is only on foot, and bags will need to be carried up). Also in Thérma, the **Anthemis Hotel** (*T: 22750 23156 or 23377*) is simple, with adequate rooms, and has helpful and friendly owners. Both hotels are inexpensive.

The island's smarter hotels are mostly in the area of Armenistís: the **Hotel Erofili Beach** (*T: 22750 71058/9; www.erofili.gr*) in the upper price range, has large, comfortable and well-appointed rooms overlooking the seafront and the pool: it is a good hotel, but the breakfast is somewhat disappointing and the reception decidedly cool. Just outside Armenistís, on the way to Nas, is the charming **Hotel Daidalos** (*T: 22750 71390/2*), looking west out to sea: next door to it, and of equivalent standard but more old-fashioned, is the **Cavos Bay Hotel** (*T: 22750 71381/3; www.cavosbay.com.gr*). Both of the above are in the medium price range. Those seeking real peace and quiet might explore **Tzamoudakis Rooms** in remote Karkinágri (*T: 22750 91217 or 91327*).

WHERE TO EAT

For a variety of local and traditional dishes, always freshly prepared, Christos Chazalas' **Taverna To Tzaki**, in Glarédo (inland 2km west of Ághios Kírykos) is much to be recommended. In Ághios Kírykos itself, the tiny **Taverna Klimataria**, under a vine pergola a couple of blocks in from the harbour, serves good soups and oven dishes, and is justly favoured by locals for its good value.

There are several good tavernas at Káto Ráches overlooking the site at Nas: **Taverna O Nas** has the best view, but the food is more imaginative and home-made in character at **Anna's Taverna**. In Karkinágri, the fresh fish is generally excellent at the **Perkas Restaurant**.

OINOUSSES

In 2004, a large, mid-4th-century BC cargo vessel, carrying around 400 amphorae of wine, was found in the channel between Chios and Oinoússes (*map p. 430*; pron: *Inoússes*) and in the same year a Roman shipwreck was identified off the west of Chios. There have been many such finds, evidence of the formidable quantity of wine traded through these waters in antiquity. The name Oinoússes (anciently Oinousa), means 'rich in wine'. The economic potential of the nine or ten islands that comprise the archipelago lay in a well-protected harbour and in their proximity to the rich markets of Chios, Ephesus and Smyrna (Izmir). Without boats, and wine to trade, the islands would have been of scant significance. Oinoússes today feels like a forgotten frontier. Its peacefulness, the wide views across to Turkey and Chios, and its dense and unusually varied vegetation, are its greatest attractions.

HISTORY OF OINOUSSES

The archipelago consists of about 10 islands: Oinoússes is the largest and the only one continuously inhabited. The islands generally followed the history of Chios. In the Middle Ages they were probably abandoned; repopulation began in the 18th century. At the time of the 1822 massacre on Chios (*see p. 434*), the inhabitants fled to Syros, then the Aegean centre for Greek shipping. They returned five years later and, within 40 years, Oinoussean families owned almost 30 ships, plying routes through the Mediterranean and Black Sea. The emergence in the 19th century of three important families or clans on the island, the Hadjipateras, Lemos and Lyras families, and their formation of a consortium, was the beginning of long-distance international shipping history for Oinoússes. The Lemos family holding is by most measures the largest private holding in Greece, and one of the largest in the world.

EXPLORING OINOUSSES

The Chora

The ferry docks at the harbour of Aignoúsa, whose port is formed by a protective chain of islets to west and south, which are crowned with churches. One islet, which has a family villa to the north end, is clearly marked 'Pateróniso' ('Pateras Island'). The main waterfront is remarkable for its lack of the customary buzz of cafés and shops; there are none. It is punctuated by several bronze statues of members of the prominent Pateras and Lemos families, as well as more symbolic memorials. In the centre of the promenade is the recently renovated Maritime Museum (*open mornings in high season only*). At the western end of the waterfront is the Naftikó Gymnásio, or Academy of Commercial Navigation, the only non-military nautical boarding school in Greece.

From this point there is a good general view of the *chora*, which lies attractively to one side of a cavea-shaped hollow in the hills.

The *chora* is large, and spreads substantially to the east onto the slopes of the next valley. The original settlement lay higher up, 2km to the northeast, just below the ridge. The modern settlement is grouped around the large church of Ághios Nikólaos, an early 20th-century building, lavishly decorated inside and well-endowed with icons. On the climb up from the port, you pass a number of fine Neoclassical buildings (many abandoned), with window frames and architectural details in stone.

Around the island

The coast road, which leaves from beside the cemetery, passes through an area scattered with houses and signs of abandoned cultivation. After 3.5km the road rises steeply towards the north: at the top of the rise, the Convent of the Evangelismós, built in 1962 at the wish of Katingo Pateras (grieving mother of a daughter of 20, who died of cancer) comes partially into view, sunk in a fold in the hills. The nunnery is meticulously constructed from the best materials, and deliberately hidden behind manicured hedges of cypress and jasmine. Above it on the crest of the hill is a landmark cross, with the church of the Análipsi just beyond (*entry to women only*). Below, nearer to the shore, are the gardens which supply the community.

The upper road runs back east along the ridge and skirts the island's summit, Voútyro (182m), with views towards Turkey. A little beyond, after a thick stand of pines, are the remains of a small settlement in a hollow: this safer, more hidden site is all that remains of the original main settlement on the island, before the development of Aignoúsa.

PRACTICAL INFORMATION

GETTING AROUND

The *Oinoussai III* (*T: 22710 25074*) runs most days from Oinoússes to Chios early in the morning, returning after lunch. Journey time 1hr. Two small water taxis go on demand between Oinoússes and Langáda on Chios.

WHERE TO STAY

Lodging is limited to the **Thalassoporos Hotel** (*T: 22720 55745*), where accommodation is basic but the owners are very friendly.

WHERE TO EAT

Eating is also very limited. The only fully-fledged taverna is the pleasant enough **Taverna Pateroniso**, set back a little way from the harbour-front; up in the town are a couple of shops that double as small eateries.

FURTHER READING

Hellas: a Portrait of Greece by Nicholas Gage has one chapter devoted to the shipping families of Oinoússes.

PSARA

Because of its position at the edge of open waters on the trade routes leading from the southwest Aegean towards the Black Sea and Asia Minor coasts, Psará (*map p. 430*) had a flourishing Mycenaean settlement in the 13th century BC. Excavations have revealed Hellenistic settlement on the site of the present town and a Roman presence at other points of the island. Its land was always poor, however, and it is little wonder that the islanders turned to the sea and became talented mariners. Famous for their skill at combating pirates, they also operated a substantial commercial navy in the 18th and early 19th centuries. In 1824 the Ottoman navy set fire to the entire island as punishment for its resistance to Turkish rule during the Greek War of Independence. Those who escaped the destruction settled in Syros, in an area of the city known to this day as Psarianá, and where they contributed their expertise to the island's important shipping industry.

Arrival at Psará is always sombre: the island's rock is barren and dark; fewer than 500 souls inhabit the main town; and being a visitor is not particularly easy: accommodation is limited and there is no public transport.

EXPLORING PSARA

The large, sheltered bay of Psará, in the southwest corner of the island, is protected to the south by the steep and looming rock of Mávri Ráchi or Palaiókastro, formerly the acropolis of ancient Psyra: traces of a Hellenistic settlement (3rd–1st centuries BC) have been uncovered on the north slope, with the cemetery occupying the lowest reaches.

The town spreads across the isthmus which joins Mávri Ráchi to the island and over the low saddle behind the port. The centre of the town circles a low rise dominated by the domed church of the Metamorphosis (1865). A walk through the neighbouring streets, which connect a myriad tiny squares, reveals an interesting variety of architecture, even though one in three buildings is a ruin.

Archontikí

By taking the north branch 500m along the road that runs from Aghía Paraskeví at the eastern edge of the settlement, you climb over a ridge and, after passing a wind farm, drop down into the Bay of Lákka. The Mycenaean cemetery of **Archontikí**, first excavated in 1962, was found at the northern end of the bay. It is from here that the remarkably rich finds exhibited in the museum on Chios were rescued. More than 50 Mycenaean graves (14th–12th centuries BC), cut relatively deeply and built with split slabs of stone, have now been investigated. They are visible from the shore-side perimeter fence at the northern end of the area. The funerary offerings found in the graves give a vivid sense of the importance and wealth of the Bronze Age settlement here, suggesting that this was a successful trading station. The finds include decorated ceramic objects, bronze weapons, seal-stones, and several kinds of metal and glass-paste jewellery of fine workmanship. The settlement itself, which reveals spacious houses with storage areas and pithoi still *in situ*, has so far been only partially explored.

Ftelió and the monastery of the Koímisis

Regaining the main road and continuing north, you come to a small, white **memorial stone** by a junction leading down to the attractive bay of Ftelió. This marks the spot where, on 21st June 1824, a large number of the local population perished—either by communal suicide or by accident—when the powder magazine in which they had taken refuge exploded. Popularly celebrated as a brave last stand against the invading Egyptian forces of Ibrahim Pasha, the tragedy is commemorated in a poem by Dionysios Solomos, the author of the words of the Greek National Anthem.

From Ftelió the road climbs across the northern side of the island as far as the **monastery of the Koímisis tis Theotókou**, a fine and compact ensemble of buildings in a magnificent position on the shoulder of Mt Profítis Ilías. The founding of the monastery is thought to date from the 15th or 16th century, although precise documentation is lacking. Most of the fabric was rebuilt after the Turkish destruction of 1824, but the form remains faithful to the old design. A celebration is held here on 1st August, when an icon of the Virgin is brought here in procession. The complex has been uninhabited since 1983, but the buildings have been sensitively restored and preserved (*the key is kept by the papás, who can normally be found around the harbour promenade in the evening*).

PRACTICAL INFORMATION

GETTING AROUND

The most regular access is from Chios, by the F/B *Nisos Thira*, which leaves Chios for Psará on most afternoons and goes in the other direction in the morning (journey time 4hrs). There is a weekly ferry from Lávrion (at the time of writing, on Mon) on the Lesbos (Sígri) and Lemnos route. In summer there is a caïque service from Limniá (Volissós) on Chios, which crosses to Psará on Sat and returns on Sun (90mins). Once on the island, transport is very limited: there are no taxis and no car rental. If you do not have your own vehicle, it is only possible to explore the island on foot—and there is no roadside shade.

WHERE TO STAY

Lodging is limited: the choice is either the clean but expensive **Psará Hotel** (*T: 22740 61180 or 61195*) at the northern extremity of town; or the **Restalia Studios** close to the port (*T: 22740 61000 or 61201; only open July–Aug*).

WHERE TO EAT

There are three tavernas on the island: the best is the **Iliovasilema** ('Sunset') on the town's south beach, Káto Gialós.

SAMOS

Samos is a large and varied island, attractive for at least two quite different reasons. It is the location of the most ambitious city of 6th-century BC Archaic Greece, with the astonishing Tunnel of Eupalinos, dozens of monuments, and its Heraion—birthplace of Hera herself. The assemblage of ex-votos from the sanctuary rivals those at Olympia and Delphi; its collection of Archaic sculpture is in itself sufficient reason to visit.

But Samos is also an island of wild mountainous landscapes, traditional villages, beaches, and a rich and unique vegetation (there are more than 60 species of wild orchid on the island). Its far west, untouched by the mass tourism that has started to affect the east, is a walker's paradise.

HISTORY OF SAMOS

Surprisingly, considering its size and resources, Samos has yielded little of significance from before the 1st millennium BC, although the island has been inhabited since the Late Neolithic (4th millennium BC). The island was settled by Ionian colonists, led by Procles from Epidaurus, around 1000 BC. It soon developed its own grain-supplying *peraia* (territory on the mainland opposite), which brought it into dispute with the cities of Priene and Miletus. The island founded colonies to the north in both the Sea of Marmara and the Black Sea; to the west on Amorgós; and to the east on the coast of Cilicia. To the south, it participated in the colonies at Cyrene and Naucratis in North Africa. Already by the 8th century BC, the island was acquiring dominance in the trade-routes across the eastern Mediterranean. Around 638 BC Colaeus (Kolaios) of Samos sailed through the Straits of Gibraltar and beyond (*see p. 492*); his journey was symbolic of the marine prowess of the islanders. The prestige of the Sanctuary of Hera increased with Samos' expansion, attracting lavish dedications from overseas.

After the overthrow of the tyrant Demoteles in the early 6th century BC, control of the city remained in the hands of a landed aristocracy until the emergence, from more popular origins, of the family of Aeaces (Aiakis) and his sons Pantagnotus, Polycrates and Syloson. By killing the first and exiling the last, Polycrates made himself sole tyrant of the island around 535 BC; during his energetic reign Samos grew to cultural, military and technological eminence. Polycrates built up a large fleet, which he used to plunder the coast and islands. He attempted to forge an alliance with the Egyptian pharaoh, and he attracted brilliant people to his court: Anacreon the lyric poet, Theodorus the sculptor and metalworker, and Eupalinos the brilliant engineer. However, he alienated others, most famously the island's greatest thinker, Pythagoras. At the height of his power, he was lured to the mainland on false pretences by the Persian satrap Oroetes, and was crucified in 522 BC.

After Polycrates' death, the island languished under the rule of his brother, Syloson, who returned to Samos with Persian support. The Persian influence was resented by

SAMOS

the islanders, and Samos participated in the Ionian revolt of 499 BC; it then defected to Persia at the Battle of Lade in 494 BC, fought for Persia at the Battle of Salamis (480 BC), and reverted once again to the Greek cause at the decisive Battle of Mycale in 479 BC. For almost 40 years after, Samos was a member of the Athenian League, paying its tribute in ships. A territorial dispute with Miletus led to the island's revolt against Athenian dominance in 440–439 BC, with difficulty suppressed by Pericles of Athens after a nine-month siege. The terms of the armistice demanded that the walls of Samos be dismantled, its fleet handed over, and the city put under direct Athenian sovereignty: in 365 BC the local population was expelled and replaced by Athenian cleruchs. This state of affairs was only reversed when the Samians returned from exile in 321 BC as a result of Alexander the Great's decree regarding exiles. Samos saw a new period of growth and stability, especially under the Antigonid rulers: probably at the instigation of Demetrius Poliorcetes, the city's walls were rebuilt. The 3rd century BC saw the island produce two brilliant astronomers, Conon and Aristarchus. From 281 BC the island was once again an important naval base, this time under Ptolemaic rule: in 129 BC it became part of the Roman province of Asia.

Under Roman rule, the island saw mixed fortunes. In 82 BC a large number of works of art were taken from the Sanctuary of Hera by Verres. In 39 BC, Antony and Cleopatra came to the island, perhaps modelling their stay on the nuptials of Hera and Zeus. Samos seemed to be favoured by the imperial family of Rome: Augustus wintered on Samos in 20–19 BC, restored some of the sculptures that had been removed and gave the islanders Roman citizenship; Caligula is said to have contemplated rebuilding the palace of Polycrates; Claudius paid for the reconstruction of the Temple of Dionysus; Nero confirmed the island's autonomy.

The Early Christian community on Samos appears not to have been particularly large, and the island may have been all but abandoned in the aftermath of 7th-century Arab incursions. In the 10th century, Leo VI, Emperor of Byzantium, created the administrative theme of Samos, its seat at Smyrna. The island was allotted to the Latin emperor after the Fourth Crusade of 1204, but within 20 years had reverted to Byzantine government from Nicaea. After 1346, it was under Genoese rule; but constant piracy forced the Genoese to move much of the population to Chios. The Turks captured the severely depopulated island in the 1470s. In 1572, the Turkish admiral Kiliç Ali Pasha obtained privileges from Suleiman the Magnificent for (Christian) settlers to the island from mainland Turkey and Greece. The island's capital was created at Chora.

Samos was briefly occupied by the Russians from 1772–74, and played a leading role in the independence movement of 1821. The Samian fleet defeated three Turkish attempts to land between 1821 and 1824. While recognising the independence of Greece, the London Protocol of 1830 excluded Samos from the Greek state; but special privileges were won by the islanders in 1832, when it became a self-governing entity within the Ottoman Empire, with a Greek prince and a legislative council of elected islanders operating from their new capital at Vathý. Repeated insurrections finally led to unification with Greece in 1912, cutting the island off from its hinterland on the mainland opposite. With the exchange of populations in 1923, the rift became permanent. During the Second World War, Samos was occupied first by the Italians, then by the British; it was heavily bombarded and finally seized by German forces, giving rise to a fierce resistance movement.

In the late 1960s the island began adapting its economy to large-scale tourism. In 2000, devastating fires destroyed almost a third of the island's forests: since then, smaller fires have become an almost yearly phenomenon.

VATHY & THE EAST

Samos is the official name for the island's capital town, in a bay on the north coast (*map p. 474, D1–D2*). This is not the site of ancient Samos, which corresponds to today's Pythagóreio on the south coast; and it is also the name for the whole island. To avoid confusion, the capital and its port are increasingly referred to as Vathý, a name which originally denoted the older settlement on the hill to the southeast. This guide follows the commonest current usage, namely: Vathý for the capital and its port, Áno Vathý for its old quarter above the main town, and Samos for the island as a whole.

EXPLORING VATHY

Vathý lies at the head of a deep bay (ancient Pánormos). It is a 19th-century port in origin; the old warehouses at its southern end were for storing and shipping the island's two most famous commodities, Samian wine and tobacco. The **waterfront** is a heterogeneous assemblage of different architectures: the abandoned remains of the 1960s Xenia Hotel stand next to a handsome Neoclassical mansion to its right; followed by a simple house façade with a protruding wooden balcony, redolent of the ports of Asia Minor and the East. To the north along the front is the Catholic church of the Virgin, in French Colonial style. One block inland, a different atmosphere prevails: narrow alleys of shops and houses, some with courtyards and gardens, have the feel of a busy, Levantine Greek town. The water side of the promenade is dominated by a monument to Themistocles Sofoulis (1862–1949), the *géros* ('Grand Old Man') of the centre of Greek politics in the period between the world wars.

The **Dimarcheíon** is part of a fine ensemble of late 19th-century Neoclassical buildings. Next to it is the exceptional **Archaeological Museum**, two blocks inland of the centre of the waterfront (*open daily except Mon, 8–5 in summer; Oct–April 8–3*). It consists of two buildings, one modern and purpose-built, the other an adapted Neoclassical mansion. Its collection of Archaic sculpture is one of the best in Greece, as is its display of votive objects from the Heraion. The exhibits are well labelled, also in English.

Archaeological Museum: First Building

Room I: Important fragments of early architectural sculpture, including part of the frieze of the 8th-century BC Temple of Hera, with a row of warriors incised.

Even though it has lost one lower leg and both its feet, and consequently does not stand as tall as it would originally have done, the dimensions of the Samos Kouros are tremendous.

Room II: Fine examples of Archaic sculpture, including an early robed female figure (c. 570 BC), its cylindrical torso betraying its origin from wooden predecessors; a lovely kore holding a bird (c. 550 BC) and most importantly, the so-called 'Geneleos Group' (against the north wall), a family group of husband and wife flanking their children, dedicated at the Sanctuary of Hera c. 560 BC. **Room III:** The centrepiece is the enormous **Samos Kouros**, the largest kouros statue to survive, found near the Sacred Way in the Heraion. It stands 4.7m tall (originally taller) and was carved in local marble c. 575 BC. A dedicatory inscription is carved on its left thigh. The mixture of stylisation and acute observation of anatomy, and the preservation of perfect proportions even at colossal scale, are the figure's most striking characteristics.

Archaeological Museum: Second Building

This part of the museum, in the Neoclassical building across from the First Building, exhibits mostly votive material from the Heraion. The ground-floor displays include good explanatory material.

Ground floor: The hallway on the ground floor contains headless statues from the Hellenistic and Roman periods. The room to the left displays prehistoric and early material from various sites, including tiny clay altars of the 3rd millennium BC. The ground-floor room to the right gives an overview of the astonishing richness of the Sanctuary of Hera and of the diverse geographical origins of the votive offerings made to the goddess (mostly 9th–6th centuries BC). The long case against the wall is a chronological display of offerings and casual finds, among them many small objects related symbolically to the goddess: small marble models of houses (domesticity), ivory poppy-heads and pomegranates, and bronze pine cones (fertility). There are objects from Cyprus, Egypt, Assyria, Babylon, the Caucasus, Iberia, the Italian peninsula and mainland Greece.

Landing and upper floor: The first-floor landing displays rare objects in wood and ivory, materials that do not usually survive. There is also a fine funerary stele depicting a nude youth carrying a box (5th century BC).

The two rooms which lead off the landing exhibit the vast range (and quantity) of votive objects dedicated to Hera. The room to the right (south) contains the bronze artefacts, many of which were produced at the Heraion. There is an exceptional quantity of bronze protomes, the heads of griffins attached to early offering bowls on tripods. The room to the left (north) displays pottery, ivory and glass objects. There are good examples of fine Corinthian pottery, and of more local Ionian and Samian wares. The central cabinets display jewellery, glass and some well-preserved pieces in carved ivory, finest among them an Egyptian jumping lion (13th century BC). Mystifying is an 8th-century BC terracotta circle (kernos) for ritual libations, on whose surface stands a heterogeneous assemblage of cups, pomegranates, a panther, a ram's head, and a toad, all realistically modelled in clay.

The Museum of Samos Wines

At the southwest corner of the inlet of Vathý, east of the main junction with the road to Karlóvasi, is the Museum of Samos Wines (*open daily except Sun, 8–8*), laid out in a former winery. The Moschato Aspro grape has been cultivated here since the late 1600s. Vineyards cluster on the slopes of Mt Ámbelos, whose ancient name, meaning 'vine', is confirmation of the antiquity of viticulture here. In antiquity, however, Samos mostly produced a dry red, which could not compete with the more highly esteemed production of its neighbours, Chios and Lesbos. The Moschato Aspro produces the sweet, golden dessert wine that Byron was thinking of when he wrote, in *Don Juan*, 'Fill high the cup with Samian wine! Leave battles to the Turkish hordes'.

Áno Vathý

A street running inland from the southern part of the waterfront leads 1km uphill to Áno Vathý, the original settlement. Its narrow streets are overhung with wooden balconies projecting from wood-frame and plaster buildings of a type common to the areas of Ottoman dominion. The most interesting monument is the double church of

Ághii Ioánnis Pródromos and Nikólaos, which is at the top of the village. The church of Ághios Ioánnis was erected in 1750; Ághios Nikólaos was added 50 years later. The result is a square and unusually compact profile, dominated by a cluster of four domes. The interiors, currently in bad condition, have 18th-century wall-paintings. The floor of Ághios Ioánnis (south) is finely laid with patterned polychrome tiles.

AROUND VATHY & THE EAST OF THE ISLAND

Two roads west climb steeply above Áno Vathý, converge, and then split shortly afterwards, with the left branch leading northeast, through Kamára, to the **Monastery of the Zoödóchos Pigí** (*map p. 474, D1; open daily 10–1 & 6–8*). The dome of the katholikon (1756) rests on four monumental ancient columns brought especially from Miletus. The surrounding buildings are mostly from the 19th century; originally housing a male community, they are now home to a small number of nuns. The belvedere in front of the monastery commands a panorama of the narrow Straits of Mycale, where the Greek revolutionary fleet defeated the combined Turkish and Egyptian navies in August 1824. On the mainland the Greeks defeated a Persian force in 479 BC.

The right branch of the road above Vathý leads to the **monastery of Aghía Zóni** (the Holy Girdle; 1695). The inside of its plain katholikon is entirely covered with 18th-century wall-paintings.

Further south, from the Vathý–Pythagóreio road, at Tris Ekklisíes (named after its three contiguous chapels), a left turn leads towards the village of Palaiókastro and on to **Poseidónio** (*map p. 474, D2*), an attractive and protected harbour, backed by olive groves. A right (south) branch just after leaving the main road gives access to **Psilí Ámmos**, in a coastal landscape of salt-flats and marshes, frequented in winter by flamingoes. There is also a long sandy beach.

PYTHAGOREIO

Pythagóreio (*map p. 474, C2–D2*) lies on the south coast, 12km from the main port of Vathý; it is the second of the island's three ferry ports. The modern town, with the character of an old-world tourist resort, occupies what was once the centre of the ancient city of Samos. From the Middle Ages until the 1950s its name was Tigáni (from the Italian word for a warehouse, *dogana*, reflecting Venetian merchant activity in the 12th and 13th centuries); thereafter it was re-named Pythagóreio in honour of Pythagoras (*see p. 497*). The surrounding area and the port itself contain the most significant archaeological sites on the island: the remains of ancient Samos would be impressive under any circumstances, but the fact that the modern town is so much smaller than its predecessor, leaving many of its monuments, not least its famous and venerable sanctuary of Hera, or Heraion, uncluttered, makes it one of the most memorable ancient sites in the Aegean.

HISTORY OF PYTHAGOREIO

The Kámbos Chóras, where the airstrip stands today, is the wide and fertile south-facing plain between mountains and shore, west of Pythagóreio. It is watered by various streams, including the Ímbrasos at its western end, and has a favourable microclimate. In ancient times there were two natural harbour inlets at the eastern end of the plain, one where the modern port of Pythagóreio is now, the other, now a small lake called Glyfáda, a little to its west. The acropolis hill, now crowned by a castle, sits between them; springs are available in the vicinity. This configuration attracted settlers early on, as indicated by a Late Neolithic (4th millennium BC) settlement on the acropolis and an Early Bronze Age one in the area of the Heraion, as well as Mycenaean activity slightly inland.

In this ideal location, on important trade routes and in helpful political circumstances, Samos was able to grow into a highly important centre by the Archaic period. It was the largest and richest city of the Aegean in the 6th century BC, still able to impress Herodotus deeply when he visited a century later. In his words, here he saw 'three of the greatest building and engineering marvels in the Greek world'. These were the Temple of Hera, the artificial harbour and its mole, and the kilometre-long Tunnel of Eupalinos. One of these survives in its entirety, the other two in parts.

The ancient harbour

The modern harbour of Pythagóreio (c. 36,000m square), with its attractive seafront, is considerably smaller in area than the ancient port (c. 66,000m square), due to sedimentation on the north and west sides. The original harbour walls on these two sides can be traced today, some way inland of the present waterfront. Under Polycrates, in 535–525 BC, the city had used man-made structures to create a larger sheltered port, protecting its large and important merchant and military fleets from the south winds. Herodotus mentions ship-sheds, but most importantly the long, artificial, protecting mole, which ran out to sea across the south side of the harbour for almost half a kilometre from its back (west) wall, into a depth of 20 fathoms of water. Laying foundations at such a depth, and building securely on top of them underwater, was an extraordinary feat for those times. The present-day mole (1862), where the ferries dock, is of considerable length; but the Polycratean one was longer and began from further west. It now lies underwater, further south out to sea. Only its base exists today, submerged at a depth of three metres near the shore, and at almost 14m at its eastern end.

Underneath the present north mole of the harbour (which runs north–south) lies a further 6th-century BC structure: this was an extension of the land fortifications and closed the harbour to the east. It is estimated to have been c. 175m long and 20m wide.

Today's breakwater, enlarged and extended in 1862, would seem to be based on a later Hellenistic mole. A 30-m stretch of its neatly cut masonry, with compact surface and finely-edged borders and paving, is preserved in the space between the Taverna Varka and the houses fronting the west of the present harbour.

The acropolis

Overlooking the port and the sea from the former acropolis hill, the only defensible position along this stretch of shore, stand the circuit walls of a large 11th-century **Byzantine castle**, partly occupied by the church of the Metamorphosis. The eastern fortifications and rounded corner towers are excellent examples of the Byzantine technique of stabilising stone walls with densely-packed brick tiles in the interstices. Beside the church is a marble bust of Lykourgos Logothetis (né Georgios Paplomatas; 1772–1850), Samian militiaman and politician who led his fellow islanders in the independence revolt in April 1821. He designed and built the church of the Metamorphosis in the 1830s, in thanks for the 1824 Greek naval victory over the Turks in the Straits of Mycale. The tower and castle to the south and west were all rebuilt after 1824.

Within the castle's circuit, east of the church, are the foundations of two fine **Hellenistic villas** of the 2nd century BC, apparently modified substantially in the course of the 1st century AD and united into one large Roman villa. Its wealth is indicated from the quantity of sculpture found here, but also from the rich polychrome marbles used for decoration—especially the two exquisite, broken columns of jasper (from Iasos, southeast of Samos on the coast of Asia Minor) framing an entrance of the north peristyle; other columns in Euboean cipollino marble can be seen to the east. The villa comprises a series of colonnaded courts. The peristyle court closest to the sea has a complex of water channels within its perimeter, and there is a cistern below an impluvium in the east of the area.

Superimposed on the centre of the area are the rough-stone walls of a small, 5th-century apsidal church. At the northern end of the site are clear sections of the Hellenistic walls; spolia from a temple building of large dimensions are visible all around the site.

The Temple of Dionysus and agorá

Three blocks in from the centre of the harbour-front, and one block north of the main street, on Efpalínou, are a corner of the crepis and fragments of fluted columns from the 4th-century BC **Temple of Dionysus**, identified only from inscriptions. Further west along the main street, towards the junction with the road north to Vathý, is the area of the ancient agorá. To the south of the street, by the junction, are the remains of a Roman temple, often referred to as the **Temple of Aphrodite**. It stood in a small courtyard bounded by stoas on three or four sides: the stone base of the colonnade of the west stoa (with visible insets for the columns) can be seen facing the rear steps of the temple platform; behind it are the lower courses of its back wall. It is likely that this is a 1st-century AD temple of Augustus and Roma, mentioned in inscriptions. Fifty metres further west along the road and to the north, behind a first row of buildings, lies what has been uncovered so far of the **ancient agorá**, which would have extended further east. The visible remains are mostly Roman. A little further along the main road on the same side, covered by a provisional roof for protection, is a nymphaeum.

The modern town hall houses the **Archaeological Collection of Pythagóreio** (*open daily except Mon, 8.30–3*), reopened after renovations in late 2009. It contains mostly sculpture and pottery from the ancient city of Samos, including numerous inscribed Archaic grave stelae and some monumental Roman portrait sculpture. The most notable objects are a marble statue of Aeaces, father of Polycrates, from c. 540 BC, and a sarcophagus in the shape of the temple from the same period.

The theatre and Panaghía Spilianí

A branch left (north and west) from the main road to Vathý, still within the town, leads along the slope to the Tunnel of Eupalinos (*described below*), passing through unexcavated parts of the ancient city. On the left, below the road, is a **Hellenistic villa** (600m; *closed at the time of writing, but visible from the outside*). The house has Archaic origins and experienced various changes through to Roman times. It features a series of airy rooms facing a central atrium, and areas of floor mosaic of exceptional refinement, with a decorative theme of waves and griffins' heads. The **ancient theatre**, 100m to the north of the villa, is covered in a semi-permanent modern superstructure for musical performances: little remains of its 4th-century BC cavea, but the vaulted Roman substructure of the stage has survived.

By the theatre, the uphill branch of the road leads to the panoramic monastery of the **Panaghía Spilianí** (*1.5km from Pythagóreio by a right branch from the road leading to the Tunnel of Eupalinos*). The buildings (of the 1880s) stand in front of a broad cave, with a small chapel to the Virgin fitted into its narrow right-hand end. This was a place of ancient cult, probably of the nymphs. To the west, ancient quarries are probably connected to the construction of the Archaic walls.

The left branch of the road continues 300m further west to the most interesting and significant site of the city, the Tunnel of Eupalinos.

THE TUNNEL OF EUPALINOS

The greatest of the 'three marvels' mentioned by Herodotus, and one of the most remarkable engineering feats of antiquity, is the aqueduct-tunnel of Eupalinos (*open daily except Mon, 8.45–2.45*), worthy of a visit not only because it is a 1036-m long double tunnel, cut by hand through the mountain, but because of what it tells us about the evolution of Greek engineering at that time. The fact that the tunnel was begun simultaneously from two points (invisible to one another) on opposite sides of a mountain and met in the centre at a depth of 170m below the surface, with an almost negligible margin of error, is evidence of an extraordinary ability to solve practical problems by the application of logic and theoretical imagination.

Purpose and date

As the city of Samos had grown to considerable size by the 6th century BC, its locally available water resources were no longer sufficient. The (still) copious spring of Aghiádes, only 2.5km from the city in a direct line, provided an obvious solution, but a mountain lay between. Instead of building a long channel around it, which would easily have been possible, a much more difficult procedure was chosen, namely to bring the water directly through the mountain, thus keeping the channel mostly hidden within the walls, which must have existed by that time. The main objective must have been to preserve a safe water supply in case of enemy attack. Archaeological evidence, as well as the testimony of Herodotus, suggests that the tunnel may have been commissioned by Polycrates, in the same period as the first circuit of walls and the harbour mole(s), i.e. around 540 BC, though some scholars place it slightly earlier.

The task

Herodotus gives the name of the engineer as Eupalinos, son of Naustrophos, from the city of Mégara, near Athens. Eupalinos may be a sobriquet, derived from the Greek word *eupalamos* ('ingenious'). Herodotus claims that the workforce consisted of prisoners of war from Mytilene. Only two men could work on each cutting face at any one time, and the lack of space and oxygen inside the tunnel precluded the presence of more than the small number of workers needed to remove rubble. Estimates vary between five and 15 years for the completion of the tunnel.

Apart from the sheer technical task of creating the tunnel, there were serious further challenges arising from the decision to begin simultaneously from opposite sides of the mountain in the hope of meeting in the middle. Eupalinos had to ensure three things: (1) that both trajectories were perfectly aligned, to guarantee meeting in the centre; (2) that the two entrances at either side of the mountain were perforated at exactly the same height above sea-level; (3) that the digging maintained both its elevation and its axial line without deviation. There were also practical problems, such as the possibility of encountering unstable rock or seams of water in the heart of the mountain. The margin for error was enormous in an age when the main surveying tools available were line-of-sight, the plumb-line and versions of the spirit-level.

Solutions

The solution to (1) was two-fold: first, the line of the tunnel had to be mapped over the surface of the hill, and then projected or extrapolated underground. The marking was done by setting up posts, positioning each new post exactly on the line projected by the alignment of the previous two. Beginning at the top of the hill, from which both the area of the spring and the general position of the city can be seen, it was not difficult to define this straight line: but projecting it underground was more complex. The mouth of the tunnel is one point of reference, but at least one other is needed, which can be perfectly aligned with it from inside, as the tunnel progresses deeper. The solution was to dig a shaft straight down to the tunnel from one of the surface posts. A beam of wood, hung on ropes down the shaft from a similar beam perfectly aligned with the posts, provided a further point of reference for direction: so long as this hanging beam was aligned with a marker in the tunnel, the workmen knew, as they looked back from their cutting-face, that the direction they were going corresponded to the line of posts on the surface.

Digging in a straight line was one thing; digging at the same height from either end was another. To monitor this, a series of posts was again necessary, this time following the contour of the hill from one side to the other. Each post was T-shaped, set into the ground and verified with a plumb-line. The first two or three had to be checked by a water-level (*chorobates*); thereafter, each new post had to be exactly at the height of the visual plane defined by the tops of the previous two. The final difference in level between Eupalinos' two tunnel entrances is about 4cm.

To maintain horizontality while digging, standing water or a water-level could possibly have been used, or, more likely, a type of hanging sighting-tube which consisted of a hollow copper pipe, about 40cm long, suspended horizontally, through which a sighting can be taken of a fixed marker.

The problem of areas of unstable rock does appear to have been encountered by Eupalinos, some way in from the north entrance. It was so bad that it forced him to deviate from his line in search of a more stable area, and this meant that the sight-line from the cutting-face to the daylight at the entrance was lost. In correcting his deviation, once good rock was again found, he appears to have over-compensated. To save the project from failure, he turned the trajectory of both campaigns slightly to the same (east) side, so that if the level of each tunnel really were identical, sooner or later they had to cross one another's path—which they did.

Subsequent completion

Once the two sections of the tunnel were successfully joined, a channel had to be excavated with the necessary gradient to allow the water to flow constantly. This was first done to one side of the floor of the tunnel; but due to what experts surmise to have been a lowering of the level of the Aghiádes spring (the water source), a subsidiary tunnel had to be dug below the existing one. This was created by sinking broad shafts down from the side of the floor, approximately every 12 metres, and connecting them below into a continuous sloping waterway; the southern exit is about 4.7m lower than the northern entrance. This lower tunnel was then lined with terracotta ducts. Next, the water had to be brought via a surface aqueduct from the Aghiádes spring to the north tunnel entrance. Finally, another aqueduct had to link the southern exit to cisterns and the network of pipes and fountains across the city. This runs parallel to the hillside and is sunk below ground; the regular shafts used for its construction are visible beside (mostly below, but latterly above) the road which leads to the site.

Visiting the site: south section

Armed with this general picture, the following elements may be observed on a visit. The two vertical shafts for fixing the direction of the south section of the tunnel can be seen from outside where they sink into the ground: one between the ticket booth and the entrance; the other just above the entrance building. Of the two, only the second is visible inside the tunnel, at the end of the first stretch of narrow passageway after the steps. Standing in the pool of light it casts, you can see down the length of the tunnel. The sides of the tunnel have a slightly serpentine irregularity, due simply to human error in cutting; but any deviation is always corrected, and the axial line remains perfectly straight. The entrance was modified, after the original opening became dangerous due to surface erosion; this is why the site is now entered by steps from above, and it means that the daylight from its entrance can no longer be seen from inside.

The body of the tunnel is roughly square in section, on average measuring 180cm by 180cm. The limestone walls and ceiling are heavily indented with the striations of the pick. As you proceed down, on the right-hand side are the regular shafts which drop down to the lower tunnel. The accessible sector of the tunnel ends after approximately 250m: rock-fall has now closed the central section. On leaving the site, the exit of the lower tunnel which carried the water pipes—at this point 8m below the upper tunnel—can be seen to the west side below the steps that lead out of the fenced area.

North section

Accessible on foot (50mins) directly across the hilltop over which the line of the tunnel was originally traced; the entrance is low down on the south side of a declivity to your left as you descend into an area of pine trees. The spring is 15mins further to the north/northwest. Alternatively, you can go by the road which branches left at the exit of Pythagóreio on the way to Vathý, climbs past the ancient walls, and drops over a brow into the broad valley of the Aghiádes spring. The church and spring are 800m along the road which branches left at the first T-junction. To find the tunnel entrance from the spring, walk back east along the road until there is a rough track bearing right, which soon begins to climb steeply up to the right to a crossing of tracks by some pine trees. The right-hand track descends into the dip, on the south side of which is the north entrance of the tunnel, somewhat hidden in undergrowth.

The Aghiádes spring rises beneath the church of Ághios Ioánnis, beside the road in Aghiádes village. The church is built directly over the ancient spring-house and cistern, whose roof—now the church floor—is supported by a forest of square marble pillars. Immediately to the south of the church can be seen the beginning of the closed channel which bore the water from here to the entrance of Eupalinos' tunnel. A hole in its roof allows the interior to be seen; originally the whole structure was hidden just below ground-level for security. The channel follows the contours of the hill, first towards the south, and then making a deep dogleg east before sharply returning west again, reaching the tunnel entrance after 900m. Shafts used to construct the channel can be located in the course of the last 300m; their openings are often hidden and unprotected.

The north entrance of the tunnel (*currently accessible, though work appears to be beginning on fitting a new gate: torch necessary*) has been restored: the original entrance is below and to the right.

The Roman aqueduct

A shallow gorge runs southwest (1.5km) from Aghiádes to the main Pythagóreio–Chóra road, joining it beside a military camp 2.8km west of Pythagóreio and a short distance west of the junction for the airport and the Heraion. A little after halfway, the gorge is crossed by the ruins of a Roman aqueduct of the 1st century AD, built to supplement the Tunnel of Eupalinos as the source of the city's water.

THE WALLS OF ANCIENT SAMOS

Much of the 6.4-km enceinte of defensive walls of ancient Samos survives, except on the seaward side. Stretches can be viewed uphill from the Glyfáda lakes (*see opposite*), or from the road to the Tunnel of Eupalinos.

There are two phases of walling. The earliest walls, erected probably in the 530s BC, were constructed at the lower levels in polygonal limestone blocks, with a superstructure of mud and brick; they had few bastions and mostly arched or corbelled gateways. The defeat of Samos by the Athenians in 439 BC led to the forced dismantling of this enceinte. The Hellenistic walls, reusing the early foundations, were built again c. 300 BC, in isodomic masonry composed of large rectangular blocks. The enceinte was endowed with over 30 towers or bastions, which protected massive lintel-and-post gateways (often preserving the slots for the massive blocking bars). In places these walls were repaired during the 2nd century BC.

Long sections of the enceinte can be walked: along the east, north and west sides over the hill behind the city. The two periods of walls and gates can be clearly seen in the eastern sector above the port (*reached by taking the left turn for Mytilinií off the Vathý road, 1km out of Pythagóreio, continuing uphill for 400m until the road returns west to the line of walls*). At the summit of the hill and down the western side (*reached from opposite the 'Dóntia'; see opposite*), the Hellenistic work displays the method of its construction, with two faces and a rubble fill between. In the lowest reaches of the western wall, a rock-cut ditch about 3–4m wide runs parallel to the walls 5m to their west; this was left by the quarrying of the stone. Most impressive is the well-preserved 4th-century BC watchtower in the northwest corner, standing to a height of over 10m.

THE WEST OF THE ANCIENT CITY

The Roman baths

By the shore just beyond the acropolis hill, south of the road to the Heraion and the airport, was an extensive 4th-century BC sports complex, one of the largest in the Hellenistic word, comprising gymnasia and a stadium. Little remains to be seen, except some of the steps of its enclosing colonnade, close to the road, and the (western end) starting-grid of the stadium which lay in the south of the area and ran parallel to the shore. A later addition to the complex was the large and well-preserved 2nd-century AD Roman baths (*open daily except Mon, 8.30–3*). The building was adapted for Christian use in the late 5th century AD. Various carved stone objects from all over town are stored near the entrance. To the south are the remains of Early Christian churches constructed over the atrium and apodyteria of the baths. The plan of a large apsidal structure is to the left; further in, the foundations of two smaller chapels are built over the octagonal pool in the centre of the main frigidarium. Traces of Roman wall mosaic are visible to the left. The caldarium lies just beyond its southwest corner, where a marble-lined pool was consecrated and turned into the baptistery of the Early Christian complex. To the south is a succession of three rectangular tepidaria, raised above a hypocaust system, their once marble-clad walls heated through cavities within their thickness. The westernmost contains five immersion pools. Further south, overlooking the shore, are the remains of the palaestra.

The basilica and Glyfáda lakes

Dominating the skyline immediately to the west are the imposing remains of a three-aisled 5th-century AD **basilica**, sandwiched improbably between the swimming pools (west door and narthex) and recreation area (apse) of a modern hotel (*access is free, either from the shore or through the hotel grounds*). The basilica was almost 30m in length and of considerable height, as is indicated by the three soaring south piers which still stand today, given the local name Tría Dóntia ('Three Teeth'), built of rough stone clad with spolia.

West of the hotel is the double lagoon of **Megáli and Mikrí Glyfáda**, all that remains of the ancient city's secondary harbour. To the east side of the inner lake are well-preserved remains of the isodomic 4th-century BC walls. To the west is the small church of the Koímisis tis Theotókou, assembled from, and surrounded by, a variety of ancient and Early Christian spolia. This is the site of the Archaic sanctuary of Artemis. A sanctuary of Demeter has also been located higher up the hill, just inside the western walls.

To the west of the lakes were the **cemeteries of ancient Samos**, used continuously from Archaic times (on the hillside further to the west) through to the Early Christian era (the area immediately west of the Sanctuary of Artemis), with the Hellenistic and Roman necropoleis between. The Early Christian cemetery centres on a Hellenistic rock-cut tomb. A Christian cemetery building was constructed around this, perhaps supporting a chapel. Two levels of burial loculi with vaulted roofs or cupolas lead off from the principal arched entrance: traces of colour (principally reds) survive on the plastered interiors.

THE HERAION

The archaeological site of the Heraion is 6.5km from Pythagóreio (*map p. 474, C3; open daily except Mon, 8.30–3; a second set of road signs beyond indicates the old site entrance, which is closed*). It lies in the southwest corner of the Kámbos plain, by the mouth of the river Ímbrasos, the mythical birthplace of the goddess Hera and also the location of her marriage to Zeus. Excavated since the beginning of the 20th century (mostly by German archaeologists), it is one of the most thoroughly investigated sanctuaries in the Aegean. The important finds are in the museum in Vathý.

The excavations have revealed a multitude of superimposed layers, from prehistoric to Early Christian. Today much has been covered over again, leaving only the upper levels of the foundations visible. Additionally, the site stands in a thicket of tall reeds, cleared only at the centre. This situation is remedied by a clear system of walkways, equipped with a series of explanatory panels.

HISTORY OF THE SITE & TEMPLE

It is not known when the cult of the Great Mother Goddess, widespread in Asia Minor, was first established here, but it may have been centuries old when Ionian colonists, around 1000 BC, identified that figure with Hera, wife of Zeus and mother of the gods, patroness of brides, marriage and female domestic life. The site rapidly developed into the main religious centre for its region and the city of Samos, but beyond that, it developed an international appeal, like Delphi or Olympia, attracting increasingly rich votive gifts from the 8th century BC onwards. Excavations have revealed a highly important succession of early temples, of which only the last, never completed, is now visible. Its predecessors were all situated slightly further east (*see plan overleaf*).

Temple 1: In the 8th century BC, one of the earliest large temples in the Greek world was constructed beside an earlier altar. It was 100ft long (hence its name, *hekatompedon*, 'hundred-footer') and 20ft wide (c. 33m by 6.6m), with a row of 13 wooden columns down the middle to support the roof.

Temple 2: Around 650 BC the *hekatompedon* was rebuilt on limestone foundations, with a modified interior. The columns supporting the roof were now pushed back to the side walls and entrance wall, forming an interior colonnade in the form of a Greek Π, thus allowing the cult statue to be viewed from the entrance. Column bases at the outside corners suggest that this was a peripteral temple.

Temple 3, Temple of Rhoikos: As the wealth and power of Samos increased, along with the fame of the sanctuary, a much grander temple was planned and begun between 570–560 BC, designed by Rhoikos (Rhoecus), who was assisted by Theodoros—the first named architects in Greek history. The design was unprecedented in terms of scale and ornamentation: the temple measured 105m by 52m; its external portico consisted of a double row of columns of 18m in height. At the time it was the largest of all Greek temples, and among the many large temples in Ionian cities that it inspired, only the Artemision at Ephesus would ever outscale it. Around 540 BC, the temple of Rhoikos either collapsed or was demolished, probably due to subsidence, as the ground could not support so heavy a structure.

Temple 4: Rhoikos' temple was immediately replaced with the structure visible today, begun under Polycrates. It was moved 40m to the west onto more solid ground, retained similar proportions and form to its predecessor, but was slightly larger (109m by 55m). The space between the columns was decreased, the columns were slimmed, and their total number increased from 104 to 155. They were almost 20m high, and the peristyle they formed was two columns deep on the long sides and three at either end. Work on the temple was interrupted by Polycrates' death in 522 BC, taken up again c. 500 BC, stopped once more after 478 BC, and resumed in the 3rd century BC, but the building remained unfinished. The columns were never fluted, and neither the floor nor roof was completed.

In Roman times a much smaller temple was placed to the east to house the cult statue of Hera. Early sources refer to this as a xoanon, an unshaped wooden plank 'not made by human hands'. Such figures were relatively common in sanctuaries of great antiquity. By the 2nd century AD, however, there appears to have been a figural statue. No trace of either cult image survives.

The sanctuary thrived throughout the Hellenistic and especially Roman periods. With the spread of Christianity, its significance faded.

THE SITE

The Sacred Way

The site is entered from the east, along the Sacred Way, which led here from ancient Samos (today's Pythagóreio). It was lined with innumerable inscriptions and statues, including the giant kouros now in Vathý (*see p. 477*). The fine stone-paved surface dates from the Roman era, as do the foundations of shops and houses to either side. Towards its western end, the Sacred Way is flanked by treasuries and shrines of various periods, of which scant foundations survive, including those of a small mid-6th-century BC peripteral **Temple of Apollo and Artemis (A)**, of unusual plan, with a row of columns in the centre of the naos (remains barely visible). The orientations of these structures are remarkably diverse, reflecting the unplanned, organic growth of the sanctuary. To the right stands a copy of the 6th-century BC **Geneleos Group (B)**, a votive offering with statues depicting a wealthy Samian family (original in Vathý Museum). Bases of other votive statues, from Archaic through to Roman times, stand in the vicinity.

The altar area

A leftward path curves round the **Altar of Rhoikos (C)**, in its present shape from about 550 BC, with minor Roman alterations. It had at least six predecessors since the late Bronze Age, all in the same spot, the sacred focus of the sanctuary. The sacred willow under which Hera was said to have been born, still visible in the 2nd century AD, may have been nearby. Foundations of the most recent **earlier altar (D)**, at an oblique angle, are visible. The 6th-century BC altar is a confusing assemblage of decorated pieces; originally it was a monumental structure (38.4m by 18.7m) in the form of a wide Greek Π, its open side fronting the temple and its arms surrounding the altar table on its raised platform. Its ornate decorative programme is indicated by the fragments around, most of which are Roman restorations.

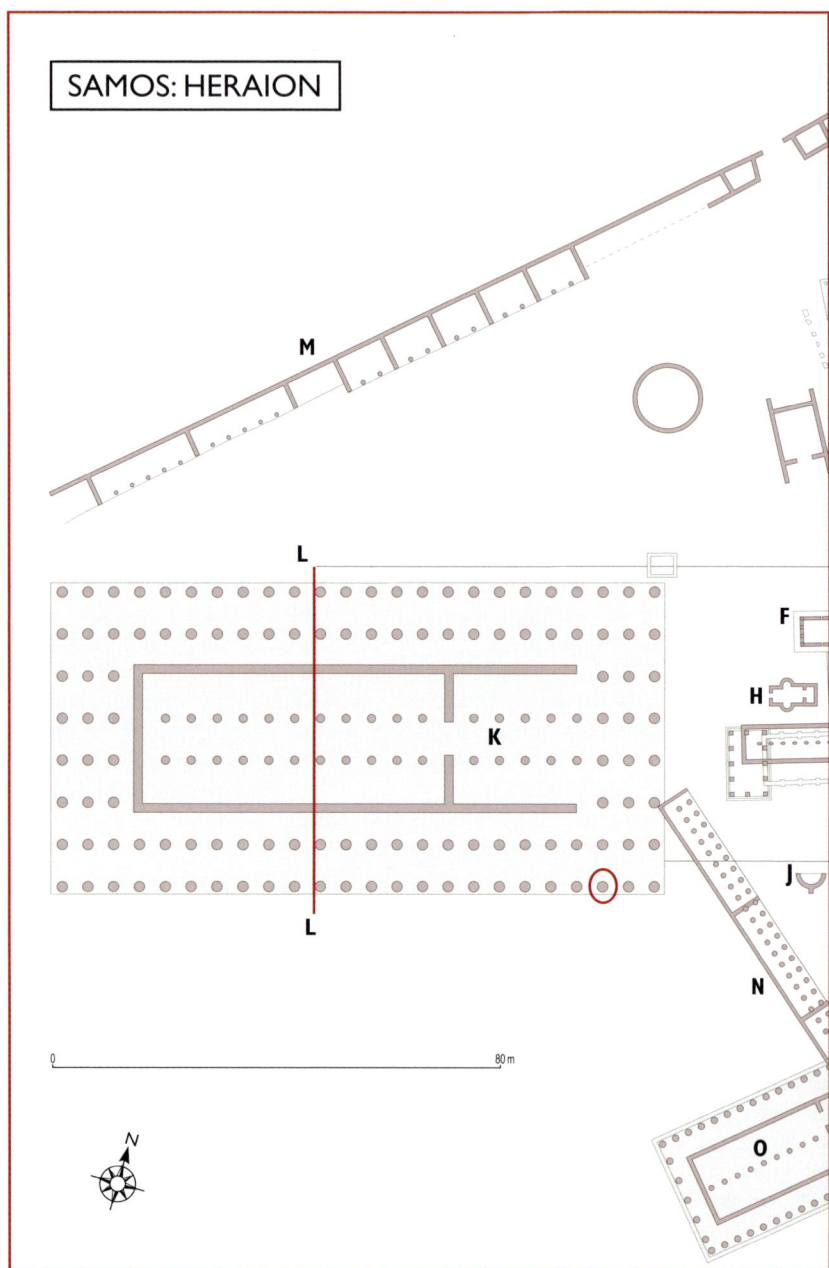

SAMOS: HERAION

M

L

L

K

F

H

J

N

O

0   80 m

N

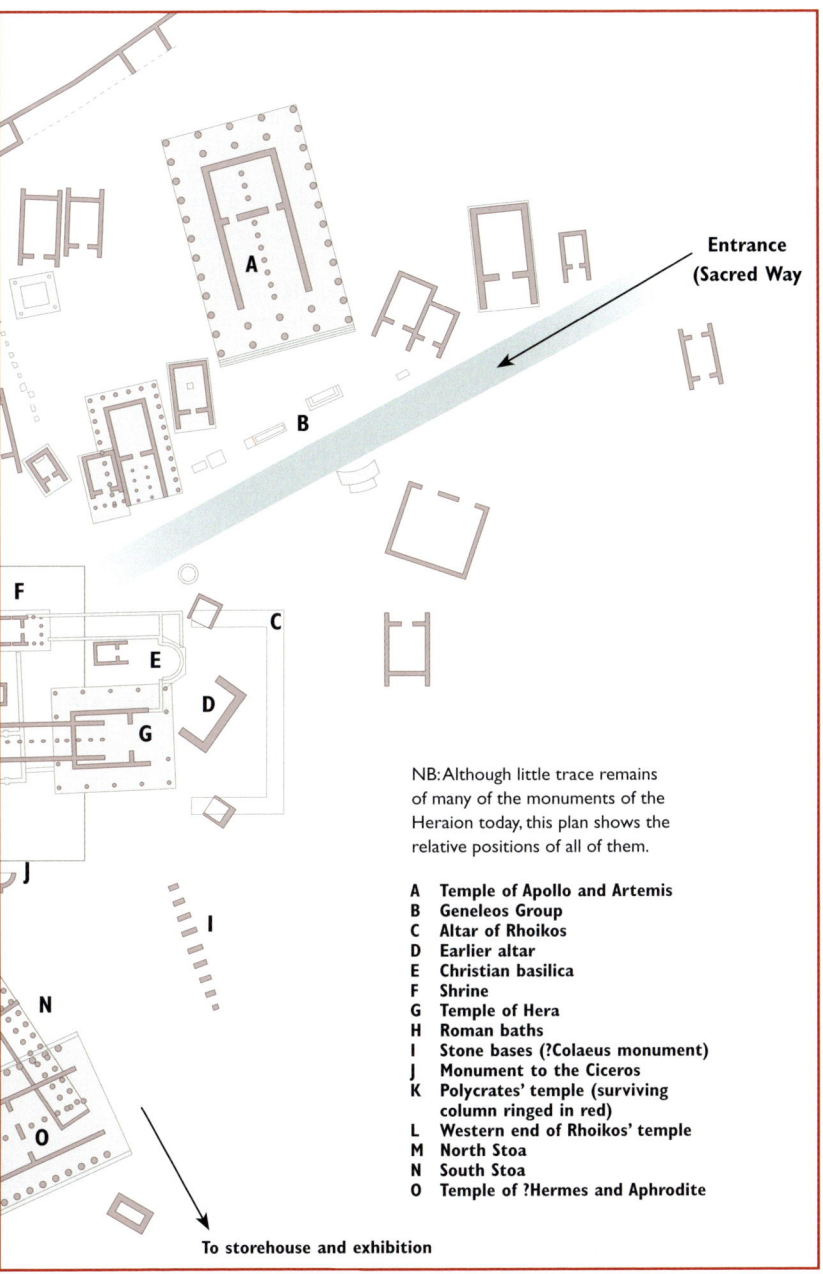

Entrance
(Sacred Way

F
E
D
C
G
J
I
N
O
A
B

NB: Although little trace remains
of many of the monuments of the
Heraion today, this plan shows the
relative positions of all of them.

A   Temple of Apollo and Artemis
B   Geneleos Group
C   Altar of Rhoikos
D   Earlier altar
E   Christian basilica
F   Shrine
G   Temple of Hera
H   Roman baths
I   Stone bases (?Colaeus monument)
J   Monument to the Ciceros
K   Polycrates' temple (surviving
    column ringed in red)
L   Western end of Rhoikos' temple
M   North Stoa
N   South Stoa
O   Temple of ?Hermes and Aphrodite

To storehouse and exhibition

The distance between altar and temple is unusually large: 60m. This is mostly due to the altar having to remain in its sacred location when the temple was moved westwards in the 6th century. The area in between is filled with a confusing jumble of remains of later periods, placed above the foundations of the earliest temples. A standing apse abutting the altar is part of a 5th-century AD **Christian basilica (E)**, constructed almost entirely from blocks and fragments from earlier structures. It is fitted snugly between two 2nd-century AD Roman buildings, incorporating their walls and floors: a small **Corinthian-style shrine** at its northwest corner **(F)** and the **Roman temple to Hera (G)** along its south side, which served as an abode for the cult statue. There are also the remains of a small complex of late **Roman baths (H)** to the west of the basilica.

One thing that impressed Herodotus about the sanctuary was the wealth and variety of its votive dedications. He mentions one piece in particular (*Histories IV, 152*): a bronze vessel, surrounded by '…griffin's heads at the rim, and supported by three kneeling figures in bronze, eleven and a half feet high'. This piece was made from the proceeds of a tithe on the profits of a trading mission undertaken by the early 7th-century BC Samian mariner Colaeus, and was dedicated by him to Hera. Colaeus' journey was remarkable in that it had penetrated into the Atlantic Ocean, beyond the Straits of Gibraltar. A series of **stone bases (I)** found about 20m east of the south stoa, and directly south of the great altar, has generally been interpreted as the support for the votive dedication of a boat. Whether the boat were that of Colaeus or not, is impossible to verify.

To the south of the path is the semicircular foundation of the **honorific monument to the Cicero brothers (J)**, erected c. 58 BC in gratitude to the orator Marcus Tullius Cicero (who had famously prosecuted the Roman governor Verres for plundering the sanctuary) and his brother Quintus, an able and beneficent governor of Asia from 61–58 BC.

The temple

What remains of Polycrates' **Temple of Hera (K)** is mostly the raised foundations for its rows of columns and the walls of its naos, laid in 13 courses to support the weight of the building. The spaces between would later have been filled with beaten earth and covered with flooring. The steps visible at two points may be no more than builders' ramps. At many points, dismantled material from Rhoikos' earlier temple, most conspicuously the beautiful column-bases with fine horizontal fluting, were incorporated into the new foundations. Two materials are used: a yellowy-white Samian marble (for details and important elements) and a grey, local limestone (for walls and steps). The low depression of the central naos area is bisected by the **foundations of the western extremity of Rhoikos' temple (L)**. The solitary remaining column of Polycrates' temple, unfluted and dislocated by seismic movement, stands only to about half its original height.

Other remains

Several other monuments were excavated in the sanctuary but are now invisible. Scant foundations of the 6th-century BC **North Stoa (M)** can be seen among the reeds north of the temple. The 70-m **South Stoa (N)**, now buried, ran at an oblique angle roughly from the present temple's east façade towards the storehouse to the southeast. Built c.

65 BC, it was the oldest such free-standing hall known from any Greek sanctuary. It was demolished by the 6th century to make room for the erection of a second substantial **temple (O)**, perhaps to Hermes and Aphrodite, of which nothing is visible.

Southeast of the temple, a path leads to the **excavation storehouse**. Its yards are used as a repository for carved stone from the site, including hundreds of fragments from the Temple of Hera, some exquisite carved sphinxes from the altar of Rhoikos, and beautiful details from the Early Christian basilica, as well as many inscriptions. A small exhibition at the back (ask the guards) displays photographs from the excavations and an informative model of all excavated remains.

WEST OF THE HERAION

The road continues past the Heraion to the coastal resort of Iraío (*map p. 474, C3*). On the road northwest from there, towards Mýli, is a fortified 15th- or 16th-century tower known as **Pýrgos Sarakinís**. Beside it is the heavily buttressed double church of Ághios Geórgios (north) and **Ághios Ioánnis Theológos** (south). The altar of Ághios Ioánnis Theológos is a superb ancient inscribed column fragment, surmounted by a capital.

Beyond Mýli (also reached by main road from Pythagóreio), a road leads west to the pretty village of Pagóndas (*map p. 474, C3*). Half a kilometre to the south, on an uphill track, is the church of Ághios Pantelémonas, amongst trees in a deep cut in the hillside. This is the site of the **ancient quarry** which provided stone for the buildings of the Heraion.

THE CENTRAL SOUTH OF THE ISLAND

Attractive **Chóra** (*map p. 474, C2*) was the capital of the island until 1834. Three kilometres to the north, at **Mytilinií** (so named because it was settled by immigrants from Mytilene), is the Natural History Museum of the Aegean (*south of the centre; open April–Oct Tues–Sun 9–2*). The (poorly-labelled) exhibition focuses primarily on fossils from 6–9 million years ago, found in a ravine nearby. They include over 60 species, among them antelope, rhinoceros and a short-necked giraffe unique to Samos (the Samotherium). A stuffed specimen of a big cat, apparently a species of tiger, was captured as late as 1862 in the forests of Samos.

From Chóra to Pýrgos

Three and a half kilometres west of Chóra, a right branch leads to the monastery of the **Tímios Stavrós,** a late 16th-century foundation, rebuilt in 1838, when its arcaded outbuildings were added. Yet more impressive for its imposing size is the monastery of the **Megáli Panaghía**, 2km northwest of Mýli, with a fine 16th-century painted katholikon. Less than 1km further downhill, the solitary 14th-century church of the Taxiárches comes into view in the valley below.

The main road from Chóra leads to **Pýrgos** (*map p. 474, B2*). The principal road through the village is crossed by a raised, arcaded aqueduct, constructed in the 18th century to irrigate the fields down the slope. Pýrgos is a network of narrow streets, with many traditional stone houses, loosely grouped around a square dominated by the uncompleted church of Ághios Geórgios (1904).

Skouréïka and Kouméïka

Five kilometres west of Pýrgos, a branch road leads south to the village of Neochóri, built against a cliff. The track towards Skouréïka (*map p. 474, B2*) crosses a stream after 1.8km. Near here are sculpted niches, perhaps related to the cult of the nymphs, and a 6th-century BC **rock-cut inscription** recording the names of the builders of a wooden bridge (*the inscription is about 3m off the ground near the east end of the existing bridge, cut into the rockface on the east side of the stream, where it passes through a narrow gorge*). Further west on the main road, another branch leads south to **Kouméïka**, which has a marble Ottoman fountain with pretty carvings.

THE NORTH COAST

At Kédros (*map p. 474, C1*), about 6km northwest of Vathý, are the remains of an Early Christian **cruciform baptismal pool** (late 4th or 5th century AD; *300m down the right/ north turn after the EKO filling station*), beside the modern church of Aghía Paraskeví. It was probably part of a basilica complex.

Kámbos, Vourliótes and Mount Ámbelos

At Avlákia (*map p. 474, C1*) the coast road turns west into the small plain of Kámbos, at the mouth of a ravine. Two 14th-century churches, **Aghía Pelagía and Aghía Matróna**, are visible among trees above the road (*access by taking the cement track uphill to the south, just beyond the signed turn for Vourliótes*). Both churches have a central, triconch plan, surmounted by an octagonal dome. Aghía Matróna, the higher of the two, is extensively decorated with fine 18th-century wall-paintings. Over the aisle to both sides are charming depictions of *Adam Naming the Animals* (left) and the *Expulsion from Eden* (right).

The 17th-century village of **Vourliótes** (*map p. 474, C1*) is characterised by its attractive balconied houses, betraying the villagers' origin from Asia Minor. Although some of the surrounding area has been damaged by fire, it is an ideal centre for walking and climbing the ridges of **Mt Ámbelos**, and to explore the valleys and villages along the north coast. Only 2km south of the village, the fires have left the **monastery of Vrontá** damaged and isolated. Founded in 1476, and therefore the oldest active monastery on Samos, it was rebuilt in 1566, fortified externally, and has graceful arcades surrounding the central katholikon inside. The mountainous area to the south of the monastery was hidden territory into which the dwindling population retreated in search of safety from seaborne attack in the 8th century. There are several late medieval summit fortifications here: 2.5km beyond the Vrontá, on the northeast-facing ridge, is the 13th-century **Castle of Louloúda** (*left-hand branch at the junction 800m south of Vrontá; the castle is* *visible on the summit to the left after 1km*); further southwest, on a peak halfway between Louloúda and the summit of Mt Ámbelos, are the earlier remains of **Lazárou Castle** (*5km along the right-hand branch at the junction 800m south of Vrontá*). Several traditional villages are scattered along the slopes south of the main road.

KARLOVASI & ENVIRONS

Karlóvasi (*map p. 474, B1*) is almost as populous as Vathý but lacks a defined centre. Overlooking the port from a hill at the western extremity of the town is the picturesque quarter of **Palaió Karlóvasi**, with its balconied houses. Below the old town is Áno Karlóvasi, inland from the sea; on the edge further behind are Mesaío Karlóvasi and Néo Karlóvasi; all loosely connected. All these different nuclei have considerable architectural variety. In the **area of Ríva**, by the shore east of the port, are many empty warehouses and tannery buildings of the 1890s and early 1900s, a memento of the town's prosperity at the turn of the last century. The mercantile families who controlled the industry constructed grand and impressive Neoclassical mansions inland; the most ostentatious example to survive is now the Samos Headquarters of the University of the Aegean, on Odós Panepistímiou Aigaíou. In a square further uphill is a ruined octagonal Ottoman fountain and the city's small Ethnographic Museum (*closed at the time of writing*). Towards the sea, on Odós Kanári, between the large church of Ághios Nikólaos and the shore, are villas of the 1920s.

The Panaghía tou Potamoú

The church known as the Panaghía tou Potamoú, in Potámi Bay, is one of the oldest and most unusual churches on Samos (1.5km west of Karlóvasi port). A track leading inland from Potámi village up the valley of a stream first passes the ruins of the early church of Ághios Nikólaos; after 150m, it reaches the Panaghía, to the left. The church is remarkable for its unusual proportions: the floorplan of the interior is approximately 5m square, while the (inside) height is about 7m; 9m to the crown of the minuscule dome. Four monolithic columns in Samian marble, surmounted by finely-carved 5th-century capitals, support the arches of the crossing; but they are only a little over a third of its total height. The church was once the katholikon of a small monastery; the vestiges of a baptistery, with an immersion font, can be seen outside the southeast corner. The columns, capitals and various other spolia must come from a 5th-century basilica. A path, climbing steeply up the east slope beyond the church, leads to a small castle with a cistern, contemporary with the church.

Inland of Karlóvasi

The long, broad valley that crosses Samos north–south between the two massifs of Kérkis (Kerketéas) and Ámbelos is one of the island's most beautiful areas: wooded, gentle and cultivated, but not rich in specific monuments. Its settlements are untouched and tranquil, good examples being the lowland village of **Léka** (northwest; *map p. 474, A1*) and the upland one of **Plátanos** (southeast; *map p. 474, B2*).

Between Plátanos and the coast is **Ydroússa** (*map p. 474, B1*). Northeast of the main church at the centre of the village is a signed track to Petaloúda. After 20mins on foot, a left turn at a T-junction leads on and eventually crosses a stream bed, shortly after which, to the left, is the church of the Koímisis tis Theotókou (12th–13th century). The simple, barrel-vaulted church preserves its original wall-paintings of exceptional quality, including saints and a *Raising of Lazarus*. Noteworthy is the scene of St Peter of Alexandria remonstrating with the tiny figure of Christ in a canopied aedicule.

THE WESTERN END OF THE ISLAND

The west of Samos is dominated by the mass of Mt Kérkis, one of the most beautiful and dramatic mountains in the Aegean, its upper slopes sometimes so pale from the colour of the chalky, bare rock that they seem covered in snow. The surrounding area is the most remote part of Samos. The only road into the area branches west of the Pythagóreio–Karlóvasi road near Ághii Theódori (*map p. 474, B2*).

Marathókambos

The sprawling village of Marathókambos (*map p. 474, A2*) stands 2km above the wide gulf of the same name. From the western end of the village, 4.2km of unsurfaced track wind westwards and uphill to the hermitic complex of the **Cave of Pythagoras and the church of the Panaghía Sarandaskaliótissa** ('Virgin of the Forty Steps'), located in a cliff-face and reached by a long stepped path, passing the 13th-century chapel of Ághios Ioánnis, on a small ledge. From just below the chapel, a rough track (indicated with red spots of paint) climbs steeply towards a natural arch and then round into the Cave of Pythagoras, which has three chambers leading off a shelf of rock. The legend that Pythagoras took refuge here with some of his students to escape the persecution of Polycrates before leaving the island for good, is an old one. It inspired a 10th-century hermit, St Paul of Latros, to live in the cave. Higher up the main footpath past Ághios Ioánnis, at the top of a flight of rock-cut steps, is the church of the Panaghía Sarandas-kaliótissa, a single-aisled stone chapel in the entrance of a deep cave (c. 80m).

A special treat is the white **beach of Psalída** on the uninhabited islet of Samiopoúla, reached in summer by small boats from Órmos Marathókambou or Pythagóreio.

Around Mount Kérkis

From Marathókambos, the road leads down to the shore and follows it west. From Votsalákia, a rough, motorable track leads north, branches twice to the left and ends at the beginning of a footpath which climbs to the convent of the Evangelístria. From here, it is possible to climb the **summit of Mt Kérkis**, reaching the lower peak, Profítis Ilías, in 90mins and, 45–60mins beyond that, the higher one, Vígla. Kérkis, an extinct volcano, is home to many rare and endemic plants, as well as various raptors, including eagles.

Beyond Votsalákia, the main road continues west, past the beautiful bay of Limnió-nas, into increasingly remote terrain. The most significant monuments in this area are the **cave-churches** on the western slope of Kérkis, above Kallithéa (*map p. 474, A2; an unsurfaced road leads up from the cemetery at the southern end of Kallithéa; after 1.7km, a left turn at the junction climbs a further 2km to the church of Aghía Paraskeví, from where a footpath leads uphill 1km east, to the first of the churches*). The church of the Panaghía Makriní is in the entrance of a shallow cave. The original 13th-century chapel was incorporated and expanded in the 18th century into the larger, domed tri-conch structure, which still preserves its original wall-paintings. At Aghía Triáda, a short distance further up the path, the church, behind a simple front, is created out of the natural rock.

Pythagoras of Samos (6th century BC)

Pythagoras was at the same time thinker, philosopher and mathematician as well as a spiritual teacher, seer and leader. His famous geometric theorem is known the world over; nevertheless, the secret teachings and symbols of the society he founded eventually undermined it, by inspiring suspicion.

Pythagoras left no writings of his own, and not all later sources can be assumed to be objective. He must have been born c. 570 BC, and probably trained on Samos in the craft of his father, Mnesarchus, as a gem-engraver. At some point he came into conflict with Polycrates, tyrant of the island, and in 530 BC he abandoned Samos for Croton in southern Italy. In Croton, led by a moral, reforming zeal, he took a leading role in politics. He is said to have given Croton a constitution and, with or through followers, governed so well that the state deserved, in a literal sense, the name of aristocracy or 'government of the best'. The Pythagoreans were given to secretive ways, however, and the assumption of superiority inherent in their behaviour eventually led to popular suspicion and discontent. Pythagoras was either banished or went into exile, meeting-houses were burned, and leading Pythagoreans were killed. Pythagoras himself appears to have taken refuge in a temple of the Muses at Metapontum, where he died c. 500 BC. The immediate influence of his teachings and of the Pythagorean School continued for at least a century more.

Pythagoras seems to have been the first to use the word *kosmos*, and it is towards unity or empathy with the divine nature of this idea that the soul of man aspires. The way was through the purification offered by *philosophia*, a reasoned understanding of the harmony of the *kosmos*, and through sympathy and harmony with all living beings which were of similar substance. Once this idea is grasped, everything else follows: the abstention from taking life and eating animals; the kinship of all beings through the transmigration of souls; the primacy of pure number as the origin of order and the expression of divine beauty and coherence; the concept that the perfectly articulated movement of the celestial bodies gives rise to a heavenly music—a music that only the enlightened can hear.

PRACTICAL INFORMATION

GETTING AROUND

There are several daily flights from Athens. Samos airport is 2km west of Pythagóreio.

Sea access is plentiful, divided between three separate ports: Karlóvasi and Vathý on the north coast are served daily by ferries from Piraeus and have somewhat less frequent connections with Chios, Lesbos and Thessaloníki. Pythagóreio, on the south coast, is served on the southern routes through the Dodecanese to Kos and Rhodes, four times a week by ferry and daily by hydrofoil. There is also a summer service to Foúrni and Ikaría, four times a week.

WHERE TO STAY

A good place to stay is the **Armonia Bay Hotel** above Tsamadoú beach, just west of Kokkári on the north coast: it strikes a perfect balance between style, comfort and simplicity, at a contained price (*open April–Oct; T: 22730 92279, www.armoniabay.gr*). In the centre of Vathý, the **Hotel Avlí**, built around an attractive courtyard, is charming and has simple rooms (*open April–Oct; T: 22730 22939*). Pythagóreio is problematic because of mass tourism and noise in high season, but if you need to stay, **Areli Studios** (*open May–Oct; T: 22730 61245*) is a pleasant hotel in a garden setting, set a little way back from the harbour.

At the southwestern corner of the island, in beautiful seclusion and with great style, is **Limnionas Village**, in the bay of that name (*T: 22730 37274,www.limnionas.net*); these are self-catering cottages on weekly lets.

WHERE TO EAT

In Vathý, **Christos** (two blocks in from the waterfront, north of the main square) serves Asia Minor specialities, interesting salads and fragrant wine. The most authentic surviving taverna is Pythagóreio is **Varka**, at the beginning of the harbour mole.

The village of Vourliótes has several tavernas offering good mountain food in its picturesque *plateía*: popular with islanders is **Pera Vrysi**, at the entrance to the village. On the shore below, at Avlákia, the **Mezedopoleio Doña Rosa** has a pleasing touch of eccentricity, but nonetheless prepares excellent Greek dishes with local ingredients. Further west at Palaió Karlóvasi, the **Oinomageireio Dryousa**, in the *plateía* where the paved road ends, is family-run, providing fresh home cooking. At the south end of Spatharéi (*map p. 474, B2*), the **Balkoni** has wonderful sunset views; while the **taverna at Koútsi** (*map p. 474, B2*), west of Pýrgos, though not remarkable for food, is an unforgettable and cool refuge on a hot day, beside a spring below plane trees in the hills.

Pure comb honey of high quality can be found at **Melissa**, a small supply-shop in Pythagórieo, a few metres up the main street from the harbour.

FURTHER READING

Graham Shipley, *A History of Samos 800–188 BC* (Oxford University Press, 1987). Hermann Kienast, *The Aqueduct of Eupalinos* (Greek Ministry of Culture, 2005). Dieter Graf, *Walking the Greek Islands: Samos, Patmos and the Northern Dodeanese*, 2005. For Pythagoreana, there is *Pythagoras and the Pythagoreans: A Brief History*, by Charles H. Kahn (2001), and, for a lighter read, *Pythagoras' Revenge: A Mathematical Mystery*, by Arturo Sangalli.

THE ISLANDS OF THE
NORTHERN AEGEAN

The group treated in this guide as the 'Islands of the Northern Aegean' is a diverse collection of islands, split between the modern administrative regions of East Macedonia/Thrace (Samothrace and Thasos) and the Northern Aegean (Lesbos, Lemnos). Historically speaking, Imbros and Tenedos (now part of Turkey and called Gökçeada and Bozcaada) also belong to this group.

NORTHERN AEGEAN ISLANDS

Thasos was settled in early prehistory; Samothrace, Lemnos and Lesbos in the Neolithic. In the Bronze Age, there was activity on all the islands, especially on Lemnos, where a complex urbanised society came into being. According to tradition, Lesbos and Samothrace were colonised by Aeolians from the east in the early 1st millennium BC. The early historical inhabitants of Lemnos were said to be of pre-Greek stock, a view potentially supported by a mysterious 6th-century inscription (*see p. 536*). On less shaky evidence, Thasos is known to have been colonised by Ionians from Paros in the early 7th century BC. Unsurprisingly, the islands followed individual historical trajectories.

Lesbos was the most prominent of the islands in antiquity, its size supporting five separate city-states. Thasos and Samothrace developed into rich mining centres. By the early 5th century, the islands had all, to varying degrees, fallen under Persian domination. After 479 BC, they came under Athenian influence, though Thasos, Lemnos and Lesbos all tried to defect. The islands flourished in the Hellenistic period. Roman and Byzantine rule was relatively uneventful, followed by upheavals in the aftermath of the Fourth Crusade, when the islands repeatedly changed hands between Byzantium, Venice, Genoa and the Ottomans—who ended up controlling all of them by the late 15th century. The islands joined Greece in 1912.

There is no generic 'Northern Aegean' character that unites the group; instead, each of the islands has its own distinct personality and its own cultural, topographical and historical peculiarities. Lesbos, home of the fabled poet Sappho, has two excellent archaeological museums, copious Early Christian and Byzantine remains, and much 19th-century industrial architecture. Its most unusual site, however, is the petrified prehistoric forest at Sígri. Lesbos also has a well-developed network of walking tracks, permitting intense and intimate exploration. Lemnos, largely neglected by modern travel, is home to one of the most significant Bronze Age sites in Greece, at Polióchni, sometimes dubbed Europe's 'oldest city'. Remote Ághios Efstrátios is among the least-visited islands in the Aegean. Samothrace, though little more than a forested mountain sticking out of the sea, is considered by many Greeks as the most beautiful of all their islands. Its Sanctuary of the Great Gods, once one of the principal religious centres in the Greek world, is among the most intriguing sites in the Aegean. The island's *chora* is a fine example of 19th-century parochial architecture. Thasos, in archaeological terms, is little short of a miracle. The modern capital sits among the remains of one of the best preserved of all Greek cities, offering visitors a sequence of beautiful, memorable and instructive sights that is second to none. The ancient sanctuary and quarry at Alykí, though overshadowed by Thasos town, would be considered a first rate site on any other island.

The North Aegean islands all preserve certain local traditions: Lesbos is known for its olive oil and distinctive pottery; Lemnos for fine soft cheeses. Thasos produces excellent fruit preserves (especially of walnut) and hosts a quasi-Dionysiac carnival festival in Panaghía; Samothrace is proud of its hard cheese, cherries and chickpea bread.

In short, each of these islands rewards more than a casual visit. Though large-scale tourism has begun to make an appearance on Lesbos, it is still quite limited and its impact is easily offset by the island's size. Samothrace and Thasos are beginning to develop a more careful form of tourism; Lemnos remains largely off the beaten track.   H.H.

LESBOS

Lesbos has a predominantly rural character that gives the island a feel of domesticity, spaciousness and calm. Water, wildlife, produce and shade are all abundant. Sappho (the first—and one of the greatest—female poets of Western literature) and her contemporaries, Alcaeus, Arion and Terpander, were all from Lesbos: the island can justly consider itself to be the cradle of ancient Greek lyric poetry and music. It is a tradition that has not died: the modern writers Stratis Myrivilis and Argyris Eftaliotis, and the Nobel laureate poet Odysseas Elytis, were also all from Lesbos.

Lesbos may appear bucolic, but it is in fact a turbulent land: the dramatic landscape of the west of the island, including its petrified forest of giant tree trunks near Sígri, is shaped and scarred by volcanic action, and the profusion of geothermic springs is testimony to continuing volcanic activity.

In spite of its size and wealth in antiquity, Lesbos has less to show in archaeological terms than its neighbours. But from the Middle Ages on, its heritage is rich and there is no corner of the island that lacks interest. Its landscape is constantly varying, offering habitats as diverse as wetland reed-beds and rocky steppes, with an accompanying diversity of bird life and flora. Lesbos is very well adapted for walking, and although its size means that it takes time to explore, this remains the ideal way to get acquainted with its beauty and spaciousness.

HISTORY OF LESBOS

Diodorus Siculus (*III, 55*) states that Myrina, Queen of the Amazons, conquered Lesbos and founded the city of Mytilene (which was named after her sister). It was a good choice for a settlement, as the island's geographical situation and many harbours had made it a centre for trade and communication from earliest times: prehistoric finds indicate occupation from c. 3300 BC until the end of the Mycenaean periods, and relate closely to finds from ancient Troy. The early inhabitants were probably Pelasgian, but in the 10th century BC the island and the mainland opposite were colonised by Aeolians under the leadership of the Penthelides, the last of whom was murdered in 659 BC. The island was divided in antiquity between five competing cities: Mytilene, Methymna, Pyrrha, Antissa and Eresos. A struggle developed between Methymna and Mytilene for the leadership of the island, and although Mytilene won and has remained the capital, western Lesbos fostered a tradition of independent resistance which was to recur at critical moments. A large fleet and wide mercantile interests (especially in Egypt) were combined with a high standard of education and a comparative freedom for women, two traditions still noticeable today.

Lesbos fell under Persian domination in 527, and was not freed until 479 BC, when it joined the Athenian League. In 428 BC, soon after the Peloponnesian War started, Mytilene tried to break away with Spartan help, but Methymna betrayed the plan

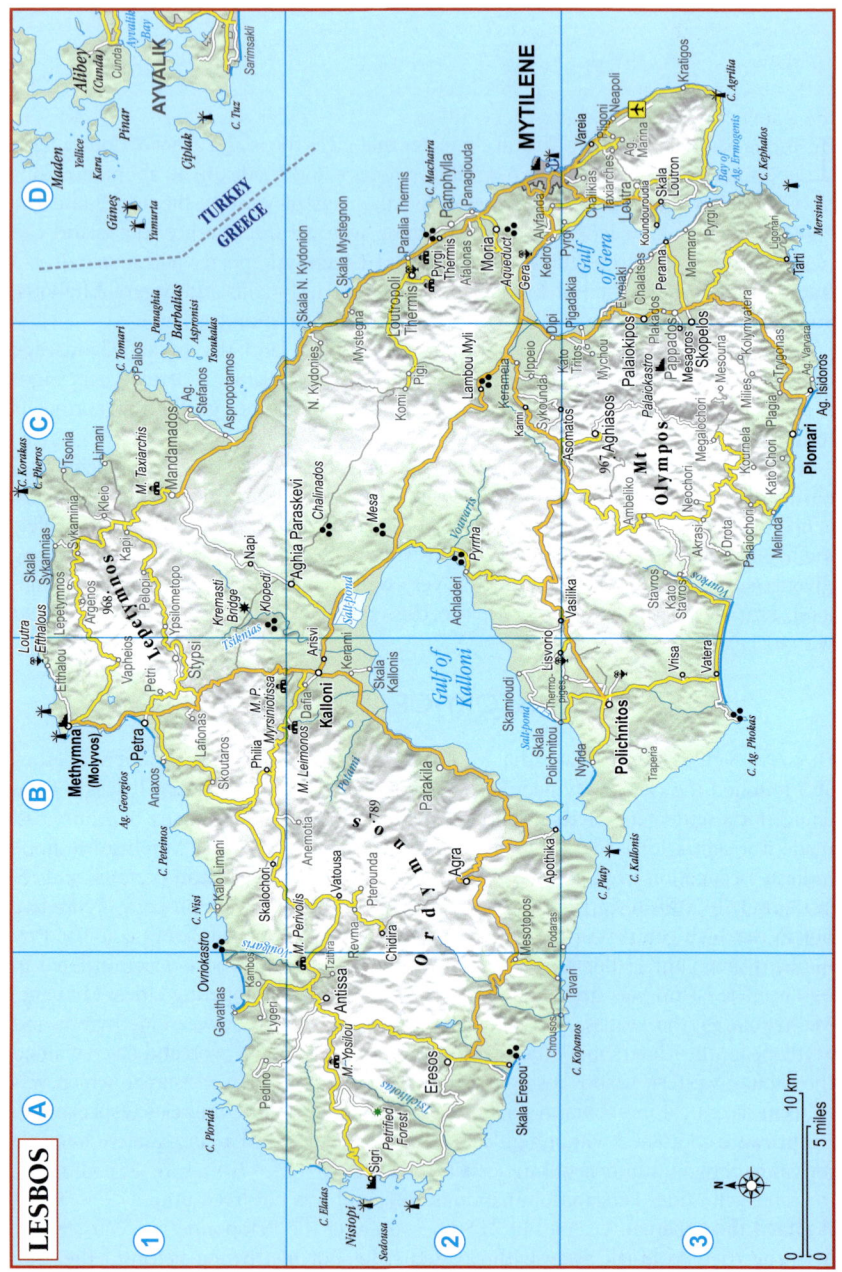

to Athens and the Mytileneans were severely punished. In 405 BC Lesbos fell to the Spartans and thereafter changed hands frequently, being ruled by Persia, Macedonia and the Ptolemies until Mithridates occupied it in 88–79 BC, only to be ousted by the Romans. According to Suetonius, Julius Caesar won his spurs during the Roman storming of Mytilene.

On his way back to Jerusalem from Greece (c. AD 52), St Paul spent a night at Mytilene before passing by Chios and Samos. By the 5th century AD Lesbos had many fine basilicas, with bishops at both Mytilene and Methymna. As a Byzantine dominion, the island was used as a place of exile, notably for the Empress Irene in 809. It suffered Saracen invasions in 821, 881 and 1055, which prompted the inhabitants to leave the coast for the mountains of the interior. Between 1085 and 1462 it changed hands between the Seljuks, Byzantines, Catalans and Genoese, finally enjoying a century of untroubled prosperity under the control of the Gattilusi family, who established an important trading principality in the north Aegean. After 12 years of paying a substantial tribute to Sultan Mehmet II, Lesbos fell to the Turks in 1462 and remained under Turkish domination until 1912, enjoying considerable privileges in the 19th century, in spite of an orchestrated revolt in 1821. The quantity of grand 19th- and early 20th-century industrial architecture around the island, and the large mansions in Mytilene and Plomári, is evidence of the island's prosperity from olive production, leather tanning and ouzo distilling before the world wars; and the many Ottoman remains bear witness to the islanders' innate tolerance. After 1912, when the island became part of the Greek state, Lesbos received large numbers of refugees from Asia Minor.

MYTILENE

The present layout of the city of Mytilene (*pron: Mitilíni*) is substantially different from its form in antiquity. Today ferries arrive in the main harbour, south of the castle, with the city centre laid out on its west shore. This was formerly the military (or 'trireme') harbour of ancient Mytilene, and was linked by a canal-like channel, referred to simply as the Euripos (Évripos; the 'Strait'), which ran north from it for 500m along the line of today's Ermoú street, to the commercial harbour on the north side of the town. This meant that the hill and eastern promontory on which the castle now stands was formerly an island, and was the heart of the ancient city. Archaeological work has revealed parts of the harbour moles, cemeteries, aqueducts, a theatre, villas of considerable size, and a sanctuary of Demeter and Persephone. The urban area was laid out according to a Hippodamian grid plan: Vitruvius observed accurately that this left the streets unprotected from the force of the north and south winds. The city was rich and seems to have been splendidly decorated in Hellenistic times; it exported metals, alum, textiles, terracottas and garum, a fermented fish paste widely used for flavouring in lieu of salt.

Ághios Therápon

The western side of the main harbour today is dominated by the eclectic church of

MYTILENE

Ághios Therápon (completed 1935; *map above, B2*). Facing its west front is the small and interesting **Byzantine Museum**, containing icons, historical documents and religious material from around the island (*open June–Sept, daily except Sun, 10–1*). Among the icons are a number of early examples including a beautiful 14th-century *Pantocrator* (from the monastery of the Taxiárchis at Káto Trítos on the west side of the Gulf of Géra) and a 13th-century *St George*.

The old Christian and Muslim quarters

The city's **cathedral** is a large, late 19th-century church halfway down Ermoú (*map above, B2*). It is dedicated to Ághios Theódoros, who was martyred at the hands of the Turks in 1795 and was chosen as the city's patron saint (his relics are preserved inside, to the right). In the immediate vicinity are four other churches, which represent the heart of the Christian area during Ottoman occupation. The oldest of these is the church of **Ághii Theódori** (50m north, down an alleyway to the east of Ermoú; *map p. 504, B1*), originally a Byzantine foundation which was rebuilt after a fire in the mid-18th century.

To the north of here was the predominantly Muslim quarter, centred on the early 19th-century **Yeni Djami** ('New Mosque') on the corner of Ermoú and Adramytíou. This fine, porticoed mosque, now gutted and roofless, was the focus of the market area in Ottoman times. The recently restored **Çarşi Hamam** ('Market Baths'), 50m to its west on Mavíli, is from the same time and part of the same complex. To the north along the shore road around the bay, opposite the DEH electricity generating plant, is another interesting Ottoman structure: the buildings of the **Kourtzi Hamam**, built as a therapeutic centre in 1883 by one of the island's richest bankers and industrialists, Panos Kourtzis, on the site of geothermic springs known and used in Roman times. Some of the interior decoration and the twin steam-rooms (one for men, the other for women; now dry) are still preserved.

The Old Archaeological Museum and Statue of Liberty

The island's archaeological collections are housed in two separate buildings, an 'old' and a 'new'. The **Old Archaeological Museum** is in the 1920s Vournazos Mansion on the corner of 8 Noembríou and Eftalióti, across from the Customs House at the north-eastern extremity of the port (*map p. 504, C2; open daily except Mon, 8.30–3; ticket also covers entry to the New Archaeological Museum; see below*). The collection is laid out on two floors, with the earliest material on the ground floor and a series of mainly terra-cotta objects on the upper. The garden contains a number of carved altars, capitals, sarcophagi and sections of Roman decorative frieze, as well as some sizeable sculptures of lions from funerary monuments of the Hellenistic and Roman periods. A small annexe at the back of the garden contains the collection's most important stone pieces: two magnificent Aeolic capitals of the 6th century BC from the sanctuary of ancient Klopedí, together with fragments of the temple's decorative sima and several inscriptions.

Just east of the Old Archaeological Museum stands Mytilene's bronze *Statue of Liberty*, created jointly in 1922 by the sculptor Grigorios Zevgolis and the local painter Georgios Iakovides. It occupies the site of the Kastrélli, a free-standing, forward bastion of the main castle, which protected the entrance to the port and which was still standing at the turn of the 20th century.

The New Archaeological Museum and Natural History Museum

The **New Archaeological Museum** (*entry as for Old Archaeological Museum; see above*), further north up 8 Noembríou on the eastern side, was custom-built in the 1970s (on a plot which was once the site of a Hellenistic temple of Aphrodite) to house a collection of fine mosaics from the period of the Roman administration of the city. The quality and condition of the mosaics give a vivid impression of the sophistication and leisured opulence of Mytilene in late antiquity. The Exhibition Room houses a rotating display of the moulded terracotta vessels that were a unique and characteristic production of the city's workshops in the 1st centuries BC and AD.

Across the road from the entrance to the New Archaeological Museum is the **Old Natural History Museum** (*map p. 504, C2; open daily except Mon, 10–2; free*). The main collection has been moved to Sígri (*see p. 522*). The permanent exhibition is on the history and cultivation of olives and the production of olive oil, including a 60,000-year-old volcanic fossil from Santorini bearing the clear impression of olive leaves.

THE CASTLE OF MYTILENE

There are two entrances to the castle (*map p. 504, C1; open daily except Mon, 8–3*), one from the south and another from the west by the Orta Kapi, 150m north of the New Archaeological Museum. The description below assumes entry by the latter.

HISTORY OF THE CASTLE

The impressive quantity of spolia incorporated in the castle walls gives an idea of the extent of the destruction wreaked on the ancient town when the castle was first built. The first post-antique fortress here is said to have been erected in the 6th century AD, under the Emperor Justinian: the innermost of the three successive gates on the west side is Byzantine, and it marks the northwestern limit of the Byzantine castle. The enceinte was strengthened and further fortified to the south and west by the Genoese Gattilusi overlords, between their coming into possession of the castle in 1355 and a catastrophic earthquake in 1384 that wrought considerable damage to the structure and killed all of the ruling family save for a single son, Francesco II. What was rebuilt was considerably damaged again by the Turkish assault of 1462. In 1501, under Sultan Beyazit II, the Lower Castle, protected by a circular bastion at the northernmost point, was added to protect the north harbour. The interior was densely inhabited in Ottoman times; many of the ruined buildings still visible inside date from the 16th–19th centuries.

The Orta Kapi and Lower Castle

The Ottoman **Orta Kapi** ('Middle Gate') is virtually invisible from the outside, and protected by a circular bastion to the left as you approach. It leads into a passage and thence through a second (medieval) gate into an enclosed area between the Ottoman and the original Byzantine/Gattilusi walls. From here a third (Byzantine) gate, with a massive ancient marble block as its lintel, leads into the wide open interior, scattered with ancient spolia. To the right is an **Ottoman fountain (1)** and to the left a deep and well-preserved **cistern (2)**, whose design is both elegant and functional. Opposite are the remains of a square Ottoman house of the 17th century. To the north, visible from stairs which give access to the top of the intermediate wall to the left, lies the **Lower Castle**, which extended the fortifications as far as the northern shore and the harbour. It was protected by a circular bastion at its northern extremity and enclosed a large

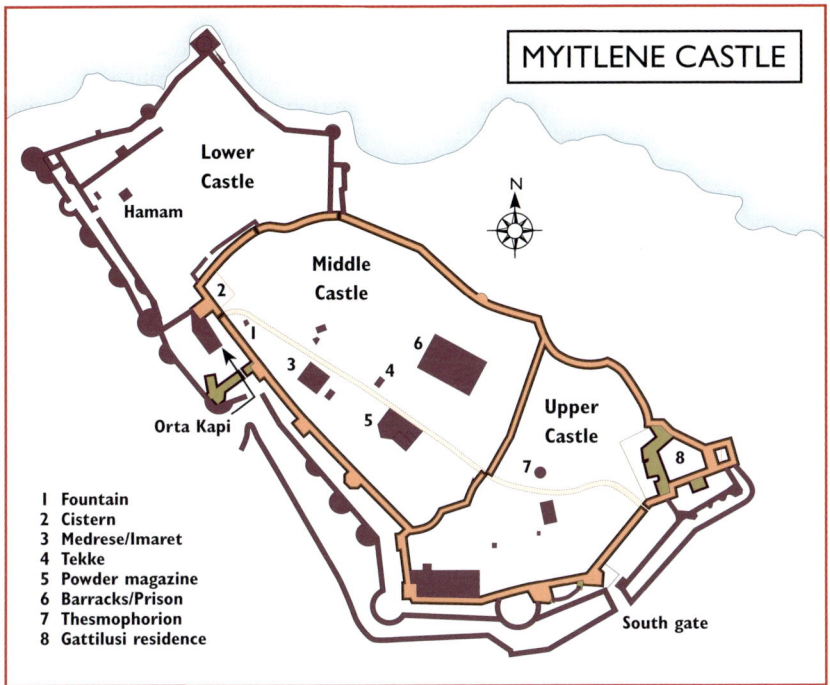

MYITLENE CASTLE

Lower
Castle

Hamam

Middle
Castle

N

Orta Kapi

Upper
Castle

South gate

1 **Fountain**
2 **Cistern**
3 **Medrese/Imaret**
4 **Tekke**
5 **Powder magazine**
6 **Barracks/Prison**
7 **Thesmophorion**
8 **Gattilusi residence**

area with a great many houses, a hamam, a fountain, a Turkish oracle-shrine, and the Christian cave-church and sacred spring of the Panaghía Galatoúsa, all of which can be reached from the road which circles the castle on the seaward side and breaches the lower walls in the north.

The Middle and Upper Castle

A paved path leads uphill to the south from the Byzantine gateway, passing the many-domed block of the **Ottoman medrese (3)** above and the **imaret** below. Immediately beyond the medrese was the hamam, and to the left of the path is a small, domed **tekke (4)**, or living quarters for dervishes, with its fireplace still intact. The three buildings together formed a complete religious unit.

The military buildings are further up: a massively-built **gunpowder magazine (5)** to the right of the path, and a large 17th-century **barracks and prison (6)**, arranged around a courtyard, to the left. Steps up to the top of the walls in the southwestern corner provide excellent views of the sharper lines of the final 17th-century Ottoman additions, the outermost walls and bastions, designed with emplacements for artillery. Below this area is an extensive undercroft of vaulted, subterranean spaces, endowed with a well-head and sanitary facilities; these were used for protecting and housing the populace during times of siege.

A massive, broken stone **sarcophagus** lies beside the path which returns towards the keep in the east. It is carved with the heraldic fish-scale motif of the Gattilusi family and may be the tomb of Francesco I Gattilusio. The area to the north and east was occupied in antiquity by a 5th-century BC **thesmophorion (7)**, or sanctuary to Demeter and Persephone. Excavations carried out by the Canadian Archaeological Institute in Athens discovered a wealth of votive objects that can now be seen in the Old Archaeological Museum (Room X).

In the southeast corner is the **fortress-keep and residence of the Gattilusi (8)**. The forbidding exterior faces are punctuated with their heraldic arms and interspersed with fragmentary Hellenistic and Roman reliefs of military duels, hunting scenes and gladiatorial matches, intended to broadcast the idea of the raw and martial nature of the power embodied here. The ensemble is built—using a lot of material taken from the ancient theatre—around an open courtyard and is fortified by five towers. It was the roofs and floors of these buildings that must have collapsed in the earthquake of 1384, killing most of Francesco's family.

The ancient theatre

Hidden among pinewoods at the top of the hill of Aghía Kyriakí (2km due west of the castle), in a panoramic position overlooking the city and the coast of Asia Minor, are the scant remains of the city's large theatre (*map p. 504, A1; open daily except Mon, 8.30–3; the climb up to it through residential streets is signposted*). It was probably built in the 3rd century BC and modified in Roman times by the addition of a high retaining wall around the orchestra, so as to enable more dangerous gladiatorial spectacles to take place. Most of the marble cladding of the theatre seats was taken away in the Middle Ages to form the foundations and the keep of the castle (*see above*). It is estimated that the cavea could possibly have held as many as 10,000 spectators.

The south of the city

Less than 250m south of the main ferry port, beside the coastal boulevard (El. Venizélou) between Karapanagióti and Pesmazóglou, are the curious remains of a 1st-century BC stone **piscina**, preserved on a traffic island. The quantity of cooking vessels and drinking cups cleared from it by archaeologists suggests that this may have been a fish-tank in a luxurious private residence; earlier it may have functioned as a water supply for commercial activity in a workshop on this site. Drains, water-channels and sluices to control flow are clearly visible in the structure.

A fine example of a **traditional *pýrgos*** (tower house) can be seen among the late 19th-century buildings to the right of the main coast road as it descends south into Vareiá Bay. These *pýrgi*, which were the second homes of wealthy Greeks or Turks, date from the late 18th and early 19th centuries and are a local variation of a kind of free-standing medieval tower found widely throughout Greece. On Lesbos they commonly have two floors in stone (small, rectangular and often with only one room per floor), with a luminous top floor freely articulated in rooms which extend out in a projecting, wooden-framed lath-and-plaster construction.

VAREIA & ITS ART COLLECTIONS

In the village of Vareiá (*map p. 502, D3*), 800m in from the shore, is a fine old *pýrgos*. From beside it, a turning leads in towards the Theophilos and Tériade museums. The largest collection (86 pictures) of Greece's most endearing and prolific folk artist are displayed in the four rooms of the **Theophilos Museum** (*open daily except Mon, 10–4; in summer 9–2.30 & 5–8*), here in his native village. The works exhibited are mostly the product of his last years; topographical views, battle scenes, tableaux of Greek traditional life, mythological scenes, and (rarer) religious images. This entire collection was donated to the city in 1964 by the art critic and publisher Stratis Eleftheriades. He left his native island in 1915 to study law in Paris, and as he began to be known and to work in that city, he adopted the name Tériade. It is to this remarkable figure that the second museum (at the end of the driveway) is dedicated.

The **Tériade Collection** (*open daily except Mon, 9–4; in summer 9–2 & 5–8*) is a concentrated display of drawings, lithographs, etchings, aquatints and woodcuts—among them many annotated artist's proofs—by Chagall, Rouault, Fernand Léger, Le Corbusier, Villon, Miró, Picasso, Matisse, Bonnard, Giacometti and other masters of the early 20th century. All the works on display were published by Tériade in the quarterly art and literary journal *Verve*, which he founded in Paris in 1937. Although this is primarily a specialist collection, the variety of work and the extraordinary quality and beauty of the production cannot fail to impress.

THE SOUTHEAST PENINSULA

South of Mytilene and Vareiá, a peninsula forms the tranquil southeastern extremity of the island. Two kilometres after passing the entrance to the airport is a solitary example of a wooden **Ottoman-style yali**, with ornate metal eaves and woodwork designs on its seaward front. Many such buildings once lined the eastern shore.

Visible across the water to the east of this point, beside the Turkish coast, are the three **Arginusae islets**, off which the Athenians won a naval victory over the Spartans in 406 bc. The Spartan admiral Callicratidas was killed and 70 of his ships were sunk or captured. The Athenians lost 25 ships and were prevented by the weather from rescuing the crews. For this omission, eight of the Athenian commanders in the battle were recalled to Athens, tried, and six of them executed.

The Gulf of Géra: eastern shore

The picturesque **bay of Ághios Ermogénis** is divided by a rocky promontory on which sits the homonymous church with its wide, canopied forecourt; just to the west is the narrow entrance into the waters of the Gulf of Géra. There are **pleasant beaches** for swimming (at Skála Loutrón) and tavernas (at Koundouroudiá). At the northern extremity of the gulf are the **Thermal Springs of Géra** which, of all the many hot waters of Lesbos, best combine a minimum of functional organisation with historic and atmospheric pools (*open daily 8–6; separate men's and women's sections;*

no bathing suits permitted and towels required; shower facilities provided. The baths are beside the shore at the northernmost point of the gulf, and lie just out of sight below the road. The turn-off, poorly signed for the 'Estiatoria Thermia', is easy to miss; the entrance is just before an abandoned stone building on the south side of the road, at the top of a low rise). The water is plentiful and of a gentle temperature (39–41°C), and pours from worn marble spouts into a large rectangular pool about 1m deep, lined with Proconnesian marble beneath a vaulted roof. The waters contain radium and their therapeutic qualities were known in antiquity, when it is believed that the springs constituted part of a sanctuary of Hera.

THE ROMAN AQUEDUCT & THERMI AREA

Three and a half kilometres to the north of Mytilene, along the east coast, a left turn leads off to the village of Mória (*map p. 502, D2*). On the left (south), as the road turns to the west, are the visible remains of **ancient quarries** in the escarpment above. This was the source of the island's grey limestone; a number of unfinished blocks (monolithic columns) and the evidence of extensive cutting with picks and wedges, dating from the Roman period, can be seen in the rockface. Stone from here was used for the construction of the magnificent **aqueduct** of the 2nd century AD, visible in the gorge to the southeast of Mória (*at the narrowest point at the centre of the village, bear left for the road that skirts the village to the south side; the aqueduct comes into view after 300m*). The aqueduct is 170m long and over 27m high: only three of the arcades still stand almost to their full height. It functioned as part of a closed system in which, after its descent down to the bridge, the water was driven uphill again, by natural pressure in sealed pipes, to a level slightly lower than that from which it started, from where it continued its slowly descending trajectory to Mytilene It covered a total distance of more than 24km, by a circuitous route from springs below the area of Megáli Límni in the foothills of Mt Ólympos, northwest of Aghiásos.

Another section of the aqueduct can be seen near Lámbou Mýli (*map p. 502, C2*). Three and a half kilometres west of the village, an unmarked rough track leads into the forest and descends for 2.6km to the aqueduct, which stands to considerable height in the pine-clad gorge to the left of the track.

The Thermí area
At Pýrgi Thermís (*map p. 502, D2*) you come to the **remains of prehistoric Thermí**, the most important Bronze Age site on the island, which lies a short distance east of the road by the shore (*after entering Pýrgi Thermís, a road signed to the New Lesbos Inn leads northeast to the shore: the excavations are 100m along, to the north of the hotel*). Even to the non-specialist eye it is clear that the foundations delineate dwellings that were spacious for their time. The contiguous houses, disposed in a seemingly well-organised plan, had pebble floors and flat roofs; they were long and narrow, with a main room and closed porch at the front. Artefacts found here show that the successive Bronze Age settlements on this site stretched from c. 2750–1400 BC and belonged predominantly

Remains of the Roman aqueduct (2nd century AD), in the olive groves near Mória.

to the cultural sphere of Troy. The final abandonment of the site may be linked to the destruction of Troy at the end of the Trojan War.

A kilometre north along the main road, a (signed) street to the west leads a short distance to the **Panaghía Troulótis**, one of the oldest functioning churches of the island. It is a handsome 14th-century stone building surmounted by a cylindrical cupola (*troulos*), from which its name derives. From outside it can be seen that the original building was square with an inscribed-cross plan and three apses; to this a narthex of large dimensions was added in the 16th century. In the exterior south wall of the narthex are two curious ancient marble reliefs, one showing a bear and a stag, the other apparently a hunting scene in which a sprawling man clinging to a pole prepares to dispatch a (?) wolf while a companion flees to the side. Given the subject matter, it is possible that these carved scenes came from the nearby sanctuary of the divine huntress, Artemis (*see below*). The once-painted interior has been plastered and redesigned; only damaged vestiges of the original murals survive on the piers and lower areas of the walls.

The Ottoman spring-house of Thermí with its iron-rich water and an Ionic capital from the ancient Sanctuary of Artemis.

A short distance further north, the **hot springs of Thermí and the remains of the Sanctuary of Artemis Thermia** are marked by the imposing buildings of the Sarlitza Palace Hotel, which used to be one of the grand spa hotels of the Aegean but is now in a state of ruinous decay. The interior has mostly been gutted, but the marble steps of the main staircase are still in place, and furniture in some of the bedrooms still poignantly remains. The hot springs which rise behind and a little to the south may later have been enclosed in a Byzantine building, but the curious spring-house which survives is mostly an Ottoman structure of the late 18th century. The low arches of the roof are supported by a central pier, surmounted by a damaged Ionic capital from the pagan sanctuary; the water in which it stands is opaque and ferrous in colour. The saline water, rich in iron, whose properties were praised by Galen, rises at 47°C. The municipal baths (next to the ruined hotel) are open from June–Oct for 15-min immersions in individual cubicles.

Fifty metres along the road inland to Loutrópoli Thermís is a small modern church (right), to the east of which is a collection of ancient pieces and **fragments from the Sanctuary of Artemis**. These include a number of fluted and plain column fragments (one of which has been reused as a mile-post, written in both Latin and Osmanli script), plinths, pedestals and a sarcophagus.

THE CENTRAL SOUTH OF THE ISLAND: PLOMARI & POLICHNITOS

The main southern projection of the island is formed by the forested massif of Mt Ólympos and defined to east and west by the gulfs of Géra and Kallonί, which cut far into the island in spite of their narrow sea entrances. The two gulfs are miniature inland seas: villages and fertile slopes face one another across calm, communal waters, while there is still the all-important access to the open sea. The surprise is that their protected environment was not home to a greater number of settlements in antiquity.

FROM GERA TO PLOMARI

The main junction on the road leading east from Mytilene is with the road to Plomári, which heads south into the rich, olive-producing landscape between the eastern slopes of Ólympos and the Gulf of Géra. The **olive plantations** in this area are amongst the oldest and most productive on the island, and the area is punctuated with a number of old olive mills and processing factories, built on a large scale in the 1930s and now mostly abandoned. The olive trees are too numerous now for the manpower available to harvest them, meaning that only a proportion of the crop is picked and many trees are left fallow.

A kilometre before Dípi (*map p. 502, C2*), the road crosses a small river draining the surrounding reed-beds: immediately south of the bridge as the road touches the shore are the remains of an **ancient harbour**, now mostly submerged.

Mesagrós, Skópelos and Pérama

Palaiόkipos (*map p. 502, D3*) is the first of a group of thriving, almost contiguous villages which spread south along the lower eastern slopes of Ólympos. **Mesagrós** is set 1km to the southeast of the medieval castle of Géra at Palaiόkastro. Beside the village's main north–south street are the ruins of an early 19th-century mosque with two minarets (one still well preserved). In the roofless interior, the ornate plaster decoration of the mihrab is still visible, and inset into the chamfered exterior corners are small white marble plaques inscribed with verses from the Koran. The street continues south to contiguous **Skópelos**, rich in mansions dating from the period of prosperity between 1890 and 1920. Above the *plateía* at its centre is the rebuilt church of Ághios Geórgios (1908), which contains the relics of St Gregory, a 12th-century bishop of Assos. Yet further uphill is the church of Aghía Magdalíni: from inside the chapel immediately to the south of the main church, steps lead down into a small network of catacombs carved by hand out of the soft volcanic tuff, and still an active focus of worship.

Pérama, on the shores of the Gulf of Géra (*map p. 502, D3*), is the modern successor to ancient Hiera, said by Pliny to have been destroyed by earthquake. Today, the harbour is dominated by the empty buildings of several late 19th-century tanneries and factories which produced soap as a by-product of olive oil. There is a small passenger ferry (no vehicles) which crosses to Koundouroudiá.

Ághios Isídoros and Plomári

A branch road off the main road to Plomári leads southeast to **Tárti** (*map p. 502, D3*), one of the island's most attractive and intimate coves, with a pleasant beach and clear waters, bordered by a couple of tavernas. The main road continues down a wooded gorge to the coast at **Ághios Isídoros** (*map p. 502, C3*), where the Varvagianni Ouzo Distillery—one of the island's most famous and respected for the quality of its produce—dominates the shoreline (*guided visits during working hours from June–end Sept*).

Plomári (*map p. 502, C3*), in spite of a drab waterfront relieved only by the dense stand of palm trees in the main square, is nonetheless an interesting town with a rich variety of architecture. It is the largest town on Lesbos after Mytilene, substantially a creation of the Ottoman period, with an economy founded on the trade of olive oil and its by-products, and on the production of ouzo. The wealth generated is displayed in the grand and often idiosyncratic mansions that line the watercourse of the Sedoúnda torrent, which runs through the town centre.

POLICHNITOS & VATERA

The main road to Polichnítos from Mytilene leads through olive groves. After Kerameía, as the road begins to climb, to the right under ancient plane trees, is the attractive—though often crowded—**taverna at Karíni** (*map p. 502, C2*), once a haunt of the painter Theophilos (*see p. 508*): a tree in which he is said to have dwelt can be seen.

Asómatos and Aghiásos

The two beautiful villages of Asómatos and Aghiásos (*map p. 502, C3*) grew rich on olive-oil production and manifested their wealth in simple but substantial stone houses. A reclusive self-sufficiency has historically characterised these two centres, and they still preserve (Aghiásos in particular) their own traditions of song, dialect, music, ceremony and *panigýria*. The feast of the Virgin (15 Aug) in Aghiásos is justly one of the most famous in the Aegean. At To Stavrí, a simple ouzeri-cum-eatery at the northern end of the village (whose walls are a treasure-house of objects, graffiti and pictures), local music and song can sometimes begin late and last well into the night.

Mount Ólympos

The road which leaves to the south from the upper extremity of the village of Aghiásos crosses the eastern side of Mt Ólympos towards the south coast. The variety of habitats on this one mountain massif make it rich in wild flowers and animals: it is the only home in Europe of the Persian squirrel and of Krüper's nuthatch (*Sitta krueperi*), often seen moving restlessly in the tops of the pine trees and emitting its distinctive calls.

The road ceases to be paved 3km beyond the abandoned sanatorium (3km above Aghiásos). Thereafter the steep descent is panoramic—but slow—as far as Megalo-chóri, from where a surfaced road leads down the Sedoúnda Gorge to Plomári.

Polichnítos

Polichnítos (*map p. 502, B3*) is a large settlement, spread across a valley between two steep rises. In the flat and marshy area 1.5km to the southeast rise several mineral springs which, at between 81°C and 92°C, are among the hottest in Europe. In the 2nd century AD, Galen observed that the locals used them for cooking food. The steam and the strong colours of the yellow, red and magenta mineral deposits beside the springs lend a fantastic touch to a forlorn landscape of tussocks and ruined bath houses. The New Baths are pleasant and well run (*open March–Dec, 8–1 & 4–7*).

Three kilometres northeast of Polichnítos are the **springs of Ághios Ioánnis** (also known as Lisvório Spa, after the nearby village of Lisvório). Notably hot (c. 70°C), ferrous and slightly sulphurous, the waters rise just to the right of the bridge and flow down to a small 19th-century bath house below, where they can be enjoyed at a more clement temperature in a couple of simple pools.

Vrísa and Vaterá

South of Polichnítos is the attractive village of **Vrísa** (*map p. 502, B3*). On the main square is a small Natural History collection, housed in a former school building, comprising an interesting display of fossilised plants, fish and early vertebrates, both from Lesbos and from elsewhere (*open winter Fri–Mon 8.30–1; summer daily 9.30–3 & 4–7*). The discovery of a large number of petrified mammal and reptile remains of gigantic dimensions in the low-lying area between Vrísa and Vaterá gave rise to the creation of this museum by the University of Athens.

The road reaches the coast at **Vaterá** (*map p. 502, B3*), whose long, sandy, south-facing strand curves towards a promontory to the west, marked by the modern church of Ághios Phokás. Beside the church are the remains of the **Temple of Dionysus Bresagenes**, orientated perfectly towards the east and crosswise to the promontory. The remaining elements reveal it to have been of an interesting design, namely monostyle in antis: the two massive marble antae and the one fluted column of its porch have been re-erected. In antiquity the temple and its headland, which would have been visible from afar, constituted the principal landmark between the entrances to the two gulfs. The waters south of here are home to the common and bottlenose dolphin, sometimes to be seen from this headland.

Ancient Pyrrha

East of Skála Polichnítou, the edge of the gulf is largely flat with salt marshes, until the knolls and headlands around Pyrrha begin to rise beside the water. The shoreline has altered with time, and the steep acropolis hill of ancient Pyrrha (*map p. 502, C2*) would probably once have been attached by only a narrow isthmus. Little remains to be seen of the acropolis of the city; there are scanty stretches of **ancient walling** at the crown of the hill, and at the highest point (or southeastern extremity), there is a small, **rock-cut crepidoma**. There appears to have been a prehistoric settlement, although the earliest burials yet found are Protogeometric. In 428 BC the city's fortifications were reinforced by Mytilene; it was a member of the Second Athenian League and was later wrested from Persian rule by Alexander the Great. Pliny mentions that the original city was 'drowned by the sea', probably destroyed by an earthquake c. 230 BC. It must have been rebuilt on the new site soon after, because it was again an active and flourishing centre in Roman and Early Christian times.

The Sanctuary of Mesa

The ancient, Pan-Lesbian Sanctuary of Mesa lies 400m north of the main Mytilene–Kallóni road (*map p. 502, C2; open daily except Mon, 8.30–3*). The name Mesa is from the ancient Greek *mesos* ('middle', 'mid-way', or 'neutral'): the sanctuary uncovered here was, by position and intention, centrally placed between the main cities of the Lesbos Commonwealth (Mytilene, Methymna, Eresos and Antissa) and it lay just outside the territory of Pyrrha. It is referred to in inscriptions relating to common decisions taken by the cities and, so as not to favour any one city over the others, the temple here—long considered to be a sanctuary of Aphrodite—appears to have been dedicated not to one divinity, but to the triad of Zeus, Hera and Dionysus. It was a place for common festivities, games and cult for all the cities of the island; for the discussion of matters which related to them all; and for arbitration in disputes.

Only the **temple** and its immediate area have so far been systematically excavated. The remains visible today date from the late 4th century BC, although the sanctuary and cult existed already as far back as the 7th century BC, in the time of Sappho and Alcaeus. The Ionic temple was large and unusually broad, with eight columns in front and 14 along the sides, and a considerable distance separating the peristyle and the naos. Clustered around the western end of the crepidoma are the remains of four improvised circular **lime kilns**, in which the temple's stones were burnt to make mortar in the late 4th century AD, at the time when the **Early Christian basilica** (whose apse can be seen to the east) was built on its remains. This in turn was destroyed and replaced much later by the humbler, medieval **chapel of the Taxiárches**, whose ruined, irregular walls now occupy the centre of the temple platform. The unattractive blanket of protective plaster which has been poured over the complex, together with the wooden walkways which keep the visitor rigorously corralled, are the result of the most recent interventions of the Ephorate of Antiquities.

METHYMNA & THE NORTH

The town once commonly known as Mólyvos (a Hellenisation of its Turkish name,

Molova) is today officially referred to by its ancient name, Methymna (*pron: Míthimna; map p. 502, B1*). That, in turn, is a word of pre-Greek, probably Anatolian, origin. Methymna clings to a rocky headland; the façades of its colourful houses fall in tiers down its south-facing slope below an all-dominating castle. Its character is infused with Ottoman remains: marble fountains at street corners and the jostling angles of projecting wooden Ottoman balconies, protected by wide horizontal eaves.

HISTORY OF METHYMNA

In antiquity Methymna was the second city of Lesbos, birthplace of the late 7th-century BC poet Arion and widely renowned for its sweet wine. Its history is dominated by rivalry with Mytilene, most significantly when it did not back the Mytilenean revolt against Athens in 428 BC. In Roman times the pre-eminence of Mytilene was confirmed, leaving Methymna with secondary status. The town became an important centre under Genoese dominion, and served as the principal Gattilusi stronghold on more than one occasion when other parts of the island were attacked. As Molova, the town maintained its importance during Ottoman times, and over a third of its population was Muslim as late as 1923.

Exploring Methymna

In the town itself, little remains to be seen of ancient Methymna, apart for a large open site revealing an **ancient cemetery** at the southern extremity of town. The main stone-cobbled thoroughfare of the old town begins just beyond these excavations and climbs steadily from southeast to northwest. Halfway up the ascent, the street reaches a junction: the street to the left leads down to the port passing the restored stone-and-timber **Ottoman mansion** now occupied by the Dimarcheíon. The nearby **Kralli Mansion** is a fine example of an Ottoman residence, with well-preserved early 19th-century wall- and ceiling paintings in the interior. It now houses a centre of the Athens School of Fine Arts (*open 9–5*).

From the top of the street it is a steep climb back towards the east, to the entrance of the **Gattilusi Castle** (*open daily except Mon, 8.30–3*). In general, the castle is well preserved and finely constructed. When seen from the west, it is clear that the walls incorporate large areas of ancient masonry, principally from Hellenistic fortifications on the same site. The interior is large and accommodates several late medieval buildings of secular function as well as an area which is currently being excavated.

ENVIRONS OF METHYMNA

A short way east of Methymna are the **hot springs of Efthaloú** (*map p. 502, B1*). The water here is clear and slightly saline, rising at 46.5°C. It has the highest radium concentration of any of the island's springs, which contributes to its important therapeutic qualities. Beyond the small modern spa is the irregular, white hump-back roof of the Ottoman bath-chamber; inside it a rock-cut pool fills constantly with the spring water and is generally accessible at all times.

Petra

Six kilometres south of Methymna, the unexpected **volcanic monolith** of Petra (*map p. 502, B1*) rises 46m almost vertically into the air behind the bland shoreline of the bay, giving the impression of a grounded meteorite. It is in fact a 'volcanic neck', a cylindrically-shaped rock formation that remains when magma solidifies in the vent of a volcano and is subsequently left exposed by the erosion of surrounding material. The present church on the rock, the Panahgía Glykophiloúsa, dates from the mid-19th century, but the cult significance of the summit is considerably more ancient. Access to the church is by over a hundred rock-cut steps on the north side. The tight complex occupies all of the limited space on top of the rock. At the foot of the rock to the north is the unadorned stone church of **Ághios Nikólaos**, a single-aisled 16th-century basilica of great simplicity, memorably decorated with a cycle of late Byzantine paintings of different periods. In the heart of the old quarter of Petra, southwest of the rock, a fine example of a 19th-century Ottoman merchant's mansion, the **Archontikó Vareltzídaina**, has survived and is now restored and open to the public (*open daily except Mon, 8–3; until 7 in May–Sept*).

AROUND KALLONI

Kalloní is contiguous, to the east, with modern **Arísvi** (*map p. 502, B2*). The remains of ancient Arisbe, from which it takes its name, lie around a knob-like hill to the north, reached by taking the track along the west bank of the Tsikniás river (directly before the bridge). The remains visible today are of the walls of the Genoese castle, which encircled the flat summit with regular bastions. Although there is much rubble and an immense quantity of sherds, none of it gives any clear evidence of an ancient presence.

East of Arísvi, a branch road to **Aghía Paraskeví** (*map p. 502, C2*) passes a small wildlife sanctuary. The village itself is one of the busiest agricultural centres on the island; its handsome streets of stone houses are home to a daily open-air market. The many stone mansions and the particularly impressive Neoclassical school building are witness to the prosperity and civic pride of the town in the 1920s. On the street corner opposite the Dimarcheíon and just south of the school is the decommissioned Ottoman hamam. The town is famous for its celebrations of the feast of Ághios Charálambos, involving the ritual slaughter of a young bull, communal feasting, parades and horse-racing—practices whose origins go back to antiquity.

The basilica of Chalinádos

The most evocative excursion to be made from Aghía Paraskeví is to the remains of the Early Christian basilica of Chalinádos (*map p. 502, C2*), in a landscape of rocky bluffs and olive groves 5.5km to the east of the town (*follow north through Aghía Paraskeví as if for Nápi, past the school to the right and the post office to the left; bear right uphill at the central junction and follow this street without turning off until it becomes unsurfaced. Further on it passes by a military camp. Shortly before the basilica, the road dips through a ravine. The remains are on the right, shaded by a number of venerable pines).* The building has the apsed, three-aisle plan typical of a 6th-century church; the threshold and posts of the stone templon are still visible. The church must once have served a now-vanished local community in the area; today it is carpeted with asphodel.

The Sanctuary of Klopedí

Less than a kilometre north of Aghía Paraskeví on the road to Nápi, a conspicuous track branches off to the northwest. On the right after 3km is the beautifully preserved **medieval bridge at Kremastí** (*map p. 502, C1*), which stands at the crossing-point of the Tsikniá river on the ancient road from Mytilene to Methymna, via the Sanctuary at Mesa. The ancient blocks incorporated in its lower parts are not necessarily an indication that there was a bridge here in antiquity; they will probably have been brought from the sanctuary at Klopedí, and re-used here so as to avoid quarrying and cutting new stone. The compactly paved carriageway has no balustrade, in order to permit the easier passage of hayricks and vehicles whose loads protruded beyond their axles.

From the bridge the road continues northwest into a valley, and branches left, back along the opposite side at a higher level through dense pines to the **monastery of the Taxiárchis**, a late 18th-century foundation, now home to a single hermit. A kilometre beyond (to the left), in a deeply rural setting, is the **Sanctuary of Ancient Klopedí**. The bases of two late 6th-century BC temples dedicated to Apollo Napaios and ?Artemis can be seen aligned parallel to one another on a southeast–northwest orientation: the upper temple has been cleared, revealing the careful cutting of the ancient blocks of its stylobate; the lower temple is still partially covered by the hillside. The boldly carved early Aeolic capitals now in Mytilene (*see p. 505*) come from here; several more examples are visible under an improvised roof at the lowest point of the site. More finds are in the museum in Nápi (*see overleaf*).

The Panaghía Myrsiniótissa and Moní Leimónos

The **convent of the Panaghía Myrsiniótissa** (*map p. 502, B1*) is the first of two closely related and important monasteries which were re-founded by St Ignatios Agallianos, a 16th-century archbishop of Methymna. To its west, accessible either by track from Myrsiniótissa (2.5km) or by the road from Kalloní to Phília, lies the second monastery, dedicated to the Archangel Michael but commonly known as the **Moní Leimónos**. It was established in 1526 with the intention of constituting the principal centre of learning on the island. Leimónos is endowed with one of the most important religious libraries and manuscript collections in the Aegean after Patmos; there is also a large collection of late Byzantine icons. The museum (*open daily 8–6*) is laid out in three rooms along the west side of the monastery complex. Ignatios laid down in his original Order that men should be forbidden to enter the Myrsiniótissa, and women the Leimónos: the first prohibition has been relaxed, and the second remains by tradition but is applied only to the katholikon.

Above Leimónos the road climbs steeply, passing the hill of Tyrannída to the right, crowned by a memorial to the last military stand of the Turkish presence on Lesbos in 1912, before descending into the plain of **Phília** (*map p. 502, B1*), an isolated village of attractively-built houses. Both Phília and its neighbouring village of **Skalochóri** (*map p. 502, B1*) have decommissioned mosques with surviving minarets.

Nápi and Mandamádos

The archaeological collection (*open in summer, daily except Mon, 9–3.30*) in the school building of **Nápi** (*map p. 502, C1*) contains finds and information about the site of Klopedí (*see p. 519 above*). About 10km northeast of Nápi is **Mandamádos** (*map p. 502, C1*). The festival of Ághios Charálambos (10th Feb) is celebrated here with the ancient pre-Christian ritual of the slaughter of young bulls, which are then prepared for a communal feast. The village is also a place of pilgrimage, centred on the large monastery of the Archangel Michael (Taxiárchis) 1km to its north, which has grown up near a sacred spring (50m east of the main buildings). To the right of the iconostasis in the katholikon is the miraculous 'black icon' of the Archangel, allegedly sculpted in high relief from a dark, aromatic wood, though it appears more to have been moulded in plastered masonry. It is believed to possess healing powers and is a focus of devotion at all times, not just at the saint's feast. The monastery is probably a foundation of Byzantine origin, but its buildings today date predominantly from the 19th century.

ERESOS & THE WEST

The volcanic origins of Lesbos are much more evident in the rugged western portion of the island. The village of **Ágra** (*map p. 502, B2*) is dramatically set in a spacious amphitheatre of mountains, hidden from the sea and sheltered from the wind. From here to the west's main centre of Eresós, settlements and farmsteads are infrequent, and the dusty volcanic soil supports little beyond bees and grazing flocks. The south-facing shore at this point is a sequence of wide, generally shadeless shingle bays backed by low hills. At **Apothíka**, 400m north of the tiny harbour, beside a creek, are the remains of the buildings and conical, stone-lined pits of an alum processing workshop of late antiquity. Alum (a complex sulphate of potassium and aluminium) is not commonly found in nature, but it is a fundamental element in the fixing of dyes in textiles. The large markets of late Roman and medieval Europe obtained alum principally from Phocaea in the Gulf of Smyrna and from Lesbos.

Eresós

Ancient Eresos, birthplace of the philosopher and botanist Theophrastus and (by general consensus) of Sappho, stood by the sea, at the eastern end of the shore. The inland Eresós of today (*map p. 502, A2*), on a steep hill at the northern extremity of the cultivated plain, was founded in the early Middle Ages when it was necessary to move inland as a refuge against pirates. The **inland town** is large, and its four-square stone houses, with low tiled roofs typical of the Levant coast, spread widely onto the plateau to the north of the centre.

On the coast, little remains of the **ancient settlement**, though a number of ancient blocks, some with inscriptions, have been incorporated into the structure of the most impressive remains in the area, namely the Early Christian **basilica of St Andrew of Crete**, which lies on the opposite (west) side of Vígla hill, possibly on the site of a pagan sanctuary of Dionysus and Apollo. The mid-5th century church's extensive mosaic floor survives both in the nave and the narthex; it carries a clear dedicatory inscription and a field of complex and varying abstract designs interspersed with panels of peacocks (symbols of immortality), all achieved with four main colours of stone. Sarcophagi, mostly of the Christian period, can be seen close to the church perimeter; others have been moved to the area in front of the school building to the side; a number of the houses also have ancient fragments in their gardens. Excavations are currently underway in a vacant lot 50m from the east end of the basilica. Another, slightly later (6th-century) basilica lies at the opposite (western) end of the shore, known generally as the **Aphendelli Basilica**, from the name of the owner on whose land the finds were made (*follow the track which passes the Aeolian Village Hotel to its end*). A beautiful area of mosaic, once again featuring peacocks, is preserved in front of the central apse.

Sappho (7th century BC)

Sappho, often called the Tenth Muse in antiquity, was a lyric poet active in the complex and often violent politics of Lesbos at the end of the 7th century BC. Her range of subject-matter was wide, but she returned again and again to the passions of the heart, which she evokes with a limpid and brilliant use of language, which has never lost its appeal and immediacy, even in translation. We have many fragments, but only one complete example of her work.

We encounter Sappho in her poems as a lover, sister, teacher, and mother of a young daughter (Cleis). Although she has become a symbol of female homoerotic sentiment, we will never know much for certain about her sexuality. She lived in an age when social mores were vastly different: women predominantly kept company with women, and men with men. Sappho's poems return repeatedly to the themes of love between women and girls; but it is the candour and beauty of their language that renders them universal and timeless.

> *Although they are*
>
> *Only breath, words*
> *which I command*
> *are immortal*
> (Tr: Mary Barnard)

The Ypsilós Monastery and the Petrified Forest

The 10km of road north from Eresós are scenic and dramatic, culminating in the sudden appearance of the monastery of Ághios Ioánnis Theológos, generally called **Ypsilós** ('lofty') because it is perched on a peak that rises into view over the top of an upland plateau. The views from the monastery are magnificent. Although the forbidding buildings date from the 19th century, the foundation goes back to the 12th century, and there is evidence of a still earlier presence. Immured into the entrance-porch, and lying inside the courtyard, are Early Christian and ancient spolia: small architectural members, capitals of all orders, a fluted pagan altar, fragments of templon, frieze and architrave; there are more spolia in the monastery's small museum, which is dedicated principally to late Byzantine icons and liturgical objects.

The Ypsilós monastery looks out over a wide, treeless succession of glens and peaks. Twenty million years ago these now bare slopes were densely forested with a variety of subtropical sequoia and cypress. At some point they were buried in volcanic ash from an eruption, and their remains can be seen in the **Petrified Forest** (*map p. 502, A2; reached by a branch road to the south from a junction 4.5km west of Ypsilós. Open in winter daily 8.30–4.30; 15 May–15 Oct 8–8*). The name, together with the assiduous signing from all points of the island, perhaps creates expectations beyond what the site delivers; but the area's scientific importance is considerable because of what it has contributed to our knowledge of the palaeoflora and climatic conditions in the Aegean 20–30 million years ago. There are similar trees in many parts of Europe, but they have only rarely been so perfectly petrified, leaving fruits, leaves, branches and fibre clearly preserved and readable, often in beautiful agate colours with fantastic glassy striations. The museum park occupies only the area of greatest interest, but the phenomenon occurs all over the surrounding valley, and petrified trunks can be seen at many points in the terrain crossed by the unmade track west from Eresós to Sígri, at Sígri itself, and in the area further to the north.

Sígri

The small port of Sígri (*map p. 502, A2*) was mostly an Ottoman creation and preserves several remains from the period of Turkish rule: an inscribed marble fountain-front in the centre of the village, the ruins of an **Ottoman hamam**, and the church of **Aghía Triáda** above the harbour, whose wide, four-square form and orientation show it clearly to be a converted mosque. The once open-arched porch on the west side was probably filled in when the building was turned into a church. The town's finest monument is its sombre, pentagonal **castle** guarding the harbour, with an imposing Osmanli inscription and the imperial tugra of Mustafa III carved on a well-preserved marble plaque over the gateway. The building dates from 1757, a time when the Ottoman administration favoured the development of this remote port as a trading entrepôt on the open-sea route from the southern Aegean to the Dardanelles and the capital.

Just south of the centre of Sígri is a **Natural History museum** (*open as Petrified Forest; see above*) where fossil finds are set in the wider context of the Mediterranean's palaeontological history.

Ántissa

Modern **Ántissa** (*map p. 502, A2*) has a story similar to Eresós: its ancient predecessor occupied a strategic position and harbour on the coast, 8km below to the north, but piracy forced its abandonment in the 7th century and the population moved to the new site in the relative protection of the hills. Ancient Antissa, known as **Ovriókastro** (*map p. 502, B2; more easily reached from the road to the northwest below Skalochóri*), commands a wide stretch of the north coast as far as the eastern extremity at Methymna. Today there is a chain of long, sweeping **sandy beaches** (Lápsarna, Gavathás, Kámbos) along this coast, backed by small communities with pleasant tavernas, and areas of cultivation behind; the headland of Ancient Antissa also projects between two wide beaches, which some traditions hold to be the shore on which the head and the lyre of Orpheus were washed up. According to Lucian, a cave dedicated to Dionysus in the hills to the west of the road from Ántissa to Gavathás was where the head subsequently pronounced accurate oracles, until it was silenced by Apollo. The remains most visible at Ovriókastro today are of the ruined Genoese castle of the Gattilusi, whose walls gird the whole of the promontory and, in part, incorporate the ancient acropolis fortifications, especially on the west side.

Moní Perivolís

Hidden from sight in a bend of the stream, 4km east of Ántissa, is a monastery dedicated to the Presentation of the Virgin. It is known as the **Moní Perivolís**, and has an intimate, walled garden shaded with planes, fruit and nut trees, surrounded by monastic lodgings and full of the sound of nightingales in spring (*map p. 502, A2; open in the morning, with no specific hours, from June–end Sept; at other times entry has to be arranged with the papás in Vatoúsa, 5km east*). Though there has been some restoration in the last 50 years, the monastery's appearance and layout is still that of its founding in 1590. The wall-paintings in the katholikon are in urgent need of cleaning, but even so they are amongst the most interesting on the island. There are two separate campaigns by different artists of the early 17th century. One of these, working in the high Byzantine tradition, executed the hagiographic images of the naos (best preserved are the faces of St Panteleimon and other saints along the south wall). The other, who was working in a more folkloric tradition, produced the striking narrative scenes of the narthex.

Two kilometres east of the Perivolís, the main road passes beside the **Voúlgaris Gorge**, a deep rocky fissure formed by a fault or crack in the rim of the large volcanic crater. The crater, averaging 6km in diameter, formed the ring of eroded and fertile hills around the village of Vatoúsa, which lies at its centre.

South of Vatoúsa are the isolated villages of Révma, Pteroúnda and **Chídira** (*map p. 502, B2*). This last produces the promising wines of the Methymneos Winery, whose particular qualities derive from the composition of the area's volcanic soil.

PRACTICAL INFORMATION

GETTING AROUND

Flights from Athens serve Mytilene throughout the year. There are also flights from/to Thessaloníki. The airport is 5km from the centre of Mytilene.

The principal ferry route from Piraeus to Mytilene is served by Hellenic Seaways, via Chios, with a daily 12.30 departure from Piraeus, arriving at Mytilene 9pm, and returning to Piraeus again overnight. GA Ferries run three times weekly along the route from/to Chios and Samos, and Lemnos and Kavála. There is a weekly Saos Ferries service from the port of Sígri (northwest Lesbos) on the route between Kavála, Lemnos, Ághios Efstrátios, and Psará and Lávrion (for Athens).

WHERE TO STAY

In Mytilene, the **Hotel Pyrgos** (*El. Venizélou 49; T: 22510 27977, www.pyrgoshotel.gr; map p. 504, B3*) is the city's smartest hotel (with prices to match): comfortable, providing a good breakfast, and open all year round. The roadside rooms can be noisy. The same company also manages the **Archontiko Mytilinis**, in an elegant 1920s house (*Vostáni 3, south of the Stadium; T: 22510 46681/2; www.archontikomytilinis.gr*). An inexpensive alternative is the **Hotel Orpheas** (*T: 22510 28523*), in a converted mansion midway between the two archaeological museums.

Methymna has a wider choice: on the shore below the town is the **Olive Press Hotel**, in a converted olive mill (*T: 22530 71205*). In the centre is the delightful **Nassos Guesthouse** (*T: 22530 71432, www.nassosguesthouse.com*).

In Plomári there is the **Hotel Leda** (*T: 22520 32507; open May–Sept*) in a fine *archontikó* in the centre of town, up a flight of steps

from the main square. The only accommodation in one of the thermal spring spas are the rooms at **Thermés Polichnítou** (*T: 22520 41201*).

WHERE TO EAT

The port area of Mytilene has many small (mostly new) tavernas serving interesting Levantine-Aegean dishes and good local bread. Two which are particularly good are: **Matzourana** ■ (*Komnináki 30; map p. 504, B2*), and **Machalas** ■ (*Mitrélia 27; map p. 504, B2*). A more folkloric setting and some good local dishes are provided by **Zoubouli** (*corner of Sarandapórou and Vernardáki; map p. 504, B2*). For traditional vegetable and fish *mezédes*, nothing can beat the **Taverna Rebetis** on the waterfront, overlooking the north harbour.

North of Mytilene, shortly after Pýrgi Thermís, is the **Taverna Aghios Georgios**, good for fresh fish and popular with locals on Sun. At picturesque Skála Sykamniás on the north coast (*map p. 502, C1*), 1km to the west along the track by the shore, is **To Kyma**, with good fish dishes. **Taverna Vapheios**, in the village of that name 6km to the east of Methymna, has good local specialities and sunset views to match. In the heart of Methymna, the tiny and basic **Ovelistirio Methymna** ■ (*past the Dimarcheíon*) servest excellent meat and delicious salads, all at very modest prices. Space is limited, especially in winter.

FURTHER READING

Richard Brooks's *Birding on the Greek Island of Lesvos* is an invaluable guide to the island's rich birdlife. The poetry of Sappho is beautifully translated by Mary Barnard.

LEMNOS

Lemnos (*pron: Límnos*) is an island of contrasts. The west is rugged and mountain-ous, Aegean in character, while in the east you find rolling eastern plains evoking Anatolia. Lemnos was sacred to Hephaistos, god of fire and the forge, appropriate for an island that is volcanic in nature and which was a centre of metalworking from pre-historic times. Its early importance gave rise to one of Europe's oldest organised cities, at Polióchni. Its attractive local architecture, its rich flora and wildlife, fragrant wine and geothermic springs, make the island a memorable place to visit.

HISTORY OF LEMNOS

Homer mentions that the people of Lemnos were the ('wild-voiced') Sintians; Herodo-tus and Thucydides say that they were Pelasgians or Tyrrhenians, indicating perhaps different stages of pre-Greek history. Whatever their identity, they were not of Greek stock in earliest times, having come from Thrace or Anatolia: the earliest Greek in-scription from the island is dated to c. 500 BC. Diodorus Siculus claims that the island capital was founded by and named after Myrina, the queen of the warlike Amazons from North Africa.

Archaeology has shown that Lemnos had an advanced Neolithic civilisation and a Bronze Age culture of Minoan-Mycenaean type, which continued without a sharp break into the Geometric period. The island fell to Persia in 513 BC and changed hands more than once before the end of the Persian Wars. During the wars the Lemnians carried off Athenian women from the Sanctuary of Artemis at Brauron in Attica and took them back as concubines. The resulting children soon began to look down on their local half-brothers, whereupon the Lemnians slaughtered both the children and their Athenian mothers. Crops failed thereafter. When the islanders consulted the Del-phic Oracle, they were told to submit to the Athenian yoke. From 477 BC the island formed part of the Delian League. It later had a cleruchy imposed by Athens, fought for Athens in a number of battles and, apart from brief periods of domination by Sparta, the Macedonians and Antiochus the Great, remained under Athenian influence; even after becoming part of the Roman Empire, the immediate governance may have been Athenian, until independence was granted by Septimius Severus. Both Theophrastus in the 4th century BC and Galen in the 2nd century AD visited and were interested in the island's renowned 'Lemnian Earth' (*see p. 530*).

The island was plundered by the Heruls in the late 3rd century AD, and later passed under Byzantine rule. In 325 a bishop of Lemnos was present at the First Council of Nicaea, and the island was raised to a metropolitan see under Leo VI (886–912). In 924 the Saracen fleet under Leo of Tripoli was defeated by a Byzantine naval force in the waters off Lemnos. In 1136 the Venetians officially obtained their first foothold on the island at Kótsinas, and from 1207 Lemnos became the fief of the Venetian Navi-

LEMNOS

gajoso family. In the 13th–15th centuries the island was disputed between Venetians, Genoese and Byzantines, the brief Genoese rule from 1453–55 being so harsh that the inhabitants begged Sultan Mehmet II to rule them instead. A papal force landed the following year as part of a crusade to repossess Constantinople. A new religious order of knights was founded on the island by Pius II; but following disputes with the Venetians, Lemnos finally fell, in 1479, to the Ottoman sultanate, which later used it as a place of exile for disgraced notables. Count Orlov's Russian force occupied the island in the war of 1770 but was driven out by the Ottoman naval commander, Hassan Bey. For a few months in 1829 Lemnos became part of free Greece, before being given back to Turkey in exchange for Euboea. In 1912 the island was liberated by the Greek admiral, Koundouriotis. The Gulf of Moúdros was the base in 1914 for the disastrous Dardanelles expedition. Under the terms of the treaties of Sèvres (1920) and of Lausanne (1923), Lemnos became an internationally recognised part of the Greek state.

LEMNIAN LEGENDS

Lemnos produced a kind of sacred, medicinal clay of volcanic origin, known throughout history as Lemnian Earth (*see p. 530*) and widely used for the curing of snakebites. Many legends are associated with the island, some of them perhaps inspired by the sulphurous odours of its soil.

As a centre of metalworking, Lemnos' patron god was Hephaistos, god of the forge and husband of Aphrodite. When the Lemnian women neglected to worship Aphrodite, the goddess punished them by making them exude a lingering stench, which caused their men to take concubines from the Thracian mainland. In revenge the women murdered all the men except Thoas, their king, who was the son of Dionysus and Ariadne. Thoas escaped through the compassion of his daughter, Hypsipyle. Soon after, when Jason and the Argonauts put in at Lemnos, the women received the men with hospitality, sleeping with them so as to ensure continuity of their tribe. Hypsipyle bore Jason twin sons.

Philoctetes, among the company of Greeks who sailed to Troy, was bitten by a snake during a stop on the journey. The ensuing wound became gangrenous and began to smell so badly that, on the orders of Agamemnon, he was abandoned on Lemnos or nearby Chryse (*see p. 533*). Eventually cured, he rejoined the Greeks at Troy and killed Paris.

MYRINA & THE EAST OF THE ISLAND

Mýrina (*map p. 526, A2*) is situated between two splendid bays, hidden behind a massive rock peninsula, crowned by the impressive curtain walls of its castle. The town is small and lively, its architecture a mixture of Ottoman and Neoclassical.

The old town and castle

In the old quarter, by the inner harbour, Odós Kýda contains two vestiges from the Ottoman past: at the end of an alleyway north of the Hotel Aktaion is an abandoned octagonal 18th-century **türbe**, and at the corner of the first block, a **fountain** still bearing its Osmanli inscription of 1771.

Far above the harbour is the **castle** (*unrestricted access*), occupying a natural fortress of rock to the west. Massive irregular stone blocks of the Archaic acropolis walls (6th century BC) are visible high up to the left amongst the volcanic folds and protrusions; they appear again at the top of the north face underneath Venetian walls. Although the inner fortress on the summit was probably erected over Byzantine foundations by the Venetians in the early 13th century, the majority of the visible fortifications were built by the Genoese and Venetians in the 15th century, later modified and added to by the Turks (especially in the north and east). In 1273 the forces of the Byzantine emperor Michael VIII Palaeologus took three years to capture the castle from the Venetian Navigajoso overlords. Today, wild deer graze in the interior.

Entrance to the fortress is through a defile of three successive gates with monolithic door-posts. Inside the gates are two Ottoman structures: an administrative building and barracks and, slightly above it, the mosque.

To the south, the castle avails itself of a deep, natural ditch for protection, while on the gentler north slope there are three (in places, four) curtain walls, the lowest (Ottoman) almost by the shore. At the highest point is the inner keep, including some ancient spolia, perhaps from a sanctuary of Athena. On the lower western face of the hill is a complex of storage buildings of Venetian origin, including a roofed cistern and large vaulted magazines. At the shore below, a natural cleft in the rocks has created a small, hidden 'harbour' with space for one boat: the sides of the rockface show roughly-cut loop-holes for mooring-ropes.

The Archaeological Museum

This interesting and unusual collection (*open daily except Mon, 8.30–3*) is displayed over two floors of a small Neoclassical mansion, formerly the Ottoman governor's offices, in the middle of the north shore of Mýrina.

The lower floor has **material from prehistoric Polióchni and Mýrina**, with surprisingly beautiful early pottery from the 4th millennium BC, including so-called 'fruit stands', a design that has remained in use for millennia. Some fine gold artefacts from Polióchni are also on display. At the rear is a collection of inscriptions and some sculpture, including a fine headless statue of Eros, a good Roman copy of a 4th-century BC bronze original by Lysippus.

The upper floor contains smaller items from the 8th century BC to Roman times, including pottery and metalwork. In the right-hand corner room is a magnificent collection of **terracotta figures of sirens** (7th and 6th centuries BC) from the Sanctuary of the Great Goddess at Hephaisteia, and a **figurine of Cybele** with a drum in her left hand and a lion cub in her lap. The central room exhibits the **burial of a sacrificial bullock** from the Sanctuary of Artemis Tauropolos at Avlónas.

Ancient Mýrina

Across the coast road from the museum is a marble **monument to the Russian naval commanders** Count Alexei Orlov and Dmitry Seniavin, whose squadrons called at Lemnos during the Russo-Turkish wars of 1770 and 1807, supporting the Greek struggle for independence. Two hundred metres further north along the shore is a large area of recent excavations, the site of **Prehistoric Mýrina**.

Polióchni in the east and Mýrina in the west were the two principal settlements on Bronze Age Lemnos. Both are exceptionally early, large-scale and proto-urban. Compared with Polióchni, Mýrina has yielded less from the 4th and early 3rd millennia BC, but flourished in the late 3rd millennium, with sophisticated architecture. The excavated area contains stone foundations of a closely-packed conurbation of houses, organised into neighbourhoods. Only a small part of the settlement has been excavated. The houses appear to have been repeatedly destroyed by earthquakes and rebuilt.

THE WEST OF THE ISLAND

The southwest corner of Lemnos is a treeless landscape of volcanic boulders, dominated by Mt Kákavos, 4km east of Mýrina. Inside a wide cave just below the summit is the whitewashed **chapel of the Panaghía Kakaviótissa**, the object of an important *panigýri* on the Tuesday after Easter. A monastic community founded in the early 14th century was preceded by earlier Christian presence. Many artificial cavities and niches and a rock-cut terrace on the summit suggest ancient cult activity (*the cave is reached either in 1½ hrs on foot from Mýrina, or by a driveable track due east from the Platý–Kornós road 1.1km north of the main road junction north of Platý. A steep path makes the final approach*).

East of Mýrina

In spite of much modern construction, the old centres of Platý and Thános preserve traditional architecture. An especially beautiful village is **Kontiás** (*map p. 526, B3*). At its centre is the 19th-century church of Ághios Dimítrios; at its south end several abandoned windmills. Further on is **Diapóri**, on the isthmus of the Phakós peninsula, a wildlife preserve where peregrine falcon and Eleanora's falcon can be seen.

At **Portianó** (*map p. 526, B2*), northwest of the centre (along 'Anzac Street'), behind a local cemetery, is the Commonwealth War Cemetery for a small portion of the British and Anzac soldiers who died on the ill-fated Gallipoli expedition in April and May of 1915.

At **Livadochóri** (*map p. 526, B2*) is the remarkable church of the Panaghía in Mitrópolis (*not signed; take the road northeast from the traffic light after the school, along the east side of an army camp. The track drops down to a farm in a hollow after the asphalt finishes; the church is in the farmyard*). The modern chapel sits on a mass of spolia from an Early Christian basilica and perhaps an earlier temple. Two enormous, ornate ancient sarcophagi make water-troughs for animals. The chapel floor incorporates Early Byzantine marble fragments. In the centre of the apse is a simple, stone episcopal throne.

At **Thérma Ifaístou** (*map p. 526, B2*), northeast of Mýrina off the airport road, are the island's principal geothermal springs (*open 11–10*).

LEMNIAN EARTH

Lemnia sphragis, also referred to as *Terra miraculosa* and *Terra sigillata*, was a medicinal soil used in antiquity to treat snakebites and wounds. Its use was revived again in the 16th century as a treatment for the plague. It is a greasy clay composed of silica, aluminium oxide, chalk, magnesia and iron, that was dug with great ceremony once a year in August from a particular depression in the Mósychlos area. In August the springs of the area would have been almost dry and thereby caused the depositing and hardening of mineral clay elements in small pools of baked mud. It was called *sigillata* or *Lemnia sphragis* (a 'seal impression'), because it was officially stamped by the priestess of Artemis before being distributed. It has a predominantly red colour (hence the former name for Kótsinas, Kókkinos, which means 'red'). Galen travelled to Lemnos in AD 167 and was convinced of the efficacy of the product. He says he returned to Rome with several thousand *sphragides*, or stamped packets, for his own patients. The active ingredient is probably an antibacterial and astringent alum salt.

Many years after Galen, Pierre Belon, a 16th-century French natural historian, visited Constantinople, where he encountered 18 different types of clay marketed as 'Lemnian Earth'. Belon later visited Lemnos and described how to find the extraction point. He mentions that it was 'not more than four arrow-shots away' from the castle of Kótsinas: 'between the port and the hill there is a small chapel called St Saviour's, where the monks gather on the 6th of August, the date set for the extraction of the earth from its vein. After leaving the church and walking towards the hillock we found two paths, one to the left and one to the right leading to two springs, one about one arrow-shot away from the other'. One of these was probably the spring of Phthelideía, which still exists today. About 20m northwest of the spring are clefts of weathered, pyroclastic rock, which in places has turned into earth displaying strong colours: white, yellow and red. The alum and other soluble elements present here may have been washed out of the higher volcanic ground into sedimentary pools in the fields below, which then dried out towards midsummer.

North of Mýrina

The road north from Mýrina along Roméikos and Richá Nerá bays drops down to the estuarial **bay of Avlónas** (*map p. 526, A2*), once the harbour for what appears to have been a Sanctuary of Artemis, worshipped possibly as Artemis Tauropolos, given the figurines of oxen and the skeleton of a sacrificial bull found at the site. The remains of the sanctuary are in the middle of a luxury hotel complex (Hotel Porto Myrina). A comprehensive view of the complex can be had from the hotel lobby. It has several construction phases: a central core of 7th–6th-century BC apsidal buildings (two overlying apsidal buildings with ancillary rooms); a Hellenistic overlay of rectangular spaces; and Roman buildings at the southern extremity. The early phase is not a standard Greek sanctuary organised around a temple and altar; it is of an Oriental, pre-Greek type generally associated with mystery cults (*see p. 542*).

The traditional village of **Káspakas** (*map p. 526, A2*) is sited precariously above a steep valley. North of Kornós, a highly scenic and panoramic branch road leads left towards the island's highest summit of Vígla (*the military zone further along the road is often closed*). The main road continues to the attractive villages of **Sardés** (*map p. 526, B2*), **Dáphni** and **Katálakkos**, where traditional foods and the island's wine can be sampled. In the village of Sardés a working blacksmith's shop survives. At Katálakkos the asphalt ends and a steep track leads a further 4km down to **Gomáti Beach** (*map p. 526, B1*), one of the island's most beautiful bays, backed by high, sweeping sand dunes.

THE NORTHEAST OF THE ISLAND

Mósychlos and environs

At Kótsinas on the north coast (*map p. 526, C2*), on a mound-like promontory, stand the ruins of a Byzantine/Venetian castle. The hills due south and southeast of Kótsinas are formed by the extinct volcano of Mósychlos. In antiquity, when it was active, it was believed to be Hephaistos' workshop. It was from here that the renowned Lemnian Earth was extracted once a year (*see box opposite*). The villages in the area are also of interest: **Kontopoúli** (*map p. 526, C2*) is known for its pottery and **Kalliópi** for its saddle-less horse-riders, who race in honour of St George in late April. Above **Romanoú** there are ruined 18th-century windmills. To the north lies the scattered rural community of **Ághios Ypátios**, in an undisturbed landscape of unexpected beauty.

Hephaisteia

Ancient Hephaisteia (Ifaistía), on the east side of Pourniá Bay (*map p. 526, C1*), was, with Mýrina, the other city of the ancient *di-polis* of Lemnos, and the larger of the two in its heyday. No metalled roads reach it; it occupies a windswept, treeless promontory overlooking an almost landlocked inlet. The settlement is widely dispersed over the hillside; only a small proportion of it has so far been explored (*most of the site has unrestricted access, except for the theatre, which is open 8.30–3*).

The site has pre-Greek origins. Its pottery carried Minoan/Mycenaean traditions into the Geometric period and imports bear witness to Macedonia, Corinth and Athens. The first (Italian) archaeological expeditions excavated a **necropolis** of the 8th and 7th centuries BC (south of the neck of the promontory) and a **sanctuary** destroyed by fire during a Persian attack in the late 6th century (west slope of promontory), comprising rectangular buildings and a room endowed with benches, containing parts of the cult statue of the Great Goddess, assimilated with Cybele. South of the sanctuary an

Archaic and Hellenistic **residential block** is being excavated (directly above the parking lot). Parts of the enceinte are visible behind the **acropolis** (eastern summit). The city reached its greatest extent in Hellenistic times, with conspicuous remains of the **theatre** (central west) from this period. The first ten rows of seats in local stone belong to the earliest, late Classical theatre, enlarged in Hellenistic times. The complex skene behind the stage is Roman. Farm buildings beside the shore near the car park incorporate the remains of Hellenistic and Byzantine **bath houses**. This long-lived city was only abandoned around AD 1400.

THE CABEIRION & THE FAR NORTH

The deserted hamlet of Ághios Aléxandros (*map p. 526, C1*) stands near the large saltwater lagoon of Límni Alykí, the largest of three such lakes on the east coast. They are important wildlife preserves with high populations of migrating birds in season, including flamingo in winter. Partridge, guinea-fowl and singing larks abound in the eastern plains, as do wild chrysanthemums. From Ághios Aléxandros, a road leads west to the attractive site of the Sanctuary of the Cabeiri, or Cabeirion ('Kavírion'), on the northeastern extremity of the bay of Pourniá (*map p. 526, C1; open daily except Mon, 8.30–3.30*). The road drops down and ends just above the entrance to the sanctuary, at the foot of a flight of steps.

The nature of the sanctuary and its buildings

The cult was of pre-Greek origin, with buildings which are not temples as such, but a specific type of structure called a telesterion, a large, rectangular, covered assembly-hall used for nocturnal rituals. Such buildings were hypostyle halls, with benches against the walls around the edge of a central space. At this site are the remains of three telesteria from the 7th and 2nd centuries BC and the 2nd century AD.

THE CABEIRI

The pre-Greek cult, probably going back to the 8th century BC, is thought to have come from Anatolia. It centred on a couple (or group) of divinities called the Cabeiri (Κάβειροι), whose identity is hard to define. Their cult is encountered principally in the northern Aegean (especially Samothrace, Lemnos and Gökçeada) and the adjacent mainland, as well as Boeotia. The Cabeiri are ancillary divinities, associated with different major deities: in Boeotian Thebes they were associated with agriculture; in Samothrace with the Great Mother Goddess; in Lemnos they appear as smiths, seen later as assistants to—and by some accounts sons of—Hephaistos.

The site

Steps lead to a wide north terrace, partially cut into the hill and almost completely occupied by the isodomic foundations of the 2nd-century BC **Hellenistic telesterion**. Its large rectangular hall, with the bases of eight Ionic columns supporting its roof, is clearly visible. To the west end the hall is bounded by a corridor and a series of four small rooms, the larger of which may have been used for ritual banquets. At the opposite end is a Doric peristyle against the hill, its north end an alcove in the natural rock. This, the largest building on the site, may never have been completed and appears to have been violently destroyed in the 2nd century BC.

There is a massive Archaic supporting wall beneath the terrace on the steep hillside to the south. This second terrace held both the earliest and the last telesteria. The remains of the **Roman telesterion**, most visible today, stand on top of the Archaic original. The design of the Roman telesterion mimics on a smaller scale that of its Hellenistic predecessor, with two rows of five columns supporting the roof, and benches on the long sides. It, too, has a lateral space and a series of small rooms at the (north) end. The cult was destroyed in Early Christian times, less than 200 years after the erection of this building. The **Archaic telesterion** lay directly below: it possessed a portico in the west, its foundation supported by the massive retaining wall, still visible.

The choice of site may be linked to a cave on the shore below (*access by the stairs beside the guardian's hut*), known as the **Cave of Philoctetes**.

North of the Cabeirion

The far north of Lemnos is a peninsula with two busy communities at its heart: **Panaghía** (*map p. 526, D1*) and **Pláka**. A track leads northeast out of Pláka to the promontory of Palaiókastro, with ruined medieval fortifications. Due east of here is the underwater Charos Reef, believed by some to be the **sunken islet of Chryse**, where Philoctetes was bitten by a water snake.

MOUDROS & POLIOCHNI

The principal centre of southeast Lemnos is **Moúdros** (*map p. 526, C2*), due east of which (500m) lies the island's largest war cemetery. The armistice between Turkey and the Allied Forces (October 1918) was signed on board HMS *Agamemnon* to the west in Moúdros Bay. Off the east shore of the bay, 1km north of Moúdros, is **Koukonísi**, attached by a causeway. The low islet has the remains of an Early and Middle Bronze Age settlement (*currently covered*) at the highest point towards the north.

To the east of Moúdros is **Kamínia**, the village where the Lemnos Stele was found (*see box on p. 536*)

POLIOCHNI

Across the ridge of hills from Moúdros, at Polióchni (*map p. 526, C3*), lies one of Europe's most important prehistoric sites, one of its earliest organised urban settlements. The settlement covers the top of a low cliff at the end of a long, curving bay. Excavations in 1931–36 by the Italian School uncovered four principal successive settlements: an unfortified town of the Late Bronze Age, beneath which lay a city of the Copper Age, with two earlier Neolithic cities below. The earliest is of the 5th millennium BC.

HISTORY OF POLIOCHNI

First inhabited c. 4500 BC by settlers from Anatolia, the site initially consisted of a village of elliptical huts. Throughout the 4th millennium BC it steadily grew, acquiring terracing, retaining walls and fortifications, streets, assembly spaces and public buildings, witness to a high level of social organisation. Dwellings began to be organised into blocks and to acquire a more structured form with a square plan and an antechamber. The site possessed good water from two wells near a fertile valley. To the north, Cape Voroskópos provided a rudimentary harbour. Around 2100 BC the settlement was abandoned after a catastrophic earthquake. During the following millennium, Polióchni was the site of a small settlement.

Visiting the site

NB: The itinerary suggested here is contrary to that indicated on site.
Heading for the furthest point below and to the right-hand (west) side of the excavated area as viewed from the entrance, one reaches the earliest monumental **city gate (A)**, of the 4th millennium BC, after passing mid-3rd-millennium BC **walls (B)**. The early gate has a paved ramp (3rd millennium BC) leading up into the city between two bastions. To the left is a deep, rectangular **grain store (C)**. Opposite it to the right (south) is the **assembly space (D)**, the earliest example of such a communal facility yet found in Europe. Roughly rectangular, with stone seats along one side, this may have been the meeting place for the 50 or so elders of the community. At the summit to the left is one of the settlement's two principal **wells (E)**, circular and lined with stones. A paved area around the well was the town's main square; to the north is one of the largest **megaron** buildings **(F)**, because of its prominent size and position often considered a ruler's residence from before the earthquake of c. 2000 BC. This hypothesis is supported by the site's only hoard of gold jewellery, found in one of its rooms. The side rooms also contain sunken storage vases. The main street continues north along the eastern edge of the hill to a second **square (G)**, this time with a square well. To the north stood a **rectangular building (H)**, conspicuous by its size and relative isolation. It is often called a temple, but no specific cult finds support this. At the northern extremity of the excavations are the bases of walls and buildings recently uncovered: a large **building with a central pilaster and a stone bench (I)** may have been the seat of the community's leader.

The far south

The landscape near the southern tip of Lemnos is tranquil and open, with the villages of Phisíni and Skandáli. East from the principal road, 500m north of Phisíni, a track

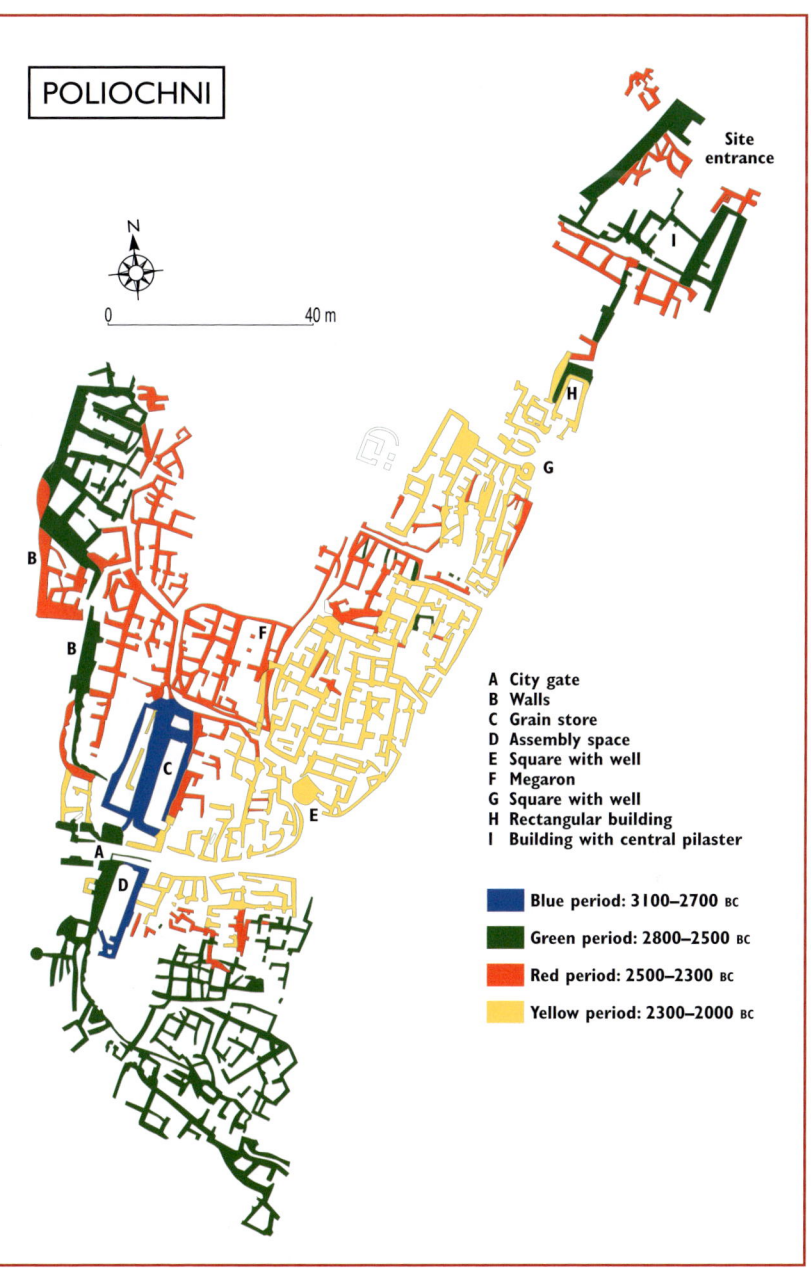

POLIOCHNI

N

0 _____ 40 m

Site entrance

A City gate
B Walls
C Grain store
D Assembly space
E Square with well
F Megaron
G Square with well
H Rectangular building
I Building with central pilaster

Blue period: 3100–2700 BC

Green period: 2800–2500 BC

Red period: 2500–2300 BC

Yellow period: 2300–2000 BC

leads north (1km) to a ridge with the collapsed **Phisíni Towers** (*map p. 526, C3*). Both were square (c. 10m by 10m), the northern one Hellenistic, the southern one medieval.

THE LEMNOS STELE

Discovered during the demolition of a church at Kamínia in 1885 and now in Athens, the Lemnos Stele is of special significance in the ongoing dispute about the origins of the Iron Age Etruscan language of north-central Italy. Herodotus claims that the Etruscans came from Lydia in Asia Minor, but is contradicted by other ancient authors. Archaeology supports the latter, but linguistically the poorly understood Etruscan language remains isolated, in spite of being part of the Indo-European family. The 6th-century stele has text in the native Lemnian language which bears close similarities to Etruscan inscriptions. It has been deciphered as the epitaph of a Myrinian. It does not necessarily support Herodotus, however, as it may be the result of Italian settlement on Lemnos.

PRACTICAL INFORMATION

GETTING AROUND

Lemnos is served by daily flights from Athens and Thessaloníki. The airport is 18.5km from Mýrina. Ferries tend to arrive and leave in the middle of the night. They go to Mýrina from Kavála six times weekly, and from Lávrion three times a week; there are less frequent ferries from Mytilene, and others from Samos and Chios, as well as Alexandroúpolis and Kavála on the mainland, and Rhodes and the Dodecanese to the south. The F/B *Aiolis* plies the route between Mýrina and Ághios Efstrátios every weekday, leaving Ághios Efstrátios at 7am and returning from Mýrina at 3pm.

WHERE TO STAY

The most characterful place to stay in Mýrina is the **Archontiko Hotel** (*T: 22540 29800/1*), one block in from the north beach, in a traditional Thracian-style mansion of 1814. There are many small pensions in the town.

WHERE TO EAT

In Mýrina, **Glaros**, by the south harbour, has good fish and serves local retsina. Just in from the north shore on Aiólou, the *mezedopoleíon* **Sinialo** probably represents the best quality in town. Wine on Lemnos is produced mostly in the area around Ághios Dimítrios (*map p. 526, B2*); it can be found in the older tavernas across the island, especially in the smaller villages. The small tavernas in the *plateías* of **Kamínia** and **Platý**, just south of Mýrina, are good places to sample it.

AGHIOS EFSTRATIOS

Á ghios Efstrátios (*map p. 499*), small, remote, unpopulated and insignificant throughout the ages, was once a place of internal exile for political prisoners, a period which ended in 1968 with a major earthquake that killed many islanders and drove still more from their homes. The island is not particularly picturesque but its remoteness guarantees tranquillity and there is good walking.

HISTORY OF AGHIOS EFSTRATIOS

The modern name of the island, commonly abbreviated locally to Aï Stratis comes from St Eustratius, a holy figure from Bithynia who took hermitic refuge in a cave here early in the 9th century. The island's name in antiquity is uncertain; in the 16th century it is mentioned by the Turkish admiral Piri Reis under the appellation Boz Papas, 'barren land of the monks'.

There is evidence of Mycenaean presence. The main centre of habitation in historic times was just east of the present port. In 1021 Basil II, the 'Bulgar-slayer', granted the island to the Monastery of the Grand Lavra on Mt Athos as a training ground for its young monks. The antiquary Buondelmonti, who passed in 1418, refers to the island as a place of pirates. In the late 16th and early 17th centuries, the settlement on the hillside north of the harbour was established. The limitations of water and fertility meant that the population was never large: in the mid-20th century, residents numbered about 800, but the island's use as a penal colony for political prisoners from 1928 pushed the temporary population to well over 3,000. The 1967–74 junta imprisoned the composer Mikis Theodorakis and the poet Giannis Ritsos here for some time. After the earthquake of 1968, many of the surviving islanders emigrated to Australia. The self-taught photographer Vassilis Manikakis documented the history of his island in the early and mid-20th century. His works are frequently exhibited.

THE VILLAGE & THE ISLAND

The **town of Ághios Efstrátios**, mostly made up of pre-fabricated concrete dwellings erected by the government after the 1968 earthquake, lies at the mouth of the principal western valley. The ancient settlement was on a hill directly east. Today it is crowned by a ruined chapel and a monument, the only ancient remains being small stretches of ancient retaining wall built in Lesbian-style masonry on the eastern side.

Since the late 16th century the main settlement has been situated on the south slope of the hill to the north of the harbour. Overlooked by ruined windmills, it has some Thracian-style houses (in ruins), a ruined church by the harbour that incorporates ancient spolia, and an impressive Neoclassical school building (1908). In the village *plateía*, a memorial modelled on the *Winged Victory of Samothrace* commemorates the islanders who died in the two world wars. Further down by the harbour is a captured Venetian cannon bearing the date 1764. On the south side of the bay are some Hellenistic rock-cut tombs.

The undulating **interior** is devoid of the churches usually found on Aegean islands. The small population lived on fishing, goat-herding and the acorn harvest. The few chapels on the shore were used by fishermen. The only two areas which were successfully cultivated, as indicated by terracing, were the gentle slopes of the northern tip of the island at Avlákia, reached by a track north from the port (*1hr*), and behind Alonítsi Bay on the east coast (*90mins on a path from the east edge of the village*). Both walks are pleasant and panoramic.

The best beaches, as remote and lonely as any in the Aegean, are on the west coast. They can be reached by caïque from the harbour (ask at the Veranda taverna), or on foot, taking any of the right-hand branches off the road south from the village.

PRACTICAL INFORMATION

GETTING AROUND

Ághios Efstrátios is served by ferries on the Kavála–Lemnos–Lávrion route (in the middle of the night). More practical is the daily weekday service on the F/B *Aiolis* to and from Lemnos (2hrs).

WHERE TO STAY

Xenonas Aï Strati (*T: 25540 93393*) overlooking the village, and **Malama Rooms** (*T: 25540 93209*) in the lower area near the harbour, both offer simple accommodation.

WHERE TO EAT

Veranda above the harbour is the only fully-fledged taverna. *Mezédes* accompanying drinks are served in the ouzeri opposite.

SAMOTHRACE

Samothrace (Samothráki), little more than the massif of Mt Sáos with a ledge of habitable land attached, has an epic solitude and grandeur. Its gorges and peaks, trees, waters, winds and shores possess a primeval simplicity. Its forests are evoked by Homer; its winds propelled and tormented Odysseus; the view from the summit of Mt Sáos is the view Poseidon had of the Battle of Troy. It is no surprise that a very ancient cult of mysterious and un-nameable 'Great Gods' evolved here.

The island offers few of the comforts of sophisticated tourism; but the walker, climber, naturalist or poet could ask for little more from a small Aegean island.

HISTORY OF SAMOTHRACE

Samothrace has always been a landmark on the busy ancient maritime trade routes of the northern Aegean. Inhabited since the Neolithic and Bronze Ages, it was first occupied by people of Thracian stock. The non-Greek Thracian language and religion for centuries survived the arrival of Greek colonists c. 700 BC. Archaeological evidence contradicts the Classical tradition that the colonists came from Samos before that date. The colonists' language has been shown to have been Aeolian rather than Ionian, probably derived from Lesbos or the Troad.

In the 6th century BC Samothrace had a silver coinage. The city reached its greatest extent and colonies were established on the mainland opposite. The Samothracian navy fought at the Battle of Salamis on the Persian side. In the 5th century BC the island's power declined, though the fame of its cult increased until the island became the chief religious centre in the north Aegean. Herodotus and Lysander of Sparta were initiated at the Sanctuary of the Great Gods; Aristophanes and Plato refer to its Mysteries. Philip of Macedon met and fell in love with his wife, Olympias of Epirus, mother of Alexander, at the sanctuary. The island was incorporated into the Macedonian kingdom in 340 BC. Samothrace was used as a naval base by the Second Athenian League, by King Lysimachus of Thrace and by the Ptolemies, Seleucids and Macedonians in turn. After the Battle of Pydna in 168 BC, Perseus, last king of Macedon, sought refuge here but was taken prisoner by the Romans.

In 84 BC the sanctuary was pillaged by corsairs but soon revived under Roman patronage. The belief that Dardanus, the legendary founder of Troy, had come from Samothrace and that his descendant Aeneas had brought its cults to Rome gave the island particular interest to the Romans. Varro and Lucius Calpurnius Piso (father-in-law of Julius Caesar) were initiates of its cult. St Paul stopped here on his way to Philippi in AD 49–50. Hadrian visited in AD 123. A severe earthquake in c. AD 200 began the sanctuary's decline, although it survived into the 4th century.

In 1431 the island was ceded by John VIII of Byzantium to Palamedes Gattilusi of Genoa, whose descendants styled themselves Princes of Aenos and Samothrace. In the

15th century the island was visited by two eminent Italian antiquarians: Cristoforo Buondelmonti in 1419 and Cyriac of Ancona in 1444. In 1457 it was taken by the Turks, who moved the inhabitants to Istanbul, and it remained an Ottoman possession (except for brief occupations by the Venetians in 1466–70 and the Russians in 1770–74) until it was liberated by the Greek fleet in 1912. The island suffered a brief Bulgarian occupation during the Second World War. It received a large émigré influx from Asia Minor between the wars: the population has fallen to 2,700 today from a recorded 4,258 in 1951.

CHORA & THE SOUTH OF THE ISLAND

Samothrace has no good harbour, and the few inlets offering refuge in antiquity have since silted up. The modern port of **Kamariótissa** occupies the site of the ancient landing of Demetrion. The remains of a 5th-century basilica lie beneath the port's principal church of the Panaghía.

A long spit of land has formed due west of Kamariótissa, culminating in Akrotíri point. Against its southern side is a small marsh. At the southern tip of this marsh, accessible by an easy walk (*2km from the port*), is the church of Ághios Andréas, mostly from the 1870s. Its west front incorporates several Early Christian marble elements.

SAMOTHRAKI CHORA & THE CENTRAL SOUTH COAST

The island's capital, 5km inland east of the port, is a beautiful example of an undisturbed island *chora*. Lying in a protected position in a natural hollow of the mountain, it is well hidden from all sides but has a fine view to the sea. It dates mostly from the 19th century. To the north, on a sheer cliff, stands the ruined medieval fortress, the **Kastro**. It has two periods of construction: the 11th-century Byzantine round tower to the east has characteristic courses of brick between the stones. The structure was incorporated into a 15th-century Genoese fortress. Genoese inscriptions, in Greek, are visible in the towers by the gate.

The **Church of the Dormition** (1875) dominates the heart of Chora. On the south side of the nave is the golden reliquary of the Five Neo-martyrs of Thrace. Originally taken hostage by the Turks in 1821 and forcibly converted to Islam, these five Samothracians re-converted to Christianity when they were returned in 1835 and were martyred for their faith in Mákri (Thrace). Below the west front of the church, in the restored Asdránia House, is the **Municipal Folklore Museum** (*open daily June–Oct, 10–1 & 6–9*).

Prehistoric Samothrace

West of Chora is the knob-like hill of **Vrichós**, site of a prehistoric acropolis of the 11th century BC. The crest is marked by the vestiges of an elongated circuit of megalithic walls. On the north slope below, three early Iron Age megalithic tombs have been identified. The road south out of Chora descends to the coast. A parallel track to the west leads to the mouth of the Polypoúdi torrent. Here, at **Mikró Vouní**, a Neolithic and Bronze Age settlement occupied the top of the mound just north of a small natural harbour. Dating back to the 6th millennium, a typical Aegean proto-urban community had formed by the 3rd millennium. Minoan clay tablets of the 19th–18th centuries BC provide important evidence of the extent of Cretan trade in metals.

Lákkoma

The south coast of Samothrace feels like a different world from the north, its outlook not Thracian but Aegean. Its minimal areas of habitation are all concentrated in the valley of the Xiropótamos stream, between the villages of **Lákkoma** and Profítis Ilías. Lákkoma is a settlement with many Thracian-style stone houses; the lower part of the village centres on a ruined olive mill. From the village a road climbs 2.5km up to the panoramic settlement of **Profítis Ilías**. The main road continues to the **beach of Pachiá Ámmos**, a long, fine, secluded stretch of golden sand.

THE SANCTUARY OF THE GREAT GODS

Due north of Chora on the coast, 5.5km from Kamariótissa, is the island's principal archaeological area: a signed pathway climbs for 300m up from the coast road, past the church of Aghía Paraskeví at the foot of a gorge. Little more than fragments of the walls of the town of **ancient Samothrace**, also called Palaiópolis, are discernible; but adjacent to the west is one of the ancient Greek world's most significant sacred sites, dedicated to the cult of a group of deities of early Anatolian origin, and known as the **Sanctuary of the Great Gods** (*open daily except Mon: winter 8.30–3.30, summer 8.30–8.30; museum open 8.30–3*).

GREEK MYSTERY CULTS

Man has always struggled to come to terms with the inevitability of death. Greek religion, literature and philosophy are reticent on the subject of the afterlife: Hades, god of the underworld, was a divinity mostly without temple or cult. To fill this gap and satisfy the need to conquer death, the mystery cults evolved, most famously on the island of Samothrace and at Eleusis, near Athens. These cults involved personal initiation and the revelation of secrets, but our knowledge of what was divulged is limited, since writers who had been initiated gave little away. The cults' origins may lie in prehistoric nocturnal festivals for the exorcism of death. Perhaps for this reason the Sanctuary of the Great Gods came to life at night, though there is still no clear understanding of the exact purpose of the buildings that composed the sanctuary. .

Herodotus refers to the mysteries as making certain things clear, but he does not say what those were. Scholars can only speculate about the nature of the revelations, but the fact that the forces and divinities venerated both on Samothrace and at Eleusis were later associated in the Greek mind with Hades, Demeter and Persephone and the cycles of natural regeneration, suggests that what an initiate experienced was related to concepts of overcoming fear of death by hope of rebirth. At Samothrace, the Earth Mother, Axieros, and the Hades/Demeter pair, Axiokersos and Axiokersa, are also accompanied by the ithyphallic Cadmilus (Kadmilos), the spouse of the Earth Mother, later identified with the Olympian Hermes.

It is impossible to reconstruct how such ideas were communicated, but it may have been in the form of a liturgy, involving the ritual acting out of religious truths, the repetition of formulae, the showing of symbolic objects, and ritual feasting.

Introduction to the site

This dramatic site, on the lower slopes of the prominent northwest shoulder of the Sáos massif, looks out towards the Thracian coast In earliest times the sanctuary was entered from the hill to the west; in the 3rd century BC Ptolemy II Philadelphus created a new monumental access from the town to the east; today access is directly from the north, which removes the original element of surprise on finding the central sanctuary hidden in a hollow. Town and sanctuary were badly affected by earthquakes in 287 BC, AD 50 and—most catastrophically—c. AD 200, resulting in reconstruction, so that much of the buildings and layout are Hellenistic, dating from the period when the royal house of Macedon embellished the site. By the end of the 1st century BC the sanctuary was of considerable splendour both in sculpture and architecture. After AD 400 it decayed.

The discovery and subsequent removal in 1863 of the famous *Winged Victory of Samothrace*, now in the Louvre, excited the imagination of European antiquarians and led to subsequent French, Swedish and (ongoing) American excavations. The 19th-century finds are divided between collections in Paris, Vienna and Istanbul.

The historian Diodorus Siculus suggests that a cult of the Great Mother Goddess was first brought to the island by Myrina, Queen of the Amazons. Throughout its history, the sanctuary continued to possess the extra-territorial character customarily accorded to sacred sites, separate from the adjacent city-state. Its remarkable openness attracted pilgrims and initiates from much of the Mediterranean and Black Sea area: attendance was open to anyone, initiated or not, and initiation itself could be obtained at any time, and made no distinctions of sex, age, social status or nationality. There appear to have been two degrees of initiation, termed *myesis* and *epopteia*. A certain moral standard seems to have been implicit in the second degree (which was not obligatory but exceptional), and some form of confession and absolution may have preceded it. Initiates wore a finger-ring of iron and carried a purple scarf as a badge of their status. The iron may have been of local origin.

The museum

The path from the entrance leads first to the small museum before entering the archaeological site (*NB: the museum closes at 3pm*).

Central Hall: This first room contains architectural fragments, mostly of Hellenistic date and often ornately decorated. They include a reconstructed segment of the upper portion or gallery of the great Rotunda of Arsinöe (c. 285 BC) and elements from the entablature and roof of the Hieron.

Hall B is dominated by the reconstruction of the impressive Corinthian capital and base from the Propylon of Ptolemy II (285–281 BC). In the corner by the entrance is a fluted, monolithic column in Thasian marble from the Hall of the Choral Dancers, surmounted by a beautiful 'collar' decorated with palmettes, giving it a vividly Oriental Ionic feel. There is also a section of the frieze that gave the Hall of the Choral Dancers its name, showing a gracious processional dance

of women (c. 340 BC). Around the walls are cases exhibiting small finds such as portable altars and figurines. In a corner are two interesting stelae, both dedicated on Samothrace by initiates resident in the city of Cyzicus on the Sea of Marmara, both depicting a circular building reminiscent of the Rotunda of Arsinoë.

Hall C displays more sculpture, including one of four large marble Nike statues (c. 130 BC), acroteria from the corners of the roof of the Hieron, and an array of ceramics and small devotional, ornamental and funerary objects, among them some fine imports from Attica.

Hall D (north of Hall A) displays a cast of the *Winged Victory of Samothrace*, now in the Louvre, and finds from graves in the area, including Hellenistic jewellery and exquisite figurines.

THE CENTRAL SACRED AREA

The site is approached up through a ravine. Across the stream-bed is the colossal base (20.2m in outside diameter) of the **Rotunda of Arsinoë (1)**, the largest Greek circular building known, dedicated to the Great Gods by Queen Arsinoë II, wife successively of Lysimachus of Thrace and of her brother Ptolemy II Philadelphus. It was probably begun after the extensive damage by the earthquake of 287 BC. Built on a site used for sacrifices, the rotunda may have continued this function. The exterior presented a marble wall surmounted by an ornamental string-course below a gallery of pilasters supporting a Doric entablature; the windowless, dark, spacious interior was covered with a low conical roof. Only the limestone foundations, surmounted by steps in Thasian marble, remain now. Beneath the floor level lies the rectangular southern end of the early 4th-century BC predecessor of the Anaktoron, the 'orthostate structure'.

More ancient is the **Sacred Rock (2)**, immediately to the southwest of the Rotunda.

Initiation to the first degree: the Anaktoron

The central hall for the first degree of initiation into the Mysteries, referred to traditionally as the **Anaktoron (3)**, is cut partially into the slope of the hill. Its walls are preserved to a considerable height. As a sacred and ancient building, it was repeatedly rebuilt in the same manner; the present structure is faithful to its predecessors although it dates from the 1st century AD. The spacious, probably windowless, interior (27m by 11.5m) was entered from the long west side by three doors. Along the back wall was a grandstand of low seats, facing a central, circular wooden platform. A wooden partition wall with doors raised on a low wall, distinguished by a layer of red stone, separated a zone at the north end, probably the inner sanctuary, its entrances marked by a stele (now in the museum) forbidding entry to the uninitiated. At the south end of the building is a small ancillary room, designated a sacristy.

Initiation to the second degree: the Hieron

Little remains of the 4th-century BC marble **Hall of the Choral Dancers (4)**. Elements from it in the museum show that it was remarkable for its fine and varied decoration. It may have housed the famous group depicting Aphrodite and Pothos by Skopas, mentioned by Pliny (*Nat. Hist. XXXVI, 25*).

Just to the south, at the heart of the sanctuary, are the re-erected Doric columns of the **Hieron (5)**, begun c. 325 BC, finished in the mid-2nd century and restored several times throughout antiquity. It was a long, rectangular, colonnaded structure which terminated in an apse at its south end, as did its 5th- and 6th-century BC predecessors. This was the place of initiation to the second and higher degree, the *epopteia*. The walls of the windowless interior were painted black and red. Along the east and west walls were stone benches, and the centre of the apse held a libation pit. An inscribed stele explicitly forbade entry to the interior to non-initiates of the second degree. An area of stone slabs framed in terracotta tile, still visible (under glass) outside the east of the building, may have played some role in the ritual.

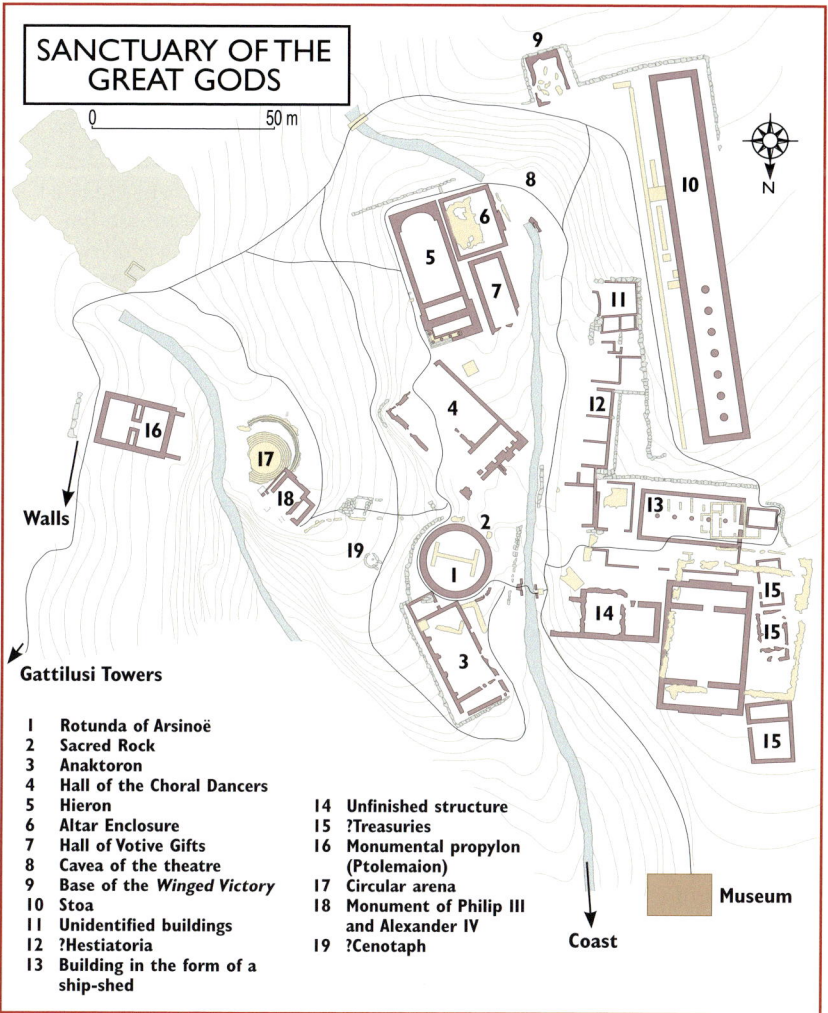

SANCTUARY OF THE GREAT GODS

0   50 m

N

Walls

Gattilusi Towers

1   **Rotunda of Arsinoë**
2   **Sacred Rock**
3   **Anaktoron**
4   **Hall of the Choral Dancers**
5   **Hieron**
6   **Altar Enclosure**
7   **Hall of Votive Gifts**
8   **Cavea of the theatre**
9   **Base of the *Winged Victory***
10   **Stoa**
11   **Unidentified buildings**
12   **?Hestiatoria**
13   **Building in the form of a ship-shed**
14   **Unfinished structure**
15   **?Treasuries**
16   **Monumental propylon (Ptolemaion)**
17   **Circular arena**
18   **Monument of Philip III and Alexander IV**
19   **?Cenotaph**

Museum

Coast

On the west side is the large main **altar enclosure (6)**, open to the skies and entered from the west. Next, to the north, is one of the oldest surviving structures, the so-called **Hall of Votive Gifts (7)**, built originally c. 540 BC. Normally votive gifts and offerings were stored in the naos or opisthodomos of a temple; but here, because of the liturgical function of the interior of the Hieron, they needed to be stored in a separate building.

Facing these two last buildings from the west is the cavea of the small **theatre (8)**. Above its southern extremity, on the crown of the ridge, once soared the sculptural complex we know as the *Nike* or **Winged Victory of Samothrace**, but only rubble from its base remains **(9)**. The sculpture was raised high above the ground on a carved ship's prow.

THE WESTERN RIDGE

The ridge to the west of the main sacred area was crowned at its southern end by a long (c. 104m) 3rd-century BC **stoa (10)**, with Doric columns and entablature, its limestone core faced with white stucco. In front of it are the bases of honorific and votive statues. This main public building provided shelter and a meeting space to visitors and pilgrims. Directly below it, on the eastern face of the ridge looking across towards the Hieron, is an area with various **polygonal and isodomic walls (11)**, also incorporating a lintel with a relieving triangle. Date and function are not clear, but it has been proposed that the structures are of the 3rd century BC and deliberately imitate earlier architectural styles. There appears to have been a spring here.

The continuation north of this area, below the eastern slope of the western ridge, is marked by a series of three adjacent **rectangular rooms (12)**, probably hestitatoria, with open porches on the eastern side. Roman marble-chip floors are preserved in parts. Just west of here, below the north end of the great stoa, is a long rectangular **building in the form of a ship-shed (13)** for the display of a consecrated warship, dedicated possibly by the Macedonian king Antigonus Gonatas after a victory in the waters of Kos in 254 BC. A couple of the marble supports which cradled the keel of the boat are still in place.

The sanctuary expanded north of here in late Hellenistic times, apparently in order to accommodate the construction of buildings dedicated by other Aegean city-states and their citizens. A large **unfinished structure (14)** bears an inscription indicating that it was the dedication of a rich lady from Miletus; it may have been destined as another hestiatorion. At the western edge, beyond the base of another unfinished building, are three small, porched buildings of the 3rd and 2nd centuries BC, perhaps **treasuries** for donor city-states **(15)**. Superimposed over this whole area was a large Byzantine fortress (c. 36m by 38m), built in the 10th or 11th centuries AD.

THE EASTERN RIDGE

The skyline of the eastern hill was in antiquity thronged with cenotaphs and monumental dedications. Across a gully is the new **monumental propylon (16)**, sometimes called the Ptolemaion, created c. 285 BC by Ptolemy II Philadelphus, through which the sanctuary could now be entered from the city. Fragments of Ptolemy's dedicatory inscription on the architrave can be seen amongst the blocks collected beside the base of the building; among the fragments is an eroded corner-stone with an elegant relief

The *Winged Victory of Samothrace* (2nd century BC), one of the most famous artefacts in the Louvre. The statue once rose high above the southern edge of the Sanctuary of the Great Gods.

of a ship on two of its sides. The substructure of the propylon is well-preserved, perforated by a barrel-vaulted tunnel allowing a stream to pass under it. The propylon had the appearance of an amphiprostyle temple with pedimented porticoes of six columns, Ionic to the east, Corinthian to the west. The latter are the earliest known example of the Corinthian order used in an exterior in Greek architecture.

The propylon led directly across to a small **circular arena (17)**, encircled by shallow rising steps (*reached by returning west across the gully and taking the path immediately to the north*). Too shallow for seats, these steps allowed people to stand and watch some ritual that took place here. The steps were constructed in the 5th century BC. The east side has eroded away, perhaps due to an earthquake, as has a third of the large **commemorative monument** the north **(18)**, with a hexastyle Doric portico. It was erected in honour of Philip III and Alexander IV of Macedon between 323 and 317 BC. At a later date, an Ionic portico was added on its north side for the display of statues. Down the slope further north are the scant remains of a late 4th-century building, possibly a **cenotaph (19)**, in the form of a tall, Doric rotunda.

ANCIENT SAMOTHRACE

Of the ancient city of Samothrace, which lay on a ridge to the east of the sanctuary, only the **walls** remain above ground. The path beyond the Ptolemaion to the northeast leads directly to them (*though their exploration appears to be discouraged officially*). They constitute an enceinte of 2400m, almost two thirds complete, climbing the ridge to the east to a look-out post at a height of 275m, after which they drop steeply down the far side, traceable only intermittently. Constructed of masonry faces with a rubble fill, they originate from the 6th century BC, but were repeatedly repaired, especially in the 3rd century BC. Five gates are identifiable, the most interesting just to the right of the main pathway.

Clearly visible are the outcrops of three early 15th-century Genoese towers further to the northeast, known, since Cyriac of Ancona saw them in 1444, as the **Gattilusi Towers** (*also reached by a path from the small car park by the shore, to the east of the site entrance*). They may once have been corner bastions in a small fortress. The highest and largest stands almost complete at nearly 18m, with the corbels for machicolations around its top still well preserved. The masonry includes many ancient blocks gathered from the city and sanctuary.

Due north of the towers at the level of the shore, inside the coast road shortly before it turns southeast, are the foundations of a small **Early Christian church**, perhaps commemorating the visit of St Paul to the island. The harbour in which he may have stopped was 150m to the west of the church, marked by a mole still visible under the water.

THE NORTH COAST

East of the Sanctuary of the Great Gods, the coast road follows the shoreline, passing below the villages of Káto and Áno (Epáno) Karyótes. Just beyond the turning to the latter, two **ceramic workshops** of the Hellenistic period have been excavated on both sides of the road. Still further east, a turning leads inland to the small settlement of **Thérma**, which takes its name from a group of small geothermic springs. The Municipal Thermal Baths (*open daily June–Oct 7–11 & 5–7*) are located to the right of the road. Just 50m uphill on a track to the right are the Psarótherma, two smaller, hotter, pools on the hillside, one of them in an improvised hut. They are open and accessible at all times.

Mount Sáos

The main path up the **north face of Mt Sáos**, towards its peaks via the springs of Kalamíthria, leaves from the southwest corner of Thérma. The Sáos massif is an impressive wilderness to explore, but it can also be dangerous because of rapid weather changes. Appropriate precautions need to be taken, and the ascent should be made in company, ideally with a guide (ask at the hotels in Thérma). The peaks of Fengári and Ághios Geórgios can be reached in just over 4hrs.

Just beyond Thérma, after the Platiá campsite (left), a track leads to the right, by a dump, leading in a 30-min climb to the ruined 14th–19th-century **monastery of Christós**, hidden among trees on a knoll, marked by a modern hut nearby. Only the ruins of the katholikon still stand, surrounded by foundations of monastic buildings. Particularly noteworthy are the massive lintel blocks of the doors in Thasian marble, bearing inscriptions listing the theoroi of the Sanctuary of the Great Gods, from where these blocks and the scattered Doric capitals must have been removed.

The Foniás river and Áno Meriá

Just under 5km east of Thérma, the coast road crosses the Foniás river. A path leads down the east bank to the 15th-century **Foniás Tower** by the shore. To the south of the road bridge, paths along the river lead 30mins inland to a gorge containing several deep pools with waterfalls.

After Foniás the road turns south with good views of Gökçeada (Imbros) and the Turkish coast. On the gentler slopes here, in the region called Áno Meriá, are some small **agricultural villages**—Isómata, Kantarátika, Remboutsádika—medieval in origin and today barely inhabited. There are ruins of several early Byzantine churches in the area. The highest and southernmost village, **Kerasiá**, now abandoned, is immersed in forest and accessible only on foot from Kantarátika.

The coast road continues along the full length of the eastern shore, to end at the pleasant beach in **Kípi Bay**.

PRACTICAL INFORMATION

GETTING AROUND

Access to Samothrace is not particularly easy, even in high season. It is principally from Alexandroúpolis in Thrace, whose airport is served by frequent flights from Athens (Samothrace has no airport). From Alexandroúpolis there are daily ferries and/or hydrofoils. There are sometimes ferry connections from Lemnos, Lesbos, Psará, Lávrion (near Athens) and Kavála, but these are not always running.

Buses from Kamariótissa serve most centres of population on the island.

WHERE TO STAY

Samothrace has few hotels, but many rent rooms and studio apartments, including especially attractive ones near Thérma, e.g. **Michail Aravis' Rooms** (*T: 25510 9841*). Just on the edge of Kamariótissa are the **Kyrkos Apartments** (*T: 25510 41620*), clean, pleasant, spacious and practical.

WHERE TO EAT

In Chora, the **Café-ouzeri 1900** in the main *plateía* is an enjoyable place to eat and is popular with locals: similarly, the **Taverna Orizontas** in Kamariótissa. **Pyrgos**, by the castle in Chora, is also pleasant for a sunset drink and *mezédes*. The best food, with many excellent local goat dishes, is to be found at the **Taverna Karydies** in Mésa Meriá, near Isómata at the east end of the island.

FURTHER READING

Samothrake: An Ecotourist and Trekking Map (available in the shops in Kamariótissa). Karl Lehmann, *Samothrace* (Institute of Fine Arts, New York University), Thessaloníki 1998.

THASOS

Something of the greenness and spaciousness of Macedonia is distilled in Thasos, a beautiful island with peaceful villages and landscapes as well as immensely important archaeology.

Thasos is rich in metal ores, including silver and especially gold. Along with wine and marble, these ores were widely traded throughout antiquity, bringing continuous prosperity to the island's single city. Its remains offer a clear feel for an ancient town in its entirety, with its walls and its sanctuaries, its ports and lighthouses, theatres, dwelling houses, meeting halls, farmsteads and workshops. Thasos also gives a vivid picture

of how the ancients sensed that a network of divine presences with different areas of influence participated in, and watched over, the daily life of their community.

HISTORY OF THASOS

The area of Liménas, or Thasos town, has been inhabited since before 10,000 BC, when the island was probably still attached to the mainland. Several Bronze Age sites are known, most importantly Skála Sotíras.

Around 680 BC colonists from Paros arrived to settle the island, on the instigation of the Delphic Oracle. Their leader was Telesicles, father of the poet and soldier Archilochus, who describes the island's appearance as like 'the back-bone of an ass, covered in dense forests'. Herodotus states that the original colonisers of the island were Phoenicians 'who came with Thasos, son of Phoenix, to colonise the island, which has borne his name ever since' (*VI, 47*). The gold mines brought prosperity, and with growing wealth and population Thasos colonised the Macedonian and Thracian mainland opposite. The island developed strong trade links with the Cyclades, Corinth, Athens and the Ionian islands. In 491, in the build-up to the Persian Wars, Thasos acceded to Darius' demands that it dismantle its walls; likewise in 480 it offered no resistance to Xerxes, but rather fêted him at public expense. After 477 BC the island was part of the Delian League, but seceded in 465 BC in a dispute with Athens over mining and trading rights. Thasos held out against Athens for over two years before surrendering her fleet, dismantling her walls and renouncing her mainland claims. A period of compliance with Athens followed until Thasos defected again in 410 BC. In 405 BC, after defeating the Athenian fleet at Aegospotamoi, the Spartan leader Lysander gathered the island's Athenian partisans in the Sanctuary of Hercules by deceit, and massacred them.

During the 5th century, Herodotus visited Thasos, and Hippocrates lived on the island for almost four years, working with the sick. The great painter Polygnotus (fl. 475–450 BC) was born here. The 4th century saw stability and prosperity and much new building. From 375 BC Thasos was part of the Second Athenian League, passing under Macedonian control after Philip of Macedon's victory at Chaironeia in 338 BC. This was the island's golden age. The island flourished also under Roman rule after 196 BC, and was rewarded for its resistance to Mithridates in 80 BC. Its wine and marble were much in demand in Rome.

The medieval history of Thasos is obscure. The island was a naval base for the Byzantine fleet, but when taken by the Genoese overlords of Lesbos, the Gattilusi, it benefited from their connections and traded produce as far afield as northern Europe. In 1455 the Gattilusi ceded the island to the Ottoman sultan in order to safeguard their rights over Lesbos. In 1770, following a defeat of the Turkish navy, Thasos became a Russian naval base. In 1813, depopulated and deforested, the island was given by Sultan Mahmud II to Muhammad Ali, Viceroy of Egypt. It was a quasi-independent apanage of Egypt for almost a century, until 1902, when it reverted to Turkish rule. In 1912 Admiral Koundouriotis liberated the island for Greece. The period between the wars was marked by an influx of refugees from Asia Minor, who settled mostly at

Liménas and Limenária, creating new centres that eventually superseded the former inland capitals of Panaghía and Theológos.

THASOS TOWN: LIMENAS

The unostentatious modern town of Liménas is built over and within the remains of what was one of the most active and prosperous ancient cities of the Northern Aegean. Its extensive ruins are a rare combination of beauty, variety and importance. They have been excavated and documented by the French School. The description below takes you on a 'tour' of the ancient city.

THE HARBOURS

Ancient Thasos had two main harbours: a commercial port to the north, and a military, or 'closed', port where the sweep of the present-day ('old') harbour of Liménas indents the shore (*see plan on p. 560*). The sea has retreated an average of 50m along this stretch, leaving the ancient sea walls well inland (below Odós Poseidónos). The **ancient commercial port** lay towards the northernmost extremity of town, and was defined and protected to the north by a 100-m mole, now submerged but visible under the water. The curve of the current 'old' harbour occupies the area of the **ancient military port**, which was bordered by deep, perpendicular ship-sheds for the storage and drying of the war triremes: their foundations can be seen below the water at the northern end of the curve. They measured about 38m by 19m and each accommodated three boats. There may have been 15 such drying sheds, for a fleet of 45 warships. Protected by a mole on the seaward side, the harbour was entered from the sea at the northern corner by a small entrance which could be closed with a chain. The delightful harbour-front is dominated today by a long, balconied 19th-century building on its eastern curve, a dependency of Vatopédi Monastery on Mount Athos.

Behind the port to the south, and just across the street from the museum forecourt, is the **Marine Gate**, one of the two principal entrances to the ancient port area, constructed in fine masonry typical of the late 5th century. The flight of steps shows support-holes for railing posts. There is a series of storage chambers with frames for doors. Just a few metres across the road is a stretch of the **ancient harbour wall**.

THE AGORA

Steps lead down into the park-like area of the ancient agorá (*open sunrise–sunset; free admission; see plan on p. 556*), one of the loveliest archaeological spaces in the Aegean. This was the main square of the ancient city, an area of about 100m by 80m, bounded by stoas and buildings on all four sides. Evolved organically over several centuries, it has a characteristic irregularity of plan: almost rectangular, yet with no perpendicular corners; apparently—but not quite—symmetrical.

The building immediately to the left on entry was added in the 1st century AD: it is a paved and **colonnaded court (1)** containing a stone exedra which supported honorific statues. Further dedications were placed on the pedestals along the east wall, left and right of the exedra. This was a type of building designed principally for meetings of the citizenry. The building backs against the outside wall of the agorá's **northwest stoa (2)**. Up the steps into the agorá proper, a threshold bears Roman perforations for the fixing of gates to close off the area when necessary. The shape of the area beyond is principally that created in the 4th century BC.

To the left, the base of the stoa's Doric portico extends for almost 100m: its original height is indicated by two re-erected Doric columns. This is an early 3rd-century BC building of simple design but fine construction. It was a shaded colonnade, surmounted by an entablature with triglyphs and a frieze with a running garland design between lion-head water-spouts (fragments visible nearby); it had a hipped roof covered with marble tiles. In front of it are the **bases of 13 altars or statues (3)**, their alignment not quite parallel to the portico. Immediately to the left at the top of the small flight of steps, this portico abuts another colonnade, the **southwest stoa (4)**, at an awkward angle, necessitating the juxtaposition of two columns a few centimetres from one another. The southwest stoa was probably built in the late 1st century BC, and contained a row of large rooms, probably administrative offices.

Both stoas gave onto the main square, which contained a number of shrines, monuments, altars and honorific statues of varying shapes and sizes. These date from different periods: a 4th-century BC **Sanctuary of Zeus Agoraios (5)**, a row of 1st-century BC **exedrae (6)**, once bearing statues and decrees, and a **monument to the family of Augustus (7)**. Northwest of this is the circular marble base of the **Altar of Theogenes (8)** (*see box opposite*). Fragments of the dedicatory inscription (now in the museum) enumerate his frequent victories in the 'heavy' sports.

The southeast side of the agorá is bounded by a third long **stoa (9)**. To the left of the path are the bases of its colonnade and a well-constructed stone drain. To the right are the foundations of a long **interior hall (10)**, with a central row of columns which may have supported a second floor above. At its far northeastern end is the base of the **Monument to Glaucus (11)**, identified by an early 6th-century inscription (now in the museum; *see p. 558*) carved in boustrophedon, declaring, 'I am the monument to Glaucus … dedicated by the son of Brentes'. This was the most venerable monument in the public area, the principal memorial to one of the city's founders.

A few metres to the west, in the corner of the open agorá, is the base of another **monument carved with a ship's prow** (or stern) decorated with stylised waves at its base **(12)**. It originally stood in the middle of a rectangular exedra. On it must have stood some naval victory monument, a common type for the 3rd and 2nd centuries BC.

Facing page: The base of the Altar of Theogenes, in the Thasos agorá.

Theogenes of Thasos

Theogenes was an immensely successful local athlete and twice Olympic victor, for boxing in 480 BC and for the *pancration*, a no-holds-barred combination of boxing and wrestling, in 476. Pausanias reports that he was censured during the 75th Olympiad for deliberate cruelty to his adversary, one of the first recorded instances of an athlete being fined.

Pausanias relates that after Theogenes' death, an opponent came each night to vent his frustrations physically, until one night the statue fell over and killed him. Since the law prescribed exile for murderers (including inanimate objects), the statue was thrown into the sea. Soon after, the island was afflicted with severe drought. Seeking advice from the Delphic Oracle, the Thasians were advised to cease neglecting the memory of Theogenes. The statue was recovered and returned to the agorá. Theogenes now received worship as a hero as his statue was believed to have miraculous powers. Hero-worship of athletic champions was by no means unusual in the ancient Greek world.

In the eastern corner, just beyond the Monument to Glaucus, the path leads out through an ancient doorway, underneath a stretch of modern street, into the so-called **Passage of the Theoroi (13)**: this is a narrow paved stretch of street

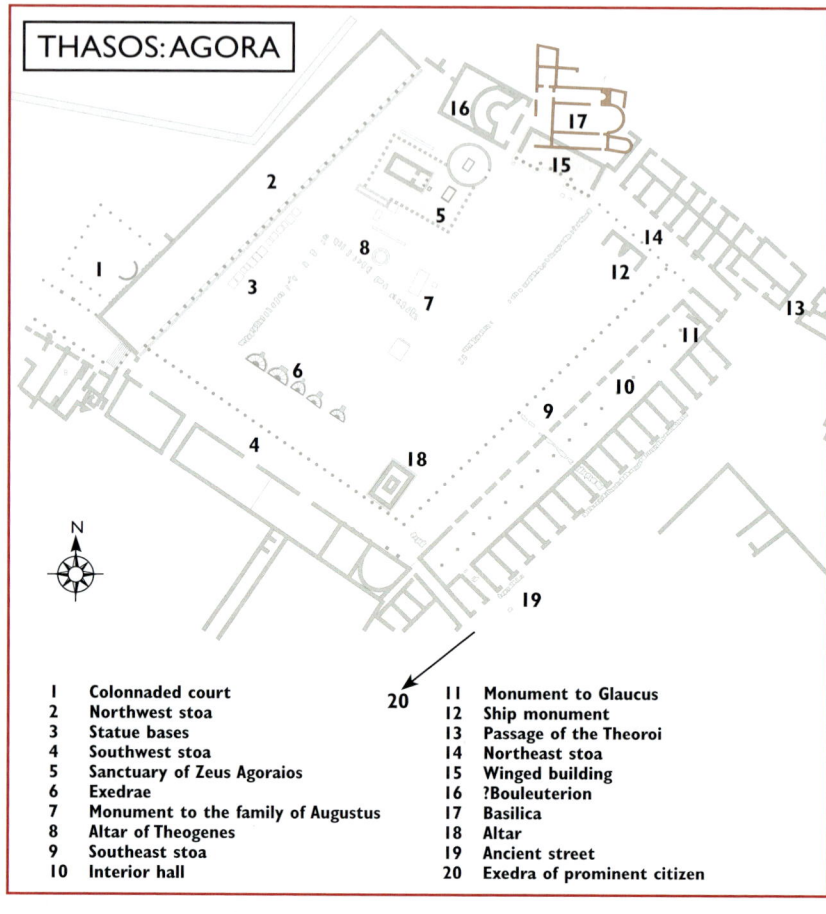

THASOS: AGORA

N

1	Colonnaded court	11	Monument to Glaucus
2	Northwest stoa	12	Ship monument
3	Statue bases	13	Passage of the Theoroi
4	Southwest stoa	14	Northeast stoa
5	Sanctuary of Zeus Agoraios	15	Winged building
6	Exedrae	16	?Bouleuterion
7	Monument to the family of Augustus	17	Basilica
8	Altar of Theogenes	18	Altar
9	Southeast stoa	19	Ancient street
10	Interior hall	20	Exedra of prominent citizen

opening out into a small area with two municipal water sources beyond—an area that was of ritual, official and practical significance in antiquity. The stretch of ancient flagstone paving marks what was a short, covered passageway (about 4.6m wide and 11m long) leading to a main artery of town joining the sanctuary of Heracles to those of Dionysus and Poseidon (*see map on p. 560*). Just before the street opened out into the square with the springs and wells, it passed by

two shrines to left and right, both decorated with fine 5th-century BC reliefs (now in the Louvre). The relief on the left depicted three nymphs, divinities of water sources, being greeted by Apollo; an inscription above laid down rules for appropriate sacrifice. On the opposite side, built into the wall on either side of the steps which led up to a recessed altar in the wall, were two reliefs showing Hermes greeting the three *Charites* or Graces, who promoted, amongst other things, civil concord. The modern name, Passage of the Theoroi, derives from an inscribed list of the theoroi of Thasos from 540 BC up to Imperial Roman times, found on the left-hand side. On the right, immediately beyond the wall, was a dedication to Athena Propylaia, 'protectress of the entrance-way'.

Returning to the main agorá square, the **northeast stoa (14)** is straight ahead: it is much shorter than the other three, due to the presence of other important civic buildings. The north side of the stoa is backed by a row of official rooms. Three of them in the middle (with the doorway positioned off-centre so as to accommodate the arrangement of couches) were banqueting rooms. Where the stoa ends, it abuts a 4th-century BC **winged building (15)**, constructed entirely of marble, the civic focus of the town; it contained engraved laws and complete lists of archons and was fronted by a row of honorific statues. The shape of its shallow 'U' and recessed, colonnaded front are discernible from the foundations; a triglyph frieze and fluted Doric columns can be inferred from the ruins lying about.

Beyond this building to the northwest (but now difficult to distinguish as it disappears under a dilapidated 19th-century mansion) was a building thought to be the city's **bouleuterion (16)**. Above it are the remains of an **Early Christian basilica (17)** of the 5th century AD, part of its narthex constructed over a corner of the winged building: it had three apses, the central one of which preserves the synthronon seating for the clergy. Attached to the church's northwest corner, the remains of a martyrion have been found, containing vestiges of mosaic and inscriptions which suggest that it may have enshrined the relics of the 4th-century Cappadocian martyr Acacius, beheaded in Constantinople in 303 AD.

Before leaving the agorá, a small detour can be made, past an **altar (18)**, out of the southern corner of the area. Here, to the right behind the southeast stoa, lies a well-preserved stretch of **paved ancient street (19)** leading southwest for about 60m. On the left, there are house foundations of the Early Christian period; further along, steps lead up to a **semicircular exedra (20)**, built by a prominent Thasian citizen of the 1st century AD for the display of statues of his family executed by a local sculptor named Limendas. To the right-hand side, the pavement was shaded by a colonnade, with a row of shops behind.

THE ARCHAEOLOGICAL MUSEUM

Open 8–3. At the time of writing the museum was being transferred into new buildings on the same site, and most exhibits were not on display.
The treasure of this collection is the colossal **kouros holding a ram**, 3.5m high, in Thasian marble, and dating from c. 600 BC. The sculpture is unfinished; it was abandoned because of the fault in the marble which appeared through the left ear and neck. It was subsequently broken up into five pieces and used as building material in the northeast terrace wall of the Sanctuary of Pythian Apollo on the acropolis.

Thasian silver coin of the early 5th century BC depicting a satyr abducting a maenad.

The collection is particularly strong in 6th-century BC Archaic works: the stylised **Wix Sphinx** (named after Adolf Wix, Austro-Hungarian consul in Kavála) stood on top of an Ionic column to mark the grave of a hero or warrior. Two further pieces both come from the Sanctuary of Hercules: the terrifying **head of a silenus**, and the front portion of a **winged horse**, of decidedly Oriental style. From a little later, the dawn of the Classical era, comes a fragment of a male torso salvaged from the sea.

From the 4th century are two works of notable quality: a **head of Dionysus** that can be ascribed to the school of Praxiteles, c. 350 BC, and which comes from the large votive monument in the Sanctuary of Dionysus. More dramatic is the large **fragment of a funerary stele** in which the life-size figure of the deceased is seen in what are perhaps her last moments in life, supported by a figure from behind, while another figure looks on.

Several of the **inscriptions** mentioned elsewhere in this text, such as the boustrophedon dedication to Glaucus from the agorá and part of the dedicatory inscription of the city's theatre, are to be found here. The museum also has some interesting early pottery, terracotta figurines, bronze and ivory items, and **coins**. For the design of its earliest coins, in the 6th and 5th centuries BC, Thasos chose the subject of Silenus carrying off a maenad, turning in the 4th century BC to a more orthodox head of Dionysus or Heracles. The finds displayed around the external courtyard are mostly Hellenistic sarcophagi and funerary monuments. Their inscriptions make poignant reading: they speak of 'the fortune of being happily married for 50 years', of 'being as blessed in death as in life'.

To the east of the museum is the broad, low church of **Ághios Nikólaos**. The nave is lined with re-used ancient marble columns supporting Early Christian capitals.

THE ODEION & THE SANCTUARIES OF ARTEMIS, DIONYSUS & POSEIDON

Not far from the south corner of the agorá area, but reached by the modern road which leads round the back of the agorá, is the **Roman odeion** (late 2nd century AD). Though bisected by the street, it nonetheless gives a sense of the intimacy of such small, covered halls, which were used for readings, concerts or meetings. The building has a brick and cement core and is finished in marble: a dozen or more rows of seats are missing from the upper cavea.

Further north along the modern street, above and to the right, are the scant remains of the terracing of the **Sanctuary of Artemis**. A hundred metres further on are the remains of the **Sanctuary of Dionysus**, surrounded by modern housing which probably obscures the temple itself. The principal foundations visible today belong to a splendid choragic monument of the mid-4th century BC, its form very similar to a tetraprostyle temple. Steps led up through the columns into a square interior where nine large statues were arranged in a semicircle: Dionysus in the centre (head in the museum), flanked by figures symbolising eight forms of drama and performance. Two small altars by the foot of the central stairs predate the monument.

Fifty metres further north, between the Sanctuary of Dionysus and that of Poseidon, the modern street passes by one of the ancient gates from the port into the city, the **Gate of the Goddess on a Chariot**, so named from the beautiful but worn relief on one of its massive door jambs. The construction dates from the very beginning of the 5th century BC and the relief from shortly after. The relief shows a goddess, almost certainly Artemis, in a chariot, her hair tied back in an elegant pony-tail, accompanied by Hermes, who holds the bridle of the horses. Elements of the securing mechanism of the doors are well-preserved and visible in the threshold.

The late 5th-century BC **Poseidonion**, a little way beyond, is another sanctuary of which today about half is visible; the rest—possibly including the temple—lies under the buildings to the east. A stone wall runs across the line of vision, with the entrance to the temenos in the centre. To the right stands a small rectangular altar to Hera Epilimineia (Hera 'of the port') with holes for the attachment of a wooden or metal superstructure. The entrance is partly bounded by two dedicatory bases bearing inscriptions. The monolithic threshold led through a short colonnaded porch into an open area with an altar (in front of the present escarpment), a statue base to the left, and the rectangular base of a shrine (perhaps to Amphitrite) to the right. Beyond this, at the far southern end of the temenos, is a series of six banqueting rooms, used principally during the midwinter Feast of Poseidon. At the opposite (north) end, outside the enclosure, are the remains of houses, some with storage pithoi still in place.

THE HERMES GATE RESIDENTIAL QUARTER

This is an area of considerable interest. The gate from which it takes its name bears a damaged, early 5th-century BC **relief showing Hermes entering the town** accompanied by three faintly discernible female figures, perhaps the *Charites*.

The **ancient street** runs along the inside of the walls. From it radiate other streets going inland, dividing the excavated area into **residential blocks**. The street plan remained in place for centuries, but the housing blocks it defined evolved constantly. There were substantial dwellings here, some two floors high with pitched roofs, built around open peristyle courtyards with paved impluvia to collect rainwater into cisterns below the buildings, still marked today by round caps and perforated flagstones at their mouths. The surface remains are mostly Hellenistic and Roman, but this area was continuously inhabited since the 8th century BC, before the colonisation from Paros. Due to the constant rebuilding over the course of time, a variety of different kinds of **ancient masonry** can clearly be seen, from the decorative, polygonal stonework of

ANCIENT
LIMENAS

Temple of
Athena

Sanctuary of
Apollo

Sanctuary of
Artemis

Theatre

Sanctuary of
Dionysus

Poseidonion

Chariot Gate

Hermes
Gate

Line of
Ship-sheds

Old
Harbour

(Ancient Military
Port)

Ancient Commercial
Port

Evraiokastro

Submerged
mole

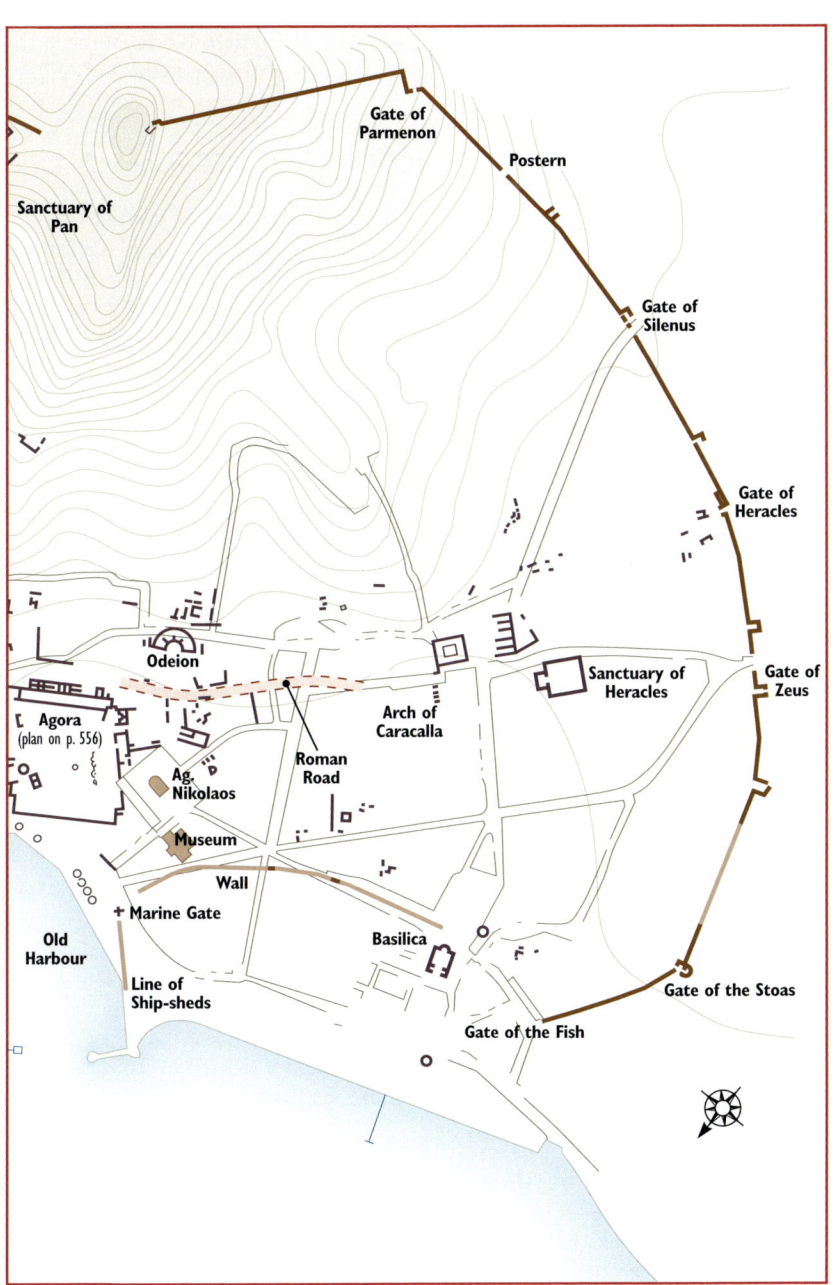

Gate of
Parmenon

Postern

Sanctuary of
Pan

Gate of
Silenus

Gate of
Heracles

Odeion

Sanctuary of
Heracles

Gate of
Zeus

Agora
(plan on p. 556)

Arch of
Caracalla

Ag.
Nikolaos

Roman
Road

Museum

Wall

Marine Gate

Old
Harbour

Basilica

Line of
Ship-sheds

Gate of the Stoas

Gate of the Fish

the 6th century BC at the base level of the southern and eastern blocks, through the smaller rectangular blocks of Hellenistic stonework on top of it, up to the 2nd-century AD alterations at the highest levels.

THE AREA OF THE SANCTUARY OF HERACLES

To the south of the modern town centre, at the southwestern end of the area that was covered by ancient Thasos, is a group of excavated sites clustered around the Sanctuary of Heracles. The cult of Heracles was of great antiquity and importance in Thasos; Herodotus says it was brought here by the Phoenicians. The sanctuary was a large, paved court surrounded by buildings on three sides and with the principal altar in the centre, facing east. The earliest temple remains are from the 6th century BC; but what is visible today dates from a 5th-century BC rebuilding on a much larger scale. The temple was at the far end from the modern entrance to the area (the northern extremity) on a raised platform. It was originally just a single-chambered naos, but at a later date it was embellished with a wide colonnade on all sides, giving it a form more square than oblong. To the west of it was the stepped and porched entrance to the temenos, probably from the 2nd century BC. It opened onto a paved court with the stepped altar in its centre and a long gallery hall forming the opposite border (by the current entrance). On the south side, opposite the temple and partially obliterated by the road, was a porticoed building containing administrative offices for the sanctuary and hestiatoria for the early summer feast of the Heracleia. It was here that the Spartan general Lysander, after defeating the Athenians at the battle of Aegospotamoi in 405 BC, deceived the Thasian allies of Athens with promises of pardon and then slaughtered them inside the sanctuary.

The Monument of Thersilochus and Arch of Caracalla

Across the road to the west, little now remains of a large and ambitious marble building, known from an inscription as the **Monument of Thersilochus**, a wealthy Thasian citizen of the 4th century who donated this structure to his city. It was a closed and roofed square hypostyle hall with a porticoed entrance on its north face. It was probably used for celebrations, banquets and meetings. Facing the entrance, less than 100m northeast of here, to the left-hand side of the road to the Odeion, are four ruined bases of an imperial Roman monumental arch of the late 2nd century AD, known as the **Arch of Caracalla** because of a later dedicatory inscription.

Across the road is the Dimarcheîon. The area behind it is used to store excavated material, constituting a fascinating collection of sarcophagi and other material of all periods and styles.

The Early Christian basilica

Outside the walls of the ancient city, but now at the heart of the modern town, in a small square two blocks in from the waterfront, are the remains of a sizeable early 6th-century Christian basilica. A considerable number of columns—mostly in local marble, but some of Thessalian green marble—occupy the area of the nave, most of which, together with the narthex, lies under buildings to the west. In the floor in front of the apse, two curious juxtaposed semicircular marble slabs with perforations for the fixture of upright elements are probably the base of the ambo. A little north of the apse foundations is an area of fine mosaic with abstract and running-vine motifs. It probably belonged to a 2nd-century AD house.

THE CIRCUIT OF THE WALLS

Evraiókastro and the Sanctuary of Demeter

The northernmost point of the town, beyond the boatyards, is a rocky promontory with remains of fortifications and the base of a **signalling tower** discernible on the northeast slope: its name, Evraiókastro ('Jewish Castle'), probably has nothing to do with Jews but is a corruption of 'Vryó-kastro' meaning simply 'Seaweed Castle'. On the slope opposite, the small, modern **Church of the Apostles** is built inside the remains of a 6th-century Christian basilica, which in turn is built over a pagan sanctuary, probably to Demeter and Kore. Remains include a 6th-century BC terrace wall, a portico and many Christian tombs. The construction of the basilica reused many spolia from earlier buildings.

Towards the theatre

The ancient **city walls** climb up from here towards the theatre, which lies about 300m further up the hill. At few other points are the walls as well preserved as here. They comprise two faces of cut masonry, the interior filled compactly with earth and stone, at an average thickness of about 2m. In places their architectural history is clear: at the lowest level there are huge, meticulously shaped and dressed blocks of the late 6th-century BC polygonal construction; above them horizontal rectangular blocks of the 5th-century isodomic masonry, in both marble and gneiss. It is worth recalling that the walls were partially dismantled on two occasions: first, as Herodotus recounts, at the order of Darius in 491 BC, and then again, as Thucydides reports, after the Athenian defeat in 463 BC. Subtle differences between various stretches of wall may be due to the individual techniques used by the teams of masons.

Thasos' ancient **theatre** is not particularly well-preserved; with its modern seating it lacks charm, except for the view towards the Macedonian mainland. Thasos had a strong tradition of drama: Aristotle considered the comic actor and writer Hegemon of Thasos to be the originator of comic parody. The earliest performances must have taken place elsewhere, as the theatre dates only from c. 300 BC. The permanent stage set, or proskenion, was like a portico of Doric columns surmounted by an architrave with decorated frieze (fragments in the museum). In the 2nd century AD the ring of orthostats in front of the first row of seats was added for the protection of the audience from the more violent Roman spectacles. Behind it can be seen holes for awning fixtures: a few of the seats still bear the inscribed names of the families who paid to have them reserved.

The site of the Sanctuary of Apollo

A stiff climb, following the line of the walls, leads up from the theatre towards the acropolis. Just before the summit, a right-angle turn in the wall can be seen on the left: here, **three types of construction** are visible all at once: the monumental Archaic masonry, the neatly-cut Classical work, and the irregular and heterogeneous medieval rubble above. Apart from its terracing, all that now remains of the Sanctuary of Pythian Apollo, his cult brought from Paros by the original colonisers, is its splendid site. It was demolished to provide material for the **medieval fortress** which now stands here, including a huge vaulted cistern, an apsidal church (both 15th century) and two towers. Its origins are Byzantine, of the mid-13th century, but additions were made by the Genoese in the 14th and 15th centuries. The southern tower contains dozens of meticulously cut ancient marble spolia, one of which is beautifully decorated with an unfinished **banquet scene from a tomb stele**. It can be located by descending the steps through the tower and passing through a narrow guard-room with stone benches within the thickness of the walls; after half a dozen steps from the exit, the relief is 5m ahead on the facing wall, below ground level and to the right.

The Sanctuary of Athena and the Cave of Pan

The path leads across the saddle, passing some rock-cut cisterns, to another eminence, a short distance to the southwest: as it rises to the top towards the Sanctuary of Athena Poliouchos ('protectress of the city'), it passes through the propylaion of the sanctuary at its northeast corner. This would have been a square, monumental staircase block, but little remains today. The extensive **artificial terracing** of the sanctuary (50m by 20m) is clearly visible as well as the **temple's stylobate**, composed of large polygonal blocks fixed to each other with bronze 'double-T' clamps. All the structures date from c. 500 BC. The temple but it had porches at either end bu no surrounding colonnade. Unusually, the altar (now just a heap of amorphous blocks) seems to have been in front of the temple's west front, not (as was normal) to the east. Just inside the north wall can be seen the remains of the stone platform of an earlier and smaller **Archaic temple to Athena**. On leaving from the southeast corner, a well-preserved section of the temple's lower rampart is visible below: the lower edge of a dislodged block near the corner, above and to the left, bears an ancient (?erotic) graffito of the 4th century BC, reading 'SKYMNOS KALOS' ('beautiful whelp'). The area offers panoramic views.

Facing you after 50m along the path is the 4th-century BC niche or **cave of Pan**, cut into an eyebrow-shaped declivity in the rock. The small relief is weathered, but a reclining Pan can be identified, playing his syrinx to a couple of goats in the apex of a shallow, carved pediment. Above this two more goats, standing on their hind legs, face each other over a kantharos. Further above again is another cut space, possibly for a votive sculpture.

Just to the south of the summit above are clear signs of surface marble-quarrying, while between here and the Sanctuary of Athena are over 200m of tunnels (*not visitable*) of an **ancient gold mine**, descending 150m below the surface, with two connected entrances.

The Gate of Parmenon

The descent from the summit is first by a precipitous rock-cut staircase which descends within what would have been a bastion of the walls. In this stretch the walls contain some blocks of remarkable size. After 80–100m, and shortly before some steps cut into the walls, a large rock to the left of the path and at right angles to the walls has, on its south face, two large eyes and a nose scratched on its surface, perhaps an **apotropaic carving**. Fifty metres further on, in a large block built into the wall to the right, and just above ground level, is the Archaic **signature of a marble worker**, contemporary with the building of the first phase of the walls and therefore dating from c. 500 BC. He carved his name, 'PARMENON', followed by a couple more letters, all deeply incised in a rising crescent. This precedes the **gate** which for convenience bears his name, complete with monolithic door posts and a massive lintel, the interior face of which bears the lateral and central cuts which held the barring mechanism. From here the line of the walls descends to the valley floor, past a postern gate, and enters the area of modern habitation.

The Gate of Silenus

None of the other gates of Thasos gives as rich a sense of the significance of an entrance through the walls of a city. The lintel is missing, as well as the wall and crenellations above; but the massive masonry, the delicate finish, the paved street, the proximity of the housing blocks and, above all, the relief of Silenus himself, create a unique ensemble. The image, carved c. 500 BC, occupies the full height of a single block of marble standing 2.5m high: it is one of the largest relief figures in Greek art. Silenus, sporting a long pony-tail and wearing nothing but leather boots, heads into the town, in a state of high sexual excitement, with a drinking vessel in his right hand. In front of him is a carved and pedimented niche for offerings. Wine was an important economic staple of the island, and Silenus' association with it must partially explain his prominence here, and on the city's coinage. His wider significance is as an associate of Dionysus, representing a form of subversive wisdom: laughter, creativity and the human need to seek physical and mental release from the sobriety of daily life.

The unusual characteristic of the residential area just inside the gate is that its buildings had to be raised on more than one occasion to avoid flooding caused by a rise in the water-table during antiquity: this is also true of the threshold of the gate. The layout of the streets and the buildings is well defined here. This was a popular area of shops, workshops and small houses.

The Gate of Heracles

NB: The path following the line of the walls at this point is not always passable due to dense vegetation. At such times the next gate is best reached by a detour, via the Sanctuary of Heracles, and then back out to the walls at the Gate of Zeus and Hera, from which the Gate of Heracles is more easily accessible.

At this point the walls are preserved to a considerable height. They run level along the floor of the plain and are therefore frequently enforced with projecting square bastions so as to increase the cover afforded to either side during an attack. The Gate of Heracles appears to have had a double dedication to Heracles and Dionysus. Reliefs depicting them were carved on either side of the gate entrance: that on the east side (now in the Istanbul Archaeological Museum) showed Heracles drawing a bow, that to the west (now lost) showed Dionysus and a procession of maenads.

The Gate of Zeus and Hera

Although not the best preserved, the Gate of Zeus and Hera shows the plan of its beautifully proportioned and constructed gate-tower particularly well. In the original construction of the walls, the gate was a simple aperture. It was adorned with two beautiful early 5th-century reliefs, of which one, the **relief of Hera enthroned**, holding a long sceptre in her left hand and resting her feet on a footstool while attended by Iris (her principal lady-in-waiting), remains *in situ*. Fragments of the pendant image of an enthroned Zeus are in the museum. The external tower was added at the end of the 4th century BC to protect and embellish the gate. Part of an **inscription** which bears the name of Pythippos, a 3rd-century BC benefactor who paid for extensions to the gate, can be seen on the left by the steps into the area. His elegant addition comprised pilasters to either side of the entrance and an architrave with triglyphs, bearing the inscription below, surmounted above by a broad Ionic colonnaded entablature below a pediment.

From here, the walls continued north to the waterfront and then turned east to the port. The city was thus entirely enclosed.

THE WESTERN OUTSKIRTS OF LIMENAS

In an area referred to both as Molos and as Tsoukalarió, 2km from the centre of Liménas just to the right (north) of the road out of the town at the point where it joins the Prínos road, are the remains of two **Early Christian basilicas**, built over the site of a Roman necropolis, from which a couple of sarcophagi still remain on the surface. Visible remains include an area of hypocaust, suggesting there may have been thermae here in Roman or Byzantine times. The smaller and older of the two basilicas (5th century) occupies the area closer to the sea on a southeast–northwest axis. As often happened, the complex was later enlarged, and a second, 6th-century basilica was built directly abutting (and partially covering) the first.

Across the ring-road from here and slightly to the east, 800m south of the road, are the interesting remains of the **Hellenistic farmstead** of Marmaromándra, Two buildings of the 4th century BC have been uncovered here: one was a two-storey dwelling built around a courtyard, the other probably a storehouse or barn. The remains of storage pithoi and a wine-press point to an agricultural use for these buildings.

THE EAST & SOUTH COASTS OF THE ISLAND

The road that leaves the centre of Liménas past the Gate of Silenus joins the ring-road that bypasses the city to the south. Just north of that junction (behind a service station) are the scant remains of another **Sanctuary of Demeter and Kore**. Beyond this point, the main road south rises swiftly to the forested watershed of a spur of **Mt Ypsárion** (1206m), the backbone of the island. There are several routes for climbing its five peaks, which afford magnificent panoramas towards Samothrace, Lemnos, Mt Athos, and into Thrace and Macedonia. Most convenient is the (signed) path which leaves from the north side of Potamiá village and reaches the summit in around 3hrs. Throughout the ages, fine-grained marble was quarried on the lower slopes by the sea.

The lighthouse of Akératos, Panaghía and Potamiá

A sequence of ancient lighthouses or signalling points punctuates the eastern seaboard of Thasos. The most impressive relic of this communication line is the late Archaic **Lighthouse of Akératos**, built c. 520 BC at the northeastern extremity of the Bay of Potamiá (*a spur of the headland descends southwards, and the tower is to be found there close to a small stand of pines, not far above the water. Take the road past the Hotel Dionysos from Chrysí Ammoudiá and follow the headland track to the point where it turns sharply up the northeast coast: a track to right leads a short distance from here through an olive grove and then finishes. At this point the tower is just visible below in the undergrowth. The last few hundred metres are without a path and are particularly hard going over rough terrain*). The tower is overgrown but stands to a height of about 2m: its drum has a diameter of 5m and is composed of carefully cut marble blocks. A dislodged block near the foot of the tower bears an inscription: 'I am the monument of Akeratos, son of Phrasierides. I am here at

The green forests of Thasos with the village of Potamiá.

the mouth of the harbour to alert and protect ships and sailors. Greetings.' Akératos was a ship-owner and prominent Thasian citizen who had remarkably been archon both in Thasos and in Paros. On the platform on top of the tower, a fire could be raised.

After the watershed (8km) the road swiftly descends to **Panaghía**, an attractive village set in the forested slopes of the mountain above the bay of Potamiá. In Potamiá Bay and north of Panaghía, at Chrysí Ammoudiá, there are good beaches. Panaghía was briefly capital of the island after 1838. The local style of Macedonian architecture is at its best here. The large 19th-century church of the Koímisis tis Theotókou reflects the relative prosperity of the village.

The main road south beyond Panaghía offers wide views of the sea and of Samothrace. After a little more than a kilometre is the village of **Potamiá**, birthplace of a Greek émigré sculptor, Polygnotos Vagis, who worked for nearly all of his life in America. The Polygnotos Vagis Museum was created in three rooms of the former village schoolhouse, in the south of the village beside the western end of the church (*open Tues–Sat 9.30–12.30 & 6–9, Sun 10–2; free*).

Koinyra

Beyond Potamiá, the main road south crosses the alluvial plain behind the bay of Potamiá and, after Skála, circles the foot of Mt Klisídi, a spur of the Ypsárion massif. It is this area, especially the southern slopes of the hill around **Palaiochóra**, which was mined for gold in antiquity. To Herodotus it seemed that the 'whole mountain had been turned upside down by the search for gold' (*VI, 47*). Many of the tunnels and shafts have been filled deliberately by local farmers and shepherds so as to prevent accidents to their animals. **Koinyra** (pron: *Kínira*) preserves its unusual, Phoenician name, supporting Herodotus' claim that it was the Phoenicians who first came here to exploit the gold deposits.

ALYKI

The fascinating site of Alykí on the south coast comprises a pagan sanctuary, two Early Christian basilicas and extensive marble quarries, in a coastal setting of great beauty.

One of the unusual characteristics of this site is the double nature of all its elements: two beaches mirroring each other on either side of the isthmus; two identical ancient, sacred buildings side by side; two similar Christian basilicas; two caves used for cult. The steep promontory attached by the isthmus is a small mountain of a pure white marble: the settlers from Paros who came to Thasos in the 7th century BC were skilled in exploiting marble, as Paros itself is a major source. They soon began to quarry this headland, establishing a working community on the isthmus itself, with its two opposite harbours (one of which was always protected from the wind), and founded a cult to their principal divinity, Apollo.

The two grottoes in the northwest corner of the promontory appear to be connected with that cult, from as early as the 7th century BC.

The pagan sanctuary

The two curious sacred buildings (by the shore at the southern end of the eastern bay) may not be connected to this cult of Apollo, as indicated by their plans, features and their pairing. The terracing of the area, its protection with a breakwater, and its first cult buildings date from the end of the 6th century BC, but the remains we see now date from a re-organisation of the site c. 470 BC. The two almost square buildings are of slightly different size but identical plan, side by side, each with a colonnaded west portico opening into two separate rooms behind: one larger room (?for ritual banqueting) with a central, stone-bordered hearth for a fire on the left, and one smaller (?treasury). The columns were fluted in the north building, but appear to have been left plain—or were still awaiting fluting—in the south building. The fine torso of an Archaic kouros (now in Istanbul) was excavated here. Our best clue to the nature of these buildings perhaps lies in the many votive inscriptions and graffiti carved on blocks and on the steps in front: these are mostly invocations of good fortune and safe-sailing for sailors and their ships (whose names are cited: the *Heracles*, the *Thessalian*, the *Artemis*, etc.): in one case, however, the ex-votos invoke the Two Saviours, or the Dioscuri (Castor and Pollux), the divine twins who protected mariners while at sea. It seems likely that the sanctuary was theirs.

The Early Christian basilicas

In the early Byzantine period, the pagan sanctuary was replaced by a centre of Christian cult further up the hill, which curiously was to develop similarly into twin, contiguous basilicas by the end of the 5th century AD. In an area that had been a cemetery in late antiquity, an elaborate three-aisled basilica was constructed c. 400–425. A small chapel of the same date, covering a martyrion, stood to its north, but was replaced at the end of the 5th century with a second basilica, also three-aisled, which incorporated the martyrion. Remains of a large atrium and narthex, as well as of a baptistery and funerary chapel, suggest that this was a centre of pilgrimage. In the west end of the south basilica is an ancient inscribed stele with a small image of Heracles resting from his labours.

The ancient marble quarries

The eastern border of the headland is, from the basilicas to the southern point, one huge ancient quarry of fine, white, crystalline marble. Alykí's marble is less compact than the dolomitic white sculptural marble quarried in the north of the island; it was used in building and for decoration.

It is worth persevering to the southern tip of the promontory, over mounds of marble debris, to observe where 200m of the headland have been cut away, shipped across the Greek world, above all to Rome. From shortly after 600 BC to after AD 600, a quantity approaching a quarter of a million cubic metres of marble was quarried here. The hill has been cut down to water-level, leaving a low barrier of rock at the southern tip to act as breakwater: around the perimeter, loading bays and moorings for barges are visible at certain points, as are carved slots for the fixing of winching machinery and pulleys. The surface of the whole area is covered with the striations of the pick and chisel and regular drill holes. Only a few column drums and bases have been left behind.

West of Alykí

A kilometre further west after Alykí, at Schídia, are the extensive ruined remains of a large **tower and ancient farm** to the left of the road. After a further 1.5km, a track leads 500m uphill to the largest of the preserved Hellenistic towers on the island, at **Thymoniá**. This is a construction of the 5th or 4th century BC. Its purpose may have been manifold: protection and supervision of the quarries; a signalling and look-out tower; and a garrison post for a small military detachment.

Further west, perched above the sheerest point of a cliff, is the **convent of the Archángelos**. There is a community of nuns here. It was originally founded in the 13th century as a dependency of the Philothéou Monastery on Mt Athos; the katholikon was rebuilt in 1834.

THE WEST & CENTRE OF THE ISLAND

Beyond Cape Pachýs, the island's northern extremity, the road runs southwest into an agricultural area which stretches for over 20km, with cultivations of olives and vines. On this side of the island, the older settlements of the last three centuries are built inland and uphill, to afford protection from pirate raids. The shoreline villages are more recent. This side of the island, especially the southwest, was the principal source of mineral ores other than gold: silver, iron, lead and minium (mercuric sulphide) were extracted in antiquity, and calamine (a carbonate of zinc) in the 19th century. The extensive forest fires of 1985 and 1989 badly affected this area and the south. At the time of writing, there were hints of slow recovery.

The traditional villages of the northwest

Roads lead from the coast to the traditional villages of **Rachóni**, **Prínos** and **Sotíras**. All three are well preserved and of exceptional beauty. The widest variety of traditional architecture, with its distinctive schist roofs and wooden balconies, is to be found at **Áno Prínos**, normally called Kasavíti. Above Sotíras is the spacious three-aisled, 14th-century church of the Análipsis; its wall-paintings mostly from the 16th century. The view of the sunset from here is unforgettable.

At **Skála Sotíras** on the coast, the remarkable remains of a fortified settlement from the Early Bronze Age have come to light. The site is awkwardly squashed underneath the modern church beside the road. Although viewing is limited by the situation, the walls, the bastions and the gates of an enceinte from the 3rd millennium BC can be seen, perhaps the fortified residence of a chief. Most remarkable are a number of life-size anthropomorphic stelae, carved in shallow relief, representing warriors or hunters, found in the walls, as well as several stylised heads.

The Mariés area

A long valley leads inland from the fishing port of Mariés Skála towards the 18th-century village of **Mariés**. After 5km, the remains of **Palaiókastro**, a fortified Byzantine settlement, are visible to the right of the road. Almost a kilometre to the other side of the road is the largely modern monastery of the Panaghoudiá or Koímisis tis Theotókou, with good 17th-century wall paintings in the katholikon.

Two kilometres south of Mariés Skála, just above the shore, are the remains of an **Archaic ceramic workshop**, probably one of many on the island. Its importance is considerable, both because of its antiquity (it was in use from the late 6th–3rd centuries BC), and for the information it provides about the processes of ceramic production. At the northern edge of the excavation, the circular base, in large blocks, of one of the kilns can be seen; at its centre is the support for the shelf on which the pots were stacked for firing. This would have been covered with a brick dome. In the southeast corner (shore side) are the decantation tanks for the washing of the clay.

Limenária and Kástro

Limenária and Potós are the principal tourist centres of the west of the island, profiting from good beaches. The southern tip of the island beyond Potós was an important area of wine production in antiquity. Thasian wines were considered among the best. At Vamvoúri Ammoudiá to the west, and at Koúkos to the east of Cape Salonikiós, workshops making wine amphorae have been excavated; at **Kamnarokaïko**, 2km south of Potós, on a rise north of the road, are the remains of a large fortified Hellenistic farmstead.

Inland to the north of Limenária is the picturesque village of **Kalývia**. Its church has some ancient funerary reliefs built into its walls.

From Limenária an arduous 11-km track through spectacular scenery climbs up to a medieval settlement, at an altitude of 550m—almost at the centre of the island—known simply as **Kástro** and mentioned by the 15th-century traveller and antiquarian, Cyriac of Ancona, under the name of Neokastro. It is extraordinarily well-hidden, coming into view only at the last moment; but it commands an almost 360-degree panorama from its exposed plateau of barren rock. The exposed village straggles along a ridge to the point of the spur, where the church of the Profítis Ilías crowns the summit. Below, an ossuary and the tiny chapel of Ághios Geórgios cling to the side of the slope. These are all built on the site of an enclosed 15th-century stronghold, its walls still visible. This was built by Uberto Grimaldi—scion of the same Genoese family as the Princes of Monaco; he was commander here on behalf of another Genoese family, the Gattilusi, overlords of Lesbos and Samothrace. This remote place was his fortress. All this is suggested by a marble plaque, immured upside down in the exterior south wall of the church of Ághios Athanásios, in the centre of the village, bearing an inscription and three escutcheons: that of the Gattilusi in the centre flanked by the Grimaldi to either side. The plaque mystifyingly gives the date of completion of the castle as 1534, i.e. a hundred years later than the Grimaldi/Gattilusi presence here, possibly an error by the carver.

Kastrí and Theológos

After Potós, a Bronze Age and Geometric settlement called **Kastrí** is reached by a 4.5-

4.5-km path from a turning (signed) to the left (west) just before entering Theológos. The delightful village of **Theológos** itself, capital of the island until 1838, lacks a discernible centre, but the main street passes a number of fine buildings and Ottoman mansions. One of these, the 18th-century Hadjigeorgiou Mansion towards the end of the village, belonged to a prominent partisan of the Independence uprising of 1821. It has recently become an informal museum (*open 11–7*). Muhammad Ali, future sovereign of Egypt, lived in this house as a young man. Two large churches, Aghía Paraskeví and Ághios Dimítrios, both 16th-century, restored in the early 19th century, lie below the street to the southeast. Just opposite the first, a Hellenistic relief of a rider is incorporated into the schoolhouse façade.

PRACTICAL INFORMATION

GETTING AROUND

There are ferries from two harbours close to Kavála, Néa Péramos to the west and Keramotí to the east, and, slightly less frequently, from the port of Kavála itself. Only the ferry from Keramotí serves Thasos Town/Liménas (1hr), with departures approximately every 90mins; there are 6 ferry services (90mins), and 3 hydrofoil services (35mins) daily from Kavála to Prínos Skála. All the above are operated by ANETH (T: 25930 24001/2). The service from Néa Péramos to Prínos Skála, is hourly (75mins). Kavála airport is served by several daily flights from Athens.

WHERE TO STAY

Thasos has no luxury accommodation, but does not lack simple places of charm, such as the **Acropolis Hotel** in Liménas, privately run with genuine hospitality (*T: 25930 22488, www.acropolis-hotel.com*).

At Panaghía is the **Thassos Inn**, in a traditional-style building (*T: 25930 61612*); below, at Chrysí Ammoudiá, is the **Hotel Dionysos** (*T: 25930 61822; dionyso1@otenet.gr*), an unpretentious and comfortable hotel just above the beaches of Potamiá Bay. All of the above are characterful and of good value, in the medium price range.

WHERE TO EAT

The *plateía* of Kasavíti (Áno Prínos) is very picturesque: the family-run **Taverna Vassilis** takes great care with both food and setting.

At Theológos, both **Kleoniki** and **Stelios** serve a variety of good dishes prepared with locally-raised meats. Nowhere especially recommends itself in Liménas, but the **Taverna Platanaki** beside the old harbour provides a pleasant setting and a good selection of fish dishes.

FURTHER READING

Yves Grandjean & François Salviat, *Guide de Thasos* (Paris/Athens 2000), an excellent archaeological guide.

THE SPORADES

Looking at a map of the Aegean, the name Sporades, meaning 'scattered', may appear something of a misnomer, as the set of islands extending to the east of central Greece is not noticeably less coherent than any other Greek island group. In antiquity, the term was used for all the Aegean islands outside the Cyclades; the archipelago currently known by the name was formerly described as the 'Thessalian' or 'Northern' Sporades.

The Sporades include over 20 islands, but only five are inhabited. The largest is Skyros, located in an isolated position just east of Euboea, while the bulk of the group,

Skiáthos, Skópelos and Alónnisos, followed by the Lesser Sporades, stretches north-eastwards in a more or less straight line from a point between Euboea and the Pelion peninsula. They are reached by ferries from Kými on Euboea, and from the ports of Vólos and Ághios Konstantínos on the adjacent coast of Thessaly.

Settlement in the islands goes back to c. 10,000 BC. There is also evidence for Neolithic and Bronze Age occupation. In historical times, the Sporades share a fairly similar history, being associated in turn with Euboea, Athens, Macedon and later, Rome. In the late Middle Ages, they passed from Byzantine to Venetian control. After their 17th-century conquest by the Ottomans, they enjoyed tax privileges that allowed for considerable prosperity. Skyros became part of newly-liberated Greece in 1821; the rest of the group followed in 1830.

Never having played a leading role in history, the islands are not adorned with famous monuments. Their most striking feature are their *choras*, or island capitals, reflecting the area's considerable wealth in the late 18th and 19th centuries, with grand *archontiká* (mansions). But there are numerous further points of beauty and interest to be discovered. Memorable sights on Skyros include the archaeological museum, as well as the grave of the English war poet, Rupert Brooke, who found his 'corner of a foreign field' here in 1915. On Skiáthos, the Kastro is a particularly fine example of a medieval citadel, while the beautifully-painted 15th-century Panaghía Kounístra is one of many interesting churches and monasteries in the islands. On Skópelos, the mysterious rock-cut graves at Sendoúkia command a view of the entire group and the mainland. The Cyclops Cave on Gioúra, near Alónnisos, is one of the most ancient settlement sites known in the Aegean.

A major attraction of the Sporades is their rich flora and fauna. Skyros is home to a unique type of feral horse, while the waters of Alónnisos and the Lesser Sporades form a National Marine Park, developed to protect the remaining habitats of the Mediterranean monk seal.

Although Skiáthos and Skópelos receive larger numbers of visitors than Skyros and Alónnisos, the group as a whole remains relatively untouched by true mass tourism. As a result, the islands preserve a distinctive intimacy and a strong sense of local identity, both as a group and individually. This is as true of architecture and folk tradition as it is of landscape and environment, which includes some of the loneliest beaches in the Aegean. The islands' overall character combines aspects of nearby Pelion, famous for its wealth and beauty, and of the Northern Cyclades. Traditional products include a variety of cheeses and unusual fish dishes. In Greece, the Sporades are increasingly perceived as a desirable destination for high-quality, low-density tourism.   H.H.

SKIATHOS

The fame of its pinewoods and magnificent sandy beaches draws many summer visitors to Skiáthos. The north of the island remains virtually untouched, however, its woods and bays preserving their peaceful beauty.

HISTORY OF SKIATHOS

According to tradition, the first settlers were from Caria, followed later by Thessalians. In the 7th century BC, colonists from Chalcis in Euboea arrived and later founded 'Palaiskiathos' in the island's northeast. In Classical times, a second city near modern Skiáthos Town succeeded it. Skiáthos played its part in the Second Persian War, providing Greek support at a geographically strategic point by relaying information signals. Skiáthos joined the Delian League after the war, becoming a subject ally of Athens. After the Battle of Chaironeia in 338 BC, the island passed under Macedonian rule, and was later devastated by Philip V of Macedon in 220 BC. Freed by Rome in 197 BC, it was bequeathed to Athens by Mark Antony in 42 BC.

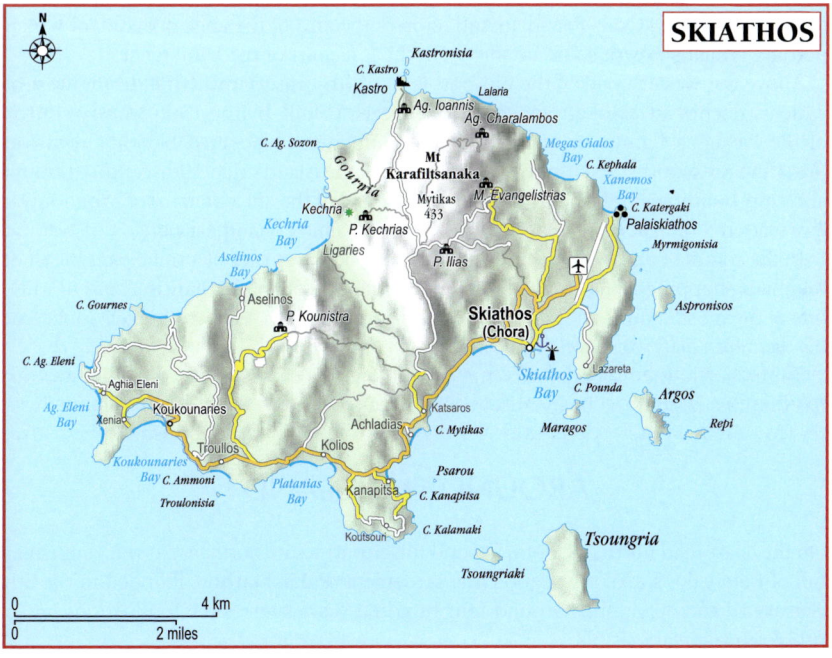

Byzantine Skiáthos belonged to the theme of Macedonia. In 1204, the Sporades came under the possession of the Ghisi family, only to be retaken by Byzantium in 1276. After the fall of Constantinople in 1453, the island was ruled by Venice, until it was captured for the Turks by Kheir ed-Din Barbarossa in 1538. Subsequently, the island was virtually deserted. Settlement returned to Kastro in the 17th century, moving to the modern capital after 1829. The island became part of the newly formed Greek state in 1830. Skiáthos was the home of the novelists Alexandros Papadiamantis and Alexandros Moraitidis in the late 19th and early 20th centuries.

During the Second World War, Skiáthos was a crucial place of refuge for retreating Allied troops (mostly New Zealanders) cut off by the German advance. Later the town was torched by retreating German troops.

SKIATHOS CHORA

The bay of Skiáthos Chora is divided into two by a promontory, with a modern ferry-port to the north and the old fishing harbour to the south. The promontory itself, the Bourtzi, was the site of a 13th-century castle, now replaced with a Neoclassical school house, used as a cultural centre.

The Chora spreads over two hills: the northern one crowned by the church of Ághios Nikólaos and a windmill; the southern occupying the site of the ancient acropolis. The town's main street, Odós Papadiamánti, crosses the area of the ancient agorá, of which nothing remains except some fragments in the forecourt of the Dimarcheíon.

Above the western end of the old port is the 19th-century cathedral, to the west of which stretches a web of attractive narrow streets. Uphill, by the 19th-century church of the Panaghía Limniá, is an impressive example of a balconied Skiáthos mansion (awaiting restoration), exemplifying the homes of the island's rich 19th-century trading and ship-building families. Further north is the hill of the ancient acropolis, but only a few scattered remains can be seen near a modern cemetery and car park.

In the centre of the town, behind the new port, on the corner of a small *plateía* east of the main shopping street, is the **house of Alexandros Papadiamantis** (1851–1911), one of the most famous Greek writers of his time, preserved as it would have looked in his day (*open daily except Mon, 9.30–1 & 5–8*).

To the north, the harbour ends in a lagoon, once a centre of boat-building. Activity has diminished, but the boatyards are well worth a visit.

AROUND THE ISLAND

On the coast road north of Chora, beyond the airport to the northeast, is the peninsular hill of Katergáki, site of the island's first settlement, **Palaiskiathos**, founded in the 8th century BC and abandoned around four hundred years later. Some foundations and a rubble enceinte are visible.

The Evangelístria monastery

Inland to the north is the peaceful **Moní Evangelístrias** (*open 8–12 & 4–8*), whose dignified 18th-century buildings surround a courtyard dominated by the 16th-century katholikon, with some 18th-century wall-paintings inside. The monastery was momentarily at the centre of Greek history in 1807, when a Greek flag (then just a white cross on blue background) was made and raised here for the first time in the presence of Theodoros Kolokotronis and Andreas Miaoulis.

A path beyond the monastery leads (*45mins; also reached by the unmade road below*) to the isolated **hermitage of Ághios Charálambos** on the slopes of Mt Karafiltsanáka, to which the novelist Alexandros Moraitidis (1850–1929), a relative and almost exact contemporary of Papadiamantis, retired shortly before his death.

Half a kilometre before the end of the asphalt road at the Evangelístria monastery, an unmade road leads off to the west by the church of the Zoödóchos Pigí. Following this, after 2km, there is a spring beneath large plane trees near the church of **Profítis Ilías**, and a taverna with panoramic views of the south of the island.

Some churches on the way to Kastro

At a junction 300m beyond Profítis Ilías (*see above*) there are two consecutive right turns: the first is for Ághios Charálambos; the second, just beyond, leads to Kastro (*described below*). This road descends and after 700m the first left branch leads to the valley of Kechriá and the 18th-century church of the **Panaghía Kechriás**, once the katholikon of a monastery whose buildings have since perished. It is decorated with late Byzantine paintings. The track soon ends and a footpath leads down beyond to the tranquil bays and beaches of Kechriá and Ligariés.

Returning to the original road, a second left branch after 1.8km leads west into the Gourniá area. A short way down it, on the right amidst some trees, is the church of **Aghía Anastasía**; beside it is the circular base of a Hellenistic watchtower. Continuing north, past the church of the Koímisis, the road ends above the promontory of Kastro. In the trees to the right is the church of **Ághios Ioánnis**: just to its west is a long, low ossuary (possibly once a fountain-head). The decorative marble plaque on its front, with a fount-of-life motif, gives no intimation that the interior is heaped with skulls and bones.

KASTRO

Kastro is one of the clearest examples in Greece of a medieval acropolis. Possibly settled in antiquity (rock cuttings by the western shore), it became the site of a Genoese fortress in the 13th century, and was the island's only major settlement. Though the location is remote and waterless, it offered safety, especially from pirates. After Kheir ed-Din Barbarossa conquered it in 1538, it was temporarily abandoned. Its final abandonment was in the 19th century.

The site

The gate, which had a drawbridge, incorporates ancient spolia in the lintels. The enceinte is visible, especially along the west side. The promontory was only the fortress of the large town; the settlement itself stretched along the bay eastwards and uphill to the south. Inside the citadel, a large cistern and fountain are on the left. All but one of the houses have gone, but the churches remain. All but one are of simple design with pitched roofs. The single exception has a dome over a square plan. It was used as a mosque during the years of Turkish occupation. The early 16th-century church of Christós sto Kastro, in the dip of the saddle, has 18th-century wall-paintings of the life of Christ and an iconostasis of the same date.

SOUTH OF CHORA

To the south of Chora, the coast road runs through modern development, but tracks lead into the forested valleys of the interior. Before Troúllos a road heads north for the bay of Asélinos and the beautiful **convent of the Panaghía Kounístra** (*open 8.30–12.30 & 4–7.30*). Its 15th-century katholikon has interesting wall-paintings, with the saints' halos not painted but made of sheets of a silver/tin alloy. The 17th-century iconostasis displays two icons: the *Presentation of the Virgin* and *Christ Enthroned*. The convent has one resident nun. The **beach of Koukounariés**, beyond Troúllos, is rightly famous. **Aghía Eléni beach**, 1km further, is less frequented.

PRACTICAL INFORMATION

GETTING AROUND

Skiáthos is reached by several daily ferries and hydrofoils from Vólos on the mainland. There are less frequent connections (5 times weekly) to Ághios Kostantínos and to Kými. All boats also go to Skópelos and Alónnisos. The airport, 2km from Chora, is served by daily flights from Athens.

WHERE TO STAY

There is a huge choice of hotels. Elegant designer luxury can be had at the **Aegean Suites Hotel**, 1km west of Chora at Megáli Ámmos (*T: 24270 24069; www.aegeansuites. com*); alternatively, good-value accommodation can be found on the seafront at the **Hotel**

Meltemi (*T: 24270 22493*). On the peninsula of Poúnda, east of town but less than 2km from the centre, is the **Hotel Emy** (*T: 24270 24119*), in the peace and quiet of its own garden.

WHERE TO EAT

Taverna Alexandros, away from the seafront on Odós Kapodístria, has good-quality traditional food.

FURTHER READING

Selected stories by Alexandros Papadiamantis are available in English translation, including his most famous work, *The Murderess*, translated by Peter Levi.

SKOPELOS

Skópelos lies beside what was a major shipping lane in prehistory and antiquity. To-day it is remotely situated and has preserved its charms remarkably well. It seems to have found a way to maintain the busy normality of its *chora*, sustain a limited amount of tourism, and preserve large areas of mountainous forest and coastline. Skópelos has the greatest depth of character of all the Sporades, with a richness of architecture and a clear identity coupled with self-sufficiency, economic importance and commercial vitality. Its attractive main town is home to many churches.

HISTORY OF SKOPELOS

The shaft-grave at Stáfilos is clear evidence of important 17th-century BC activity. Its rich finds give some credence to the legend that the island's first notable ruler was Staphylos, son of Ariadne. His brother was Peparethos, the name of the city and island of Skópelos throughout antiquity. Since *stafili* (σταφίλι) is Greek for a grape bunch, and Peparethos may be cognate with the verb meaning 'to ripen', they may simply embody the mythical explanation of the island's fame as a producer of a highly-prized wine. In historical times, much of the island's history is identical to that of Skiáthos: the city of Peparethos (modern Skópelos Chora) was founded in the 7th century BC by colonists from Chalcis in Euboea, along with two other cities on the island, Pánormos and Selinous (modern-day Loutráki). Skópelos joined the Delian League, paying a substantial tribute, indicative of its prosperity, based on the export of wine. In 427 BC Peparethos was damaged by earthquakes and tidal waves. After the Battle of Chaironeia in 338 BC, the island passed under Macedonian rule. It was freed by Rome in 197 BC but in 42 BC, after the Battle of Philippi, was presented by Mark Antony to Athens.

Christianity came to the island most notably in the person of the bishop-saint Reginus, who was martyred under Julian the Apostate in AD 362 or 363. In the 6th century the island's name emerges as Schepola in Byzantine chronicles. Together with Skiáthos, it belonged to the Byzantine theme of Macedonia. In 1204, after the Fourth Crusade, it fell to the Ghisi family, who were driven out in 1276 by the Byzantine fleet. After the fall of Constantinople, it was governed by the Venetians until its capture for the Turks by Kheir ed-Din Barbarossa in 1538, which left the island devastated and depopulated. Under Turkish control, however, the islanders enjoyed some privileges and freedoms. During the 1820s Skópelos accepted refugees from Thessaly and Macedonia, and in the 1920s from Asia Minor. The island became part of the new Greek state in 1830.

SKOPELOS CHORA

From the sea, the ascending, theatre-like *chora* of Skópelos (*map p. 580, C2*) is a memo-

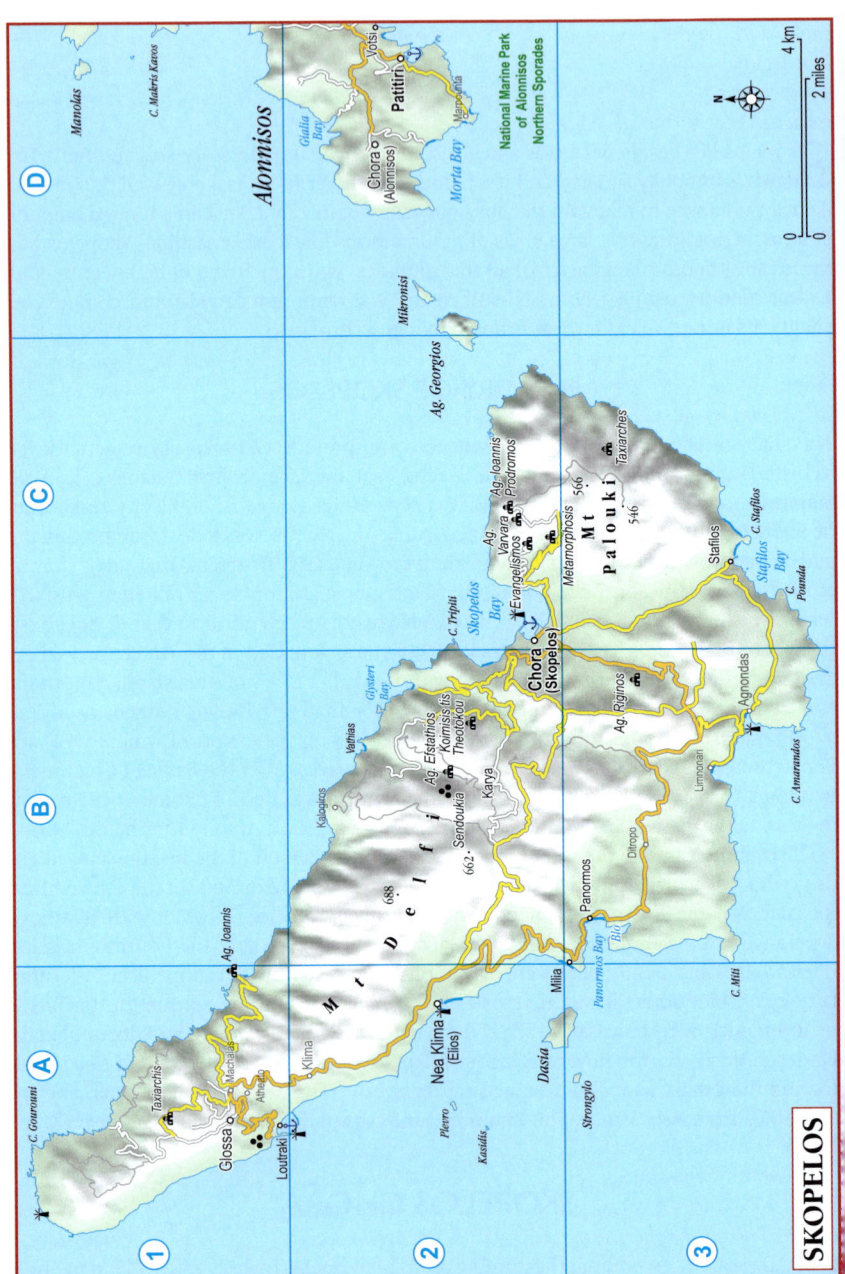

SKOPELOS

rable sight, with its distinctive traditional architecture, the roofscape constantly broken by the towers and cupolas of its five dozen churches. The town is best explored by ascending from the north end of the promenade, returning eventually to the Dimarcheíon at the centre of the waterfront.

The ascent to the castle

Above the northern end of the seafront promenade is the 15th-century Panaghía tou Pýrgou (the narthex and bell-tower are 19th-century). Immediately seaward of it stands the tiny chapel of **Ághii Pándes**, with rare tile-work in the wall of its eastern apse. Above these two churches, to the left of the path, is **Ághios Nikólaos**, another small church of domed inscribed-cross plan; part of an ancient column is displayed on the exterior of the east end. Further up along the edge of the hill is the 15th-century church of the **Evangelismós**, entered through an enclosed courtyard to the south. Its screen has beautiful 16th- and 17th-century icons. The characteristic 'fish-scale' schist roof and the pleasing octagonal drum are best appreciated from the stairs behind. They lead up to a higher level and the 11th-century church of **Ághios Athanásios tou Kástrou**. Its wall-paintings are of the 16th century, its carved iconostasis is 200 years later. Not far above is the summit with a small 13th-century **Genoese castle** (it may originally have extended to the north and west). By the steps at the rear (west), large masonry blocks of the 5th-century BC walls of the **acropolis of ancient Peparethos** are visible in the foundations. Other vestiges of ancient walls can be glimpsed higher up the hill to the west and northwest: here were the terraces on which temples of Athena and Dionysus stood.

The churches of Chora

A narrow street descends from south of the castle round the hill, leading to the two churches of Ághios Antónios (right) and the domed **Ághios Geórgios** (left), of the 11th or 12th century. The interior has a beautiful pebble floor and wall-paintings. Further along the same street, on the opposite side through a gated courtyard, is another remarkable church, dedicated to the **Panaghía** (Zoödóchos Pigí) and with fine frescoes, including a *Virgin and Child*.

Near Ághios Geórgios and Ághios Antónios, steps lead down to the unusual church of the **Génnisis tou Christoú** (Nativity of Christ). Its core is from the late 15th century, but a broad parallel nave, or parecclesion, was added on the north in the 19th century, along with an arcade to the south. The interior is dominated by eight columns: two monolithic ones with early Byzantine capitals, two with undecorated capitals, and four extraordinary columns composed of drums.

Nearby are several smaller churches of varying dates and shapes, some with paintings and carved iconostases.

Downhill from the Christoú, by a small terrace, is the 11th-century church of the **Ághii Apóstoli**, similar to Ághios Athanásios and with 17th-century wall-paintings of saints. The plain exterior of the east end, facing the harbour, is relieved by the inclusion of five identical 16th-century Iznik tiles.

Down an alleyway from the south corner of the terrace beside the church, then 100m to the left, is one of the most remarkable churches in Chora, **Ághios Michaïl**, its exterior a veritable museum of ancient spolia, sarcophagi, column sections and inscriptions. Many of the fragments can be identified as having been carved at Assos in Asia Minor.

The Panaghía Pap ameletíou and Folklore Museum

The large church of the **Panaghía Papameletíou**, recognisable by its high octagonal drum with double rows of arches above the window-lights in the cupola, lies in the upper central area of town. It was built in the 1670s; inside there is remarkable wood carving in the iconostasis and the throne. To its north are many substantial and prosperous houses with characteristic wooden balconies.

The **Folklore Museum** (*open daily 10–1*), in the centre of town, northwest of Plateía Plátanos, illustrates the island's customs, including striking traditional garments.

THE SOUTH & EAST OF THE ISLAND

A group of five monasteries is located on the panoramic and scenic slopes of Mt Paloúki, the eastern extremity of the island.

The **monastery of the Evangelismós** (*map p. 580, C2; open daily 8–1 & 4–8*) is a 17th-century building on the site of an older foundation, with views over the bay of Chora. It now has three resident nuns. The outside of the cupola drum of the katholikon is studded with Ottoman ceramic plates; its door has elaborate carved lintels. The most unusual element of the interior is the polychrome tile floor. The kitchen on the north side has a fine large bread oven.

Across the valley is the **monastery of the Metamorphosis** (*open daily 8–1.30 & 5.30–8*), founded about 1500. The katholikon contains a beautiful, carved 17th-century iconostasis. Beyond the Metamorphosis, the road reaches a plateau containing the mid-17th-century fortress-like **Aghía Varvára**, its katholikon with three curious apses, and beyond it again, the nunnery of **Ághios Ioánnis Pródromos** (*open daily 8–1 & 5–8*). It was founded as a monastery in 1612 and later enlarged and restored. It became a nunnery in 1920, and has three resident nuns today. In the katholikon, the painted iconostasis with beautifully carved animals and an icon of St John the Baptist are worthy of note.

Beyond Ághios Ioánnis, a track with fine views of Alónnisos continues for a further 2km, passing a junction which leads down to the modern chapel of Aghía Triáda and then coming to a point where a path leads steeply downhill to the east (left) towards the church of Aghía Ánna. It then branches right for the tiny monastery or hermitage of the **Taxiárches** (*30mins south from the beginning of the path*). It is built beside the entrance of a cave-like gap in the hillside, by two springs.

Stáfilos and Ághios Rigínos

South of Chora is the fertile valley of Stáfilos. Beyond Stáfilos Bay to the east (*map p. 580, C3*), by a conspicuous headland, a Middle Bronze Age **shaft-grave** (c. 1500 BC) complete with rich Mycenaean burial gifts was uncovered in 1936. There are good beaches around the bay.

Also south of Chora, on another road, is the monastery of Ághios Rigínos (*map p. 580, B3*). The church is 18th century, but numerous Early Christian columns in the forecourt indicate a much earlier predecessor. A first church here may have been built shortly after Reginus' 4th-century martyrdom. Cut into one of the columns beside the steps in the forecourt is a curious version of the sacred acronym 'ΙΧΘΥΣ', in which the five letters are compressed and joined into a monogram.

North of Ághios Rigínos, you come to the outskirts of Chora, where the massive, buttressed façade of the ruined Episkopí monastery looms above the road (*normally closed, except by arrangement with the owners*). Once the residence of a bishop, it is now privately owned. The present 17th-century single-aisled church of the Panaghía inside the walls is built on the site of the northern aisle of a much larger three-aisled Early Christian basilica of the 5th or 6th century.

THE NORTH OF THE ISLAND

From the northern extremity of the ring-road around Chora, a narrow road leads north and west into the island's interior towards its highest peak, Mt Délfi, and its densest woods, the Váthia Forest (*follow signs for Sendoúkia and for the monasteries*). After 1km the road reaches a valley with the monastery of the Koímisis tis Theotókou. At its western head, a track leads off the asphalt road to the west towards Mt Délfi, climbing through dense pinewoods, past springs at Karyá; 600m after the springs, a right-hand fork leads down to the extensive complex of the **monastery of Ághios Efstáthios** (7km), a well-preserved foundation of 1596.

Sendoúkia

From the junction for Ághios Efstáthios, the road climbs on towards the summit. At a fork in the tracks (6.5 km), the path to Sendoúkia (meaning 'boxes' or 'chests'; *map p. 580, B2*) is signed to the right and thereafter marked by small stone cairns. It leads to the northern tip of a long limestone outcrop, ending in a sudden drop to the east (magnificent views). Just by the edge are four empty graves: three deep and precisely carved loculi with solid stone roofs with a highly pitched profile, and one shallower rectangle, probably an unfinished grave. All are orientated due east and each has a shallow 'ledge' at the western end; the rims are carefully cut to fit the lids. Dates as various as the Neolithic and the Early Christian have been suggested for the graves. They may be part of a larger monumental or cult area: on the eminence above them (100m due west), a conical limestone mound might represent an altar or shrine.

Pánormos, Glóssa and around Cape Gouroúni

The west coast is characterised by azure bays, pinewoods descending to the shore, and a sparseness of settlement. In a coastal valley beside a bay, ancient **Pánormos** (*map* *p. 580, B3*) was founded by colonists from Chalcis in the 7th century BC. The settlement was clustered around an acropolis on the rise about halfway along the shoreline. Stretches of Classical walling can be seen on the north slope, just above the Panormos Beach Hotel. The hidden inlet of Blo in the south was the site of the city's harbour.

North of Pánormos, past Miliá (with a good beach), the road passes Élios or **Néa Klíma**, created in the 1970s after the 1965 earthquake devastated the village of Klíma, a small traditional settlement of balconied stone houses with panoramic views. **Glóssa** (*map p. 580, A1*), with similar architecture, sits just above the rise occupied by the acropolis of ancient Selinous—a third, Chalcidian colony of the 7th century BC. Remains of the ancient city's walls are clearly visible before reaching Loutráki (27.5 km).

The scant visible remains of **ancient Selinous**, spread around Loutráki, are mostly of Roman date. At the southeastern end of the shore are the badly eroded ruins of 3rd-century AD Roman baths, including areas of pebble mosaic and hypocausts. Inland from the port are the remains of an arched stoa from the town's agorá, the upper part of which carried an aqueduct. There are fragments of early Byzantine architectural sculpture in the forecourt of the church of Ághios Nikólaos beside the harbour.

On the road to the northern extremity of the island is the deserted **monastery of the Taxiárchis**, with a 17th-century katholikon and Byzantine columns from a 7th-century church. An archaeological survey of **Cape Gouroúni** (*map p. 580, A1*) has revealed that the 19th-century lighthouse is only the latest in a long tradition of lookout posts: there was a network of fortified agricultural buildings and towers as early as the 4th century BC. The chapel of Ághios Ioánnis (*map p. 580, A1*) features in the film *Mamma Mia*.

PRACTICAL INFORMATION

GETTING AROUND

Skópelos is reached by ferry (4–5hrs) and hydrofoil (approx. 2hrs) from Vólos, from which there are daily services both to Glóssa, and to the main port: there are also less frequent connections from Ághios Konstantínos (4–5hrs), and Kými on Euboea. Skópelos is only 70mins by ferry or 45mins by hydrofoil from Skiáthos, where the nearest airport is.

WHERE TO STAY

Skópelos Chora offers a good choice of accommodation in all price ranges, from rent rooms such as **Thea Home Studios**, at the top of the ring-road west of the port (*T: 24240 22859*), to the luxurious **Hotel Prince Stafilos** (*www.prince-stafilos.gr, T: 24240 22775 or 22744*). Studios are also available in some of the villages.

WHERE TO EAT

The most creative taverna on Skópleos is **Agnanti** at Glóssa. Simpler homemade dishes and fresh wine can be found at the garden taverna **Terpsis**, just outside Stáfilos on the road to Chora.

ALONNISOS & THE
LESSER SPORADES

Fragrant with pine and wild oregano, Alónnisos (*map pp. 573 and 580*) and its smaller neighbours are distinguished by their varied topography and vegetation, which form a marine landscape of exceptional beauty and intimacy. A fruitful equilibrium between the natural protection afforded by an island and the ease of communication and commerce by sea attracted human settlers here in prehistory.

Along with the islets to the north and east, Alónnisos has been designated the largest marine conservation area in Europe, with the particular aim of protecting the monk seal. The Northern Sporades Marine Park aims to create an alternative kind of tourism based on respect for, and interest in, the environment. Walkers, snorkellers and sailors frequent Alónnisos in large numbers during the summer, most of them staying either in the busy port of Patitíri or in the more tranquil hilltop Chora.

HISTORY OF ALONNISOS

Some of the earliest evidence of human presence in the Aegean, from c. 10,000 BC, has been unearthed in the Cave of the Cyclops on Gioúra, northeast of Alónnisos. Neolithic settlements exist around the bay of Ághios Pétros on Kyrá Panaghiá and at Kokkinókastro on Alónnisos. The island was later settled by Carians and Dolopians. Alónnisos, called Ikos throughout Classical antiquity, was, like Skiáthos and Skópelos, a 7th-century BC colony of Chalcis on Euboea. Allies of Athens in the Peloponnesian War, the Sporades were subsequently occupied by Sparta. Ikos regained independence and was a member of the Second Athenian League until its dissolution in 346 BC. After the battle of Chaironeia in 338 BC, the Sporades came under Macedonian supremacy. Ikos, along with Skiáthos and Skópelos, was devastated by Philip V of Macedon in 220 BC in his attempt to thwart the Romans, who became masters of the region after 146. Mark Antony later ceded the islands to Athens in gratitude for the city's military support.

Christianity reached Alónnisos in the 4th century. The island was sorely affected by the Slav and Arab incursions into the Aegean during the 7th and 8th centuries. In 1204, after the Fourth Crusade, along with the other Sporades, Alónnisos, now called Chelidromia, came under Venetian rule. From 1276 until 1453, the island reverted to Byzantine control. After the fall of Constantinople, it was governed by the Venetian Republic, except for a decade of Turkish occupation between 1475 and 1486, until it was finally captured for the Turks by the corsair Kheir ed-Din Barbarossa in 1583. During the following centuries, the outer Sporades suffered from piracy but enjoyed tax privileges bestowed by Osman III in 1756. In 1821, during the Greek War of Independence, a free Dimos Alonnísou, under the jurisdiction of the new Greek administration of the Sporades, was declared. The island was officially ceded to Greece in 1830. In 1965 it was severely damaged by earthquake. The National Marine Park of Alónnisos–Northern Sporades was established in 1992.

CHORA & PATITIRI

In March 1965 an earthquake damaged over 80 percent of the buildings on Alónnisos. As a result, **Chora**, the picturesque hilltop capital, was abandoned and its population moved to Patitíri. Much of the old settlement, its setting one of the finest in the Sporades, has been sensitively restored as a summer retreat for visitors. The short distance to Chora from the port can be covered on foot along an old mule-path (*30mins*).

The main part of the settlement is preceded by a charming *plateía*, across which to the left is the main church, Christoú (late 17th-century), dedicated to the Nativity of Christ: it is a simple domed chamber with a small narthex but no apse, roofed in schist slabs from Pelion. Inside, the wooden balcony for women is still *in situ*. Beyond, the path climbs steps to a higher level, the area of the old Kastro, with shops and tavernas and varying dramatic views. To the north, among abandoned houses, is the oldest of Chora's surviving churches, Ághios Geórgios, probably from the 15th century.

About 600m east of Chora, along the road to Patitíri, the modern church of Ághios Ioánnis stands above the scant remains of one of the island's two ancient settlements. Further east, after the church of Profítis Ilías, a by-road to the north followed by two successive right forks leads to the beautiful, rural 15th- or early 16th-century monastic church of the **Panaghía sto Vounó**, with fine paintings on the ceiling.

Mikrós Mourtiás is a sandy beach reached from Chora by a southward path through olive groves.

Patitíri

The island's main harbour, Patitíri, is an unpretentious port, built in the late 1960s and '70s with no particular architectural merit, but in a pleasing and intimate setting around the attractive harbour-front and the steep slopes encircling it. Its name reflects the island's economic history: a *patitíri* is a place where grapes are trodden. Alónnisos produced and exported wine in antiquity (*see Tsoukaliá, opposite*).

The **Kostas and Angelas Mavriki Museum** (*open daily June–Oct, 11–7*) is housed in a large stone building above the western side of the harbour. The collection covers three floors, with a 'Pirate Museum' on the upper floor, a modern historical section with documents and objects pertaining especially to warfare on the ground floor, while the basement houses a folklore exhibition, focusing especially on the implements of traditional wine production and saddle-making.

FROM PATITIRI TO THE WEST COAST

Patitíri is the westernmost of a series of three coves in the sheltered southeast corner of the island: the settlement now extends east beyond Rousoúm Bay (the next cove east), and incorporates the separate neighbourhood of Vótsi beyond. A little to its west are the ruins of the Early Christian church of **Ághios Andréas**.

In the valley north of Vótsi is the island's most abundant spring, **Megá Neró** (turning north off main road, 2.1km from Patitíri waterfront). Beyond the spring, a track leads

1.5km across the width of the island to the small **bay of Tsoukaliá** on the north coast. On the east slope of the bay are remains of an ancient installation, partially hidden among pines. This was the site of a substantial wine-making installation of the Classical and Hellenistic periods, with associated pottery workshops producing the amphorae for transportation (the name *tsoukaliá* means 'pots' in modern Greek). A number of amphora handles, stamped with the legend 'IKION' have been found here, confirming the ancient name of the island as Ikos. Amphorae bearing that stamp have been found throughout the East Mediterranean and Black Sea.

The right-hand branch off the main track, 1km before Tsoukaliá, leads north and slightly east for a further 1.5km, at which point a narrow path continues a further 400m to the hermitage chapel of the Ághii Anárgyri, possibly from the 15th century, on a cliff overlooking the sea. Downhill from here, on the summit of the steep hill due east of lovely Megáli Ámmos cove, are the remains of the **Hellenistic watchtower** of Kastráki.

THE EAST COAST

The **site of ancient Ikos** is at Kokkinókastro, a long peninsula projecting into the sea in the middle of the lower eastern half of the island, between two large beaches. At sunset the headland turns deep orange, hence its name, 'Red Castle'. The point of the promontory where the city stood is marked by steep seaward cliffs and is attached to the island by a high and inaccessible razor-thin isthmus of eroding sandstone. The site can only be reached by boat, or by swimming out from the south beach (*c. 20mins*) and climbing ashore at the southeastern point where the headland slopes down to the sea.

The tip of the headland is indented by a deep cove, which served as an anchorage. Cutting transversely across the lower slopes is a fine 5th-century BC Classical fortification wall. Buried foundations and walls are further up the slope to the west.

On the east coast lies **Stení Vála**, a tranquil creek with a harbour, fronted by excellent tavernas. The principal monk seal rescue centre is based here.

The northern half of the island is mostly uninhabited. The main road across the island terminates in the deep creek of Gérakas Bay, where one of the biological research stations of the Marine Park is located.

THE LESSER SPORADES

To the north and east of Alónnisos is a scattering of diverse uninhabited islands (*map p. 573*) which form a marine landscape of exceptional beauty. They are all part of the Northern Sporades Marine Park. It key focus is the protection of the habitat of the Mediterranean monk seal (*Monachus monachus; see box overleaf*); but corals, cetaceans, birds, goats and rare plants are also found here. The area is of great archaeological importance, as the islands were a centre of Neolithic and earlier settlement, and the waters are rich in ancient, Byzantine and later shipwrecks. Off **Peristéra**, a barren islet east of Alónnisos, an important 5th-century BC shipwreck was explored in 1991. It was a sizeable Athenian trade-vessel, with a cargo of several thousand amphorae of wine from Macedonia, Alónnisos and Skópelos.

THE MEDITERRANEAN MONK SEAL

There are probably fewer than 500 pairs of Mediterranean monk seal (*Monachus monachus*) in the world today. Traditionally they were hunted for skins and oil, and killed by fishermen, who saw them as competitors. Recent human encroachment on their coastal habitats has had catastrophic effects. The main cause is the vulnerability of the female when gestating and nursing her young, as a litter usually consists of only a single pup. The seals used to bask and even pup on open beaches, but industrial fishing and coastal development have driven them to remoter locations and sea-caves.

The monk seal appears to have been present throughout the Mediterranean and Black Sea littoral in antiquity, but is now confined to two principal colonies: the northwest Aegean and the Atlantic coast of Mauritania and Madeira. Mature animals may travel far in pursuit of food. They are very occasionally sighted in the Dodecanese (Kárpathos, Tilos and Rhodes) and elsewhere in the Aegean.

A 1st-century BC grave excavated in 1999 in the area of the Commercial Harbour of Rhodes contained the skeleton of a monk seal, buried with funerary honours in a family inhumation, together with the remains of humans, a dog and some small grave gifts, just as if the seal had been a family member. The remarkable finds are displayed in the Rhodes Aquarium (*see p. 278*).

The fertile island of **Kyrá Panaghiá** may be ancient Halonnesos. Its main feature is the large 16th-century monastery of Kyrá Panaghiá (recently revived). On the west side of the island is the bay of Ághios Pétros, with a Neolithic settlement. Mountainous **Gioúra**, further northeast, has revealed human presence from c. 10,000–6000 BC in the Cave of the Cyclops in the south of the island (the cave is so named because according to myth it is here that Odysseus blinded Polyphemus). Gioúra's unusual limestone landscape is home to a variety of unique plants. An endemic species of goat, *Capra aegagrus*, roams the island. The northernmost island is **Psathoúra**. Its northern end is crowned by a tall lighthouse (26m; 1895).

Pipéri, to the east, is the most protected zone of the Marine Park, as it is a breeding ground for the monk seal and for various birds, including populations of raptors. **Skántzoura**, south of the group, is one of the most important Aegean breeding habitats for the rare Audouin's gull.

PRACTICAL INFORMATION

GETTING AROUND

There is no direct boat from Piraeus, but car ferries sail from Vólos (6 hrs, daily) and Ághios Konstantínos (6 hrs, five times a week). The island is also connected by a rapid hydrofoil service in 2½ hrs from both of the above ports with varying frequency throughout the year. All services stop at Skiáthos and Skópelos en route. In the summer months, the hydrofoil connection is more frequent and the network extends to include Thessaloníki to the north and Kými and other destinations on Euboea to the south. Access to the outlying islands in the Marine Park (with the exception of Pipéri) can be arranged from Patitíri.

WHERE TO STAY

Various options are available on Alónnisos, especially in picturesque and quieter Chora and more lively Patitíri. A comprehensive list is found at www.alonissos.gr. Chiliadrómia in Chora is a charming guesthouse in a restored traditional home with panoramic views (*www.chiliadromia.gr*).

WHERE TO EAT

The two main villages on Alónnisos offer a range of tavernas. A good place to sample the island's traditional spiral *tyrópita* (cheese pie), called *striftí*, is at **To Paradosiako** at Stení Vála, where they are freshly made. The place also serves a variety of good fish dishes and local wine.

WALKING

Walking is popular on Alónnisos. An informative guide, *Alonnisos through the Souls of your Feet* (sic), Chris Browne, 2008, is available on www.alonnisoswalks.co.uk. For more on the Marine Park, see www.alonissos-park.gr.

SKYROS

There is a tenacity to tradition on Skyros which comes of the island being so isolated. Here the islanders proudly preserve their music and dance, their style of domestic decoration, their customs of cheese-making and horse-breeding and their traditional festivals. It is still possible to see sandals that would have been familiar to Theocritus on the feet of goatherds, or to watch carnival dances that might have come straight from a comedy of Aristophanes. The mainland feels a long way away, because the great wall of the mountains of Euboea blocks the island's view of the rest of the world. Skyros is large (more than 200km square) and the inhabitants are few (2,700); for this reason it feels quiet, spacious and self-contained.

Its geography is almost that of two different islands: the fertile, wooded and densely inhabited north is not unlike the other Sporades; the empty, mountainous, wild south resembles the Cyclades. With its varied and beautiful scenery of shore and mountains, its archaeological wealth and its pretty *chora*, and the evocative grave of the poet Rupert Brooke, Skyros lacks little to suit a traveller's changing moods and needs.

HISTORY OF SKYROS

In myth, Achilles hid on Skyros, disguised as a girl, to avoid joining the Trojan War, but was discovered by Odysseus. It was also on Skyros that Lycomedes treacherously killed Theseus, King of Athens, by pushing him off a cliff.

Important Neolithic and Bronze Age sites bear witness to the island's prehistoric settlement, which continued through the Geometric and Archaic periods. In 476–475 BC, Cimon of Athens conquered the island, enslaved the inhabitants and planted Athenian settlers; the bones of Theseus were disinterred and brought to Athens. Skyros thereafter remained an Athenian cleruchy, with interruptions when it was ceded to Sparta (404–394 BC) and again when it was held by the Macedonians (322 and 197 BC). It was captured by the Romans in 197 BC, but only finally taken for Rome by Sulla in 86 BC.

Invading Goths pillaged the island in AD 276, and Arabs in the 9th century. In the 4th century, Skyros was promoted to a Christian bishopric. After the Fourth Crusade of 1204, Skyros came under Frankish domination, but returned to Greek Byzantine control in 1276. After the capture of Constantinople in 1453 by Sultan Mehmet II, the Byzantines ceded it to Venice. In 1538, the Turkish admiral Kheir ed-Din Barbarossa captured the island, which remained Turkish until Greek independence in 1821.

SKYROS CHORA & ENVIRONS

Skyros Chora and its acropolis (*map p. 591, B2*) occupy a steep and dramatic site, chosen because it could be easily defended and is virtually hidden from the sea, providing

SKYROS

A   B   C

N

1

Podia

Aloni

C. Aloni

C. Markesi

C. Agalipa
Agalipa Bay
Air Force
Base
Palamari
Trachi

Katounes

Kyra Panagia
Gyrismata

Kambos   Ag. Nikolaos
Plain   Pouria
Molos

Kalogrias
Bay
367

Atsitsa

Mt
Olympos   Skyros   Magazia
(Chora)

Kalogeratsi

Klouthros

Oros
316
Aliko   Aspous   Bay of Achili
Bay
Ag. Phokas   Achili

Koulouri   Ag. Phokas   Katholiko
Bay   Bay   C. Katergo
Ag. Panteleimon   Loutro

C. Souliotis   Acherounes
Pefkos   Pefkos
Lakonissi   Bay   Linaria   Kalamitsa

Rinia   Mt Kochylas
792

Valaxa
Kalamitsa Bay   Nyfi

Mt Vouva

Exo
Diavates   Mt Gligori

C. Fanari   Mt
Mesa   Grave of R. Brooke   Fanoftis
Diavates
Vales   Tris Boukes Bay   C. Lithari
Bay   (Naval Base)

Renes   C. Xiloparatis
Bay
C. Marmaro   Plateia

Sarakino

0   5 km
0   2,5 miles

protection against piracy. In addition to its natural defences, the acropolis was repeatedly fortified and re-fortified. Most visible today are the 13th-century Frankish fortifications at the summit. Mainly on the southern and seaward sides, they are built on top of ashlar masonry of the late 5th-century BC walls. The most visible remains are of the gates and towers on the east side of the acropolis, halfway between the summit and the sea, and at the north end below Plateía Brooke. The *plateía* itself, open and windswept and with impressive views, has a statue of *Immortal Poetry* (Michalis Tombros, 1930), commemorating Rupert Brooke (*see p. 595*).

Three churches

A visit to the upper town of Skyros is best started on foot from Chora, or from Plateía Brooke, halfway between Chora and the Kastro. A stepped street towards the summit passes (50m) the tiny 13th-century **church of the Pénde Mártyres**, built on one of the city's ancient cemeteries, with rock-cut grave loculi by the door and inside. Further up the street, the main path to the centre of Chora leads off down to the right. The uphill path twists to the left, and after a further 20m rises alongside the large 17th-century **church of the Panaghía**, with an interesting carved arch on the south exterior. Adjacent to the south is an older church, **Ághios Athanásios**, which contains wall-paintings and marble columns with early Byzantine capitals.

The Town House Museum and Aghía Triáda

On returning to the axial path leading up the hill, beside a small shaded *plateía* on the right, is the **Skyrian Town House Museum** (*open July and Aug daily except Mon; erratic opening times otherwise*), a typical example of Skyrian dwellings of the 19th century and before. Skyrian houses are based on a single small unit, usually separated from the street by a small courtyard. The interior is divided vertically into two parts by a wooden partition, often ornately carved. The front half of the house, occupying the whole height of the building, is the reception area, with a conical fireplace and shelves displaying precious pottery, metal and glass objects. The rear half is divided into a kitchen and storage area (with sunken jars) below and a sleeping area above, reached by a steep and often ornate stair. The entire family would sleep here, on low couches. The roof was insulated by a covering of branches, seaweed and earth.

Shortly beyond the museum, the street doubles back on itself. Opposite you as you climb up is the interesting 14th-century church of **Aghía Triáda**. In front of it stand two ancient columns, one in Euboean cipollino marble (*if locked, the key is held in a nearby house: lower door at no. 93*). The interior is a simple domed square, apsidal in plan. Almost every surface is painted and decorated following the traditional iconographical scheme: a *Christ Pantocrator* in the dome surrounded by seraphim and archangels; the four Evangelists in the pendentives; and scenes from this world on the walls. In front of the iconostasis stand two Byzantine candlesticks in cipollino marble.

The Kastro

The gate to the Kastro (*closed at the time of writing due to earthquake damage*) at the top of the street is surmounted by a marble lion, placed here by the Venetians; it is probably an ancient fragment. Through the gate is the **monastery of Ághios Geórgios**, founded in 960 under the emperor Nicephorus Phocas. Beside the steps to its church is a fresco of St George saving a lady in a tower from the dragon. The katholikon has a high dome supported on slender monolithic columns, extensive 16th-century wall-paintings on the north wall and an 18th-century wooden iconostasis incorporating minute scenes along the rail below the icons.

A tunnel leads to a narrow staircase giving onto the upper Kastro. In front are the three apses of the large **church of the Episkopí**, founded in 895 and once the seat of the Bishop of Skyros. Ninth-century churches of this magnitude are rare. Originally the church was domed and extended as far as the thresholds to the west. The central apse contains the synthronon, tiered seating for the clergy, with a central throne for the bishop. Higher up the hill, a huge vaulted **Venetian magazine** crowns the rise to the north. Nothing remains of the ancient structures.

The museums

The **Archaeological Museum** is below Plateía Brooke to the east (*open 8.30–3; closed Mon*). Prehistoric finds include a Mycenaean vase decorated with a ship. The museum is most significant for its rich collection of finds from the Geometric period, including some domestic material but mainly high-quality finds from graves. Especially noteworthy is a circular ritual object comprising eight ducks in a circle, with two snakes winding over them and devouring a dove, and an 8th-century diadem in electrum, beautifully embossed with designs of warriors and shields.

Below Plateía Brooke to the north, the street ends after 30m above the impressive semicircular remains of the 'Palaiópyrgos', or northern bastion of the late Classical enceinte of the acropolis. Nearby to the east is the **Manos Faltaïts Museum** (*open daily March–Nov 9–2 & 6–8*), with a rich variety of displays. This private collection is dedicated to Skyrian traditions and to the 20th-century painter Manos Faltaïts. The upper part of the house exhibits furniture, textiles (some exquisite nuptial embroideries), costumes, woodwork etc, illustrating the particular Skyrian synthesis of Ottoman, Venetian and Byzantine influences. There is an example of the goat costume used in the pre-Lenten festivities and dances on Skyros, a tradition perhaps surviving from antiquity: it weighs nearly 60kg. Also displayed are typical Skyrian pottery jugs, left unglazed to allow their contents to remain cooler.

ENVIRONS OF CHORA

The lower part of Chora stretches in a chain of tiny squares and spaces along its curving main street. Below it to the west lies a beautiful river valley with good views of the town.

Below the south precipice of the Kastro is the modern cemetery, and behind it to the south rises the hill of Foúrka, named after the gallows erected by the Turks. On its summit is the **platform of the Archaic Temple of Apollo** (6th century BC), cut out of the bedrock. The temple is orientated on a north–south axis and was unusually broad

(17.5m) in relation to its length (24m). This hill may be the 'place which had the appearance of a mound', mentioned by Plutarch as being the site of the tomb of Theseus, from which Cimon took the hero's bones, returning them triumphantly to Athens in 476 BC.

The fertile plain of the Kámbos, stretching north of Chora towards the coast, has yielded many archaeological finds as it was an important place of continuous settlement and burial from pre-Mycenaean times onwards. At its easternmost point are the ancient **sandstone quarries of Pouriá** (*map p. 591, B2*). The road ends by a windmill on the promontory, in front of a large rectangular outcrop, the last remaining piece of the soft poros stone which once constituted the whole promontory. A chapel dedicated to Ághios Nikólaos has been hewn out of it. The quarries continue southwards along the waterfront, where stone could be easily loaded onto barges.

The coast extending south of Chora has yielded rich finds from the Mycenaean, Neolithic and even Mesolithic periods. The **Bay of Achíli** (*map p. 591, B3*) is said to have been the point of Achilles' departure for Troy.

AROUND THE ISLAND

Palamári and Markési

North of Chora is the once-large village of **Katoúnes** (*map p. 591, B2*), a whole hillside scattered with deserted 18th- and 19th-century houses. A kilometre or so beyond it, a track to the right leads to the early **Bronze Age town at Palamári** (*map p. 591, A1*), founded on this low headland in middle of the 3rd millennium BC and inhabited continuously until c. 1650 BC, after which it seems to have been abandoned. The site was well fortified and was built to a sophisticated design. The ring of its walls, with a ditch outside, is preserved to a height of nearly 3m in places and is regularly punctuated by the bases of semicircular towers. Directly behind the walls are storerooms and hidden corridors communicating between the bastions. Further inside the site lie excavated houses. Although they seem relatively cramped and small, their hearths, storage areas, doorways, stone benches and ovens are all well built, and the drainage channels are carefully constructed. A considerable part of the town has been eroded by the sea; it may originally have been twice the surviving size. It is assumed to have had a port.

The **ancient site of Markési**, at the northwest tip of the island, is unfortunately inaccessible due to its location in a military zone. The site, continually inhabited and used from the Early Bronze Age through to Christian times, is located on a promontory. The hill is marked by the church of the Theotókos; beneath it are remains of an Early Christian church, built over a Classical temple to Poseidon.

The west coast

Atsítsa (*map p. 591, A2*) occupies a sheltered bay, with a pleasant taverna and a small hotel. The pale green colour in the cliff to the south shows the presence of iron ore in the area; the overhead viaduct and the stone buildings of a loading station at the shore are the remains of an early 20th-century mining plant. South from here, a dirt road traverses a beautiful landscape of forest and seashore. It reaches the sea at **Ághios Phokás** (*map p. 591, A3*; taverna on the shore). The eponymous chapel, at the top of the low rise at the south end of the bay, occupies the site of some ancient structure. Outside it are large dressed blocks of the colourful, brecciated marble for which Skyros was famous in Roman times and which was quarried near here (a splash of water on the marble surface immediately enhances its kaleidoscopic colours).

Several marble quarries of varying size and age are to be found all around this area. Those north of Ághios Phokás produce a largely white marble with orange veining, but at the top of the track to the south there are those that yield the high-quality, polychrome stone. The area of the quarries is protected by the church of Ághios Panteléimon, which stands beside the road overlooking the sea.

The attractive **bay of Péfkos** (*map p. 591, A3*) was the ancient Roman harbour for the loading of marble. At the south end of the shore, the rockface has been perforated in two parallel rows of deep square holes for the wooden posts used to winch the heavy blocks into barges. The shore is littered with huge rectangular blocks of all colours of marble.

Mount Kochylás and the south of the island

Between the reedy bays of Kalamítsa and Achíli, at the island's narrowest point, stretches a thin band of alluvial land, probably once submerged, thus dividing the island in two. Its east side is fed by numerous springs. The road hugs the west shore of the Kochylás massif and then climbs onto an open mountain plateau. In winter, these wild slopes are the domain of the Skyrian Horse.

THE SKYRIAN HORSE

In the central and southern valleys of the island it is common to see the wild Skyrian horse grazing. Though wild in the sense of freely roaming, the animal is notably placid. Never standing much more than a metre at the shoulder, the horses may be descended from the smallish horses of ancient Greece. They winter in the wilder southern half of the island and migrate to the northern part in search of greenery and shade during the hotter months. They number fewer than 150, which causes concern for their survival as a breed.

Tris Boúkes Bay and the grave of Rupert Brooke

A single road cuts across the southeastern tip of the island. The northern branch of it runs high above the coast, eventually reaching the wild cliff scenery of the island's southeast corner. The southern branch descends to **Tris Boúkes Bay**, another Roman quarry harbour, today inaccessible due to the presence of a naval base.

About 100m before the entrance to the base, in a grove of olives below the road, is the solitary **grave of Rupert Brooke** (*map p. 591, C4*). The young English poet (1887–1915), commissioned into the navy in the First World War, was buried here during the night of the 23rd April 1915, having died of septicaemia the same afternoon aboard a French hospital ship. The expeditionary force of which he had been a member sailed the following morning for the Dardanelles.

Brooke's valediction in *The Times* was written by Winston Churchill, who was First Lord of the Admiralty at the time: he described Brooke as 'joyous, fearless, versatile, deeply instructed, [and] with classic symmetry of mind and body'. At the time of his premature death, his personality and writing had begun to make a considerable mark. His striking stature and good looks caught the attention of many, amongst them Henry James, who encountered Brooke on a visit to Cambridge in 1909. His circle of friends and acquaintances included E.M. Forster, Virginia Woolf, and the Prime Minister's vivacious daughter, Violet Asquith. He was only 27 when his battalion set out for the Aegean. His friend Frances Cornford, with her keen and compassionate sense of irony, later wrote of Brooke as 'A young Apollo, golden-haired … dreaming on the verge of strife/ Magnificently unprepared/ For the long littleness of life'.

The first grave here was an improvised pile of stones with two wooden crosses, but there is now a simple stone sarcophagus. At its foot is inscribed Brooke's famous sonnet, *The Soldier*, written in 1914. There is a poignantly prophetic quality in the words of the poem. Few landscapes would seem more 'foreign' to Brooke's beloved English fenlands. The remoteness of the setting and the peaceful animals grazing here constitute one of the most indelible images of the island.

PRACTICAL INFORMATION

GETTING AROUND

Skyros is reached by daily ferries from Kými on Euboea (Skyros Line, T: 22220 22020 at Kými and T: 91789 or 91790 at Skyros; 2hrs). Less frequent (generally twice-weekly) services also operate to/from the other Sporades, and Ághios Kostantínos on the mainland. All boats dock at Linariá on the west coast, 9km from Skyros Chora (*map p. 591, B3*). There are twice-weekly flights from Athens. The airport is 10km north of Chora.

WHERE TO STAY

At Magaziá, the peaceful area below and north of Chora, the **Hydroussa Skyros Hotel** (*T: 22220 91209 or 92063, www.hydroussahotel. gr/Skyros.htm*) offers comfortable and luxurious accommodation. Also in Magaziá, simple rooms and kindly hospitality can be found at the **Hotel Deidameia** (*T: 22220 92008*). On the coast road, right under the Kastro is the panoramic **Paliopirgos** (*T: 22220 91014*). Both are inexpensive.

WHERE TO EAT

In the upper part of the main street of Chora, the popular *mezedopoleíon* **O Pappous** has excellent local specialities as well as Skyrian cheeses. At Gyrísmata (north of Chora, beyond the church of Ághios Nikólaos), the **Stelios** taverna has good fresh seafood.

EUBOEA

Lying so close to the body of Greece, Euboea (pron. Évia) maintains many of the characteristics of mainland life coupled with the tranquillity and individuality of an island. There is no airport, and the several harbours are small and informal. Access from the mainland is either by ferry or by car, across the Euripos bridge. And once out of the busy capital of Chalkída, you can be in forests and gorges and mountains within a matter of minutes; some of Greece's remotest villages are to be found at the island's southeastern corner. The grandeur and beauty of Euboea's landscapes are matched only by their constantly unfolding variety.

HISTORY OF EUBOEA

The long, beetling ridge of the island is like a mountainous breakwater protecting the eastern flank of Greece. In the placid stretch of safe water in its lee it has nurtured a number of rich, productive and very ancient centres—Lefkandí, Eretria and Chalcis—which flourished in prehistoric and early historic times. Fertile Euboea was sometimes called the 'larder of Greece': its very name implies the quality of its livestock (*eu boia*: 'good cattle'). It later exported grain to Rome, together with the largest quantity of decorative marble from any single place in the Mediterranean (*see p. 628*).

The island shared the culture of the Cyclades in the Bronze Age, and in remote antiquity was peopled by colonists from Thessaly who settled in the north (Ellopians), in the west (Abantes) and in the south (Dryopes). According to tradition the early settlers were joined by Ionians from Attica, Aeolians from Phthiotis and Dorians from the Peloponnese. The island, also called Makrys ('Long') because of its length, was divided between seven independent city-states, of which the most important were Eretria and Chalcis, rivals for the possession of the fertile Lelantine Plain. After the expulsion of the Peisistratids, Chalcis joined Boeotia against Athens. In consequence, in 506 BC, the Athenians crossed the strait, defeated the Chalcidians and divided their land up between 5,000 cleruchs (Herodotus, *Histories V, 77*).

After the Persian Wars (5th century BC) the whole of Euboea became subject to Athens, where it mainly remained until it was incorporated by Macedonia after the battle of Chaironeia (338 BC). Aristotle retired to Chalcis in 323 BC and died there the following year. In 194 BC the island was taken by the Romans, who restored its cities to nominal independence. The island later came under the sway of Byzantium.

In the wake of the Fourth Crusade, the island came under Frankish and Venetian control: the Venetians held the ports and Frankish nobles occupied the interior, which they filled with their castles. By 1366 the Venetians were masters of almost the whole of Euboea. It was they who gave it the name of Negroponte ('Black Bridge'), which referred to the bridge over the Euripos (*see p. 608*). Under the Venetians, Negroponte ranked as a kingdom, and its standard was one of the three hoisted in St Mark's Square.

EUBOEA North

EUBOEA South

After the expulsion of the Venetians from Constantinople by the Genoese, Negroponte became the centre of their influence in the western Greek area. In 1470 the island was conquered by the Turks and was governed by a Kapitan Pasha, or high admiral of the Ottoman Empire. In 1833, Euboea passed to Greece. By special decree, a certain number of Muslims, nearly all ethnic Albanians, were permitted to remain on the island.

By the early 20th century, Euboea had become a backwater supplying timber and building materials to Athens, but the development of mining led to some industrialisation. There was bitter resistance to the Axis Occupation and strong support for the popular forces of ELAS, the Greek People's Liberation Army, and the Democratic Army in the mountains during the Civil War period between 1944 and 1949. Northern Euboea was controlled by ELAS as early as June 1943.

AIDIPSOS, OREI & THE NORTHWEST

Loutrá Aidipsoú

A verdant setting, the generally calm waters of the Euboean Gulf, and a variety of stately 19th- and early 20th-century buildings make Loutrá Aidipsoú (*map p. 598, A3*) a characterful and increasingly popular place to stay. Ancient Aedepsus and its waters

Thermal waters flowing into the sea at Loutrá Aidipsoú.

were popular with the Romans, who were the first systematically to develop a **thermal station** here. Evidence of this can be seen in the hill, crowned by the church of Ághios Phanoúrios, directly behind the new Municipal Thermal Baths, about 400m in from the south shore. The main springs originally rose in a grotto known as Sulla's Cave. The source was covered in Roman times: the cruciform design of its four vaults can still clearly be seen. Two inscribed statue bases lying at the entrance commemorate two imperial patrons of the waters, Hadrian and Septimius Severus.

THE THERMAL WATERS OF AIDIPSOS

The hot springs were a centre of cult from ancient times and were probably linked to the worship of Heracles (Strabo in fact refers to them as 'The Springs of Heracles'). The town grew up in the Hellenistic period and was visited by later Macedonian kings. One of the most famous visitors in the Roman period was Sulla, who came here to cure his gout; Plutarch describes the great banquets he gave. The spa achieved its greatest prosperity between 100 BC and AD 400, when numerous emperors and dignitaries visited, including Hadrian, Septimius Severus and Constantine the Great. The spa suffered with the arrival of Christianity, when early Christians attacked what they saw as a cause of the dissipation of the inhabitants. It revived after the establishment of a bishopric in the 8th century, under the Metropolitan of Athens. In the later Middle Ages it went into decline as a result of the growth of piracy. After Greek Independence, little happened until the end of the 19th century when the spa was gradually developed under the influence of a new European predilection for 'taking the waters'. It became the most fashionable resort in Greece for a time after World War I, when the poet Cavafy was a visitor.

The water can be taken today in any of the larger spa hotels, such as the Avra or the grander Thermae Sylla (Sulla), founded in 1896 and which has received in its history such illustrious guests as Greta Garbo, Maria Callas and Winston Churchill; or else in the main Municipal Thermal Baths. Alternatively, the waters can be enjoyed on the main south-facing beach, where there are underwater hot springs in addition to the water which flows from the sources into the sea: the warmth and sulphur attract a unique diversity of fish and marine life. The waters rise at temperatures between 34° and 71°C and enjoy a reputation for curing gout, rheumatism, sciatica and arthritis. The ancients believed, probably correctly, that the springs were connected with those of Thermopylae on the opposite, mainland coast.

A small **Archaeological Collection** (*notionally open July–Sept 10–1 daily except Sun; closed at the time of writing for lack of staff*) is gathered in two rooms on the upper floor of the Municipal Baths. Also exhibited in the upper floor of the hallway of the building, and freely accessible whenever the baths are open (*daily 7am–9pm*), are two pieces of note: a headless 1st-century AD statue of a man wearing a himation (the missing head was originally part of the single piece of marble) and a fine Roman relief showing the bow and pelt of Heracles.

Next door to the Municipal Baths stands the former **Neoclassical bath house** with its horseshoe of private, marble bathing tubs, and a high central hall (at the time of writing in a perilous state of disrepair).

Licháda and Ília

To the west of Loutrá Aidipsoú stretches the tranquil **Licháda peninsula** (*map p. 598, A3*), dense with pines and olive groves. It takes its name from the hapless servant, Lichas, who delivered the Shirt of Nessus to Heracles and was hurled down into the sea here by the hero (Ovid, *Metamorphoses IX, 211*). The two largest settlements of Giáltra in the east, and **Licháda** towards the western point, both have old centres with pleasing stone houses and extensive views. **Giáltra** has a harbour with its own therapeutic springs, Loutrá Giáltron. The water is of milder temperature than at Aidipsós (39°–42°C). From Licháda the road leads down to **Cape Kínaion**, a beautiful spot, popular for bathing. Little remains of the Temple of Zeus Kinaios, which stood to the north of here, other than an eroded piece of frieze lying beside the church of Sts Helen and Constantine, as you turn back to Ághios Geórgios from the cape.

To the southeast of Loutrá Aidipsoú, the road to Límni hugs the shore beneath the steep slopes of Mt Teléthrion (969m). The small fishing village of **Ília** (*map p. 598, A2*), once accessible only by boat, is spread along a protected beach with a number of attractive fish tavernas. At the eastern extremity of the beach an abundant hot spring (65°C) of highly ferrous water gushes from the rock and disperses in the sea, depositing an orange-coloured mud of therapeutic qualities. A track (in poor condition) leads 8km up the mountainside to the remote and dramatic site of the 18th-century monastery of **Ághios Geórgios Ilíou**, occupying possibly the same location as the oracle of Apollo Selinountios, which Strabo mentions. The katholikon is decorated with late Byzantine wall-paintings and a carved wooden iconostasis of 1834.

OREI & ISTIAIA

The road north from Loutrá Aidipsoú reaches the north coast at Aghiókambos, where the small car ferry for Glýfa runs every 2hrs. Shortly beyond is the small port of **Oreí** (Oreoi; *map p. 598, A2*), one of the most interesting towns in northern Euboea.

The attractively laid-out town, planned in 1833 by the Bavarian architect Georg Schumayer, probably follows the ancient street plan. In the harbour, the submerged line of the ancient mole can be made out. A little behind the church of the Sotirás, by the water, stands the ***Bull of Oreí*** (late 3rd century BC), a bold and remarkable piece of Hellenistic funerary sculpture, found by the shore in 1965. The definition of the surface—of the tail, and especially around the neck and shoulders—is beautiful. The horns were fitted separately, and were possibly of bronze or ivory.

Inland to the east of the shore rises the **hill of Kastro**, the ancient marine acropolis of Oreos, now crowned by the ruins of a Venetian fort, built over successive Byzantine and Hellenistic fortification walls which are visible in places below. Below the castle to the southwest is the interesting church of **Ághios Vasíleios**: in the crypt are the remains of an Early Christian place of worship cut down into the rock, with a curious rock-hewn niche behind the altar forming the central liturgical focus.

HISTORY OF OREI & ISTIAIA

The modern settlement occupies the site of ancient Histiaea—called *polystaphylos* ('rich in vines') by Homer—which controlled the lucrative passage between the Euboean Gulf and the open sea. Its strategic location led Pericles to banish the Histiaeans and install 2,000 cleruchs here in 446 BC. The city became known thenceforth as Oreos, which appears to have been previously a deme of Histiaea, on a site very close by. After the banished Histiaeans were called back to their former city after the Peloponnesian War, the city was subsequently known by both names. It was destroyed by the Romans in 199 BC. According to Livy, Oreos had two citadels separated by a valley: a maritime acropolis which dominated the port, and an inland acropolis, Oreos Apanos, hence the modern plural 'Oreoí'. As a bishop's seat since as early as the 5th century, Oreí remained the centre of northern Euboea through Byzantine times. A prosperous small town existed under the Ottomans, which came under the rule of Ali Pasha, the 'Lion of Ioánnina', in the late 18th century. After his assassination in 1822, the area was important as the scene of some of the first battles in the Greek War of Independence. Modern Istiaia (4km inland) received numerous refugees from Asia Minor: the new settlement of Ághios Geórgios, 1km south of the town, was built for them.

Istiaía

A little way inland, to the east of Oreí, lies modern Istiaía (*map p. 598, A2*), which has a number of fine old houses and middle-Byzantine churches. Of these, **Ághios Nikólaos**, south of the main square, is the most interesting: a modern narthex leads into a very low interior with three aisles and apses, supported in part on monolithic stone columns. The scattered remains of painted scenes inside are executed in the simplest and fewest of colours (local earth pigments); they are the work of local artists working probably in the late 16th century.

Around Cape Artemísion

East of Istiaía the landscape becomes hilly and verdant. A branch to the left leads to the rural chapel of the Panaghía Dinioús, in a setting of great tranquillity. Beyond, the road touches the shore again at the villages of **Asmíni and Artemísio** (*map p. 598, A1*), where there are good, shaded beaches. The village of Artemísio and the cape to the west both take their name from a shoreside temple of Artemis Proseoia, mentioned by Plutarch in his *Life of Themistocles* (*VIII, 1*), surrounded, he says, by a wall of a kind of marble that imparted the odour and colour of saffron when rubbed. The ruins of the small 6th-century Byzantine complex of Ághios Geórgios on an isolated spur of the hills east of Péfki and west of Goúves is probably built over the ancient temple. It was here, in the **bay of Péfki**, that the Greek fleet based itself during the three days of crucial fighting in the straits, in which they succeeded in blocking the advance of the fleet of Xerxes, early in the second Persian invasion of 480 BC. The sea off **Cape Artemísion** also yielded two of the most spectacular underwater archaeological finds of all time, found at the site of a shipwreck which had occurred in the 2nd century BC. These are the magnificent, mid-5th-century BC bronze statue of Zeus hurling a thunderbolt (sometimes wrongly referred to as an image of Poseidon); and the Hellenistic bronze *Horse and Jockey* (probably 2nd century BC). Both are now in the National Archaeological Museum in Athens.

At **Goúves** (*map p. 598, A1*), a village with many attractive wooden balconied houses, is the so-called Drosinis Tower, a fortified Ottoman house built in the early 1800s by Ibrahim Aga. It belonged for a time to the Athenian poet Georgios Drosinis (1859–1951) and now houses a small Ethnographic Museum.

AROUND LIMNI & PROKOPI: NORTHERN CENTRAL EUBOEA

Límni

Gathered in front of a south-facing shore surrounded by hills and with beautiful views across the water into Boeotia and Phthiotis, Límni (*map p. 598, B2*) is an attractive centre from which to explore the rural areas of northern central Euboea. Understated and quietly elegant, the town has retained much of the dignified architecture and planning of its late 19th-century design.

Little remains of ancient Elymnion, to which Límni is the modern successor. The earliest vestiges are to be found at the curious **church of the Panaghítsa**, which stands in a small square about three blocks inland of the waterfront from the statue of Lela Karayiannis (a martyr of the underground resistance movement in the Second World War). Inside the church is an area of late Roman mosaic floor from an ancient bathing complex. In the floor of the apse, visible through two low arches, it has decorative representations of fish and marine animals. A marble statue of Heracles (now in the museum in Chalkída) was found on the site in 1856.

At the opposite end of the waterfront, set back from the northern extremity of the beach and cut into the cliff-face, is the 11th-century **hermitage of Hósios Christódoulos**. Here tradition relates that Christodoulos, the founder of the Monastery of St John on Patmos (*see p. 417*), died in March 1093, after he had been forced to flee Patmos in the face of Turkish incursions. The interior, filled with censers and icons, is a minute grotto of hermetic simplicity.

The other churches of the town, often richly decorated and furnished, date mostly from the last 130 years. The small **Municipal Museum** (*open in summer Mon–Sat 9–1,*

Sun 10.30–2; weekdays only in winter) exhibits a collection of ancient and Byzantine antiquities found locally, as well as examples of local costume, furniture and domestic articles, in the setting of a restored Limniot house of the late 19th century. A large area of mosaic from the Roman baths by the church of the Panaghítsa (*see above*) is displayed on the ground floor.

Mount Kandíli and Moní Galatáki

The coast road to the southeast of Límni passes by the former magnesite minehead and loading-bays at **Katoúnia**. Today the defunct buildings have become dwellings immersed in flowering vegetation. The road ends below the western face of Mt Kandíli (1236m), which drops over 600m sheer into the water, dispatching strange currents of wind onto the sea below. Here, set back from the shore, is the 16th-century **monastery of Ághios Nikólaos Galatákis** (*map p. 598, B2; open summer 9–12 & 5–8; winter 4–7*), purportedly founded in the 8th century on the site of a temple of Poseidon. The dedication to St Nicholas, patron saint of sailors, may be a carry-through from that cult. The monastery (today inhabited by nuns) has a compact form dominated by the sturdy tower (now sleeping quarters for guests) built between 1555 and 1562 by Hosios David Gerontos as a defence against pirate raids. The katholikon was built in 1566. The dome is supported by four columns, which on the south side have early capitals: one Ionic, the other early Byzantine. The walls have areas of painting executed in 1586. The best preserved and most complete, showing scenes of the miracles of St Nicholas, are in the narthex. The *Ladder of Ascent to Heaven* on the south wall is particularly noteworthy. The later wall-paintings in the parecclesion on the south side, dedicated to St John the Baptist, are in good condition and include decorative details such as the unusual guinea-fowl below the window in the south wall. At several points, graffiti of boats have been scratched into the surface by grateful mariners.

Roviés and its hinterland

Set back behind a wooded shore of great beauty, **Roviés** (*map p. 598, B2*) lies near the site of ancient Orobiai, which, according to Thucydides (*Peloponnesian War III, 89*), was destroyed by a tsunami in 426 BC. The centre is dominated by a medieval Frankish tower built by Guillaume de Villehardouin, Prince of Achaia, between 1255 and 1258 during his successful war against the Venetian lords of the island. From Roviés a pleasant loop can be made into the forested interior in order to visit the much-frequented 19th-century **monastery of Hosios David Gerontos** (with fine early 20th-century wall-paintings); the gorge and **waterfalls of Drymóna**; and the picturesque village of **Kokkinomyliá**.

Kírinthos and Mandoúdi

The attractively wooded village of Kírinthos (*map p. 598, B1*) was created in the 1830s around the stately Villa Averoff (*see p. 630*). It takes its name from nearby **ancient Kerinthos**, the site of which lies 5km to the east on the coast at Kastrí, close to the tiny resort of Krýa Vrýsi (at the east end of the beach, beyond the fast-flowing Voúdoros stream). Directly beyond the stream, a series of walls confront you, which were the western limit of the settlement: an outer enceinte in large, polygonal blocks of the 6th century BC, and an inner wall constructed of smaller elements. The site extends over three successive rises, terminating at the eastern end in a natural precipice. The base of a small temple, orientated to the cardinal points, can be detected at the highest point above this eastern limit. The line of the fortifications running east along the north side is clear, with the base of a bastion clearly visible; to the south, the ruins (mostly walls of Hellenistic construction) are immersed in undergrowth. On the saddle between the central and western hills are the remains of public buildings of the Hellenistic era, bordering a wide street. Kerinthos drew considerable wealth from the fertile land of its interior, in the plain watered by the Kiréas river (*see below*). It figures in the Homeric Catalogue of Ships, and is mentioned by Strabo. Early on, probably in the 5th century BC, it lost its independence to Histiaia.

Mandoúdi (*map p. 598, B1*) stands in the low land at the mouth of the valley of the River Kiréas, which nurtures several kilometres of plane woods to the south. Three kilometres south of Mandoúdi, opposite the church of the Koímisis tis Theotókou, a small sign points east to the **Megálos Plátanos** ('Great Plane'), 800m down the east side of the river. This vast and remarkable tree, now slowly dying, is perhaps one of the oldest planes in Europe.

Prokópi

The often busy activity of Prokópi (*map p. 598, C2*) centres on the large church of **Ághios Ioánnis Roússos**, 'St John the Russian', the town's miracle-working patron saint. Greek refugees from Ürgüp in Cappadocia colonised this village in the mid-1920s, bringing with them the body and relics of their guardian saint, a hermit and healer, born in Russia in 1690, and taken as a captive to central Anatolia in 1711, during the wars between the Sultan and Peter the Great. He died in Ürgüp in 1730 at the age of 40. His presence in the church in Prokópi is the focus of an active and widespread cult, which culminates on his feast day, 27th May. The relics—including the saint's beret, which the faithful still put on their heads when they visit—are in the small chapel on the left on entering: further inside the church on the left is his embalmed body. Up until the arrival of the refugees, Prokópi was known by its Ottoman name, Achmetaga. Its recent history is closely intertwined with the Noel family, relatives of the poet Byron, who purchased the surrounding land in the 1830s and whose manor house, in a curious hybrid of Greek, colonial, hacienda and English suburban styles, overlooks the village from a wooded hill to the northwest.

From just south of Prokópi centre, a branch road leads to the east coast, touching the shore at the crescent **bay of Píli** (*map p. 598, C1*). A few metres before the harbour, to the left of the road, is the tiny, mid-14th century church of **Ághios Ioánnis Theológos**, whose single-vaulted interior is completely covered with later wall-paintings, in places hard to read because of a layer of dirt and soot. A particular curiosity is the bizarre frieze of hellish tortures depicted in a running frieze, low on the south wall: some of the artist's inventions are worthy of Bosch.

CHALKIDA & ENVIRONS

Chalkída (*map p. 598, D2*), Chalcis to the ancient Greeks and Negroponte to the Venetians, is the capital of the *nome* of Euboea. The city itself and its architecture—built and rebuilt after countless earth tremors and sprees of destruction—would win few beauty contests, but it is a busy, historically important place, and beautifully sited on both sides of one of the most curious channels of seawater in the Aegean. Although there is now a new suspension bridge that spans the channel for through traffic, any exploration of Chalkída needs to start at the old bridge over the Euripos: it was this that gave the city life, significance and wealth, as well as two harbours and dominance of one of the most lucrative trading hubs in Greece after Corinth and the Piraeus.

HISTORY OF CHALKIDA

According to the ancients, the name of Chalcis (from χαλκός, copper, and hence bronze) reflected the importance of its chief industry. The exact site of the Mycenaean city of Homer's 'great-hearted Abantes' (*Iliad II, 540*) remains unknown, but the present site was occupied from late Geometric times. The situation of the city as the outlet of a rich island, with two harbours on the Euripos, made for its early development into a commercial and colonising centre. It was on the trade route between Thessaly (horses and corn), Thrace and Macedonia (gold from Thasos, timber, corn) and Attica and central Greece. In the 8th century BC Chalcis colonised the Sporades and settled so many cities (32 in all) in the Macedonian peninsula between the Thermaic and Strymonic gulfs that the whole peninsula was called Chalcidice (Chalkidikí in modern Greek). Later it founded colonies in Sicily: Naxos (Giardini-Naxos), Messana (Messina) and in mainland Italy: Rhegion (Reggio Calabria) and Cumae. The city fought many wars with Eretria for possession of the Lelantine Plain (*see p. 609*), and in the 7th century BC emerged victorious. Its last king, Amphidamas, a contemporary of Hesiod, was killed in one of these wars, and the government passed to the aristocracy, who were themselves overthrown when the Athenians overwhelmed Chalcis in 506 BC. In 480 BC the city sent 20 ships to the Greek fleet at Salamis, and its soldiers took part in the Battle of Plataea.

The city's subsequent history is largely that of Euboea. In 1210 it was seized by the Venetians, who made it the capital of the kingdom of Negroponte. When the Turks acquired Euboea in 1470, Chalcis became the headquarters of the Kapitan Pasha.

The old town

The mainland approach via the old road to the Euripos is guarded by the **Karababa** ('Black Father') Castle, an Ottoman fortress of 1686. The walls give a comprehensive view of the strait and the whole town. The unusual bridge that carries the old road over the Euripos opens by a double action; the carriageway descends just sufficiently to allow each half-span to roll on rails under its own approaches. The channel is only 38m wide at this point. The bridge leads into Kastro, the older part of Chalkída and the area of the Venetian town of Negroponte, whose northern walls ran along the line of the modern Leofóros Venizélou.

THE EURIPOS

The Euripos is notorious for its alternating currents, which change direction six or seven times a day and sometimes as often as 14 times in 24 hours. The current flows from north to south for about three hours at a rate which can vary between 6 and 12 knots. It then suddenly subsides; and, after a few minutes of quiescence, it begins to flow in the opposite direction. The currents are driven by the gradient which forms between the respective water levels to either side of the narrows, caused by the restriction of tidal movement at the bottleneck in the strait. The exact mechanics and timing of the water flow are still not fully understood. Its behaviour was widely speculated on from ancient times. Socrates (*Phaedo, 90*) uses the variability of the Euripos as a metaphor for that which is in a constant state of flux. The phenomenon is alluded to by Aeschylus (*Agamemnon, 190*), as well as by Livy, Cicero, Pliny and Strabo. According to popular tradition, Aristotle, in despair at his failure adequately to explain the phenomenon, flung himself into its heaving waters.

The narrows were first spanned in 411 BC. Since then there has been a succession of bridges; the current one dates from 1962 (it closes to allow boats to pass). Some way further south is the newer suspension bridge, open permanently.

On the further side of the bridge, on the left, is a **sculpture** by the Sicilian artist Carmelo Mendola (1980), a skeletal, cobweb-winged version of the *Victory of Samothrace*. It was donated to Chalkída by its ancient colony of Giardini-Naxos in eastern Sicily (where another, earlier version of the statue also stands). To the right (south) a narrow alleyway (Kállia) leads past an old, wooden-framed **Ottoman house**, whose protruding first floor is supported on gracefully curving beams. One block further south (across Kótsou and Papalouká) stands the late 17th-century **mosque of Emir Zade**, whose dome rises from a broad octagonal drum. The carved marble surround of the door has beautiful calligraphy and design. Substantially later in date is the decorative fountain facing the mosque. The 19th-century **synagogue** is nearby, back on Kótsou (one block north).

From the southwest corner of the square of the mosque, Stamáti leads to the church of **Aghía Paraskeví**. It was built in the mid-13th century as the Catholic priory church of St Mary of the Dominicans, as one of the early mission centres of the itinerant branch of the order, probably on the site of a pre-existing Byzantine church. It is an unusual example in Greece of early Dominican architecture that has survived largely undamaged and little modified. The interior is grand and spacious, punctuated with cipollino (*see p. 628*) and Hymettian marble columns (two of which are deeply fluted) surmounted by a variety of carved capitals. The chancel arch is carved with Gothic foliage and with the figures of two principal saints of the Dominican order, St Dominic himself and St Peter Martyr. The heavy marble iconostasis is modern.

The Archaeological Museum

North of the bridge, Leofóros Voudoúri leads along the shore to the broad Leofóros Venizélou, which runs southeast past the Neoclassical law courts to the Archaeological Museum (*open daily except Mon, 8.30–3*). The collection is small but of high quality. Much of the **sculpture** is in the courtyard and garden, with the best pieces under two covered porticoes. At the left end of Portico A is a marble panel of the 2nd century BC, delicately carved with three rows of victorious athlete's wreaths, with inscriptions at the centre of each noting where the athlete was from and which contest he won in the games of the Heracleia.

Inside there are three rooms: to the right are the earliest finds, including **pottery from Mánika**, an important Early Helladic site on the coast north of Chalkída (there is little to see *in situ*), and examples of the characteristic **Early Cycladic incised frying pans** (*see p. 54*). The Mycenaean artefacts include a bronze sword and pots which are exuberantly decorated with lily and vine-leaf designs. A rare **funerary group** of Geometric bronze figurines (two humans leading a dozen oxen) comes from a grave at Dokós (east of Chalkída). The central room is dominated by the two **Roman statues** of Dionysus and an elegiac, heavy-headed Antinous, the beautiful, youthful favourite of the emperor Hadrian. Also here is part of an exquisitely carved and delicately stylised 5th-century BC relief of the sacrifice of a ram, from Lárymna on the mainland. The room to left contains other sculptural pieces. A central case exhibits a 1st-century BC **athlete's gold wreath**. Beside it is a cup in clear glass of the same period, which has miraculously survived entire.

To the east of the city centre, the main north–south ring-road is traversed by the arcaded **Ottoman aqueduct** which supplied Chalcis with water from two springs on the slopes of Mt Dírfys, 24km away.

SOUTH TO LEFKANDI & ERETRIA

The road south from Chalkída crosses the rich and fertile Lelantine Plain, mentioned in the Homeric *Hymn to Apollo* as famous for its vineyards. It was the object of deadly rivalry between ancient Chalcis and Eretria, and its value was also appreciated in later epochs: the landscape is punctuated with Venetian towers and forts, which combined to guard its agricultural activity and inhabitants as well as to protect the southern approaches to Chalcis.

LEFKANDI

The importance of Lefkandí (*map p. 598, D2*) lies in the fact that the finds made here have dramatically illuminated a hitherto little understood period of early Greek history (referred to pejoratively as the 'Dark Age') between the 11th and 9th centuries BC. In precisely this period, Lefkandí, which had been inhabited from the Early Bronze Age, became a flourishing and important centre for a wide area of eastern Greece and the islands, with trade contacts with Cyprus and the Levant. The wealth of the finds and the scale of one of the funerary buildings uncovered here contrast markedly with what little has been found from this period elsewhere in the Greek world. Around 700 BC, however, probably as the result of the Lelantine war with neighbouring Chalcis (*see above*), Lefkandí was abandoned and is heard of no more. It was superseded by the city of Eretria, and most scholars now identify Lefkandí with 'Old Eretria', the city Homer mentions together with Chalcis in the Catalogue of Ships (*Iliad II, 537*). The fascinating finds from Lefkandí are in the museum in Eretria (*see opposite*).

The site

On the top of the flat-topped promontory of Xirópolis, to the south of the bay, the remains of a **settlement** with a complex of three cemeteries has been excavated by the British School (*little for the visitor to see*). In the modern residential area, 200m uphill to the north of the harbour (between Chrysánthemon and Plateón streets, on Toúmba Hill), is the so-called **Heroön**, a large area now covered by a protective roof. This is what remains of a once-imposing peripteral building, constructed from timber and mud brick over the burial of an important 'prince' or warrior of the early 10th century BC. The building was unusually large, approximately 14m wide by almost 50m long, with an apsidal end to the west, and an entrance from the east. It appears to have possessed internal and external wooden colonnades supporting a steeply raking roof—a new form of monumental architecture which in some respects prefigures later Greek temple design. The ashes of a man, wrapped in a linen tunic with embroidered bands and placed in a bronze urn, were interred inside. Close to that was found the burial of a woman (not cremated as the man had been), wearing a gold pectoral and a gold

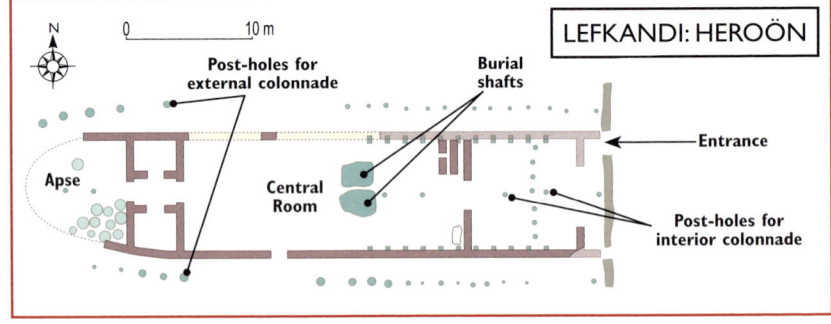

disc over each breast. The presence of a knife beside her head has led some to surmise a ritual sacrifice. Four horses were also buried in the same complex. The fact that the building was only used for a very limited period before it was covered by the mound makes it difficult to determine what function it originally fulfilled.

ERETRIA

From Lefkandí the coast road soon leads to Erétria (*map p. 599, A3*). The modern settlement, founded as Néa Psará in 1824 by refugees from the island of Psará, overlies much of the ancient city, whose ruins are the most extensive on Euboea. Three kilometres north of the town are the ancient quarries (now reactivated) of the beautiful maroon-red and white marble, known as *marmor chalcidicum* (Chalcidian marble) to the ancients and as *Fior di pesco* ('peach flower') during the Renaissance.

HISTORY OF ERETRIA

Eretria was one of the chief maritime states of Greece and is included in the Homeric Catalogue. Together with Chalcis, it joined in trade with Syria, and in the 8th century BC settled colonies in Italy, Sicily and the North Aegean. The city sent troops to burn down the Persian capital at Sardis in 498 BC, a gesture which drew upon it the wrath of the Persians, who some years later razed the city to the ground and enslaved the inhabitants. The city made a partial recovery, sending contingents to Salamis in 480, and to Plataea in 479 BC. In 377 BC it joined the Second Athenian League. In 198 BC it was plundered by the Romans; and after its destruction in 87 BC in the Mithridatic wars, the city was never rebuilt until modern times. A school of philosophy was founded at Eretria in 320 BC. Excavations have been carried out since 1964.

The museum

The principal archaeological sites lie scattered to both sides of the main road. A visit best begins at the museum (*open daily except Mon, 8.30–3*), which stands just to the south of the road. There are two rooms, one dedicated to exhibits from prehistoric times to the beginning of the 6th century BC, the other containing the pedimental sculpture of the Temple of Apollo Daphnephoros and later Classical and Hellenistic pieces.

Room 1: The cases to the left exhibit the extraordinary finds from Lefkandí, bearing witness both to its wealth and to the extent of its commercial trade overseas. Of particular note are the broad alabastron in clay with magnificent designs of griffin, deer and roe-buck in a light slip on dark background (c. 1100 BC); vases imported from Italy and Palestine; and an elegant clay centaur with fine Protogeometric decoration, which was curiously found broken in two halves and buried in separate burials. Note also the curious cup, whose steadying handle ingeniously ends in a leg wearing a fine laced boot. Also exhibited here are some simple but refined items of gold jewellery. The showcases to the right exhibit a wide variety of pottery, including a number of large, decorated funerary amphorae characteristic of the Geometric period.

Room 2: The sculpture fragments from the west pediment of the Temple of Apollo Daphnephoros ('Bearer of Laurel') date from the end of the 6th century BC. The scene, presided over by a central, standing figure of Athena with the Gorgon's head on her breast-plate, depicts Theseus carrying off Hippolyta, also called Antiope, Queen of the Amazons. The pieces are typical of the aristocratic art of the late Archaic period. The showcases exhibit objects mostly from Classical and Hellenistic Eretria.

The site: north of the road

Western walls and West Gate: A circuit of nearly 4km of walls surrounded and protected the city, joining the acropolis hill in the northwest with the harbour in the southeast corner. The first enceinte was built in the 8th century BC; what you see today dates from c. 400 BC and is well preserved, with the moat and the bases of external bastions. At the point where the ancient road from Chalcis entered the city, is the **West Gate (1)** and barbican. The ample vaulted drainage passage is finely constructed, with a round arch at one end and a corbelled support at the other.

Palaces: Between the entrance and the West Gate, you will have crossed an excavated area of large residences or **palaces (2)**, some contiguous with the west wall. Although there are several superimposed layers of construction here, the design of the houses around a central peristyle court is always discernible. A well-preserved clay bath remains *in situ* in one. Many different colours and types of stone were used for the threshold blocks.

Temple of Dionysus and theatre: The 4th-century BC **Temple of Dionysus (3)**, whose base survives, was a Doric peripteral structure with an altar to the east. The temple precinct abuts—as is appropriate for the deity—the 5th-century BC **theatre (4)**, whose form is clear, although it has largely been left covered. It retains its seven lower rows of seats, much defaced; the upper tiers were nearly all removed to build the modern village. The design has unusual innovations: from the orchestra, steps descend through a square opening into an underground vaulted passage leading to the hyposkenion; it was used for the sudden appearance and disappearance of agents of the underworld, as well as for the facilitating of special sound effects.

Gymnasium: Further east, above an area identified as the site of a stadium, is a **gymnasium (5)**. Near its west end was found an inscribed stele set up in honour of a gymnasiarch and benefactor. At the eastern extremity is an extensive series of water conduits which supplied the bathing troughs, still clearly visible

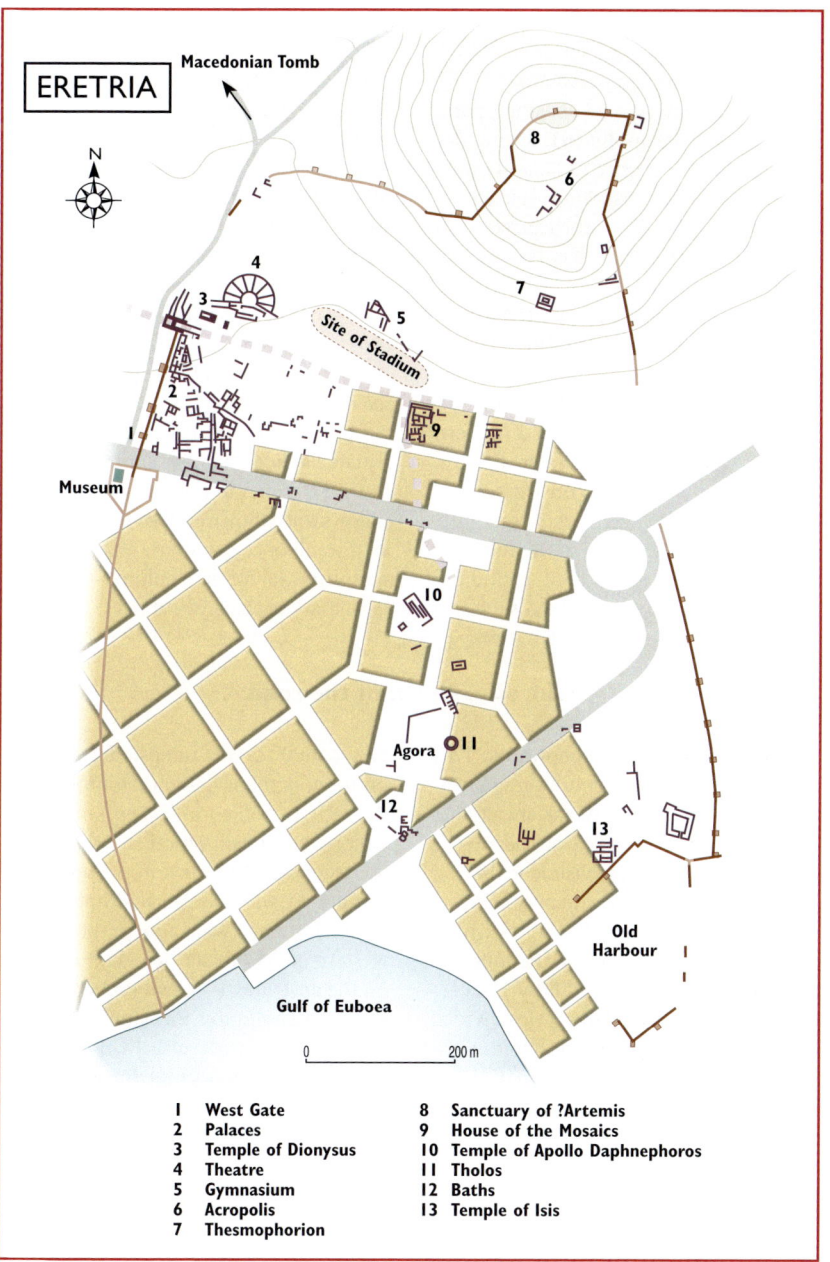

ERETRIA

Macedonian Tomb

N

Site of Stadium

Museum

Agora

Old Harbour

Gulf of Euboea

0   200 m

1 West Gate	8 Sanctuary of ?Artemis
2 Palaces	9 House of the Mosaics
3 Temple of Dionysus	10 Temple of Apollo Daphnephoros
4 Theatre	11 Tholos
5 Gymnasium	12 Baths
6 Acropolis	13 Temple of Isis
7 Thesmophorion	

along the side of a room with a plain mosaic floor.

Acropolis: Above the gymnasium, paths lead up to the **acropolis (6)**, where the late 5th-century BC enceinte and its well-preserved towers in isodomic masonry are visible, especially to the east side. On the way up are the remains of a **thesmophorion (7)** (sanctuary to Demeter and Kore) and the **sanctuary of a female deity (8)**, perhaps Artemis Olympia.

House of the Mosaics: Recognisable because it is partly covered by a modern building and roof, this is a large and important residence **(9)** constructed c. 370 BC with private quarters and an ample public area. Much of the furniture and small objects found here, including the exceptional terracotta gorgon's head, are now in the museum. The figurative mosaics are preserved *in situ*. They are executed mostly in black and white, soberly highlighted with colour. The house appears to have been destroyed by fire a hundred years after it was built.

Macedonian Tomb: On a hill 1km west of the theatre, a tumulus encloses a Macedonian tomb (*key from museum. Not signed. Take the asphalt road parallel to west side of the archaeological area; then first fork left. Road climbs; as it turns sharply right, the tomb is at the summit of the hill crowned with pines*). The neatly cut dromos on the north side leads to a square vaulted chamber containing two funeral couches in marble with carved pillows and draperies, two thrones and a table, all once coloured. A funerary sculpture—a lion or a sphinx—would have marked the grave above.

The site: south of the road

Temple of Apollo Daphnephoros: This is Eretria's most significant monument **(10)**, and was the hub of the ancient city. The most recent excavations are covered over; all that is visible is the large stylobate of the Doric peripteral temple, erected c. 530–520 BC, to which the pedimental sculpture in the museum originally belonged. It had 6 by 14 columns, with a cella of three aisles divided by a double row of columns. Noteworthy is the beautiful dressing of the blocks of the lowest level, which retain their natural irregular profile underneath and are finished to a perfectly flat, lipped ledge on the upper surface. Below what is seen however, archaeologists have identified two earlier buildings: the first, c. 800 BC, was an apsidal Daphnephorion, perhaps designed to imitate the early hut of laurel (*daphni*) branches which traditionally stood at Delphi; the second, built over it in the mid-7th century BC, was a longer building, again terminating in a wide apse at the northwestern end, with six (wooden) columns on the ends and 19 down each side. In plan and design this building has affinities with the Heroön at Lefkandí and with the early hekatompedon at Samos (*see p. 488*). It lies partially under the north edge of the visible temple base.

Agorá and baths: A meticulously cut circular base with a central circular pit is visible in the area occupied by the ancient agorá. This **tholos (11)** dates from the 4th century BC and is possibly the sanctuary of a hero. Beyond it, on what was the edge of the harbour in ancient times, are **baths (12)** of the 4th century BC, probably belonging to a gymnasium complex. To the east of these are the ru- ins of a **Temple of Isis (13)**, whose cult was introduced into the Greek world by mariners and merchants returning from Egypt. The broken cult statue in terracotta was found *in situ* when the building was excavated in 1917.

AROUND MOUNT DIRFYS & MOUNT OLYMPOS

The two peaks of central Euboea are Mt Dírfys (1743m), the island's highest mountain, and the gentler Mt Ólympos (1171m). The area between them is one of the loveliest landscapes in all of Greece, forested with many varieties of trees, generously watered, and dotted with castles, medieval churches, springs, gorges and simple villages.

A good base for exploring is (Áno) **Stení** (*map p. 598, D1*), an attractive village of balconied houses and stone dwellings in a valley of plane trees at the mouth of the pass across the east shoulder of Dírfys. At c. 600m it remains pleasantly cool in summer. There is a delightful shady square and the sound of running spring water is everywhere.

Above Stení, the road climbs rapidly and unrelentingly to the watershed through forests of chestnut, pine, spruce, wild cherry and plane. At the top the views are magnificent into Boeotia and towards Mt Parnassus, and over the east coast towards Skyros. The bald, conical **peak of Mt Dírfys** rises clear to the northwest. The mountain's presiding deity was Hera, who assumed the epithet Dirphya. A track climbs from the ridge to the northwest above the tree-line to the Fountain of Liri Refuge (*information from E.O.S. Halkidas, Angelí Govíou 22, Chalkída; T: 22210 25230*). From the refuge a marked path leads to the long ridge of the summit in under 2hrs.

On the northern side the road descends tortuously to **Strópones** (*map p. 598, D1*), with many traditional stone houses, continuing beyond through magnificent scenery to the isolated shore at **Chiliadoú** (*map p. 598, D1*). To the southwest of the mountain extends a wide, sloping apron of watered valleys. In medieval times this fertile landscape was parcelled out amongst local feudal lords, hence the many **Frankish and Venetian towers**. There are particularly well-preserved examples at Pisónas (*map p. 598, D2*) and at Amfithéa and Pýrgos further northeast.

Around Kambiá

The springs which rise beneath these mountains were often in antiquity the site of shrines to the nymphs and other deities. These later became churches: then more chapels and churches were built in their own right. The area of **Kambiá** (south of Stení via Káto Stení) is especially rich in both water and churches. In the densely wooded valley above the village is a trout farm. The water was collected by an aqueduct in antiquity: at the southwest corner of the gorge, a deep, natural split in the rockface has been dressed and enlarged to form a water conduit (best seen from the road that descends the east side of the valley below Kambiá). At **Aghía Kyriakí** (5km below Kambiá), by a waterfall beneath mature planes, the church is built into a cave, with the apse in the natural rock. An aghiasma, or pool of sacred water, is cut into the north side of the floor, behind which the rushing of an underground stream can be heard.

Around Loútsa and Kathení

The wide area below Dírfys is dotted with 12th–14th-century rural churches, many with painted interiors. Several lie in the area of Loútsa and Kathení (respectively 6km and 8km west of Stení; map p. 598, D1). In **Loútsa**, take the road which drops down southwest of the church of the Theotókos in the main square and follow it for 600m to find the 13th-century church of Aghía Paraskeví, a small and isolated barrel-vaulted chapel with three arches, heavily buttressed to the south side (*the door is opened by pulling the wire to the right-hand side*). The interior contains fine paintings of the 16th century. The clearest are on the west wall, where the *Last Judgement* unfolds in every detail, with the presence of the Almighty ingeniously represented by the small window through which the light enters the church, and from which a river of fire descends.

To the north of Loútsa is the entrance to the majestic **Agáli Gorge**, whose waters descend straight from the southern slopes of Dírfys, which rise unimpeded to the summit directly above.

A short distance to the southwest of Kathení, a sign points west down a track 2.5km to Eriá (**Moní Erión**), which lies amongst trees beside the lower reaches of the Koumbés torrent, which descends originally from the Agáli Gorge. The tiny 13th-century church, c. 4m by 4m, is surmounted by a disproportionately high dome. All the surfaces inside are painted, but much blackened with candle soot. The monastery buildings were destroyed in 1840, and only the church now remains. The springs here once fed the Ottoman aqueduct to Chalkída (*see p. 609*).

Voúni

A different design of church, but one particular to Euboea, is encountered in the two beautiful 13th-century churches at Voúni (5km southwest of Stení), to the south side of the main village road: the churches of the **Metamorphosis** and, further west, of the **Ághii Apóstoli**. Both are of substantial size, built on a rectangular plan with an apse. The cruciform element of their design is intimated by the elevated transverse vault which bisects them and gives the buildings greater height. The first has had a later narthex added and possesses an early example of a free-standing belfry, an innovation which may be an example of Western, Frankish influence in Orthodox architecture of the 13th century.

Makrychóri and the Manikiótis Gorge

This area (*map p. 599, A2*) is accessible by the scenic road which rises north from Amárynthos (*see p. 620*) through a sea of olive groves into the eastern foothills of Mt Ólympos. The road levels off at the attractive mountain villages of **Séta and Káto Séta**, where there are country tavernas with good wine. At **Machrychóri**, the early 14th-century cemetery church of Ághios Dimítrios lies in the centre of the village, just below the level of the road. The design has the characteristically Euboean elevated transverse vault in the centre. The interior, with its simple altar and stone floor, is decorated with 15th-century paintings of considerable quality, although darkened with soot.

Beyond Machrychóri is **Maníkia**, after which the road begins to descend the impressive gorge of the Manikiótis river. The valley is deep and tranquil, hemmed by vertical scarps that rise to 800m on its north side. The gorge ends abruptly just west of the village of **Koíli**: on the northern bastion of cliff at its entrance are traces of well-constructed polygonal walling, suggesting that the entrance was marked by a fortified lookout in antiquity. These are high up on the precipice above the entrance to the gorge, just below the summit: they can best be seen from a point on the last level stretch of road, before the final descent by hairpin bends. Further west, a **medieval tower** still stands on the crest. From the gorge the road drops into the lush, hilly country of the eastern corner of central Euboea, whose natural centre for exploration is Kými.

KYMI & THE CENTRAL EAST OF THE ISLAND

Kými

In common with other towns which were founded or re-founded in the 18th century and knew modest prosperity during the 19th, Kými (*map p. 599, A1*) has a stately air, with gardened villas and stone houses. It is famous for its figs and honey, and had a strong maritime tradition; in 1821 it put to sea a fleet of 55 merchant ships, which earned it a bombardment from the Turks. Much of the town is a loosely connected series of semi-rural neighbourhoods, stretching over the hills and looking out to Skyros. In the outlying districts to the north, graves of the 4th and 3rd centuries BC have frequently come to light. The spirit of the place is pleasingly captured in the **Kými Folklore Museum** (*open daily 10–1 & 5–7.30*), in a Neoclassical town house to the right of the road as you exit the centre for the port.

To the north of Kými a road descends through a valley of plane trees to the **springs** (1.5km) of the town's homonymous mineral water, which is now bottled and distributed all over Greece. The road which leaves the town to east and then heads north terminates at the **Convent of the Metamorphosis** (4km), founded in the 17th century on what has been claimed as the site of ancient Kyme. The setting is panoramic and protected, well-endowed with water, and has a natural acropolis, now occupied by the remains of the Venetian castle of Ághios Geórgios. Below Kými to the east is the port which serves the ferry crossing to Skyros.

Áno Potamiá

From Platána on the bay of Kými, a road leads uphill for 3km to the archaeological site of Áno Potamiá, on the summit of a steep, conical hill (*access is easiest by the west slope; the east slope, which preserves substantial stretches of wall, is densely covered with undergrowth*). The **ruins** extend over a large area: at the crown of the hill is the well-preserved base of a Hellenistic fortress, with the remains of adjacent buildings (possibly barracks) and dwellings, one with a baking oven. The area is scattered with potsherds, broken tiles and fragments of white marble. The earliest habitation on the site goes back to Neolithic times (4th millennium BC), when the settlement was located in the saddle between this and the hill to the south. The small **museum** (*no fixed opening times; ask locally for the 'fílakas'/custodian*) in a converted hall beside the church in the nearby village of Potamiá, contains the artefacts found at the site, from various periods.

SIX BYZANTINE CHURCHES

The wide, fertile valley that stretches south from Kými Bay as far as Lake Dýstos knew considerable prosperity in the 13th and 14th centuries. As a consequence it is dotted with churches from this period, many of which have wall-paintings. Six of the most important are described below. They are grouped around two principal centres: Oxý-lithos and Avlonári.

Churches near Oxýlithos

The scenic village of Oxýlithos (*map p. 599, A1*) clusters around the sharp conical peak of an extinct volcano (now crowned by a modern church). The road south out of the village makes a sharp bend around a modern church: down the hill which leads out of the curve of the bend is the tiny 13th-century chapel of **Aghía Ánna**, decorated with wall-paintings of different periods. The fine *Pantocrator* in the ceiling is by a more sophisticated hand than the later scenes on the south wall. Close by, and of greater architectural interest, is the **church of the Theotókos** (*left of the main road, 300m beyond the modern church*). The unusual design is articulated in several successive developments: the nucleus is a small, domeless 13th-century vaulted chapel of rectangular plan, with the characteristic Euboean elevated transverse barrel vault bisecting the space and a small faceted apse; in the subsequent century a square, cross-vaulted narthex was added to the west; finally, in the last 50 years, a modern vestibule was added yet further west. The interior has wall-paintings of the 15th century, interesting both for their quality and subject-matter: in the cross-vaults of the narthex, *Christ at the Well with the Woman of Samaria* (north) and a very literal interpretation of the text, 'Take up thy bed and walk' (east). In the same narthex, a *Dormition of the Virgin* (north) faces *St John Dictating the Revelation to Prochoros* (south), with *Abraham and Sarah with the Three Angels* (west). The floor, with elements in a yellow stone, is also of considerable age.

Churches around Avlonári

The principal centre of this area of the island is the attractive village of **Avlonári** (*map p. 599, A1*). Its narrow streets of balconied houses wind up to the summit of a hill, crowned by one of Euboea's best-preserved Frankish towers, erected in 1260 over ancient foundations on the site of what is believed to have been an ancient sanctuary of Apollo. In the vicinity are two churches with noteworthy paintings. In the centre of the village of **Pyrgí**, 2km north of Avlonári, is the 14th-century church of the Metamorphosis, which has small areas of painting in good condition: the *Archangel Michael* and the *Entry into Jerusalem* (north wall) reveal a high quality of workmanship, which must be almost contemporary with the church's construction. In the area of Achladerí (*map p. 599, B1*), the monastery church of **Ághios Ioánnis Pródromos Karión**, in an isolated site, stands amid the ruins of its former conventual buildings. There is a spring of excellent water with a fountain-head of Byzantine design. The plan of the church is more traditionally Byzantine, with the central dome supported on four monolithic columns with antique capitals. Other pieces of reused ancient marble in the vicinity suggest the presence of an earlier pagan structure. The interior, with its flagstone floor, is vividly painted with 15th-century murals of high quality.

The church of Ághios Dimítrios

The most important and remarkable church in the area, and one of the finest in Euboea, is the large 13th-century basilica of Ághios Dimítrios at **Chánia** (*map p. 599, A1*), just to the west of Avlonári. It is a church with a splendid presence both inside and out and has several unusual elements, such as the pointed arches of its interior, which reveal a marked Western or Frankish influence: indeed this feature tends to suggest that the elevated transverse vault with pitched roof in lieu of a dome, which is encountered so frequently in churches on Euboea, may be influenced by the transept-crossing of contemporary Gothic structures in the West. As a design, it certainly represents a significant deviation from the traditional Byzantine circle (dome) on square. It must also have reduced the complexity—and therefore the cost—of construction.

The dedication to St Demetrius is possibly significant: the saint often supersedes Demeter in the Christianisation of pagan sanctuaries. This church lies in a rural position at the heart of a low-lying, fertile area of cultivation, a configuration typical in ancient times for sanctuaries to Demeter. Demetrius was a Roman soldier turned Christian, and is often depicted slaying a fellow (heathen) Roman soldier, neatly symbolising the victory of Christianity over the pagan.

The **exterior** has beautiful features at both the east and west ends: an apse in fine cloisonné brick and stonework with a three-lobed window, and an attractive surround to the west door with further brick embellishments, which are echoed in the surround of the niche above and in the brickwork below the eaves of the cupola. The **naos** is entered through a narrow, steeply arched doorway, with two antique columns and capitals to either side. Not much remains of the wall-paintings, except for a fine face of St George (centre north wall) and a graphic Last Supper table, laid with delicacies, visible above the templon screen to the south side: their style would date them to the mid-15th century. Two 17th-century candlesticks in cipollino marble (*see p. 628*) stand before a masonry templon-screen incorporating carved marble reliefs in the lower area.

Aghía Thékla

The hidden, 13th-century chapel of Aghía Thékla stands in a delightful setting of plane trees, running water and nightingales (*map p. 599, A1; branch left 1km north of Chánia; after a further 1km, take the first left turn to the village of Aghía Thékla. Just before the mod-*

ern church in the village, a narrow road leads 50m steeply down to the chapel by a stream). The design is a simple, apsed rectangle with an elevated transverse barrel vault. The hands of two artists can be detected in the murals: the artist of the *Presentation of the Virgin* in the northwest corner has a much less sophisticated style than that of the talented 14th-century artist of the figures to the south of the apse.

AMARYNTHOS, LEPOURA & ALIVERI

A number of the Early Helladic artefacts in the museum at Erétria come from excavations in the area of **Amárynthos** (*map p. 599, A2*), which was an important centre in antiquity. A kilometre and a half beyond the eastern limit of the town is the **hill of Palaiochóra**, between the main road and the shore, crowned by two 12th-century churches. Both have the characteristic Euboean design with rectangular floorplan, and an elevated transverse barrel vault to create the crossing. Closest to the water is the church of the Koímisis tis Theotókou, which has wall-paintings of considerable quality but in poor condition; the church of the Metamorphosis has no painting: the simple dignity of the design is revealed in the plain stone interior.

Beyond Lépoura (*map p. 599, B2*) and approximately halfway from there southwest to Alivéri, clearly visible on a hill 2km to the south of the main road, are the remains of one of the island's oldest Frankish strongholds, the early 13th-century **Rizókastro**, consisting of a well-preserved enceinte of walls surrounding a pre-existing tower. The castle was fiercely contended between the Turks and Greek independence fighters in the summer of 1823. Four kilometres due north of it, in the hilly area of the interior, is a church of Ághios Dimítrios, generally known as the **Kókkini Ekklisía**, or 'Red Church', because of the preponderance of red tiles in its masonry (*best reached by the right/north turn signed 'Ághios Dimítrios', 1km east of the municipal limit of Alivéri. The road leads through olive groves and a functioning lignite and stone quarry; after 2.4km, the church is to the left, hidden on a low hill*). The church exemplifies the 14th-century delight in decorative tile patterns: a cross pattern at the east end and a half-moon over the door. An ancient offering-table with three shallow depressions and a fragment of an Ionic capital are incorporated in the west front, with other ancient elements elsewhere. There are vestiges of murals in the apsidal conch.

KARYSTOS & THE FAR SOUTHEAST

The grand sweep of the setting of Kárystos (*map p. 599, D2*) is unexpected, with the majestic rise of Mt Óchi behind and the theatrical openness of the space between the mountain and the curve of the sheltered gulf. The modern town is spacious, peaceful and pleasantly indolent, and makes a good base for exploring the south of the island. The site of ancient Karystos lies a little to the north of the modern town; its acropolis is still prominently marked by the pinnacle of Castel Rosso, the rambling fortress from which the Venetians held the south of the island.

HISTORY OF KARYSTOS

Karystos is first mentioned in Book II of the *Iliad*: it took part in the Trojan War under the command of its king, Nauplius. In Classical times it became the principal commercial and cultural centre of southern Euboea, issuing its own coinage in the 6th century BC. Remembering its destruction in 490 BC at the hands of the Persians, the city allied with Xerxes in the second Persian invasion, and was treated punitively for its medising by Themistocles as a result. It was part of the First and Second Athenian Leagues, and after 338 BC came under Macedonian control. Apollodorus, a comic dramatist, and Antigonus, a bronze sculptor and writer, were 3rd-century BC natives of Karystos. The Romans took the city in 198 BC; their later exploitation of the marble quarries made the city into an important and prosperous provincial centre.

After the liberation of the city from the Turks in 1833, the centre was laid out on a grid pattern by a Bavarian architect, at the request of King Otto, who desired that the city be named 'Othonoupolis' in his honour. The focus was to be the square where the church of Ághios Nikólaos (1912) now stands. The plan languished.

One block north of the harbour (intersection of Kótsika and Sachtoúri) are the remains of a 2nd-century AD **Roman funerary monument** of a wealthy official in charge of the marble quarries. It had the appearance of a small, peripteral Ionic temple, with 6 by 7 columns and an entrance on the east side: its base and the cella threshold are visible. Some of its decorative elements (a carved tondo depicting the bust of a man with a bridled horse) is now incorporated, along with other antique marbles, in the east side of the 13th-century tower on the harbour esplanade (east of Aiólou), known as the **Bourtzi**. The tower is a fortress, of irregular hexagonal form, with two cannon embrasures on the seaward wall and well-preserved machicolations high up on the south wall.

Opposite is the city's small **Archaeological Museum** (*open daily except Mon, 8.30–3; free*), which displays the finds from the Drakóspito on the summit of Mt Óchi (mostly pottery from the 4th and 3rd centuries BC, but also an early Archaic bronze earring and other pieces showing earlier use of the site); finds from Neolithic through to Byzantine times from Plakarí, to the west of Kárystos; interesting evidence from a metallurgy workshop at Archámpoli (east coast); and Megarian bowls of the 3rd century BC with beautiful relief designs.

North of Kárystos

In the gorges to the north of Kárystos are several important sites and monuments. At the top of the village of **Kalývia** (*map p. 599, D2*) is the attractive, late medieval church of the Taxiárches. The luminous interior incorporates some antique elements:

the steep drum of the dome sits on four monolithic columns, each surmounted by a double capital: Byzantine on top of Ionic. The whitewash has been removed to reveal a *Pantocrator* over the apse.

Due north of Kárystos is **Grabiá**, where there are mineral springs of considerable force at the church of Aghía Triáda, on the east side of the hill. Finds going back as far as Palaeolithic times have been made in the cave (*closed*) above the church, from one of the earliest human settlements on Euboea. In the depths of the cave is a watercourse with falls and pools.

The site of the **Castel Rosso** (*accessible either from Grabiá or from Mýli*), dominating the plain and bay of Kárystos, has impressive natural defences to the north and east. It was the acropolis of ancient Karystos, and the lower courses of the existing faceted west tower are composed of large, rectangular poros blocks and courses of polished marble taken from ancient buildings and fortifications. The castle, the largest on the island, was built in the first decades of the 13th century by Ravano dalle Carceri, the triarch who had been awarded the southern third of Euboea by the Frankish overlord Boniface of Monferrat. In 1261, the Latin emperor Baldwin II took refuge here when he was driven out of Byzantium. The castle was effectively under Venetian control from 1365 until the Turkish conquest of 1470. Why it became called 'Castel Rosso' is not known. Behind the castle to the northeast, the medieval aqueduct brought water from the springs on the hillside opposite. The conduit would always have been vulnerable to attack; for this reason there are cistern complexes in the north corner of the enceinte and a well beneath the floor of the chapel of Profítis Ilías at the summit (lift the metal trap). The impressive gateway and the five-sided eastern bastion have been to some degree rebuilt; the square tower in the southwest corner, with artillery embrasures, is an Ottoman addition. Across the expanse of the bailey is an immense quantity of collapsed rubble, indicating that the interior was densely constructed, with an eye to withstanding long sieges.

Mýli and Kýlindri

The road north from Kárystos, past the hospital, leads into the area of Palaiochóra, the site of ancient Karystos, at the foot of the acropolis hill now crowned by the castle. It continues beyond, into the valley of **Mýli** (3.5km), named from its water-mills. The village is a welcome retreat in summer heat, with a couple of shaded tavernas. At the top of the village are vigorous springs of water.

The road ends at the church of Ághii Theódori, where a path continues up the slopes of Mt Óchi to the ancient quarry at **Kýlindri** (*map p. 599, D2*) and eventually to the summit of the mountain (*from the end of the cement road, go straight and cross the stream bed. Ahead, you can see a first quarry to the right of the gorge and stream, then a second face much higher up; on top of this, you can make out the supine, abandoned columns. This is the objective: it is 40mins uphill to the right/northeast, about 300m higher than the point of departure*). Kýlindri is a truly remarkable and evocative site. The half-dozen abandoned monolithic columns, some detached from the rock bed, others still at a more protean stage, are of massive dimensions: approximately 12m long, with a diameter of over a metre: they already have a gentle, swelling entasis and cuffs at either end. They await a

Abandoned columns at Kýlindri, on the lower slopes of Mt Óchi. Kárystos can be seen in the distance: the columns would have been destined for the harbour there, where they would have been taken by ship to adorn a temple or basilica in Rome or elsewhere in the Empire.

shipment that never materialised. The square holes in the bedrock are for fixing pegs and capstans to lift and manoeuvre the columns. From this vantage point the port of Kárystos, where the monoliths would have been loaded for export, looks despairingly far away over a terrain that presents seemingly insurmountable problems. The sheer size of such columns made transportation very difficult. Yet by the construction of pistes of beaten earth, and by the use of a combination of braked sledges and calibrated rolling, such blocks were moved down in large numbers. From the port they were shipped, slung just below water-level between two barges lashed together in the form of a catamaran. Although this provided the best hope of stability at sea, many never made it to their destination.

All around are other quarries, cutting faces and assays: it was the quarry-master's expertise that selected the best veins. Below, as you descend, you see a flat-topped rectangular knob which remains from the surface quarrying of thin decorative plaques of marble, cut from the bedrock.

MOUNT OCHI

There are several routes up to the summit of Mt Óchi (1399m): it can be reached with some difficulty in 3hrs from Kýlindri. The easiest and safest route is from the northwest, where the mountain road which continues high above Grabiá eventually brings you to above 900m, from where the peak is visible and can be reached with a further climb of just over an hour. The path, latterly very steep, is hinted by stone cairns. Cloud can suddenly and unpredictably envelop the summit, and care should be taken to ensure that weather conditions and pressure are stable before attempting the climb.

The summit is marked by the chapel of Profítis Ilías. Fifty metres further east, right on the ridge, is the **Drakóspito**, the finest of all *drakóspita* (*see box opposite*) and one of the most extraordinary and unexpected sights in Greece. It camouflages itself so well against a background of the rock from which it is made, that it can be missed at first. Symmetrical, pleasingly proportioned, and precisely constructed in horizontal courses of blocks with often beautifully drafted borders, it is almost certainly a Hellenistic construction. The posts and lintels of the doorway are magnificent, and the long interior space is beautifully corbelled. There are windows and niches in the double south wall. All around are pieces of stone with perforations or shapes that have been worked by hand. For a military surveying point, the views over the commercially crucial straits between Euboea and Andros could not be better. Very frequently, however, nothing at all can be seen from this point except the inside of a cloud.

THE FAR SOUTHEAST

The eastern seaboard of Euboea was one of the most important maritime traffic corridors in the ancient Aegean, on the route between the Black Sea and the commercial centres of Athens and Corinth. It was also well known for being one of the windiest and most tempestuous channels in the region, funnelling the wind just as effectively as it funnelled the commercial traffic. The ancient city of Geraistos, at the southern end of this coast, profited richly from the tariffs it levied on passing merchant vessels. Its site, which corresponds to the protected **Kastrí Bay** (*map p. 599, D2*), is hard to reach today (*take the unmade track descending from the asphalt road just after it turns sharply north, 11km from Kárystos*). By the bay, in a field to the right, c. 400m before the track ends at the church of the Zoödóchos Pigí, are the vestiges of a Classical temple. Large architectural blocks, one with a clearly preserved triglyph, mark the site of what may have been a temple of Poseidon: other material from the site has been taken to the museum in Kárystos.

To the ancient seaman this was a welcome haven in bad weather. Today it is a wild and inaccessible place. Maps which breezily show roads crossing the corner of the Óchi massif, or circumnavigating its lower slopes, should be treated with caution. Time and patience, and strong legs or a strong vehicle, are needed to explore this area: there are no signs. Those who have the energy to explore, however, will be rewarded—especially on the north side of the mountain—by some grand and beautiful valleys, rich in flora, butterflies and fauna. Medieval mule-paths and stone *kalderímia* can be followed along the scenic **Dimosári Gorge**. From the point mentioned above for beginning the climb to the summit of Óchi, a path to the north leads down into the gorge: at least 8hrs should be allowed for the journey down to the shore and back. There is fresh water running in falls almost all the way down to the sea.

DRAKOSPITA

These remarkable megalithic constructions are unique to Euboea. Over 20 of them have been identified on the island, mostly in the areas of Mt Óchi and Stýra. Most are rectangular: some have windows and indented niches or shelves inside. They are mostly solitary, and intentionally panoramic, though at Palli-Lakka they exist in a small group and in a position with limited visibility.

Before wildly surmising, as many have, about prehistoric places of cult, it should be recalled that this whole area was dedicated in antiquity to quarrying stone, and that a community would have lived on site. The mountains are subject to sudden storms for much of the early part of the year, and solid refuges would have been a real boon. The limestone quarried here naturally splits into large slabs or schists, which lends itself to a technique of superimposing and corbelling them for a roof. The drakóspita are unlikely to date to before the 4th or 3rd centuries BC. They may well have been used in more recent times for penning animals. None of the above precludes the possibility of an additional cult aspect to the buildings; we know little about the people who worked in the quarries.

STYRA, MARMARI & LAKE DYSTOS

(Palaiá) Stýra (*map p. 599, C2*), a pleasant enough village grouped around a *plateía* with trees, can make a good base for exploring the fascinating hinterland, still of interest in spite of the ravages of the fires of 2007. On the coast 3.5km below is the port of Néa Stýra, with ferries to Aghía Marína on the mainland.

HISTORY OF ANCIENT STYRA

Styra is mentioned in the *Iliad* (*II, 540*) as participating in the Euboean expedition to Troy under the leadership of Elephenor. Although Herodotus sees its inhabitants as of Dryopian origin, Strabo relates that the city was settled by colonists from the Marathonian Tetrapolis (*Geog. X, 6*). In 490 BC it was taken by the Persian commander Datis and the offshore island of Aigilia was used for the safe-keeping of Persian hostages. Styra contributed two ships to the Greek force at Salamis in 480 BC and soldiers to the Battle of Plataea; as a consequence its name was engraved with those of other participating Greek cities on the serpentine bronze trophy, formerly at Delphi and now in the Hippodrome in Istanbul. After 477 BC Styra was part of the Athenian League, and in 415 BC fought with Athens in the Sicilian campaign. In Roman times the acropolis area may have been used as a settlement for the quarry-workers. The Venetians erected their fortress of Larmena or 'Armena', remains of which are visible today, on the site of the ancient fortifications.

THE SITE

The site of ancient Styra, still largely unexplored and unexcavated, lies inland of the shore. The ancient city's remarkable and remote acropolis, however, can be seen from many points on the road up to inland Stýra, its megalithic portal silhouetted against the light, over 600m above, on the summit of the ridge to the southeast. It is here that the most fascinating remains survive.

The archaeological area (*unsigned*) of the quarries, the acropolis and the remarkable drakóspita or 'dragon's houses' (*see p. 625*) is reached by taking the main road north from the square of Stýra. *After 800m, on a bend, take the asphalt road to the right; after a further 800m turn left onto a track, and then after 100m turn right. This track climbs for 1.5km, at which point turn right at the first opportunity. After 500m, fork left. After a further 500m the track splits: a left turn takes you, after 400m, to the foot of the hill where the drakóspita can be visited (10mins); a right turn leads on (20mins) up to the principal quarries and (1hr) the acropolis.*

The Pálli-Lákka group of drakóspita

This group of buildings is found after a short climb up from where the left-hand track ends, in a dip in the hillside As you approach you encounter two parallel rectangular buildings with impressive pitched and corbelled roofs constructed from large schists, which at first sight have the appearance either of communal dwellings or large animal pens. A shallow-cut stone basin sits by the corner of the nearest building. Above and behind is a square building with a concentric corbelled roof with an open oculus in the centre, which could perhaps be covered, if necessary, with ephemeral material. There is a stone corner shelf inside.

As you climb higher, you pass two rectangular basins cut in the rock: the one to the left has a small circular depression carved on its front; further up again is an elliptical stone construction built up against the wall of natural rock behind, with two small loculi to north and south, and a wall and doorway in front. Substantially higher up, after crossing a scree of stones, is a vertical rockface (clearly cut by hand, as evidenced by the chisel striations all over its surface) fenced by a wall and doorway in front. This would appear to be one of many quarry faces in the area.

The main quarry area

The track and path up to the acropolis of Styra passes through the centre of the main ancient limestone quarry. As you climb (*15mins*) there are channels in the stone and terraces cleared in the rock. A number of shaped architectural pieces are still *in situ*: a finely tapered column (note the ring of circular indentations around the 'collar' for transportation); an abacus; several blocks of architrave with precise indentations. The rough-hewn dromos, the long horizontal cuts and cart ruts, are evidence of the laborious task of transportation. Other ancient surface quarries and screes of refuse can be seen on the hillsides opposite.

The acropolis

The acropolis (*reached after a 50-min climb*) is entered through a magnificent portal, which commands views of the whole of the Gulf of Euboea. It is composed of large monoliths of veined limestone and its lintel is still in place. To the left, as you face it from outside, are vestiges of the ancient enceinte, probably dating from the 5th century BC or earlier. This site is composed of a natural ridge of limestone tors, running northeast–southwest: the southwest tor has steps carved in its lower north side, which provided access to the lookout post on its summit. As you skirt the east side of the ridge towards the northeast tor, there are deep-cut post-holes in the rock and other cuts for gate imposts. Further north, you come to the tiny chapel of Ághios Nikólaos (with a rock-cut cistern in front of its west end) and the remains of the 15th-century Venetian stronghold, the Kastro Ármeno, now much dilapidated. The view takes in the sea to east and west, the three peaks of Attica in front, the Sounion peninsula, the islands of Makrónisos, Kea and Skyros, the Boeotian coast, the Euripos, and Mts Óchi, Dírfys and Kandíli—in short, everything.

Kokkinómylo Hill

Almost opposite the first turning towards the sites described above (*800m north from the plateía of Stýra*), a road to the left leads less than a kilometre northwest to the hill of Kokkinómylo, where a small marble monument enshrines the bones of Elias Mavromichalis (b. 1795), who died on this spot in January 1822. Mavromichalis, who hailed from a famous clan of patriots from the Mani in the Peloponnese, was a redoubtable fighter for Greek independence. He had arrived in Euboea in early January to give support to the island's resistance movement and died a matter of days later. He made his last stand against the Turks here in a windmill on this hill, remains of which can still be seen, and died for his cause together with a group of fellow revolutionaries.

MARMARI

The town of Marmári (*map p. 599, D2*) takes its name from the local crystalline veined marble, known since the Renaissance as cipollino, and which enjoyed immense popularity in imperial Rome (*see box below*). It is found in varying quality over the whole area from here to Kárystos and beyond: mostly grey and white in undulating veins, sometimes blue-grey, and sometimes (the type most prized by the Romans) in a beautiful sea-green and white. Strabo mentions a temple to Apollo Marmarinos nearby. Today Marmári is a quiet resort, served by a busy crossing from Rafína.

CIPOLLINO MARBLE

Of all the decorative marbles that the Romans extracted from the length and breadth of their empire, none had such apparent popularity or was so widely employed as *marmor carystium*, which was plentifully available in the foothills of Mt Óchi. Elegant and cool in colour, with long, green-blue veins on a translucent background, it enhanced any other marble combined with it, and above all set off the white marble of sculpture with exemplary elegance. It was abundant, resilient, adaptable to construction, and not difficult to work. The Renaissance stone-workers called it cipollino ('onion-like'), not so much because of its appearance, but because the veins of mica which colour it cause it to be easily cut, onion-like, along the seams.

Its illustrious career in Rome began, according to Cornelius Nepos (cited by Pliny, *Nat. Hist. XXXVI, 48*) when it was introduced by Mamurra of Formiae, Julius Ceasar's chief engineer in Gaul. It was extensively used in the Roman and Imperial fora, its translucence and colour being preserved and refreshed by annual applications of a solution of chalk and milk.

On the quarry at Kýlindri on Mt Óchi are some columns, around 12m high, which have been left unfinished (*see p. 623*). The Romans also extracted asbestos from these hills. The official who oversaw all this activity was a figure of some importance, as is suggested by the lavish funerary monument of the local quarry-master, whose ruins are still visible in the centre of Kárystos (*see p. 621*).

Cipollino is rarely seen properly polished today, and it appears dull when not regularly maintained. Pieces can be gathered easily in the area of the quarries and are of a rewarding lustre and elegance when polished even by the most basic machinery.

From Marmári a road leads into the interior of the island, to the attractive village of **Paradeísi** (*map p. 599, D2*), which has many stone houses in the local vernacular style and pleasantly shaded tavernas. The road continues below the western slopes of Mt Óchi, past **Ághios Dimítrios** (good taverna), and down the deep Porphýras Valley, emerging onto the steep Aegean coast at Kalérgo.

DYSTOS & AGHIA TRIADA

The landscape around **Lake Dýstos** (*map p. 599, B2*) appears as a strange cone of limestone rising from the middle of a sea of green, surrounded by bald hills. The alluvial lake itself, encircled by swallow-holes, is filled with water in spring and summer, and then recedes to a verdant reed-bed in summer and autumn. The isolated hill on the lake's east side is the **site of ancient Dystos**, inhabited since the Neolithic period, and settled in earliest antiquity by Dryopians (*access is by any of the tracks that lead west from the main road, south of the turn for Kóskina. Dense vegetation has engulfed many of the remains still on the surface and makes exploring the site arduous. The walls and terraces alone stand above the vegetation*). The walls of the 5th-century BC city, of polygonal construction, 3m high and 2m thick, with eleven towers, once described a semicircle eastward from the west cliff. The main entrance on the east, between two towers, led north to the area of the agorá. On the slopes of the hill, especially the north slope, where there are also protrusions of terraces in a later, isodomic construction method, are the remains of houses, considered important examples from the 5th century BC. They generally possessed an entrance passage, an inner court, a living room, bedrooms, and in some cases an upper storey. On top of the hill, overlooking the lake from the west, is the acropolis, the north part of which became a Venetian fortress.

Some of the remains from Dystos have made their way to the curious, ruined medieval **church of Aghía Triáda,** just to the north (*to the left, 1.2km south of Kriéza, about 200m before the descending road finally flattens out into the floor of the Dýstos valley*). The lower areas of the apse and walls still stand. The altar is a fluted column stump. The central door of the templon screen, an ancient sarcophagus standing on end, its bottom cut out to create a rectangular entranceway, is an ingenious example of recycling.

PRACTICAL INFORMATION

GETTING AROUND

Access to Euboea is either by road via the Euripos bridges (1hr from Athens, take the Schimatári exit from the Athens/Thessaloníki motorway) or via short ferry crossings from

Rafína (Attica) to Marmári (c. every 3hrs, 4 times daily, more often at weekends); from Aghía Marína (Attica) to Néa Stýra (c. every 2–3hrs); from Skála Oropoú (Attica) to Erétria (every 30mins); Arkítsa (Phthiotis) to Aidipsós (hourly); Glýfa (Phthiotis) to

Aghiókambos (every 2hrs from 7am–9pm daily). A hydrofoil service, four times weekly in the summer also links Chalkída with Límni, and Límni with Loutrá Aidipsoú and Ag. Konstantínos.

WHERE TO STAY

North Euboea
The spa hotels in Aidipsós are the luxurious **Thermae Sylla** (*T: 22260 60100, www.thermaesylla.gr*) or the **Avra Spa Hotel** (*T: 22260 22226*). Alternatively, the **Hotel Aigli** (*T: 22260 22215*) is comfortable, but without spa facilities.

In Límni, choice is limited: the **Hotel Plaza** (*T: 22270 31235*) on the waterfront is quiet and simple, and is probably the best option.

For those seeking a luxurious base for a longer period, these two historic houses are excellent solutions: **Villa Averoff** at Kírinthos (*www.villa-averoff.com*); and the house on the **Candili estate** at Prokópi (*www.candili.gr*), owned by the Noel-Baker family, who number Olympic athletes, socialist politicians, early philhellenes and Lord Byron among their ancestors.

Central Euboea
At Stení, the **Hotel Dirfys** (*T: 22280 51217*) is tranquil, very basic, but delightful. Chalkída is not an obvious choice to stay, but if necessary, the **Paliria Hotel** (*T: 22210 28001*) near the museum is a pleasant option. At Kými the **Hotel Corali** (*T: 22220 22212, www.coralihotel.gr*), a little way outside the harbour, is modern and comfortable.

South Euboea
In Kárystos, the **Apollon Suites Hotel** (*T:*

22240 22045, www.apollonsuiteshotel.com) is an Italian-run hotel on the beach, with large rooms, to the eastern end of town. Closer to the centre is the **Hotel Karystion** (*T: 22240 22391, www.karystion.gr*), less spacious, but a little more stylish, and with pleasant service.

WHERE TO EAT

In Aidipsós, the central **Mezedopoleion Armenizontas** often has good, live rebétika music. In Límni, **To Kyma**, in a handsome stone house on the waterfront, serves a delightful variety of classic Greek dishes. The well-established **To Astro** at Katoúnia, south of Límni, is good for fresh fish. **To Neon**, 1km below Stení, delightfully spread out beneath immemorial planes by a stream, specialises in local sausage and char-grilled vegetables and meats.

Geroplatanos in Mýli, near Kárystos, is somewhat similar in setting, with a good choice of dishes, especially at lunchtime on Sun. In Kárystos itself, Odós Kótsika is lined with simple, inexpensive places; they may look uninspiring, but do not underestimate the quality of meat and the freshness of the wine at the minuscule **I Melissa**, at no 27.

Otherwise, where villages have good tavernas, this is mentioned in the text.

FURTHER READING

Sarah Wheeler, *An Island Apart*, 1992. Barbro Noel-Baker, *An Isle of Greece: The Noels in Euboea* (2000), Archaeopress, Oxford.

PRACTICAL INFORMATION

The Greek islands of the Aegean are well-established as tourist destinations. Visiting them is rarely very challenging: the infrastructure exists and, especially in season, there are plenty of places to stay and eat. The following pages offer some practical tips on how to get the most out of your visit.

PLANNING A TRIP

The islands provide the opportunity for various styles of holiday, from traditional resort tourism, staying in one location the entire time, to island-hopping. In most parts of the Aegean, even if you have decided to base yourself in a single location, you can relatively easily make day trips to other nearby islands or to parts of the Greek or Turkish mainland (for Turkey a visa may be required).

Choice of island(s), choice of season

Only you know how touristy an island you want to stay on, how many archaeological sites you have an appetite for, whether Byzantine church architecture is a particular interest, whether you want to go on hikes into the hinterland or spend most of the day at the beach. All these things are possible in the Aegean, and some islands allow you to combine them all. The introductory sections to each island group in this guide will help you decide where to base yourself. The most authentic experiences are, unsurprisingly, to be had on the smaller, airport-less islands, and more generally, outside the main tourist season. It is often said that May is the finest time to travel in the area, but it should be borne in mind—at least by those who want to swim—that the Aegean only fully heats up around the beginning of June. It may also be worth noting that the August winds are the best argument to make a pebble beach seem, occasionally, superior to a sandy one.

This book attempts gives a general idea of how far the individual islands are affected by mass tourism. Larger islands may well combine huge tourist resorts with areas that are essentially untouched. Smaller islands are rarely as varied in this regard. Even the smallest Aegean island deserves some time to be truly enjoyed, however. The Blue Guide approach, albeit based on the hope that readers will be able to visit many places on their travels, is aimed at helping you to see and experience as much as possible wherever you are.

Further sources of information, literature and maps

The maps in this book are for planning purposes and are not intended as a substitute for a detailed road map of any given island. Towns, villages and sites described in detail appear in black type. Other places, including those mentioned simply for a good taverna or hotel, appear in grey. Detailed maps, especially for the walker or sailor, are not always available locally, and it is wise to stock up before you go. The best regional maps of the islands, available through good specialist shops or online, are by Road editions (www.road.gr), Skaï (shop.skai.gr) and Anavasi (www.anavasi.gr).

It is rare to find detailed information about individual Greek islands in bookshops in the English-speaking world. This guide is probably the most detailed and comprehensive Aegean islands book available. On the islands themselves, you will find a variety of more or less professionally produced books on locally relevant topics. Most Greek island municipalities have their own websites, the URL of which is usually www.name.gr, with 'name' standing for the name of the island. These sites tend to be partially aimed at the local community, and also vary in quality and organisation, but they usually offer one or two useful pieces of information on local sights, accommodation, etc.

GETTING AROUND

All the permanently inhabited islands are accessible by public ferry. Some islands also have airports, but many do not. The information about flights and ferries at the end of each chapter in this book was correct at the time of going to press, but is not detailed as timetables are subject to constant variation. The aim has been to give a general idea of routes and their frequency, to help with planning. Before travelling, always check that the service you require is running.

By air
Direct international flights to the Aegean islands tend to be charters, exclusively serving the more touristy islands, and operating only during the tourist season. Affordable ways to get to the eastern islands or the Dodecanese also include charter flights to airports on the west coast of Turkey, such as Izmir or Bodrum, while the Cyclades can in some cases be reached from Crete, with its main charter airport, Herakleion, operating plenty of flights each summer.

Scheduled flights will involve changing planes in Athens (www.aia.gr) or Thessaloníki (less frequent service but often cheaper). Any Greek Aegean island that has an airport is served by domestic flights from one or both of these cities.

By boat
All Greek Aegean islands are served by a dense and usually frequent network of ferry services, mostly at very affordable prices. Up-to-date timetables can be found on various websites, including the Greek Travel Pages (www.gtp.gr). Most islands of the central and southern Aegean are served from Greece's main port at Piraeus, which is essentially part of Athens and is serviced by a direct bus connection from Athens airport. It is important to check which berth of this large port (it serves the largest number of individual passengers of any port of Europe) a ferry moors in, as this can add up to 30mins to the connection time. In the northern Aegean, Thessaloníki also serves as a

major port. Some of the islands also have more than one main port, which the Blue Guide always points out. Some islands are more regularly, or even entirely, served by local ports, such as Rafína near Athens for the western Cyclades; Ághios Konstantínos, Volos or Kými for the Sporades; and Xánthi, Kavála or Alexandroúpolis for Samothrace or Thasos. Needless to say, many ferry services cover whole strings of islands.

Obviously, the ferry services can be affected by uncontrollable factors, the most important being the weather. The high winds of August occasionally ground shipping for a day or so, but this is not a very common occurrence.

Some islands are also served by caïque, i.e. local fishing boats that also transport passengers. These may be available reasonably regularly during high season, but otherwise depend on personal negotiation.

Organised tours

It is also possible to experience the islands through organised tours or cruises. Two of the editors of this book work for Peter Sommer, which offers culturally-focused tours on Turkish gulets (see www.petersommer.com). There are a number of other companies offering tours or packages—if you want to be part of a group, this can be a good way to see Greece. Accommodation and access to the islands will all be taken care of for you. Cachet Travel is a travel company specialising in the Eastern Aegean (Samos, Ikaría and Foúrni). They can help with hotel bookings, or even tailor an entire holiday (*see www.cachet-travel.co.uk*).

TRAVELLING WITHIN AN ISLAND

Getting around

The larger, more densely inhabited or more touristy islands usually have pretty good (and cheap) internal bus services linking the main settlements, and sometimes sites, to the main harbour or main town. In smaller islands, walking can also be a highly enjoyable way to explore. For bigger islands, though, renting a car is the best (often the only) way to get full access. This can be arranged either on the internet or locally. Taxis are also available, but be careful with them: in many cases, official rates for key trips are displayed at bus or ferry terminals. If they are not, do insist that the driver uses the meter, unless the fare he quotes seems a brilliant deal.

Accommodation

If you are pre-booking your trip, you will find a broad range of accommodation of varying cost, depending on the island or islands you choose to stay on. Plenty of on-line reviews are available.

Island-hoppers will want to be spontaneous. At the end of each chapter, a handful of suggestions are given, with websites (if they exist) and phone numbers. During high season, touts are often pushily present in harbours or airports, offering easily-organised accommodation of varying quality. If you are quite flexible and your budget is irrelevant, they are fine and you may well find somewhere very pleasant. If you prefer to be safe and not sorry, it is better to book ahead, or persevere into the centre of town and make enquiries.

The range of places to stay includes resort hotels, usually lacking character but rich in amenities. They almost always take large groups. A range of boutique hotels also exists and is a growing sector. For the most casual traveller, virtually any Greek island has *domátia*: simple, affordable rooms in the bottom price bracket. Greece also has a rapidly developing agrotourist market (www.agrotravel.gr). The properties on offer in this sector tend be restored traditional dwellings, making use of local traditional produce in terms of food and drink, and often offer additional information on the local area and how to explore its amenities. A hotel which styles itself an *archontikó* will be in an old building, typically an elegant 19th- or early 20th-century town house.

BLUE GUIDES RECOMMENDED

Hotels, restaurants and tavernas that are particularly good choices in their category—in terms of excellence, location, charm, value for money or the quality of the experience they provide—carry the Blue Guides Recommended sign: ▬. All these establishments have been visited and selected by our authors, editors or contributors as places they have particularly enjoyed and would be happy to recommend to others. To keep our entries up-to-date, reader feedback is essential: please do not hesitate to contact us (www.blueguides.com) with any views, corrections or suggestions, or join our online discussion forum.

OTHER INFORMATION

Food and drink

The local culture of each Greek Aegean island is the outcome of a long and complex cultural history. One of the best ways to appreciate this individuality and diversity is to enjoy the local food and drink. It is always advisable to enquire what local specialities exist, even in high season and even on a highly frequented island. When choosing tavernas to eat in, it is best to look out for the most likely informed crowds, namely locals, followed by non-local Greeks, followed by the French. If the menu on display at a taverna includes as a central factor any non-Greek dishes—pizza, hamburgers, bacon and eggs—go somewhere else. Touting, in other words using individuals of varying charm to talk visitors into choosing a restaurant, is very common and can be intimidating. It usually happens in the main tourist centres, and often reflects poor quality—but not always. Follow your instincts. If you speak some Greek, it is often a good idea to ignore the written menu and just ask what they have freshly cooked. Even better, in many simple, unpretentious tavernas, you are welcome to go into the kitchen and look.

Greece is one of the first regions of Europe where wine was grown, many millennia ago. Recently it has begun to produce high-quality wines of more-than-local significance. Its grapes are amongst the oldest varieties in the world, and are now part of an active process of rediscovery. It is always worth asking for local wines, either bottled or loose. Ouzo (grape-spirit flavoured with aniseed) and grappa-like spirits (Tsípouro or Tsikoudiá) are also common, as are sweet wines.

Walking and other activities

Some islands offer a variety of sporting activities in a more or less organised way, ranging from coastal paragliding in the large resorts to spelunking in gorges and caves. It is beyond the scope of this guide to deal with these. Walking, however, is one of the greatest pleasures of the islands, within the reach of everyone, with minimal skill or preparation necessary. Many of the smaller islands can be explored entirely on foot: this can mean mountaineering, hill-walking or simply strolling through the towns or across the hillsides. Many of the less developed islands offer grand and inimitable scope for pure exploration of the untouched or mostly untouched.

Sites, museums and churches

Archaeological sites and museums represent one of the key attractions of the islands. Their on-site presentation varies hugely, from none at all to detailed noticeboards, heavy use of fencing, and custodians who clearly consider the visiting public a menace. None of this is connected to the interest or beauty of the individual site. Whatever an island has to offer in terms of ancient archaeology is worth visiting and thinking about, and the same applies to medieval castles, Byzantine churches or Ottoman monuments. This guide describes all such sites in considerable detail, and gives opening times. Sadly the latter are notoriously capricious. Before you set off, it is always best to check with a local source. The Greek Ministry of Culture website (www.culture.gr) is not always kept up to date, and the official opening times it quotes are often not adhered to *in situ*.

Note that church descriptions use liturgical east, west, south etc, and not compass east. The 'east end', therefore, refers to the end of the church where the sanctuary is situated, behind the iconostasis.

CHRONOLOGY

Compiled by Heinrich Hall

NB: The Aegean is a large and immensely varied region. Non-specific dates listed here should be seen as broad approximations, reflecting general trends and developments.

Palaeolithic and Mesolithic
(before 7000 BC)

During the last ice age, c. 16,000 BC, sea levels in the Aegean were much lower than today. The Sporades and Euboea, as well as most of the north Aegean and Dodecanese, were still attached to the mainland, while the Cyclades formed a single large island. By 7000 BC the present configuration had more or less come into existence. Human communities of hunter-gatherers began to visit the sites in the Upper Palaeolithic (when Melian obsidian was taken to the Argolid) and Mesolithic (e.g. Cave of the Cyclops on Gioúra, c. 10,000 BC).

Neolithic
(7000–3200 BC)

The dawn of permanent settlement in the islands sees the introduction of agriculture, animal husbandry, pottery, village-like settlements and maritime trade. Activity in the islands is quite limited initially (mainly Chios, Lesser Sporades, Cyclades), but by the 4th millennium most islands are settled.

Bronze Age
(3200–1100 BC)

Early Bronze Age (3200–2000 BC)
Following the introduction of metal, activity continues to increase. In the Cyclades, an important civilisation develops (Early Cycladic), creating large settlements, sometimes fortified, with complex cemeteries as well as distinctive pottery and marble sculpture. Trade contacts exist with Crete, the Greek mainland and Asia Minor. Outside the Cyclades, proto-urban communities develop e.g. on Lemnos, Lesbos and Chios.

Middle Bronze Age (2000–1650 BC)
The Cyclades and the islands of the East and North are subject to increasing influence from Minoan Crete. The Minoans may have established political or military dominance in part of the Aegean, perhaps colonising some islands. Major settlements flourish e.g. on Milos, Kea, Aegina and Euboea, but especially at Akrotiri on Santorini.

Late Bronze Age (1650–1100 BC)
In c. 1609 BC, a massive volcanic eruption destroys Akrotiri on Santorini and causes widespread damage, especially around the southeastern Aegean. Crete remains the dominant cultural influence in the region until the 14th century, when this role is increasingly assumed by the Mycenaeans from the mainland. From now on, the general developments of the islands mirror those of the mainland. The upheavals leading to the demise of Mycenaean civilisation (still poorly understood), are reflected in the islands by the physical destruction of various sites, as well as by changes in aspects of culture and settlement patterns.

Early Iron Age/Geometric Period
(1100–700 BC)

In later Greek legend, the 'Dark Age' at the beginning of this period is the time when most Greek islands are colonised by the Greek tribes (Ionian, Dorian and Aeolian), perhaps reflecting major changes during the Bronze Age/Iron Age transition. Euboea begins to flourish at this time.

The Geometric period sees the reappearance of complex, increasingly urbanised societies, leading to the development of a recognisably Greek culture and identity in mainland Greece, on parts of the west coast of Asia Minor and also on the islands. The Aegean is a core area in a network of wide-ranging trade contacts, participating on both the active and receiving ends of Greek colonisation, and contributing to the development of Geometric pottery. Major settlements thrive on Euboea, throughout the Cyclades, on Rhodes, in the Dodecanese and in the east Aegean. Some of the most important sanctuaries of later periods have their origins now, including the Heraion on Samos, the sanctuary of Apollo and Demeter on Delos and that of Poseidon on Poros.

The institution of the panhellenic Olympic Games in 776 BC is a legendary milestone for the coming together of Greek culture.

Archaic Period
(700–480 BC)

The city-state emerges as the most typically Greek form of political organisation, ideally suited to a region that is fragmented into numerous small units by mountain chains and by the sea. Most islands now form states of their own, participating in broader cultural developments through internal and external competition, co-operation and conflict.

For many Aegean islands, the Archaic period is a golden age of unsurpassed wealth,

power and influence. This applies especially to Naxos and Paros, major contributors not least to the development of Archaic sculpture throughout the 6th century; to Lesbos; to Samos, a cultural and political superpower in the later 500s; to Siphnos, fabulously wealthy until its metal resources dwindle before 500 BC; and to Aegina, which briefly rivals Athens at this time.

In the late 6th century, increasing conflict with the Persian Empire, which by now controls Greek cities in Ionia and the islands off its shore, leads to the unsuccessful Ionian revolt, which in turn triggers the Persian Wars, forcing the island Greeks to choose sides. In the aftermath of the conflict, the individual power of the Aegean city-states is severely restricted.

c. 700: Greeks settle Samothrace
c. 680: Thasos is settled by colonists from Paros
c. 630: Thera founds the colony of Cyrene in North Africa
c. 589–579: Lesbos thrives under the rule of the lawgiver Pittacus
c. 570: A dozen Greek states found a collective trading colony at Naucratis in Egypt. Among them are Rhodes, Chios, Mytilene, Samos and Aegina
c. 550: Aegina is the first Greek state to mint its own coins
543: The Athenian tyrant Peisistratus undertakes the first ritual purification of Delos
538–522: During the reign of the tyrant Polycrates on Samos, the island reaches a cultural, political and military zenith, including raiding campaigns in the Cyclades
506: Naxos withstands a siege by the Milesians. Athens conquers Chalcis
527: Lesbos conquered by the Persians
499–493: Ionian revolt. Aristagoras of Miletus foments a revolt against Persian dominance in Ionia. In spite of support from Euboea and Athens, it eventually fails.

Chios is conquered by the Persians, Samos sides with them

490: Rhodes conquered by the Persians

490–489: First Persian War. In an attempt to gain dominance over Greece and the Aegean, Darius I sends an expeditionary force. After conquering various Cycladic islands, including Naxos, and destroying Eretria on Euboea, he is defeated at the Battle of Marathon near Athens

480: Second Persian War. Darius' son Xerxes attacks the Greek mainland by land and sea. Initially he is successful, securing the surrender of several cities and islands, defeating a Spartan army at Thermopylae, and forcing the Athenians to evacuate their city. His fleet is damaged by a storm near Euboea. The Greek allies, led by Athens and Sparta, defeat the Persians in a major naval battle off Salamis, in which many island fleets participate

479: After the Persian land army is defeated by the Greeks at the Battle of Plataea, the allies defeat the remains of the Persian fleet and another Persian army at the Battle of Mycale, thereby liberating Lesbos and Chios and placing Euboea under Athenian control. Samos reverts to the Greek side.

Classical Period
(480–338 BC)

During the 5th century, the Aegean is mostly dominated by Athens and its Delian League, leading to considerable prosperity in places such as Chios and Samos, but largely stifling the cultural, political and economic independence of the islands. Those who have second thoughts about league membership are cowed into submission, culminating in the massacre of the Melians in 415. After the Athenian defeat by Sparta in 404, some islands see a short period of renewed independence, but most end up embroiled in the various conflicts of the 4th century. Many join a short-lived Second Athenian League. As Macedon gains control of virtually the entire mainland, most islands end up under its sway.

478: Foundation of the Delian League. After Sparta has withdrawn from further action against the Persians, the Athenians take a leading role in founding of the League, an alliance including city-states in Asia Minor and the vast majority of the Aegean islands. Its headquarters are on Delos; its purpose is the further defence of Greek states against the Persians. League membership entails accepting—at times unwillingly—a democratic constitution, submitting to the Athens-based jurisdiction of the League, using Athenian coins, weights and measurements, and paying an annual tribute to the League's coffers on Delos, which fund the continued fighting

476/5: Skyros is forced to join the League

c. 470: Karystos on Euboea, having supported the Persians ten years previously, is attacked and forced to join the Delian League

c. 470: Naxos attempts to leave the League, but is defeated and forced to pay a high tribute as well as to accept Athenian settlers

469 or 466: At the Battle of the Eurymedon, the League defeats a large Persian fleet, effectively ending the role of Persia as a sea power in the Aegean

c. 465: Metal-rich Thasos attempts to leave the League but is forced after a two-year siege to rejoin and pay a heavy fine

454: The Athenian politician Pericles moves the League Treasury to Athens, ostensibly to keep it safe from Persian attack. This marks a milestone on the gradual transformation of the League into an Athenian Empire

458/7: After a naval blockade, Aegina is forced to join the Delian League

450: Andros comes under Athenian control

449: Peace of Callias: Persia refrains from further action in the Aegean. The Delian League, its original objective now attained, remains in existence

446: Euboea revolts and ends up directly controlled by Athens. Athens and Sparta sign the '30-year peace', recognising each other as leaders of alliances. Hereafter, Athens refers to League members as 'ruled by the Athenians'

440–439: Having defected from the League, Samos is besieged and punished

431: Athens banishes the wealthy class of Aegina from their island

431–404: Peloponnesian War. The rivalry between Athens and Sparta eventually turns into all-out war. The intermittent conflict lasts nearly three decades and eventually embroils Sicily and the eastern Aegean. It ends in Athenian defeat

428: Lesbos is severely punished for an attempt to leave the League

426: The Great Delian Festival is reinstated by the Athenians. Second purification of Delos

422: Athens banishes the Delians from their island

415: After resisting pressure to join Athens, Milos is conquered, its population massacred or enslaved

412: Chios defects from Athens but is defeated

411: Euboea successfully defects

410: Rhodes switches from the Athenian to the Spartan side

411: Kos sacked by the Spartans

410: Kos sacked by Athens. Thasos defects

408: Synoecism of Rhodes: the island's three cities join to found a single new one, ushering in a long period of affluence and power

406: Athens defeats a Spartan fleet at the Battle of Arginusae, off Lesbos

405: The Spartans totally destroy the bulk of the Athenian fleet at the Battle of Aegospotamoi in the Hellespont

404: Athens surrenders and barely escapes destruction. The islands end up either under short-lived Spartan control or briefly independent

c. 400: Rhodes takes Tilos, heralding a long period of Rhodian expansion and dominance in the southern Dodecanese

378: Following the decline of Spartan power and the increasing unpopularity of its rule, Athens founds the Second Athenian League, which again includes most of the islands but affords Athens less dominance

377: Athens defeats a Spartan fleet at the Battle of Naxos: Naxos and Paros are forced into the Second Athenian League

371: The Battle of Leuctra, a major Spartan defeat, establishes a short-lived Theban hegemony. Theban control of Euboea

366: The synoecism of Kos

365: Athens expels the Samians from their island

363: Kea is forced to remain in the League

358: Euboea back under Athenian rule

357–355: Social War: Chios, Rhodes and Kos overthrow their democracies and defect from the Athenian League, with assistance from Byzantium. Eventually Athens is forced to disband the League. In the following decades many islands, now nominally independent, effectively end up under the control of the ascendant mainland power, Macedon

357: Rhodes falls under the rule of the Persian satrap Mausolus of Halicarnassus.

Hellenistic Period
(338–133 BC)

The rise of the Macedonian Kingdom as the dominant power of mainland Greece effectively spells the end of the city-state as the main political unit. From now on, independence, where acknowledged, is merely nominal. After the conquests of Alexander the Great, the islands are part of an immensely expanded Greek world, but their political role mostly decreases after his death, when they become pawns in the power struggles between his successor kingdoms. Rhodes develops as a major regional power and forges an early alliance with Rome, which begins to threaten the Greek world in the 2nd century and rapidly becomes dominant in the region. Some islands, such as Thasos, Samos and Kos, experience a cultural flowering during this time.

338: Battle of Chaironeia. Philip II of Macedon defeats Thebes and Athens, the two major remaining powers in the mainland. Virtually all the islands now form part of Philip's Corinthian League, and are thus under Macedonian control

334–323: After Philip's death, his son Alexander embarks on an unprecedented series of campaigns, conquering the Persian Empire, including all of Anatolia, the Levant and Egypt

333: Chios is conquered by Macedon

323: Alexander dies. His empire fragments into successor kingdoms, controlled by dynasties founded by his generals. Rhodes, freed from Persian rule, forges and alliance with the Ptolemies of Egypt

315: In his doomed attempt to reunite Alexander's empire, Antigonus I (Monophthalmus), based in Asia Minor, prepares to attack Greece, controlled by Alexander's Macedonian successor, Cassander. To do so, he founds the short-lived 'League of the Islanders', supported by Rhodes and ostensibly uniting most of the Aegean islands

305: Siege of Rhodes. As part of his various campaigns, Demetrius Poliorcetes, Antigonus' son and later king of Macedon, lays siege to Rhodes but is driven away by Ptolemy I of Egypt

c. 250: First establishment of Roman traders on Delos. The island rapidly develops as an important trading city

227: A major earthquake destroys much of Rhodes and the powerful city receives help and support from throughout the Greek world

214–205: The First Macedonian War between Rome and Philip V of Macedon. Rome is allied with the Aetolian League, which includes much of the southern and western mainland, many of the eastern islands, including Rhodes, Chios and Lesbos, and Pergamon in Asia Minor. Rhodes becomes an important Roman ally

200–197: Second Macedonian War. Pergamon and Rhodes appeal for Roman help against Philip. At the Battle of Cynoscephalae, Macedon suffers a massive defeat, ending its status as a major power. Macedon has to surrender its fleet

192–188: Roman-Syrian War. Rome defeats its last major opponent in the east, the Seleucid Empire. In the aftermath, Rome has hegemony over the Mediterranean. Western Anatolia is distributed among its allies

171–168: Third Macedonian War. At the Battle of Pydna, Rome defeats Philip's son, King Perseus. Rome now controls mainland Greece

166: Rome cedes Delos to Athens and declares it a free port

164: Rhodes signs a treaty of friendship with Rome and becomes an important centre of education for Roman nobles

153: Cretan pirates raid Siphnos

146: Corinth, the most important trading centre on the mainland, is destroyed by Rome. Refugee traders settle in Delos

133: Attalus III of Pergamon dies, bequeathing all his possessions, including some of the islands, to Rome.

Roman Period
(133 BC–AD 330)

By the late 2nd century BC, Rome is in the process of replacing its control of the East Mediterranean through allies and client kingdoms with direct incorporation into the Roman state. In the Aegean, this process is completed after the Mithridatic Wars. Not least through the elimination of piracy, the Aegean enters a long and relatively uneventful period of stability as a backwater of the Roman Empire. Some islands thrive as trading centres, e.g. Delos in the earlier part of the period, Samos and Kos later on. Small or remote islands are sometimes used as places of exile for various undesirables. This period also sees the first appearance of tourism in Greece and its islands, as many sites attract visitors from around the Empire. The School of Rhetoric at Rhodes is attended by many prominent Romans, including Cicero and Julius Caesar.

89–85 BC: First Mithridatic War. King Mithridates VI of Pontus in northern Anatolia attempts to turn the tide of Roman dominance in the region. After conquering Roman Asia and massacring all Romans present, he styles himself the new champion of Greekness and gains the support of some cities, including Athens. After a siege by Sulla in 86, Athens falls and Roman rule over the Aegean is re-established

82 BC: The Roman governor of Asia, Verres, plunders Samos and Chios. He is later tried by the famous orator Cicero

74 BC: Julius Caesar is abducted by pirates and held at Farmakonísi. After his ransom and release, he has his captors arrested and crucified

69 BC: Delos is devastated by the infamous corsair Athenodorus. In spite of Roman support and aid, the island never recovers

43 BC: During the civil war following the murder of Caesar, Rhodes sides against the 'liberators' and is plundered by Cassius, never fully to recover

42–41 BC: During the conflict between Mark Antony and Octavian (the future Augustus), the Aegean is briefly controlled by the former

50s AD: St Paul travels in the Aegean and visits several islands

70s AD: Rhodes is formally incorporated into the Empire

95–96 AD: St John the Apostle is in exile on Patmos and has his vision of the Apocalypse

120s AD: The emperor Hadrian, an ardent hellenophile, travels in Greece and visits various islands, including Samothrace

260s AD: The Heruls, a Germanic tribe, raid much of mainland Greece, but also Lemnos and Skyros

324 AD: St Helen, mother of the emperor Constantine the Great, founds a Christian church on Paros. Christian communities already exist in many of the islands

325 AD: Constantine convokes the Council of Nicaea, thereby giving the Christian religion official status. Bishops from many islands attend

Byzantine Period–Fourth Crusade
(330–1204)

With Constantine's division of the Roman Empire and his establishment of Constantinople as the eastern capital, the Aegean becomes part of the Greek-speaking East, which is to outlast Rome by a millennium. The region is christianised rapidly. During an initial phase of stability, Christian cities thrive throughout the islands, and Early Byzantine art constitutes a major departure from ancient predecessors. This is followed by increasing unrest, as the empire loses its grip. Piracy, incursions by Arabs in the south and Slavs in the north lead to Byzantium being caught between Turkish expansion into Anatolia and increasing Western ('Frankish' or 'Latin') activity in the course of the Crusades. The islands suffer from a collapse of urban civilisation and frequent raids, which lead to major changes in settlement patterns as security becomes a dominant issue. Only islands with large interiors, such as Naxos, manage to maintain some stability.

330: Constantine re-founds Byzantium as Constantinople, the 'New Rome'

4th–8th centuries: Christianisation progresses at speed: churches and basilicas are founded throughout the islands, and bishoprics established, as the pagan cults are suppressed and gradually die out

380: Theodosius I declares Christianity the only legitimate religion of the Empire. In subsequent years, he proceeds to outlaw pagan worship

476: The last Western Roman emperor, Romulus Augustulus, abdicates

7th–11th centuries: Arab raids affect virtually the entire Aegean, leading to a massive loss of population and the abandonment of several (smaller) islands

672: Arab forces briefly occupy Rhodes

727: In the Cyclades, a rising against the Byzantine emperor Leo is suppressed

730–787: Iconoclastic period. The depiction of human figures in sacred art is banned, church decorations have to be limited to decorative patterns and images of animals or plants

769: Slav raids on the Cyclades

9th–11th centuries: The Byzantine Empire temporarily reasserts control and somewhat stabilises the Dodecanese and eastern Aegean

934: The Byzantines defeat a large Saracen fleet near Lemnos

1054: The Great Schism. After centuries of conflict, the Western (Roman Catholic) and Eastern (Orthodox) churches separate

1071: At the Battle of Manzikert, Seljuk Turks defeat the Byzantine army. The Turkish advance through Anatolia now seems unstoppable

1088: With the patronage of Emperor Alexius I Comnenus, the Blessed Christodoulos founds the monastery of St John the Divine on Patmos. It is granted property in many of the surrounding islands. According to legend, the monastery of the Chozoviótissa on Amorgós is founded at the same time, with similar privileges

1089–1091: The Turkish emir Chaka Bey briefly conquers Lesbos, Chios, Samos and Rhodes, but is eventually repulsed by Byzantium

1095–1099: The First Crusade. With papal approval and following an appeal from Byzantium, Western Christians mount a military campaign in the east Mediterranean, aiding the Byzantines against the Turks and taking control of Jerusalem. Byzantium retakes Rhodes. The West is now directly involved in Eastern affairs. The Byzantines uneasily allow passage to the Second (1147–49) and Third (1189–92) Crusades The port of Rhodes is used as a staging post

12th century: Genoa and Venice compete for trading privileges in the East Mediterranean; at the same time Genoese and Venetian pirates undertake raids against various islands

1202: Beginning of the Fourth Crusade.

Venetian and 'Latin' Period
(1204–1453)

After the 'Latin' conquest of Constantinople in 1204, the Aegean becomes the theatre of increasing conflict between the mercantile republics of Venice and Genoa, the former gaining control of most of the islands and establishing itself especially in the Cyclades, which now receive Catholic settlers and enjoy a period of relative stability. After a short resurgence, Byzantium falls to the Ottoman Turks in 1453. Under the control of the Knights, Rhodes and the Dodecanese briefly embark on a separate historical trajectory.

1204: The Fourth Crusade leads to the first Fall of Constantinople. Venice manipulates the crusaders into conquering and sacking the city. The Byzantine emperor is allowed to retain part of the Anatolian mainland, with Nicaea as capital. The remaining Byzantine territories are divided between various Western powers, nominally as vassals to the newly-created Latin Empire based in Constantinople. Most Aegean islands are placed under Venetian control, including Euboea, the Sporades and the Cyclades. Rhodes becomes a Greek despotate

1207: In the aftermath of 1204, the Venetian adventurer Marco Sanudo creates the Duchy of the Archipelago, incorporating all the Cyclades and Sporades, with its capital on Naxos. Naxos and part of the central and western Cyclades are ruled directly by Sanudo and his descendants; the rest are given as fiefs to other Venetian families. This is the beginning of Catholic settlement in the islands

1224: Lesbos returns to the Byzantine Empire of Nicaea

1261: With Genoese help, Michael VIII Palaeologus retakes Constantinople, putting and end to the Latin Empire. Rhodes is also nominally rejoined to Byzantium, although it is effectively ruled by the Genoese. Chios is ceded to the Genoese. A pre-Byzantine revolt in Milos is put down. The Venetians are expelled from Constantinople and make Euboea their main base in the region

1270s–80s: Under Michael and his successor Andronicus, Byzantium briefly reconquers various Cycladic islands, but only manages to retain permanent hold of Alónnisos

1309: The Knights Hospitallers, having arrived in Rhodes as refugees three years earlier, capture the island, styling themselves the Knights of Rhodes and gaining control of the Dodecanese

1316: Catalan raid on Milos

1319: The Knights of Rhodes put down a rebellion on Leros

1334: A Turkish raid leads to the depopulation of Astypálaia

1346, 1347, 1431: Samos, Lesbos and Thasos are ceded to the Genoese by Byzantium

1444: Rhodes withstands a siege by the Sultan of Egypt

1453: Mehmet II conquers Constantinople and makes it his capital, recognising the Greek Orthodox patriarch. Refugees from the city settle on Patmos.

Ottoman Period
(1453–1821)

Whereas mainland Greece is already under full Ottoman control by 1453, the islands are virtually all in Latin hands. It takes the Ottomans over two centuries to conquer the entire Aegean archipelago.

1461: Pope Pius II grants protected status to the Monastery of St John on Patmos, which is also respected by the Ottoman sultans

1462: The Turks take Lesbos

1470: The Turks take Samothrace and Euboea

1479: The Turks take Lemnos

1480: On Rhodes, the Knights withstand a major siege by the Turks

1502: The Knights expel all Jews from Rhodes

1522: The Turks under Suleiman the Magnificent take Rhodes and the rest of the Dodecanese, but preserve the privileges of Patmos. In the aftermath, many Sephardic Jewish refugees from Spain are settled in Rhodes

1530s: The dreaded Turkish corsair Kheir ed-Din Barbarossa raids and devastates the Cyclades. He conquers Ios, Paros, Amorgós, Sériphos, Astypálaia, Skyros and Alónnisos for the sultan

1566: Sultan Selim II takes Chios as well as Naxos, Andros, Milos, Santorini and Kea. The Duchy of the Archipelago is no more

1617: The Turks conquer Folégandros, Siphnos, Kythnos and Kímolos

1648: The Venetians briefly conquer Leros

1645: The Venetian captain-general Francesco Morosini captures Aegina for the Serene Republic

1648: Morosini plunders Patmos

17th century: Christian refugees from the Turkish advances in the Balkans settle in parts of the Argo-Saronic islands

1669: Refugees from the Turkish conquest of Crete settle on Patmos

1675–78: Milos enjoys a brief independence

1713: The Theological School of Patmos is established and soon becomes a hotbed of Greek nationalism

1715: Tinos is the last Cycladic island to fall to the Turks

1718: The Turks reconquer Aegina

18th century: The northern Cyclades and Sporades flourish, enjoying extensive Ottoman trading privileges, as do the Argo-Saronic islands

1768–74: Russo-Turkish War. The Russian navy under Count Orlov establishes a base on Paros and briefly occupies Naxos, Milos, Ios and Folégandros, as well as Thasos and Samothrace

1797: Pirates from the Mani in the Peloponnese devastate Amorgós

1813: Thasos is ceded to the Pasha of Egypt

1814: Foundation of the Philikí Etaireía ('Society of Friends'), involving island and mainland Greeks as well as members of the Greek diaspora. Its goal is the establishment of an independent Greece.

Greek War of Independence to the Second World War
(1821–1941)

The islands play a major and heroic role in the Greek War of Independence, but not all of them benefit immediately. Some islands suffer infamous reprisals and when the fledgling Greek state is recognised; many remain Ottoman. The Kingdom of Greece grows in fits and starts throughout the 19th century. In the First Balkan War, Greece gains the islands of the north and east, while Italy occupies the Dodecanese. In the aftermath, the Anatolian 'Catastrophe' forces Greece to accept the permanent loss of its Anatolian and Constantinopolitan claims, and to accept over a million refugees. A mid-19th–early 20th-century economic boom is followed in many islands by a long phase of depression, accompanied by mass emigration to Athens or abroad.

1821: The Greek rebellion begins. Virtually all islands participate, with the notable exceptions of Kea and Tinos, who soon receive refugees from reprisals on other islands, notably Chios, where a large part of the population is massacred

1822–24: Relative success by the Argo-Saronic fleets at sea is not matched by advances on land

1824: The Ottomans call on Egypt for aid against the Greek insurrection. Their forces are led by Ibrahim Pasha, governor of the Morea (Peloponnese). The Massacre of Psará, when the Turks kill a large number of Greek refugees, causes widespread shock across Europe

1825: The Great Powers (Britain, Russia and France), initially hostile or indifferent to the uprising, begin to change their stance, influenced both by philhellenism and by self-interest. Western philhellenes participate in the fighting

1826–28: Aegina serves as the capital of the new Greek state

1827: Battle of Navarino. The Great Powers finally intervene. Their combined fleets inflict a devastating defeat on the Ottoman navy, severely limiting Turkish ability to manoeuvre and supply troops in Greece

1828: Ioannis Capodistrias is made President of Greece. The ambassadors of Britain, Russia and France meet on Poros. The ensuing Poros Protocol lays down borders for the Greek state, and insists that it must be a monarchy

1829: London Protocol. As the tide of war turns in favour of Greece, the Great Powers initially opt to offer autonomy to Greece under Turkish suzerainty, which Turkey accepts

1831: Battle of Poros. Infighting in the young Greek state leads to the sinking of the navy's flagship

1831: Capodistrias is assassinated in Náfplion

1832: Treaty of Constantinople. In a final settlement, the new independent Kingdom of Greece is recognised, incorporating the Peloponnese, Attica, parts of the southern mainland, the Cyclades and the Sporades. The capital is moved to Athens, and the Bavarian prince Otto of Wittelsbach is proclaimed king

1832–1912: Samos is granted partial autonomy under Ottoman suzerainty

Mid-19th–early 20th century: Some of the islands thrive under the new regime, developing new industries and exploiting mineral resources

1863: Otto is removed from the throne and replaced with George I of the Danish House of Schleswig-Holstein-Sonderburg-Glücksburg, whose descendants will remain monarchs of Greece until 1973

1911–12: First Balkan War. In the aftermath of an Italian invasion in Turkish North Africa, Greece, Serbia and Bulgaria attack the Ottomans. Greece gains Samothrace, Thasos, Lemnos, Lesbos, Chios and Samos

1912–48: Italy uses the weak Turkish position to occupy the Dodecanese. During its 36-year presence, it moves to suppress all expressions of Greek identity in the islands

1920: Treaty of Sèvres. In the aftermath of the First World War, the Western Allies plan to divide the collapsing Ottoman Empire. Greece is to receive part of Ionia on the Anatolian mainland

1921–22: The Anatolian 'Catastrophe': Greek armies attempt to take the promised Anatolian territories. After initial success, they are routed and flee to Greece, followed by hundreds of thousands of refugees

1923: Treaty of Lausanne. The Greek leader, Venizelos, and the head of the emerging Turkish state, Kemal Atatürk, agree on fixed borders. Greece renounces all claims on the Anatolian mainland and eastern Thrace, but is assured sovereignty over all non-Italian-held Aegean islands except Imbros and Tenedos (Gökçeada and Bozcaada). They also agree on an 'exchange of populations', leading to the displacement of hundreds of thousands. In total, Greece absorbs well over a million refugees, some of whom settle in the islands. The Turks in the Italian-held Dodecanese are not affected

1933: Kos Town is destroyed in an earthquake. It is rebuilt and major excavations are undertaken by the Italians in the aftermath

1935: The Italians suppress rioting on Kálymnos.

Second World War to the present

Only a generation after the 'Catastrophe', the country suffers gravely from a Second World War it has no stake in, enduring first Italian, then German occupation. After the War, the Dodecanese are joined to Greece. But liberation is followed by a long civil war and a longer period of instability, ending only in 1974. Since the 1970s, tourism has developed as a major industry in the islands, leading to environmental devastation as well as cultural initiatives and localised wealth. In recent decades, European structural funds have also had a visible effect on many islands. The tide of emigration has been stemmed and awareness of the natural and cultural resources offered by the islands is growing.

1940: The Second World War. Greece, ruled by dictator Ioannis Metaxas, attempts to stay neutral in the growing atmosphere of conflict. In August, the Greek gunboat *Helle* is sunk in the harbour of Tinos by an Italian submarine. In October, Mussolini invades Greece from Albania, but is repulsed by a staunch Greek defence

1941: Aiding the ailing Italians, Nazi Germany invades, and in spite of assistance from a British expeditionary corps, Greece has to capitulate. Italy occupies most of the mainland and all the islands except those of the east and north Aegean, which fall to Germany and Bulgaria

1943: After Italy's surrender, Germany takes over her occupied territories, often using violence against remaining Italian forces. A reign of terror is instituted and an active Greek resistance develops. A British attempt to occupy the Dodecanese fails amid heavy fighting

1945: Remaining German troops surrender; Greece is liberated

1945–49: The long and bloody Greek Civil War mainly takes place in the mainland. Euboea is its only island theatre. During its course and in its aftermath, various small islands are used as 're-education' camps for Greek communists

1948: Italy cedes the Dodecanese to Greece, marking the most recent territorial expansion of the country

1952: Greece joins NATO

1956: A major earthquake destroys much of Santorini and Astypálaia

1967–74: After a military coup, the right-wing junta of the Colonels takes power. Again, small islands are used as places of internal exile for dissidents

1973: The monarchy is abolished

1974: The junta collapses. For the first time in history, Greece is a fully democratic republic

1981: Greece joins the EEC (later EU)

1987, 1996: Greece and Turkey come to the brink of hostilities in an ongoing dispute over territorial rights in the Aegean

1999: Rapprochement between the Aegean neighbours

2000s: Serious forest fires repeatedly ravage the islands.

GLOSSARY

Compiled by Annabel Barber

Abacus (pl. *abaci*), flat block above the capital of a column, on which the horizontal architrave linking the columns rests

Abaton, literally the 'place of no stepping'; an inner sanctuary for the sole use of initiates or priests

Acrolithic, statue where the head and extremities are of stone while the rest is made of wood and covered by drapery

Acroterion (pl. *acroteria*), plinth surmounting the apex of a pediment and its two corners, often topped by a statue

Adyton, inner sanctum of a temple with no natural light, from where oracular pronouncements were made

Aeolian, an ethnic group of the Greek people, originally from the northern mainland, who migrated to Lesbos and northwest Asia Minor (Aeolia)

Aeolic, a type of column capital (*see p. 653*)

Aghiasma (pl. *aghiasmata*), a sacred pool

Aghía Triáda, church dedication to the Holy Trinity

Ághii Anárgyri, literally the 'penniless saints', Cosmas and Damian, doctors who refused to accept payment for their ministrations

Ághii Pándes, All Saints

Ághios, (*m.*), aghía (*f.*), ághii (*m.pl.*), aghíes (*f.pl.*), saint(s), holy

Agorá, public square or market-place of an ancient city

Akathist Hymn, four-part paean to the Virgin, traditionally sung on the first four Fridays in Lent

Alabastron, small vase in alabaster, glass or clay, used for oils and perfumes

Amazonomachia, depiction of a battle between Greeks and Amazons

Ambo (pl. *ambones*), elevated reading platform in a Christian basilica; the two pulpits on opposite sides of the nave from which the Gospel and Epistle were read

Amphiprostyle, of a temple, meaning that it has a colonnade at front and back

Amphora (pl. *amphorae*), large two-handled vase for storage and transport

Análipsis, the Assumption of the Virgin (the ascent of the Virgin to Heaven) or Ascension of Christ

Andreion, public building or hall where men and youths ate communal meals

Aniconic, material symbol of a deity (pillar or block) not shaped into an image of human form (icon)

Anta (pl. *antae*), pier or piers at the front of a temple formed when the side walls project beyond the front wall. Columns placed between these piers are said to be *in antis*

Antigonids, Hellenistic dynasty that gained control of part of Alexander the Great's empire after his death. The son of its founder, Antigonus, was Demetrius Poliorcetes (*see p. 259*)

Apodyterium (pl. *apodyteria*), changing room in a baths complex

Apotropaic, pertaining to an object or ritual intended to ward off evil spirits or bad luck

Apse, vaulted semicircular end wall of the sanctuary of a church or chapel

Archaic, period in Greek civilisation preceding the Classical era (*see Chronology, p. 637*); sculpture of this period is characterised by large eyes, a stiff smile, and stylised posture

Architrave, the lowest part of an entablature (*qv*); the horizontal beam or band of stone blocks spanning the top of a colonnade

Archon, the chief magistrate in some ancient Greek city-states

Archontikó (pl. *archontiká*), mansion house,

typically of the late 19th or early 20th century

Arcosolium (pl. *arcosolia*), a tomb where the sarcophagus or funerary bed is in a recessed niche surmounted by an arch

Ares, the Greek god of war and bloodshed, son of Zeus and Hera, equivalent of the Roman Mars

Aryballos (pl: *aryballoi*), small jar for carrying oil, typically used by an athlete

Ashlar, masonry consisting of blocks of stone precisely cut with even faces and square edges, laid in regular courses

Asclepeion (also Asklepieion), a sanctuary dedicated to the healing god Asclepius, where patients would seek cures

Askos (pl. *askoi*), vessel for oil, often used for refilling lamps

Attalids, one of the successor dynasties of Alexander the Great, whose territory centred on the city of Pergamon

Basilica, originally a Roman hall used for public administration; in Christian architecture an aisled church with apse(s), the nave separated from the aisles by columns supporting the central raised roof

Blachernae, icon of the Hodighitria type (*qv*), in encaustic bas-relief, originally from the Blachernae quarter of Constantinople, now on Mt Athos

Bothros, a pit used in sacrifices and libations

Bouleuterion, a public building where the council of citizens (*boule*) met

Boustrophedon, a system of writing that involves alternating lines of left-to-right and right-to-left, like an ox ploughing a field (the derivation of the term)

Bucranium (pl. *bucrania*), originally an ox skull, sometimes covered in plaster and used for ritual purposes. Later a sculpted ornament representing an ox skull

Caldarium, the hot room of a baths complex

Cardo, the main north–south street in a Roman town; it crossed the decumanus (*qv*)

Caryatid, female figure used as a supporting column

Cavea, the seating area of a theatre, named from the semicircular hollow dug out (exCAVated) from a hillside

Cella, enclosed interior part of a temple, also known in Greece as the naos

Chamfer, a cut-off corner. A chamfered square becomes an octagon

Charites, Greek name for the Three Graces

Chiton, sleeveless linen tunic falling in vertical folds, secured at the waist or bustline with a girdle

Chochlákia, a style of pebble-mosaic paving typical of the Dodecanese

Choragic monument, monument to a *choragos*, the person who paid for the choir at an ancient Greek festival or who funded a choir in a musical competition

Chryselephantine, describes a statue or figurine in which ivory is used for the flesh parts and gold leaf (from the Greek *chrysós*, gold) is used for garments and armour. Other materials ranging from glass to precious stones were used for the eyes, jewellery and weapons

Chthonic, 'of the earth'. The Chthonic divinities are deities of fertility and the soil

Ciborium, casket or tabernacle containing the Host (the Communion bread or wafer)

Cipollino, a marble from Euboea much prized in ancient Rome (*see p. 628*)

Cippus, an inscribed stone pillar used as a grave marker or boundary stone

Classical, of the period from 480 BC (second Persian invasion) to 323 BC (death of Alexander the Great)

Clerestory, the part of the wall of a church nave that rises above the side aisles, with windows

Cleruchy, colony founded by Athens, whose members enjoyed Athenian citizenship. Each colonist, or cleruch, received a plot of land, in return for which he was bound to render military service to Athens. Cleruchies were political satellites of the mother city;

essentially the system was a means whereby Athens exported her own loyalists to fractious parts of Greece

Cloisonné, metalworking technique in which objects are decorated with areas of multicoloured enamel partitioned by thin strips of metal; in masonry, a style where the stone blocks are set off by thin courses of brick

Codex (pl. *codices*), a medieval manuscript bound in book form

Conch, dome over an apse or recess, in the form of a quarter sphere

Corbelling, building system which gives support by the superimposition of projecting courses, each bearing the load of the next; used in tholos (*qv*) tomb vaulting

Corinthian, an order of architecture characterised by a capital with the shape of an inverted bell decorated with two or more rows of acanthus leaves sprouting scrolls at the top, and surmounted by an abacus (*qv*) with concave sides (*see illustration on p. 653*)

Crane Dance, a dance of labyrinthine choreography supposedly performed by Theseus at Delos after his slaying of the Minotaur on Crete

Crepidoma (or crepis), stepped platform (usually of three steps) on which an ancient temple stood. The top flat surface is the stylobate (*qv*)

Cross-domed, Byzantine church type in which a square central bay, with four arms of equal length (Greek Cross), is surmounted by a dome (*see illustration on p. 654*)

Crossing, the part of a church where the nave meets the transepts (side arms)

Cross-in-square, a form of Byzantine church architecture consisting of intersecting barrel-vaulted naves of equal length (Greek Cross). The central section is surmounted by a dome, with smaller domes in each of the four corners (*see illustration on p. 654*)

Cycladic, Early Bronze Age culture of the Cycladic region (*see box on p. 651*)

Cyclopean, type of masonry consisting of huge blocks, so large that they appear to have been laid in place by giants (the Cyclopes)

Daidalic, sculpture of the Bronze Age and Archaic period characterised by large, staring eyes, wig-like hair and stiff drapery. The term derives from Daedalus the mythical Bronze Age craftsman, builder of the Cretan Labyrinth

Decumanus, the principal street of a Roman town, normally running east–west

Deësis, iconographical composition of petition or intercession, showing Christ appealed to by the Virgin and (usually) St John the Baptist

Delian League, association of Greek city-states, led by Athens, formed in 478 BC as a bulwark against Persian ambitions

Deme, unit of local government in the ancient Greek world

Dendrochronology, dating system involving the study of tree rings

Dentillated, articulated or decorated with a row of small, narrowly-spaced carved blocks

Dimarcheíon, the Greek word for a town hall

Dioscuri (also Dioskouroi), Castor and Pollux, twin sons of Zeus

Distyle, of a temple or porch, having two columns

Dokathismata (*see Cycladic figurines, overleaf*)

Dorians, ancient people surmised to have invaded Greece around 1100 BC

Doric, an order of architecture developed in Greece before the 6th century BC. It is characterised by fluted columns standing close together directly on the stylobate (*qv*), with no base. Capitals have a convex moulding topped by a square abacus (*qv*) (*see illustration on p. 653*)

Dormition, the 'falling asleep', in other words death, of the Virgin Mary, in Greek the Koímisis tis Theotókou

Dragoman, in the Ottoman world, an interpreter between the Sublime Porte and the courts of Europe; by association any interpreter or guide

Dressed stone, stone worked to a surface finish

Dromos (pl. *dromoi*), literally 'road', used to denote the entrance passage to a tomb

Dryopians, a Pelasgian (*qv*), pre-Hellenic people of obscure origin

Eclectic, of architecture, betraying the influence of a variety of disparate styles

Eisódia, literally 'entry', used in a theological context to denote the entry of the Virgin into the Temple, known in the West as the Presentation

Emblema (pl. *emblemata*), the central panel of a mosaic or ancient wall-painting, often showing a scene from mythology while the space around it is decorated with geometric designs, fruit and foliage, etc

Entablature, the horizontal elements above a colonnade, divided from the bottom upwards into architrave, frieze and cornice (*see illustration on p. 653*)

Entasis, a design technique used to counteract the optical illusion of inner sagging created by the parallel sides of a column. Entasis (meaning 'stretching') involved giving the column a slightly convex curvature, with the result that the diameter at the bottom was marginally larger than that at the top

Ephebos (pl. *epheboi, ephebes*), Greek youth under military or academic training

Epitaphios, icon, funeral montage, or embroidered cloth used in the services of lamentation on Good Friday and Holy Saturday

Evangelismós, the Annunciation, that is, the Archangel Gabriel's message to Mary that she is to bear a son

Evangelistary, book containing excerpts from the Gospels, for readings in church

Evangelists, the writers of the four Gospels, Matthew, Mark, Luke and John, often represented in Christian art by their symbols, respectively a man, a lion, a bull and an eagle

Exedra, semicircular or rectangular recessed area, often with seats

Exonarthex, outermost vestibule of a church, followed by the narthex (*qv*) and then the naos, or church proper

Ex-voto, votive offering left at a temple, shrine or other holy place

Firman, a decree from the Ottoman government

Foricae, in the ancient Roman world, public lavatories

Fresco, wall-painting executed while the plaster is still wet

Frieze, strip of decoration, usually along the upper part of a wall; in a temple of the Ionic or Corinthian order, this refers to the horizontal feature above the architrave (*see illustration on p. 653*)

Frigidarium, the room with the cold pools in a baths complex

Frying pan vessels, Cycladic objects of uncertain function, named from their distinctive shape (*see p. 54*)

Geometric, pottery style with complex, abstract decoration (900–700 BC)

Glykophilousa, the Virgin of the 'Sweet Kiss'. Icon type showing Mother and Child snuggled in a tender embrace

Graffito (pl. *graffiti*), scratched design or date on a wall

Greek cross, a cross with all four arms of equal length

Gutta (pl. *guttae*), small peg-like projections carved on the underside of a Doric cornice (*see illustration on p. 653*)

Hamam, a Turkish bath

Helladic, term denoting the Greek Bronze Age on the mainland and Euboea, covering the same period as the Cycladic on Milos et al or the Minoan on Crete, c. 3000–1050 BC

Hellenistic, denoting the period from the death of Alexander the Great (323 BC) to the defeat of Antony and Cleopatra (31 BC)

Herm, quadrangular pillar decreasing in girth towards the ground, surmounted by a head,

CYCLADIC FIGURINES

Some of the most admired and important artistic output of the Early Bronze Age in the Aegean is represented by the 3rd-millennium BC figurines of the Cyclades, usually (but not always) depicting female humans, in marble, in heights varying from a few centimetres to over a metre. Scholars have subdivided the figurines into various stylistic types, which are thought to reflect chronological development.

Broadly speaking, the sequence begins with highly schematic figures, typified by the violin-type idols (*fig. 1*), depicting an anthropomorphic female body (reminiscent of Man Ray's *Le violon d'Ingres*) with a long neck but no defined head. Anatomical details are only rendered occasionally. These are followed by more naturalistic—but still highly stylised—forms, typically named after the findspots of significant deposits. The earliest of these is the Plastiras type (from Plastíras on Paros), the first fully to represent the female form in a nature-identical fashion. Modelling is crude and the emphasis tends to be on hefty thighs and chubby bottoms. The Louros type (from Loúros on Naxos; *fig. 2*), occurring a little later, ignores facial features and bodily details, and renders the arms as mere stumps. These early types are followed by the phase that scholars call 'canonical', implying that the sculptors followed set rules or canons: a backwards-tipped head, arms folded left over right, etc. Examples from this phase include the Spedos variety (from Spedós on Naxos; *fig. 3*) and the Dokathismata type (from a cemetery on Amorgós; *fig. 4*). The latter is characterised by a particularly refined and elegant kind of abstraction.

A similar level of artistry is aimed at, but not achieved, in the later, so-called 'post-canonical' figures. Here the canons are not always followed, modelling is crude and composition less skilful. The proportions of the human body are ignored (legs are often very short) and the head appears merely as a flat triangle lying obliquely on the neck (*see illustration on p. 54*). Many items from this phase were found at Chalandrianí on Syros.

More rarely, Early Cycladic figurines can also depict males. The most celebrated examples are the 'musician' types, showing seated figures playing the harp or lyre (*see illustration on p. 197*). The candid whiteness of all the figurines today is misleading. Many retain traces of pigmentation, showing that they would originally have been painted, with fully rendered details such as eyes, mouths, hair and eyebrows.

From left to right:

1 Schematic figurine (violin-type)
2 Louros-type figurine
   (schematic–figurative transition)
3 Spedos-type figurine (canonical)
4 Dokathismata-type figurine (canonical)

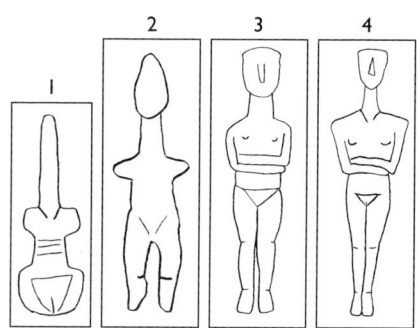

sometimes with a phallus halfway down the pillar itself

Hermax, a pile of stones with one projecting upright from the middle, serving as a marker of a boundary or landmark, or as a grave mound

Hestiatorion (pl. *hestiatoria*), in an ancient sanctuary, a ritual dining hall

Heroön, a shrine to a deified hero

Heruls (or Heruli), a nomadic, barbarian people from northern Europe

Hexastyle, having six columns

Hierarchs, the three pre-eminent Doctors of the Eastern Church, St Basil the Great, St John Chrysostom and St Gregory of Nazianzus

Hieron, a sacred building

Himation, a cloak; an outer garment worn by men and women in ancient Greece

Hippodamian, refers to the regular grid plan for city streets named after the 5th-century BC town planner Hippodamus of Miletus

Historical, the period beginning with written records, in a Greek context c. 700 BC

Hodighitria (also written Hodeghetria, Odighitria), icon type representing the Virgin with the Child seated on her lap. It functions as a 'guide', presenting the infant Christ as 'the way'. Traditionally based on the prototype said to have been painted by St Luke

Hydria, a vessel for water

Hymettian, marble from Mt Hymettus near Athens

Hypocaust, ancient Roman heating system in which hot air circulated under the floor and sometimes also between double walls

Hyposkenion, the front wall of the stage in an ancient theatre, often adorned with statues

Hypostyle hall, a large room with the ceiling borne by rows of columns

Iconoclastic, in the Byzantine world, the period in the 8th and early 9th centuries when representations of the human form (icons, graven images) were banned from sacred art

Iconostasis, screen holding icons in a Byzantine church, separating the sanctuary from the laity

Imaret, in the Islamic world, an almshouse

Impluvium (pl. *impluvia*), in an ancient Roman building, a tank or pool for collecting rainwater from the roof

Impost, block or projecting corbel above a capital or pier from which an arch springs

Inscribed cross (*see Cross-in-square*)

Incunabulum (pl. *incunabula*), any book printed in the same century as the invention of movable type, i.e. between 1450 and 1500

Insula (pl. *insulae*), the basic unit of the Hippodamian (*qv*) system; a block of housing

Ioánnis Pródromos, St John the Baptist

Ioánnis Theológos, St John the Evangelist

Ionia, ancient region of coastal Asia Minor. The Ionians colonised much of the Aegean

Ionic, order of architecture developed in Ionia (*qv*) in the late 6th century BC, and identified primarily by its capital with paired volutes supporting a moulded abacus (*see illustration opposite*)

Isodomic, masonry made up of blocks of very similar size, with the vertical joins coming in the centre of the block below and above. The variant known as pseudo-isodomic has alternating taller and lower courses (*see illustration on p. 657*)

Ithyphallic, with an oversize, erect phallus

Kalathos, a vase in the shape of a basket with handles

Kalderími (pl. *kalderímia*), a paved road dating from before the modern era

Kámbos (also Kámpos), a fertile plain; typically the cultivated area where produce was grown to feed a town

Katholikon, a monastery church

Kernos (pl. *kernoi*), a cult vessel in stone or clay with several hollow receptacles. No firm interpretation exists. Some scholars have suggested that they may have been gaming boards; others believe they were for ritual offerings

THE CLASSICAL ORDERS

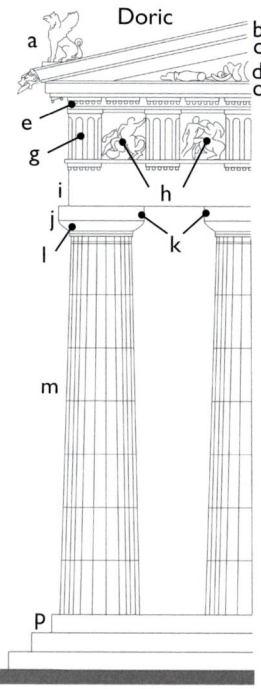

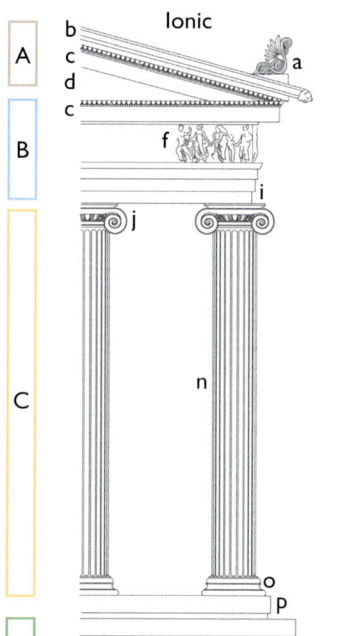

A	Pediment	B	Entablature	C	Column	D	Crepidoma

a	Acroterion	e	Mutules & Guttae	j	Capital	p	Stylobate
b	Cyma	f	Frieze	k	Abacus	q	Stereobate
c	Cornice	g	Triglyph	l	Echinus		
d	Tympanum	h	Metopes	m/n	Shaft:		
		i	Architrave		(m) flutes meet in		
					sharp ridges (arrises);		
					(n) flutes lie between		
					flat ridges (fillets)		
				o	Base		

The Aeolic capital developed in northwest Asia Minor in the Archaic period. It is closely related to the Ionic capital, the difference being that the volutes of the Aeolic capital are separated by a downward-pointing central wedge.

The Corinthian capital, with its distinctive decoration of acanthus leaves.

Keros-Syros Culture, Early Cycladic culture dated 2700–2300 BC and named from two islands where important deposits were found, particularly of figurines

Koímisis tis Theotókou (pron: *kee-misis*) Dormition (*qv*) of the Virgin

Kore (pl. *korai*), from the Greek word for young girl, used to describe a standing female figure in the Archaic (*qv*) style. It is also a name for Persephone

Kouros (pl. *kouroi*), from the Greek word for young man, used to describe a standing nude male figure in Archaic (*qv*) style

Krater, large, wide-mouthed vessel used for mixing wine and water

Larnax (pl. *larnakes*), chest or rectangular tub, normally in fired clay, used as a coffin

Latin, in medieval Greece, pertaining to Western Christianity

Latin cross, a cross where the vertical arm is longer than the horizontal

Lebes, deep bowl typically used for mixing, supported on a stand

Lesbian masonry, polygonal (*qv*) masonry type where the visible, projecting surfaces of the stones have been smoothed into curved shapes (*see p. 657*)

Loculus (pl. *loculi*), small niche or compartment for the placing of a dead body or cinerary urn

Machicolated, of a parapet, having holes in the floor through which stones, boiling oil etc. could be dropped on attackers

Maenads, female followers of Dionysus who worked themselves into a ritual frenzy during his festivals

Martyrion (pl. *martyria*) building or chapel commemorating the death of a saint or martyr, or built over his or her tomb

Medise, a term used at the time of the Persian Wars meaning to favour the Mede or Persian side

BYZANTINE CHURCH DESIGN

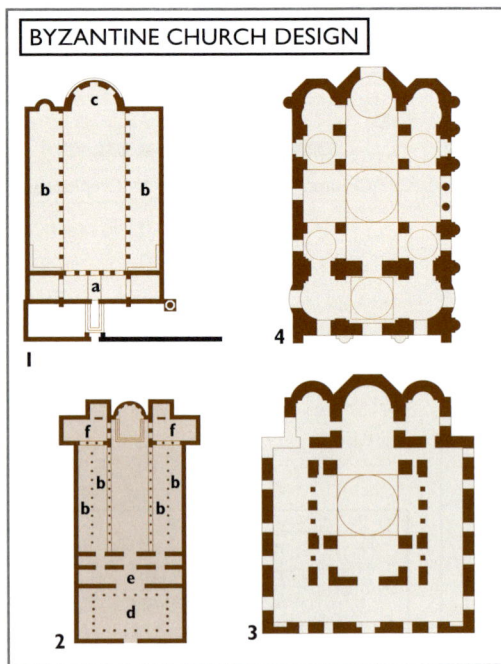

1 Simple basilica on the model of Roman meeting halls. It has a narthex (a), aisles (b) and an apse (c)

2 As the basilica evolved in Early Christian times, it acquired multiple aisles (b), an atrium (d), exonarthex (e) and transepts (f)

3 Cross-domed basilica. A square central bay with arms of equal length (Greek cross) is surmounted by a dome

4 The cross-in-square or inscribed-cross model, where a Greek-cross core, surmounted by its dome, is flanked by side bays all bearing smaller domes

TEMPLE DESIGN

Early temple. This example is distyle in antis, meaning that the entrance has two columns nestling between the projecting piers (antae) of the side walls. The inner chamber (naos) is preceded by an antechamber (pronaos).

More complex temple design, again with two columns in antis, but this time also amphiprostyle, meaning that each end has a colonnaded porch (prostyle). The temple and its porches are built onto a crepidoma, a stepped platform.

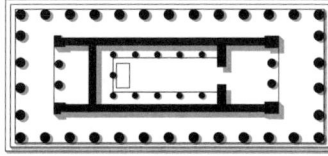

Peripteral temple, with peristyle (colonnade surrounding the naos). Access to the inner chamber (the naos) is through the pronaos (antechamber). The room at the back (with no access to the naos) is the opisthodomos.

Medrese, an Islamic theological school

Megaron, a large rectangular hall, typically the chief building of a Mycenaean city, with a roofed entrance lobby at one end

Meltemi, the north wind

Metamorphosis (tou Sotíros), the Transfiguration (of the Saviour)

Metope, square ornamental relief on a Doric frieze, alternating with triglyphs (*qv*); (*see illustration on p. 653*)

Metropolis (also Mitropolis), the Greek word for a cathedral

Mihrab, prayer niche in the wall of a mosque, indicating the direction of Mecca

Mimbar (also Minbar), pulpit in a mosque

Minoan, term coined by Sir Arthur Evans to describe the Bronze Age culture of Crete

Moní, the Greek word for a monastery or convent

Monostyle, of a temple porch, having only a single column

Mycenaean, the latter Bronze Age in ancient Greece, named after the people of Mycenae on the mainland (*map p. 4*)

Naïskos, piece of funerary architecture in the form of a small temple with a statue or relief of the deceased

Naos, enclosed interior part of a temple; the main body of a church

Narthex, vestibule of a church or basilica stretching across the façade before the west entrance to the nave

Naumachia (pl. *naumachiae*), mock sea battle as staged in amphitheatres; also, by association, the area that was flooded for such a mock battle to take place

Neorion (pl. *neoria*), gallery or hall for the display of a victorious warship

Nicopoea (also Nikopoia), epithet for the Virgin as 'Bringer of Victory'

Nomarcheíon, in a Greek town, the seat of the district government or prefecture

Nymphaion (in Latin, nymphaeum, pl. *nymphaea*), in the Greek and Roman world, a grotto filled with streams and springs considered the habitat of the nymphs. It came later to designate buildings or a room in a villa with fountains, plants and statuary

Obsidian, a natural glass occurring in volcanic areas when lava comes into contact with water. It was used for tools from early antiquity

Octastyle, having eight columns

Odeion, small theatre, occasionally roofed, typically used for musical performances

Oikos (pl. *oikoi*), house. Also oikia, singular and plural

Opisthodomos, the back room of a temple

Opus alexandrinum, Byzantine style of revetment for floors and other surfaces in which small pieces of stone and glass paste are arranged in expansive geometric patterns interspersed with larger discs of marble and other coloured stone

Opus caementicium, Roman wall-building technique in which pieces of brick and stone were mixed with cement

Opus sectile, floor or wall covering made of coloured pieces of marble or glass (larger than mosaic tesserae; *qv*) arranged in geometric or figurative designs

Orans, with the arms raised in prayer

Orientalising, decorative style originating in the Near East. It reached the Aegean in the second half of the 8th century BC and exercised a profound influence on the figurative arts. It is characterised by an almost baroque exuberance contrasting with the native, more austere Geometric (*qv*) style

Orthostat, large stone slab set vertically in the lower part of a wall

Osmanli script, Perso-Arabic script in which Ottoman Turkish was written

Ostrakon (pl. *ostraka*), a potsherd used in antiquity as a writing medium

Palaestra, public space for the training of athletes

Panaghía, the 'All Holy' Virgin

Pancration, from *pan-kration*, literally 'all holds': a boxing contest in which no holds were barred

Panigýri (pl. *panigýria*), public festival in honour of a saint's feast day

Pantocrator, literary 'He who Controls All', a representation of Christ in Majesty traditionally featured in the central dome of Orthodox churches and in the main apse of an Early Christian basilica

Paraskenion (pl. *paraskenia*), projecting wing or wings attached to the skene (*qv*) of an ancient theatre

Parecclesion, a subsidiary chapel in a Byzantine church with a variety of functions, often funerary

Peak sanctuary, a Minoan cult place in an elevated position

Peisistratids, autocratic ruling dynasty of Athens of the 6th century BC

Pelasgian, pertaining to a pre-Hellenic people variously regarded to have settled in the northeastern mainland and in Ionia (*qv*)

Pendentive, one of four concave spandrels (triangular spaces) descending from the 'corners' of a dome, in Christian architecture decorated with images or symbols of the Evangelists (*qv*)

Pentelic marble, high-quality marble from Mt Pendeli, near Athens, used for both construction and statuary

Peribolos, the enclosure or court of a temple. The word may refer either to the perimeter wall itself, or to the space enclosed

Peripteral, surrounded by a colonnade

Peristyle, colonnade surrounding all four sides of a courtyard or a building

Pilaster, a shallow pier or rectangular column projecting only slightly from the wall

Pithos (pl. *pithoi*), large ceramic container used for storage, often taller than a man

Platytera, representation of the Virgin and Child as a symbol of the Incarnation. The Christ Child is placed in the centre of the Virgin's lap or abdomen. She holds her hands out wide

Polyandrion, funerary monument commemorating the fallen in battle

Polygonal, a style of masonry in which blocks of irregular shape are roughly hewn to fit

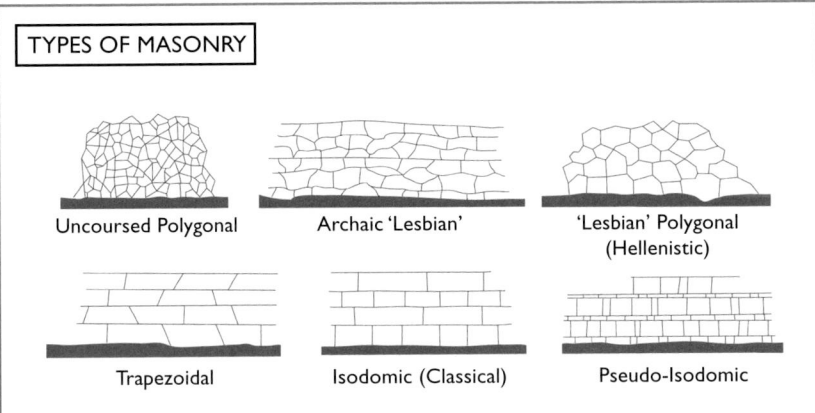

TYPES OF MASONRY

Uncoursed Polygonal   Archaic 'Lesbian'   'Lesbian' Polygonal (Hellenistic)

Trapezoidal   Isodomic (Classical)   Pseudo-Isodomic

(*see illustration above*)

Poros, a soft, coarse, conchiferous limestone

Pothos, in mythology a youth, the personification of sexual yearning and a follower of Aphrodite

Predella, the panel below an altarpiece, usually decorated with a series of small painted scenes

Pronaos, temple vestibule or antechamber, preceding the naos (cella) or sacred inner room

Proconnesian, a marble from the island of Marmara, modern Turkey

Propylon (also propylaion; pl. *propylaia*), monumental entranceway to a sacred enclosure or major public space. Propylaia have more than one entrance door or arch

Proskenion, raised performance area in front of the skene (*qv*) of a Hellenistic or later theatre

Prostyle, of a temple, with columns on the front only

Prothesis, the part of a Byzantine church dedicated to the preparation of the Communion bread and wine. This may be a separate room or recess or simply a table

Protogeometric, pottery style with simple, non-figurative decoration (1050–900 BC)

Prytaneion, a public building in which the governors of the city conducted their business and took their meals

Pseudo-isodomic (*see Isodomic*)

Ptolemies, one of the successor dynasties of Alexander the Great, who became rulers of Egypt

Pýrgos (pl. *pýrgi*), literally, a tower; also a type of dwelling-house, with stone lower storeys and a top floor of wood

Pyxis (pl. *pyxides*), small, round lidded box made in pottery, stone, ivory, metal or wood

Ravelin, fortification with two sloping faces built outside the walls, beyond the moat

Relieving triangle, three-cornered empty space above a lintel, designed to lessen the load that it has to bear. It is a characteristic feature of tholos (*qv*) tombs

Rhyton (pl. *rhyta*), vessel made of clay or metal, sometimes moulded at one end in the shape of an animal head, with a small opening for the liquid to run through when making libations

Sabil, in the Islamic world, a public fountain

Saracen, term used in Early Christian and medieval times to refer to Arabs or indeed any Muslim

Scagliola, substance typically made from ground alabaster or gypsum, pigmented and used as a kind of imitation marble

Sealing, impression left by a seal stone or a signet ring

Sgraffito, technique for decorating a plastered wall entailing scraping a pattern in the outer surface allowing the contrasting colour of the surface below to show through

Silenus, a familiar of Dionysus, his mentor and tutor. In the plural form, sileni are the paunchy, drunken followers of the god

Sima, the upturned edge of a roof acting as a gutter; made of fired clay or stone, it may be continuous or broken by spouts

Sistrum (pl. *sistra*), a percussion instrument like a rattle

Skene, the permanent buildings behind the orchestra or stage, the backdrop or set of an ancient theatre

Spedos (*see Cycladic figurines, p. 651*)

Sphendone, the curving end of a hippodrome or racetrack

Spolia, building material reused from an earlier ruined or demolished structure

Stele (pl. *stelae*), upright stone slab with a commemorative function

Stoa, a covered, free-standing, colonnaded portico, often with a row of shops under the arcade

String course, thin band of projecting brick or stone running horizontally around a building

Stylobate, the surface upon which the columns stand in an ancient temple

Synoecism, the banding together of individual city-states into a single polity

Synthronon, semicircular bench for the clergy in the apse of a basilica

Talus, retaining or sloping wall of a fortress

Taxiárches, the Archangels. In church dedications in the singular (Taxiárchis), this is typically the Archangel Michael

Tekke, in the Ottoman world, a lodge for dervishes

Temenos, a sacred precinct

Templon, a partition or screen separating the laity from the clergy in an Orthodox church

Tepidarium, the warm room in a baths complex

Tessera (pl. *tesserae*), a small cube of marble, glass etc. used in mosaic work

Tevah, elevated reader's platform in a Sephardic synagogue

Theoros (pl. *theoroi*), sacred envoy of an ancient Greek city-state

Thermae, baths

Thesmophorion, temple of Demeter Thesmophoros, goddess of fertility and the fields; normally situated outside the city and connected to the ancient fertility festival celebrated by women

Tholos, circular building, in a funerary context roofed in a domed 'beehive' shape either by stone corbelling or by an organic structure

Tondo, a circular painting or relief

Trabeation, term used in architecture when

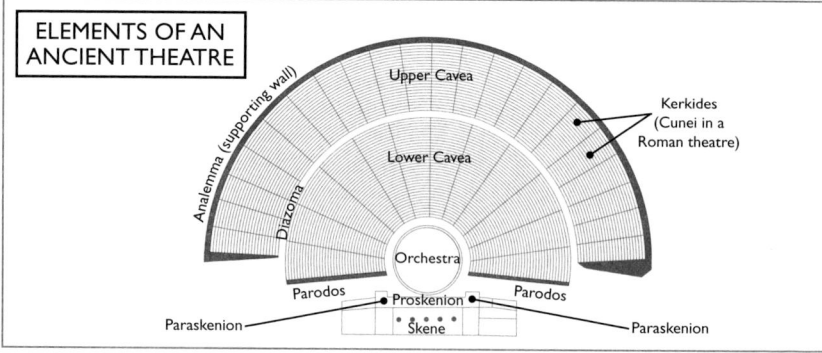

ELEMENTS OF AN ANCIENT THEATRE

Analemma (supporting wall)

Upper Cavea

Kerkides (Cunei in a Roman theatre)

Lower Cavea

Diazoma

Orchestra

Parodos

Proskenion

Parodos

Paraskenion

Skene

Paraskenion

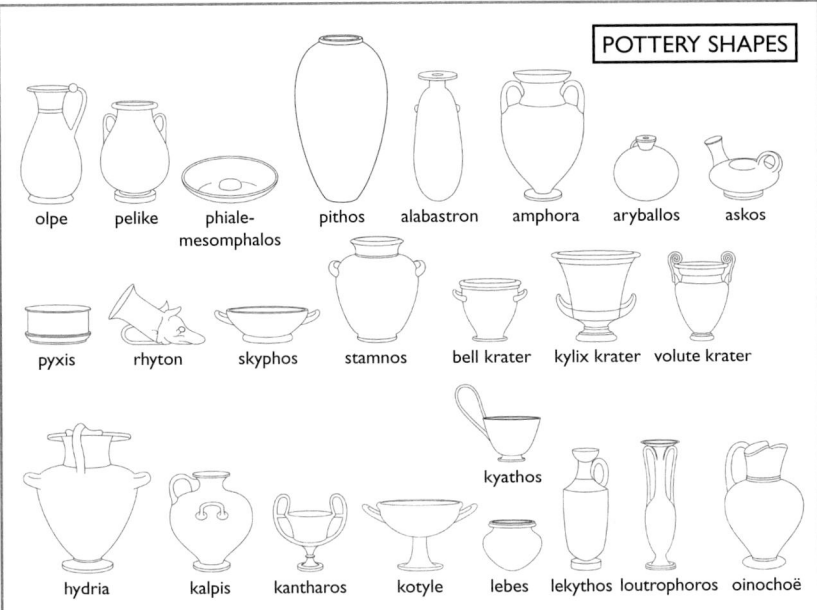

POTTERY SHAPES

olpe · pelike · phiale-mesomphalos · pithos · alabastron · amphora · aryballos · askos

pyxis · rhyton · skyphos · stamnos · bell krater · kylix krater · volute krater

kyathos

hydria · kalpis · kantharos · kotyle · lebes · lekythos · loutrophoros · oinochoë

apertures (doors, windows, niches) are closed at the top with a horizontal lintel as opposed to an arch

Triarch, one of three rulers sharing power

Tribute Lists, inscriptions recording the financial contributions made by the members of the Delian League (*qv*) to the Treasury of Athena at Athens

Triclinium, in a Roman house, specifically a room with three couches; by association, the 'dining room'

Tri-conch, a church structure with three apses set at right angles

Triglyph, a small decorative panel on a Doric frieze carved with three vertical channels (*see illustration on p. 653*)

Tugra (also Tughra), the elaborate calligraphic signature of an Ottoman sultan, appearing on all official documents

Türbe, in the Ottoman world, a mausoleum

Tyrant, in ancient and medieval times, an autocratic ruler; not necessarily (despite modern connotations) an evil one

Volutes, scroll-shaped decorations, e.g. on an Ionic capital (*see illustration on p. 653*)

Voussoirs, wedge-shaped stones forming the curved part of an arch, fanning upwards from the side piers; the central voussoir is the keystone

Xoanon (pl. *xoana*), a cult image in wood

Xysta, the scratched wall decorations of the Mastic Villages of Chios

Xystos (pl. *xystoi*), a covered running track or portico for exercising

Yali, gracious summer home of a high-ranking Ottoman official, often built on a waterfront, hence its name, from the Greek *gialós*, 'shore'

Ypapantí, Candlemas; the feast of the Purification of the Virgin and the Presentation of Christ in the Temple

Zoödóchos Pigí, popular church dedication to the Virgin as the 'Fount of Life'

INDEX

Islands with detailed coverage are given in bold capitals. Ancient place names are rendered in italics. Page references in italics indicate illustrations. Where many pages are listed, those where principal content appears are given in bold. Churches and monasteries are listed as 'Ag. Name'. Towns and villages bearing the names of saints are listed as 'Ághios/Aghía Name'.

contd. from p. 6

Editor-in-Chief: Annabel Barber
Co-editors: Heinrich Hall, Michael Metcalfe

Regional maps: Dimap Bt and Kartext
Site plans: Imre Bába and Blue Guides © Blue Guides 2010

Photo research, editing and pre-press: Hadley Kincade
Photographs by Roger Barber: pp. 119, 122, 511, 512, 600; © Shmuel Magal/Sites & Photos:
pp. 149, 167, 289, back cover; Duby Tal/Albatross/Topfoto: pp. 78, 163, 190;
© Duby Tal/Albatross: p. 445; Yann-Arthus Bertrand/Corbis/Red Dot: pp. 134, 157, 216, 299,
391; Annabel Barber: p. 20; © INTERFOTO/Alamy/Red Dot: p. 137; John Hicks/Corbis/Red
Dot: p. 139; © Bettmann/Corbis/Red Dot: pp. 235, 283; Bernd Kohlhas/Corbis/Red Dot: p. 255;
Hubert Stadler/Corbis/Red Dot: p. 295; © terry harris just greece photo library/Alamy/Red Dot:
pp. 354, 402; Bildarchiv Monheim GmbH/Alamy/Red Dot: p. 362; Robert Morris/Alamy/Red
Dot: p. 377; © Art Directors & TRIP/Alamy/Red Dot: p. 418; Vanni/Corbis/Red Dot: p. 547;
Hoberman Collection UK/Alamy/Red Dot: p. 558; Mark Shenley/Alamy/Red Dot: pp. 623, 625;
Alinari Archives-Alinari Archive, Florence: p. 271; The Art Archive/National Archaeological
Museum Athens/Gianni dagli Orti: pp. 54, 197; The Art Archive/National Archaeological
Museum Mykonos/Gianni dagli Orti: p. 87; The Art Archive/Gianni dagli Orti: p. 555;
Wikicommons: p. 59; Nadia Prigoda/Wikicommons: p. 177; © istockphoto.com/PEDRE:
p. 66; © istockphoto.com/asiafoto: p. 98; © Simon Whitehouse/Dreamstime.com: p. 204;
© Newphotoservice/Dreamstime.com: p. 236; Vlas2000/Shutterstock: p. 567.

Cover photograph © istockphoto.com/Fanelli Photography
Spine © istockphoto.com/Ljupco.

Line drawings pp. 653, 655, 657, 658, 659: Gabriella Juhász & Michael Mansell RIBA;
p. 654: Imre Bába; p. 651: Annabel Barber.

Every effort has been made to contact the owners of material reproduced in this guide.
We would be pleased to hear from any owners we have been unable to reach.

Nigel McGilchrist would particularly like to thank Ivan de Jesus Tabares-Valencia, for constant
inspiration and support; Professor Robin Barber, author of the previous general *Blue Guide Greece*,
for considerable assistance; Peter Cocconi, Marc-René de Montalembert, Geoffrey Cox, Valentina
Ivancich, Charles Arnold and William Forrester, for different kinds of research and help generously given; John and Jay Rendall for unstinting hospitality in Athens; and Graziella Seferiades,
Matthew Kidd, Martin Leon and Iain McGilchrist, for inspiring company on many island journeys,
as well as the Louisianan friends who kindly helped with journeys to Chálki, Alimniá and Saría.

Thanks from the editor to Pierre MacKay, for information on the Dominicans in Chalkída.

Material prepared for press by Anikó Kuzmich,
Printed in Hungary by Dürer Nyomda Kft, Gyula.

ISBN 978–1–905131–35–8